D1572867

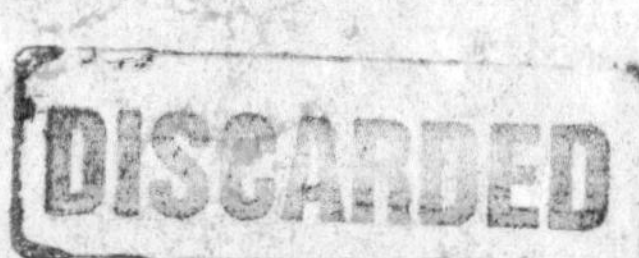
DISCARDED

# The Complete Visitor's Guide to Mesoamerican Ruins

# The Complete Visitor's Guide to Mesoamerican Ruins

by Joyce Kelly

Photographs by Jerry Kelly and by the author

Drawings and Maps by the author

University of Oklahoma Press NORMAN

Library of Congress Cataloging in Publication Data

Kelly, Joyce, 1933–
The complete visitor's guide to Mesoamerican ruins.

Bibliography: p. 517
Includes index.
1. Indians of Mexico—Antiquities. 2. Indians of Central America—Antiquities. 3. Mexico—Antiquities. 4. Central America—Antiquities. 5. Excavations (Archaeology)—Mexico. 6. Excavations (Archaeology)—Central America. 7. Mexico—Description and travel—1951– —Guide-books. 8. Central America—Description and travel—1951– —Guide-books. I. Kelly, Jerry. II. Title. III. Title: Mesoamerican ruins.
F1219.K44 917.2'04 80–53853
AACR2


Manufactured in the U.S.A. First Edition.

This book is affectionately dedicated to the people who inhabit the remote areas of Mesoamerica—to the Juans, Adelaidos, and Marios who graciously assisted my husband and me in reaching *their* ruins. Without their help and encouragement we would have had fewer adventures, would have missed seeing many interesting sites, and this guide would have been much less thorough. We have enjoyed their company tremendously and all of them would be rated four stars as hosts. We are eternally grateful for having met them.

# Contents

# Illustrations

Color Plates



*Drawings*



*Black-and-White Photographs*

*Maps and Site Plans*

# Preface

I suppose that my interest in archaeology began when I was a child. I clearly remember being fascinated by stories of the pyramids in Egypt and the archaeologists who discovered the ancient tombs of the Pharaohs.

Many years later my interest shifted geographically when I learned that there were also pyramids in Mexico. This information came as quite a surprise, and I wondered why I hadn't learned of it earlier.

My husband and I visisted Mexico for the first time in 1957, and one of our top priorities was to visit the "pyramids." We drove there on a rainy day and were almost the only visitors. With official guidebook in hand, we investigated the site (and the old museum), which only then did I learn was called Teotihuacán. The name sounded enchanting and exotic.

My notes indicate that to get to one of the outlying areas of Teotihuacán we drove a short distance over "dirt roads." How adventurous that seemed at the time, and how little did I realize the many hundreds of miles of much worse dirt roads we would travel in the coming years.

I was awed by the massiveness of the Pyramid of the Sun and intrigued by the strange sculptured serpent heads on the Temple of Quetzalcóatl. What I found most interesting was that these ancient structures were in ruin when the Aztecs entered the Valley of Mexico. I had never stopped to think about who occupied the area before the Aztecs.

The next day we visited the "old" Museum of Anthropology near the Zócalo in Mexico City. Artifacts from throughout the republic were displayed in a rather haphazard fashion in both an outdoor patio and an indoor section. I viewed these with some interest, but soon my attention was attracted by one particular display, a replica of a tomb found beneath the Temple of Inscriptions at Palenque.

Although the sarcophogus was a copy, the jade jewelry and small sculptures in the burial were original, and there appeared to be a ton of them.

Questions flooded my mind: "Where is Palenque?" "Is it nearby?" "Can we drive there?" I was ready to leave immediately.

Our guide's answers were very disappointing. "It's very far, and there are no roads going there. It's very difficult to reach."

Nevertheless, I knew that someday I would see Palenque—wherever it was. During the morning hours of Saturday, September 28, 1957, I became an obsessive ruin buff, even though I had seen only one archaeological site and two poorly arranged museums.

I was becoming somewhat aware of my ignorance of Mexican archaeology and sought to rectify this immediately upon my return home. I phoned every bookstore in New Orleans and succeeded in finding exactly *one* book on the subject: Miguel Covarrubias's then recently published *Indian Art of Mexico and Central America.* Although I now treasure this volume, it was too advanced for me at the time that I bought it.

The shelves of the public library gave me some of the basics, and later, paperbacks filled in more of the gaps. I periodically returned to Covarrubias and began to get more out of it.

Most of my study of Mesoamerican art and archaeology has been done independently, although I did take a course on "High Civilizations of Middle America" at Tulane University in 1966. Taught by Robert Wauchope, then director of Tulane's Middle American Research Institute, this excellent course tied together many loose ends and introduced me to some important sites of which I had been unaware. More important, however, it made me appreciate the interrelationships among the various cultures, a subject that I find endlessly fascinating.

In addition to formal and informal study of the subject, I have been fortunate in having been able to visit many of the more interesting sites during the past two decades. Yet, on each trip, there are always a couple of sites that we miss and that we have to save for the next time.

Often I am asked how I find out about all these places. I read anything I can find on the subject. I pore over maps. I discuss the subject with professional archaeologists and fellow enthusiasts at every opportunity. I also write a lot of letters and ask a lot of questions.

This inquisitiveness has enabled me to collect

much useful information, which is often difficult to come by. Since I feel our lives have been greatly enriched by our experiences in ruin hopping, I decided to write this book and make the information generally available to those with similar interests.

Visiting the major sites, especially those in Mexico, is a simple matter. They are accessible by paved roads, have first-class accommodations nearby, and are well publicized. You can visit them on conducted tours, with your own private guide, or on your own. These are the sites that you will want to visit first, of course.

Once you get interested in seeing the less-often-visited sites, the going gets harder. Tourist departments of the various countries are generally of little help since they deal mostly with the average tourist, who is interested in seeing only the "big" sites.

For this reason the slant of this guidebook is basically "how to get there" and the best way of doing so when there are choices. Also included are suggestions on what to bring and photo hints where they seem appropriate. It has been my experience that ruin buffs are generally also photography buffs, who are interested in the visual aspects of the sites. Although this guide is intended primarily for the serious enthusiast, who has probably visited many of the major sites, I hope it will be useful for those whose interest is just beginning. For this reason, I have included the major sites as well.

What I have above all tried to do is produce the kind of guidebook that I wish had been on the market when I became interested in ruins twenty years ago.

We have reached sites by car, Jeep, light aircraft, dugout canoe, on foot over muddy trails, and combinations thereof. Since I am basically lazy, I prefer to do things the easiest way. Never walk if you can ride. Don't use a Jeep if a more confortable car will get you there. Recommendations on "Getting There" will follow this philosophy.

Many sites that seem remote turn out to be relatively easy to reach once you know how. Remoteness is actually a relative term. The only places I consider really remote are those I haven't been to: once I get there, they will not seem remote either.

Surprising though it may seem, almost all the sites rated in this guide can be reached within two days from major cities within the United States, if you are able to make good connections. It is true, however, that it is sometimes impossible to make arrangements ahead of time. It is a matter of getting to the general area and then making plans, but this method can be amazingly successful. We have had few disappointments along these lines. Having alternatives is, of course, always wise.

I have personally visited all the 119 sites and 41 museums rated in the text, many on several occasions, and have visited all but 13 of the sites and museums at least once since 1974. Nevertheless, as with all other guidebooks, the material presented becomes outdated. New roads get built, and existing dirt roads get paved (or deteriorate into impassable muddy trails). New airstrips are cut in the jungle, making additional sites accessible, and new information from sites being excavated changes our ideas about the archaeology of the area.

For instance, for a long time it was believed that the sites were ceremonial centers without a large permanent resident population. New evidence suggests that many were indeed cities. Likewise, it was thought that slash-and-burn agriculture was the only kind practiced. Now we know that irrigation was also practiced.

In this guide I do not give comprehensive coverage of hotels and restaurants, but I will mention some where they are few and far between and not well known, or where there is some special reason to do so. Neither is this intended as a scholarly work emphasizing the fine details pertaining to the various cultures that built the fascinating structures and carved the amazing monuments. Excellent comprehensive guides and scholarly tomes are readily available on bookstore shelves and in libraries. Some of these are mentioned in the "General Advice" section, and in the Selected Readings. Care has been taken, however, to ensure the accuracy of the material presented, as far as is possible, with regard to both existing conditions and archaeological data.

The mileages listed have been compiled from various sources, generally from odometer readings corrected after calibration, but also from maps and published material. They have been double- and triple-checked where possible. They may be considered accurate to within a margin of error of $\pm 5$ percent. In most cases, the margin of error will be even less.

Although this guide covers more sites and museums than does any other book on the market, some important ones are not included. For example, major Maya sites Piedras Negras and Altar de Sacrificios have been omitted because most of their monuments have been removed, and there has been no restoration of the architecture. All information indicates that only overgrown rubble mounds are to be seen there today. Some potentially interesting sites that are difficult to reach are not covered simply because we have not yet seen them, and I decided to avoid the pitfalls of using secondhand information. I apologize if I have left out one of your personal favorites. Some sites that we visited are not included. Mostly these are one- or two-star sites on private property or sites we got to by a set of lucky circumstances that may not be repeatable.

In the text the arrangement of the sites and museums is by country. In the sections on Mexico and Guatemala subdivisions within these countries are used. In nine of the thirteen subdivisions, where there is a major museum, it is covered first; the sites and other museums then follow. In section 1 (Mexico–Northern, Western, and Central) and section 3 (Mexico–Gulf Coast) the sites and museums are covered state by state. I have tried to arrange all the material in a logical geographical sequence.

Joyce Kelly

*New Orleans*

# Acknowledgments

In the preparation of this guide a number of individuals were helpful in various ways. I am indebted to the late Robert Wauchope, former director of the Middle American Research Institute of Tulane University, whose informative class led me even deeper into a study of Mesoamerican archaeology and who offered suggestions and advice on many occasions.

Over several years E. Wyllys Andrews V, present director of the Middle American Research Institute, has been very kind and generous with information. I am especially appreciative of his suggestions that I visit certain sites in Yucatán that I might otherwise have overlooked.

I consider the rating of the sites an important feature of this book, and I would like to thank those who assisted in this task. E. Wyllys Andrews V, Ellie and Taylor Caffery, Don Cornelsen, Alice and Bill Desrosiers, Ed and Jo Dunn, Helen Johnson, Ron Ranson, Jr., Ivan Ruzicka, and the late George Zuckerman.

For editorial suggestions, and a fine job of typing a long and difficult manuscript, I am indebted to Eileen Mintz.

I would like to thank Fritz Grannan for his advice and assistance in preparing the maps and chronological chart, and Barbara Paikert and Roy Kelly for their help with proofreading.

My sincere thanks to my husband, Jerry, for accompanying me to the sites, for taking most of the black-and-white photographs used in this guide and printing all of them, and especially for his consideration and encouragement while this book was in preparation.

Joyce Kelly

*New Orleans*

# PART ONE : *Introduction*

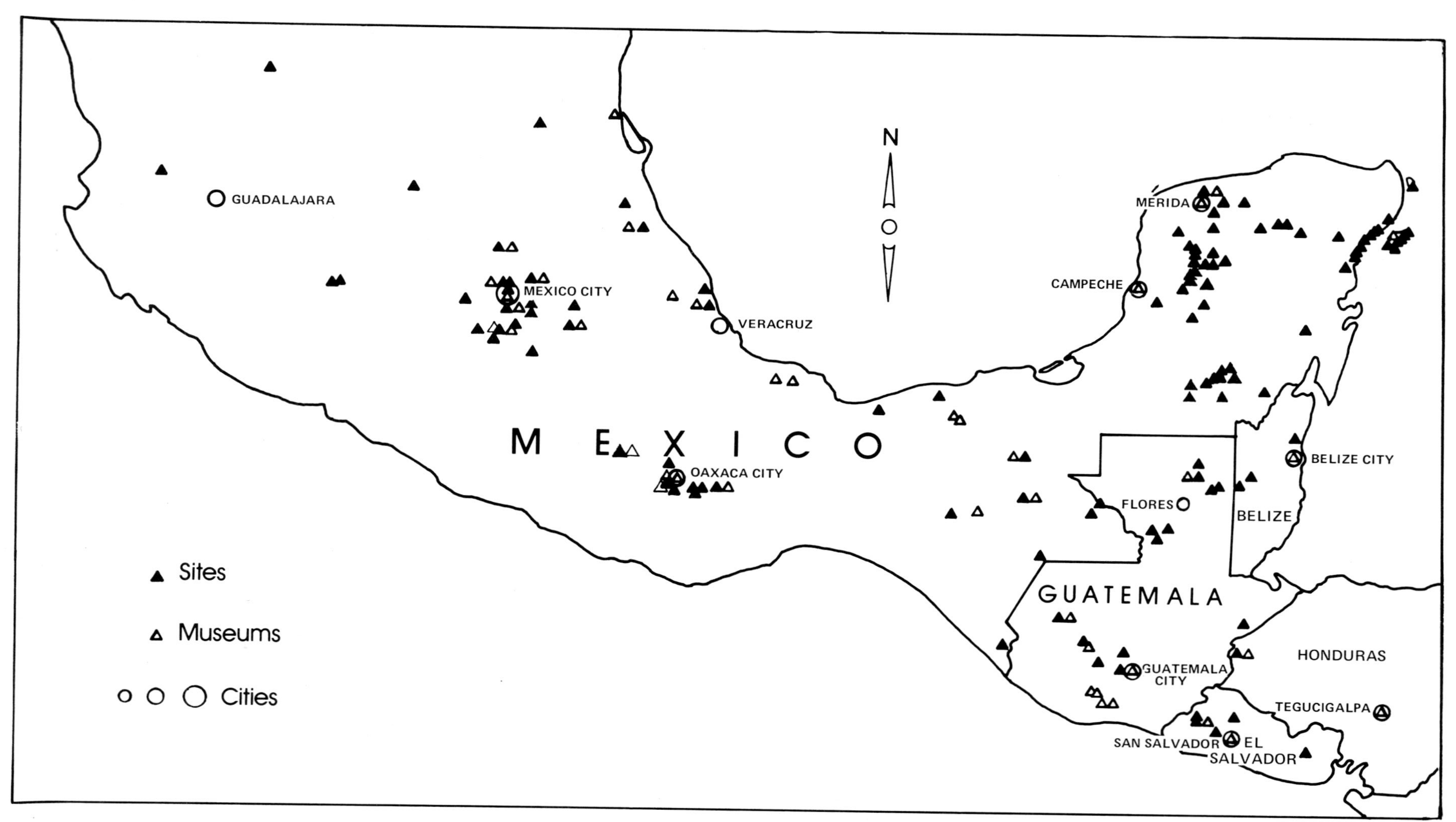


*Mesoamerica*
Sites and museums covered in the text

# *The Origins of Man in the New World*

Authorities generally agree that man entered the New World at least 20,000 and perhaps more than 40,000 years ago. Man came, in several waves, over a period of thousands of years until about 8000 B.C.

These migrations from Old to New World took place across the Bering Strait at a time of glacial advance, when a land bridge formed. Two physical types immigrated; the earlier had long flatsided heads, and the later arrivals were more Mongoloid, with large faces and a more yellowish pigmentation. Both groups were fully developed *Homo sapiens.* These immigrants were hunters, who followed game across the land bridge. Once across, they followed the ice-free routes in present-day Alaska and Canada, heading south and eventually spreading through what are now the American continents. There is firm evidence that man occupied the Valley of Mexico at least by 10,000 B.C., and reached the southern tip of South America at least by 7000 B.C.

The monumental work of Richard MacNeish in the 1960s, carried out in the Tehuacán Valley of Central Mexico, has added greatly to our knowledge of the early stages of man's progress in America. MacNeish discovered that in the earliest period (12,000–7000 B.C.) man lived in caves and seasonal outdoor camps in small groups. He hunted some big game but relied more on hunting and trapping small game and gathering wild plants for his food supply. Chipped-flint tools were in use.

When the larger animals became extinct, man relied even more on small game and plant collecting. Some of the plants were later domesticated, and the idea of cultivation probably occured between 7000 and 5000 B.C. The tool assemblage now included ground and pecked stone, mortars, and pestles.

Around 5000 B.C. agriculture began in earnest and accounted for 10 percent of man's diet. Stone water jars and bowls were manufactured. Sometime between 5000 and 3400 B.C., corn was domesticated, and agricultural products became an ever-increasing part of the food consumed. About 2300 B.C. a crude pottery was manufactured, and fine obsidian blades were produced.

Between 1500 and 900 B.C. we find man a full-time agriculturist living in small villages. There is evidence of a complex religious life, shown by the existence of a figurine cult. This is the Early Preclassic period and the early part of the Middle Preclassic, when the Olmec culture of the Gulf Coast began. Indeed, the figurines found in the Tehuacán Valley from this period show Olmec influence.

During the latter part of the Middle Preclassic and in the Late Preclassic periods, ceremonial constructions were built throughout Mesoamerica. Various cultural groups were developing at different rates, but many proceeded to an eventual peak during the Classic period (A.D. 300–900), when there was a proliferation of activity in architecture and sculpture.

There was a decline in the arts and architectural endeavors during the Postclassic period, from A.D. 900 until the Spanish conquest, and many earlier Classic cities were virtually abandoned (the archaeology of the individual sites is covered in the text).

One theory remains to be mentioned: the possibility of outside influence that may account for—at least in part—man's development in the New World. The Spaniards who conquered the land were indeed impressed by the civilization they encountered and the material arts it produced. Some early writers could not believe that it developed indigenously and sought to account for it by looking for culture bearers from the Old World. Some thought the Lost Tribes of Israel were responsible, while others looked to traveling Irish monks. There was talk of seafaring Phoenicians, Scythians, Scandinavians, and refugees from the lost lands Atlantis and Mu. In time these fanciful theories were discarded, and a more scholarly approach to investigation was undertaken. It was concluded that American cultures did indeed develop in situ.

In recent years, however, there has been a resurgence of interest in the question of outside influence. Speculation now includes visitors from China, India, Japan, Egypt, and even outer space. Scholars, of course, reject the more outlandish of these theories, and most of them, while admitting *possible* trans-Pacific contacts (probably accidental), generally see no evidence that these contacts were more than

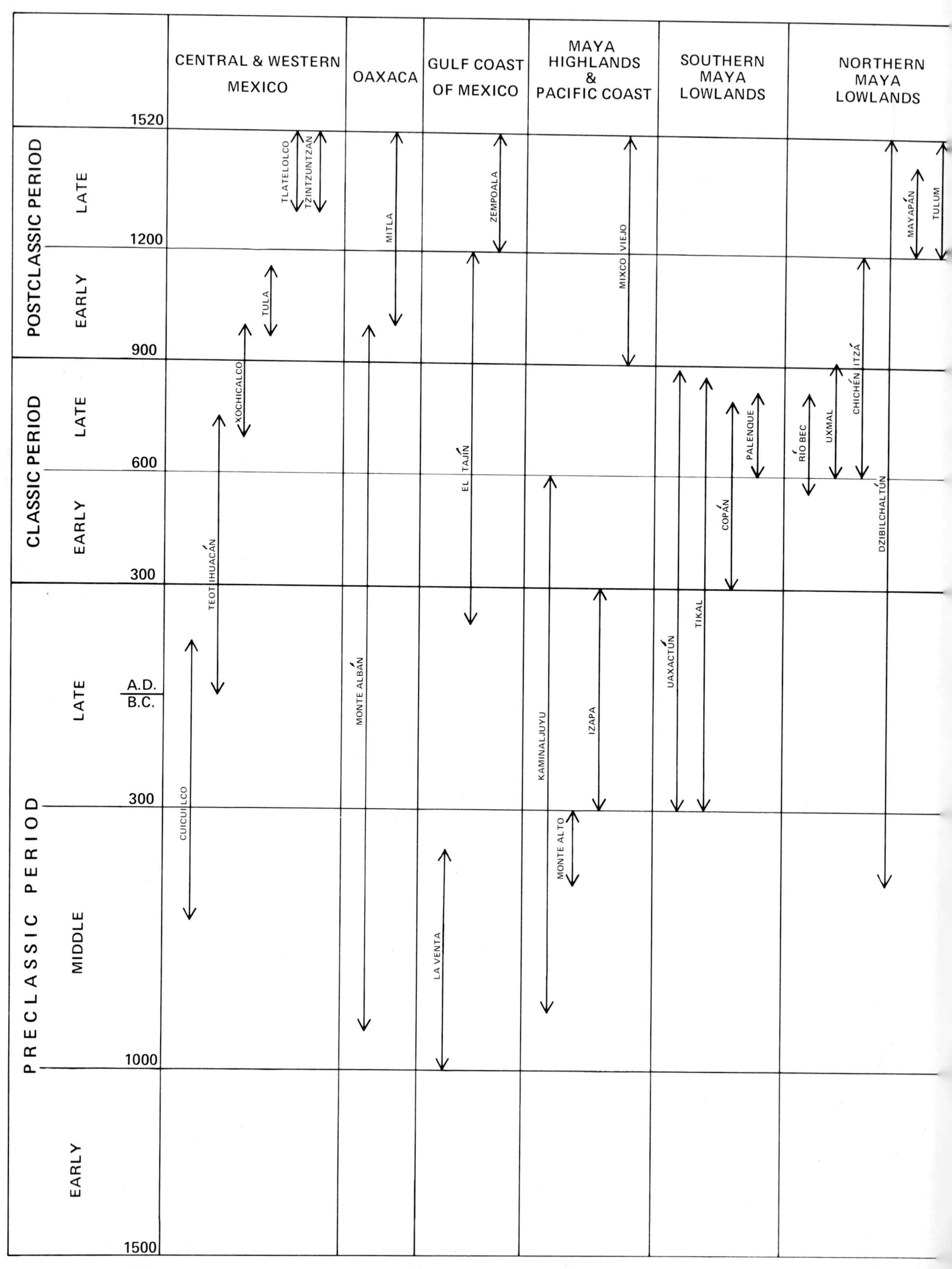

CENTRAL & WESTERN MEXICO
OAXACA
GULF COAST OF MEXICO
MAYA HIGHLANDS & PACIFIC COAST
SOUTHERN MAYA LOWLANDS
NORTHERN MAYA LOWLANDS
1520
POSTCLASSIC PERIOD
LATE
1200
EARLY
900
CLASSIC PERIOD
LATE
600
EARLY
300
PRECLASSIC PERIOD
LATE
A.D.
B.C.
300
MIDDLE
1000
EARLY
1500
TLATELOLCO
TZINTZUNTZAN
TULA
XOCHICALCO
TEOTIHUACÁN
CUICUILCO
MITLA
MONTE ALBÁN
ZEMPOALA
EL TAJÍN
LA VENTA
MIXCO VIEJO
KAMINALJUYU
IZAPA
MONTE ALTO
UAXACTÚN
TIKAL
COPÁN
PALENQUE
RÍO BEC
UXMAL
CHICHÉN ITZÁ
DZIBILCHALTÚN
MAYAPÁN
TULUM

incidental or that they had an important or lasting effect on the development of the indigenous cultures.

The best information we have indicates that the pyramids, temples, sculpture, painting, and other arts we see today in Mesoamerica, as well as the advancements in calendrics, astronomy, and hieroglyphic writing, were products of the people whose ancestors migrated across the Bering Strait thousands of years ago.

### *Chronological Chart*

Twenty-five key sites are shown on the Chronological Chart. The temporal extensions approximate the major period at the site, but not always its total time of occupancy. For instance, Mitla and Palenque were occupied earlier than indicated (as shown by ceramic evidence), and Palenque somewhat later, but the architectural remains seen today date to the time indicated.

Although the breakdown of periods is one that is popularly used, it is not accepted by all authorities. Some prefer somewhat different dates. Nevertheless, the chart should serve the purpose for which it was intended, that is, to show in graphic form when the various centers flourished.

It should also be pointed out that the last part of the Late Preclassic period (ca. A.D. 100–300) is sometimes referred to as the Protoclassic period. For simplicity this short period is included as part of the Late Preclassic rather than as a separate period.

For some sites Maya hieroglyphic dates were used to determine the latest time of occupancy. These dates are converted to the Christian calendar according to the GMT (Goodman-Martínez-Thompson) correlation, which is also used in the text.

# *General Advice and Miscellaneous Notes*

## MAPS

One of the most important items for the ruin buff is a good map. Better are several maps. My policy is to try to have at least three whenever possible. Some back roads are not shown on all maps, but may show up on at least one.

*General:* Texaco publishes road maps of Mexico and the Central American republics. Its Mexico map is available from Texaco Travel Service, P.O. Box 1459, Houston, Texas 77001. See the other specific countries for further information.

The American Automobile Association has road maps of Mexico and Central America available to their members through any of their offices in the United States. There are some inaccuracies in the depiction of the more remote regions of Mexico and not enough detail for Central America, but mileages are shown even for back roads.

In 1968 the National Geographic Society published an archaeological map of Mesoamerica (central and southern Mexico, Belize, Guatemala, El Salvador, and Honduras). It pinpoints hundreds of sites and includes extensive text. It has the high degree of accuracy that one expects of the society. It is available for a modest charge plus postage from the National Geographic Society, Department 60, Washington, D.C. 20036.

*Mexico:* Exxon publishes a road map of Mexico. It is available from Exxon Touring Service, P.O. Box 2180, Houston, Texas 77001, or at the Touring Service Desk in the lobby of its building at 800 Bell Street, Houston. Exxon and Texaco maps of Mexico are not available in Mexico.

The Mexican Tourist Department has road maps available at its tourist delegation offices in major cities in the United States and in Tourismo offices in Mexico.

A variety of road maps of Mexico is sold in bookstores and hotel shops in Mexico. The quality varies from excellent to almost useless. Look them over before you make your selection.

*Guatemala:* Texaco road maps of Guatemala are available at some Texaco service stations in Guatemala; important archaeological sites are shown. Maps published by Guatemala's Tourist Department are lovely to look at but less useful in travel.

*Belize:* The Tourist Board in Belize City has a large tourist map, reasonably priced. In addition to roads and cities it has site plans for Altun Ha and Xunantunich. The address is Belize Tourist Board, P.O. Box 325, Belize City, Belize. Texaco road maps of Guatemala include Belize.

*Honduras:* Texaco road maps of Honduras are available in Honduras at some service stations.

*El Salvador:* Texaco road maps of El Salvador are available in El Salvador at some Texaco Service stations.

## GUIDES—THE PAPER KIND

*Mexico:* As with maps, there are more general guidebooks for Mexico than there are for the Central American republics. Two excellent ones (although there are many others) are *Terry's Guide to Mexico,* by James Norman (Doubleday and Company, Inc.,

Garden City, New York, 1972), and *Fodor's Mexico* (Eugene Fodor, editor, revised annually, David McKay Company, Inc., New York, New York).

For years *Terry's Guide*—the 1972 and, before that, the 1965 edition—has been my bible. I never travel without it. James Norman has collected a wealth of information and admirably presents it. An out-of-date *Terry's* is more useful than current issues of most general guidebooks.

I have also come to like *Fodor's*, which has the advantage of annual revisions and a removable map. Both give excellent information on hotels, restaurants, sights, and so forth. *Terry's* is more accurate on the archaeological information and is better indexed.

The Mexican government's National Institute of Anthropology and History (Instituto Nacional de Antropología e Historia, INAH—pronounced "*een-*ah") publishes excellent small guides to the major archaeological sites of the republic. The availability of these guides is in a constant state of flux, however, and certain issues may be out of print at any given time. If you see one for a site you plan to visit, do not pass up the chance to get it. The guides are not always available at the sites themselves. Check for them at the museum in Mexico City and at hotel and airport bookstores.

Richard Bloomgarden has a series of small guides called *The Easy Guide to . . .*, which cover cities and environs and, recently, specific archaeological sites. They are updated each year and are inexpensive. You will find them useful, even though the site plans are not too clear, and the archaeological data are not always completely accurate.

*Note:* There are no general guidebooks for most of the Central American republics that approach the thoroughness of *Terry's* or *Fodor's*. A few thin volumes are available in the United States and they generally cover all of Central America (occasionally excluding Belize).

The American Automobile Association's *Guide to Mexico and Central America*, available to its members, covers all the countries in this book and the other Central American republics as well. When you get to the country of your choice, you can sometimes find small guides at hotel bookstores.

*Guatemala:* A recent and welcome general guidebook for Guatemala is *Guatemala Guide*, by Paul Glassman (1978). It can be ordered directly from Passport Press, Box 596, Moscow, Vermont 05662. It is up to date and well organized.

Another general guide, *Discover Guatemala for Vacation, Investment, and Retirement*, by Phillip Schaeffer (1974), is published in Guatemala and is available there in bookstores and hotels where tourist publications are sold.

Of crucial interest to the ruin buff is *Tikal: A Handbook of the Ancient Maya Ruins*, by William R. Coe (1969), with a removable map of the site. It is published by the University Museum of the University of Pennsylvania and is available at Tikal and in bookstores in Guatemala. It is well written and profusely illustrated with photographs and drawings. Although larger than most guides to individual sites, it is paperback and small enough to carry with you when you visit the site.

Also well done is *Guide Book to the Ruins of Quiriguá*, by Sylvanus Morley, published by Carnegie Institution of Washington in 1935 and reprinted in 1947. It is still available from the institution. Although the information on getting to Quiriguá is outdated, it makes interesting reading. The data on the site, however, are extensive. Maps and plans are included, as are excellent sharp photos by Jesse L. Nusbaum.

Mixco Viejo, in the highlands near Guatemala City, is the subject of a small guidebook by Henri Lehmann. It is available at the site and sometimes at bookstores in Guatemala City.

*Belize:* Pamplets with tourist information are available from Dee-Jay's Travel Service, P.O. Box 432, Four Queen Street, Belize City, Belize; and Coral Beach Travel Service, P.O. Box 614, 172 North Front Street, Belize City, Belize.

Guides are available for the two major archaeological sites in Belize. The guide for Altun Ha was written by David M. Pendergast (1964), the archaeologist responsible for the recent work at the site, and is nicely printed and illustrated. The Xunantunich guide is less professionally done and is undated. The original text is by A. H. Anderson and was revised by P. J. Schmidt, the former archaeological commissioner of Belize. Both are most useful and are available at the Tourist Board in Belize City.

*Honduras:* There is an excellent guide for Copán by the late archaeologist Jesús Núñez Chinchilla. The title is *Copán Ruins* (1970), and it is available in the town of Copán at the museum, at the Hotel Marina, at the site, and perhaps in bookstores in Tegucigalpa.

*El Salvador:* A volume called *El Salvador*, by Tsuyoshi Nakagawa, is available in El Salvador. It is more a travelogue (with lovely photos), however, than a guidebook with detailed information.

## GUIDES—THE HUMAN KIND

*Type 1:* Whether to hire a guide at the more visited sites is strictly a matter of personal preference. I am speaking here of such sites as Teotihuacán and other four-star sites.

I prefer doing these sites alone. If you have studied the site and are carrying along a guidebook plus a site plan (see below), you will be able to get around and see just as much without help. You can also linger in the spots that interest you most rather than being hurried along. If you are a serious ruin buff and have done your homework, you probably know at least as much as most guides you might hire. If you are less well informed, you won't retain many of their rambling statistics anyway. Nevertheless, on the rare occasions when we have hired a guide at such a site, we have found them pleasant and conscientious. Usually they are also happy to help you carry your excess camera gear.

Guides in this category are bilingual and, at least in Mexico, are bonded by the government. They carry identification to this effect. Rates for a tour of a site are sometimes set by the government and should be discussed beforehand. If the guide has been especially helpful, you may want to include a small tip, although it is not essential.

*Note:* I recommend copying the site plans for the places you intend to visit. Mark any special points of interest, and carry the plans with you. If they get rumpled or torn, they can be copied again.

*Type 2:* At some sites, such as Yaxhá, Chacmultún, and Muyil, if you don't have a specific guidebook or map for the site, a *guardián* or *vigilante*—(pronounced gwahr-dee-*ahn,* vee-hee-*lahn*-teh)—or his young son will offer to show you around, and while their assistance isn't crucial, you will probably see some things that you might miss on your own and will cover the area faster. These guides generally do not speak English, and that is one of the nice things about them. They don't bore you to death with excess information and misinformation. Of course, if you are fluent in Spanish, that may be another matter. What little information you do glean from them you will probably retain, and you can check the accuracy of it later when you return home, if you are interested.

For such guides there is no set price; generally prices are not discussed beforehand, although there is nothing wrong with doing so. Tipping (or better, paying) the guide depends, of course, on the time they spent with you, how helpful they were, and their relative age. An adult who has to use his machete and spend the better part of the day with you would deserve a good deal more than a seven-year-old who entertained you on a tour of an hour. Let your conscience be your guide, but remember that inflation has hit the peso and quetzel as well as the dollar and that what was an appropriate tip (or payment) five years ago will leave you looking like a cheapskate today.

*Type 3:* For certain sites, such as Río Bec, Dos Pilas, Chalcatzingo, and Hochob, a guide is essential just to get you there. The guides are very like those of type 2 mentioned above. They have no set price, they speak no English, and so forth. Tip or pay on the same scale. The only difference is that you are likely to spend more time with these guides, since "getting there" can take more time than visiting the site.

While I try to avoid gross overtipping, I feel it is preferable to err in that direction when in doubt.

## ASKING DIRECTIONS

No matter how many maps and guidebooks you carry along, you will be faced with asking directions—not occasionally, but frequently. You need not be the least bit bashful about doing so. People in this part of the world are extremely friendly and helpful and will do their best to assist you. You often hear that the people, in an effort to please, will make up something if they don't know the answer to your questions. In practice we have seldom found this to be the case, especially if you know how to ask.

Assume that you are at point A and wish to proceed to point Z, (about fifty miles away) and your map shows villages B, C, and D in between. Don't ask whether you are on the right road to Z—the local you are asking may never have heard of a place so far away. Ask if you are on the road to B (the closest spot shown on your map). That he will be familiar with. When you get to B, ask how to get to C, and so on. If the directions you get are lengthy and complicated and your Spanish is less than fluent, listen to the first part only and deliberately forget the rest. Follow the first turn or two (no more) and ask again. This may take a lot of asking, but, believe me, in the long run you'll save time by not having to do a lot of backtracking.

## LANGUAGE

If your goal is only the four-star sites, lack of

Spanish will not be much of a hindrance because guides and key hotel personnel speak English. If you plan to see some of the more remote spots, a little Spanish will help considerably, especially when combined with sign language. Pointing fingers and waving hands can get a lot across in both directions. Don't worry if your pronunciation is a bit off and your grammar less than perfect. The people you are talking to will appreciate your trying. Sprinkle all conversations liberally with *por favor* ("please") and *muchas gracias* ("thank you"). Smile and shake hands a lot, and you will do just fine.

You should, however, at least be able to ask directions and understand the replies. You should also be able to negotiate the cost of a trip, ask for a hotel room, order a meal, and be able to answer questions when crossing an international border. That really doesn't require a lot of Spanish, and if you know more, so much the better; it will make your trip more pleasant.

I recommend carrying one of the small Spanish–English phrase books and dictionaries. Berlitz's is the best known. If you are driving, you will want to know the Spanish for the parts of the car in case you should need a mechanic.

Also helpful is knowing the pronunciations of the names of the sites. How else can you ask to get there? Many of the names are in one of the Indian languages; they may seem like tongue twisters at first, but they can be learned with a little practice. Pronunciation is given for each site in the text, and the local people will politely correct your pronunciation if it is a bit off.

## TRAVEL IN THE RAINY SEASON

The rainy season in Mexico and Central America is roughly from late May to October, with some regional variation. Even in this season the mornings are generally clear. Don't let fear of rain keep you from a visit during that time of year. One of the two times we actually got stuck in the mud and missed seeing a site was in February in Belize, on one of two trips we have made during the dry season. Our other "dry season" trip was to El Salvador in March—and it really was dry and extremely dusty. I then decided that I prefer traveling in the rainy season, although, admittedly, one of the roads we traveled (not to a ruin) may be impassable in the rainy season.

It will be necessary to check locally about the conditions of dirt roads and go in by Jeep or on foot when necessary. Don't be satisfied if you are told that a road is *malo* ("bad"). Ask whether it is *posible* ("possible") to make it in your particular vehicle. Of course it's bad—you already knew that. The point is whether you can *make* it.

If you are roaming around the jungle, you will be soaking wet from perspiration anyway, and a little rain will only cool you off. Just make sure your camera gear is protected.

The only danger in the rainy season is going somewhere, getting a hard shower, and not being able to get out. Use common sense. Many of the unpaved roads are of crushed limestone and drain very rapidly. Others can turn to a sea of mud. Road conditions are covered in the text relating to each site and in "A Note on the Petén and Belize."

## IS IT DANGEROUS?

Two questions we are often asked are, first, "Is it dangerous to travel alone in the remote areas?" I assume the questioner wants to know whether one is in any physical danger from the people. The answer is emphatically no. Maybe we have been inordinately lucky, but we have never felt the least bit threatened or even uncomfortable. In fact, the more remote the area, the nicer the people. Our friends are often surprised that we will take off on foot for miles in the jungle with a guide we have just picked up. What would they do? Chop us to pieces with their machete and steal our camera gear? Not likely.

I admit that I probably would not have attempted that sort of trip on my first one or two visits, but as you get used to the area, you feel more comfortable about trying trips that previously seemed wildly adventurous. Just as in the United States, you are in more danger in the larger cities than in the rural areas.

On the other hand, use common sense, and don't invite trouble. Do not leave luggage or camera gear visible, even in a locked car. Keep the items out of sight in the trunk and keep your car locked whenever you are not in it.

The second question is, "What about snakes?" Yes, there are snakes, but we have run into precious few—no more than half a dozen, and half of those were dead and lying across the highway. When you walk through the jungle, you will be making lots of noise and will effectively scare off most snakes that may be around. You will find insects to be much more of a problem.

## WHAT TO TAKE

*Footgear:* A ruin buff's best friend is good comfortable footgear. Splurge on this. For many of the sites, tennis shoes or the equivalent are adequate. Wear heavy cotton socks for extra comfort. Other sites require heavy-duty equipment. It took me three tries to find the right boots, and until then I preferred tennis shoes for any site. But when you will be walking over muddy trails and climbing over loose rubble, boots are preferred. Mine are ankle high, are made of sturdy brushed leather, and have a padded waterproof lining. I now find that I like them better than tennis shoes for almost any site. Army-surplus jungle boots are ideal for men.

Two things are important. Your boots should not restrict ankle movement, and they should have definite heels to help when you have to dig in to keep from slipping while climbing. They should not be too tight since your feet may swell during long hikes. Wear them with one pair (or two, if you know it's going to be a whole-day affair) of heavy cotton or wool socks.

*Clothing:* The most comfortable clothing is lightweight but fairly sturdy cotton. Denim jeans or khaki work pants are fine. I recommend pants with belt loops whether or not you use a belt (see the section "Camera Gear"). Cotton or cotton-synthetic blends are best for shirts. Those that are 100 percent synthetic are hot as Hades and cling to you uncomfortably when you get wet—which is always. Long sleeves offer more protection from the sun, insects, and thorny bushes while short sleeves are cooler. I use both; it depends on the trip. Make sure your shirts have pockets—the more the better.

*Guayaberas* (shirts worn outside the pants) are available throughout Mexico and Central America. They come with long and short sleeves, in cotton and blends, in sizes for men, women, and children, in various colors, with or without decorations, and generally with four pockets. They are ideal. You will find a few large cotton handkerchiefs or bandanas useful to wipe the sweat from your brow. Facial tissues just won't do.

Bring a lightweight windbreaker for the few occasions when it gets cool in the jungle or when you are traveling by dugout. In the highlands you will need a heavier jacket or sweater at night.

Other items you should have are sunglasses—always—(preferably glare-free) and a sun hat (lightweight and with good ventilation) for the larger, cleared sites.

Some notes for the women: Leave your purse behind in your hotel or out of sight in your locked car. You'll want both hands free for climbing and picture taking. If you insist on a bit of glamour even in the boondocks, use waterproof eye makeup. The other kind will melt off in the first half hour of steamy jungle travel, and even the waterproof kind will not last all day. If your hairdo is wash-and-wear, you'll be more comfortable. If not, carry a wig to wear when you get back to the cities or until you can go to a beauty shop. I have never found a beauty shop that did not do a good job, even when the equipment is more primitive than what I am used to at home.

A note for the men: If you use an electric razor, you'll do fine in most places. If you are going to, say, Tikal, Copán, or Sayaxché for an overnight trip, take along a safety razor. Do the same if you are planning to stay in the Xpuhil area and sleep in your car. In these spots the electricity is either nonexistent or is on only a few hours in the evening. It will never be on when you need it.

*Miscellaneous Gear:* If you are traveling by car (yours or a rented one), by all means take a plastic-foam ice chest. It will repay you a thousandfold. Such chests are becoming available in some of the cities, but it would be safer to bring one from home. Don't worry about it looking silly when you collect your luggage at the airport. Everyone will realize that you are heading for the boondocks. When you are ready to go home, leave the ice chest for the bellboy, maid, or garage attendant at your hotel. You will leave the recipient in ecstasy, and it will have cost you only a few dollars *minus* what you would have to pay in overweight baggage. If you are driving home, keep it for the return trip. Ice, water, and cold drinks whenever you want them can extend your endurance considerably. Ice is available in cities and some smaller towns. Try to keep a supply wherever you go.

Take one or two terry-cloth hand towels. When dipped in the cold water in your ice chest and applied to the face and the back of the neck, they can be incredibly refreshing, especially on long drives and when you return to your car after a few hours of walking.

To get rid of bugs on your windshield, take along a pot cleaner, the sponge kind covered with a plastic-mesh scraper. The sponge holds enough water to make the job easier, and the plastic won't scratch the glass.

You will also want a plastic bottle (one-gallon size) for carrying drinking water. These are available in *tiendas* ("shops") in even the smallest towns. In Yucatán the water is very alkaline. Add the juice of a lime to the water to make it more palatable or carry bottled water. There are times when beer and *refrescos* ("soft drinks") just won't do.

You should carry a small supply of food. Canned

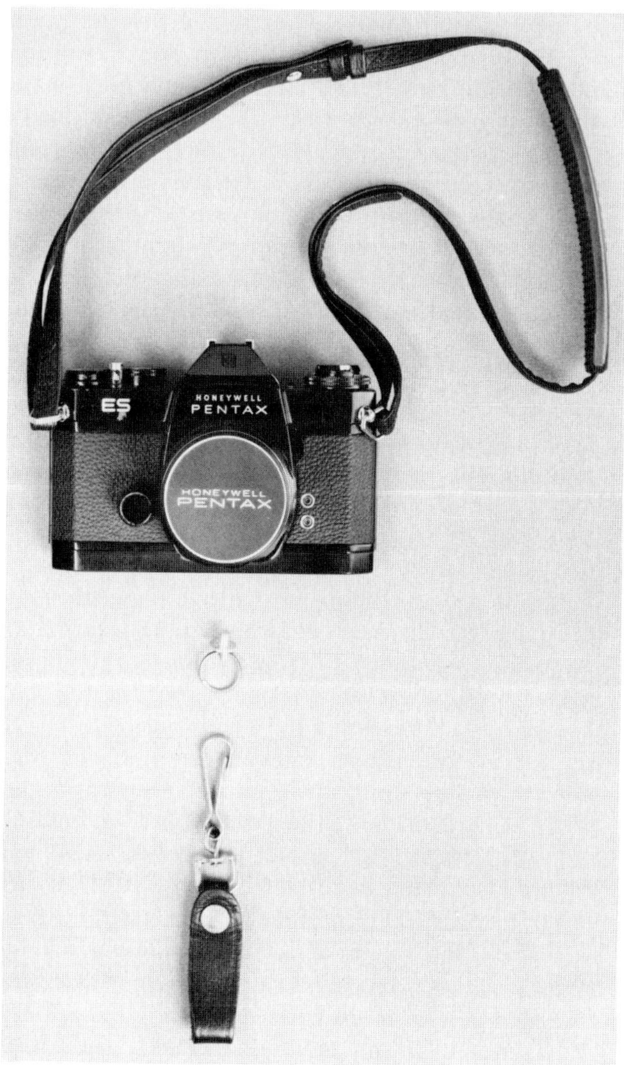


*Top to bottom: Camera. Screw that fits into camera bottom with attached metal loop. Snap clip attached to leather loop to be connected to belt or belt loop. Photographs by Jerry Kelly unless otherwise noted.*

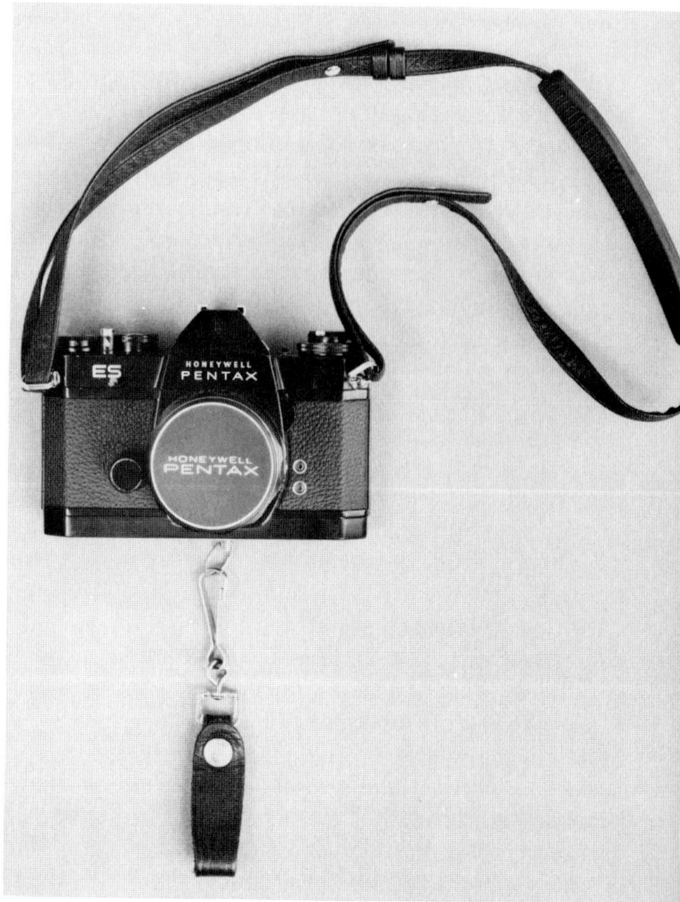


*Camera, screw and metal loop, and snap clip and leather loop, as they should be assembled.*

tuna, deviled ham, and crackers are available everywhere and can be eaten while you are driving if necessary. This supply can be rounded out with packaged chips and sweets and will get you by nicely and safely. They are also easy to carry in a camera bag or backpack if you are on foot. Don't forget a small can opener; better yet, get a good Swiss knife with multiple gadgets including can and bottle openers. The other gadgets will also be useful.

Insect repellent is important for most of the jungle sites and is absolutely essential if you visit the highlands of Guatemala and southern Mexico, where a small, gnatlike creature can drive you wild. We generally carry a spray can or bottle in the car and have extra packets of the repellent-saturated towelettes in our camera bag for use on the trail.

*Camera Gear:* Since every camera buff will have his own favorite equipment (preferably already well tested), only general recommendations are made here. You will have a normal lens, of course, and a telephoto will sometimes be useful; but absolutely essential is a wide-angle lens, especially for the more remote sites. Often it is impossible to back off far enough from a temple to get an over-all shot with a normal lens. My favorite lens is an extreme wide-angle 20-mm. (not a fish-eye). It is also useful for photographing stelae that are lying on the ground. Hold the camera as high as you can and point it down. Who cares if your feet get in the picture—it's better than not getting *any* head-on shots of the carving.

We devised a method of eliminating the feet but

have rarely used it since the monopod needed was generally back in the car. Nevertheless, the method does work. Attach your camera (with a wide-angle lens) to the telescoping monopod at an angle. Hold it over the monument on the ground and get someone to stand on the side to help you get the proper alignment. Use your self-timer and the fastest speed you can to minimize the effect of camera shake, which will be considerable. You will have to prefocus the lens, but you should be able to estimate that accurately enough. You may have to try a couple of times before getting this setup properly adjusted.

If you are visiting a site that requires a long hike and you have a lot of camera gear, carry it in a waterproof backpack. For added protection take a sheet of plastic to cover it. The backpack is more comfortable than a shoulder-strap bag on long hauls.

While we are at a site, we wear the cameras around our necks and attach them to our belts or belt loops, which leaves our hands free for climbing. This way you don't have to worry about an expensive new lens banging against a stone. We attached metal loops to screws that fit into the bottom of the camera—the case may have to be removed. A machinist can make it for you. To our belts we attach a leather loop with a snap. To this is attached a spring-type clip. The clip can be hooked through the loop hanging from the camera. It is easy to engage and disengage (see illustrations). It is extremely helpful, especially if you are carrying more than one camera. The lens caps should be kept in place, except while actually shooting.

Your gear will get dirty, and you should have lens-cleaning liquid, tissue, and brush. Sunshades are a help, and a flash unit can be useful.

Bring your film from home. It is available in the cities and the larger towns, but is more expensive. If you have to buy a roll of color-slide film, however, don't panic at the cost. The cost *includes* processing—even if you lose the envelope that comes with it. The canister is marked and the "Great Yellow Father" will process it for you without extra charge when you get home.

Keep exposed film in its original container and in a plastic bag. Store it in a cool place. Use your ice chest if necessary, and have it processed as soon as possible. Mailing your film home immediately in prepaid mailers is a possibility, but I'd hesitate to trust the mails with valuable film.

In general, photography is freely permitted at the archaeological sites and museums. Exceptions are noted in the text. Tripods may not be used at the archaeological sites and museums in Mexico, and the use of flash equipment is prohibited in some museums. Ask before using it. Avoid taking pictures of military installations in any of the countries.

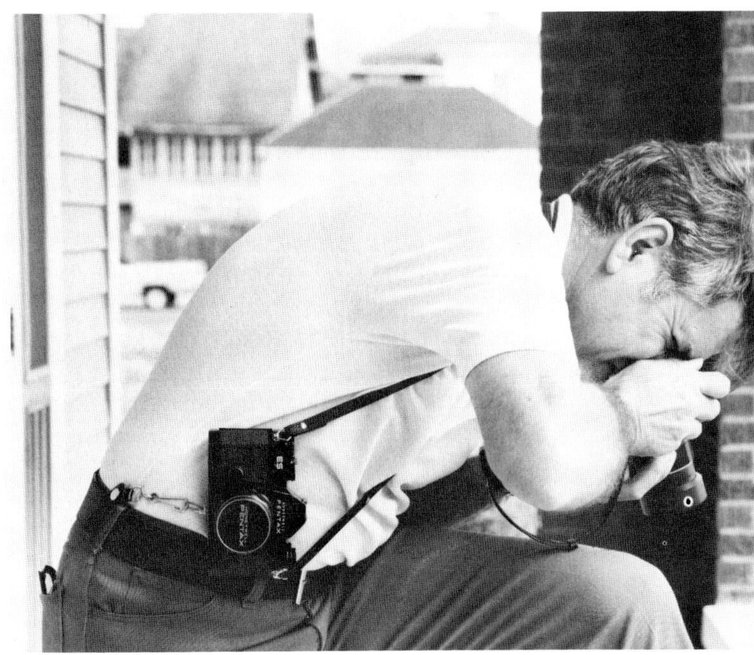

*Camera, screw and metal loop, and snap clip and leather loop, attached to belt. Shown as used. Photograph by author.*

If you are carrying cameras, lenses, tape recorders, or any other equipment of other than United States manufacture, you should have it registered with United States Customs *before* you leave home. You will be given a certified list that you can present upon your return. Otherwise, you may be required to pay duty on them.

## ENTRY REGULATIONS FOR UNITED STATES CITIZENS

*Mexico:* You must have proof of United States citizenship and a tourist card. If you enter Mexico from Belize or Guatemala, you are sometimes asked for proof of sufficient funds to maintain you while you are in the country. You should have your tourist card with you at all times, since officials at certain check points will want to see it. Sometimes you are asked for it when you cash a traveler's check.

*Note:* If you are driving from the United States *through* Mexico and into Central America, you are considered a transient in Mexico, and you should have a transient card rather than a tourist card. Transient cards are available from Mexican consulates in the United States for a small charge. Tourist cards are free and are available from Mexican tourist delegations in major cities in the United States. Both cards can be obtained from immigration offices in Mexico when you enter from the United States.

If you fly from the United States to Mexico, your airline can provide you with a tourist card.

*Belize:* A birth certificate is acceptable, but a passport is encouraged. A tourist card is given you upon entry. Proof of sufficient funds is sometimes required. If you fly in, you need a ticket for ongoing travel.

*Guatemala:* A tourist card is required. It is best also to have your birth certificate.

Guatemala tourist cards are good for two entries into the country. For instance, if you enter Guatemala from Mexico, drive on to El Salvador or Honduras, and reenter Guatemala later, you can retain your tourist card when you leave the first time and use it when you return. Tell them at the immigration station that you will be reentering, and they will allow you to keep your card.

*Honduras:* You must have a properly visaed passport. A birth certificate or voter's registration as proof of United States citizenship is no longer sufficient. A tourist card will be issued to you when you enter the country, whether you drive in or fly in.

*El Salvador:* You will need a tourist card or a visaed passport as well as a birth certificate or other proof of United States citizenship.

*General:* Business travelers are required to use passports, while tourists may use tourist cards (except to enter Honduras). The latter are preferable because less red tape is involved.

When possible, try to get your tourist cards ahead of time. Check with your closest consular office. Regulations tend to change.

Proof of smallpox vaccination is no longer required for entry into Mexico and Central America or reentry into the United States.

Citizens of countries other than the United States should check with the nearest consular office of the countries they plan to visit for current requirements.

## AUTO INSURANCE AND INTERNATIONAL CROSSINGS

If you are driving your own car in Mexico and Central America, get insurance coverage for those countries; your United States policy is not valid. Three separate policies are needed, one for Mexico, a package for Central America (excluding Belize), and the third for Belize.

Sanborn's, one of the best-known agents, can provide a policy for Mexico and the Central American package. The company has several offices in the United States near the Mexican border. If you want your policy (or policies) ahead of time, write to Sanborn's Mexican Insurance Service, P.O. Box 1210, McAllen, Texas 78501. They will also give you excellent road logs for your trip.

The American Automobile Association will provide coverage for its members for Mexico and Central America (except Belize). Most of its United States offices can give you coverage for Mexico, and the offices in Brownsville, Laredo, and El Paso can also write a Central American package. The address in Brownsville is 2534 Central Boulevard, Brownsville, Texas 78520. Your local AAA office can give you the addresses of the other two.

Insurance is mandatory in Belize and can be bought *only in Belize.* If you enter Belize from Guatemala, you can get a policy at Ruby's Saloon, near the Belize Immigration Station. If you enter from Mexico, Gevy's Restaurant and Bar, across the street from the immigration station, can give you coverage for Belize. A Sanborn's office is nearby that can provide you with a Central American package.

If you fly in and rent a car, your rental agent can give you coverage for the country where you rented it. If it is one of the countries covered by the Central American package, you are also covered for the other countries included in that package but not for Mexico or Belize, for which you must buy separate policies from other agents.

When you are taking a rented car across an international frontier, you must have a letter from the rental agency saying that you have its permission to do so. Hertz is prepared to give you a letter that will specify the length of time you expect to be out of the country where you rented the vehicle. Other agents are not as well prepared for this sort of paper work. No rental agent will allow you to rent a car in one country and drop it off in another.

Crossing internation borders by car is always a bit of a hassle. I'm never sure which desk to proceed to next or what documents the officials will want to see, and no one seems to be eager to tell me what to do. It can be frustrating, but, remember, it probably won't lose you more than an hour if you arrive during regular hours and the station is not too crowded. Some helpful information on procedures is covered in Sanborn's logs, though sometimes procedures change.

The border stations are generally open from 8:00 or 9:00 A.M. to 5:00 or 6:00 P.M. and close for lunch between 12 noon and 2:00 P.M. (weekdays). They are generally open in the mornings only on Saturday and are closed on Sundays and holidays. You may cross at other times for an extra charge.

Sometimes small fees are charged for entering or leaving a country, for fumigating tires, and so on. The fees vary from country to country, and requirements change.

## SERVICE STATIONS AND CAR REPAIRS

Service stations are not as numerous in Mexico and Central America as they are in the United States, but with a little planning you should have no trouble. State and department capitals and larger towns generally have gas, as do smaller towns on highway junctions. In the less heavily visited areas, fill up at every opportunity. Unusually long stretches without gas are mentioned in the text. In some places you may have to get gas from a drum. Don't let that bother you—it is just as good as gas out of a modern pump. When there are power failures, the modern pumps don't work, and you may have to hand-pump your own.

There are mechanics even in the small towns—look for a sign saying Taller Mecánico. They can handle minor repairs on the spot with only a minimum of equipment. If your problems are major, of course, you'll have to get to the nearest large town or city.

Drive carefully and avoid night driving. The hazards include people walking along the edge of the road, cattle occupying the center of the road, and slow-moving vehicles without taillights.

## ARCHAEOLOGICAL SITES AND ARTIFACTS

Fees for entry into the archaeological sites and museums are minimal or nonexistent. They will be your smallest expense. In Guatemala and El Salvador there is no charge; in Belize, and Honduras a small fee. In Mexico the fee varies with the site, and Sundays are sometimes free. Remote sites are free. Sites are generally open during the daylight hours. They close at 5:00 P.M. in Belize. Check locally if in doubt.

All the countries covered in this guide have laws prohibiting the removal of pre-Columbian artifacts. These items are considered part of the national patrimony, and United States Customs is now cooperating in preventing the entry of such items into the United States.

Looting of the ancient sites has reached alarming proportions, and all governments are enforcing their regulations more stringently to halt this illegal traffic. An incredible amount of information is lost to the world of archaeology because of this illicit digging and thievery. High-quality reproductions, sold as such, are available in Mexico City and in Guatemala City.

## A NOTE ON SITE NAMES AND HEADINGS

The current name of each site is listed at the beginning of each section. Derivation of the current name is listed for the sites where the information is available. If the derivation heading is not included, I was unable to find the information. Sometimes sites are simply named for the closest town, such as Castillo de Teayo and Playa del Carmen If earlier names are known, they are also listed. In a few cases where the original name is known, that is likewise mentioned. If it has been established that the original name is "unknown"—for instance, Tikal—then that is mentioned. If the heading "Original Name" is omitted, it means that I was unable to learn the original name and it is probably "unknown."

The culture with which each site is identified is given for the sites where it has been clearly defined. For sites that are primarily identified with one culture but have received strong influence from, or were occupied at some point by, another culture, only the major culture is listed in the heading, followed by "see text."

Some sites are not clearly identified with a specific culture, but often were influenced by one or more cultures. In these cases the culture heading is followed by "see text." In a few instances it has not been determined with which of two cultures a site should be properly identified; both are given, separated by "or."

The general location of the site is given at the beginning of each section. An exact location is given later in the section under "Connections."

## MUSEUM NAMES

In each museum section the formal name of the museum is listed first, followed by the popular name when it differs from the formal name. The popular name generally indicates the city or site of the museum. When it does not, the city is listed after the popular name.

The popular name is used in the Contents, in the "List of Sites and Museums by Country and Ratings," in the photograph captions, and in the text.

GLOSSARY

Many specialized words and foreign words and names of deities are used in the text. Those that occur frequently are explained in the Glossary at the end of the book. Those used infrequently are explained in the text.

## *The Rating System*

As soon as I decided to write this guide, I also decided to attempt a system of rating the sites. It seemed to me that it would provide useful information in a nutshell for the prospective visitor.

I wrote up a list of sites and museums and an explanation of the rating system and dispatched copies to several knowledgeable friends, both professionals and dedicated ruin buffs. Everyone I queried had visited quite a number of sites and had a good general background on the subject. When the rating sheets were returned, I was pleased by the general agreement of the scores and, frankly, a bit surprised at how close they were. While I attempted no statistical analysis of the data, it was obvious that the idea of rating was valid.

Since the participants rated only those sites that they had personally visited, the ratings for specific sites reflect the opinion of differing numbers of people. On some sites I had twelve votes (including mine and my husband's), and on others only the two of us made the decision. Nevertheless, my own ratings—determined before the others were tabulated—were so close to the rest that I feel safe in using them.

I did occasionally run into a problem on certain sites that no one else rated. A few seemed to be better than the average two-star site but not as good as the average three-star site. When this happened, mention is made of it in the text. I decided that this procedure was preferable to confusing the situation by introducing a two-and-a-half-star category.

RATINGS

★★★★ An absolute must for the ruin buff and of great interest to the average visitor.

★★★ Very important for the enthusiast and of some interest to the tourist.

★★ Of some importance and interest to the ruin buff, especially if it can be combined with visits to nearby three- and four-star sites. Not too interesting for others.

★ Only for superdedicated ruin buffs. "Average tourists," please ignore.

No stars Of minor importance. If you are absolutely avid about ruins, are passing right by, and have a little time, you might want to spend five minutes and get a couple of pictures.

The rating does not necessarily indicate the relative importance of a site in ancient times but reflects a combination of factors, of which relative importance is one. Other considerations are the degree of preservation or restoration and ease of access compared to the visual rewards received. For instance, Uaxactún is rated one star even though archaeologically it is a most important site and the one upon which Maya chronology is based. One interesting structure has been recently restored there—the rest are overgrown—but the site is difficult to get to. Uaxactún and other visually exciting but hard-to-reach sites would receive a higher rating if access were easier.

Another example is Dzibilchaltún, which is rated two stars. This large site, with an almost continuous occupation of two thousand years, is of immense importance in the archaeological record and is easy to get to, but since very little restoration has been done, the visual rewards are limited.

# LIST OF SITES AND MUSEUMS BY COUNTRY AND RATINGS

## Mexico

*Above all ratings:*

Mexico City Museum

*Four stars* ★★★★

Chichén Itzá
El Tajín
Jalapa Museum
La Venta Park Museum (Villahermosa)
Mitla
Monte Albán
Oaxaca Museum (Oaxaca City)
Palenque
Teotihuacán
Tulum
Uxmal
Villahermosa Museum

*Three stars* ★★★

Becan
Bonampak
Campeche Museum (Campeche City)
Chacmultún
Chicanná
Cholula
Cobá
Comalcalco
Cuernavaca Museum
Dainzú
Etzna
Izapa
Kabáh
Kohunlich
Labná
Malinalco
Mayapán
Palenque Museum
Sayil
Tamayo Museum (Oaxaca City)
Teotihuacán Museum
Tula
Xochicalco
Xpuhil
Yagul
Yaxchilán

*Two stars* ★★

Acancéh
Aké
Archaeological Museum in Situ (San Miguel de Allende)
Balankanche (Cave)
Calixtlahuaca
Castillo de Teayo
Chalcatzingo
Chinkultic
Cholula Museum
Cuicuilco
Dzibilchaltún
Dzibilchaltún Museum
Dzibilnocac
El Tajín Museum
Hochob
Hormiguero
Huamelulpan
Huamelulpan Museum
Ikil
Ixtlán del Río
La Quemada
Lambityeco
Loltún (Cave)
Mérida Museum
Mitla Museum
Monte Albán Museum
Mul-Chic
Muyil
Na Bolom Museum (San Cristóbal de las Casas)
Quiahuiztlán
Río Bec B
Santa Cecilia
Santa Cecilia Museum
Santiago Tuxtla Museum
Tampico Alto Museum
Tamuín
Tenayuca
Teopanzolco
Tepozteco
Tepoztlán Museum
Tizatlán
Tlatelolco
Toniná

Toniná Museum
Tres Zapotes Museum
Tula Museum
Tzintzuntzan
Xkichmook
Xlapak
Zaachila
Zempoala

*One star* ★

Chakalal
Chiapa de Corzo
Cozumel Museum (San Miguel de Cozumel)
Culucbalom
El Cedral
Huexotla
Huitzo
Ihuatzio
Isla Mujeres
Itzimté
Izamal
La Venta
Manos Rojas
Oxkintok
Payán
Playa del Carmen
Puerto Rico
Tancah
Temple 1
Temple 3 (El Real)
Tlapacoya
Tohcok
Xcaret
Xcavil de Yaxché
Xelha
Yalku
Yaxché-Xlapak
Zempoala Museum

*No stars*

Akumal
Cobá-Yaxuná Sacbé
Cuicuilco Museum
"La Ruinita"
Limones
Temple 2
Temple 4

## Guatemala

*Four stars* ★★★★

Guatemala City Museum
Tikal

*Three stars* ★★★

La Democracia Plaza
Mixco Viejo
Quiriguá
Seibal
Tikal Museum
Zaculeu

*Two stars* ★★

Chichicastenango Museum
Finca El Baúl
Finca Pantaleón
Iximché
Kaminaljuyú
Utatlán
Yaxhá
Zaculeu Museum

*One star* ★

Aguateca
Dos Pilas
La Democracia Museum
Topoxté
Uaxactún

## Belize (British Honduras)

*Three stars* ★★★

Altun Ha
Xunantunich

*One star* ★

Belize Museum (Belize City)

*No stars*

Floral Park

## Honduras

*Four stars* ★★★★

Copán

*Three stars* ★★★

Copán Museum

*Two stars* ★★

Tegucigalpa Museum

## El Salvador

*Three stars* ★★★

San Salvador Museum
Tazumal

*Two stars* ★★

Campana-San Andrés
Tazumal Museum

*One star* ★

Cihuatán
Quelepa

*No stars*

Casa Blanca

# PART TWO : *The Sites and Museums*

## MEXICO

### Northern, Western, and Central

*The 200-ton sculpture generally called Tlaloc, Mexico City Museum. Carved near the village of Coatlinchán and moved to its present location in 1964. Probably Classic period.*

# *The National Museum of Anthropology (Mexico City Museum)*

The Mexico City Museum is probably the finest of its type in the world and so far surpasses any other museum in this guide that I made the decision not to use the rating system. If this museum were rated four stars, then the Guatemala City Museum and the excellent regional museums in Mexico would have to receive a lower rating, which would not give a fair idea of their worth.

The Mexico City Museum is indeed in a class by itself. Even the visitor who does not generally care for museums and who is not particularly interested in ancient or modern cultures cannot fail to be impressed by this one. For the ruin buff, it is like a visit to heaven. The only problem is that there is so much to see that you are torn between lingering over each exhibit and hurrying on to the next fascinating section.

For the most casual tourist a good half day is needed for a visit. The ruin buff could spend months here. I would suggest a once-over-lightly on your first visit to get an idea of the layout, then several return trips to absorb properly what is presented. This way you can pay special attention to the sections that interest you most. I have visited the museum on five occasions but do not feel that I have begun to cover it thoroughly.

There are several guidebooks in English for the museum, ranging widely in price. They are available at the museum bookstore, as are other archaeological publications in Spanish, English, French, and German.

## HISTORY OF THE COLLECTION

In 1790, while the Plaza Mayor (Zócalo) in Mexico City was being paved, three monumental Aztec sculptures were uncovered: the now famous Aztec Calendar, or Sun Stone; the statue of Coatlicue; and the monument to the victories of Tizoc. The first was placed beside the cathedral, and the others were installed at the university.

In 1825, Mexican historian Lucas Alamán organized the first legally established National Museum at the university, and more pieces were collected. This first museum included pre-Hispanic and colonial period materials, as well as exhibits of natural history. The collections grew, and the space soon became inadequate.

In 1865, Archduke Maximilian gave the old mint (Casa de Moneda) to the National Museum to house its materials.

The natural science and colonial-period collections were removed to other quarters some time later, while the archaeological specimens remained at the Casa de Moneda. In 1947 the exhibits were reorganized, and the building's interior was modernized. The displays still left a lot to be desired, and the shortcomings eventually led to the creation of the remarkable museum in Chapultepec Park.

## MUSEUM STATISTICS

Once the decision was made to build a new museum, many lengthy studies were undertaken. Pedro Ramírez Vásquez was selected as the principal architect, and his design of the huge umbrellalike roof with a single support is truly outstanding. This freestanding cantilever-type roof, the largest in the world, covers an area of over 70,000 square feet and protects part of the central patio. It is made of aluminum and weighs 2,000 tons.

A single column, 40 feet high, supports the roof. The column, sheathed in sculptured copper, depicts pre-Columbian motifs; it was designed by Mexican artist José Chávez Morado. Around the column is a shower of water—a sort of raining fountain.

Part of the patio is occupied by a large, reed-garnished reflecting pool whose focal point is a huge stylized conch shell symbolizing the wind. This and the other Indian elements of water and earth are admirably fused to accomplish the architect's goal of combining function with pre-Columbian folklore.

The exhibit rooms surround the patio, and each has individual access, allowing the visitor to select any path he chooses. Benches provide a resting place for the visitor in a parklike setting that achieves the indoor-outdoor experience sought by its designers.

There are over 400,000 square feet of covered area, including exhibition space, offices, auditorium, bookstore, and restaurant, and almost as much open patio and plaza space. The library contains some

12 million documents and a quarter of a million books, with space for twice that many. It draws about 1,500 students a day, while the museum itself attracts about a million visitors a year.

Of all the statistics associated with this building, perhaps the most incredible is that its construction—from groundbreaking to inauguration and opening in September, 1964—took only a brief nineteen months. Its cost was about $20 million.

## OUTSIDE THE MUSEUM

Before entering the museum, you will want to stop for a look at the two-hundred-ton sculpture near the entrance. The identity of this figure is still a bit controversial. It is popularly called Tlaloc, the rain god, but most authorities believe it is more likely Chalchihuitlicue, his female counterpart, the water goddess. She is variously listed as his wife, sister, or mother. Earlier the sculpture was thought to date to Aztec times; however, some scholars now date it to the period of Teotihuacán. Carmen Cook de Leonard, who undertook a comparative study of the statue, believes it to represent a sun god intended for placement on the Pyramid of the Sun at Teotihuacán.

The statue was carved near the village of Coatlinchán (about 17 miles east of the center of Mexico City), where its sculptors left it attached to bedrock. It is assumed that they lacked the engineering skill to remove and transport it. In 1964 it was cut loose and moved to its present location on special flatbed trucks.

During the 18-hour trip from old home to new, an unseasonable rainstorm occurred. It was April—during the dry season. The statue had hardly been put in place when a second storm broke. That was enough to convince the general populace that indeed the statue did represent Tlaloc. Otherwise, why did it rain?

## THE MUSEUM PROPER

The main entrance to the museum is at ground level. That level houses the archaeological exhibits surrounding the patio described above. It also contains an area for temporary exhibits, an auditorium, a bookstore, and a checkroom.

Above this level, on the second floor, are the ethnographical section, the library, and an area occupied by the National School of Anthropology and History.

A basement level houses a restaurant, which can be reached from the stairways on either side of the adjoining Halls 11 and 12.

Just as you enter the museum, you will see the dais of the orientation theater. You enter at this level but go downstairs to the theater proper. There is a small charge for the twenty-minute film (in Spanish), which presents the history of mankind in Mesoamerica in chronological order beginning with man's arrival in the Valley of Mexico thousands of years ago.

The museum was designed with a particular visiting sequence in mind for best and most rapid comprehension, and that is the one presented here. As you enter the ground level, go to your right to Hall 1—Introduction to Anthropology. Circulate in a counterclockwise direction through this hall and the following ones completely around the patio. This takes you through Hall 2—Mesoamerica; Hall 3—Origins; Hall 4—Preclassic Central Highlands; Hall 5—Teotihuacán; Hall 6—the Toltec; Hall 7—(at the far end of the patio) the Mexica (Aztec); Hall 8—the Cultures of Oaxaca; Hall 9—the Gulf Coast Cultures; Hall 10—the Maya; Hall 11—the North of Mexico, and Hall 12—Western Mexico.

To begin your tour of the ethnographical section on the next level, return to Hall 1 and take the stairway up. It leads to Hall 13—the introductory hall to this section. Continue again in a counterclockwise direction. Next are Hall 14—Cora-Huichol Indians; Hall 15—Tarascan; Hall 16—Otomí; Hall 17—Puebla; Hall 18—Oaxaca; Hall 19—Gulf Coast Cultures; Hall 20—Maya; Hall 21—Northwestern Mexico, and Hall 22—the Salon of Indigenous Arts. The last hall displays Mexico's contributions to architecture, the visual arts and crafts, literature, and dance throughout its pre-Hispanic, colonial, and modern periods.

If you prefer to have a guide, ask for one at the desk when you buy your ticket. Tours in various languages begin frequently.

Since it would take a volume the size of this book to describe the multitudinous exhibits in the museum, only a general summary will be given here. The museum is so well laid out that, if you follow the path indicated, you won't miss anything and will do little or no backtracking.

The ground-floor exhibits include original ceramics and sculpture in various materials; where copies are displayed, they are plainly labeled. The smaller pieces are in glass cases, the larger on platforms or pedestals. There are many scale models of reconstructed ancient cities, maps, dioramas, murals, and charts. There are displays of carved

*Stucco mask panel from southern Campeche or Quintana Roo, Mexico City Museum. The panel is similar to the mask panels at Kohunlich, Quintana Roo. Maya Culture, Late Classic period. Photograph by author.*

jade, flint and obsidian tools, and figurines. All are well labeled in Spanish and dramatically lighted. There is even a full-scale copy of part of the Temple of Quetzalcóatl at Teotihuacán shown in the full color of the original.

Several of the halls have adjacent outdoor exhibits (Halls 4, 5, 6, 9, and 10). You will want to be sure to see all of them. The most interesting, however, are the replicas of the Maya architecture and sculpture outside Hall 10 and the colossal Olmec head outside Hall 9. Two halls have basement sections. These are reconstructions of tombs and are found in Hall 8 (Tomb 7 at Monte Albán) and Hall 10 (Tomb under the Temple of Inscriptions at Palenque).

In the basement section of Hall 10 is a small theater that shows a short movie (in Spanish) about the Maya Calendar.

The second-floor ethnographical exhibits include displays of art, crafts, costumes, customs, dance, and daily life of the various present-day ethnic groups in the republic. These areas are explored, explained, and depicted with artifacts, photographs, graphs, and charts. Folk music typical of each area is played in each of the halls.

Restrooms are conveniently situated in various locations on all levels.

## MISCELLANEOUS NOTES

The museum is closed on Mondays.

Wheelchairs are provided for those who need them, and the gentle slope of the ramps and elevators were designed with this in mind.

There are two large parking lots near the museum.

You are generously allowed to photograph the exhibits; however, tripods are prohibited. The dramatic illumination will make you want to take many pictures. Bring fast film, of course, and the fastest lens you own. A polarizing filter will help cut down the glare on objects in glass cases but reduces the effective film speed.

Since there are indoor and outdoor exhibits, if you use color film you'll need two cameras—one with daylight film and one with film balanced for tungsten illumination—unless you don't mind an orange cast to your tungsten-lighted objects (somehow I don't) or excessive blueness in your outdoor shots (which I do object to). You can also get some great black-and-whites.

The museum can be easily reached by private car, peso cab, regular taxi, bus, or metro (subway) from almost anywhere in Mexico City.

*Front (west) side of the Palace, La Quemada. Early Postclassic period.*

★★

# *La Quemada*

(lah keh-*mah*-dah)

# *(Chicomoztoc)*

(chee-koh-*mohs*-tohk)

DERIVATIONS: *La Quemada* is Spanish for "The Burned One." The site was named after a nearby hacienda. *Chicomoztoc* means "Seven Caves" and is the name of a legendary place from which the Aztec and other Nahua tribes claim to have come.

EARLIER NAME: Tuitlán.

ORIGINAL NAME: Unknown.

CULTURE: Chalchihuites or Malpaso.

LOCATION: East-central part of the state of Zacatecas, Mexico.

---

## THE SITE

The hilltop-fortress site of La Quemada is in a rather arid zone at an elevation of about 6,500 feet. The northwest part of the hill is surrounded by a stone wall.

There are three areas of major importance at the site for the visitor:

1. Southwest of the parking area (on the lower level of the hill) is an architectural complex called the Palace or the Cathedral. It is composed of a large platform supporting a building with eleven huge columns and a western stair facing a large open plaza. The entrance to the building is flanked by two more columns. The columns are made of slablike stones, as are the remaining walls of the structure; the dimensions of both are truly impressive. On the northwest exterior corner of the Palace is a passageway with a corbeled vault. There are remains of small structures in the plaza that today are simply rubble mounds.

2. A short distance north of the Palace and on the same level is a small platform with a southern stair that leads to a ball court. It is one of only two ball courts known in the northern area of Mesoamerica and is by far the more impressive. At the north end of the ball court is an unusually steep, plain-sided pyramid, the lower portion of which has been restored, including a southern stair. The top of the pyramid is missing, and at one time it was thought that this was a true nontruncated pyramid. The pyramid is sometimes called the Votive Pyramid or the Temple of the Sun.

3. The next area of interest lies west of the Votive Pyramid, on the upper levels and the top of the hill. It is called the Citadel or Acropolis, and it includes a number of structures. Easily followed foot trails lead up the hillside, and the climb is not too difficult. I recommend climbing to the top, stopping along the way to see the various buildings and catch your breath.

Partway up the hill you can look down on a large courtyard surrounded on all four sides by platforms (or remains of some low construction). Higher up are remains of many interconnecting rooms that almost form a maze.

Near the top of the hill is an open sunken courtyard with a stepped pyramid—locally called the Temple of Sacrifices—on the north side. The pyramid has an inset stairway on the south side, which faces a small rectangular two-tiered altar and a nearby circular structure in the plaza. The other three sides of the courtyard have stairs leading to the lower level. Remains of high walls border the east and south sides of the courtyard and were part of structures that must have been two stories high. On a still higher level, northeast of the Temple of Sacrifices, is another structure with a steep south stair flanked by balustrades. This building, locally called La Terraza, is perched on a portion of the top of the hill. From atop La Terraza there are great views of the courtyard and its surrounding structures and of the Palace and the Votive Pyramid far below. Bring along a telephoto lens for good shots of the Palace from various places on the hill and a wide-angle lens for over-all views of the upper courtyard.

In addition to the structures already described, there are others on the hill that are in a more ruinous condition. Roadways extending out from La Quemada and leading to smaller sites have also been discovered.

La Quemada occupies the northern periphery of what we know today as Mesoamerica. Less advanced peoples lived beyond its frontiers, and they are not considered to have been part of Mesoamerican civilization.

It is possible that La Quemada had beginnings as early as the Early Classic period, but it is more

*Southwest corner of the Votive Pyramid, La Quemada. Early Postclassic period.*

certain that the culture that built the site was in the area during the Late Classic period. La Quemada's heyday, however, was in the Early Postclassic, and the strongest influence it received was Toltec. The greatest concentration of occupation was A.D. 900 to A.D. 1000, though the site remained active for many years after. By 1350 to 1400 Mesoamerican culture had deserted the area, and La Quemada was depopulated. There is archaeological evidence that at the end of its period of occupation the site was burned.

La Quemada is generally listed as belonging to the Chalchihuites culture (or the neighboring Malpaso culture), and the site is thought to have been deliberately constructed to defend the frontier of Mesoamerica against the less advanced groups on the north.

## RECENT HISTORY

La Quemada was visited by early Spanish explorers. A letter dated 1535 gives a description of the site and mentions that it was unoccupied. In 1650, Fray

*Over-all view of the fortified hilltop called the Citadel, La Quemada. The Votive Pyramid is on the far right. Early Postclassic period.*

*View from the Citadel looking southeast, La Quemada. The Votive Pyramid is on the left, a maze of rooms on a lower level of the Citadel is at the right of center, and the distant Palace is above. The ball court is seen as a line running between the Votive Pyramid and the Palace. Early Postclassic period.*

Antonio Tello, in a history of Nueva Galicia, (northwestern Mexico), described the site. He used the name Tuitlán for La Quemada.

In the 1830s a map of the Malpaso Valley was made by the mining engineer C. de Berghes; it showed La Quemada and other sites. It was published in part in 1839 along with a description of the site by Carlos Nebel. Thirty years later a map of La Quemada itself was published by Edmond Guillemín Tarayre.

Early-twentieth-century visitors who described the site were Leopoldo Batres, Eduardo Noguera, and Agustín García Vega, who also cleared much of the site.

La Quemada was excavated by Carlos Margain and Hugo Moedano and later by Pedro Armillas in the mid-twentieth century. In 1955 the lower stairway of the Votive Pyramid was reconstructed by José Corona Núñez, and in 1963 additional work was carried out by Armillas, who directed a group from Southern Illinois University.

## CONNECTIONS

1. 30 miles by paved road from Zacatecas to the cutoff, or
2. 169 miles by paved road from Guadalajara to the cutoff, then 1.6 miles of good blacktop and rock road to the site.

## GETTING THERE

From Zacatecas go northwest on Highway 45 for 4 miles, to the junction with Highway 54. At the junction take Highway 54 southwest for 26 miles to the cutoff. The cutoff is marked with a sign saying "Ruinas de Chicomoztoc" and heads east to the site. Driving time from Zacatecas to La Quemada is about 40 minutes.

From Guadalajara head north on Highway 54 to the cutoff and on to the site. Driving time is about 4 hours.

Other possible stopovers are Durango (202 miles), Aguascalientes (111 miles), and San Luis Potosí (146 miles). Paved roads connect all these cities to Highway 54 and the junction for La Quemada.

The parking area is about 100 yards from the lower level of the ruins.

There is no food at La Quemada, but lukewarm soft drinks are available. Tennis shoes are fine. Allow about two hours for a visit—that will give you time to climb to the top of the hill and take a look at a few fragments of stucco floors and walls from the site, housed in the office, where tickets are sold. A guide is not necessary.

*View of the circular building from the northeast, Ixtlán del Río. Postclassic period.*

★★

# *Ixtlán del Río*

(eesh-*tlahn* dehl *ree*-oh)

DERIVATION: *Ixtlán* is Nahuatl for "Where There Is Obsidian"; *del Río* is Spanish for "of the River."

ORIGINAL NAME: Unknown.

CULTURE: See text.

LOCATION: Southern part of the state of Nayarit, Mexico.

## THE SITE

As you enter the site of Ixtlán del Río, proceed to the end of the road and park near the circular structure—the best-known and best-preserved building at the site.

This structure rises in two tiers and has projecting access stairways rising in two levels on the east and west sides. The stairs are flanked by balustrades, and vertical upper zones still remain on those on the second level. The wall that forms the upper level of the structure has cross-shaped perforations as decorations around the circumference. Enclosed within the wall are two rectangular platforms, each with a single stair. The stairs of these structures face each other, and each has balustrades with vertical upper zones. The platforms are made of cut-stone slabs, and the same material is used in the circular portion of the structure along with boulders and stone blocks.

Northeast of the circular structure and connected to it by a cobblestone walkway is a rectangular building with an eastern stair. The building sits on a three-tiered platform, and the remains of the lower walls and rectangular columns can still be seen. Of special interest here is a carved slab on the south face of the structure near the west end. It is set at an angle between the second and third tiers of the platform. Although another carved slab is reported from this structure, we did not see it.

A similar structure with rectangular columns lies southeast of the one just described. On the north is a small rectangular platform with a western stair that faces the structure with the carved slab. Another small two-tiered platform is found south of the circular structure.

From this area you can drive back toward the highway and park near the other buildings of interest. Most impressive in this second area is a large L-shaped building resting on a low platform. Except for the circular structure, this seems to be the most elaborate building at the site. There are remains of many rectangular columns, and in one area a low stair leads to what appears to be an inner chamber.

West of the L-shaped structure is another small two-tiered platform, this one with stairs on all four sides. Beyond it on the west is another platform.

While Ixtlán del Río is not one of Mexico's more spectacular sites, it is one of the most interesting ones in the western part of the republic and is certainly worth a visit if you are passing nearby.

During the Early Classic period—and perhaps as far back as the Preclassic—an unusual type of shaft tomb was constructed in the area around Ixtlán del Río and as far south as southern Colima; some tombs have been found on the outskirts of the site itself. There has been no stratigraphic work at Ixtlán del Río, but a surface collection of ceramics has failed to turn up evidence for this early period, although it is represented at nearby sites.

The Late Classic occupation of Ixtlán del Río is also a matter of question. The picture is clearer for the Postclassic period, the major period at the site. The remains seen today at Ixtlán del Río date to that period, but it is unknown whether the site was still occupied at the time of the Spanish conquest. There is evidence of some influence from central Mexico during the Early Postclassic period.

## RECENT HISTORY

Although there has been some restoration of the architectural remains at Ixtlán del Río, little intensive work has been carried out, and even that has been intermittent.

In 1950, E. W. Gifford published a paper based on his collection of surface sherds, and two years later José Corona Núñez described one of the site's structures. E. Contreras worked at the site and in 1966 reported on the reconstruction of some of the architecture.

The art of the Ixtlán del Río region is well known to collectors, however. Many large, hollow ceramic figures from the area are in private collections and probably come from looted tombs. Several types are represented; Gifford believes that they date to the phase called Early Ixtlán (Late Preclassic and Early Classic periods).

## CONNECTIONS

1. 84 miles by paved road from Guadalajara to the cutoff, or
2. 55 miles by paved road from Tepic to the cutoff, then 0.3 mile of fair dirt road to the site.

## GETTING THERE

From Guadalajara take Highway 15 west to the cutoff, which is a little past (west of) the kilometer 135 marker. The cutoff heads north (right) and is marked with a sign indicating the archaeological zone. If you come in this way, you will reach the cutoff for the site before you reach the town of Ixtlán del Río. From Tepic take Highway 15 southeast to the cutoff and on to the site.

Shortly after you take the cutoff you will cross a railroad track; continue straight ahead to the site.

No refreshments are available at the site—bring your own. Allow an hour for a visit. Tennis shoes are fine since the site is kept cleared. A guide is not necessary.

Other possible stopovers are Mazatlán (236 miles), San Blas (100 miles), and Puerto Vallarta (160 miles via Tepic or about 20 miles less if you take the toll road and bypass Tepic).

A bus can drop you off at the cutoff.

★★

# *Archaeological Museum in Situ (San Miguel de Allende)*

CULTURE: See text.
LOCATION: San Miguel de Allende, on campus of Allende Institute, in the east-central part of the state of Guanajuato, Mexico.

---

## THE SITE

I was not sure whether to list this spot as a site or as a museum. It is actually both. The final decision was to treat it as a site since some of the remains are in situ.

There are three burials in a sort of pit a few feet below the floor level of the museum. In one burial the skeletal and ceramic remains have been left untouched except for the removal of a top layer of dirt. In the other two burials the pottery was carefully removed, cleaned, restored, and replaced in the locations assumed to be the original ones. This gives the visitor a good idea of how the burials looked when first excavated, as well as how the objects were placed originally. There are also skeletal remains—mostly in situ—in the burials with the restored pots. During excavation ten other burials were encountered, and artifacts from some of them are in display cases in the museum.

As far as can be determined, all the interred were adults, but the skeletal remains were not sufficiently well preserved to determine the sex or age of the individuals.

One especially interesting discovery was a skull found in association with some obsidian blades and a ceramic pipe. The skull was apparently a secondary burial, and the blades were found at its base. It could not be determined whether the blades were placed at the base of the skull at the time of interment or whether there was a postinterment shift in the soil, which caused the close association. A relative dating of the obsidian is planned when equipment becomes available.

Three or four *florero*-style ceramic vessels were found in the burials. They relate to the type produced at Teotihuacán during the Early Classic period. On the basis of these finds the burials were dated to that period.

Other interesting ceramic finds were a couple of flat platterlike objects, each with an elongation forming a sort of handle. The original use of these unusual artifacts remains unknown. Round-bottomed bowls with incised geometric patterns and bowls painted with red-orange designs were also uncovered, as were pots. Other finds were vessels covered with nubbinlike projections. There are neatly arranged photo displays in the museum showing the progress of the excavations.

It is hoped that the museum displays will be enriched by donations from private individuals whose collections include artifacts from nearby sites. That would make the museum more fully representative of the archaeology of the area.

Although there are many sites in the vicinity, few have received careful study, and the area remains poorly known archaeologically. The Archaeological Museum in Situ would be an ideal nucleus for an expanded museum and a central collection point for artifacts yet to be uncovered.

*Note:* If the museum is not open when you arrive, check at the office of the Allende Institute (Instituto Allende). The office is closed from noon to 3:00 P.M.

## RECENT HISTORY

In March, 1975, workmen on the campus of the Allende Institute began digging up an area near the theater to install a water tank. Soon after the work began, some pre-Columbian remains were uncovered, and the institute stopped the digging.

The National Institute of Anthropology and History (INAH) was informed, and Emilio Bejarano, the institute's chief archaeologist for the state of Guanajuato, duly visited the site. Permission was then granted for scientific excavation of the site under Bejarano's technical direction. The project was financed by the Allende Institute and private contributors; INAH provided assistance, lending equipment and supplying information.

It proved to be a unique experience for the archaeology students at the Allende Institute. They were able to take part in a dig without having to leave the campus. Work was supervised by Don Patterson, professor of archaeology at the Allende Institute, and Al Desmond.

About 50 cubic meters of dirt were sifted during

*Three burials, Archaeological Museum in Situ (San Miguel de Allende). Left, remains in situ; center and right, ceramics cleaned, restored, and replaced. Early Classic period.*

the excavation, and some 200 human teeth were recovered, as well as obsidian, ceramics, and human bones. Part of a colonial wall was also unearthed. A building was erected around the burials and forms the museum as it is seen today.

## CONNECTIONS

1. 183 miles by paved road (154 miles are toll road) from Mexico City (via Celaya) to San Miguel de Allende.

## GETTING THERE

From Mexico City take Highway 57D northwest to Querétaro, then Highway 45D (two-lane toll road) west toward Celaya. At a junction just north of Celaya take Highway 51 north for 29 miles to San Miguel de Allende. The campus of the Allende Institute is on Highway 51 (east side) on the south end of town.

From Querétaro there is another route to San Miguel; take Highway 57 north for 18 miles to a junction with an unnumbered paved road heading west (left) to San Miguel (22 miles). This is 18 miles shorter than the route via Celaya, but not much faster, since none of the section is toll road and the second part has many curves. Nevertheless, this entry offers a spectacular view of the town as you approach it from high above. If you come in this way, take Highway 51 heading south from San Miguel to the Allende Institute.

The Allende Institute is seven blocks from the Jardín—the main plaza in the center of town—and is a pleasant walk. Driving time from Mexico City to San Miguel is 3½ to 4 hours no matter which route you take from Querétaro.

The colonial town of San Miguel is a perfectly delightful place with a flavor all its own and a generally fine climate. It is a great place to spend a couple of days as a visitor or to stay for an extended period if you have a special goal—for instance, studying Spanish, writing, arts, or crafts. It is not really a place to spend a two-week vacation; you will run out of things to see after the first couple of days. I have spent several months there off and on (for painting), and I am always eager to return.

There is a large resident population of United States citizens in San Miguel, and the Allende Institute and other schools register many students from the United States and Canada. The town is also a major tourist attraction for the casual visitor.

Some purists consider the town "spoiled" because of the many foreigners, but their presence is an important factor in the town's economy and also accounts for the many hotels (in various price ranges), restaurants, and night spots (likewise) and a couple of good drugstores and foodstores. Few other towns of comparable size in Mexico can boast such amenities.

San Miguel is, of course, the best stopover for the Archaeological Museum in Situ. Others are Querétaro and La Mansión—a lovely motel on Highway 57D, 4 miles north of San Juan del Río.

In addition to visiting the site museum and the picturesque campus of the Allende Institute, there are two things that are musts while you are in San Miguel:

1. Spend an hour just sitting in the Jardín absorbing the atmosphere and watching the world go by. If you can't just "sit," then buy a copy of the *News* (an English-language daily) hawked by boys in the area and read it while you relax.

2. Visit Colibrí Bookstore (across the street from the southwest corner of the Jardín). It has a large selection of books on Mexico and pre-Columbian art and archaeology.

*Northernmost of the five yácatas, partly restored, Tzintzuntzan. Tarascan Culture, Late Postclassic period.*

★★

# *Tzintzuntzan*

(tseen-*tsoon*-tsahn)

DERIVATION: Tarascan for "Place of the Hummingbirds."
ORIGINAL NAME: Tzintzuntzan.
CULTURE: Tarascan.
LOCATION: West-central part of the state of Michoacán, Mexico.

---

## THE SITE

The archaeological site of Tzintzuntzan lies about 0.5 mile uphill from, and north of, the town of the same name.

It is famous for a large rectangular platofrm, some 1,400 feet long and 850 feet wide, surmounted by five unusual structures called yácatas (*yah*-kah-tahs). The shape of the yácatas differs from other pyramidal substructures found in Mesoamerica, but they served the same purpose, bases for temples. The shape is generally described as that of the letter T, with a short stem and rounded bottom. The bodies of the yácatas rise in several stepped levels to a height of over 40 feet and it is thought that the circular portion originally supported temples of perishable materials. The yácatas are tightly packed in a more or less north-south line and each originally had a stair on the east side, opposite the rounded portion. There has been some restoration of the yácatas at either end that gives you a good idea of their original shape.

The platform below, very wide on the east side, served as an open area for ritual activity. It is now occupied by a soccer field and grazing horses.

There is a parking area on the north end of the platform. From here you can head south past the rounded portions (west side) to the far end, circle around part of the east side, and then climb one of the yácatas to get a better idea of their shape. This also affords lovely views of the town and lake below.

As you begin your tour at the north end, you will see what appears to be evidence of earlier construction on the rectangular portion of the first yácata. Along the west side over the edge of the large platform, near the central yácata, is a small, rectangular one-room enclosure.

Construction methods of the yácatas can best be studied on the west side. They were built of rough stone slabs and rubble, without the aid of mortar, and then faced with large cut stones of volcanic lava joined by a mud mortar. Near one of the yácatas on the west side is a pile of stone—one of which has the remnants of a carved spiral. There are also a couple of other carved slabs in place in the walls. As you circle around the last yácata, you will find the remains of the stair on the east side. There are footpaths on top of the unrestored yácatas, and you might like climbing around these for various views of the restored sections. After you leave the site, you can get some over-all shots of it from the highway below. Yácatas are a development of the Tarascans and have not been found in other areas of Mesoamerica.

According to their own traditions, the Tarascans moved into the area in the fourteenth century, first establishing their capital at Pátzcuaro, then at Ihuatzio, and finally at Tzintzuntzan. They were occupying Tzintzuntzan at the time of the Spanish conquest. There is archaeological evidence of earlier occupancy, however, probably by a group that was linguistically related. Wigberto Jiménez Moreno sees Teotihuacán influence in the area from around A.D. 650. This is supported by certain lapidary work. Chac Mool–type statues are also known from this area, perhaps indicating Toltec influence.

The culture of the Tarascans was less well developed in most regards than those of central and southern Mexico and the Maya area. They were, however, outstanding craftsman in the metallurgical arts, especially when working in copper. They were also noted as workers of obsidian and fine potters. Excavation of graves in and around the yácatas has brought to light many of their lovely creations.

The Tarascans were one of the few cultural groups that successfully defended their frontiers against the Aztec. When the Spaniards came in 1522, however, the Tarascans apparently offered little resistance, even though the population of Tzintzuntzan was reportedly 40,000.

Many puzzles remain in Tarascan archaeology, including an apparent linguistic relationship to South American languages, and production of pottery vessels with stirrup-spouted handles, also of a kind found in South America.

## RECENT HISTORY

The earliest written references to the archaeological remains of Tzintzuntzan are found, as might be expected, in Spanish colonial documents of the sixteenth century.

Excavations (apparently disastrous) were attempted in 1852 by a priest, Ignacio Trespeña, and in 1902, Nicolás León described the monuments. It was only in 1937 and 1938, however, that serious work began at the site. It was conducted by Alfonso Caso, with the help of Jorge Acosta, D. F. Rubín de la Borbolla, and Hugo Moedano. In the 1960s further work was carried out by Román Piña Chan. These excavations were sponsored by the National Institute of Anthropology and History.

## CONNECTIONS

1. 31 miles by paved road from Morelia to the town of Tzintzuntzan, or
2. 11 miles by paved road from Pátzcuaro to the town of Tzintzuntzan, then 0.5 mile of dirt road to the site.

## GETTING THERE

From Morelia take Highway 15 west to Quiroga (26 miles), then turn south for 5 miles to the town of Tzintzuntzan. Keep an eye out to the left (east) for a view of the yácatas on a hill and for a dirt road leading to them.

From Pátzcuaro, head north to Tzintzuntzan and the same dirt road. Bus service can also get you to the town of Tzintzuntzan, and you can do the last 0.5 mile to the site on foot.

There are no accommodations, food, or drink at the site, but soft drinks are available in the town of Tzintzuntzan.

If you plan to climb around the unrestored yácatas, boots would be best. Allow an hour or a bit more to visit the yácatas.

The rounded portions of the yácatas are lighted in the afternoon. Though these are actually the backs of the structures, they are the best-restored and most interesting sides. An afternoon visit is recommended.

You can easily visit Ihuatzio—9 miles away—when you visit Tzintzuntzan. While neither is spectacular, you might just as well make a day of it (or half a day) and see them both.

Other nearby stopovers are Uruapan and Zamora.

★

# *Ihuatzio*

(ee-*what*-see-oh)

CULTURE: Tarascan.
LOCATION: West-central part of the state of Michoacán, Mexico.

## THE SITE

The structures of main interest at Ihuatzio are a pair of pyramids at the west end of a large, enclosed plaza. These twin pyramids—sharing a common base—are rectangular. Although yácata-shaped mounds have been reported at Ihuatzio, we did not see any.

When you park your car at the end of the dirt road, you have to crawl over the loose stone fence on your left (west). From here the pyramids, some 200 yards in the distance, are visible. They are approached by what seem to be the remains of an ancient causeway.

The construction of the pyramids is the same rough slab-and-rubble core with cut-stone facing seen at Tzintzuntzan, although little of the outer surface has survived in place. It is still possible, however, to see that the pyramids rose in several tiers.

Climb the left (south) pyramid for views of the remains of mounds that formed a plaza in front of the pyramids. There are also enclosing mounds in the rear. From here you also can see the Island of Janitzio in the distance, with the gigantic statue of Morelos on top, and additional pre-Columbian mounds closer by. The whole area surrounding the pyramids is cultivated in neat rectangles, although the immediate area and the causeway from the fence to the pyramids is kept cleared.

## RECENT HISTORY

According to traditions, Ihuatzio was the capital of the Tarascan culture before it was moved to nearby Tzintzuntzan.

See "Tzintzuntzan" for more on the Tarascans. The site has hardly been touched archaeologically, although some work was carried out there by Alfonso Caso and his associates in the 1930s for the National Institute of Anthropology and History. An interesting Chac Mool figure in the Mexico City Museum is attributed to Ihuatzio.

## CONNECTIONS

1. 36 miles by paved road from Morelia to the cutoff, or
2. 6 miles by paved road from Pátzcuaro to the cutoff, then about 4 miles of dirt road to the site.

## GETTING THERE

From Morelia take Highway 15 west to Quiroga (26 miles), then turn south for about 10 miles to the cutoff for the town of Ihuatzio. The cutoff, which is marked, is on your right (west) and is a fair dirt road. When you arrive at the town of Ihuatzio, you take a right turn. Ask directions to make sure you get the correct turnoff. This part is very rough and begins with a steep incline. The road is also strewn with boulders and, sometimes, covered with puddles that go completely across it. Nevertheless, if you drive slowly, it can be negotiated in a regular car. Drive to the end of the road and park.

From Pátzcuaro, head north to the cutoff to Ihuatzio (then see above).

A bus could get you to the cutoff and probably to the town of Ihuatzio, but, frankly, the walk to the site would hardly repay you. Better skip this one if you don't have your own car, or, try for a taxi in Pátzcuaro.

There are no accommodations, food, or drink at the site. Bring cold drinks along. Wear boots if you plan to climb one of the pyramids because part of it is loose rubble.

Allow ½ hour from the time you leave your car till you return.

The pyramids are lighted in front in the morning so this would be the best time for a visit.

A visit to Ihuatzio can be easily combined with a visit to Tzintzuntzan, 9 miles away by road.

Other overnight stops in the area are Uruapan and Zamora.

*Conical altars and bench, with remains of red-painted frescoes, Tamuín. A small pyramidal platform is at the rear. Postclassic period.*

★★

# *Tamuín*

(tah-moo-*een*)

CULTURE: Huastec.
LOCATION: Southeastern part of the state of San Luis Potosí, Mexico.

## THE SITE

Tamuín is recognized as one of the major Postclassic centers of Huastec culture. It covers an area of almost 0.1 square mile. Only one small section of the site has been cleared, however, and another part partly cleared. As you approach the site on foot from the east, you will see foot trails that branch to the right and left. The one leading to the right (north) goes uphill and leads to an area with small mounds arranged around what appears to be a plaza. This area is partially overgrown, but you might want a quick look.

From here, return on the foot trail toward the south to another small hill. The trail passes the caretaker's house on the way up.

This second area is well cleared and there are structures on the north, west, and south sides of a plaza. These structures are platforms of varying sizes. All have a stairway facing the plaza. The west building is the largest and appears also to have had a stairway on the west side facing the Tamuín River—a tributary of the Panuco. This structure rises in a couple of tiers, and there are remains of small circular constructions adjacent to the upper stairs on the east side. These, as well as the platform itself and the other structures at Tamuín, are made of river boulders, which were originally covered with plaster.

The south platform has some remaining (or restored) plaster, and also has a stairway on the west side. The stairs of this structure have sloping balustrades with vertical upper zones.

The most interesting part of the site, however, is the central part of the plaza. There is a small pyramidal platform with an eastern stair, topped by low, stepped masonry constructions that look more like decorative elements than the remains of walls meant to enclose a room.

Abutting the bottom of the stair, and running to the east, is a long, low bench, interrupted by one truncated conical altar and terminating with another. The altar near the steps is smaller at the top, while the reverse is true of the other. The platform, bench, and altars retain much of their plaster surfaces, and red-painted frescoes are found on the altars and parts of the sides of the bench. The altars and bench are protected by a thatch-and-tin roof and barbed wire, but you can get close enough for detail photographs of the paintings.

Some authorities feel the style of the frescoes is related to the style used in the Mixtec Codices. Others see more of a Toltec influence. The Huasteca, where Tamuín is located, is known to have received influences from both groups and Huastec culture flourished during the Early Postclassic period.

The Gulf Coast of Mexico and the Yucatán Peninsula are believed to have been occupied in ancient times by a people speaking a common Mayance language. At one point, there was an intrusion of another group (or groups) of Totonac-Zoquean speakers. They pushed into the southern Gulf Coast area, effectively splitting the Maya group into two parts—the Huastec Mayas on the northwest and the Yucatec Mayas on the east.

On the basis of glottochronology, it is believed that the Huastecs were separated from the rest of the Maya group as early as 1400 B.C. and that, at a later date, other groups intruded into the area. The stratigraphic ceramic sequence for the Huasteca runs in an unbroken line from 1100 B.C. up to the Spanish conquest.

Architecturally, the Huastecs were no match for their southeastern Maya cousins. Nevertheless, they did develop their own characteristic architectural style—notable for many circular structures—and an important culture of their own, distinguished by fine stone statuary, beautifully carved shell, and excellent pottery.

One of the gems of Huastec sculpture was found at El Consuelo ranch, near Tamuín. Popularly called "The Adolescent," it is now in the Mexico City Museum. This figure, carved in the round, depicts a nude young man with tattoos covering almost half his body; some of the tattoos are glyphs. He carries an infant on his back, which is perhaps associated with the sun or wind god—Éhecatl—a manifestation of Quetzalcóatl.

Quetzalcóatl was a major deity in the Huasteca, and it may be Quetzalcóatl or his priests that are depicted in the frescoes at Tamuín. Some authorities even believe that Quetzalcóatl had his origins in the Huasteca.

## RECENT HISTORY

The major work at Tamuín was that of Wilfrido du Solier, who explored the site in 1946 under a project sponsored by the National Institute of Anthropology and History. Du Solier is known for his work in the Huasteca, and he reported on the frescoes at Tamuín in 1946. The site is also mentioned in Ignacio Marquina's *Arquitectura Prehispánica*, published in Mexico in 1951.

The statue, however, was discovered many years before the major work at the site, and was in a local collection in 1918. Later it was sent to the Mexico City Musem.

## CONNECTIONS

1. 23 miles by paved road from Valles, or
2. 70.5 miles by paved road from Tampico, then 0.5 mile by foot trail.

## GETTING THERE

From Valles, take Highway 70 east to the town of Tamuín. Go through the town until the highway makes a curve to the right (19.5 miles). Shortly after the curve, there is a cutoff on the right, marked for San Vincente. Take this cutoff for 3.5 miles to the gate at the entrance to the site, where there is a small sign indicating the archaeological zone. Park at the gate and walk the last part on an easily followed trail.

From Tampico, take Highway 70 west for 67 miles to the San Vincente cutoff. Turn left, and proceed as above.

There are no accommodations, food, or drink at the site, but cold drinks are available in the town of Tamuín. Boots are better than tennis shoes as the trail is rocky. Bring insect repellent.

Allow 1½ hours from the time you leave your car until you return.

If you are without a car, you can get a bus to the town of Tamuín from Valles or Tampico. There you might get a local taxi to the site.

★★★

# *Tula and Tula Museum*

(*too*-lah)

DERIVATION: Nahuatl for "Place of the Bulrushes." It also implies "Metropolis" or "Capital City."
ORIGINAL NAME: Tollán (a variant of Tula).
CULTURE: Toltec.
LOCATION: South-central part of the state of Hidalgo, Mexico.

## THE SITE

Tula is one of the most interesting and accessible sites in central Mexico, exceeded only by Teotihuacán, and equaled only by Xochicalco and Cholula. In recent years, it has become a favorite attraction for Mexican families, who go there on Sundays for an all-day outing. On our first visit on a weekday in 1959, the place was deserted.

If you drive to the site, there is a parking area near the museum. From there, head to the Great Pyramid (Mound or Building C) east of the Main, or Central, Plaza. This pyramid is the largest structure at Tula, and it was found in a very ruinous state. It was similar in design, however, to the restored Pyramid of Tlahuizcalpantecuhtli.

Much of the stone facing of the Great Pyramid was removed in pre-Columbian times, and the lower part of its stairway and the lower tiers on the west side, facing the plaza, were all that could be restored.

You can climb the Great Pyramid by a foot trail on the north side. From the top you can get good over-all and telephoto shots of the Pyramid of Tlahuizcalpantecuhtli.

Now descend the Great Pyramid by its western stairway, and head west across the Central Plaza. On the way, stop for a look at the small platform (adatorio) in the center of the Plaza. This was perhaps an altar, and had stairs on all four sides. It is similar in design to, but smaller than, two platforms found at Chichén Itzá—the Maya-Toltec city in Yucatán. Continue west to Ball Court No. 2, which bounds the plaza on the west side. This court and some adjacent structures have been partly restored in recent years.

From here head northeast to the Burnt Palace (Building 3) and the Great Vestibule. The Burnt Palace is a complex of structures made up mainly of three rooms in an east-west line. All are worth a look, but the most interesting is the central room. Here are two remnants of polychromed bas-relief sculptures on a bench. Both are protected by modern roofs. The best-preserved is the one in the northeast corner. It shows a procession of richly attired individuals in the lower section; above is a cornice depicting an undulating serpent. Much of the original color remains.

A Chac Mool statue (my absolute favorite) was found in the same room in front of an altar on the east side. Actually, the original Chac Mool has been moved to the Mexico City Museum and a copy has been placed at the site. The copy is a good one and very photogenic.

Throughout the chambers of the Burnt Palace and the Great Vestibule (which fronts the Burnt Palace and the Pyramid of Tlahuizcalpantecuhtli) are numerous pillars, which originally supported beam, pole, and mortar roofs. The pillars are all restorations; the originals were dismantled in ancient times though impressions of their placement remained.

Walk through the Great Vestibule to the stairway of the Pyramid of Tlahuizcalpantecuhtli. This pyramid, and the sculptures that surmount it, form the most interesting part of the site.

The Great Atlantean statues for which Tula is famous are found on top, along with the remains of sepent columns and carved pillars. All originally supported the roof of the temple. Three of the Atlantes (also called Telemones) are original; the fourth is a copy, replacing one that was moved to the Mexico City Museum. The Atlantes are truly some of the masterpieces of Toltec sculpture. The statues are nearly 15 feet tall and were carved in four sections, which were then tenoned together. There are still some remnants of paint adhering to the surfaces. The Atlantes depict Toltec warriors, who represent Quetzalcóatl in his manifestation as the planet Venus as the morning star. In this guise, the deity is called Tlahuizcalpantecuhtli; hence the name of the pyramid. It is sometimes called—more prosaically—Building B or, simply, the Pyramid of Quetzalcóatl.

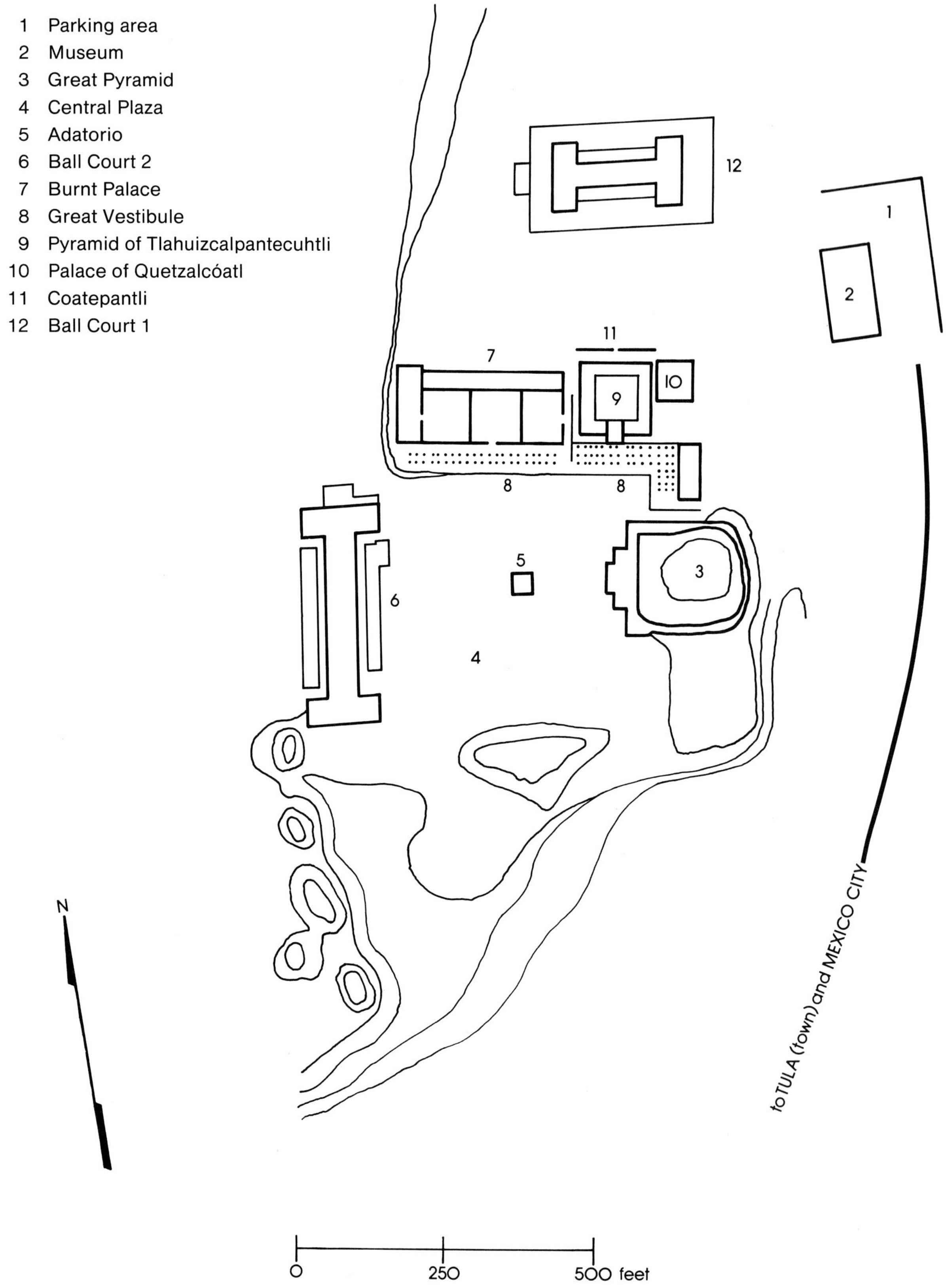
1 Parking area
2 Museum
3 Great Pyramid
4 Central Plaza
5 Adatorio
6 Ball Court 2
7 Burnt Palace
8 Great Vestibule
9 Pyramid of Tlahuizcalpantecuhtli
10 Palace of Quetzalcóatl
11 Coatepantli
12 Ball Court 1
12
1
2
11
7
10
9
8
8
5
3
6
4
N
to TULA (town) and MEXICO CITY
0
250
500 feet

TULA

*Front (west) side of the Great Pyramid, Tula. Early Postclassic period. Photograph by author.*

The warrior figures are shown in full regalia with elaborate headdresses, butterfly-shaped breast plates, ornamented aprons, and decorative sandals. Each holds an atlatl in his right hand and darts in his left. The eye sockets and mouth may have originally had inlays.

At the waist in the rear are large discs with a human face in the center; below are bare behinds.

The pyramid on which the statues rest rises in four tiers, which originally were covered with panels of bas-reliefs. Some of these remain on the north and east sides.

In the twelfth century, when Tula was destroyed, a great trench was dug into the north face of the Pyramid of Tlahuizcalpantecuhtli and the Atlantes, serpent columns, and pillars were thrown in. When the pyramid was excavated, the statues and other carvings were discovered in and around it. They were eventually reassembled, and placed on top of the pyramid in what were assumed to be their original positions.

Climb down to the Great Vestibule, and follow it east and then south. Here is another polychromed bas-relief bench showing a procession of figures. These are similar to those in the Burnt Palace, and likewise are sheltered by a modern roof.

Now head north to the Palace of Quetzalcóatl (Building 1). This is a complex of several structures erected against the east side of the Pyramid of Tlahuizcalpantecuhtli. This addition, fortunately, preserved the bas-relief panels on this side of the pyramid. The Palace of Quetzalcóatl is presumed to have been residential—perhaps for the priests of the adjoining pyramid-temple or perhaps for the great priest-king, Ce Acatl Topiltzin Quetzalcóatl.

The bas-relief panels on the east side of the pyramid are best studied from this area. They depict a procession of jaguars in a row. On the row below are a series of eagles, in profile, eating bleeding hearts; this motif is occasionally interrupted by a frontal depiction of a human emerging from the mouth of an animal.

From here, turn the corner at the rear (northeast corner) of the pyramid, and head west for a look

*Pyramid of Tlahuizcalpantecuhtli fronted by the Great Vestibule, view looking north, Tula. Early Postclassic period. Photograph by author.*

at more bas-relief panels on the north side of the pyramid and the adjacent Coatepantli, or Serpent Wall. The Serpent Wall originally extended along the entire north side of the pyramid, but was thrown down when Tula was destroyed. Fortunately, some parts fell in such a way that they could be accurately restored.

The wall is composed of five sections. On top are open-work, stylized, and connecting shells; below is a solid bas-relief in three parts; and below this is plain section, reaching to ground level.

The center section of the bas-relief is the most interesting, complex, and frankly, gory. It depicts a human skull in the open mouth of a serpent, which presumably devoured the human. Bones are intertwined with the undulating body of the serpent. The sections above and below have carved meanders. There are some remains of paint on the three central sections and all sections are separated by a simple cornice. The wall reaches more than 7 feet, to the top of the bas-relief section, and the same motif is repeated on the other side. The openwork shells on top—found only on one part of the wall today—added perhaps another 2 feet to the height.

The wall is over 130 feet long, and is separated from the face of the pyramid by a sort of alley, 15 or 20 feet wide.

Now head north to Ball Court No. 1. This large I-shaped court is sunk below ground level. Several stairs give access to the playing area. The sides of the playing area are flanked by platforms joining

*Atlantean statues and carved pillars atop the Pyramid of Tlahuizcalpantecuhtli, Tula. Early Postclassic period. Photograph by author.*

vertical walls, which originally supported rings.

One carved panel was found in situ when the ball court was excavated. It depicts the lower part of a ball player, and is found just around the corner from the central playing section, on the southwest, at ground level.

From the ball court, head to the museum area for a cold drink and a rest before you view the collection.

Several native chronicles mention the Toltec capital of Tollán (Tula) in glorious terms. It is said that there were many rich palaces decorated with turquoise, jade, and red and white shells, and that rare birds of precious feathers filled the air. Pumpkins and ears of maize grew as large as a man, and cotton was grown in various colors. Hunger and want were unknown among the people. Legend says that the Toltecs were physically larger than any people known today and that they excelled in science and art.

Many myths are told about the founding of the city and its various leaders, and, as you might expect, there is more than a little contradiction. What we can glean from these confusing stories is a rough outline of the history of the Toltecs. Even today, however, all authorities are not in agreement about the dates; some prefer dates a few years different from those given below; others prefer dates some two centuries earlier.

Sometime after the fall of Teotihuacán, in the seventh century, less advanced Nahua groups from the north entered central Mexico. One group, under the leadership of a certain Mixcóatl, settled at Culhuacán on the southern outskirts of present-day Mexico City, shortly before A.D. 900. It is Mixcóatl that gave his group the name Toltec. At Culhuacán, the Toltecs mingled with the more civilized groups already living in the area, and Mixcóatl married a local maiden named Chimalma.

Mixcóatl was later killed by his brother Ihuitimal, who took over leadership of the group. Chimalma fled for her life, only to die a short time later at the birth of her son, Ce Acatl Topiltzin.

When older, Topiltzin was sent to Xochilcalco to study with the priests of Quetzalcóatl. He later returned to Culhuacán, recovered his father's bones, and reburied them. He then visited his Uncle Ihuitimal, killed him, and took over leadership of the Toltecs. He moved the capital to Tulancingo and finally to Tula, which he founded in A.D. 968. A portrait of Topiltzin is carved on a rock overlooking the site and is accompanied by a date believed to be A.D. 968.

Ce Acatl Topiltzin attempted religious reform, and introduced the worship of Quetzalcóatl to his people, adding the deity's name to his own. Under his leadership, the arts and sciences flourished. He encouraged his people to end human sacrifice and substitute symbolic sacrifices of jades, butterflies, and snakes, which were entirely satisfactory to the deity Quetzalcóatl.

Some of the Toltecs, however, preferred their old tribal god, Tezcatlipoca (Smoking Mirror), god of the night, a more bloodthirsty deity, who demanded human sacrifice. The followers of Tezcatlipoca allegedly tricked Ce Acatl Topiltzin Quetzalcóatl into becoming drunk and neglecting his religious duties. He left Tula in disgrace in A.D. 987.

He traveled to the Gulf Coast with some of his followers, stopping at Cholula on the way. There are two versions of what happened when he reached the coast. One says that he set himself afire and ascended to the sky to become the morning star; the other says that he traveled east on a raft made of snakes, promising to return.

Certain Yucatec legends record that at this time there arrived in their land a certain Kukulcán, and the coast of the Yucatán Peninsula does indeed lie to the east of where Quetzalcóatl supposedly embarked. Kukulcán means "Feathered Serpent" in Mayan, just as Quetzalcóatl means "Feathered Serpent" in Nahuatl. Kukulcán became the major deity at the Maya-Toltec city of Chichén Itzá.

Whether Ce Acatl Topiltzin Quetzalcóatl was the founder of the new order at Chichén Itzá, or whether a later Quetzalcóatl was responsible, is still uncertain. The whole is wrapped in myths and allegory that may never be fully untangled.

At any rate, Tula remained the major center in central Mexico until it was destroyed and sacked by invading tribes from the north around A.D. 1156. During its life-span in the Early Postclassic period, Tula exerted a great influence on many parts of Mesoamerica. Later groups were quick to claim the Toltecs as their ancestors.

## RECENT HISTORY

The first modern report on Tula was that of Antonio García Cubas, a Mexican who presented his findings to the Mexican Society of Geography and History in 1873. French traveler Désiré Charnay visited the site, carried out limited excavations, and published his results in 1885.

For many years scholars sought to determine the location of the legendary Tollán or Tula, a question made more complex by the existence of many Tulas in Mexico. Some thought the ancient Toltec capital was Teotihuacán.

Mexican historian Wigberto Jiménez Moreno diligently studied the old sources, and came to the conclusion that Tollán was the Tula in the state of Hidalgo. Excavations were carried out beginning in 1940, primarily by Mexican archaeologist Jorge Acosta. This work, plus information presented at a round table conference of the Mexican Society of Anthropology in 1941, proved once and for all that Jiménez Moreno was correct.

Nevertheless, others must have held similar views even earlier since Tula, Hidalgo, is identified as the Toltec capital of Tollán in a 1911 edition of *Terry's Mexico,* and a captioned photo in a 1914 issue of the *National Geographic Magazine* states that Teotihuacán was built before the Toltec entered the Valley of Mexico. Work at Tula continued off and on during the 1950s and 1960s.

## CONNECTIONS

1. 57 miles by paved road (43 miles are toll road) from Mexico City.

## GETTING THERE

From Mexico City, take toll Highway 57D north for 43 miles to a junction near Tepeji del Río. Get off the toll road, go past Tepeji, and you will shortly pick up Highway 126 heading north. It is 10 miles to the town of Tula. The archaeological site is a short distance away, across the river and perched atop a hill overlooking the town. Driving time from Mexico City is about 1½ hours.

Tula may also be reached from the Pan American Highway number 85 by taking the cutoffs: (1) a bit south of Ixmiquilpan, or (2) at Actopan. These join at the town of Progreso, and Highway 126 continues to Tula.

Stopovers in addition to Mexico City are (1) a lovely place called La Mansión, 4 miles north of San Juan del Río, (2) Querétaro, or (3) the charming San Miguel de Allende. Driving times to Tula are 1½ hours from La Mansión, 2 hours from Querétaro, and 3 hours from San Miguel.

In addition to private car, you can reach Tula by bus, train, or on specially conducted tours from Mexico City. There is no food at the site, although soft drinks are sold. There are some small restaurants and groceries in the town of Tula, but I would recommend bringing a picnic lunch. Tennis shoes are fine. Allow about 3 hours for a visit to the site and museum. The fronts of the Atlantes get sunlight in the afternoon.

## TULA MUSEUM

The most interesting objects in Tula's Museum are displayed on the outside. All come from the site. Included are a stela depicting a warrior in frontal view, with a mask of Tlaloc in his headdress, a headless Chac Mool, and the lower portions of huge Atlantean figures.

Inside the museum are displays of ceramics, sacrificial knives, pieces of jade, and stone sculpture. It is definitely worth a look when you visit the site.

*South side of the Temple of Quetzalcóatl (Structure 3), Calixtlahuaca. Late Postclassic period.*

★★

# *Calixtlahuaca*

(kah-leesh-tlah-*wah*-kah)

DERIVATION: Nahuatl for "House on the Plain."
ORIGINAL NAME: Probably Calixtlahuaca.
CULTURE: Matlatzinca; see text.
LOCATION: Central part of the state of Mexico, Mexico.

## THE SITE

Calixtlahuaca is another of those places difficult to rate. Perhaps two and a half stars gives the best idea of its worth.

There are four separate sections at Calixtlahuaca of interest to the visitor, and all should be seen. Three of these are on various levels of an artificially terraced hill and the fourth is on ground level. I recommend seeing those on the hill first.

At the site there is a parking area at the base of the hill. From here you climb through fields of maguey to the Temple of Quetzalcóatl (Structure 3), the most interesting and most publicized building at the site. This is visible from the parking area and is approached by well-defined foot trails.

This circular structure has a single stairway facing east, and it was presumably dedicated to Quetzalcóatl in his form of the wind god, Éhecatl. A life-size statue of this deity was found in the building.

There are three earlier structures inside the temple, and these may be seen by using tunnels dug during excavation. All the earlier structures were round and had a single east stairway. Some of the earlier remains, including crude stone serpent heads, may be seen from the outside as you circle the temple. These belong to the third construction.

You will want to spend the bulk of your time in and around the temple. On the lower level of the south side are a couple of carved stones embedded in the structure. From this section you climb higher up the hill to the second section. If a boy offers to show you the way, take his help. It will save some time.

The second section is composed of three partially restored structures around a small plaza. The most interesting is the Altar of the Skulls. It is in the shape of a T, with a circular extension on the top. The outside walls are covered with projecting skulls and knobs. The skulls are in a poor state of preservation. Good over-all shots of the altar are possible by climbing the other two structures (Numbers 4 and 7) facing the plaza. The last are rectangular platforms with a single stairway facing the plaza. From this vantage point you can also get good telephoto shots of Structure 17 at ground level.

The third section is still higher up the hill, and the trail going there is not so well marked. This section is often overlooked, and the sparse architectural remains of Structures 5 and 6 (two platforms) are partially overgrown with weeds. It is worth the climb, however, to see the two carved stone slabs lying on the ground. Also in this area are smaller carved stones incorporated into the wall of what our guide said was a tomb. You are not likely to find these on your own as they lie a bit below ground level and are obscured by vegetation. Our guide had to pull up and push back weeds so we could get photos.

From here head downhill and return to your car. When you reach the level the Temple of Quetzalcóatl look north to ground level for a view of a ball court unstudied by archaeologists. Your guide may have to point this out to you.

Drive north to the junction with the main road, turn left (west), and go a few hundred yards. This takes you to the fourth section (Structure 17). You will pass the ball court on the way, but there is not much to be seen at ground level.

Structure 17 is an architectural complex of many rooms and platforms. It is thought to have been a sort of seminary and is called the Calmecac (Nahuatl) or Seminario (Spanish). Part of it is constructed of adobe and part of stone. One of the major features is a large platform with a triple stairway facing a large plaza.

In addition to the four sections and the ball court already mentioned, there are other remains at the site, mostly unexcavated or only partially excavated, but not restored. These include those at the top of the hill and some at ground level, bordering the town of Calixtlahuaca. They are reportedly not worth the effort to see them. It is worthy of note, however, that a statue of Coatlicue was found at

*Altar of the Skulls, Calixtlahuaca. Late Postclassic period.*

the top of the hill, and is now in the Mexico City Museum.

Excavation at Calixtlahuaca has brought to light a great deal of interesting information, which has resulted in a determination of five occupational periods. The site was occupied as early as the Preclassic period, which is represented by figurines and a few remains of vertical walls, constructed to support some terraces half way up the hill. The second period of occupation dates to the third period of Teotihuacán (A.D. 300–600), when Calixtlahuaca was the home of people connected with the former site. The earliest building inside the Temple of Quetzalcóatl dates to this time. The third period shows pronounced influence from Tula. During this time, the second building of the Temple of Quetzalcóatl was constructed.

In the fourth period (A.D. 1200–1474), the Matlatzincas, a Nahua group related to, but enemies of, the Aztec, became the predominant force in the area (although they had occupied it during the previous period), and the third building of the Temple of Quetzalcóatl was undertaken. Excavation shows that this structure was destroyed by earthquake in 1474. During the fifth period (A.D. 1474–1510) Calixtlahuaca was conquered by the Aztec, so this is referred to as the Azteca-Matlatzinca period. During this time, final enlargement and reconstruction were made on the Temple of Quetzalcóatl. Also dating to this period are the Altar of the Skulls and the adjacent Structure 4. The Calmecac (Structure 17) was built during the third and fourth periods and was burned in 1510, on the orders of Moctezuma II, to quell the rebellious Matlatzincas. The inhabitants then left the area, but returned after the Spanish conquest, when they founded the new town near their ancient center.

## RECENT HISTORY

Excavation at Calixtlahuaca was undertaken by the Mexican government's Department of Monuments (now the National Institute of Anthropology and History [INAH]) in 1930, and continued for about eight years. Most of the work was done under the direction of Mexican archaeologist José García Payón.

## CONNECTIONS

1. 5 miles by paved road from Toluca.
2. 45 miles by paved road from Mexico City.

*Carved slab, in the third section, partway up the hill, Calixtlahuaca.*

## GETTING THERE

From Mexico City take Highway 15 west to Toluca. From Toluca take Highway 55 north. Just past the kilometer 7 marker, you come to a well-marked cutoff for the town of Calixtlahuaca heading west (to your left). The road is paved to the town. Here you will find signs pointing out the direction to the archaeological zone, which is on the edge of town.

There is no food or drink at the site. Bring something cold along in your car. Tennis shoes are okay.

A special point to keep in mind is that Calixtlahuaca is one of the highest sites in Mexico, with an altitude of over 9,000 feet. This—plus the fact that the visit entails climbing—is likely to leave you a bit breathless. Having a guide for the higher sections is recommended, not only to show you things you might miss on your own, but also to help you carry your excess camera gear.

Calixtlahuaca can also be reached by taxi or bus from Toluca. Allow about 2½ hours for a visit.

*Temple of the Eagle and Jaguar Knights, the front (south) side, Malinalco. Late Postclassic period.*

★★★

# *Malinalco*

(mah-leen-*ahl*-koh)

DERIVATION: Nahuatl, from *malinalli*, meaning "grass," or a certain weed used for cordage.
CULTURE: Aztec; see text.
LOCATION: East-central part of the state of Mexico, Mexico.

---

## THE SITE

Malinalco is one of the most unusual sites in Mexico. Some of its temples are carved into living rock. The only other place in Mexico where something similar is known is at Texcotzingo, where rock-cut baths and canals are found at the summer palace of Nezahualcóyotl, king of Texcoco. These latter date perhaps a bit earlier but certainly are nowhere as impressive.

The most interesting building at Malinalco is Temple I, also called the Temple of the Eagle and Jaguar Knights. This circular building, with all its sculptural decorations, its pyramidal base, and its balustraded stairway, is a single unit carved into the mountainside. It is really quite a fantastic achievement, and is best thought of as sculptured architecture.

There are remains of a sculptured jaguar to the right of the stairway, and a few remains of one on the left. Little is left of the carving in the center of the stairway.

At the top of the stair is a low platform in front of the doorway to the temple. Flanking the doorway are three-dimensional sculptures of a serpent head, with an Eagle Knight seated on top (east or right side), and a drum covered with a jaguar skin, surmounted by remains of a Jaguar Knight, on the left (west).

On the exterior wall of the temple, next to the doorway, are bas-relief carvings representing the open mouth of the serpent; its tongue protrudes from the doorway, and lies on the platform, stretched out like a mat. Each half of the serpent relief can be seen as a serpent head in profile, while together they depict a front view. Some authorities believe this mouth-doorway represents Tepeyolotl, the earth monster.

The interior chamber is almost 19 feet in diameter, and contains a semicircular bench. Three sculptures adorn the bench; a stretched-out skin of a jaguar is in the center, and eagle skins are found on either side. Another outspread eagle skin adorns the center of the floor of the shrine. Behind this is a circular hole—perhaps a receptacle for offerings. Originally, the whole building (including the sculptures) was covered with a thin layer of stucco, and then painted.

A modern conical thatched roof tops the temple and is probably like the original roof. A channel at the back of the roof was carved into the living rock to carry off rain water. Bring a flash unit to get photographs of the interior of the temple. A two-flight stairway to the east of the temple gets you to a higher level, where you can see the drain.

Structure or Temple II, a truncated pyramid with a western stair, lies a few feet southeast of Temple I. Climb Temple II for over-all shots of Temple I; a wide-angle lens is useful here.

About 15 feet west of Temple II is Temple V—a circular structure with an eastern stair built of stone and mortar, and set upon a small platform.

From here walk northwest between Temples I and II to Temple III. Temple III is composed of two chambers, one circular and one rectangular; each has a rectangular altar of dressed stone surrounding a cistlike depression.

You first enter the rectangular room through openings formed by the remnants of two pillars and lower masonry walls. When this chamber was excavated, remains of a mural painting were found on the western wall, but little of this can be seen today.

The mural depicted three warriors in full regalia, carrying shields and lances, and according to José García Payón, represented souls of warriors transformed into a stellar god under the guise of Mixcóatl.

From the rectangular room there is a single entrance to the large circular chamber of Temple III; the whole is formed of thick masonry walls.

Temple IV lies to the north of Temple III, and is partially carved into the living rock. This huge single room has a bench running around three of its sides upon which are found two altars. In the

*Jaguar sculpture east of the stairs of the Temple of the Eagle and Jaguar Knights, Malinalco. Late Postclassic period.*

center of the room are stone bases that originally supported wooden posts that upheld the roof. Archaeological evidence indicates that the roof was solid rubble made in two sections, and resting on beams.

Farther north is Temple VI, carved from living stone. This temple is incomplete. It was being worked on at the time of the Spanish conquest, which apparently put a halt to it. During excavation, a large number of stone chisels were found in the debris.

Malinalco was occupied by the Matlatzinca, a branch of the Nahua, who were conquered by the Aztec during the reign of Axayácatl (around 1469, according to native and early Spanish documents). Matlatzinca ceramics have verified their presence at the site. It was the Aztec, however, who carved and constructed the temples. The work began in 1476 or 1501, depending on your choice of authority, and was carried out under the Aztec rulers Ahuizotl (who followed Axayácatl) and Moctezuma the younger.

Temple I was closely associated with the elite military orders of the Eagle and Jaguar Knights, organizations described in early Spanish colonial documents as being composed of warriors of noble birth. The whole site may have been reserved for their rituals.

Although Temple I is circular, it is not connected with the cult of Quetzalcóatl, as are many other circular edifices in Mesoamerica.

Two beautifully carved wooden drums were found at the site. Both are in museums, one formerly in Toluca and one in Mexico City (the collection of the Toluca Museum has been moved to Tenango—about 15 miles south). Both drums bear representations of eagles. The one formerly in Toluca also depicts jaguars with headdresses, symbolizing the warrior knights, further verifying Malinalco as an important center of the Eagle and Jaguar Knights.

## RECENT HISTORY

Malinalco was conquered in 1521 by Andrés de Tapia, who led a detachment sent by Cortés. Some of the buildings were burned and destroyed. Two decades later the Augustinians used stone from the site to construct their church. There is little to be said for the period from then until the National Institute of Anthropology and History began research and reconstruction in 1936. Most of what we know of the site is due to the efforts of García Payón, who undertook work there in the 1940s and 1950s.

## CONNECTIONS

1. 66 miles by paved road from Mexico City to the town of Malinalco, or
2. 48 miles by paved road from Toluca to the town of Malinalco, then 1 mile of rock road.

## GETTING THERE

From Mexico City, take Highway 15 west to La Marquesa (22 miles from the center of Mexico City). At La Marquesa there is a cutoff to the left (south), marked for Chalma—a renowned pilgrimage center. Take this cutoff and continue to Chalma (37 miles from La Marquesa).

*Note:* About 3 miles south of the La Marquesa cutoff, you will be faced with a choice of roads. The right fork is marked "Chalma via Atlapulco" and the other is unmarked. We opted for Atlapulco, since that way obviously would get us to Chalma. The other fork may have also gone to Chalma, but it was not shown on any of our maps.

At Chalma the road turns to the west, but con-

*Jaguar-skin sculpture on the bench in the interior of the Temple of the Eagle and Jaguar Knights, Malinalco. Late Postclassic period.*

tinues to the town of Malinalco and is paved to the edge of the town (7 miles). Drive into the town and on to the Main Plaza, where you will see "pyramid" signs directing you to a parking area near the archaeological zone (1 mile).

From Toluca take Highway 55 southeast to Mexicalcingo (6.5 miles). Then take the cutoff to the left (east) to Tianguistenco (8 miles). From there proceed to the town of Coatepec (5.5 miles), where you join the La Marquesa-Chalma road described above. From Coatepec it is 28 miles to the town of Malinalco. Driving time to Malinalco is 2 hours from Mexico City and 1½ hours from Toluca.

From the parking area at Malinalco it is a 30-minute climb (400 feet) to the archaeological zone, and the way is paved with stone paths and steps installed in 1975. There are lovely views on the way up, so you may want to take a bit longer to enjoy them—and to take a breather.

A guide is not really necessary to reach the site (the way is well marked), but you may want to take along one of the youngsters from town who will invariably show up to point out the way.

Allow at least 2 hours from the time you begin your climb till you return to your car. Tennis shoes are fine.

Soft drinks are available in the town, but there are no accommodations.

Malinalco can also be reached by bus.

*Note:* The roads described above are rather narrow and curvy, but with good surfaces. They traverse some exquisite scenery and pass through several small towns. None of the roads are numbered. The mapping of this area leaves a lot to be desired—of four maps I consulted, none agreed. Nevertheless, if you take the cutoff at La Marquesa and follow the signs directing you to Chalma, you should not have any problems. There are many other connecting roads in this area, but check locally before attempting them. One road you definitely do *not* want to take is the 8-mile rock and dirt road directly from Tenancingo to Malinalco. This used to be the major access to Malinalco, but was always a bad road. It apparently has been allowed to deteriorate in recent years since other access has been improved. This is a treacherous road best used only by those with nerves of steel and four-wheel drive.

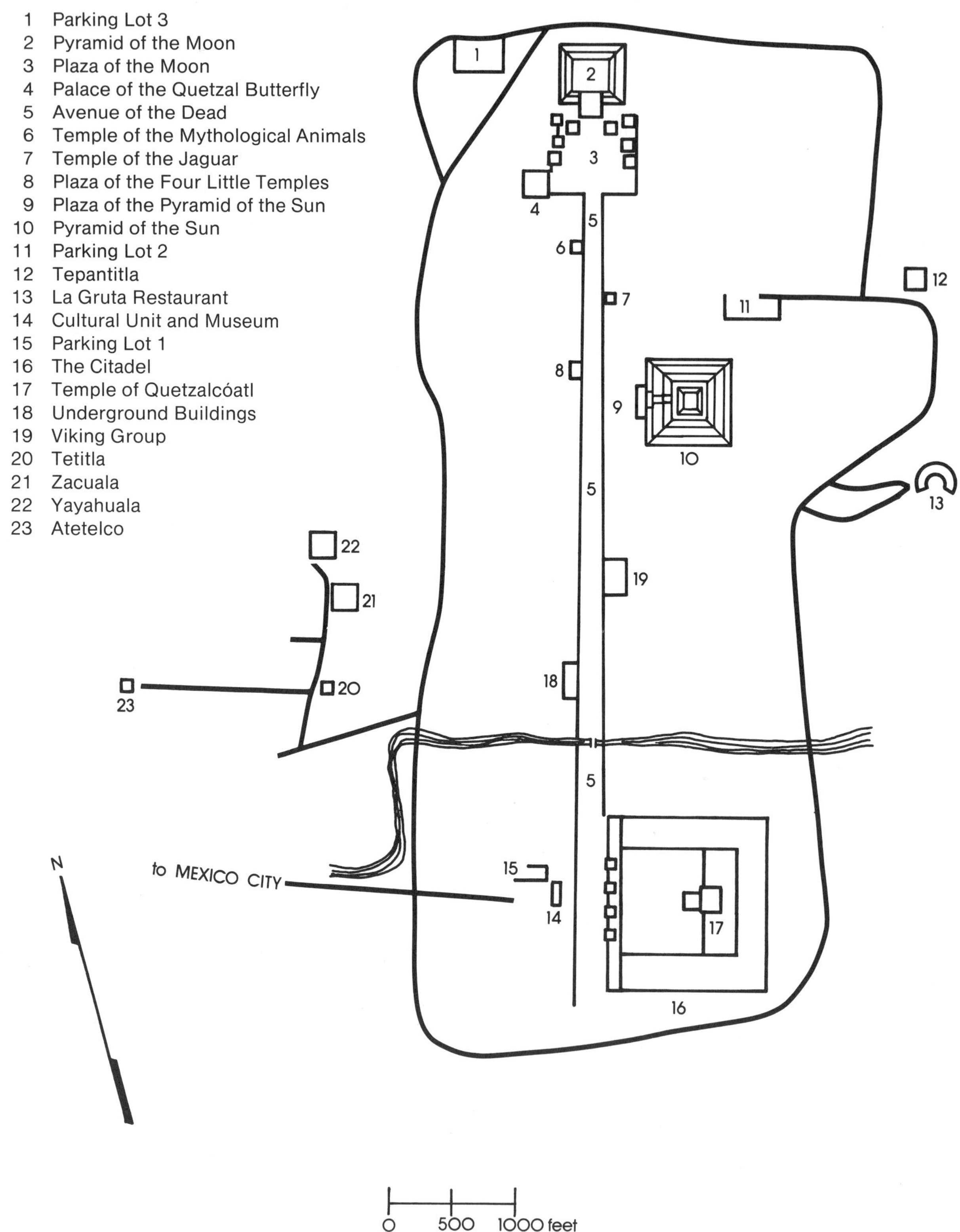


TEOTIHUACÁN

★★★★

# *Teotihuacán and Teotihuacán Museum*

(teh-oh-tee-wah-*kahn*)

DERIVATION: Nahuatl for "Place of Deification" or "Place of the Gods."
ORIGINAL NAME: Unknown.
CULTURE: Teotihuacán; see text.
LOCATION: Northeast part of the state of Mexico, Mexico.

## THE SITE

Teotihuacán is one of the largest, most-visited, and most easily accessible sites in Mesoamerica. Even the most casual visitor generally sees the pyramids.

A great deal of excavation and restoration was undertaken in the 1960s, and a road now encircles the site. There are parking lots strategically placed, which makes getting around a simple matter if you have a car. You can do it on foot, but it will take a bit more time.

There are several possible itineraries. The following one is an efficient way to spend your time. It differs from the one recommended in the excellent National Institute of Anthropology and History (INAH) guide.

When you enter the archaeological zone, take the road heading north to Parking Lot 3, near the Pyramid of the Moon. See the pyramid, its plaza, and the adjacent structures. Proceed to the Palace of the Quetzal Butterfly, whose entrance is found at the southwest corner of the Plaza of the Moon. Then head south on the Avenue of the Dead to the Temple of the Mythological Animals, which lies on the right (west) of the avenue. Continue south to the Temple of the Jaguar, on the left (east) of the avenue. Again head south along the avenue to the Plaza of the Four Little Temples on the right (west), and farther south to the Plaza of the Pyramid of the Sun, and to the pyramid itself to the left (east) of the avenue.

From here return to your car the same way you came. Follow the road east and south (clockwise) to Parking Lot 2. Walk east to Tepantitla, and return to your car.

It is probably time for a lunch break. There are two choices: the older La Gruta Restaurant, housed in a cave, or the more modern Las Pirámides, inside the cultural unit, which also houses the museum.

In either case, continue clockwise on the road from Parking Lot 2. The cutoff for La Gruta is some 800 yards south of Tepantitla. If you decide on Las Pirámides, continue clockwise to the entrance to the site and turn right (east), to Parking Lot 1 near the museum. If you eat at La Gruta, then proceed to Parking Lot 1 after lunch.

Now cross the Avenue of the Dead and see the Citadel and the Temple of Quetzalcóatl. Proceed north on the avenue to the Underground Buildings (to the left [west] of the avenue), then farther north to the Viking Group on the right (east) of the avenue. Return to the museum for a visit and on to your car.

If you have some energy left, you might want to see some of the outlying groups. If so, head north on the main road until you cross a bridge. Shortly after this there is a cutoff to the left (west). Take this for a few hundred yards and then another cutoff to the right (north). This one takes you to Tetitla, Zacuala, and, at the end of the road, Yayahuala. Then retrace your path to Tetitla and look for a cutoff to the right (west). This goes about 0.3 mile to Atetelco. From here return to the main entrance-exit to pick up the road back to Mexico City.

The main ceremonial structures of Teotihuacán lie along the Avenue of the Dead, which runs in a north-south line for about 1.3 miles. If you are doing the whole tour on foot, begin at one end of the avenue and proceed to the other end. This will take you past everything covered above except Tepantitla and the four outlying groups.

Teotihuacán was occupied from around 100 B.C. and experienced fantastic growth. By the period designated as Teotihuacán I (A.D. 1–150), it had an estimated population of 30,000. It was during this time that the Pyramids of the Sun and Moon were constructed. Certainly this was an outstanding achievement for any period, but especially so for such an early time. The early builders are unknown; they are simply referred to as the Teotihuacanos. There are, however, some indications of influence from or affinities with the Gulf Coast area.

Other theories hold that Teotihuacán got its impetus from the existing centers of Cuicuilco and Cholula. Some authorities believe there was great

*Pyramid of the Moon (end of the Late Preclassic period) with smaller structures flanking the Avenue of the Dead, Teotihuacán.*

continuity in customs and beliefs from Aztec times back through Toltec times to Teotihuacán. A linguistic continuity is also assumed that would make the Teotihuacanos perhaps an early branch of the Nahua. None of this is certain.

By the end of Teotihuacán I, Cuicuilco, the earlier dominant ceremonial center of the Valley of Mexico, had been eclipsed by the young giant, Teotihuacán. The city's growth continued until it reached its population peak of around 85,000 (some say as many as 200,000) sometime during the period A.D. 450–650, making it the largest city in the preindustrial world. It covered a larger area than Imperial Rome.

During this time, and even a bit earlier, Teotihuacán exerted a great deal of influence throughout Mesoamerica. Evidence from Kaminaljuyú indicates that this Maya site was taken over by an aristocracy from Teotihuacán. Other Maya sites showing Teotihuacán influence in sculpture, ceramics, lithics, or architecture are Tikal, Yaxhá, Altun Ha, and Becan. New evidence of this influence is regularly uncovered in Maya excavations. Closer to home, Teotihuacán influenced the centers of Cholula, Monte Albán, and El Tajín.

After A.D. 650, the population declined somewhat, and the city was destroyed, perhaps around 750. Who was responsible for the destruction is unknown, although several theories have been proposed. After this, the bulk of the population departed. Only about 2,000 to 5,000 people remained. Teotihuacán was never totally unoccupied, nor was it completely forgotten.

The Aztecs revered it as a holy city and also believed that it was a burial place. It is their names for the site and some of the structures that are used today. The great Moctezuma is said to have made pilgrimages there.

Let us begin our own pilgrimage at the Pyramid of the Moon. This structure and its plaza form the northern extremity of the Avenue of the Dead. Restoration in the 1960s has converted the grass-covered mound that I first saw in 1957 to an intriguing architectural complex. The base of the pyramid rises in four sloped tiers, though only the lower three have been restored. A projection of three tiers lies on the southern side, and this in turn is fronted by a five-tiered pyramidal platform of *talud-tablero* design. A stairway in three sections (the fourth or top one has not been restored) gives access on the southern side. It is a steep climb, but you should try to get at least as high as the top of the first platform. From here you get a comprehensive view of the Plaza of the Moon and of adjacent structures

*Pyramid of the Sun (end of the Late Preclassic period), at left of center as seen from the Pyramid of the Moon, Teotihuacán. The Plaza of the Pyramid of the Moon and its surrounding structures are in the foreground. The Avenue of the Dead is at right center.*

in the same style as the tiered platform abutting the front of the Pyramid of the Moon.

The remains of the lower portion of a structure containing ten altars, and beyond this a low platform with stairways on all four sides, are found in the central area of the Plaza of the Moon. To the south of the platform is a crude and eroded piece of three-dimensional sculpture. It has been proposed that the plaza was used for ceremonial activities.

Go now to the Palace of the Quetzal Butterfly, a magnificent structure discovered in 1962 when this section of Teotihuacán was being intensively excavated. Access is up a broad stair to a columned hall. At the top of the stair, on the right, is a huge serpent head with some remnants of paint. Some remnants of mural painting are found in the hall. A doorway on the northwest corner of the hall leads to an open courtyard, surrounded by bas-relief carved pillars. Mythological creatures and water

*Serpent head at the top of the stairs leading to the Palace of the Quetzal Butterfly, Teotihuacán. End of the Late Preclassic or Early Classic period.*

symbols are depicted and some inlaid obsidian discs are still in place. The carvings were originally polychromed. Painted decorations in an inset panel are above the pillars, and the whole is topped by merlons in the design of the Teotihuacán Yearsign. Mural paintings are found on the lower walls of the structure.

There are two other areas of interest that are part of this structural complex, though I must admit that I did not see them. Return to the hall where you entered, and head through the doorway on the southwest corner. A narrow stairway and alley lead to a series of rooms around a courtyard. This is the Jaguar's Palace, so named for painted jaguars found on the lower walls. On one side of the courtyard is a stairway, with remains of carved snake rattles at the bottom of the balustrades. Another group of rooms—with more murals—surrounding a large courtyard connects to the first group. Access is from a passage in the northwest corner of the first group.

The other area of interest in this complex is the substructure of the Feathered Shells. This structure was built between A.D. 100 and 200, and was later filled in to form a platform that supported the Palace of the Quetzal Butterfly. Access is by a modern tunnel in the northwest corner of the large courtyard. Polychromed bas-reliefs of feathered shells give the structure its name. They are accompanied by four-petaled flowers. There are also murals on the platform that supports the temple.

Proceed now to the Temple of the Mythological Animals. The murals that give the temple its name are part of an older building and access is by a modern door in the back of the structure. This may not be open to the public.

Continue to the Temple of the Jaguar. An interesting mural painting of a jaguar can be seen behind a modern protective fence and roof, but you can take pictures over them from an adjacent stairway.

Now head to the Plaza of the Four Little Temples. This is composed of a low platform with remains of four small temples on top.

We now go to the major monument at the site—the Pyramid of the Sun. To reach it, we pass through the plaza that fronts it and some palace-type structures.

The Pyramid of the Sun is not only the largest structure at Teotihuacán, but it has the most interesting history—and mythology. The Aztecs gave it its name; we do not know what it was called by the Teotihuacanos who built it. Some early native sources say that the pyramids were built by giants, others that they were erected by the gods before man existed. A more modern myth is that the Pyramid of the Sun is bigger (that is, greater in volume) than the Pyramid of Cheops in Egypt. This is patently incorrect. It is perhaps understandable that earlier writers made this error. Even today, different authorities give slightly different measurements. It is hard to understand, however, how modern authors continue to make this error or why they wish to perpetuate this myth. The facts are that the base of the Pyramid of the Sun is almost identical to the Pyramid of Cheops, but Cheops is almost twice as tall. The Pyramid of the Sun, including the original temple that topped it, is 243 feet high (according to Jorge Acosta, who wrote the INAH guide for Teotihuacán). Cheops originally rose to a height of 476 feet. The square bases of both pyramids are about 740 feet on each side.

The Pyramid of the Sun was the first major structure to be excavated at Teotihuacán, and in 1905 methods were still primitive. The work was carried out by Mexican archaeologist Leopoldo Batres, who—the story goes—having done his homework, expected to find earlier pyramids beneath the existing one. He peeled off the badly ruined outer surface of three faces and found to his dismay (at least I assume he was dismayed) that

*Interior courtyard of the Palace of the Quetzal Butterfly with carved and obsidian-inlayed columns, Teotihuacán. Note merlon decorations on the roof. End of the Late Preclassic or Early Classic period.*

there were no earlier structures beneath. By this time tons of stone had been removed.

Rocks were used to re-cover the pyramid, but large projecting stones that originally were used to anchor stone slabs and the stucco finish may still be seen. They were once part of the core of the pyramid and were never meant to be visible.

For this reason, the Pyramid of the Sun as seen today is not what it looked like originally; the reconstruction presents "various defects."

It is true that deep inside the core of the Pyramid of the Sun there is a very small earlier platform, but the huge mass that we see today was built in one great effort. Its interior was mostly adobe brick, the same material used for the construction of the Great Pyramid at Cholula. A projecting platform at the west side of the base of the pyramid may have been added somewhat later.

A stairway in several sections gives access to the top of the pyramid. Whether to climb it I leave up to you, but, as always, the higher you go the better the view of the other structures.

If you nostalgia buffs would like to see the remains of the old museum of Teotihuacán, you will find them to the south of the Pyramid of the Sun. All that is left is its paved floor and some old decorative metal columns lying in a heap. Some remains of pre-Columbian stone sculpture are found lying around. There is also a bench, and you may want to rest before returning to your car.

Drive to Parking Lot 2 and visit the nearby Tepantitla.

*Pyramid of the Sun (end of the Late Preclassic period), view from the northwest, Teotihuacán. Remains of small structures are in the foreground.*

Tepantitla is not part of the ceremonial center of Teotihuacán, but one of the site's suburban residential areas. A house here has been restored, but the reason for a visit is to see the remains of the mural paintings that adorn the walls.

Motifs include depictions of Tlaloc (the rain god), and many small figures are shown singing, dancing, catching butterflies, and cutting flowers. These happy individuals are carvorting in "Tlalocan," Tlaloc's earthly paradise, a place of fertility and abundance. This is probably one of the "happiest" murals in pre-Hispanic art.

From here drive to the restaurant of your choice.

After lunch, begin at the south end of the Avenue of the Dead and cross it to reach the Citadel. This is a large quadrangular complex, bordered on all four sides by a broad raised area, which supports pyramidal bases. The raised area encloses a lower courtyard. A stairway gives access on the western side to the top of the raised area, and another descends to the courtyard below.

In the center of the courtyard is a small rectangular platform, and behind this is a four-tiered structure that was built to cover the front of an earlier tiered structure. The earlier structure is the Temple of Quetzalcóatl, and it is the gem of this complex. The rear of the newer structure has been cut away from the front of the earlier one, forming a narrow passage that you can walk through. The face of the Temple of Quetzalcóatl is covered with magnificent sculptures—both three-dimensional and bas-relief—found on four tiers (it is assumed that there were six tiers originally). Huge projecting serpent heads with feathered collars alternate with stylized geometrical sculptures, which may represent Tlaloc or a corn deity. In between, in bas-relief, are undulating serpent bodies with rattles on their tails. The remaining space is filled with sea shells—all Caribbean varieties—and the whole was originally painted. Some paint remains, but the inlays of obsidian that decorated the eyes

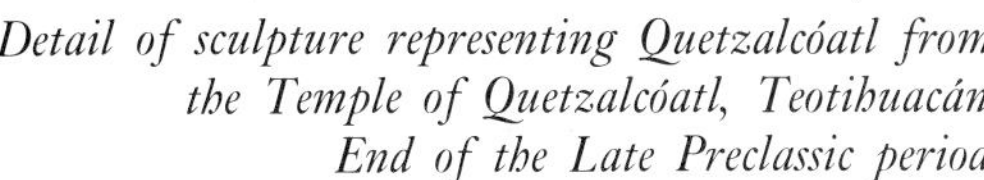

*Detail of sculpture representing Quetzalcóatl from the Temple of Quetzalcóatl, Teotihuacán. End of the Late Preclassic period.*

*Temple of Quetzalcóatl, south portion of main (west) face, Teotihuacán. End of the late Preclassic period.*

*Detail of sculpture—possibly representing Tlaloc or a corn deity—from the Temple of Quetzalcóatl, Teotihuacán. End of the Late Preclassic period.*

of the sculptures are little in evidence today. A stairway divides the façade and more serpent heads are found on the flanking balustrades.

The whole is truly spectacular, but must have been more so when it was built. Evidence indicates that originally all four sides of the pyramid were covered with such sculptures. Those were removed when the new tiered structure was added at the front. Some remnants of extra sculptured decorations lie on the ground north of the passageway. On the north side of the newer addition are remnants of painted stucco.

Leave the Citadel the way you came in and head to the Underground Buildings.

This complex was excavated in 1917, and was restored and reconstructed in such a way that you can see some earlier buildings beneath the later structures that covered them. Modern beams support the upper buildings and a metal stairway gives access to the earlier ones below. Some remnants of painted decorations are still visible.

The next group to see is the Viking Group, named for the foundation that provided funds for its exploration. An unusual feature in this complex is the use of two layers of sheet mica to cover the floor of one of the rooms. They were found below a floor of ground lava rock, a more commonly used material.

Return now for a look at the museum and back to your car at Parking Lot 1.

I have not visited the remaining four sections, but certainly Atetelco should be the most interesting since a great deal of restoration has been undertaken there. All four of these sections were residential. Remains of mural paintings are found at Atetelco and Tetitla. Zacuala and Yayahula are complexes of rooms, porticoes, and courtyards surrounded by huge walls.

## RECENT HISTORY

Teotihuacán's large pyramids had been well covered with vegetation for centuries by the time of the Spanish conquest. Nevertheless, their existence was known and they are mentioned in several early chronicles. Sculpture from the site was described as early as 1687.

In 1760 Ypólito Guerrero, an Indian who claimed Moctezuma as an ancestor, was the owner of the pyramids, and he was given permission to excavate. The results of this work have not come to light.

The first reported work was that of R. Almaraz, published in 1865. He was a geologist occupied in mapping the zone of Teotihuacán, and he undertook limited excavation. He also reported that most of the "dilapidation which is noted" was caused by people who were excavating the mounds in the hope of finding treasure. Looting is obviously not a recent problem.

In 1885, Désiré Charnay reported on his excavations at Teotihuacán (and a host of other sites). He hired thirty-five workers, who dug trenches, and he discovered burials containing figurines, masks, obsidian knives, and other artifacts.

Shortly afterward, Leopoldo Batres began excavating around the Pyramid of the Sun. This was some years before he began his assault on the pyramid itself.

Other large-scale investigations were undertaken by Manuel Gamio in 1917. Work on a smaller scale by Eduardo Noguera, Pedro Armillas, Sigvald Linné, Laurette Séjourné, Jorge Acosta, and many others, followed.

In 1962 more large-scale excavations were begun with the "Teotihuacán Project," under the direction of Ignacio Bernal for the National Insitute of Anthropology and History (INAH). These continued for two years. During this massive effort the Pyramid of the Moon, its plaza, and adjacent structures were restored. One of the most interesting discoveries was the Palace of the Quetzal Butterfly, which likewise was restored. During this time, William T. Sanders, of Pennsylvania State University, conducted an intensive study of the ecology and rural settlement patterns of the valley, and René Millon began a detailed mapping project. The Cultural Unit was also built during the Teotihuacán Project, as was the road that encircles the site.

## CONNECTION

1. 32 miles by paved road (all toll road) from Mexico City.

## GETTING THERE

Take toll Highway 85D north from Mexico City. After about 17 miles, a branch of the toll road heads east to Teotihuacán. The junction is marked "Pirámides," and it is marked the same way at following junctions. Follow this to the entrance gate of the archaeological zone.

You can also get to Teotihuacán by taking the older Highway 85 to Venta de Carpo, then going east to the site. This road is free and it is about the same distance. The toll road is recommended since it is faster.

The site can be reached by bus (they leave frequently), taxi, or on conducted tours from Mexico City. A train also runs to the town of San Martín Teotihuacán, but is very slow and not recommended. Sometimes it is difficult to arrange transportation from the train station to the site.

A guide is not necessary at Teotihuacán if you are carrying a plan of the site. If you prefer having a guide, however, you can bring one along from Mexico City or hire one at the entrance booth where tickets are sold.

There is an extra charge (nominal) for bringing your car into the archaeological zone. The parking lots inside the zone are free.

In addition to the two restaurants already mentioned, you can get soft drinks from stands at Parking Lots numbers 2 and 3. Various and sundry tourist junk is also sold. If you are looking for better quality, check the INAH-approved reproductions in shops in the Cultural Unit.

From October to June, there is a light-and-sound pageant in the evening in Spanish and English.

Many guidebooks recommend 3 to 5 hours for a visit. For the ruin buff, this really isn't enough time to see everything. I would suggest getting a good night's sleep beforehand and arriving at the site as early as possible—it opens at 8:00 A.M. You really need a whole day there. Don't plan to do much that evening. Otherwise, plan visits on two separate days.

Tennis shoes are fine.

★★★

# TEOTIHUACÁN MUSEUM

The museum at Teotihuacán is delightful, and a far cry from the old museum at the site. It is well-laid-out and lighted, and a great deal of information can be rapidly comprehended. It was designed (as was the Mexico City Museum) with a particular path in mind. As you enter, bear to the right, pass the bookstore, and continue around, counterclockwise.

Included in the displays are diagrams of the Valley of Mexico, showing the location of Teotihuacán, and others showing the geology of the area, chronological tables, and illustrations of the climate and topography of the area.

The various industries, flora and fauna, pottery, food, and items of dress used are the subjects of other displays. Religion, social and political organization, and urbanization are also covered. Outstanding is a scale model of the site. The second half of the museum covers architecture, mural painting, and plastic arts. The museum closes at 5:00 P.M., while visitors are given until 6:00 P.M. to leave the archaeological zone.

*Massive wall partly enclosing Huexotla. Late Postclassic period.*

★

# *Huexotla*

(weh-*shoh*-tlah)

ORIGINAL NAME: Huexotla.
CULTURE: Acolhuacán.
LOCATION: Eastern part of the state of Mexico, Mexico.

---

## THE SITE

The ruins of ancient Huexotla are nestled among the more modern structures of the town of the same name. The most impressive feature here is a wall some 15 feet high that borders a part of the site. It rises in several layers and is topped by wedge-shaped constructions, with spaces in between. It was reportedly built in A.D. 1409. In profile view, the wall tapers toward the top; its design is attractive and its mass is impressive.

It is the only known wall of its type in the Valley of Mexico, although one early chronicle mentions a great wall that surrounded the Palace of Nezahualcóyotl at Texcoco. This, however, is no longer in existence. The wall at Huexotla may have had a defensive function in addition to its use in partially defining the site. Behind the wall are some modern residences, a soccer field, and a church, the foundation of which is probably the remains of a pyramid. Near the church there are two other pyramids. One is a mound that is mostly overgrown with weeds, but there are remains of a couple of steps on the west side. When you climb to the top of this mound, you will see another structure to the east that is in somewhat better condition, though not as large as the first. The eastern structure is a pyramidal base with a western stair. The upper parts of the corners of the pyramid flanking the stairs are cleared and the top of the structure is paved. There are a number of low stone and plaster platforms built on top of the pavement, and these are thought to be the remains of small rectangular shrines. There are other mounds at Huexotla, but these are mostly unexcavated.

## RECENT HISTORY

During the late part of the late Postclassic period, Huexotla was one of fourteen dependent city-states that formed the nucleus of the kingdom of Acolhuacán. Texcoco was the capital of this kingdom, and its king was the supreme ruler. He appointed the rulers of the city-states and was assisted by them in his duties. According to William T. Sanders, who studied the settlement patterns in central Mexico, "each of these states consisted of a central urban town and a constellation of rural villages." After the Spanish conquest, the city-states became pueblos. The Spaniards, in general, preserved the basic settlement pattern and built churches in each of the pueblos.

## CONNECTION

1. 22.5 miles by paved road from the center of Mexico City, then a little over 1 mile of fair to rough dirt road.

## GETTING THERE

From Mexico City take Highway 190 southeast for 11 miles to Los Reyes. (Do not get on the toll road to Puebla, which begins shortly before Los Reyes.) At Los Reyes take the cutoff to the left (Highway 136) that is marked for Texcoco. Proceed on Highway 136 for about 11.5 miles till you come to a pyramid sign on the right indicating the cutoff for Huexotla. Take this dirt road and follow it as it curves to the right after 0.7 mile. It continues for another 0.4 mile, up to the wall that it passes on the west.

After you have seen the wall, drive to the far end and turn left. Go 0.1 mile and park. The pyramids are a few yards to the right though they are hidden by trees. Ask if you can't find them—there will be plenty of people around.

Huexotla can also be reached by bus or taxi from Mexico City. Soft drinks are available in the town.

Allow half an hour to see the wall and pyramids. Tennis shoes are fine.

*Pyramid, Tlapacoya. Middle–Late Preclassic period.*

★

# *Tlapacoya*

(tlah-pah-*koh*-yah)

CULTURE: See text.
LOCATION: Eastern part of the state of Mexico, Mexico.

## THE SITE

Tlapacoya is located near the town of the same name and is considered a transitional site between Late Preclassic Cuicuilco and the Early Classic Teotihuacán, although it overlapped both in time. It may have inherited the earlier site's function of serving as a religious center. The architecture at Tlapacoya indicates experimentation, and is believed to have served as an inspiration for the builders of Teotihuacán.

Though modest in size, the pyramid at Tlapacoya is a complex one. It rises in several tiers and has miltiple stairways facing in different directions. There is no evidence of a permanent temple on top. Although Tlapacoya has been nicely reconstructed, and the area around it kept cleared and planted with flowers, it is difficult to get a good descriptive photo of the pyramid. The front of the structure is just a few feet away from the edge of the hill on which it is built, so you cannot back off very far. A wide-angle lens will help, but will not entirely cure the problem. Morning light is best. On top of the pyramid are two vertical openings, the entrances to the remains of excavated tombs.

Man has apparently lived in the area of Tlapacoya for many thousands of years. Finds of some hearths, animal bones, and stone artifacts are currently dated to 19,000 B.C., but this has yet to be confirmed by additional work. At one time Tlapacoya was an island or peninsula, depending on the fluctuations of a lake that has since dried up.

There is evidence of Olmec influence during the Middle Preclassic period in the ceramic pots and figurines, but even earlier ceramics of local manufacture were discovered. Some ceramics discovered in three burials at Tlapacoya demonstrate a transition to Classic forms. The pyramid at Tlapacoya shows evidence of three phases of construction, dating from around 400 to 200 B.C., although the site continued to be active for some time thereafter.

## RECENT HISTORY

Tlapacoya was discovered only recently, and the major work of excavation and restoration at the site was undertaken by the Mexican archaeologists Beatriz Barba de Piña Chan and her husband, Román. They published the results of their work in 1956 in Mexico. Later, some stratigraphic work was carried out at the site by Paul Tolstoy and Louise Paradis, the results of which were published in 1970. Results of this work were a new classification of phase names for the basin of Mexico—which replaced an earlier system of overlapping subphases—and the discovery of a previously unknown Early Preclassic phase.

## CONNECTION

1. 16.5 miles by paved road from the center of Mexico City, then 0.6 mile of rough dirt road.

## GETTING THERE

From Mexico City take Highway 190 (the old Mexico City–Puebla Highway, not the newer toll road) southeast. Proceed to Los Reyes (about 11 miles) and continue on Highway 190 toward Ayotla. A bit over 5 miles past Los Reyes you will come to kilometer marker 10. Some 0.3 mile past this you will see a water tower and a basketball court on the right—and though it doesn't look like it, this is the cutoff you want. Turn right and go straight in for 0.4 mile till you reach a church. (You will cross a railroad track shortly after you turn off the highway.) Turn left at the church and go 0.1 mile, then turn right (this road doesn't look like much either) and go another 0.1 mile. This will bring you to a wall surrounding a cemetery, and, opposite it, the entrance gate to Tlapacoya. You can park nearby.

*Note:* The 0.6 mile of bumpy dirt road is actually through an inhabited area, so the roads are best thought of as streets. If you have doubts about any of the turns described, the people in the area will be happy to direct you. When you reach the site, you may not immediately realize it since you notice the cemetery wall first. When you are facing the wall directly, the gate to the site is behind you.

There is no food or drink at the site, but you will pass some small grocery stores that sell cold drinks on the first part of the dirt road. Allow about 20 minutes to see the pyramid. Tennis shoes are fine.

You could reach the dirt cutoff by local bus (this is actually the outskirts of Mexico City, though technically it is the state of Mexico) and walk to the site, or taxi all the way from Mexico City.

★★

# *Tenayuca*

(teh-nah-*yoo*-kah)

DERIVATION: Nahuatl for "Fortified Place."
ORIGINAL NAME: Tenayuca.
CULTURE: Chichimec; see text.
LOCATION: State of Mexico, Mexico, just north of Mexico City.

---

## THE SITE

Tenayuca is a very fine two-star site—perhaps two and a half stars would be a fairer description.

The site includes a large double pyramid, rising in four tiers, that has been partially restored, and a few small structures surrounding it. The whole is enclosed by a low modern wall and forms a plaza.

As you enter the gate on the south, you will see one of the long rows of serpents for which Tenayuca is famous. They surround three sides of the base of the pyramid and have stone carved heads. The rather fat S-shaped bodies are made up of small stones and mortar and were originally plastered and painted. While hardly graceful, they are plentiful. In addition to those at the base, more serpent heads project from the slope of the pyramid.

The most interesting sculptures at the site, however, are two coiled serpents, found at ground level on the north and south sides of the pyramid. As with the other serpents, only the heads are carved, but these have a crested decoration on top identifying the sculptures as Xiuhcóatl, the fire serpent. They are accompanied by low platforms.

Also of interest at ground level is a trench near the rear of the pyramid where remains of a wall or building can be seen.

When you circle around the front of the pyramid, you will want to climb the steps—some of which are made of blocks of carved stones. At the top of the steps you can get a good view of the inner stairway of an earlier structure. A wide-angle lens is good here. You can also climb to the top of this inner structure by a path at the back of the pyramid, and I recommend this since from that vantage point you can get a comprehensive view of the serpents below. To the right (south) of the outer stairway at ground level is a projecting platform with some interesting sculpture. There are depictions in bas-relief of crossed bones and three-dimensional projecting skulls. Several tunnels were cut into the pyramid during excavation but most are barred. Perhaps the caretaker could let you in.

Historical tradition speaks of the founding of Tenayuca by Xolotl, a Chichimec lord, in A.D. 1224, although ceramics from a somewhat earlier period have been found there. Tenayuca was perhaps the principal center in the Valley of Mexico between the fall of Tula and the rising of Tenochtitlán, but it never reached the size of the latter, by whom it was conquered.

There are at least six major construction phases at the site and perhaps a couple more showing minor alterations. The original double pyramid was covered over and enlarged on five occasions, probably beginning in A.D. 1299 and continuing at 52-year intervals, until the last building was erected in 1507.

Aztec influence becomes evident on the third reconstruction in 1351. The following three stages are purely Aztec. This is made clear by sloping rather than vertical walls on the tiers that make up the body of the pyramid and the walls of the temple that top them.

Nothing remains of the temples today. Tenayuca's double pyramid served as a model for the larger "Great Temple" at Tenochtitlán.

Vertical upper zones on the balustrades flanking the stairway occur on the two latest reconstructions and are visible on the inner stairway of the fifth stage.

Tenayuca was a living town at the time of the Spanish conquest, and fighting occured there in 1520. Bernal Díaz del Castillo refers to it as the "Town of the Serpents."

## RECENT HISTORY

Tenayuca apparently was forgotten for many years. It was generally believed that the mound was of natural origin. This was disproven during excavation by Mexican archaeologists starting in 1925. Among those working at the site were Alfonso Caso, Eduardo Noguera, Ignacio Marquina, and José Reygadas Vertiz. Later studies were undertaken by Jorge Acosta. A great deal of restoration has been

*Double stairway of the inner pyramid (fifth stage), Tenayuca. Late Postclassic period. Photograph by author.*

done and this is one of the best places to see typical Aztec architecture.

## CONNECTION

1. 7 miles by paved road from the center of Mexico City.

## GETTING THERE

Tenayuca can be reached by private car, taxi, or bus from Mexico City.

Take Calzada Vallejo north toward the industrial suburb of Tlalnepantla. As you near the town, you cross a small bridge. Take a right just after you cross the bridge, then a left at the first opportunity. This is a cobblestoned street that continues straight ahead for a couple of blocks to the pyramid.

There are several small grocery stores on the plaza facing the pyramid where cold drinks and packaged snacks may be purchased.

Tennis shoes are fine. Allow about 2 hours to visit the site.

*Row of serpents as seen from above, Tenayuca. Late Postclassic period. Photograph by author.*

*Coiled fire serpent, Xiuhcóatl, Tenayuca. Late Postclassic period. Photograph by author.*

*Restored one-room Aztec-period temple fronted by a long low platform, Santa Cecilia. Photograph by author.*

★★

# *Santa Cecilia and Santa Cecilia Museum*

(*sahn*-tah seh-*seel*-ee-ah)

DERIVATION: Spanish for "Saint Cecilia."
ORIGINAL NAME: Unknown.
CULTURE: Chichimec, Aztec.
LOCATION: State of Mexico, Mexico, just north of Mexico City.

---

## THE SITE

Santa Cecilia is a gem, the only place where a fully restored Aztec temple tops its pyramidal base. It serves to give a good idea of what other Aztec-period architecture must have looked like originally.

The main pyramid and temple are abutted by a lower pyramidal base, whose temple is not restored. A low platform is found in front. The whole sits on the rear of a large flat area (presumably a plaza) that has been restored with cobblestones. The main pyramidal base rises in four tiers, and almost its whole width in front is occupied by the stairway and flanking balustrades with vertical upper zones. A plain pillar, or stela, stands in the center at the top of the stair and banded drum-shaped sculptures are found on each side. The temple itself is composed of a single chamber with one doorway. Within is found a headless figure of the Chac Mool type.

Two sides of the plaza are now flanked with trees and well-kept grassy areas, giving a nice parklike atmosphere, and forming a pleasant setting for the temple.

Santa Cecilia is of Late Postclassic date and is typical of Aztec construction. It was apparently once a district of the Chichimec capital at Tenayuca.

## RECENT HISTORY

There is little in English about Santa Cecilia beyond the fact that it was restored a few years ago by the National Institute of Anthropology and History (INAH).

## CONNECTIONS

1. A little under 2 miles (mostly paved) north of Tenayuca, or
2. 9 miles from the center of Mexico City.

## GETTING THERE

First, follow the directions that take you to Tenayuca. Then follow the same road to the town of Santa Cecilia. When you get to the town, you will soon come to the church. Take the road on the side of the church to the pyramid.

Santa Cecilia may also be reached by taxi from Mexico City, and probably by bus.

There is no food or drink at the site, but you can get packaged snacks and cold drinks in town.

Tennis shoes are fine.

A visit here can be easily combined with a visit to Tenayuca. The two make a pleasant half-day trip from Mexico City. Allow 1½ hours to visit the temple at Santa Cecilia and the museum.

*Small Aztec-period sculpture, Santa Cecilia Museum. Photograph by author.*

## SANTA CECILIA MUSEUM

This small museum is a nice surprise. It is located in a building (and patio) to the right of the cobblestone plaza as you face the pyramid. Somebody will show up to let you in. If you are here to see the pyramid, you really should visit the museum as well. The indoor section was without lights at the time of our visit but the displays seemed well arranged. Included were pre-Columbian ceramic models of Aztec temples very much like the temple at Santa Cecilia. Carved skulls adorning a portion of a wall made another interesting exhibit. In the same room was a large drum-shaped carved stone.

The patio section is a delight. Various pieces of Aztec sculpture are charmingly displayed among potted plants and lush gardens. They are crying to have their pictures taken. There are standing and seated standard-bearers, glyph-carved panels, and other sculptures. They are unlabeled, but no matter. I don't know if all are from the site of Santa Cecilia, but all are certainly of Aztec style and date. Fast film would be good for the museum.

A locked glass bookcase had a surprisingly good selection of INAH guides. The caretaker will be happy to sell you some.

★★

# *Tlatelolco (Plaza of the Three Cultures)*

(tlah-tehl-*ohl*-koh)

DERIVATION: Nahuatl for "Artificial Mound of Sand."
ORIGINAL NAME: Tlatelolco.
CULTURE: Aztec.
LOCATION: North-central part of Mexico City.

---

## THE SITE

Tlatelolco, the rival sister-city of Tenochtitlán, the Aztec capital, has in the end won out. While Tenochtitlán lies buried under the center of Mexico City, Tlatelalco's ceremonial precincts have been reclaimed. It is one of the places where you can see the three major periods of Mexico's long history at a glance; the pre-Hispanic temple bases, a colonial church built in 1536, and modern office and apartment buildings; hence the new name of the Plaza of the Three Cultures.

There are raised walkways threading among the ancient buildings, and from them you get good views of the various temple bases. Just follow the indicated path.

One of the largest structures is the double pyramid opposite the church. The pyramid is of typical Aztec design, having double balustrades with vertical upper zones. It now tilts at an odd angle, apparently because of settling of the soil.

Other small pyramids and platforms, some circular, lie adjacent to the walkways. The most interesting is the Templo Calendárico, which has individual carved panels depicting dates. They form a frieze around the top of the first stage of the temple on three sides and total thirty-nine in all. Unfortunately, only the panels on one side are easy to see and photograph from the walkway. A telephoto lens is useful here for detail shots of the panels.

There are two higher sections of the walkways and from both you get good over-all views of the site. Here you will want to use a wide-angle lens.

*Note:* Although there are no signs saying so, you are not allowed to leave the walkways and traverse the grassy areas. It is tempting to do so for a closer look at some of the structures, but guards will promptly ask you to return to the walkways.

Tlatelolco was probably founded in the fourteenth century—although there is some evidence for occupancy of the area a century or more before—by a branch of the Aztec, sometime before another branch founded Tenochtitlán in 1325. The two rival centers grew and prospered, but remained independent until 1473 when Axayácatl, the Lord of Tenochtitlán, conquered Tlatelolco. He then installed his own governors.

The city that the Spanish conquistadors entered in 1519 was actually the double metropolis of Tenochtitlán-Tlatelolco, occupying an area of 20 square miles and having an estimated population of 200,000.

Tlatelolco had a long reputation as a great mercantile center even before its subjugation by Axayácatl. It still had the largest market at the time of the Spanish conquest.

The Spaniards were amazed at the size, variety of merchandise, and orderliness of the market. Conquistador Bernal Díaz del Castillo wrote a lengthy description of it in *The Discovery and Conquest of Mexico.* He ends by saying, "one would not have been able to see and inquire about it all in two days."

It is estimated that between 20,000 and 25,000 people attended the daily market at Tlatelolco, and that twice that many assembled for the special market held every fifth day.

This was also the site of the last battle of the Spanish conquest in central Mexico. It took place on August 13, 1521, when Tlatelolco fell to Hernán Cortés. A marble plaque near the church records this date and further informs that, "It was neither triumph nor defeat, but the painful birth of the Mestizo people that is the Mexico of today."

## RECENT HISTORY

Although numerous artifacts were dug up in Tlatelolco many years ago, it was only with the inauguration of a large urban renewal project in the 1960s that the site was restored to its present condition. Some excavation was undertaken, however, and ceramic reports were published during the 1940s

*Tlatelolco, showing pre-Columbian structures from the Late Postclassic period, a colonial church, and modern office and apartment buildings. Photograph by author.*

and 1950s. Work was sponsored by the Mexican government.

## CONNECTION

1.3 miles north of the Zócalo in Mexico City.

## GETTING THERE

Tlatelolco can be reached by private car, taxi, or bus from anywhere in Mexico City.

There is a small restaurant located behind the church. Tennis shoes (or even sandals) are fine.

Allow 1 hour to visit the site.

★★

# *Cuicuilco and Cuicuilco Museum*

(kwee-*kweel*-koh)

DERIVATION: Nahuatl for "Place of Singing and Dancing."
ORIGINAL NAME: Unknown.
CULTURE: See text.
LOCATION: On the southern extremity of Mexico City.

## THE SITE

The "Pyramid" of Cuicuilco (actually a stepped, truncated cone approached by ramps on the east and west sides) is of interest to the ruin buff primarily because of its massiveness and age rather than for any strong aesthetic appeal.

The structure is some 370 feet in diameter at its base and it rises to a height of 60 feet. Encased in the visible pyramid are two earlier constructions of a similar circular plan. Both lava blocks and river boulders were used to face the pyramid and its ramps.

Cuicuilco's heyday dates to the Late Preclassic period, and it has the earliest monumental and ceremonial architecture found in the Valley of Mexico. This fact alone makes a visit worthwhile.

As you leave the parking area, you head east toward the pyramid. A recommended tour would be to take the trail to the north and walk around the base of the pyramid. After you return to the west side, climb the ramp to the top. When you follow the trail to the north you get good over-all views of the pyramid and its main western ramp. From a distance the pyramid seems unusually squat, but its impressive dimensions become more apparent as you approach. You are actually walking on top of a lava flow that covered the base of the pyramid. As you circle the base, you can clearly see the four terraces that make up the structure.

Halfway around the base you come to the eastern ramp, which is not as well preserved as its western counterpart. From here take a short side trail to the southeast for a look at a small stone platform with steps. This lies some feet below the general level of the lava flow, so you have to get right to it before you see it. From here return to the base of the pyramid and continue your circle tour around the south side. In this area you can most easily appreciate the depth of the lava (25 to 30 feet) that covers the base; it has been cut back from the pyramid, leaving a sort of trench.

From here it is but a short detour to the southwest to the Cuicuilco Museum.

Return to the base and follow it around to a small vaulted construction covered by a modern roof. This is composed of large slabs driven deeply into the ground and tilting inward. On the inner surface of the slabs are remains of red paint applied in spirallike designs.

Head now to the western ramp and climb to the top of the pyramid. Under another modern roof are the remains of a horseshoe-shaped altar covered by river boulders. Beneath this latest altar are two earlier ones, covered over when the pyramid was enlarged.

The area around Cuicuilco was occupied by simple farmers, perhaps as early as 900 B.C., a time when other villages appeared around the lake in the Valley of Mexico. Its monumental constructions, however, date to 600–200 B.C., when Cuicuilco was the major center in the valley.

During the following period (200 B.C.–A.D. 300), various outside influences were felt in the valley and Cuicuilco's importance diminished. By A.D. 150 the emerging Teotihuacán had eclipsed Cuicuilco. At this time the site was abandoned, or at least the structures were no longer maintained and enlarged. The stone veneer became weakened by rains, allowing the sides to slump.

The final death knell occurred around A.D. 300 or 400 with the eruption of Xitle, a nearby volcano. Its lava flow covered the base of Cuicuilco's pyramid and formed what today is known as the Pedregal, a volcanic desert, on the southern extremity of Mexico City. This same eruption also engulfed the earlier site of Copilco—a Preclassic cemetery 2 miles north of Cuicuilco.

The principal deity at Cuicuilco seems to have been Xiuhtecuhtli (or Huehueteotl), the old fire god. Depictions of him in clay were found during excavations at the site. He is represented as an old man seated with bowed head; upon his head and shoulders he supports a brazier for burning incense.

*"Pyramid," showing the main western ramp, Cuicuilco. Late Preclassic period. Photograph by author.*

He was thought to control the volcanoes. Perhaps he quit doing his job when his subjects no longer maintained his temple. He was continuosly worshiped into Aztec times and it is their name for him that is used today.

Although Cuicuilco's pyramid is circular, there is no particular evidence to indicate that it was dedicated to Quetzalcóatl, as were later circular structures in Mesoamerica.

## RECENT HISTORY

In 1922, Byron Cummings, of the University of Arizona, and Manuel Gamio, Mexico's director of anthropology for the Mexican government, visited a hill in the Pedregal. They felt there were indications that the hill might not be natural and decided to excavate. What they uncovered was the Preclassic pyramid. Work was carried out under the direction of Cummings as a cooperative venture between the Mexican government and the University of Arizona, and later with the aid of the National Geographic Society, during the years of 1922 through 1925. In 1955 further investigation was undertaken by the University of California.

## CONNECTION

1. 8 miles by paved road from the central part of Mexico City.

## GETTING THERE

From Mexico City take Avenida Insurgentes Sur (this is also Highway 95) south. Continue past University City to the cutoff for Cuicuilco. The cutoff heads left (east) and is found 2.5 miles past (south of) the University Stadium. A few hundred feet of paved road gets you to the site.

There is no food or drink at the site. Tennis shoes are fine.

It would be best to plan for an afternoon visit as the sun then hits the main western ramp. A wide-angle lens is good to have along for over-all shots of the structure.

Allow about 1½ hours to visit the site and museum.

Cuicuilco can also be reached by taxi or bus from Mexico City, the obvious stopover.

# CUICUILCO MUSEUM

You might want to spend 5 minutes here since you are already at the site.

The most interesting display is found at the museum entrance, an oversized photo of one of the fire-god figures excavated at the site. The original figure is in the Mexico City Museum. Other items are rather poorly displayed and labeled pottery and figurines.

Previously the museum was located under the lava on the east side of the pyramid, and you can still see remnants of its construction. For some reason the museum was moved. At least the earlier one had an interesting location.

This is not one of Mexico's best, and you will not miss much if you pass it by.

*Remains of columns and glass-encased painted altars, Tizatlán. Late Postclassic period.*

★★

# *Tizatlán*

(tee-sah-*tlan*)

DERIVATION: Nahuatl for "Place of White Stone."
CULTURE: Tlaxcalan.
LOCATION: Central part of the state of Tlaxcala, Mexico.

---

## THE SITE

There are a few vestiges of architectural remains at Tizatlán, but the real reason to visit the site is for a look at some murals (of which there are precious few in Mesoamerica).

The murals are found on the sides of two altars, which sit on a platform. The altars measure approximately 6 feet by 3½ feet and are a bit over a foot high. They were painted on smooth unpolished lime in true fresco technique, and the colors used were yellow, red, blue, and black. The style is called Cholula-Puebla and it is similar to that in the *Codex Borgia* (a famous Aztec manuscript).

Depicted in the murals are the Nahua deities Tezcatlipoca (Smoking Mirror) and Tlahuizcalpantecuhtli (Lord of the house of dawn—the planet Venus as morning star). Other motifs represent the fire serpent, Xiuhcóatl, skulls, hearts, and hands. There is a border of the stepped fret design on the lower part of the altars. One of the clearest is a sort of patchwork-quilt design with a different motif in each rectangle.

Alfonso Caso believes that, in accordance with the mythological concepts of the Nahua, the altars represent the west, both the region of the land and the death of the sun.

Unfortunately, the altars are covered with glass cases (none too clean) making photography difficult. Even a polarizing filter did not help much.

Also found on the platform near the altars are the lower sections of large columns. Both columns and altars are shaded by modern roofs.

West of the platform (left as you face it) are a few architectural remains of walls and another small platform.

After you visit this area, head east to the nearby church for a look at the large stone statue on a pedestal, found near the northeast corner on the outside. Presumably, it was found at the site.

Also worth a look is the sixteenth-century open chapel adjoining the church. There are remains of murals, one of which depicts the baptism of Xicotencatl, the King of Tizatlán at the time of the Spanish conquest. At this time there was a Tlaxcalteca Confederation made up of four Dominians of Tlaxcala; Tizatlán was the third Dominion. After the conquest the church was built—possibly over part of the pre-Hispanic site. The part of the site with the altars and murals became overgrown and forgotten.

Although the architectural remains of Tizatlán are Late Postclassic, ceramics dating to an earlier time have been found at the site.

## RECENT HISTORY

According to a local story (of which I have been unable to learn the date), some years ago one of the villagers had a dream in which King Xicotencatl appeared to him and told him of treasure buried in the mound near the churchyard. He and his friends began digging, and located a wall. Further secret digging at night ensued and more of a temple was uncovered—but not the treasure they were hoping for. The Mexican government got wind of this and stopped the illicit excavation in time to preserve the remains.

Tizatlán was studied by Alfonso Caso, who published his findings in 1927 in Mexico.

## CONNECTIONS

1. 22 miles by paved road from Puebla to Tlaxacala, then 2.5 miles of paved road to Tizatlán, or
2. 75 miles by paved road (all toll roads) from Mexico City to the Tizatlán cutoff, then 0.3 mile of paved road to the site.

## GETTING THERE

Oddly enough, Tizatlán can be difficult to reach—especially if you drive to Tlaxcala from Puebla on Highway 119. We asked directions in Tlaxcala and drove around for an hour, so I couldn't possibly tell you how to get there the way we did. There

are many strange turns and cutoffs involved. Your best bet would be to get on the *autopista* (toll road) that runs in a northeast-southwest direction a couple of miles north of Tlaxcala. This is Highway 136D. Between kilometer markers 3 and 4, there is an unmarked paved cutoff heading north. (On some maps the site is shown as being south of the autopista; this is incorrect.) This cutoff goes for about 0.3 mile to the church. You can park in the churchyard beyond. Behind a wall on the far side is the site. This is not readily apparent, however, as the wall blocks the view of the ancient structures.

*Note:* A right fork of this road continues uphill. Make sure you stop just past the church.

From Mexico City take toll Highway 190D (150D) to San Martín Texmelucan (59 miles). Here you turn left (north) on toll Highway 136D and go for about 16 miles. The cutoff (to your left) is shortly after the kilometer 3 marker. Tizatlán is actually in the village of San Esteban Tizatlán, some 2.5 miles north of the central part of Tlaxcala.

You could also get to Tizatlán by taking a bus to Tlaxcala, and then a taxi to the site.

Best stopovers are Puebla or Mexico City, or, in an emergency, Tlaxcala.

There is no food or drink at the site, but a nearby grocery can provide soft drinks and packaged snacks.

Tennis shoes are fine. No guide is needed. At the time of our visit, an elderly man was selling garish carved walking canes, and he showed us around the church.

Allow half an hour to see Tizatlán and the church.

If you are staying in Puebla, a visit to Tizatlán can be combined with a visit to Cholula.

*Free-standing sculpture on the side of the colonial church, Tizatlán.*

★★★

# *Cholula and Cholula Museum*

(choh-*loo*-lah)

DERIVATION: "Place Where the Waters Spring From."
ORIGINAL NAME: Cholula.
CULTURE: See text.
LOCATION: North-central part of the state of Puebla, Mexico.

---

## THE SITE

What with fairly recent excavation and restoration, Cholula has become a most interesting site. Of prime importance of course, is the Great Pyramid—the largest in volume on the American continent—and the surrounding structures and sculptures. Remains of paintings may be seen inside the body of the pyramid on the face of earlier construction.

When you leave your car, cross the road and take a trail uphill toward the east to an area where there are some burials. They are inside small platforms covered with glass. The skeltons and pottery offerings are in situ. One of the platforms has carved skulls on the outside. There are a few other architectural remains in the vicinity.

From here head west toward the front of the pyramid (you are about halfway up) for views of the charming town of Cholula and of the restored architecture below on the west and south sides.

A trail and steps lead to the top of the pyramid and to the colonial church crowning the summit. From here you get more gorgeous views, making the tiring climb worthwhile. It is also worth a few minutes to visit the inside of the church for a look at its lovely gilt and white interior.

After you have caught your breath, head down the south side of the pyramid by foot trail and road for a look at the remains (there are plenty) on ground level.

Centered on the south side of the pyramid is the Patio of the Altars, flanked by the Southeast and Southwest Plazas. Stop for a look at the architectural remains of the Southeast Plaza first, then continue west to the Patio of the Altars. As you enter this patio, take a look at the small glass-covered Aztec shrine standing by itself in the southern part of the patio. It was constructed many centuries after the abandonment of the complex and contains pottery offerings and two human skulls.

Then proceed to the eastern part of the patio.

The Patio of the Altars is surrounded on three sides by typical Cholula-style architecture, which has been restored. There is a curved lower element—peculiar to the site—with fret designs supporting a *tablero* ("tablet" or "panel"). Wide stairs also flank the patio. Two of the four altars that give the patio its name are accompanied by stelae that have bas-relief designs in the style of El Tajín. These are found on the east side of the patio and at the foot of the north stairway. The altar on the east has carved edges.

There is another altar—a plain stone atop a small platform—in the northeast corner of the patio. Nearby on the patio floor are two pieces of three-dimensional sculptures. One is a rather crude head, the other seemingly part of an animal.

Continue around the patio to the west altar, a large slab with carved edges depicting a serpent.

You now leave the Patio of the Altars and go west to the Southwest Plaza. In this area are remains of construction from various periods. It is quite fascinating, but, I must admit, rather confusing. Some skeletal remains under glass are found in this area.

From the Southwest Plaza look up the side of the pyramid near the southwest corner to see a bit of construction that was once part of the pyramid. Most of the rest of the upper portion of the pyramid is grass-covered and unrestored.

Continue now to the north for a look at the west face (front) of the pyramid. Here is found the Stone Building. It is composed of three sloped tiers with a *tablero* atop each one and a broad central stairway. Construction was faced with large well-cut and fitted stone blocks. The inset panels of the *tablero* are decorated with a braid motif. This structure formed a part of a platform projecting from the body of the pyramid. It is one of the best constructed buildings at the site, which perhaps accounts for why its severe crispness almost makes it seem overrestored.

All of Cholula's other buildings were constructed of an adobe brick nucleus faced with small stones,

*Patio of the Altars showing the north stairway, Cholula. Classic period. The Great Pyramid rises behind the stairway and supports a colonial church.*

and then stuccoed. This building method allowed rapid deterioration once maintenance was discontinued.

There is an interesting tradition about the adobe bricks used in constructing the pyramid. It is said that the bricks were made at Amecameca, over 30 miles away as the crow flies. The bricks were reportedly transported by 20,000 prisoners, who stood in line and passed them along. This means it would have been necessary for them to have stood about 8 feet apart—a figure that doesn't sound unreasonable.

Facing the stairway is a plain stela with a rectangular perforation of unknown significance.

Return now to the parking area and get a cold drink (sold at stands) and have a short rest. Then cross the road to the entrance of the tunnels. Several miles of tunnels were cut into the pyramid in the 1930s, and they revealed several earlier pyramids within. The tunnels are illuminated—though hardly brilliantly lighted—and you can see remains of paintings and the surface of the earlier structures. Bring a flash unit along.

When you leave the tunnels, cross the road again and head a bit east for a look at the Cholula Museum.

Ceramic evidence indicates that the area of Cholula was occupied from the Middle Preclassic period (ca. 500 B.C.) to the Spanish conquest, and up until today.

The pyramid, however, and the earlier structures it encloses were erected from around the time of Christ until the eighth century. At this time (accord-

*View of the east side of the Patio of the Altars, Cholula. Altar 1 and its stela and two crude three-dimensional sculptures are at center. Classic period.*

ing to some authorities), for unknown reasons the site was abandoned. The city of Cholula that the Spaniards found in 1519 was located more to the northeast.

From its beginning, Cholula has been a place of religious pilgrimage and, therefore, shows influence from various areas. There are indications of connections with Monte Albán in the Middle Preclassic period. In the Early Classic period (starting around A.D. 200–300) Cholula was an urban city-state under the domination of Teotihuacán. According to native histories, around A.D. 700–800 the city was conquered by the Olmeca-Xicalanca, who in turn were expelled in A.D. 1168 by the Toltec. Evidence of these various influences is found in the ceramics from the site. The Late Postclassic wares show a fusion of the earlier traditions resulting in the famous Cholula polychrome.

## RECENT HISTORY

The Mexican government's Department of Pre-Hispanic Monuments (now the National Institute of Anthropology and History) initiated archaeological investigations at Cholula in 1930, under the supervision of Ignacio Marquina. During this period the tunnels were dug. The findings were reported in Mexico in 1939.

In 1966, Project Cholula was begun; the aim was further exploration and restoration of some of the structures. In 1967, Marquina was again put in charge, and was assisted by several Mexican archae-

*Northeast corner of the Patio of the Altars, Cholula. Classic period.*

*Detail of the west side of the Patio of the Altars showing curved element typical of Cholula architecture, Cholula. Classic period.*

*Stone Building projecting from the west side of the Great Pyramid, Cholula. Classic period.*

ologists and a group of architecture and engineering students from the University of Puebla. Work continued until 1970 and resulted in the restoration seen today. This work is a remarkable achievement when you consider that in some places 30 feet of debris—accumulated as a result of the erosion of the Great Pyramid—had to be removed. Both mechanized equipment and hand labor were used. In 1975 we were told that in a few more years, when funds are available, further investigations will be undertaken.

## CONNECTIONS

1. 8 miles by paved road from Puebla, or
2. 78 miles by paved road (59 miles toll road) from Mexico City.

## GETTING THERE

From Puebla take Highway 190 (150) west for 6 miles to the cutoff for Cholula. The cutoff heads south 2 miles to the site. There is also a new road connecting the two points, but it will be difficult to find in Puebla. It would make a good route back.

From Mexico City take toll Highway 190D (150D) east to San Martín Texmelucan (59 miles). Then take the old Highway 190 (150) (to your right) to the Cholula cutoff (17 miles), and turn right for 2 miles to the site.

Cholula may be reached by bus from Mexico City and by bus or taxi from Puebla—the only recommended stopovers.

Soft drinks and snacks are sold across the road from the north side of the pyramid and a short distance east on the same road are several roadside restaurants.

I preferred boots for this one, but you could probably get by in tennis shoes. Allow 2½ hours to visit the site and museum. Afternoon hours offer best lighting on the restored structures.

While a guide isn't essential, you will see more, in less time, if you have one along. They will be found in the area where you park (across the road from the side of the pyramid) and some speak English. Settle on a price beforehand.

*Cutaway model of the Great Pyramid showing the crowning colonial church, an earlier inner pyramid, and the Stone Building at the bottom, Cholula Museum.*

★★

## CHOLULA MUSEUM

The small, well-lighted museum at Cholula is worth a visit to see the model of the Great Pyramid. It is shown partially reconstructed and in cross-section, giving a good idea of the earlier construction phases.

Other displays include ceramics and reconstruction drawings.

The lighting is such that you can get hand-held photographs of the model, even with medium-speed color film.

★★

# *Tepozteco*

(teh-pohs-*teh*-koh)

DERIVATION: Nahuatl for "Place of the Ax."
CULTURE: Tlahuica or Tepozteca; see text.
LOCATION: Northern part of the state of Morelos, Mexico.

## THE SITE

The one point of interest at Tepozteco is a Late Postclassic shrine perched atop a pinnacle some 1,200 feet above the town of Tepoztlán. Only you can decide if you think it is worth the climb, but let me say that if you attempt it, it will seem like three times the recorded 1,200 feet. This one is definitely not recommended for anyone with heart or respiratory problems.

The climb takes only 1 hour, but it is an exhausting hour. Nevertheless, the footing is generally good, and the trail goes through some lovely scenery on the way. There is also a tall metal ladder to negotiate as you near the site. It is sturdy and not a problem.

The Temple of Tepozteco rests on a pyramidal base and is composed of two chambers, with a stairway giving access on the western side. Although there is no longer a roof, the massive walls of the temple rise over 6 feet. The inner chamber—with a bench running around three sides—is the most interesting since it contains remains of sculptured decorations. The jambs that formed the doorway to the inner chamber are also carved. The inner chamber reportedly originally contained a statue of Tepoztecatl, the god of pulque (an indigenous intoxicating beverage still imbibed in Mexico) to whom the shrine was dedicated. He is described as a sort of patron saint of Tepoztlán.

During the early colonial period a certain Fray Domingo de la Asunción sought to destroy this statue in an effort to convert the local inhabitants to Catholicism. Many legends have sprung from his act. One says he cast the statue over the cliff, but that it landed intact, whereupon it was demolished by hand, the fragments being used in the foundations of a church in a neighboring town.

The Tlahuicas or Tepoztecas, both Nahua groups related to the Aztec, are generally credited with building Tepozteco. They were later conquered by the Aztec. A carving with a glyph for the Aztec king Ahuitzotl was found in the debris of the temple, and he is known to have reigned from 1486 to 1502. The temple was built before this and perhaps before the Aztec capital of Tenochtitlán, but is still relatively late. It shows many Aztec architectural characteristics. Pottery found at Tepoztlán also confirms this late date.

The shrine of Tepozteco was a place of pilgrimage in pre-Hispanic times, and, with the town of Tepoztlán below, was a living entity at the time of the Spanish conquest.

Views of the town below and the countryside are superb.

## RECENT HISTORY

Knowledge of Tepozteco was never lost, but the first archaeological report of the site was that dated 1895 by Mexican architect Francisco Rodríguez.

He did a plan of the temple and sketches of the reliefs, and discovered that the terrain at the top of the pinnacle was leveled to accommodate the temple. There has been no systematic excavation in the area, but apparently Eduard Seler studied the reliefs.

## CONNECTIONS

1. 45 miles by paved road (all toll roads) from Mexico City, or
2. 17 miles by paved road (all toll roads) from Cuernavaca.

## GETTING THERE

From Mexico City take toll Highway 95D south for about 40 miles. Then take toll Highway 115D east to the Tepoztlán cutoff (5 miles). Then, less than 1 mile of paved road gets you to the town of Tepoztlán. Drive through the town to its far end. There is a parking area near the park where you begin your climb.

From Cuernavaca take toll Highway 95D north for 12 miles, then toll Highway 115D to the Tepoztlán cutoff.

*Back view of the Temple of Tepozteco and the pinnacle on which it is perched, Tepozteco. Late Postclassic period.*

There is also an old road to Tepoztlán that connects with 95D some 6 miles north of Cuernavaca. It has a good surface but is narrow and curvy. It is the same distance as going by toll road 115D and, therefore, not as good a choice.

In addition to Mexico City or Cuernavaca, you could spend the night in Tepoztlán at the Posada de Tepozteco on a hill overlooking the town, or at one of the resorts near Cuautla.

There is no food at the site, but the caretaker has soft drinks available (kept cool in pine straw). I could not help but wonder who carried them all the way up.

This is one trip where you will want to strip down your camera gear to bare essentials. A normal lens will get you by. You can make the climb in tennis shoes but boots would offer more support. Allow about 3 hours from the time you leave your car till you return. Soft drinks and prepackaged munchies are available at grocery stores in town, or you can get lunch at the Posada de Tepozteco.

A visit to Tepozteco can be combined with a visit to the Tepoztlán Museum and the ruins of Teopanzolco in Cuernavaca. Unless you are a masochist, do not try to combine it with another exhausting site like Chalcatzingo.

You can get to Tepoztlán by bus from Cuernavaca or Mexico City if you are without a car.

*Detail of carved stones that form the bench in the back chamber of the Temple of Tepozteco. Late Postclassic period.*

★★

## *Tepoztlán Museum*

The museum in Tepoztlán is located behind the convent in the center of town. It houses the collection of Carlos Pellicer. (See "La Venta Park Museum" for more on this man.)

It contains artifacts from all over the republic, and they are reasonably well displayed. It is particularly strong on Maya antiquities. Unfortunately, the labeling is not as careful as one might wish.

Allow ½ hour or a bit more to visit the museum. It is worth a stop if you are here anyway to see Tepozteco.

★★★

## *Cuernavaca Museum*

The Cuernavaca Museum is housed in the Palace of Cortés on the east side of the plaza in the center of Cuernavaca. The construction of the palace was begun by Cortés in 1530, and it is said that it was his favorite residence in Mexico. From it he supervised the vast domains that were granted him by the Spanish Crown.

The palace served as the administrative center

*Stone carving of a female figure in a niche, from Xochicalco, Cuernavaca Museum. Classic period. Photograph by author.*

of the area until the late 1960s, when it was converted into an art museum. Later it became a museum of archaeology and history.

The first floor contains the archaeological collection, which covers a time span dating from the Asian migrations through the Postclassic period. There are several rooms arranged in chronological order in a counterclockwise direction.

Among the various well-labeled displays are interesting stone carvings, some from the nearby site of Xochicalco. In addition, there are charts and diagrams and ceramic displays. Various publications are sold at the desk on the first floor.

The second floor houses the historical collection and represents the colonial period through modern times. Also on the second floor, in an open gallery, are the murals painted by Diego Rivera in 1930, depicting the history of Cuernavaca.

During a 1973 restoration of the palace, the remains of a Tlahuica structure were uncovered. (See "Tepozteco" for more on the Tlahuica.) Remnants of this structure can now be seen in front of the palace and in the archaeological section inside.

Allow 1½ hours to see this delightful museum.

★★

# *Teopanzolco*

(teh-oh-pahn-*sohl*-koh)

DERIVATION: Nahuatl for "in an old (or abandoned) temple."
CULTURE: Tlahuica; see text.
LOCATION: West-central part of the state of Morelos, Mexico, within the city limits of Cuernavaca.

## THE SITE

The double pyramid of Teopanzolco is a typical example of Aztec period architecture. The building is composed of two pyramidal structures, one built over the other, a Mexican custom.

The inner pyramid has a double stairway broken by projections on the balustrades. The lower walls of the two temples are found on top. The outer pyramid has a similar double stairway on the west side, but without the projections. A wide-angle lens is useful here for photos of the inner stairway.

The double pyramid faces a plaza, as do several small, low platforms, a couple of which are circular. In the back of the double pyramid is another structure, which appears to have been built in more than one construction stage.

Teopanzolco was originally built by the Tlahuica, according to most sources. This Nahua tribe was later conquered by the Aztec, although the Tlahuica still occupied the area at the time of the Spanish conquest and were paying tribute to the Aztec.

The ceramic evidence seems to indicate an Early Postclassic date, but probably postdating the Toltec complex. The pottery may be contemporaneous with "Aztec II" ceramics, though some authorities date this ware to around A.D. 1200–1350.

## RECENT HISTORY

The story goes that Teopanzolco was discovered in 1910 during the Mexican Revolution, when an artillary emplacement on a mound shook loose some dirt and revealed stone construction below. What was below was the double pyramid.

In the 1920s the Mexican government undertook some excavation of the site and in 1956–57, Eduardo Noguera and Román Piña Chan reported on its stratigraphy.

## CONNECTIONS

1. 52 miles by paved road (all toll road) from Mexico City.
2. The site is in the northeastern part of the city of Cuernavaca near the railway station.

## GETTING THERE

From Mexico City take toll Highway 95D south to Cuernavaca.

The site may also be reached by bus from Mexico City to Cuernavaca, then by taxi or local bus.

There is no food or drink at the site itself, but you are in Cuernavaca where food, drink, and accommodations are readily available. Tennis shoes are fine.

*Double stairway of the inner pyramid, Teopanzolco. Postclassic period.*

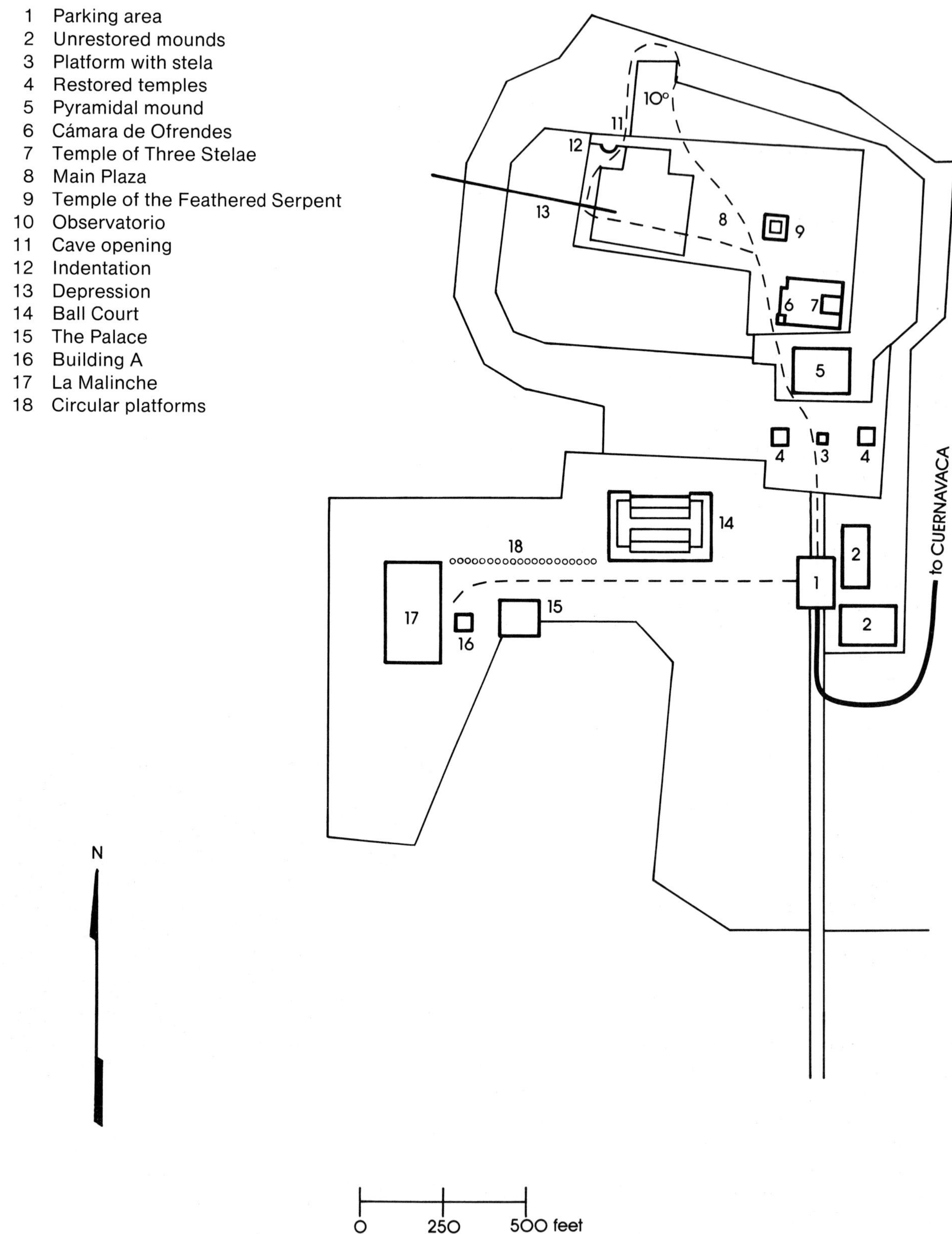

1 Parking area
2 Unrestored mounds
3 Platform with stela
4 Restored temples
5 Pyramidal mound
6 Cámara de Ofrendes
7 Temple of Three Stelae
8 Main Plaza
9 Temple of the Feathered Serpent
10 Observatorio
11 Cave opening
12 Indentation
13 Depression
14 Ball Court
15 The Palace
16 Building A
17 La Malinche
18 Circular platforms
to CUERNAVACA
N
0
250
500 feet


XOCHICALCO

★★★

# *Xochicalco*

(soh-chee-*kahl*-koh)

DERIVATION: Nahuatl for "House of Flowers."
ORIGINAL NAME: Unknown.
CULTURE: See text.
LOCATION: Western part of the state of Morelos, Mexico.

---

## THE SITE

Xochicalco is one of the most interesting, important, and thoroughly delightful sites in central Mexico. It is located on an artificially terraced and partially leveled hill called the Acropolis, overlooking a beautiful green countryside and some small lakes, although the area can become barren in the dry season.

When you arrive at the parking area, climb one of the unrestored mounds nearby for some good overall views of the lower sections. An impressive number of remains, still unstudied, surround you; however, the stone walls of some structures are clearly discernible.

As you head north from the parking area, you come to a plaza with a low platform in the center. On the platform is a badly eroded stela. Flanking the plaza on the east and west sides are two restored temples. They are similar in design and each is composed of sloped pyramidal base, the lower portion of sloped temple walls and pillars, and a single stairway with balustrades facing the plaza.

Bounding the plaza on the north is a large pyramidal mound with a partially restored lower stairway. I recommend climbing this on your way to the Main Plaza for a good view of the other structures.

Beyond the mound, continue north. This trail will take you past a large structure on your right (east). The pyramidal base rises in two tiers and supports a broad stairway. A small sanctuary, the Cámara de Ofrendes ("Chamber of Offerings"), lies to the south of the stairway and there are other architectural remains nearby. A double row of pillars at the top of the stairway provided openings to a large paved patio and another small temple at the rear, called the Temple of Three Stelae. In 1961 three beautifully carved, but broken, stelae were excavated in the debris of the temple, giving it its name. They are now in the Mexico City Museum. Other carved monuments from Xochicalco are found in the Cuernavaca Museum.

A bit farther north is the Temple of the Feathered Serpent (also called the Higher Monument), the real gem of the site. This single-chambered temple with lower walls intact rises on a pyramidal base and is approached by a western stair. Its fame lies with the multitude of carvings on its outer surfaces. There is no evidence of earlier construction beneath the existing one.

On the lower talus slope there are depictions of the feathered serpent, Quetzalcóatl, stylized shells—a symbol of this deity—and seated figures in Mayoid style. There are also glyphs, and dates in the bar-and-dot system used by the Maya and Zapotec. Also found on the monument are glyphs and dates in the system used by the Mixtec and Nahua groups—dots without bars. The reliefs average some 3 inches deep, and the whole was originally painted.

The panel above the talus has some carved remains, and the projecting cornice forms a border of stylized seashells.

After a tour of the lower part of the structure—and you will want to spend a lot of time studying the reliefs—climb the stair for a look at the top. The lower part of the ramps flanking the stairs have a design representing scales of the serpent. The remains of the lower temple walls and the jambs have more carvings of sandaled figures, glyphs, birds, animals, and warriors with shields and darts. This temple and others at the site, are thought to have had flat roofs originally. A wide-angle lens is good here since you cannot step back very far from the reliefs. One theory is that the motifs on the Temple of the Feathered Serpent, with calendric glyphs in two styles, represent some adjustment in the calendar. In the Main Plaza, near the Temple of the Feathered Serpent, is a pile of carved stones, which apparently originally adorned this or another temple.

From here head across the plaza toward the northwest, and take the trail that heads downhill. This eventually leads to a cavelike opening in the side of the hill. You pass more unexcavated mounds

*Temple of the Three Stelae at the top of the stairway, and the Chamber of Offerings at the right of the base of the stairway, Xochicalco. Late Classic–Early Postclassic periods.*

*The Temple of the Feathered Serpent, view from the southwest, Xochicalco. Late Classic–Early Postclassic periods.*

*Detail of the lower talus of the Temple of the Feathered Serpent showing a depiction of Quetzalcóatl, Xochicalco. Late Classic–Early Postclassic periods.*

and a small opening in the ground labeled Observatorio (see below) on the way.

Bring along a flashlight if you want to visit the cave—and it is worth a few minutes. Inside are remains of a broad stairway and, farther along to the east, a vertical hole (rather like a chimney) leading to the outside. This may have served for astronomical observations or may have been used as a ventilating shaft. It is this opening that is visible at ground level above. The upper part of the shaft is lined with boulders. There are also remains of stucco floors in the cave.

When you leave the cave, take the other trail back uphill. This leads to an area west of the Main Plaza. After a short but steep climb you come to an area with remains of a stucco floor and a small rectangular platform. This area forms an indentation in the hillside and may lie above the stairs in the cave below. I have been unable to learn anything about it.

From here continue to the south towards a depression in the terraced hillside. This depression is several feet wide and runs in an east-west direction from the rear of the unrestored structure that faces the Main Plaza on the west downhill over terraces for many hundreds of feet. Part of it has remains of stucco lining and again, I must confess, I have been unable to learn more about it, although it may have been one of the ancient roads or causeways. It is easily seen on aerial photos of the site.

Follow the depression uphill (east) for a while till you are treated to nice views of the Main Plaza. From here you can see the ball court and remaining structures off to the south. Trails are few in this area, but you can climb downhill through the vegetation to the ball court. If this looks too steep,

*Detail of the lower talus of the Temple of the Feathered Serpent showing a seated Mayoid figure, Xochicalco. Late Classic–Early Postclassic periods.*

return to the Main Plaza, go south to the parking area, and take the trail west to the ball court.

Xochicalco's impressive ball court is over 200 feet long and is in the typical shape of the letter I The walls flanking the playing area are sloped and meet vertical walls with stone rings. It is sometimes compared to the main ball court at Tula.

From the ball court, proceed west to an architectural complex called "The Palace" (El Palacio or Calmecac). Here you see the lower walls of many interconnecting rooms and patios. This is thought to have been a residential area, and it included a sweat bath.

A bit farther west is Building A—a small structure that may have been an altar. There are some remains of lower walls and a stucco floor.

Again to the west is the large pyramidal mound called La Malinche; although partly excavated, no restoration has been attempted. It is worth a climb for views of the other structures.

From the top of La Malinche you can see a row of low circular platforms paralleling the road you have just walked. There are more easily seen if the vegetation is not too lush. Their function is unknown, but they may have been altars. Their diameter is too great for them to have been remains of columns.

From La Malinche proceed back to the parking area and caretaker's house for a well-deserved cold drink.

Archaeologically Xochicalco is a most interesting site, although even today it is far from thoroughly understood. The Temple of the Feathered Serpent, and probably most of the other visible architectural remains, date to a period called Xochicalco III (A.D.

*View of the Palace (left center) and La Malinche (upper center), looking west, Xochicalco. Late Classic–Early Postclassic periods.*

700–1000), although there was some occupancy of the area as early as 200 B.C.

In addition to the ceremonial structures occupying the main portion of the Acropolis, there is an extensive complex of buildings on the neighboring hill (Cerro de Bodega), to which the Acropolis is connected by a causeway. The structures on Cerro de Bodega were probably ceremonial, but may also have acted as a fort given that the area is walled.

The lower slopes of the Acropolis are circled by moats and dry stone walls, which also were probably fortifications. There is evidence of heavy occupancy on the slopes of the Acropolis and on the plateau to the north. It is estimated that Xochicalco had a population of 10,000 to 20,000 people in its heyday.

Xochicalco was influenced by various other cultural groups during its history. There may have been influence from the Maya area as early as A.D. 300, but certainly there was some in the eighth century A.D. Other influences proceeded from Teotihuacán, the Zapotec and Mixtec areas of Oaxaca and Puebla, and perhaps from El Tajín on the Gulf Coast. It is possible that Mixtec speakers settled at Xochicalco in Late Classic times.

Xochilcalco is sometimes thought of as a connecting link between Classic Teotihuacán and Postclassic Tula, with which it was contemporaneous in part.

Xochicalco also exerted influence upon Mesoamerica for years to come. This is evident in the sculptural style of the Toltec and even, in a few instances, in sculpture as late as the Aztec period.

Some authorities believe that Xochicalco is the legendary "Tamoanchán" of Toltec-Mexica traditions. The name, apparently of Mayance origin, means "Place of the Bird-Serpent." Tamoanchán was regarded in pre-Columbian religion as a sort of primordial terrestrial paradise occupied by the gods.

Robert Chadwick believes that an early dynasty (seventh century A.D.) of Quetzalcóatl ruled at Xochicalco and that this group may have been responsible for the intrusive foreign traits found in Yucatán some two centuries before the Toltec period at Chichén Itzá.

In summary, we know that Xochicalco received and transmitted many influences during its history, but much is still to be learned about some of the connections.

## RECENT HISTORY

The ruins of Xochicalco were first explored and described by Antonio Alzate in 1777 and illustrations were published by Alexander von Humboldt in 1810. The site was visited by the ill-fated Maximilian while he was emperor of Mexico. In 1910 Leopoldo Batres restored the Temple of the Feathered Serpent. Eduard Seler made some study of the sculpture in the early twentieth century and in 1928 Marshall Saville compiled an annotated bibliography of works on the site.

Major work at Xochicalco, including excavations and restoration, was conducted from the 1940s to the 1960s by Mexican and American arhcaeologists. Of primary importance are the ceramic studies of Eduardo Noguera, published in 1947, and the discovery of three stelae by C. A. Sáenz in 1961, as well as his later work at the site.

## CONNECTIONS

1. 76 miles by paved road (68 miles are toll roads) from Mexico City, or
2. 24 miles by paved road (16 miles are toll roads) from Cuernavaca.

## GETTING THERE

From Mexico City or Cuernavaca take Highway 95D (toll road) south. Proceed to the Alpuyeca cutoff some 16 miles south of the Cuernavaca cloverleaf. Turn right (west) on Highway 421 and cross the older Highway 95 about a mile later. Continue west on Highway 421 (see below) for about 5 more miles to the cutoff for Xochicalco. The cutoff is marked and is located a little past (to the west of) the kilometer 7 marker. The cutoff heads north for about 2 miles to the site.

If you are without a car, a bus can get you at least as far as the last cutoff, but you will have to do the last 2 miles on foot. A taxi from Cuernavaca is another possibility.

There are neither food nor accommodations at the site, but soft drinks are sold.

If you plan only to visit the more restored sections of the site, then tennis shoes are fine, but if you plan to follow the recommended tour over the west area, boots would be better.

Bring plenty of film; Xochicalco is a most photogenic site. Sun hits the front of the Temple of the Feathered Serpent in the afternoon, but since all four sides are carved and equally interesting, no special time of day is recommended for a visit.

Allow 3 hours at the site if you plan to see the whole area, including the cave.

If you are driving between Cuernavaca and Taxco and visit Xochicalco in the morning, stay on Highway 421 (heading west) after you leave the site. (Highway 421 is how the highway is labeled at the Alpuyeca cutoff and while its route is shown on road maps, it is generally not numbered. On one map it is numbered 166.) This will take you past the interesting caves of Cacahuamilpa. There is a picnic area here where you could eat a box lunch (brought along). Soft drinks are available. You can then visit the caves—if you miss one of the regularly scheduled tours you can sometimes get an *especial* for just a few pesos extra—and drive on to Taxco.

Cacahuamilpa is one of the largest caverns in Mexico and is still not completely explored. It is well worth a visit.

Other possible overnight stops near Xochicalco are Hacienda Vista Hermosa, some 5 miles southeast of the Alpuyeca interchange, or Hotel Tequesquitengo, on the lake of the same name, about 14 miles farther on.

★★

# *Chalcatzingo*

(chahl-kaht-*seen*-goh)

# *(Chacalzingo)*

CULTURE: Olmec; see text.
LOCATION: Far-eastern part of the state of Morelos, Mexico.

---

## THE SITE

Chalcatzingo is a most interesting site in a lovely setting. Unfortunately, it is seldom visited. If you are an Olmec fan, rate this one three stars.

After you arrive in the town of Chalcatzingo, ask around for a guide. The *vigilante* will probably show up to take you. In 1975 this was the helpful Filemon Pérez Morales.

Having a guide here is essential since it is something over a mile from the town to the site—where there are several areas of interest—and the trail goes through *milpas* part of the way. The vigilante told us that a road was passable for cars for part of the distance until a bad winter rain in 1974 washed it out. Perhaps it will be eventually repaired, but in the meantime you have to do the whole distance on foot.

The first thing he takes you to is a carved stela called La Reina (the Queen), lying on a cement platform in somebody's milpa. Although incomplete, it is most interesting. It depicts a figure in profile wearing a skirt; whether it is a female, as the name implies, is not certain. A wide-angle lens is useful here.

The next stop is a recently excavated architectural assemblage—only the lower part remains—protected by a wire fence. You can get shots, through or over the fence, of the carving on the lower portion. Some plain stone stelae are also found in this complex.

A bit farther on is a partially restored, small circular structure, seemingly an altar.

You then are taken to another fenced-off architectural complex with remains of a broken carved stela. Next is another carved stone lying against a tree.

As you begin to climb, you come to Relief IV carved on a large boulder. It depicts a jaguar and a human in battle and the motif is shown twice. Your next stop is Relief III on another boulder. This one shows a sort of plant with a feline figure at the bottom. The surface of both these boulders is irregular, making it a bit difficult to discern the designs. The same is true of the next boulder carved with Relief V.

Relief V depicts a feathered serpent, with a figure—perhaps the young sun god—emerging from his mouth. Some authorities believe the figure is being devoured. Michael Coe sees this as evidence of the worship of Quetzalcóatl by the Olmec. Peter D. Joralemon labels the reptile god VII, a serpent deity with avian atributes; in other words, a feathered serpent. In his conclusions, Joralemon identifies god VII as Quetzalcóatl. Other carved and painted depictions of a feathered serpent are known from Olmec and Colonial Olmec sites.

You climb a bit more and finally come to the well-published Relief II, with its depiction of four human figures. This represents a ceremony (perhaps a fertility rite), or a scene of conquest—depending on which authority you prefer. The two central figures are standing and carrying what appear to be clubs. The figure on the left faces away from the others, is likewise standing, and is carrying what may be a maize plant. All three wear Olmec (or Olmecoid) masks. The fourth figure, a bearded man bound at the wrists, is seated on the far right and is nude—which may indicate that he is a captive, perhaps about to be sacrificed. This relief is sometimes compared to the large Stela 3 from La Venta because of iconographic similarities.

It is impossible to get a good over-all shot of this scene even when it is lighted by late afternoon sunlight. It is carved on the lower portion of a boulder that curves under and is partially blocked by another boulder on which you sit (or lie) to see it. A wide-angle lens is necessary even for detail shots since you can only get a couple of feet away from the carving. In any case, it is a magnificent piece of sculpture. Below this carving are some restored remains of a stairway, flanked by more boulders and rock outcrops.

You resume your climb and continue to Relief I, some 9 feet high, the most interesting carving at the site. The stone surface is relatively flat (for a

*Architectural assemblage with plain stela and carved steps, Chalcatzingo. Middle Preclassic period.*

change) so the sculpture is easier to make out and photograph. The scene depicts a richly attired person seated on a throne. Some feel the figure represents a female because of the skirt and long hair. The figure—holding a rectangular object similar to the "ceremonial bars" depicted by the Classic Maya—and throne are shown inside a cave or perhaps a monstrous mouth (maybe of a jaguar). Sprouting maize plants, stylized clouds, and rain drops are also part of the scene. Scroll-like designs issue forth from the cave (or mouth), which may represent clouds of mist, smoke, or incense. Relief I perhaps symbolizes a rite of fertility or rain invocation. The left edge of the relief is partially blocked by another boulder. A wide-angle lens is good here to get over-all shots of the relief, which, according to our guide, is lighted by direct sunlight around 11:00 A.M. (this was in August).

Off to the left of Relief I, on an almost horizontal rock outcrop, is another very faint relief. Your guide may have to point it out to you. Also found in this area are some curious small circular depressions carved into the living rock.

From your vantage point at Relief I, you have a beautiful view of the countryside below. You will notice a pyramidal mound on the plain, in the middle of a milpa. It is partially covered with trees. Your guide will take you there on the way back. About all to be seen there are partially restored lower walls and stairs, but it is not much out of the way so you might want a look.

Chalcatzingo's relief carvings date to the Middle Preclassic period and are in "purest Olmec style," according to some authorities. The ceramics of the site also show pronounced Olmec influence. Ignacio Bernal, however, considers the site to have been occupied into the Postclassic period.

Several theories have been proposed to account for an Olmec presence in this area; religious missionaries, location on a trade route, and military conquest. The truth may involve all three.

The motifs on the reliefs seem to be mostly of a religious nature although Relief II may also imply a military theme. It has been well demonstrated that Chalcatzingo was an important point on a trade route. Michael Coe believes the main item of commerce was jade, a substance highly prized by the Olmec, but unavailable in the "Olmec Heartland" on the Gulf Coast.

## RECENT HISTORY

Chalcatzingo was archaeologically discovered by Eulalia Guzmán in 1934 while she was a student exploring the remote sections of Morelos. More recent study of the site was conducted by Román Piña Chan, Carmen Cook de Leonard, Carlo Gay, and David Grove in the 1950s and 1960s. Several of the reliefs were discovered during the more

*Detail of Relief V depicting the feathered serpent with a figure emerging from its mouth, Chalcatzingo. Middle Preclassic period.*

recent work and numerous publications in Spanish and English have appeared.

## CONNECTIONS

1. 79 miles by paved road (57 miles are toll roads) from Mexico City,
2. 51 miles by paved road (34 miles are toll roads) from Cuernavaca,
3. 42 miles by paved road (none are toll roads) from Cuernavaca, or
4. 72 miles by paved road (none are toll roads) from Puebla, then 2.5 miles of good dirt road to the town of Chalcatzingo and a little over a mile on foot to the site.

## GETTING THERE

In addition to the cities mentioned under "Connections," you can use one of the resorts near Cuautla as a closer stopover.

From Mexico City take toll road (Cuota) 95D south for about 40 miles. Then get on toll road 115D east for 22 miles, where it ends. Head south on Highway 115 to Cuautla (3 miles), then east on Highway 140 for 13 miles. (Some maps show this last stretch as Highway 160.) This brings you to a junction with a paved road heading south (on your right), shown as Highway 115 on some maps; on other maps it is not numbered at all. This junction is near the town of Amayuca. Highway 115 leads some 3 miles to Jonacatepec (not shown on all maps) and another 3 or 4 miles to Atotonilco (generally shown). The towns are mentioned so you can locate the right road, but you take it for only 1 mile. Then you pick up the dirt cutoff for Chalcatzingo. The cutoff heads east (left) and is well marked, but neither it nor the town of Chalcatzingo are shown on road maps.

From Cuernavaca you can get as far as Cuautla

*Detail of Relief II showing the head of the seated figure, Chalcatzingo. Middle Preclassic period.*

*Relief I showing the throned personage inside a cave or mouth, Chalcatzingo. Rain symbols are at the top. Middle Preclassic period.*

in two ways: (1) on Highway 95D north for 12 miles, then Highway 115D east for 22 miles, and Highway 115 south for 3 miles, (2) on Highway 138 east for 26 miles, then Highway 115 south for 2 miles. From Cuautla, follow directions given above.

From Puebla take Highway 190 south to Izúcar de Matamoros (42 miles), then Highway 140 (160) west to Amayuca (29 miles), then south (to your left) for 1 mile to the Chalcatzingo cutoff.

Although these directions sound a bit complicated, they can be easily followed with a good road map.

When you approach Amayuca, you will see three huge stone outcrops. One is north of Highway 140 (160) and two lie to the south. The site of Chalcatzingo is located at the base and part way up one of the southern outcrops. The outcrops are thought to be the cores of ancient volcanoes that have since eroded away.

When you arrive in the town of Chalcatzingo, drive through it as far as you can before trying to locate a guide.

If you are without a car, you can get a bus to Cuautla. From there a taxi could get you to the site, or a local bus could get you to Amayuca.

There is no food or drink at the site and it may be a problem finding them in the town of Chalcatzingo. It is best to have soft drinks along in your car for when you return from the long, tiring hike to the site.

Hiking boots are best. Allow 2 to 2½ hours from the time you leave your car until you return to it.

## MEXICO

### Oaxaca

*Stucco head of Cocijo, the Zapotec rain god, in place at Lambityeco. Late Classic–Early Postclassic periods.*

# *A Note on Oaxaca*

(wah-*hah*-kah)

The city of Oaxaca, the centrally located capital in the state of the same name, is one of the most delightful places in Mexico. It is situated in a valley a bit over 5,000 feet above sea level, and is blessed with a springlike climate and low humidity. The surrounding mountains form a scenic background. Whenever I leave Oaxaca it is with the feeling that I wish I had a few more days there—a reaction shared by most visitors.

In addition to the archaeological sites, most of which are nearby, there are interesting craft villages specializing in certain types of pottery and weaving, beautiful colonial churches, and one of the most colorful markets in the country. Allow a minimum of two or three days—more are better.

Oaxaca City is the only recommended base for visiting the ruins in the area. It has hotels in various price ranges. Two of the nicest are on the edge of town (Hotel Victoria and Misión de los Angeles—formerly Oaxaca Courts). You might prefer being in town in the center of activity, though parking there can be a problem. The recently opened El Presidente is near the Oaxaca Museum and is reportedly excellent. It is housed in an old colonial structure.

The big market day is Saturday and people start coming in the day before. If you plan to arrive on Friday, either have reservations or arrive early as the town can get packed. The smaller villages have their markets on other days. An interesting one is at Tlacolula on Sunday.

You will also want to see Teotitlán del Valle, where beautiful handloomed ponchos, rugs, and blankets are made. The wool is colored with both natural dyes and synthetics. Those with the natural dyes are more expensive.

The town of San Bartolo Coyotopec is famous for its distinctive black pottery, which is widely exported. An ancient lady called Doña Rosa is the town's best known citizen and leading potter. She and her family operate a workshop a couple of blocks off the highway. As you enter the town, you will see a sign directing you there.

It is best to visit the villages other than on Saturday since on that day all the craftsmen are in Oaxaca selling their wares at the big market.

Oddly enough, you will pay about the same for a Teotitlán del Valle blanket whether you buy it in the village, in the Oaxaca market, or from a street vendor in Oaxaca City. The vendors quote a higher price originally, but will bargain quite a bit. In the market or village workshop the price is lower to begin with, but they will bargain only a little. The final price you settle upon is about the same.

There are numerous restaurants surrounding the city's pleasant Zócalo, and having coffee or lunch there is a must. Service can be incredibly slow, but you will enjoy the leisurely pace. You can get your shoes shined while you wait, and just generally watch the world go by.

## CONNECTIONS

Oaxaca can be reached from Mexico City by car or bus over all-paved highways, by airlines, or by rail.

If you are driving, there are several choices: (1) the shortest and fastest is, Mexico City to near Cuautla by toll roads 95D and 115D, then 3 miles to Cuautla proper on Highway 115, to Izúcar de Matamoros on Highway 140, to Oaxaca on Highway 190. Total about 320 miles. (2) Mexico City to Puebla on toll road 150D (190D), to Izúcar de Matamoros and on to Oaxaca on Highway 190. Total about 330 miles. (3) Mexico City to Puebla and Acatzingo on toll road 150D (190D), 5 miles on Highway 140 to connect to Highway 150, to Tehuacán on Highway 150, to Huajuapan de León on Highway 125, to Oaxaca on Highway 190. Total about 340 miles. One interesting feature of this last route is the abundance and variety of cacti between Tehuacán and Huajuapan de León.

Allow about 7 or 8 hours for the drive as much of it is mountainous. Best stops along the way would be Cuernavaca or one of the resorts near Cuautla, Puebla, or Tehuacán, depending on your route. In an emergency, there is the Hotel Laredo in Huajuapan de León, and another that we spotted in Acatlán, right on the highway.

Buses leave Mexico City for Oaxaca almost hourly and take 8 or 9 hours.

Airlines connect the two cities with one or more

flights daily. Oaxaca can also be reached by air from Acapulco.

There is daily train service from Mexico City to Oaxaca, which takes about 15 hours. I have had conflicting reports about this trip. Some say it is ghastly, others that it is not bad at all. In any case, the bus is certainly faster and, since the service is first-class and hourly, it is probably to be preferred. The train travels at night, however, so you could sleep along the way and save time.

Cars can be rented in Oaxaca, and there are bus and taxi services to the archaeological sites and villages.

## CHRONOLOGY OF THE ARCHAEOLOGY IN THE VALLEY OF OAXACA

The archaeological sequence of this area and of most of the sites covered in this guide is designated by periods called Monte Albán I through V. The exact dates of these periods in our calendar differ somewhat from one authority to the next.

For consistency and simplicity, I have followed the chronology used by Ignacio Bernal in "Archaeological Synthesis of Oaxaca," an article in the *Handbook of the Middle American Indians*, edited by Robert Wauchope.

## RECOMMENDATIONS FOR VISITING THE SITES

If your time in Oaxaca is limited (an unhappy thought), you will find that the following recommendations will help you use your time more efficiently.

On one day, visit Monte Albán in the morning (best light on the Danzantes). Return to Oaxaca for lunch, then visit the Oaxaca Museum and the Tamayo Museum. On another day, visit Mitla in the morning (best light on the façade of the Hall of the Columns), the Mitla Museum, and have lunch there. On your way back see Yagul, Lambityeco, and Dainzú in the afternoon (best light on the Ballplayer Slabs). If you plan to see the Tule Tree, it is more convenient to stop in the morning on your way out. If you have more time, then use another day to see Zaachila and the Monastery at Cuilapan, and maybe the pottery village of San Bartolo Coyotepec. If only two days are available, you can skip Zaachila, or see it late in the afternoon of the day you visit Monte Albán and the museums. You can visit Huamelulpan and Huitzo most easily when you are driving between Mexico City and Oaxaca City.

★★★★

## REGIONAL MUSEUM OF OAXACA (OAXACA MUSEUM) (Oaxaca City)

The Oaxaca Museum is another of Mexico's fine archaeological museums. It is located in the convent adjacent to Santo Domingo Church, 6 blocks north of the Zócalo. Some years ago it was housed in a building closer to the Zócalo, but its new quarters are better.

The collection is made up of numerous artifacts from throughout the state of Oaxaca, as well as of displays of present-day costumes and crafts from the area. It is especially famous, however, for the priceless jewelry excavated from Tomb 7 at Monte Albán by Mexican archaeologist Alfonso Caso in 1932. This ranks as one of the most spectacular discoveries in Mesoamerican archaeology.

Over 500 items were found in Tomb 7 and catalogued, according to Caso, "at times including under one number necklaces of gold, pearl and turquoise, composed of hundreds of beads each." A rare rock-crystal urn and more than 300 carved jaguar and deer bones, some inlaid with turquoise, were also part of the treasure trove. After the artifacts were excavated, they were moved to Mexico City. Subsequently Oaxaca sued the federal government for their return and won. They are now on display in a special section in the Oaxaca Museum. Copies of the more impressive pieces of jewelry are sold throughout the city.

Santo Domingo Church is one of the gems of Spanish colonial architecture in Mexico and is definitely worth a visit.

Allow a couple of hours to visit the museum and a bit extra to see Santo Domingo.

★★★

## MUSEUM OF PREHISPANIC ART OF MEXICO RUFINO TAMAYO (TAMAYO MUSEUM) (Oaxaca City)

In 1974 the Tamayo Museum opened its doors at 503 Morelos Street in Oaxaca City. The museum itself is a lovely colonial building, and it houses the collection of the Mexican artist it is named for. Tamayo collected pre-Hispanic art for over twenty years "for his own pleasure," but also with the idea of protecting the pieces from exportation and, most important, with the idea of donating them to the people of his native state of Oaxaca.

The governor of the state of Oaxaca donated the building, but Tamayo bore the cost of its restoration and adaptation. It is admirably done, with black marble floors and attractive lighting, and the pieces are imaginatively displayed.

A sign near the entrance informs you that "this is a museum of art" and the displays bear this out. There are five *salas* ("exhibit halls") around three sides of a pleasant patio and each sala is a different "color." That is, the background color for the display cases is different from room to room and this color code is used in the small guidebook for the museum. There are also some pieces displayed on the corridor walls that face the patio. The collection is surprisingly extensive. It covers everything from Middle Preclassic Olmec pieces to Late Postclassic Aztec. Practically all parts of Mexico where Mesoamerican civilization developed are represented. There is an especially fine selection of ceramic figures from Western Mexico, and Veracruz is well represented with numerous carved stone yokes, *hachas* and ceramic smiling heads and figures.

For me, the most exciting part of the collection

*Maya stela from Campeche, Tamayo Museum. Classic period.*

is in the Green Sala (Number 4), where much of the Veracruz material is displayed; also in this sala are several major Maya monuments. There are two complete Classic Maya stelae from Campeche set on pedestals and a portion of another—showing the upper part of a figure—in a showcase. Another case houses a beautiful glyph-carved stone from Chiapas and yet another stela fragment from Campeche.

One particular item gave me a start—a bas-relief stone carving of Tlaloc labeled as coming from Campeche. I had seen this before (or so I thought) in the National Institute of Anthropology and History guide for Uxmal, where it is said to be in the lower part of the Adivino. I was never able to find it and was told at Uxmal that it was no longer visible. When I was later able to compare photos carefully, the Tlaloc in the Tamayo Museum proved not to be the Tlaloc from Uxmal. They are so similar, however, that they might have been carved by the same artist.

Another very interesting Maya monument is found in a niche in the outside corridor. This Classic period stone panel is well preserved and shows a main figure seated on two captives. The style of the carving and the motif depicted seem very related to monuments from Palenque.

This brings up the one flaw at the museum—most objects are rather vaguely labeled. The one just mentioned is designated only as "Classic Maya, seventh to eighth century." Other items are labeled with the state from which they come, but rarely is a specific site given.

In any case, when you are in Oaxaca you will not want to want to miss this excellent museum. Allow 1½ hours for a visit.

★★

# *Huamelulpan and Huamelulpan Museum*

(wah-meh-*lool*-pahn)

## *(San Martín Huamelulpan)*

ORIGINAL NAME: Unknown.
CULTURE: See text.
LOCATION: West-central part of the state of Oaxaca, Mexico.

### THE SITE

The archaeological site of Huamelulpan is located on a hill, above the town of the same name, and is composed of five groups of structures extending for a distance of about 0.5 mile. Visitors today see only a portion of this.

There are remains of stone walls, tombs, and huge stone blocks—between three and four tons each—that are part of a platform. Some of the cornerstones are carved with calendric hieroglyphs and numerals, and are well preserved. On one block, above two glyphs, is a rather naturalistic carving of a lizard or iguana.

From this area a trail leads to a church where there are some interesting sculptures. To the right of the church, as you face it, is an arch that gives entrance to a courtyard. There are four carvings embedded in the face of the arch—two on each side—a little above eye level. On the right is a naturalistic human head and, above it, a more abstract piece that could be a stylized head. On the left is another naturalistic human head and, above, a more grotesque head, perhaps representing an animal.

You now enter the courtyard through the arch, go to the far end, and turn left. You will be facing the exterior side wall of the church, where there is embedded a large carving depicting a stylized jaguar. It stands upright in an almost human pose; the head is three-dimensional, while the body is in low relief. We were told that this interesting carving has been in place in the church wall for about forty years.

### RECENT HISTORY

Although the existence of a pre-Columbian site above the town of Huamelulpan apparently was known for some time, it was only in the late 1950s and early 1960s that excavations were undertaken. This work was conducted by Lorenzo Gamio and Alfonso Caso. Reports were written, but they remain unpublished manuscripts in the archives of the National Institute of Anthropology and History (INAH).

In the late 1970s, additional work was undertaken by INAH, and in 1978 a small museum was opened in the town (see below).

From the work at the site, we know that Huamelulpan was occupied for 1,000 years, from 400 B.C. to A.D. 600. This span is broken into three periods; Huamelulpan I (400–100 B.C.), Huamelulpan II (100 B.C.–A.D. 200), and Huamelulpan III (A.D. 200–600).

During Huamelulpan I, the site was founded, probably as a small hamlet, the extension of which is unknown.

During the second period there was an increase in activity, and civic-religious buildings were constructed. Huamelulpan is considered the most important site in the Mixteca Alta at this time and for the latter part of the preceding period, and it maintained relations with other major sites of the Mixteca Alta. There were also relations with the Valley of Oaxaca, demonstrated by the use of common calendric glyphs, urns of similar form, and gray ceramics.

Huamelulpan reached its maximum residential extension in Huamelulpan III and there is evidence of a differentiation in the social structure. Possibly the site functioned as a control center for small urban hamlets in the nearby regions.

### CONNECTION

1. 105.5 miles by paved road and 0.7 mile by fair rock road from Oaxaca City.

### GETTING THERE

From Oaxaca City take Highway 190 northwest for 83 miles to the junction with Highway 125 (well-marked). Then take Highway 125 left (south) for 22.5 miles to a junction with a rock road that heads left (east) to the town of Huamelulpan. A nice sign indicating the museum and archaeological zone marks this junction. From here proceed to the town

and the easily spotted municipal building. Driving time from Oaxaca City is about 2½ hours.

I recommend seeing the museum first, then getting the caretaker there to take you to the site. It is about a 10-minute walk uphill. Allow about 45 minutes to see the museum and the site. There is no food or drink around—carry your own.

Tennis shoes are adequate.

If you are traveling to Oaxaca City on Highway 190 from central Mexico, you can visit Huamelulpan by taking Highway 125 and following the directions above. The drive from the junction of Highways 190 and 125 to Huamelulpan takes about 35 minutes. Adding the time to visit the site and museum, and the return to Highway 190, figure it as a side trip of just under 2 hours.

*Stone carving of a jaguar embedded in the church wall, Huamelulpan.*

★★

## HUAMELULPAN MUSEUM

The Huamelulpan Museum is located in one room of the municipal building of the town, facing the plaza, and is marked with a sign. Although small, it contains some interesting items.

Huamelulpan's fame (at least in the literature) rests with an Olmecoid, cigar-shaped statue that reportedly was rolled down to the town from the hill above some time ago. The statue—which has been widely published—is about 3 feet tall, and, before the museum was opened, it stood outside the entrance of the municipal building. It is now inside. While authorities agree that the figure is in Olmecoid style, there is some question about its age. Caso believes that it dates to the period Monte Albán I (900–300 B.C.), and it is believed that some ceramics from the site could date to the end of this period. Ignacio Bernal also believes that the statue may date to this period, while Charles R. Wicke thinks, on the basis of its style, that it could be considerably older.

Another interesting piece is a rectangular slab with the hieroglyphic date "13 Flint" carved in bas-relief. This carving was seen by Caso in 1933 in place in a wall of the school building, and he reported it in a 1956 publication. It dates to the period Monte Albán II (300–100 B.C.), as do the glyphs and numerals found on the large blocks at the site.

*Note:* These datings were made in the Monte Albán sequence apparently before the sequence for the site of Huamelulpan was established.

A smaller slab with a carved numeral and another with a figure of an iguana are also housed in the museum. In addition, there are glass cases containing ceramic specimens from the site, a chronological chart showing Huamelulpan's relationship to the Nochixtlán Valley of Oaxaca, and a sign relating a description and chronology of the site.

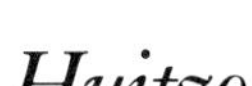

# *Huitzo*

(*weet*-soh)

EARLIER NAME: Cuauhxilotitlan.
ORIGINAL NAME: Unknown.
CULTURE: Zapotec; see text.
LOCATION: Central part of the state of Oaxaca, Mexico.

## THE SITE

The most interesting feature at Huitzo is a tomb with some carved slabs set in its exterior face. There are remnants of red paint in the deeper grooves of some of the carvings.

On the far right (as you face the tomb) is a depiction of a stylized animal head with the number 1 represented by a dot—perhaps indicating a date. The head and dot are partially enclosed by a simple border. Below and to the left is a larger slab that is difficult to interpret, but it appears that an animal is depicted.

To the left of the entrance of the tomb is a panel that is more abstract and geometrical, and a couple of feet above this is a fragment showing a realistic animal head—perhaps a coyote—framed by remains of a border. On the far left is another rather abstract panel.

In between the carved slabs, the face of the tomb is made of plain stones. The whole has been restored and covered with a cement roof.

The tomb is entered through a low doorway and is composed of two chambers. At the top, on the left side of the first chamber, is another carved slab that is worth a look. Bring a flashlight and a flash unit for your camera.

The rest of the architectural remains visible today at Huitzo are not impressive and are partly covered with vegetation. They are composed of the lower remnants of walls that formed a hall, which runs a short distance from the left of the tomb. In one part there is a large circular depression. There are also remains of a stair on the side of the mound on which the structure rests.

The part of Huitzo that the visitor sees today is apparently only a small portion of the whole. In earlier times the now independent towns of Suchilquitongo and Telixtlahuaca were considered barrios of Huitzo. According to Ignacio Bernal, the site of Huitzo-Suchilquitongo is nearly as large as Monte Albán and has numerous buildings and great plazas.

## RECENT HISTORY

Huitzo was formerly known as Cuauhxilotitlan, and under this name (spelled various ways) it is mentioned in Spanish chronicles of the sixteenth and seventeenth centuries. These early works refer to the town as having both Zapotec and Mixtec residents and it remains a living town today.

Little work has been done at the site. Therefore, not much mention of it is found in the English-language literature.

Huitzo and Suchilquitongo were two of 251 sites visited by Bernal on a pottery-collecting expedition, and he notes that ceramics from Suchilquitongo are fundamentally Zapotec or earlier, with a thin surface layer belonging to a Mixtec invasion. This invasion occurred shortly before the Spanish conquest and is corroborated by early Spanish writings.

Bernal further says—in a work published in 1965—that the architectural remains at the sites he visited were similar to those at Monte Albán, Mitla, and Yagul.

In 1966, John Paddock published photos of some ceramics from Huitzo (called Huitzo Polished Cream), and notes that it is rarely found at other sites in the Valley of Oaxaca. On his chart he dates this ware to A.D. 800.

## CONNECTION

1. 22 miles by paved road from Oaxaca City to the cutoff, then less than 1 block of fair dirt road to the site.

## GETTING THERE

From Oaxaca take Highway 190 northwest. You will come to a sign marking a cutoff for the town of Huitzo. It is possible to get to the site this way, but it necessitates negotiating the bumpy streets of the town. It is better to pass up this cutoff and proceed 0.9 mile along to the highway to another cutoff

*Carved slab—possibly depicting an animal—in the face of the tomb, Huitzo. Probably Classic period.*

(unmarked). Both cutoffs are on the left (south) and the second one is much closer to the site. After you take the second cutoff, the dirt road crosses a railroad track. The site is located just past the track on a mound on the left of the road. Take the footpath that leads uphill and follow it a short distance to the site. The ruins are not visible from the road.

There is no food or drink at the site, but cold drinks, at least, could be found in the town. Tennis shoes are fine and a guide is not necessary. Bring a wide-angle lens for over-all views of the front of the tomb.

If you are without a car, a bus can drop you off at the junction.

See "A Note on Oaxaca" for accommodations and general information about the area.

★★★★

# *Monte Albán and Monte Albán Museum*

(*mohn*-teh ahl-*bahn*)

DERIVATION: Spanish for "White Mountain."

EARLIER NAMES: An earlier Aztec name was Ocelotepec, Nahuatl for "Hill of the Jaguar." An even earlier Mixtec name was Yucu-cui. A still earlier Zapotec name may have been Danipaguache or Danipaan, Zapotec for "Sacred Mountain."

CULTURE: Zapotec; see text.

LOCATION: Central part of the state of Oaxaca, Mexico.

---

## THE SITE

Monte Albán is perched atop an artificially flattened mountain about 1,200 feet above the city of Oaxaca. This superb location makes it a worthy setting for a city of the gods. It is a large site and one of the most intensively studied in Mexico. Its well-developed chronology forms the basis for the dating of the other sites in the state. The sequence in brief is as follows.

The earliest period at Monte Albán is designated Monte Albán I (900–300 B.C.). The culture that produced the remains of this period was already well developed. Who its members were exactly is not known, but that they were influenced by the Olmec is generally agreed. They are referred to as Olmecoid, although they were more advanced than the Olmec in some respects. They already had a form of hieroglyphic writing—the earliest known in Mesoamerica—a knowledge of calendrics, still undeciphered, and stone architecture with stucco floors. They constructed tombs and their pottery is of a fine quality and very abundant.

A pantheon of at least ten deities has been identified, including Cocijo, the rain god. The inner building of the Danzantes was constructed during this period and most of the Danzantes themselves were carved during this time.

The following period, Monte Albán II (300–100 B.C.), shows evidence of new arrivals. This is thought to be an aristocracy, perhaps from Chiapas or Guatemala. They brought new traits that mingled with the older ones. By this time the Great Plaza was completely planned and the mountain top leveled. New glyphs are used and new deities are added. Mound J and its carved slabs were produced during Monte Albán II. A transitional period, Monte Albán II-III (100 B.C.–A.D. 200), follows and is known mainly from ceramic changes.

With Monte Albán III A (A.D. 200–550) begins the great classic period at the site. This continues through a short transitional phase (A.D. 550–650) and Monte Albán III B (A.D. 650–1000). The culture that produced the remains of Monte Albán III was influenced by Teotihuacán; it is thought that the culture bearers came from the Mixtec region or from south of Puebla. Jorge Acosta says, "With their arrival begins what we can call the true Zapotec period."

The period of Monte Albán III is divided into phases on the basis of ceramics. It is not clearly distinguishable in the architecture. Most of the structures seen today at the site belong to Period III. During Monte Albán III B, the site reached its population peak. It is estimated that a population of 50,000 to 60,000 people occupied an area of about 3 square miles surrounding Monte Albán.

After that no large buildings were constructed by the Zapotecs, and the site went into decline. The period Monte Albán IV (A.D. 1000–1521)—actually a continuation of III B in many ways—is used to label the culture of the Valley Zapotec. Monte Albán itself was virtually abandoned and the Mixtec were entering the area.

Monte Albán V (A.D. 1300–1521) is typically Mixtec, and overlaps the end of the Zapotec Monte Albán IV. Mixtec invaders used Monte Albán as a burial place for their lords, reusing earlier Zapotec tombs. It is the Monte Albán V Mixtec culture that produced the fabulous grave goods found in Tomb 7.

A great deal of restoration has been undertaken at Monte Albán, making it extremely rewarding visually.

As you arrive at the site, you enter the northeast corner of the Great Plaza (some 1,000 feet long and 650 feet wide). Various structures cover the perimeter of the plaza and more are found on the central axis.

A logical tour would be clockwise around the

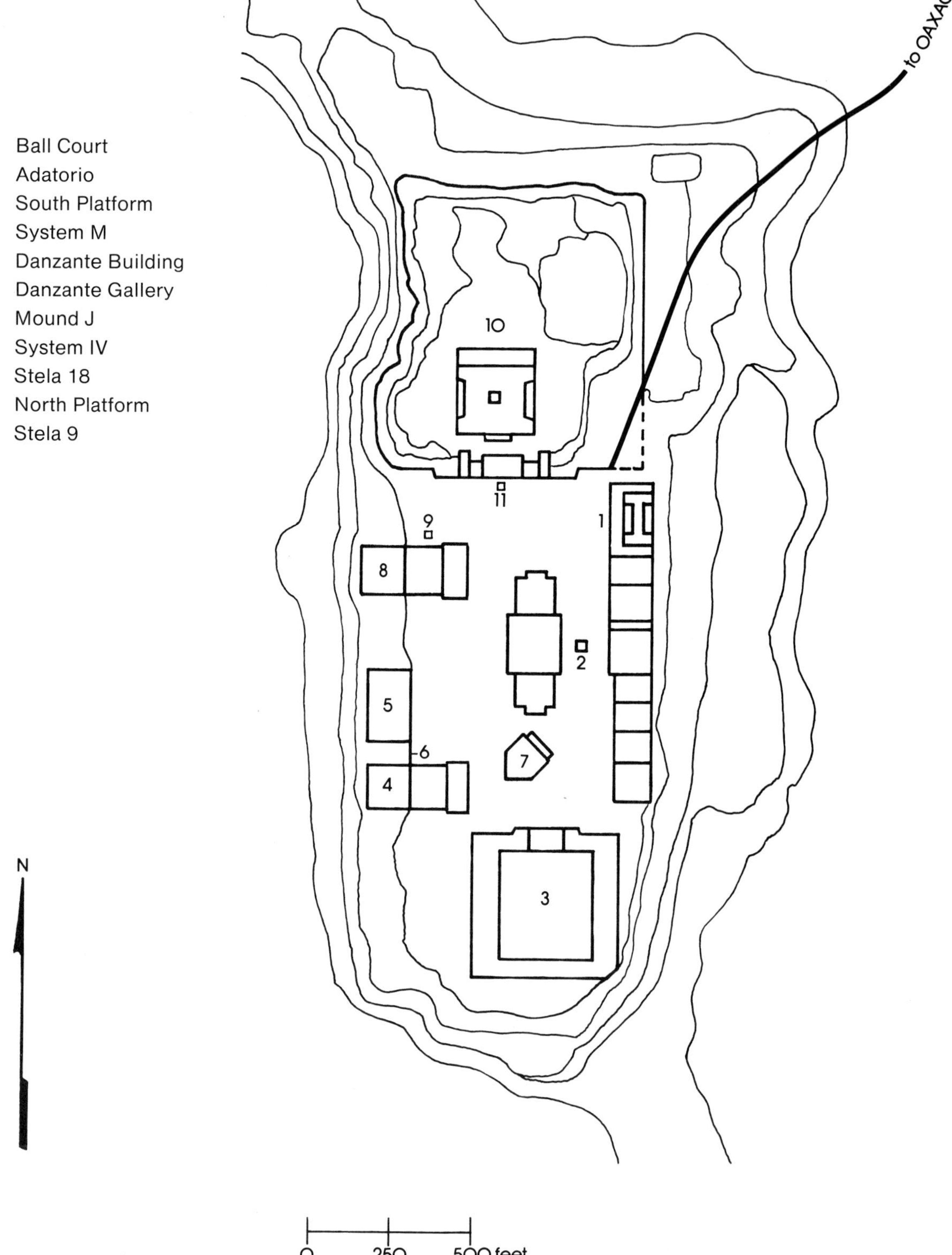
1 Ball Court
2 Adatorio
3 South Platform
4 System M
5 Danzante Building
6 Danzante Gallery
7 Mound J
8 System IV
9 Stela 18
10 North Platform
11 Stela 9
to OAXACA CITY
N
0
250
500 feet

MONTE ALBÁN

*View of the northeast corner of the Great Plaza with Classic-period structures, Monte Albán.*

plaza to its southern extremity, then zigzagging between the structures on the central axis and those on the western edge. Then proceed to the northern area. If you have time, you can visit some tombs that are away from the main area.

Following this plan, the first structure to visit is the ball court. This large, well-restored court, is in typical Zapotec style. A stair on the north side leads down to the playing level. To the south of the ball court are substructures and platforms, also in Zapotec style, which may have been used for dwellings. These date to Period III. The structures are approached by broad stairs. Lying between the central structure of this group and the buildings on the central axis is a small adatorio. When excavated, it revealed a magnificent mask of the bat god. It is made of twenty-five pieces of jade, with shell for the teeth and eyes. Pendants hanging from the mask are of a common green stone. The mask is dated to Monte Albán II and is now in the Mexico City Museum.

The south end of the Great Plaza is bounded by

*Northeast corner of System M and part of the Danzante Gallery, Monte Albán. The structure is Classic period. The carved slabs and stelae are mostly Middle Preclassic.*

the unexcavated South Platform. The stairway has been restored, however, and it is worth a climb for views of the other structures. The South Platform is also interesting for the numerous carved stelae incorporated into its base and others found in the surrounding area. Some have glyphs and all are worth some study, even though a few are copies. The originals of these are in the Mexico City Museum. Alfonso Caso believes that these sculptures date to the period Monte Albán III A.

From the South Platform continue clockwise to the west for a look at System M and a carved stela found in front of it that dates to Monte Albán III A.

System M is composed of a large pyramid rising in four terraces, with remains of the lower part of a temple, which included four columns, on top. It is fronted by a patio and, farther east, a low mound with a broad stairway.

To the north of System M is one of the most interesting parts of the site, the Danzante Gallery and Danzante Building. The Danzantes are stone slabs carved with figures in dynamic poses thought to resemble dancers; hence the name Danzantes (the Spanish equivalent). We know that the figures do not represent dancers but may depict captives—perhaps dead, since the eyes are often shown closed. Some of the slabs are incorporated into the building of the Danzantes and others are lined up between it and System M. Also in the area are found copies of Stelae 12 and 13. The originals are in the Mexico City Museum. Stelae 12 and 13 date to the earliest period, Monte Albán I. Although the inner building of the Danzantes is one of the earliest structures at Monte Albán, a restoration was undertaken later in Period III B. A tunnel gives access to the earlier structure.

*Danzante figure with glyph in the upper right corner, Monte Albán. Middle Preclassic period.*

From the Danzantes, head east to Mound J, the southernmost structure on the central axis. Mound J differs in both shape and orientation from the other structures at Monte Albán; it resembles an arrowhead and points southwest, while the other structures at the site are aligned to the cardinal points.

This interesting building has a stairway on the northeast side, a vaulted tunnel, and is built of large slabs, many of which are carved. A few Danzante-style figures from Period I have been incorporated, but more prevalent is another style. The motif in each is similar; a human head faces downward beneath a glyph for "hill," indicating a place. This is accompanied by glyphs that probably indicate the name of the place, and, sometimes, a calendric notation. These carvings may depict towns conquered by the people of Monte Albán. It is also theorized that Mount J may have been an astronomical observatory.

North of this structure on the central axis is a group of three connected buildings in typical Zapotec style approached by stairs on all four sides.

From here head west to System IV, similar in layout to System M. Under the main pyramid of System IV is an earlier structure dating to Monte Albán I or II. It may be visited by means of a modern tunnel on the north side. To the north of the Patio of System IV is Stela 18, dating to Period II; this huge monument is broken and partially eroded, but worth a look.

Proceed north to the broad stairway that ascends the North Platform. At the level of the Plaza, near the center of the stairway, is Stela 9—carved on all four sides and dating to Period III B. Climb the stairway for a look at the sunken patio and the sur-

*Mound J, view from the west, Monte Albán. Late Preclassic period.*

*System IV, view from the northeast, Monte Albán. The visible building is Classic period, but it covers an earlier, Preclassic structure. The Late Preclassic Stela 18 is at right of center.*

rounding structures. There are stairs leading down into the patio on all four sides and an altar is found in the center.

From this area you can return to the entrance via the Great Plaza. If you wish to see some of Monte Albán's famous tombs, however, follow a trail heading north from the rear of the North Platform and going downhill to Tomb 104. This tomb has a niche that contains an urn bearing a depiction of Cocijo in the headdress of the figure. There is a slab with carved glyphs and the interior of the crypt is covered with murals. Unhappily, a gate blocks the entrance to the crypt, and there is no artificial lighting, so the murals cannot be appreciated.

Trails lead from here to other tombs in the area, but they are kept locked. On one, however, there are some carvings visible through a metal gate.

The best access to the famous Tomb 7 (also locked) is via a trail that heads north from the road to Monte Albán (west side) and joins the road near the restaurant.

On the east side of the road another trail leads to Tomb 105. This tomb can easily be spotted from the restaurant and is worth a visit to see the huge stone lintel—reminiscent of those at Mitla—at the entrance. Tomb 105 also contains mural paintings but, unfortunately, is also kept locked. You pass a partially excavated ball court on the way to the tomb.

## RECENT HISTORY

Guillermo Dupaix visited Monte Albán in the early nineteenth century and uncovered some of the Danzantes.

The first description of Monte Albán, however, was published in Mexico in 1859 by J. M. García, as an appendix to a work by José Murguía. It included a sketch of the Great Plaza. In 1881, A. F. Bandelier visited the site, as well as others in the area, and published a report of his tour in 1884. William Holmes superficially studied the site in 1895 and left a panorama of Monte Albán. The first serious exploration of the site was undertaken by Leopoldo Batres in 1902.

Most of what we know about the site, however, is due to the work of Alfonso Caso and his collaborators. This began in 1931 under the auspices of the Mexican government and lasted for eighteen seasons. This work resulted in many publications in both Spanish and English. Monte Albán has still not been completely excavated.

*Stela 9, view of the back and side, at the base of the stairway to the North Platform, Monte Albán. Late Classic period.*

## CONNECTION

1. 6 miles by paved road from Oaxaca City.

## GETTING THERE

You can reach Monte Albán by private car, taxi, or bus from Oaxaca. Check current bus schedules at your hotel.

If you are driving, take Calle 20 de Noviembre south from central Oaxaca and cross the Río Atoyac. Shortly after crossing the river, the road forks. The right branch leads directly to Monte Albán. Although it is paved, drive slowly, for the road is narrow and winding, and sometimes there are people along it trying to sell reproductions of artifacts.

Allow 3 to 4 hours for a visit once you arrive. Tennis shoes are fine. A building housing a restaurant, bookstore, and small museum has recently opened at the site.

Bring plenty of film; Monte Albán is a very photogenic site. A wide-angle lens will be useful for shooting some of the Danzantes in the wall by the tunnel.

## MONTE ALBÁN MUSEUM

The collection at the Monte Albán Museum is rather small and consists mostly of ceramics from the site and a large, but eroded, stone carving. The meagerness of the collection is not surprising since most of the important monuments that were removed from the site were taken to the museums in Oaxaca City and Mexico City some time ago. Nevertheless, the items in the Monte Albán Museum are nicely displayed and labeled. It is worth a few minutes to see since you will be parking just outside.

★★

# *Zaachila*

(sah-*chee*-lah)

DERIVATION: Zapotec for "Sky Dragon."
EARLIER NAME: Teozapotlán.
CULTURE: Zapotec; see text.
LOCATION: Central part of the state of Oaxaca, Mexico.

## THE SITE

Zaachila, the last capital of the Zapotecs, seems a sad place when compared to the magnificent earlier capital of Monte Albán. There is only one area of interest, a rectangular patio with the remains of adobe walls and two tombs in the patio floor. Tomb 1 has a stepped fret design over the doorway of the antechamber and remains of sculptured plaster figures on the interior walls. This tomb has several niches, which originally contained pottery offerings. If you want shots of the sculpture, bring along a flash unit, but ask permission before using it. The people of Zaachila do not like outsiders fooling around their ancient graves. In 1947, when Alfonso Caso tried to excavate there, he was forced to flee for his life. The same thing happened to Ignacio Bernal in 1953. Finally, in 1962, Roberto Gallegos managed to do some work at the site, but only under armed guard.

The ruins of Zaachila are near the church in the center of town. Park on the street to the right of the church (as you face it). Then look for a stone stairway (on the right) and hard-to-find sign at its foot, announcing the archaeological zone. The stairway leads directly to the ruins. When you arrive, the caretaker will open the tomb for you.

There are two Zapotec urns embedded in the top of the clock tower near the church.

## RECENT HISTORY

At the time of the Spanish conquest, Zaachila was a living town. Although it was originally Zapotec, by the time of the conquest the Mixtecs were in control of the area. The Zapotec king of Zaachila at this time was Cosijoeza, who welcomed the Spaniards, hoping with their aid to rid himself of his Mixtec and Aztec enemies. He died in Zaachila in 1529. By that time the Zapotecs, as well as the Mixtecs and Aztecs, had been crushed by the Spaniards.

*Plaster figure on the wall of Tomb 1, perhaps representing the Lord of the Netherworld, Zaachila. Late Postclassic period.*

What we know of the site archaeologically comes mainly from the excavations of Gallegos for the Mexican government, although certain carved stones from Zaachila and the surrounding area were known and studied earlier by Caso. Stone 1, now in the Mexico City Museum, is dated by Caso as perhaps coming from the period of Monte Albán III A.

The contents of Tombs 1 and 2 at Zaachila are similar to the objects found in Tomb 7 at Monte Albán. The carved bones and gold jewelry found in both places show that they were very close in time. Both belong to the period Monte Albán V.

## CONNECTION

1. 10 miles by paved road from Oaxaca City.

## GETTING THERE

Leave Oaxaca by the same road that takes you to Monte Albán. Shortly after you cross the Río Atoyac, there is a fork. The left branch is the road to Zaachila. On the way there you pass through the village of Xoxocotlán and then Cuilapan, with its fascinating, unfinished Dominican monastery and church dating from 1555. This is worth a stop, either before or after you visit Zaachila, as it is most photogenic.

Inside the church is the grave of the Zapotec princess Donaji, daughter of Cosijoeza, and her husband, the Mixtec prince of Tilantongo. Their tomb stone is inscribed with the Spanish names they took, "Maioana Cortés" and "Diego Aguilar."

There is no food or drink at the site of Zaachila, but soft drinks are available in the town. Tennis shoes are fine. Bring along a flashlight to see the tomb sculptures as the caretaker may not have one. Allow ½ hour to visit the site and 1 hour or more to visit the monastery at Cuilapan.

You can also get to Zaachila by bus or taxi from Oaxaca.

★★★

# *Dainzú*

(daheen-*soo*)

ORIGINAL NAME: Unknown.
CULTURE: See text.
LOCATION: Central part of the state of Oaxaca, Mexico.

---

## THE SITE

Dainzú reportedly occupies the southern section of a huge archaeological area. It may have actually been an independent site. The area of interest for the visitor is the relatively small excavated part. The road that enters the site divides it into two sections. The main pyramidal mound lies to the left (east) of the road, and Group B and the ball court lie to the right (west).

The mound measures 150 feet along its north–south axis, is some 25 feet high, and has been partially restored. It rises in three stepped tiers and is divided by a stairway. The southern wall of the stairway and the lower tier of the mound have inlaid stones with bas-relief carvings. Most are found on the right (south) of the stairway, but there is one on the left (north) as well. If you have seen the Danzantes at Monte Albán, you will immediately recognize a similarity.

Other carved slabs lie on the ground nearby. Fifty in all have been discovered, twenty-seven of which were found in place. One represents a god, and two others depict humanized jaguars.

It seems fairly certain that the figures on the remainder of the slabs depict ball players. Each of these figures wears a mask or face shield and most have a collar and protective gear on the hands and sometimes on the knees. Each holds a small ball in the right hand, which would indicate a different kind of ball game than that played in the Classic period, where players were not allowed to touch the ball with their hands. The dynamic poses depicted also support the theory that they were ball players. The carvings are most interesting and many are well preserved.

The carved slabs and most of the structure date to the very end of the period Monte Albán I (ca. 300 B.C.). This is corroborated by ceramic evidence. The present stairway, however, dates to a later period (perhaps to the seventh century A.D.). A tomb is also found in this structure, and the whole is built into the side of a hill. There are nice views from the top of the structure. The National Institute of Anthropology and History guide mentions some bas-relief sculptures in living rock at the top of the hill, and we asked the *guardián* at Dainzú about them. He said it would take over an hour to reach them and implied that it was a difficult climb. Since there was no visible trail, and since he was unable to take us as there were other visitors at the site, we made no attempt to see them.

Group B has been partially excavated and restored, and there are a number of interesting remains there. This complex also dates to around 300 B.C. The first excavations in the central and southern part of Group B uncovered remains of a stairway and the lower portion of stone walls. More recent work in the northern part of the group brought to light a tomb, the façade of which is made of three large stones, carved in bas-relief, with a frontal depiction of a crouching jaguar. The relief is an excellent state of preservation. Use the widest-angle lens you have for a head-on shot.

A bit to the north of the tomb is an eroded carved boulder under a protective roof and nearby, to the east, is a stairway that descends to a lower chamber. On a portion of a wall, abutting the stairway on the north, is a carved slab, and two more carved slabs are found inlaid in the walls of the lower chamber. The *guardián* will point them out to you. One slab depicts a man who seems to be running and holding a bag.

Return to the upper level and head west and then south for a look at some restored stairs, a sunken patio, and the lower walls of a plastered structure with two columns in the doorway. Farther south are the remains of what appears to be a sunken chamber, and nearby is a sort of drain.

From here head west to the ball court, found on a lower level. The south half of the ball court has been restored and it is interesting to compare this part to the unrestored amorphous mound that faces it and forms the other half. This court is similar to the one found at Yagul and dates to around the same time period, A.D. 1000.

*Part of Group B in the foregroun Dainzú. Late Preclassic period. T main pyramidal mound is in the bac ground. Late Preclassic period w Classic-period additio*

*Carved slab representing a god, reset in the south wall of the stairway of the main pyramidal mound, Dainzú. Middle Preclassic period.*

There is little in the literature about Dainzú, at least in English, so I do not know if the site was continuously occupied from the time of the earlier structures to the time of the ball court. Since the stairway on the main mound falls in between, perhaps it was.

Ignacio Bernal considers the ball-player carvings part of the Olmec world, as are the Danzantes at Monte Albán. He finds both "Olmec in spirit, if not in detail." He labels this "Olmecoid," meaning a high culture showing Olmec influence but not being purely Olmec. The Danzantes and ball-player carvings date to roughly the same time period.

Since Monte Albán is not considered Zapotec until Period III, it seems safe to assume that the same is true at Dainzú. In other words, we cannot credit the ball player carvings to the Zapotec, but must assign them to another and an earlier culture.

## RECENT HISTORY

Dainzú was reportedly discovered in the 1960s and excavation began under the direction of Ignacio Bernal, in late 1966, for the Mexican government. It has been open to visitors since 1970.

## CONNECTION

1. 13 miles by paved road from Oaxaca City, then 0.7 mile of good dirt road to the site.

## GETTING THERE

Take Highway 190 southeast from Oaxaca to the junction with the dirt road to Dainzú. The junction is marked and the dirt road is on the right and heads south to the site. If you are without a car, you can get a bus to drop you off at the junction and walk to the site, or you can get a taxi in Oaxaca. There is no food or drink at Dainzú. Tennis shoes are fine. Allow 1½ hours to visit the site. Afternoon hours are best since the carved slabs are then better lighted.

*Recently excavated jaguar carving on the face of the entrance to a tomb, Dainzú. In the northern part of Group B.*

★★

# *Lambityeco*

(lahm-beet-*yeh*-koh)

ORIGINAL NAME: Unknown.
CULTURE: Zapotec.
LOCATION: Central part of the state of Oaxaca, Mexico.

## THE SITE

Lambityeco, like Dainzú, is part of a large archaeological zone, but only a small portion on the edge of the site has been excavated. The whole site comprises two or three dozen mounds, some of which extend to the nearby village of Tlacolula. An accurate count is impossible since some of the mounds in the village have been leveled.

The excavated portion is made up of an architectural assemblage running in an east-west line, and a separate structure a bit to the south. The whole is part of a residential construction. The architectural remains are not terribly impressive, but the sculptural decorations make a visit very worthwhile.

On the east end of the main assemblage is a patio with carved stone friezes, each depicting an aged couple with their accompanying name glyphs. Between the two friezes is a small altarlike structure. All of these are at the present patio level. In front of and below the altar a tomb has been excavated in the patio floor and another ancient couple is represented in stucco on the façade. Some remains of red paint border the faces. It is theorized that the couple depicted on the tomb were the owners of the house. The area around the friezes and tomb is kept fenced off, but generally the caretaker will open up the fence so you can get a closer look and better shots.

Lambityeco was occupied for a relatively brief time during the period of late Monte Albán III B and early IV. Even so, the excavated house shows several construction phases. It is thought to have been built during the population peak of the community. Carbon-14 dates from Lambityeco are around the seventh and eighth centuries, but as with

*Carved-stone frieze in the patio on the east, Lambityeco. Late Classic–Early Postclassic periods.*

*Stucco façade on the tomb entrance in the patio on the east, Lambityeco. Late Classic–Early Postclassic periods.*

other carbon-14 dates from Oaxaca, they seem too early.

The structure to the south of the main assemblage also contains a tomb. Of more interest here, however, are the nearby stucco heads of Cocijo, the Zapotec rain god. One of these large sculptures is in almost pristine condition.

The west end of the main assemblage is occupied by a fair-sized plaza, with low stepped platforms bordering three sides, and a taller pyramidal base, with a stairway on the fourth (east) side. There is a low rectangular altar in the plaza.

Both stone and adobe were used in the construction at Lambityeco and some cut-stone, stepped fret designs are found in the wall facing the east patio.

## RECENT HISTORY

Lambityeco was reportedly rediscovered in 1961. This seems strange as it is just a few feet off the highway, which has been in existence for many years. Excavation was begun later in the decade by John Paddock for the University of the Americas, which is connected with the Institute of Oaxaca Studies. Much of the site remains unstudied.

## CONNECTION

1. 18 miles by paved road from Oaxaca City.

## GETTING THERE

From Oaxaca take Highway 190 southeast to the site. If you are without a car, a bus could drop you off at the site, which is on the south side of the road and from which it is visible. Lambityeco is located less than 2 miles before (northwest of) the town of Tlacolula as you drive away from Oaxaca.

There is no food or drink at the site, but these are available in Tlacolula. Try La Fiesta Restaurant on the highway at the cutoff for Tlacolula (across the cutoff from a Pemex station). It has good regional food.

Tennis shoes are fine for Lambityeco.

# *Yagul*

(yah-*gool*)

EARLIER NAME: Gui-y-Baa.
CULTURE: Zapotec; see text.
LOCATION: Central part of the state of Oaxaca, Mexico.

## THE SITE

A relatively large site, Yagul is set in lovely surroundings. It lies at the base of a hill that was partially leveled to accommodate the buildings forming the Acropolis. This group is made up of several patios and their surrounding buildings, a huge ball court, and several interesting tombs.

The other group of interest, the Great Fortress, is located on the highest point of the hill overlooking the valley and can be reached by a rather steep foot trail. It is definitely worth the effort for views of the Acropolis and the surrounding countryside. The builders of Yagul certainly had an eye for beauty when they selected their location.

When you arrive at the site, proceed first to Patio 4, a bit to the southwest. There are several tombs in the floor of the patio; the most interesting is number 30, which, with the adjoining Tombs 3 and 29, forms one of several triple tombs found at Yagul. The façade is decorated with carved stepped fret designs and small three-dimensional heads. You may have to ask the caretaker to open the door to the tombs for you. Patio 4 also has a squat statue of a toad near the mound on the east end.

From Patio 4, a short climb to the northwest will get you to the ball court. This court, larger than that at Monte Albán, has been completely excavated and restored, and is a beauty. It is considered of Zapotec style, although it differs from the ball court at Monte Albán in that there are no niches or central marker stones.

West of the ball court is Patio 1 and its surrounding buildings. The best preserved are those bordering the patio on the west and north. The northern structure, called the Council Hall, is similar in dimension to the Hall of the Columns at Mitla, but no columns were used.

When you leave this area, make sure you see the back of the Council Hall. Here are the remains of a stepped fret design in a panel that is over 120 feet long. There are two variations of the motif, both of which are also found in the Group of the Columns at Mitla.

*View of the ball court, Yagul. Postclassic period.*

From the rear of the Council Hall, head north across a narrow street to the Palace of Six Patios. This is a veritable maze of residential structures that was altered and added to several times. The earlier constructions were in Zapotec style and the later are similar to the Mitla palaces.

The trail to the Great Fortress takes off from the north of the Palace of Six Patios and goes up the hill.

Certain stone implements collected at Yagul may indicate that the site was occupied in preceramic times. By Monte Albán I, occupation is certain. A carbon-14 date for Yagul is 390 B.C. and comes from material associated with the later part of the period. Yagul continued to be occupied until around the time of the Spanish conquest.

The similarities with Mitla are pronounced, though the structures and decorations at Yagul are less refined. Use of the stepped-fret mosaics is also

*Stone mosaic panel at the rear of the Council Hall, Yagul. Postclassic period.*

*Partial view of the Palace of Six Patios, Yagul. Postclassic period.*

*Large pictograph on the face of the cliff, Caballito Blanco.*

less extensive, and Yagul probably lacked the huge stone lintels used at Mitla. This would probably partially account for the poorer state of preservation of the structures.

Like Mitla, Yagul had an earlier Zapotec occupation followed by a Mixtec or Zapotec-Mixtec blend. Again, the preponderance of the architecture is civic and residential rather than religious in nature. It is possible that some of the latest Mitla-style constructions at Yagul are a little later than those at Mitla.

## RECENT HISTORY

The first report of Yagul was that of A. F. Bandelier in 1884. He had visited the site some three years earlier when he also visited Mitla, Monte Albán, and several other places.

There is nothing to note about Yagul from that time until the 1953 investigations by Ignacio Bernal. Nevertheless, I found it interesting that a 1911 edition of *Terry's Mexico* mentions the site by its old name, Gui-y-Baa, states that the ruins are inferior to Mitla, and, "will scarcely repay one for the time spent in visiting them." I cannot help but wonder if this scant notice caused anyone to visit the site.

Bernal began excavating Yagul in 1954, and, because it proved to be a particularly interesting site, work continued for over a decade. Students of the University of the Americas assisted in the work under the direction of Bernal, John Paddock, and Charles Wicke.

In 1960, three tombs of Monte Albán I style were excavated by Robert Chadwick for the University of the Americas. They are located near the Great Fortress and are the only Period I tombs known at Yagul. An unusual feature is their adobe construction.

## CONNECTION

1. 20 miles by paved road from Oaxaca City.

## GETTING THERE

Take Highway 190 southeast from Oaxaca City to the Yagul cutoff, then head north (left) for 1 mile to the site.

A bus could get you as far as the junction, which is marked, although you would have to walk the last mile. Car or taxi would be easier as the last part is uphill.

There is no food or drink at the site; tennis shoes are adequate. Bring a wide-angle lens for front shots of Tomb 30. Allow about 2 hours for a visit.

*Note:* As you turn off the highway onto the Yagul cutoff, look to the right (east) at the upper part of a nearby cliff. On the face is a white pictograph that is part of the archaeological site of Caballito Blanco. According to Alfonso Caso, the pictograph is difficult to interpret, but is probably one of the oldest-known paintings in Oaxaca.

You can get good photographs of it from the road with a telephoto lens.

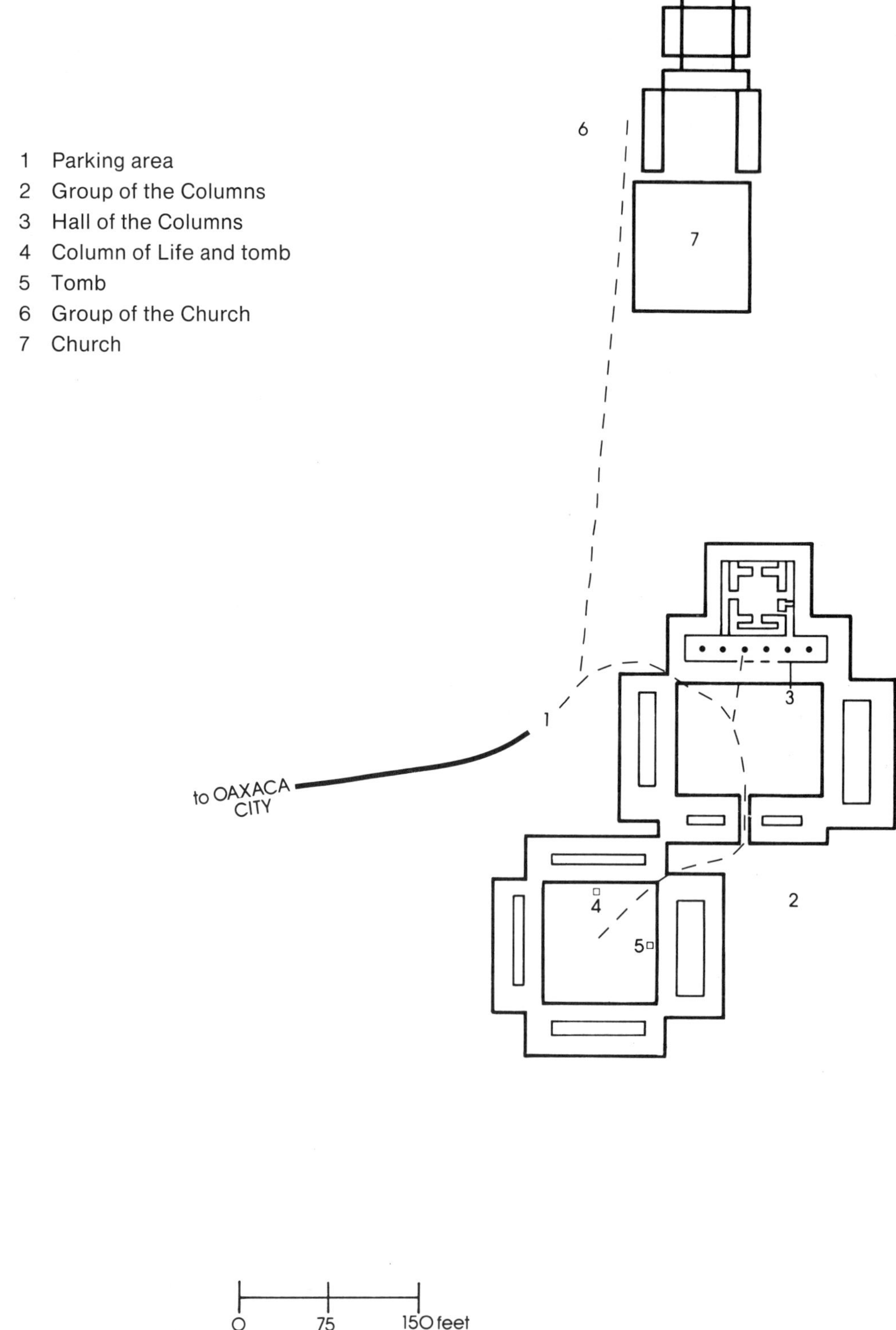
1 Parking area
2 Group of the Columns
3 Hall of the Columns
4 Column of Life and tomb
5 Tomb
6 Group of the Church
7 Church
6
7
1
3
2
4
5
to OAXACA CITY
N
0
75
150 feet

MITLA

★★★★

# *Mitla and Mitla Museum*

(*meet*-lah)

DERIVATION: From the Nahuatl Mictlan ("Place of the Dead").
EARLIER NAME: Lyobaa, Zapotec for "Tomb" or "Place of Rest."
CULTURE: Mixtec; see text.
LOCATION: Central part of the state of Oaxaca, Mexico.

---

## THE SITE

There are five groups of structures at Mitla, although only two are of real interest to the visitor. Most important is the Group of the Columns made up of one small and two large square patios and the building surrounding them. Next is the Group of the Church, some 150 feet to the north. The other groups are the South Group, the Arroyo Group, and the Adobe Group. These have been less studied and no restoration has been attempted.

When you arrive at the site, you can park near the Group of the Columns. An enclosed market was recently erected in this area and a variety of merchandise is for sale. As you enter the Group of the Columns, you will find the caretaker selling tickets.

From the first patio you get a gorgeous view of the Hall of the Columns. Its façade is broken by three centrally located doorways, interrupted with panels of the stepped-fret design in many variations for which Mitla is duly famous. This long, low building rests atop a platform with vertical walls and a central inset stairway. The stairway leads to the Hall of the Columns, a room some 120 feet by 21 feet, with 6 huge monolithic columns, 3 feet in diameter, arranged along the long axis. These originally helped support the roof. The interior of the room is undecorated. Near the eastern end of the room, a low doorway, formed by huge stone jambs and a lintel, gives access to a small patio. This patio is surrounded by four rooms in an excellent state of preservation, and all are decorated (both inside and out) with panels of the stepped-fret design. There are many variations of this motif. The designs are formed by inlaying the cut stone in mosaic

*Hall of the Columns, main façade, Mitla. Late Postclassic period.*

*Hall of the Columns, interior room showing the columns, Mitla. Late Postclassic period.*

fashion into the core of the wall. It was done with great precision, and then painted. A few remnants of paint remain. The total effect is sometimes referred to as "frozen lace."

In a few places the stepped-fret design was carved into large stone blocks, but the mosaic form is decidedly more prevalent. It is generally agreed that this motif is a stylized version of the Sky Serpent and, therefore, a symbol of Quetzalcóatl. The beam, pole, and mortar roof of one of the rooms around the small patio has been restored to give the visitor an idea of the original construction.

From here you return to the first large patio for a look at the other architectural remains surrounding it. Then proceed to the second large patio adjacent to the southwest.

The structures around the second large patio are not as well preserved, but are well worth some time to see. Especially impressive are the huge stone lintels and jambs, some of which are still in place. The decorations are similar to what have already been described.

Of interest in this area are the cruciform tombs (in front of and below the east and north buildings), which are accessible from the patio floor. The interior of both are decorated with carved stepped-fret designs, and a large monolithic column is found in the tomb of the north building.

This is popularly called the Column of Life. If you hug the column, the distance left between your hands indicates how long you have to live. I have never found out if the calculation is based on years left per inch, foot, centimeter, or what, or whether by embracing the column you simply know.

From here, return to the parking area and head north to the Group of the Church. This group is made up of three patios in a north-south line with some remains of surrounding rooms. The patios are smaller than those in the Group of the Columns and not as well preserved.

The southernmost patio is occupied by the Catholic church built in the colonial period of stones from the pre-Columbian structures.

The central and northern patios are similar to those in the Group of the Columns, and small bands of paintings are found in the inset panels above the doorways in the north patio.

Ceramic evidence indicates that Mitla was occupied from a period relating to Monte Albán I (900–300 B.C.), but the structural remains date to later periods, Monte Albán III A-V (A.D. 200–1521). The structures in the Group of the Columns and the Church Group belong to the last period, Monte Albán V (A.D. 1300–1521), before the Spanish conquest. The Arroyo Group is similar in construction and apparently dates to the same period.

Although somewhat different architecturally, the badly ruined Adobe Group was also constructed during Monte Albán V. The South Group provides a longer sequence. It contains a burial dating to Monte Albán III A with a typical Zapotec tomb, although the contents were of Monte Albán V date.

The earlier structures at Mitla are credited to the Zapotec, while the later are Mixtec or a Zapotec-Mixtec blend. There was certainly some interchange between the peoples and an interesting sequence

*Interior room with stepped fret designs, Mitla. The room opens onto the small patio in the Group of the Columns. Late Postclassic period.*

*Detail of the tomb entrances of the north building, located in the second large patio in the Group of the Columns, Mitla. Late Postclassic period. Photograph by author.*

was discovered in the South Group. It was occupied by the Zapotec, then the Mixtec, then again by the Zapotec, who had a mixed culture at that time.

Some of Mitla's structures were still occupied at the time of the Spanish conquest and continued in use during part of the sixteenth century.

## RECENT HISTORY

Mention of Mitla is made by early Spanish friars, just a few years after the conquest. The earliest account is apparently that of Fray Martín de Valencia, who visited the site and in 1533 gave a short description. Better known is the seventeenth-century work of Fray Francisco de Burgoa. This native of Oaxaca praises the skill of the ancient architects and comments on the monolithic columns and stone mosaics. Equally enthusiastic were the eighteenth-century reports of Fray Juan de Torquemada.

In the nineteenth century, there were many visitors. Although Alexander von Humboldt did not personally visit the site, he published (in 1810) plans made earlier (1802) by Luis Martín and Pedro de Laguna, working for the Mexican government. Then came Guillermo Dupaix, A. F. Bandelier, Désiré Charnay, Eduard Seler, William Holmes, Marshall Saville, and many others. Mitla became one of the most visited sites in Mexico and remains so today.

Although a few attempts at preserving the structures were made at the end of the nineteenth century, it was not until the work of Leopoldo Batres in 1901 that the existing restoration was carried out. Although imperfect, it succeeded in preserving the buildings.

The bulk of this work was exploratory and descriptive. The first modern excavation of the site was that of Alfonso Caso and Daniel F. Rubín de la Borbolla in 1934 and 1935. In the early 1960s, additional work was carried out by Ignacio Bernal and John Paddock, all sponsored by the Mexican government.

## CONNECTION

1. 27 miles by paved road from Oaxaca City.

## GETTING THERE

Take Highway 190 southeast from Oaxaca for 24 miles to a paved cutoff heading northeast (left side of highway). This continues 3 miles to the town of Mitla and to the site. There are frequent buses from Oaxaca to Mitla.

Food is available in the town of Mitla at the small inn connected to the Mitla Museum (see section on the museum for more details). Soft drinks are available at one of the stands in the market.

Mitla is the easiest major site to get around that is covered in this guide. You can do it in sandals if you like. Allow 1½ to 2 hours for a visit.

In addition to the archaeological sites between Oaxaca and Mitla, you should also stop for a look at the giant tree called El Tule. It is located in a churchyard just off the north side of the highway about 4 miles out of Oaxaca. It is a species of cypress called ahuehuete and is reputed to be 2,000 years old. The circumference at its base is 160 feet. A 10-minute stop should do it.

# MUSEUM OF ZAPOTEC ART (MITLA MUSEUM)

This was originally a private museum based on the collection of the late E. R. Frissell, but it is now operated by the University of the Americas Center of Regional Studies.

The items come from the state of Oaxaca and most are from the Valley of Oaxaca. They were purchased and donated over a period of years. The collection includes some small stone carvings, a display showing the evolution of the Zapotec urn from the periods Monte Albán I through IV, stone idols, censers, stone implements, and other objects. They are displayed along the sides of a pleasant patio and in one interior room.

The Posada La Sorpresa, connected to the museum, rents a few rooms and also serves food. If you make this a lunch stop, you will certainly want to visit the museum. Allow ½ hour to view the collection.

The posada and museum are located across the street from the Main Plaza in the town of Mitla.

## MEXICO

### Gulf Coast

*Colossal Olmec head; El Rey, or Monument 1 from San Lorenzo, Jalapa Museum. Middle Preclassic period.*

★★★★

# *Museum of Archaeology of the University of Veracruz*

# *(Jalapa Museum)*

The Jalapa Museum is one of Mexico's most delightful museums. It has both indoor and outdoor sections.

The outdoor part has many stone monuments placed seemingly at random on a well-kept lawn. They are well-spaced, making photography easy, and you are sure to want a picture of each one.

Included are stelae and other sculptures from Cerro de las Mesas and other sites in Veracruz, and three Olmec colossal heads from San Lorenzo. One (Number 5) is inside the museum. Another (Number 1) is outside near the entrance, and one (Number 3) is in the outdoor lawn section. A fourth San Lorenzo head (Number 4)—which in 1968 was inside the museum—has since been removed. I was unable to verify its present location. The museum staff speculated that perhaps it had been taken to Mexico City.

*Note:* Of the remaining heads from San Lorenzo, two are in the Mexico City Museum. Number 6 is inside and Number 2 is on a mound outdoors, adjacent to the hall with other Olmec remains. I am unable to account for Numbers 7 and 8. Drawings (but no photos) of these two heads—the most recently discovered at the site—are presented by Beatriz de la Fuente in *El Arte Olmeca* (1972). They are listed as being in the Mexico City Museum. As of 1979, however, they were not on display (nor was Number 4). Other Olmec sculptures, as well as objects from later cultures of the Gulf Coast, are also represented in the Jalapa Museum. The indoor section contains some large stone pieces, as well as smaller sculptures, ceramics, and figurines. They are well lighted and labeled.

Jalapa—the capital of the state of Veracruz—is on Highway 140 and can easily be reached from Mexico City, Puebla, or the city of Veracruz by car or bus. Jalapa is a pleasant town and makes a good stopover.

The museum is on Avenida Xalapa, near Highway 140, as you approach from Puebla. When you come in this way, take the Avenida Xalapa turnoff, and proceed straight ahead a few blocks to the museum, which is on the right.

If you approach Jalapa from Veracruz, stay on Highway 140, which bypasses most of the city (passing up a couple of Centro signs) until you come to the Avenida Xalapa turnoff at the far end of town. Turn left (almost a U turn) and go straight ahead (as above) to the museum.

Allow at least 2 hours to see the museum, more if you want to take a lot of photos. To get the best light on all the outdoor monuments, you need some morning and some afternoon hours.

*Huastec sculpture from the state of Veracruz, Jalapa Museum. Late Postclassic period.*

★★

# *Tampico Alto Museum*

The town of Tampico Alto, where this museum is located, is on Highway 180 some 8 miles south of the city of Tampico. The cutoff from the highway to the center of town and the museum is marked with a sign. Follow the cutoff for a few blocks to the Main Plaza, where you will see a colorfully painted church. The museum is housed in a building—nearly hidden by vegetation—to the right of the church (as you face it).

The main features at the museum are some interesting sculptures carved in a rather flat style and unimaginatively arranged in a single row down the center of the room. Included are stylized depictions of humans and animals, and most are well preserved. Unfortunately, they are unlabeled, but they come from the general area and are Huastec sculpture of the Postclassic period. Display cases along the walls house an abundance of ceramics—mainly figurines—and these too are poorly displayed and unlabeled, and covered with cobwebs. A couple of interesting carved yokes are on pedestals in between some of the cases. A sign at the museum indicates that it is also a museum of paleontology and geology. These displays have fared worse than the archaeological specimens.

At one end of the museum are reproductions of paintings—including the Mona Lisa—a garish tapestry, gnarled tree roots, and a very interesting primitive carved wooden crucifix. On the outside of the building are a couple of carved stones, and a glass case with a variety of cacti.

The museum would be greatly improved if it would settle on the subject of archaeology, cull and better display the collection, and afford the visitor some written information. It is still worth a half hour to see. There is enough natural lighting for photography.

*Slablike female figure, Tampico Alto Museum. Huastec Culture, Postclassic period.*

★★

# *Castillo de Teayo*

(kahs-*tee*-yoh deh teh-*ah*-yoh)

CULTURE: Toltec; see text.
LOCATION: North-central part of the state of Veracruz, Mexico.

## THE SITE

The Postclassic archaeological site of Castillo de Teayo is mainly a well-preserved pyramid in the town of the same name. The pyramid faces southwest, so the afternoon hours are the best for photography.

This Toltec-style pyramid consists of three superimposed units and is adjacent to the town's Main Plaza. The structure is some 42 feet high, with a broad stairway on one side and a small temple with a thatched roof on top.

According to Mexican archaeologist José García Payón, Castillo de Teayo was probably originally founded in A.D. 815. It was one of the fortified towns in this general area built by the Toltecs of central Mexico. This Toltec invasion is confirmed by both archaeology and sixteenth-century records. The archaeology of the area shows remains of Huastec culture—a group linguistically related to the Maya—both below and above Toltec remains.

Around the base of the pyramid are a number of well-preserved sculptures. Just circle the entire base of the structure to see them. They include both stelae and panels and are definitely worth a look. In fact, you will probably find them more interesting than the pyramid.

*The pyramid, Castillo de Teayo. Postclassic period.*

*Stone sculpture at the base of the pyramid, Castillo de Teayo. Postclassic period.*

## RECENT HISTORY

Most of the archaeological work at Castillo de Teayo was conducted by García Payón, who published his reports in the 1950s and 1960s. Earlier, Eduard Seler studied the site and felt the remains were Aztec. Although sculpture in a provincial Aztec substyle is found at the site, the site itself is attributed to the final Toltec period. Apparently the ceremonial precinct was never wrecked by the Spaniards.

## CONNECTIONS

1. 25.5 miles by paved road from Poza Rica, or
2. 38.5 miles by paved road from Tuxpan.

## GETTING THERE

The highway that goes from Tuxpan to Poza Rica is numbered both 130 and 180. The cutoff for Castillo de Teayo is located along this highway, 11 miles north of Poza Rica and 24 miles south of Tuxpan. The cutoff heads east from the highway; the junction is marked with a pyramid sign and another sign indicating the town of Zapotalillo. The cutoff is a paved, but narrow, road that winds 14.5 miles to the pyramid. This part takes about 30 minutes to drive. Reaching the site by bus is a possibility, but connections might be difficult. There are no accommodations at Castillo de Teayo, but cold drinks are available. Allow ½ hour for a visit. Tennis shoes are fine.

Stopovers besides Poza Rica and Tuxpan are Papantla (23 miles south of the cutoff), Veracruz (163 miles south of the cutoff), or Tampico (145 miles north of the cutoff). All are on Highway 180.

★★★★

# *El Tajín and El Tajín Museum*

(ehl tah-*heen*)

DERIVATION: Totonac for "Lightning." Also the name of the Totonac rain god.
CULTURE: Classic Veracruz (or El Tajín).
LOCATION: North-central part of the state of Veracruz, Mexico.

## THE SITE

The ruins of El Tajín are beyond question the most spectacular on the Gulf Coast of Mexico. Although the central nucleus of the site occupies only about 0.3 square mile, architectural remains—mostly unexcavated—cover a much wider area. There are temples, palaces, and several ball courts.

As you enter the site, proceed first to the famous Pyramid of Niches and the surrounding structures. The Pyramid of Niches, 60 feet high, is not huge as Mesoamerican pyramids go—but its design is exquisite. It rises in six terraces and supports a central stairway on its east face. A temple once crowned its summit, but little of that remains today. The entire structure is covered with nichelike openings numbering (some authorities say) 365. This perhaps had some connection with the number of days in the solar year. Other authorities, however, list a different number of niches, and propose the idea that they had only a decorative function, and no calendric connotation. Nevertheless, the architects of this structure surely took into consideration the interesting and changing effects of light and shade produced by the niches—the feature that emphasizes the dynamic quality of the pyramid. Try for a morning visit to the site if you want front-lighted shots of the Pyramid of the Niches.

It was once thought that the niches originally held pices of sculpture, but this theory has been discarded. Likewise discarded is the idea that El

*Pyramid of the Niches as seen from Building 5, from the southeast, El Tajín. Late Classic period.*

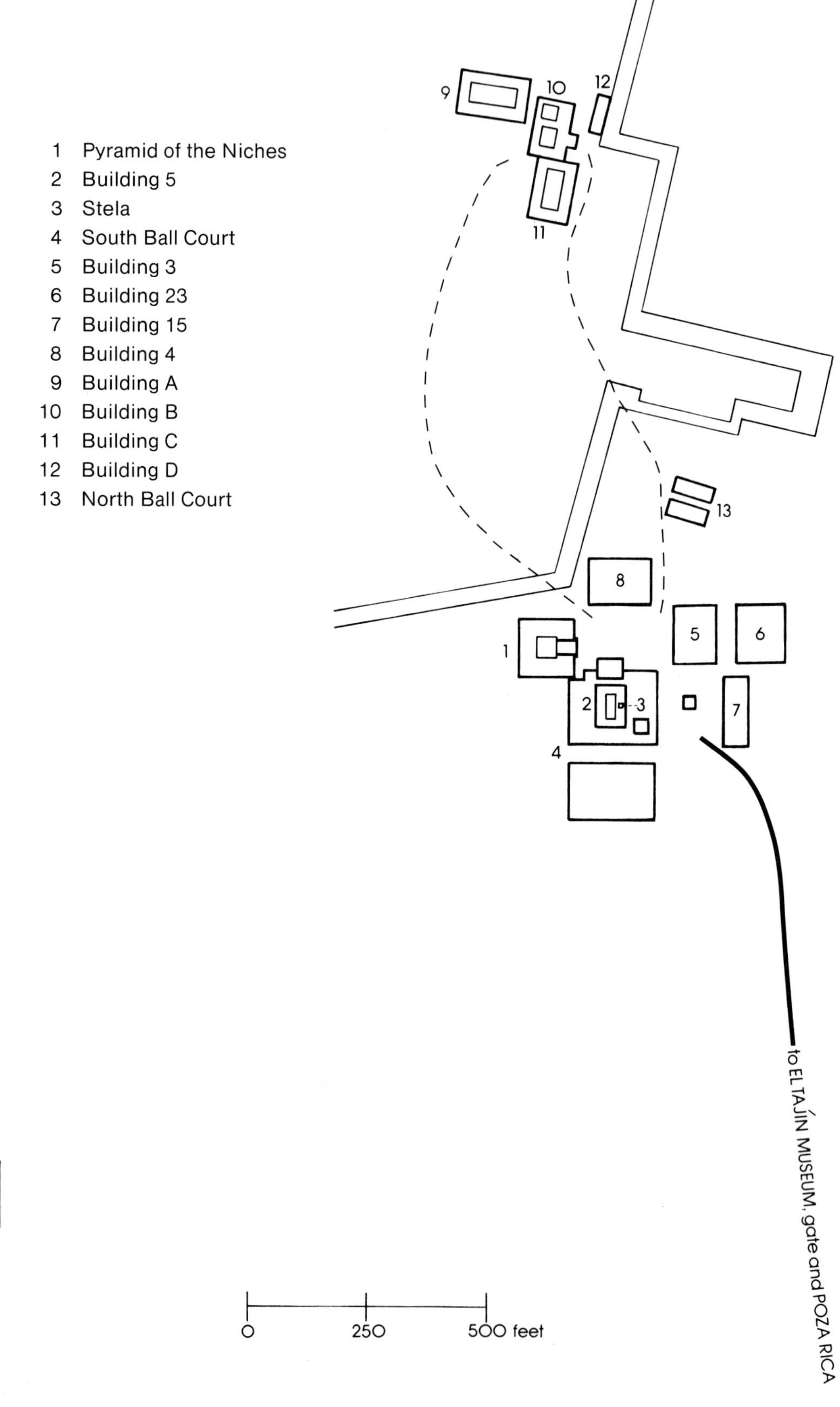
1 Pyramid of the Niches
2 Building 5
3 Stela
4 South Ball Court
5 Building 3
6 Building 23
7 Building 15
8 Building 4
9 Building A
10 Building B
11 Building C
12 Building D
13 North Ball Court
N
0
250
500 feet
to EL TAJÍN MUSEUM, gate and POZA RICA

EL TAJÍN

Tajín was built by the Totonac. We now know that although they inhabit the area today, and even gave the site its present name, the Totonac only migrated to this area late in the history of El Tajín. The preferred nomenclature for the builders of the site now is the culture of El Tajín or the culture of Classic Veracruz. An earlier pyramid of almost identical design has been discovered inside the Pyramid of the Niches.

Two small figurines found at El Tajín have been attributed to the Late Preclassic period. The site was occupied from around A.D. 100, when the first small constructions were inaugurated.

The interior structure of the Pyramid of the Niches was built around A.D. 300, while the pyramid seen today was completed some three or four hundred years later at the beginning of the site's peak period (A.D. 600–900).

El Tajín flourished and building continued until its abandonment around A.D. 1200. Tradition has it that the site was conquered and burned by the nomadic Chichimec from the highlands to the north at about this time. Nevertheless, there was still some occupation of the area until the mid-sixteenth century, when El Tajín was reclaimed by the tropical vegetation.

There are several other restored and partially restored structures near the Pyramid of the Niches and all are worth careful scrutiny. There is some interesting variation in the architecture but the use of niches—sometimes enclosing the stepped fret pattern—is almost universal.

Of special interest is Building 5 to the southeast of the Pyramid of the Niches. Building 5 rests on a large platform, which also supports two smaller restored structures. An interesting freestanding sculpture (or stela) representing Tajín or the death god—depending on your choice of authority—is

*Building 5, front (east) side, El Tajín. Late Classic period.*

*Free-standing sculpture or stela on the steps of Building 5, east side, El Tajín. Late Classic period.*

found on the stairway of Building 5 on the east side.

The south edge of the platform that supports Building 5 also forms one wall of the South Ball Court. Both walls of the ball court are made of large squared stone blocks and the ends and the center parts of the walls are decorated with intricate and well-preserved bas-relief carvings—some of the sculptural gems at the site.

These carvings probably date to around A.D. 1150, and depict scenes of rituals connected with the sacred ball game. In one, a man is practicing self-mutilation and, in another, a victim is being sacrificed. The death god, in his skeleton form, is repeatedly represented. There are representations of *palmas,* being worn by both sacrificing priest and sacrificial victim.

Palmas, along with *hachas* and yokes of stone are found in the El Tajín area and well beyond. This complex apparently was related to the sacred ball game although how the heavy stone objects could have been worn by the ball players is a puzzle. Some speculate that the stone objects were ritual copies of protective gear made of a lighter material that was actually worn by the players. At any rate, there is no question that these items are depicted on the bas-reliefs at the South Ball Court of El Tajín.

The style of the sculptures is typical of El Tajín, but the subject matter is the same as that found on the walls of the Great Ball Court at Chichén Itzá. This latter is due to Toltec influence, and it is proposed that the same is true at El Tajín.

Buildings 3 and 23 lie to the east of the Pyramid of the Niches across a plaza. Both are simpler in design than the Pyramid of the Niches but both rise in several stepped tiers and have stairways facing south. There are some remains of painted stucco in the niches in the lower part of the stairway of Building 3 and some on the east side of the structure.

*Bas-relief carving from the South Ball Court, El Tajín. The figure at the lower right is practicing self-mutilation. Early Postclassic period.*

The best vantage points for shots of the Pyramid of the Niches are found on tops of Buildings 5 and 3. Both are easy to climb.

Other remains in this general area are the partly restored north end of Building 15 and a low rectangular platform found in a plaza bounded by Buildings 5, 3, and 15.

Very little restoration has been done on Building 4, which lies to the northeast of the Pyramid of the Niches.

Now head to Tajín Chico, about 300 yards north and on a higher level. There are two foot trails leading there. I recommend taking the one that starts from between the Pyramid of the Niches and Building 4 to get to Tajín Chico, then returning by the other, which connects to the main area between Buildings 4 and 3.

The major cleared and partially restored structures at Tajín Chico are Buildings A through D, though there are also remains of stairs and terraces in the area. Buildings A, B, and C are visible at once where the trail enters the area.

Building A—the westernmost structure in this group—has an unusual doorway as access on the south side. It is covered by a corbeled vault and concrete slabs and through it a stair leads to an upper level. The inside walls of the upper level bear many well-preserved stucco decorations in the stepped fret pattern and other geometrical motifs.

Building B—which lies east of Building A—is a complex structure. In the southern part of this structure a rear stair and a front entrance both lead to a room with remains of rectangular columns. The northern part of Building B is on a higher level and is in a more ruinous condition.

East of Building B is Building D. Remains here include stucco decorations in a geometrical pattern and a doorway that leads to a terrace on a lower level.

The well-preserved Building C abuts Building B on the south. It is in typical Tajín style, with niches enclosing a stepped fret motif and a stairway facing west.

Actually, Buildings A through D are rather bunched together and sometimes it is hard to tell where one begins and the other ends, especially between B and D.

A trail from the back of Building C leads over a terrace with stairs, back to the area of the Pyramid of the Niches. On the way it passes the North Ball Court, well worthy of investigation.

This court—like the South Ball Court already described—is made of large stone blocks, and also has bas-relief carvings on the ends and center parts

*Building C at Tajin Chico, front (west) side, El Tajín. Early Postclassic period.*

of both walls. The North Ball Court is thought to date to around A.D. 800. The other ball courts shown on published site plans of El Tajín are in areas that are now overgrown.

El Tajín was the recipient of influences from other cultures throughout its history; Teotihuacán, Maya, and Toltec. In some cases the influence was reciprocal, especially in the case of Teotihuacán. Even while incorporating foreign traits, however, El Tajín retained its identity.

## RECENT HISTORY

El Tajín was discovered by an engineer, Diego Ruiz, who reported his findings in Mexico in 1785. The site was visited by Guillermo Dupaix (who is better known for his work at Palenque), Alexander von Humboldt, and Carlos Nebel, all in the early nineteenth century.

The first extensive work at the site, however, came many years later and was conducted by Mexican archaeologist José García Payón, who published reports from 1943 through 1963. Ceramic studies conducted by Wilfrido du Solier were published in 1945. The restoration at the site was undertaken by the Mexican government, and work is continuing.

## CONNECTIONS

1. 10.5 miles by paved road from Poza Rica to the cutoff for El Tajín, or
2. 8.5 miles by road (5.2 miles bad and 3.3 miles paved) from Papantla to the cutoff for El Tajín, then 0.9 mile of poor dirt and rock road.

## GETTING THERE

Although it is shorter to go to El Tajín from Papantla, it will take more time than going from Poza Rica. The first part of the road from Papantla was at one time blacktopped, but it has deteriorated drastically over the years. There are huge hunks missing, and part is rough dirt and rock. You would probably hit the bottom of a low-slung car.

Even if you are driving through the country, I would recommend returning to Poza Rica to rejoin Highway 180 rather than continuing through to Papantla on the bad road. This will cost you 15 extra miles, but it is well worth it until the road to Papantla is improved.

The cutoff for El Tajín is on the north side of the paved road (on your left as you approach the site from Poza Rica). The cutoff is marked with a sign for the archaeological zone. As you drive in, you come first to the gate, the nearby museum, and the "dining room." You can drive in even farther, to the ruins proper, where there is a parking area.

There are hotels in Poza Rica and Papantla. Other stopovers are Tuxpan (47 miles) and Tampico (168 miles) to the north, and Veracruz (163 miles) to the south. There is also a hotel right on Highway 125–180, El Palmar. It is located 33 miles south of Papantla and 15 miles south of the toll bridge over the Río Tecolutla.

There is a nice thatch-sheltered "dining room" at El Tajín where packaged snacks and cold drinks are sold.

A guide is not necessary at the site, and tennis shoes are fine. Allow 3 hours to visit the ruins and museum.

## POSTSCRIPT

At the time of our second visit to El Tajín in 1976, we were fortunate to see a performance by the famous Voladores. As far as I know, it was not a special occasion so maybe this is now being performed on a regular basis.

If you see that a performance is about to take place—do not miss it.

This acrobatic "dance" has pre-Columbian roots and a religious and ritual significance. Five costumed men climb a tall metal (formerly a wooden) pole. Four are attached to the top with ropes and the fifth performs a stomping dance, accompanied by flute music and drum beats, atop a small platform. As the dance progresses, the four men "fly" from the top of the pole by their ropes, slowly descending while upside down, in ever-widening circles, as the platform atop the pole gradually turns.

They are said to represent macaws, which symbolize the sun; they make thirteen revolutions as they descend, before righting themselves at ground level. The four flying men, times thirteen revolutions equals fifty-two—a number that represents a major cycle of time (in years) in the Mesoamerican calendar.

A sixth costumed young man circulated among the viewers and collected donations, perhaps a modern addition to the ceremony.

The area around El Tajín is noted for the production of vanilla carried on by the present-day Totonac. Vanilla is actually the seed pod of a certain orchid that is hand-pollinated. A popular regional curio is made from the pods; they are woven together into various forms: flowers, scorpions, vases, and so forth. They are called *figuras de vainilla* locally and make unusual souvenirs. They are sold at El Tajín and at stores in Papantla.

It is sometimes suggested that you place the *figuras* in your sugar bowl to impart a vanilla aroma.

*Voladores with the Pyramid of the Niches in the background, El Tajín.*

*Detail of a carved column from the Building of the Columns, El Tajín Museum. Early Postclassic period.*

## EL TAJÍN MUSEUM

The El Tajín Museum is located on your left, just beyond the gate, as you enter the archaeological zone. It is one large warehouse-type room with only skylights for illumination. It contains a wealth of bas-relief and other carved-stone decorations from the site, including panels and a stela. Although there is no labeling, the multitude of artifacts makes a visit worthwhile.

In a fenced-off area outside the museum, and a few feet from it, are remains of numerous columns made of drum-shaped stones. All are beautifully carved in bas-relief. They come from the Building of the Columns—an unrestored structure located uphill to the west of Tajín Chico.

In 1968 a foot trail led to this structure where some of the columns could be seen. Since the removal of the columns to the museum area, the trail has been allowed to become overgrown.

★★

# *Quiahuiztlán*

(kee-ah-wees-*tlahn*)

ORIGINAL NAME: Quiahuiztlán (?)
CULTURE: Totonac; see text.
LOCATION: Central part of the state of Veracruz, Mexico.

---

## THE SITE

The archaeological remains that the visitor sees today at Quiahuiztlán consist of two groups of miniature temples. The first group is near the top of a hill and is made up of some twenty or so temples and a larger platform (with a stair flanked by balustrades with vertical upper zones). The top of the platform is smoothly paved and partly surrounded by merlon decorations. There are no remains of a temple on top. The platform is located at one end of the temples, which run in a couple of irregular rows.

The miniature temples vary in height but generally do not exceed 4 feet. They are similar in design and all sit on small stepped platforms mounted by one stairway. These stairs are also flanked by balustrades with vertical upper zones and each temple has a single doorway at the head of the stair. All the temples have sloping roofs with a flat top, and all are covered with a well-preserved cementlike coating.

The second group of temples is a short distance away at the top of the hill, from which you get a gorgeous view of the Gulf of Mexico.

In this section the temples are roughly arranged around the north and east sides of what appears to be a small plaza. They are similar in style to those in the first group. To the north of the temples on top of the hill is a low rubble mound.

You can get some good shots of the eastern temples with the Gulf in the background.

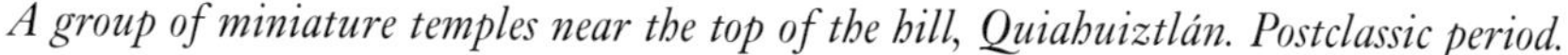

*A group of miniature temples near the top of the hill, Quiahuiztlán. Postclassic period.*

*One of the miniature temples from the group near the top of the hill, Quiahuiztlán. Postclassic period.*

## RECENT HISTORY

Quiahuiztlán is mentioned in the account of conquistador Bernal Díaz del Castillo as a fortified town, "which stands amid great rocks and lofty cliffs." It was a living city at the time of the Spanish conquest and it was near here that Cortés founded the first Spanish settlement on American soil. He called it Villa Rica de la Vera Cruz.

What is seen today is thought to be a cemetery, and there is apparently some question about the exact location of historic Quiahuiztlán. Perhaps the present remains were on the outskirts of the town seen by the Spaniards.

A pottery type bearing the name Quiahuiztlán—and having three phases—dates from the Early Postclassic through the Late Postclassic period. The style of the architecture of the small temples is certainly of late date.

There is little in English about the site, although its location is shown on several maps. It is thought that Quiahuiztlán was the recipient of some Toltec influence and the site is near, and existed at the same time as, the Totonac capital of Zempoala.

## CONNECTION

1. 18 miles by paved road from the cutoff for Zempoala, then 25 minutes on foot uphill to the site.

## GETTING THERE

See "Zempoala" for getting that far, and for accomodations in the area.

From the Zempoala cutoff, head north on Highway 180 to Quiahuiztlán. The stopping place is marked by a small sign, but it is sometimes illegible and partially covered with weeds, so you will have to look closely. The caretaker's house is a few feet off the highway on the west side and this is easier to spot than the sign. Park here and ask someone at the house to guide you to the temples.

As you drive along Highway 180, keep an eye out for a tall rocky peak on the west side of the road. It is a prominent landmark, and the temples lie on the lower hill just north of the peak. The caretaker's house is about 1 mile south of a sign saying Villa Rica, which can be used as another checkpoint. A bus could probably drop you off at the caretaker's house.

There is no food or drink at Quiahuiztlán. There is a small grocery 1.5 miles to the north, on the east side of the highway. They have cold drinks and packaged snacks.

Climbing boots would be advisable, especially if it has been raining. It is a rather tiring, though not too difficult, climb to the temples. Allow about ½ hour to see the temples plus the time for the climb. Bring insect repellent.

★★

# *Zempoala and Zempoala Museum (Cempoala)*

(sehm-*poah*-lah)

DERIVATION: "The Place of Twenty Waters." Twenty tributaries of the Actopan River pass nearby.
ORIGINAL NAME: Zempoala.
CULTURE: Totonac.
LOCATION: Central part of the state of Veracruz, Mexico.

---

## THE SITE

Zempoala was founded by the Totonacs at the time of Toltec expansion in the Postclassic period, probably around A.D. 1200. As the Toltecs moved into the former Totonac territory, there was an exodus by the Totonacs. They established new towns, the most important being Zempoala, their last capital. It was a living city of considerable size at the time of the Spanish conquest in 1519.

The ruins of Zempoala cover about 2 square miles and have ten groups of buildings. The visitor today, however, sees only the central area, a small portion of the whole.

As you enter the site from the south, most of the interesting structures are visible on the west, north, and east sides of and within the plaza. The most impressive is the Great Temple bounding the plaza on the north. It is formed of a large pyramidal base, rising in several tiers, that supports a central stairway; two or more construction phases are visible on the left (west) side of the stairway. The remains of columns and stepped merlon decorations are found on top.

These merlons are found on several of Zempoala's structures and are locally called *almenas.* According to the caretaker at the site, they are purely decorative and have no symbolic meaning, but they are typical of Totonac architecture. There are also remains of a wall, formed of merlons, enclosing the main ceremonial precinct.

In the plaza in front of the Great Temple is a low rectangular platform with stairs on all four sides—seemingly a dance platform or altar. To the south of the platform are two circular structures. The smaller of the two has a stair, while the larger is perhaps best described simply as an enclosure formed by stepped merlons.

On the west side of the plaza is a small pyramidal base with remains of lower temple walls on top, and beyond this, to the west, are more pyramidal bases rising in several tiers. One of these structures has a semicircular extension at the rear, and the temple is thought to be dedicated to Éhecatl, the wind god—an aspect of the feathered serpent Quetzalcóatl.

The Temple of the Chimneys lies to the east of

*The Great Temple from the southeast, Zempoala. Late Postclassic period.*

*Large circular enclosure with merlon decorations, near the Temple of the Chimneys, Zempoala. Late Postclassic period.*

the plaza. Although smaller, it is similar in design to the Great Temple. It differs, however, in that there are remains of lower temple walls and columns at the foot of the stairway.

From the top of the Temple of the Chimneys you get a good view of the structures around the plaza, including a similar but smaller temple to the south. Also visible (to the east) from this vantage point, is another temple a couple of hundred yards away and accessible by foot trail.

The trail is easy to follow and runs through sugarcane fields. It is definitely worth the short walk to this temple as there are painted stucco decorations on both the inside and outside walls. A Chac Mool statue is reported from the site but is no longer there.

Four construction periods have been identified at Zempoala. The earliest shows some Toltec remains and the latest exhibits strong influence from central Mexico, both in the Aztec-style architecture and the Mixteca-Puebla–style ceramics typical of Cholula.

Zempoala occupies an ecological niche in the form of an arid wedge that interrupts the tropical rain forests along the coast of Veracruz. It is probably for this reason that irrigation was necessary. There is both documentary and archaeological evidence for an elaborate drainage system consisting of canals, aqueducts, and subterranean masonry, although this is not readily discernible today.

The central area of Zempoala is kept well cleared and it is easy to roam around the various structures.

*Temple of the Chimneys from the southwest, Zempoala. Late Postclassic period.*

## RECENT HISTORY

Shortly after Cortés landed on the coast of Veracruz, he visited Zempoala. At the time it was the largest native city he and his men had seen, with a population of about 30,000.

The conquistadors were much impressed with what they saw. In the words of Bernal Díaz: "We were struck with admiration. It looked like a garden with luxuriant vegetation, and the streets were so full of men and women who had come to see us, that we gave thanks to God at having discovered such a country."

The freshly whitewashed structures gleaming in the tropical sunlight led one of Cortés's scouts to believe that the buildings were covered with silver.

Although Zempoala once represented the apogee of Totonac culture, at the time of the Spanish conquest it had been under Aztec control for some time. Mexican archaeologist José García Payón believes that had the Spanish conquest occured fifty years later, the Totonac culture probably would have been extinguished. Aztec exploitation of the Totonac made the latter receptive to an alliance with Cortés. This alliance—Cortés's first with a native group—was one of the major contributing factors in the success of the conquest of the Aztec capital of Tenochtitlán and, thereby, all of Mexico.

Just sixty years after the conquest, Zempoala consisted of only thirty households, most of the inhabitants having been killed by smallpox brought in with the conquistadors. By 1600, only two inhabitants survived.

The site was explored and reported upon by Francisco del Paso y Troncoso in 1891, but the bulk of the work at the site was done in the 1940s by García Payón.

## CONNECTIONS

1. 27.5 miles by paved road (22 miles are toll road) from Veracruz, or
2. 128 miles by paved road from Poza Rica.

## GETTING THERE

Best stopovers near Zempoala are Veracruz on the south and Poza Rica or Papantla on the north. Jalapa is another possibility. Zempoala is 2 miles off Highway 180, and the cutoff to the town and site is marked, heads west, and is paved. The cutoff is a little over 4 miles north of José Cardel and 70 miles south of Nautla.

There is no food or drink at the site, which is on the edge of the town of Zempoala.

A guide is not necessary, and tennis shoes are adequate. Allow about 1½ hours to visit the site.

## ZEMPOALA MUSEUM

The Zempoala Museum is located at the entrance to the site. It is housed in a small room, where publications are also sold. The collection (all from the site) is poorly arranged and unlabeled. It really resembles a small warehouse where excavated items were placed for protection. There are fragments of painted stucco, figurines, and stone artifacts. Five to 10 minutes is ample time to see it.

★★

# *Tres Zapotes Museum*

(trehs sah-*poh*-tehs)

One of Mexico's newest small museums is located in the village of Tres Zapotes. This is somewhat off the beaten path, but the trip is worthwhile if you are a fan of the Olmec.

The museum consists of four small wings, open on all sides, and a small enclosed section where tickets are sold. The lack of walls on the wings is an advantage because of the amount of light it affords. All the large monuments are in this area (and all are from the site of Tres Zapotes, though they are unlabeled).

The Tres Zapotes colossal head (Monument A) is the prize of the collection, but it shares honors with Stelae A and D, some smaller stone monuments, and most important, the recently discovered upper portion of Stela C (see below). Oddly enough, the side of the stela with the Cycle 7 date is displayed toward the outside of the museum; facing the interior is the side of the stela with remains of a carved figure. With a wide-angle lens you can get a photograph of the date on the back while standing "in" the museum, or, with a normal lens, you could step down to the grass below for a shot.

The Tres Zapotes head was the first colossal

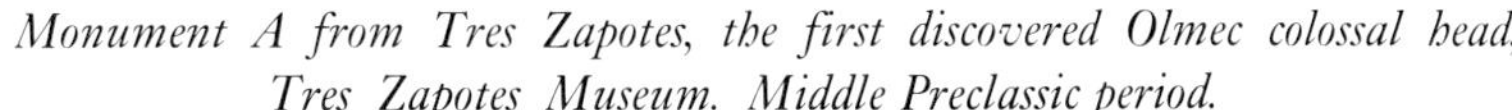

*Monument A from Tres Zapotes, the first discovered Olmec colossal head, Tres Zapotes Museum. Middle Preclassic period.*

Olmec head to be discovered. It was seen by one José María Melgar in 1862 when he was visiting the region of San Andrés Tuxtla. He had heard of the unearthing of a head in 1858 by a workman on a nearby hacienda and went to see it. In 1869 he published a short note in the *Bulletin of the Mexican Society of Geography and Statistics*, accompanied by an engraving of the head.

In 1905 Eduard Seler and his wife visited the Tres Zapotes region and saw and photographed the head and an elaborately carved stone box. They reported their findings in 1922.

The most serious work at Tres Zapotes was undertaken by Matthew Stirling, who perhaps did more than any other person literally to "uncover" the Olmec. He visited the site in 1938 and found, uncovered, and photographed the head. These photos won him the support of the Smithsonian Institution and the National Geographic Society, who sponsored further investigations. Stirling worked at Tres Zapotes in 1939 and at La Venta, San Lorenzo, and Cerro de las Mesas in the following years, making one stupendous discovery after another.

One outstanding monument discovered in the 1939 season was Stela C, with a bar-and-dot date in the Maya style, but without the usual period glyphs. Although the carving was incomplete, Stirling was able to calculate a date of 31 B.C. for the stela. (Actually, Mrs. Stirling did the initial calculation.) This created a great controversy since it was earlier than any date from the Maya lowlands, where dating was then thought to have originated. In 1972 it was reported that a farmer had found the crucial missing portion of Stela C, which confirmed beyond doubt the date that Stirling had calculated, though by this time most authorities already tended to agree with his interpretation.

Many of the monuments from Tres Zapotes are in the museums in Mexico City and Jalapa, but the new museum in the village should become an attraction for the ruin buff, if not for the average tourist.

The town of Tres Zapotes and the access roads leading there are not generally shown on road maps. A few years ago, access to the town was by nasty dirt roads from Lerdo de Tejada or Angel Cabada—fortunately, it is no longer necessary to use these roads. The best access now is from Santiago Tuxtla. In Santiago Tuxtla ask directions for the highway to Isla (paved and known locally as the Via Isla and shown as an unnumbered road on maps).

Take this road southwest for 5.7 miles. This brings you to a junction with a good new rock road on the right (known locally as Dos Caminos) that leads directly to the town of Tres Zapotes, 9 miles away. In 1978 there were no bridges on this road, but the detours were easily passable. By now bridges may have been installed. In any case, this route is definitely to be preferred over the older ones. There is a parking area on the side of the museum. Driving time from Santiago Tuxtla to Tres Zapotes is about 40 minutes and buses connect the two towns.

Soft drinks are available in the town of Tres Zapotes, but there are no accommodations. Best stopovers near Tres Zapotes are Veracruz to the northwest and Catemaco to the southeast. Others would be Acayucan and Coatzacoalcos farther southeast. All are on Highway 180.

Allow half an hour to visit the Tres Zapotes Museum.

*Note:* There is little to see at the site of Tres Zapotes itself, but in 1978 new excavations were in progress and a tomb had been discovered. Some stone objects from the tomb had been brought to the museum and more work was planned. At that time the tomb was covered with a sheet of plastic at the bottom of a deep pit and was inaccessible to visitors. The tomb is a couple of miles from the museum but you will need a guide to get there. Ask at the museum.

★★

# *Tuxteco Museum*

(toosh-*teh*-koh)

# *(Santiago Tuxtla Museum)*

(*toosh*-tlah)

The recently opened Santiago Tuxtla Museum is in a building facing the Main Plaza. There are both indoor and outdoor sections. On the inside there are nicely arranged and well-lighted displays of ceramics—including a large selection of the famous Veracruz "smiling heads"—and stone artifacts. Labeling, however, leaves a bit to be desired. There are photo displays and sections devoted to ethnological materials and to the colonial period.

Some larger carved stones are attractively exhibited in the outside section. The most impressive is one of the colossal Olmec heads. This head is from Nestepe, although it was formerly listed as coming from Tres Zapotes, and was called Tres Zapotes Monument 2 or Q. The new designation was made when it was discovered that it actually came from another site (provisionally named Nestepe). Until a few years ago, this head resided on a cement platform on the other side of the plaza, accompanied by Monument F from Tres Zapotes. Monument F has since been moved to the Jalapa Museum, but a copy is displayed in the Santiago Tuxtla Museum.

In the Main Plaza, across the street from the museum, is another important monument—the most recently discovered colossal Olmec head. The Cobata Head is more than 9 feet tall and is installed under a special shelter surrounded by a moat. It is one of the most unusual of the heads because the eyes are shown closed. It is less refined than the other heads and, frankly, has a face that only a mother (or an Olmec fancier) could love. You will not want to miss it. In fact, if you are an Olmec fan, rate the museum and the plaza display three stars.

Even though the Cobata Head is under a shelter, it is not difficult to photograph. Try "overexposing" a stop if you are using a camera with an averaging meter. This will better bring out the details.

Santiago Tuxtla is on Highway 180 about 87 miles southeast of Veracruz and 17 miles west of Catemaco. Those are the two best stopovers, but others would be Acayucan (68 miles) or Coatzacoalcos (106 miles) farther to the east.

A sign on the highway marks the entry into the town of Santiago Tuxtla.

*Note:* If you are driving Highway 180 in the area, you will pass through the town of Angel Cabada (17 miles northwest of Santiago Tuxtla and 5 miles southeast of Lerdo de Tejada). There is an interesting bas-relief stela facing the highway as it passes the Main Plaza of the town. The stela is located on the north side of the highway adjacent to some soft drink and snack stands. This large monument is known as El Mesón Stela and it dates to the Late Preclassic period. Matthew Stirling believes it is probably Late Olmec, and he notes that it shows some Izapan traits. It is definitely worth a look and a few photographs.

*The Cobata Head, the most recently discovered Olmec colossal head, Plaza of Santiago Tuxtla. Middle Preclassic period.*

★★★★

## *La Venta Park Museum (Villahermosa)*

This unique park-museum, planned and executed under the able direction of Carlos Pellicer, is located near the old airport, just off Highway 180 as it skirts the city of Villahermosa.

Somewhat more than two dozen stone monuments are set in a jungly park environment. They were transported some 80 miles from La Venta and comprise the finest pieces found at the site.

Included are three of the colossal heads (Numbers 1, 3, and 4), seven huge altars, four stone stelae, and two huge floor mosaics (each consisting of 485 pieces of serpentine). These mosaics represent stylized masks of the jaguar. The pieces were carefully numbered so they could be accurately reassembled when they were installed in the park.

The mosaics form pavements, apparently of a sacred nature, as they were buried almost immediately after completion. Colored clays originally filled the spaces between the serpentine slabs. Some authorities believe that the serpentine came from the Pacific Coast, 150 miles away.

It is now generally agreed that the basalt used for the colossal heads, altars, and stelae came from the Cerro Cintepec in the Tuxtla range, 60 miles west of La Venta. Undoubtedly, the Olmec were excellent engineers as well as artists: moving basalt boulders averaging 18 tons apiece through such terrain would be difficult even today.

When you visit the park, simply follow the well-marked trails. Take any short side trails that you see before continuing along the main trail, as all these lead to interesting monuments.

Having the monuments in this jungle setting is appropriate, since it is in this sort of environment that they were found. Huge pieces of sculpture seem to be at their best in an outdoor setting instead of confined within museum walls. It is altogether an excellent idea.

Allow 1½ hours to see the monuments and a little more if you want to spend some time looking at the zoo that is included in the park.

Soft drinks and packaged snacks are available near the entrance to the park.

A guide is not needed, but by all means bring and use insect repellent. Tennis shoes are okay if it has not been too wet. Otherwise, boots would be better because the trails can get muddy. In 1978, work was in progress to turn some of the trails into stone walkways. This will be a nice improvement when completed. Villahermosa can be reached by plane from Mexico City or by car or bus on Highway 180.

*Altar 5 from La Venta, side view, La Venta Park Museum. Middle Preclassic period.*

★★★★

# *Regional Museum of Tabasco (Villahermosa Museum)*

The Villahermosa Museum, located on the northeast corner of the Plaza de Armas in the center of Villahermosa, is one of the outstanding regional museums in Mexico.

It has twelve exhibit halls, with representative samples of archaeological specimens from throughout the republic. Especially fine are the objects from La Venta exhibited in Halls 1 and 2, which include some large sculptured monuments.

*Note:* Formerly, Colossal Head Number 2 from La Venta rested on a platform at the end of Hall 1. In 1978 it was no longer in place and was reported to be in storage until a new wing of the museum (or a new museum) was finished. Presumably it will then be put back on display.

Other special features are copies of existing Maya codices in Hall 5 and full-scale copies of the famous murals at Bonampak in Hall 12. Several well-preserved Maya stelae are found in Hall 11. Allow 2 hours to view this excellent collection.

★

# *La Venta*

(lah *vehn*-tah)

DERIVATION: Spanish for "The Roadside Inn."
ORIGINAL NAME: Unknown.
CULTURE: Olmec.
LOCATION: Extreme western part of the state of Tabasco, Mexico, near the border with Veracruz.

## THE SITE

The best place to see La Venta is in Villahermosa because the large carved monuments have been removed from the site to the museums in the state capital. The finest specimens of Olmec jade carving from La Venta are found in the Mexico City Museum. (See those museums for details.)

Nevertheless, if you are fond of the Olmecs, you may want to see the site of one of their ancient ceremonial centers. The only thing to be seen today at La Venta is a fluted clay "pyramid," which all sources list as being around 100 feet high. It does not seem anywhere near this tall. It has eroded some since it was cleared, and its gentle slope probably also gives the illusion of a more modest height. Nevertheless, it stands out rather dramatically from the flat plain.

If you climb to the top, you can easily see the ridges that form the fluting. One theory holds that the Olmecs built this "pyramid" in the form of volcanoes in the Tuxtla Mountains, 60 miles to the west. It is further postulated that there was a ritual significance to the shape.

The site of La Venta was occupied during the Middle Preclassic period, and, more specifically, from 1000 to 400 B.C. The "pyramid" was probably built around 800–700 B.C. It is also probable that this is the largest construction in all of Mesoamerica dating from this early time period and the largest construction ever built by the Olmecs (unless the plateau at San Lorenzo with its ridges and ravines should be considered a single man-made construction).

Today the oil boomtown of La Venta has grown to the very base of the pyramid, and many ancient mounds have been bulldozed.

## RECENT HISTORY

Frans Blom and Oliver La Farge, working for Tulane University in 1925, discovered the site of La Venta after they heard local reports about its existence. Their expedition was largely exploratory, but during the one day they spent at the site, they discovered six interesting stone monuments, one a colossal head (Number 1). They were only able to excavate a portion of the head due to their limited time, but it was enough to suggest to Blom a relationship to the head previously reported from Tres Zapotes.

In 1940, Matthew Stirling, working for the Smithsonian Institution and the National Geographic Society, visited La Venta. He found all the monuments reported by Blom as well as fourteen others, among which were three more colossal heads (Numbers 2, 3, and 4). He returned to do additional excavation in 1942, assisted by Philip Drucker, and in 1943, with the help of Waldo Wedel. Other work at the site was undertaken by Drucker, Robert Heizer, and R. J. Squier during the 1950s and 1960s. In 1968 Heizer briefly excavated the Stirling Group, which lies about 0.3 mile southeast of the La Venta Pyramid. He reported that this group appears to be separate from and physically unconnected with La Venta. Twenty-three new sculptures were discovered; one, of a head with elaborate head gear, is almost an exact duplicate of that found by Blom on the summit of San Martín Pajapan in the Tuxtla Mountains.

The Stirling Group seems to be a complex of earth-and-clay fill with basalt columns set in rows, and it probably overlapped La Venta in time.

In 1958 most of the known monuments from La Venta were moved to Villahermosa, thanks to the efforts of Carlos Pellicer, founder and director of the Villahermosa Museum, who also designed the La Venta Park Museum. The monuments were transported by Petróles Mexicanos, a national oil company with operations in the La Venta area. Most of the monuments are now found in the outdoor La Venta Park Museum, but some are also in the Villahermosa Museum.

## CONNECTIONS

1. 32 miles by paved road from Coatzacoalcos to the town of La Venta, or
2. 80 miles by paved road from Villahermosa to the town of La Venta, then 0.5 mile of dirt road to the pyramid.

## GETTING THERE

There is a paved cutoff from Highway 180 (near kilometer marker 105) that leads north for about 3 miles to the town of La Venta. The cutoff, which is marked, is 29 miles east of Coatzacoalcos and 77 miles west of Villahermosa. These are also the best overnight stops in the area, but others are Acayucan and Catemaco farther west, and Palenque farther east.

When you arrive in the oil boom town of La Venta, look to the right (east) for occasional views of the pyramid. Drive through the town until you come to an air strip on the right. Just before the air strip there is a dirt road to your right, heading east. Take this for about 0.5 mile. Look for the short cutoff to the right (south) that takes you to the base of the pyramid.

A visit to La Venta can be combined with a visit to Comalcalco, whether you are driving east or west on Highway 180. The cutoff from the highway to the town is heavily trafficked due to the oil industry in the area.

There is no food or drink at the site, but these are available in the town of La Venta.

No guide is needed, and tennis shoes are fine. Allow 15 or 20 minutes to climb the pyramid and look around.

1 Parking area
2 Acropolis
3 Tomb
4 Temple IV
5 Temple V
6 The Palace
7 Temple VI
8 Temple VII
9 Temple I
10 Temple II

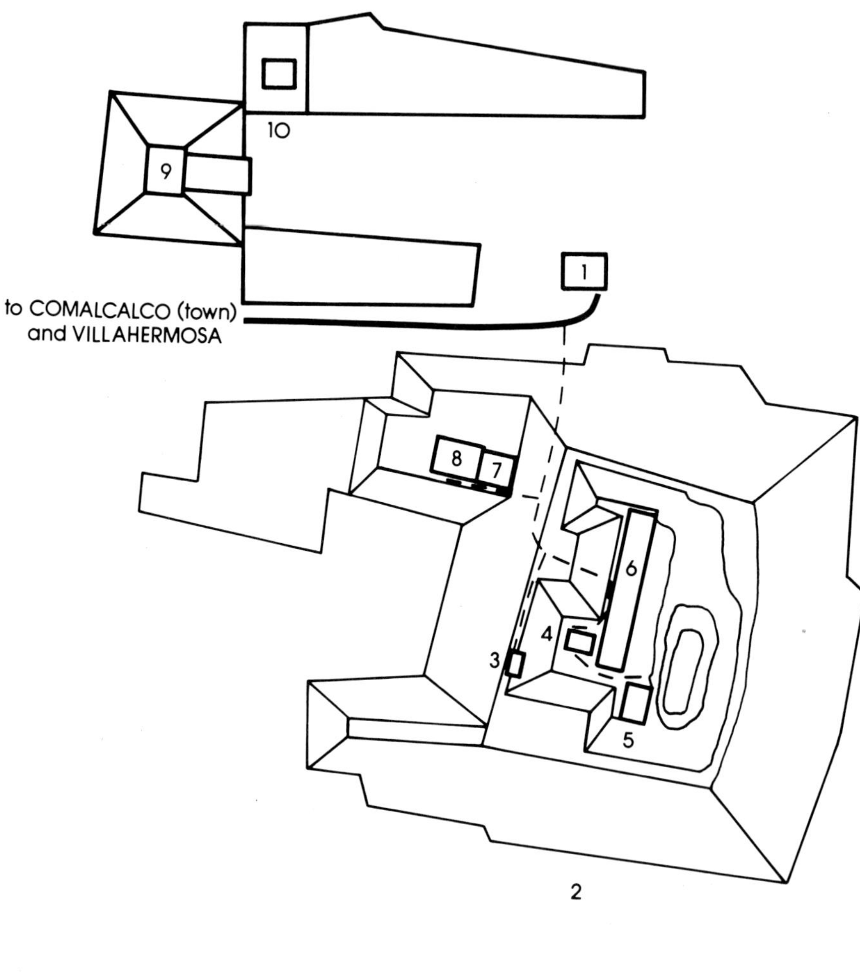

COMALCALCO

★★★

# Comalcalco

(koh-mahl-*kahl*-koh)

ORIGINAL NAME: Unknown.
CULTURE: Maya.
LOCATION: North-central part of the state of Tabasco, Mexico.

## THE SITE

Comalcalco is a medium-sized site lying on the westernmost edge of the Maya area. As of 1978 some restoration had been completed and work was continuing, making a visit there very worthwhile.

As you arrive at the site, you pass a large pyramid, which is being restored, and some mounds. Proceed to the archaeologist's camp a bit farther on and park your car. Try for a spot under the tree. There are three main groups to see at Comalcalco, all easily accessible and visible from the parking area.

Begin your tour by crossing the road and climbing up a path to the Acropolis. This large artificial platform supports the remains of two small temples (Numbers IV and V—unrestored) and a larger, partially restored palace-type structure, as well as the well-known tomb with the sculptured figures. The tomb has been restored: a locked gate prevents entry, but you can shoot pictures over it. It is located a little to the south of Temple IV. When Frans Blom discovered the tomb, the figures were painted red, but no evidence of color remains today.

The nine bas-relief figures, three on each of three walls of the tomb, may represent the Nine Lords of the Underworld. This arrangement of nine figures is also found on the inside of the tomb below the Temple of Inscriptions at Palenque. A good portion of the Comalcalco figures is intact and two physical types are depicted, only one of which is typically Classic Maya.

The tomb was sacked before archaeological discovery, but presumably it originally contained a sarcophagus. Blom also excavated a large number of squared and perforated clam shells from the dirt on the floor of the tomb. They had once formed a necklace.

After you visit the tomb, just roam around the other structures of the Acropolis (Temples IV and V and the Palace).

One unusual feature at Comalcalco is the use of kiln-fired brick rather than stone for construction. This is understandable since no stone is found in the Tabasco Plains, where Comalcalco is located. The bricks are perhaps better described as slabs since they are so thin. In one wall of the Palace, the mortar forms thicker layers than the bricks it binds together.

From the top of the Acropolis you get good views of the other two groups. This a good spot for some telephoto shots.

Descend to the second group on a lower level. This group consists of the restored remains of two temples (VI and VII) atop a stepped platform. The one you reach first (Temple VI) has remains of a beautifully modeled stucco mask on the steps

*General view of the Acropolis, with the Palace at upper left and center, Comalcalco. Temples VI and VII are on the lower level. Late Classic period.*

*Temple IV of the Acropolis, the front (north) side, Comalcalco. Late Classic period.*

facing south. The mask is protected by a tin roof, but is not too difficult to photograph.

Temple VII also has stucco decorations on the south face and they are likewise protected by a roof. The stucco remains show some seated figures in profile and other motifs. This is a bit more difficult to photograph because the roof is close to the top of the decorations. On the north side of the second temple is another fragment of stucco decoration. You are not permitted to climb either of these structures.

From this area you cross the road to where you parked and enter a large plaza bounded on the north and south sides by mounds. Facing the plaza on the west is a large pyramid with a central stairway. The pyramid rises in several levels and supports remains of a temple on top (Temple I). You are not permitted to climb the pyramid, but perhaps this will be allowed when the restoration is finished.

Recently uncovered at the base of the pyramid (to the left of the stairway as you face it) are remains of some stucco figures protected by a shelter.

The only other standing architecture in this area is part of Temple II on top of the mound immediately to the northeast of the pyramid.

Comalcalco shows certain similarities to the much larger site of Palenque, 100 miles southeast. These similarities lie in the plan of its temples, the use of stucco decorations and their style, and in the tomb with the nine figures. The visible structures at Comalcalco date to the Late Classic period, as do those at Palenque.

## RECENT HISTORY

Apparently the first visitor of note to see Comalcalco was Frenchman Désiré Charnay. He explored Comalcalco in 1880 and reported his findings, which included a sketch map, five years later. An English translation followed in 1887.

*Temple VI, the front (south) side, Comalcalco. Late Classic period.*

*The stucco mask on Temple VI, on the front (south) side, Comalcalco. Late Classic period.*

The site was further explored in 1925 by Frans Blom and Oliver La Farge, working for Tulane University. Their report was issued in 1926–27 and included Blom's discovery of the tomb with the nine figures.

Recent work at the site was undertaken by Gorden Ekholm for the American Museum of Natural History and Román Piña Chan for the National Institute of Anthropology and History.

*Temple I, partly restored, Comalcalco. Late Classic period.*

## CONNECTION

1. 55 miles by paved road from Villahermosa, then 1 mile of dirt road to the site.

## GETTING THERE

The ruins of Comalcalco are located on the northeast side of the town of the same name. From Villahermosa, the best stopover, drive west on Highway 180 for 29 miles to Cárdenas. Here you take a paved road to the right (north) for 24 miles, to the entrance of the town of Comalcalco. Continue skirting the edge of town for 2 miles to the north side. A Zona Arquelógica sign marks the dirt cutoff to the right that goes 1 mile to the site. It is not necessary to go through the main portion of the town of Comalcalco, which lies off to the left (west). Just stay on the road you came in on until you get to the Zona Arqueológica sign.

There is another road that leads directly from Comalcalco to Villahermosa and this shortcut is reportedly now paved.

From the site head back to the paved road and turn left. Proceed for 2.5 miles (this is the road you came in on). Here you will find a cutoff for Jalpa on your left (east). Take the cutoff to Jalpa and continue to Villahermosa. The distance from the cutoff to Villahermosa is shown as approximately 33 miles on some maps.

A guide is not necessary at Comalcalco and tennis shoes are fine since the site is kept well cleared. Allow about 2 hours for a visit. Soft drinks are sometimes available at the site and always in the town.

If you are driving Highway 180 either east or west and pass Cárdenas, you are only 30 minutes or so from the site.

Other stopovers are Palenque farther east and Coatzacoalcos, Acayucan, or Catemaco on the west.

*Pyramid of the Sun (end of the Late Preclassic period), Teotihuacán. View from the northwest. Remains of small structures are in the foreground. Unless otherwise noted, color photographs by the author.*

*Detail of Relief II showing the head and torso of one of the standing figures, Chalcatzingo. Middle Preclassic period.*

*Pyramid of the Niches, El Tajín. The front, or east, side. Late Classic period.*

*Temple VI (right foreground), Temple VII (center), and Temple I (center background), Comalcalco. Late Classic period. View from the southeast.*

*Aerial view of Palenque.*

*The recently restored Structure 33 (the House of Hachakyum), Yaxchilán. Late Classic period.*

*The Governor's Palace, Uxmal. View from the northeast. Late Classic period.*

*West face of the Labná Arch, Labná. Late Classic period.*

*Edifice 5, Cabalpak, Chacmultún. East wing of the front, or north, side. Late Classic period.*

*El Castillo, Chichén Itzá. View from the northwest. Early Postclassic period.*

*Structure II, Chicanná. Central portion of the front, or west, side. Late Classic period.*

*Temple B, Río Bec B. The front, or east side. Late Classic period.*

*Pyramid with the mask panels, Kohunlich. This panel is south of the stairway on the lowest level. Late Classic period. Photograph by Jerry Kelly.*

*Structure 1 (El Castillo), center, and Structure 5 (Temple of the Descending God), left, Tulum. View from the northwest. Late Postclassic period.*

*Mother and child at the Sunday market, Chichicastenango. Photograph by Jerry Kelly.*

*Zoomorph P, the back, or south, side, Quiriguá. Late Classic period.*

*Stela 9, south side, Tikal. Early Classic period. Situated in the Great Plaza.*

*Stela 7 depicting a ballplayer-clad ruler, Seibal. Late Classic period.*

*Three stelae in the Ceremonial Plaza, Copán. Stela 4, left; Stela C, center; Stela B, right. Late Classic period.*

*The major pyramid at center and the structures bordering the east side of the plaza on the left, Campana–San Andrés. Classic-Postclassic period.*

## MEXICO

### Chiapas

*Stone bas-relief in place at Palenque, south side of the east stair of the Eastern Court in the Palace complex. Late Classic period.*

★★★★

# *Palenque and Palenque Museum*

(pah-*lehn*-keh)

DERIVATION: Spanish for "Palisade."
ORIGINAL NAME: Unknown.
CULTURE: Maya.
LOCATION: Northeastern part of the state of Chiapas, Mexico.

---

## THE SITE

Here I must admit a personal bias. Although I have enjoyed all the sites I have visited, Palenque remains my favorite. It is the site that attracted me to Mesoamerican archaeology—even before I saw it. It is the site that I most wanted to see for the longest time, and it is the first Maya site I actually visited. I was also fascinated with thoughts of Copán and Tikal, but fifteen years ago they seemed less accessible than Palenque.

I attempted to get to Palenque in 1959, but only succeeded six years later. Even after this long anticipation, I was not disappointed. On my first visit I could only catch my breath at the sight of its exquisite temples. Oddly enough, subsequent visits have produced the same effect.

If there is such a thing as a previous life, then I am sure I lived it at Palenque.

It is not a huge site, but the design of its architecture, its state of preservation, and its setting in the green foothills of the Sierra of Chiapas make it a veritable jewel in the crown of Maya cities. Mayadom's finest architects and sculptors surely worked here.

There is some ceramic evidence for occupation of Palenque as far back as the Middle Preclassic period, though this and the following Late Preclassic are poorly represented. Better represented is the Early Classic, but the full florescence of Palenque took place during the Late Classic period. Most of the visible remains date to this period, from A.D. 600 to 800 or 830, when the site collapsed as a major ceremonial center. There was some occupation by peasant groups for a few more years before it was totally abandoned to the jungle.

There is only one carved stela known from Palenque; most of Palenque's sculpture is on panels used as part of the architectural decoration.

There is much to be seen at Palenque, so if you can arrange to spend two days there, you will enjoy it more. The climate is hot and humid and climbing around can be exhausting. One plan would be to visit the Palace complex, the Temple of the Lion, the Temple of Inscriptions and its tomb, and Temple XII on one day. Next day see the aqueduct, the Temple of the Sun, Temple XIV, the Temple of the Cross, the Temple of the Foliated Cross, the Temple of the Count, the North Group, the ball court, and the museum. This plan divides up the tiring climbs. All these structures, with the exception of the Temple of the Lion, are in the area that is kept cleared.

If you only have one day, skip the Temple of the Lion, the aqueduct, and ball court, and pass up climbing the Temple of the Cross, the Temple of the Count, and Temple XII—you can get photographs of these from other structures—but do try to climb the rest.

The tomb of the Temple of Inscriptions is now open all day, but the museum is only open during certain hours. Check the hours when you enter the site so you can work this into your schedule.

When you arrive at the site, you will find the paved parking area and ticket office. If you want a guide, that is where you will find one. If you are carrying a map of the site or the National Institute of Anthropology and History (INAH) guidebook to the site, you will not really need a guide, for it is easy to find your way around. The following tour of the ruins assumes that you have two days to spend at the site.

When you enter the gate, follow the path to the Palace directly ahead. This path passes Temple XII, two ruined structures, and the Temple of Inscriptions.

The Palace is a large complex of buildings rising on an artificial platform 300 feet long, 240 feet wide, and 30 feet high. Access today is by the recently restored stairway on the west side. Another broad stair, recently excavated, originally gave access from the north side. This stair is flanked by a large stucco head, and nearby is a large stucco fragment—apparently part of some architectural decoration—that still bears remnants of red and blue paint. The

1 The Palace
2 Tower
3 Western Court
4 Eastern Court
5 Temple of the Lion
6 Temple of Inscriptions
7 Temple XII
8 Temple of the Sun
9 Temple XIV
10 Temple of the Cross
11 Temple of the Foliated Cross
12 Aqueduct
13 Otolum Creek
14 Restaurant
15 Stone Bridge
16 Museum
17 Ball Court
18 North Group
19 Temple of the Count
20 Temple X

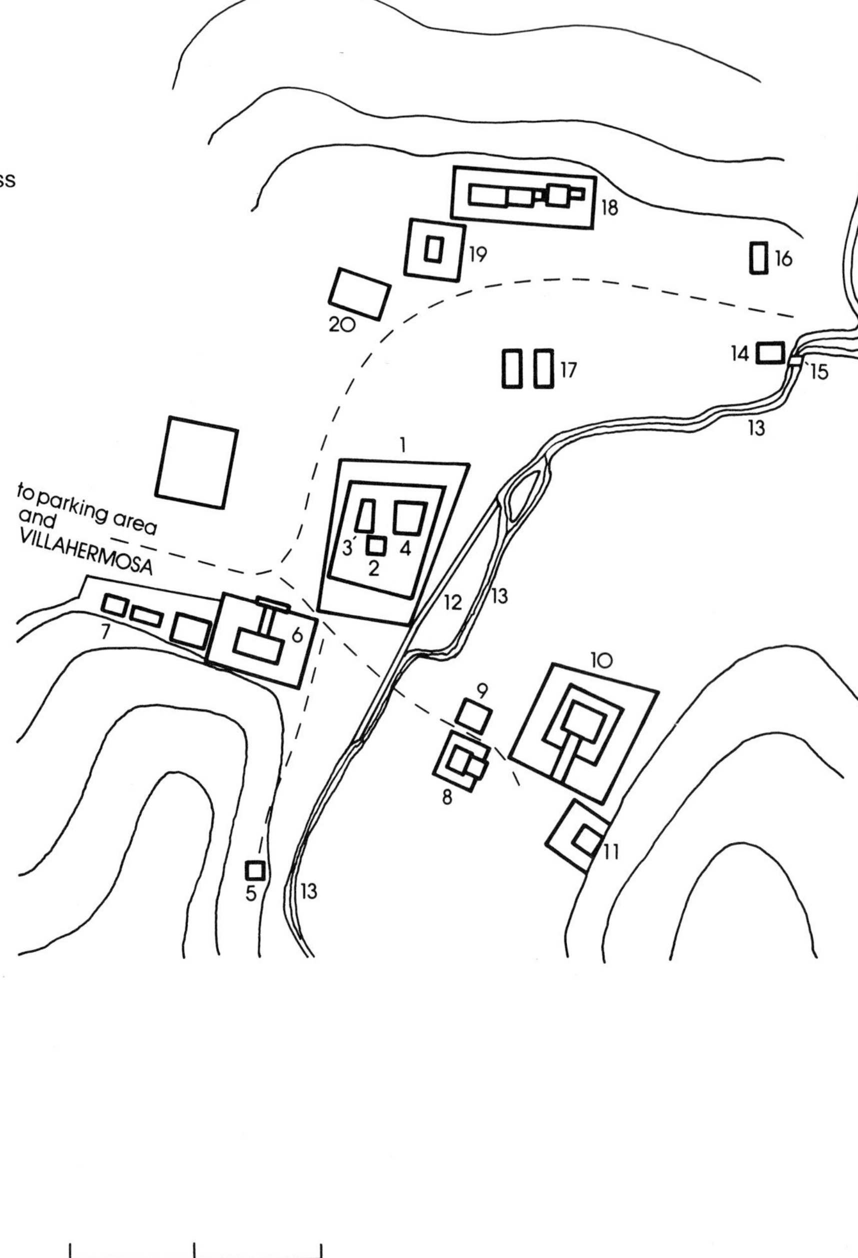

PALENQUE

*The Palace from the southeast, Palenque. Late Classic period.*

fragment is protected by a plastic roof and a wire fence. There are a few other remains of stucco decoration on the north face of the Palace platform.

The structures of the Palace complex were erected at different times, and the plan seems informal. There are four courts or patios, and the unique four-story tower dominates the whole. An entire day could be profitably spent in this area; there are interesting architectural and sculptural remains everywhere.

By all means, climb the interior stairway to the top of the tower. This is a great vantage point for views of the other structures—and generally there is a nice breeze. The tower probably served the dual function of astronomical observatory and watch tower. From here you can see for a great distance across the plains that lead to the Gulf Coast.

Other features of the Palace are the stucco bas-reliefs on the pillars on the east and west exterior surfaces and on the interior of the Western Court.

The larger Eastern Court has several large stone bas-reliefs of figures flanking the east stairway and some beautifully preserved glyphs on the risers of

*Detail of stucco decoration on one of the pillars of the Palace, Palenque. Late Classic period.*

*Glyph-carved steps on the west side of the Eastern Court, Palenque. Late Classic period.*

*Bas-relief sculptures and glyphs in the Eastern Court, west side, Palenque. Late Classic period.*

the west stairway. Other bas-reliefs in stone are found on the vertical walls above the court, both here and in the Western Court.

There are remains of stucco decorations on the interiors of many of the buildings. Three stairways descend to the "cellars," which lie in the southern part of the complex. These parallel underground galleries were probably employed for religious ceremonies, although this is not certain. Some slablike tables are found here that may have been altars or thrones. One near the south entrance has its edges carved with glyphs.

You will enjoy just roaming around the Palace complex.

If you leave by the south entrance, look for some nearby sculptured stucco decoration on the south face of the Palace platform, protected by a corrugated plastic roof. This was also just recently uncovered.

As you leave the south entrance of the Palace, look for a trail that heads south and uphill, passing the side of the Temple of Inscriptions. This leads about 200 yards to the Temple of the Lion (sometimes called the Temple of the Beautiful Relief). This is the only temple included here that is not in a cleared area. The trail through the jungle, however, is easy to follow. This small temple has lost its front façade, but it is worth a look for the remains of a stucco relief on the rear wall. Unfortunately, much of this was destroyed during the last hundred years. It represented a priest seated on a throne decorated with two jaguar heads. At the rear of the room a stairway leads to a lower chamber, which probably once contained a burial, although no traces of such have been found.

From the Temple of the Lion, head back to the Temple of Inscriptions—one of Palenque's most impressive structures. The temple itself rests on a stepped pyramid; its floor is 75 feet above the level of the Plaza. The back of the pyramid is partially supported by a hill covered by tropical green, which contrasts nicely with the pale gray architecture.

This structure has been known for as long as the site has been known but only gave up one of its secrets in 1952. Mexican archaeologist Alberto Ruz Lhuillier, while investigating the structure, noticed some holes in a large slab that formed part of the floor of the temple. He also noted that the walls of

*The Temple of Inscriptions, the front (north) side, Palenque. Late Classic period.*

the temple did not end at floor level, but went deeper. This suggested that there was some sort of chamber beneath the floor. And, indeed there was.

When the floor slab was lifted, a rubble-filled stairway was found. It took four field seasons of two and a half to three months each to remove the rubble. The stairway was found to make a U turn part way down and the remains of five or six youths were found near the end. They were probably sacrificed to accompany their master. Beyond this was a large triangular stone slab, fitted neatly into the slope of the vault. When this was removed, a fantastic sepulchral chamber came into view, and was looked upon by human eyes for the first time in over 1,200 years.

The chamber measures 30 by 13 feet, and has an unusually high vault (23 feet), reinforced by stone beams. The bottom of the chamber is 80 feet below the floor of the temple and some 5 feet below the floor of the Plaza. Its walls are covered with bas-reliefs of nine figures thought to represent the Nine Lords of the Underworld. Most of the area of the chamber is taken up by a stone slab (measuring 12½ feet long, over 7 feet wide, 10 inches thick, and weighing some 5 tons) beautifully carved in low relief and resting upon a stone block. When this lid was raised—a difficult job in these cramped quarters—a smooth slab was found fitted into the stone block. This slab had holes fitted with stone stoppers: these were removed and the slab was duly lifted. On the interior of the stone block were found the remains of a tall man literally covered with jade. There were jade rings on each finger, multiple jade necklaces made of hundreds of pieces—many in the form of flowers and fruits—many jade bracelets, earplugs, and a jade mosaic mask over the face. A small jade statue of the sun god was found, and the personage held a large jade in each hand and one in his mouth.

On the floor of the crypt under the tomb were found clay vessels, apparently containing food and drink for the deceased, and two beautiful life-size stucco heads that were originally part of the decoration of some other temple at Palenque.

The objects found in this tomb, except for the carved sarcophagus lid, are now on display in a replica tomb in the Mexico City Museum. The tomb was obviously built before the pyramid. Otherwise, it would have been impossible to get the lid down the stairway.

It was originally thought that the man entombed had died at age 40 or 50, but recent research has led to the decipherment of some of the glyphs on the edge of the sarcophagus lid, and they indicate that he died at age 80. We now know that he was Pacal (meaning Shield)—probably the greatest ruler of Palenque—who reigned from age 12 until his death. He was born in A.D. 603, ascended to the throne in 615, and died in 683. Glyphic evidence found elsewhere at Palenque corroborates this decipherment.

Along the stairway that descends to the tomb is a hollow molding that connects with the sarcophagus. It is believed that this was a sort of magic connection so the dead Lord could communicate with those in the temple above.

The temple itself is also of great interest. It contains three large stone panels carved with 620 hieroglyphs, some of which have been deciphered. It indicates a date of A.D. 692 for the temple. These inscriptions give the temple its name.

The pillars on the outside of the temple are deco-

*Stucco decoration depicting one of the gods of death, on the bottom of a pillar in Structure XII, Palenque. Late Classic period.*

rated with stucco bas-reliefs of figures of men and women carrying small children.

From here, proceed west to Temple XII. You can do this without going all the way down the steps of the Temple of Inscriptions. On the way, you pass the substructures of two ruined temples.

Although Temple XII is partially ruined, it is worth a visit to see the well-preserved stucco decorations at the foot of one of the remaining pillars of the façade. It is a representation of one of the gods of death.

From Temple XII you can climb down directly to the road—watch out for loose rubble.

On your second day at Palenque, proceed first to the group making up the Temple of the Sun, the Cross, and the Foliated Cross, and the recently excavated and partially restored Temple XIV. The first three temples face the Plaza and Temple XIV lies next to the Temple of the Sun.

All four structures are similar in design and rise on pyramidal bases. The Temple of the Sun is the best preserved and has been partly restored. It is one of the most beautiful small temples ever erected by the Maya. This elegantly proportioned structure is sheer perfection, making it one of the most photographed buildings at Palenque. On the back wall of the interior shrine is a magnificent carved panel. It depicts the ascension of Chan-Bahlum, son and successor of Pacal, in A.D. 684. Pacal is the figure on the left and he is shown deified and acting after death (according to his dress and certain symbols that accompany him). Chan-Bahlum is on the right receiving his dynastic rights.

The panel was dedicated in A.D. 692, as were those in the Temple of the Cross and the Temple of the Foliated Cross.

There are remnants of stucco decorations on the exterior pillars of the Temple of the Sun as well as

*Temple of the Sun, the front (east) side, Palenque. Late Classic period.*

*Temple of the Sun at left, Temple XIV at center, and part of the Palace at right, from the east, Palenque. Late Classic period.*

on the mansardlike roof and on the perforated roof comb.

Temple XIV has had its two-tiered base and some of its walls restored, although it lacks a roof. It houses another beautifully carved panel in its inner chamber. This is protected by metal bars, but you can get photographs from over the bars or in between them. There are some remnants of paint on this panel.

The Temple of the Cross rises on the tallest pyramidal base in this group. The only carved stela found at Palenque was discovered on the upper part of the slope in front of the temple. This eroded, rather three-dimensional monument depicts a man standing on a large hieroglyph. (It may be worthy of note that a stone column still standing was reported by Frans Blom and is located on his map a little less than a mile west of the ceremonial precinct of Palenque. It was called La Picota by the native who showed it to him, and it was accompanied by two stone drums apparently serving as altars. Blom describes it as a stela and mentions that it was uncarved.)

Neither its base nor the Temple of the Cross itself has been restored, and most of the front of the temple has collapsed. The carved panel that originally graced the rear wall, and gave the temple its name, is now in the Mexico City Museum, though two carved slabs flanking the door of the shrine are in place.

From here you get excellent views of the rest of the site and an especially nice one of the Temple of the Sun. Try for morning hours for front-lighted shots of the Temple of the Sun.

The Temple of the Foliated Cross has also lost its front façade, but its carved panel is still in place and it, too, is a beauty. This temple and its base are also unrestored.

From this area head west (toward the Palace) for a look at the aqueduct. There is a vaulted section that you can walk through—watch out for bats—and an open channel. The vault is some 9 feet high and huge stone slabs were incorporated into its construction. The aqueduct connects with the Otolum Creek and you can follow the creek to the museum area.

There is a small restaurant and soft drink stand in this area where you might want to take a break before visiting the museum. Remains of an ancient stone bridge are found near the restaurant.

From here follow the main trail heading west. A couple of hundred yards ahead on your left (south)

*Temple of the Cross, the front (south) side, Palenque. Late Classic period.*

is the ball court. It is in a badly ruined condition, and is unrestored and generally overgrown, but you might want a quick look. On the right side (north) of the road directly opposite the ball court is the North Group.

This is a complex of five structures sharing a common base, although they were not built at the same time. The two small temples (the easternmost is totally collapsed) and the larger central one were later additions. They were all originally decorated with stucco reliefs, but little of this remains today.

Just to the southwest of the North Group is the Temple of the Count. This temple gets its name from the fact that it was used as a residence by Count Jean Frédéric Waldeck during the time he worked at Palenque. There has been some restoration of this temple and the stairs of its pyramidal base. It is a rather typical Palenque temple in design. There are some remains of its roof comb, and a few fragments of stucco decorations on the pillars flanking the central doorway.

This covers the major structures at Palenque. If you still have some energy left, however, you might want to visit Temple X on your way out. It lies to

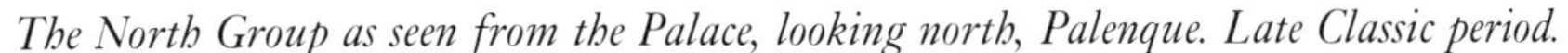

*The North Group as seen from the Palace, looking north, Palenque. Late Classic period.*

the southwest of the Temple of the Count. Large stone steps and the remains of lower walls of the temple are all to be seen today.

## RECENT HISTORY

Palenque was known in limited circles from the middle of the eighteenth century, and has been one of the most visited and reported upon sites in all Mayadom.

The relatives of Antonio de Solís—the curate of the nearby town of Tumbala—explored the area and reported their findings to the padre, who died before being able to visit the site himself. The stories, nevertheless, were repeated to the families involved.

Some years later a boy told the story to Ramón Ordóñez, a friend who later became a priest. When Ordóñez was working at his clerical duties in Ciudad Real (now San Cristóbal de las Casas) and had the opportunity to do so, he sent his brother to investigate the site. In 1773, Ordóñez wrote a *memoria* about Palenque from the information his brother provided and sent a copy to Josef Estachería, president of the Royal Audiencia of Guatemala. (Both Ciudad Real and Palenque were part of Guatemala at that time.) Eleven years later (1784), Estachería commissioned José Calderón to investigate.

Calderón, the mayor of the town of Santo Domingo de Palenque—the nearest town to the ruins—reported to Estachería. Estachería wanted more information and in 1785 he commissioned Antonio Bernasconi, the royal architect of Guatemala City, to investigate further.

Still dissatisfied, Estachería sent the two reports to Spain, where a royal historiographer, Juan Bautista Muñoz, read them. He, too, wanted more information, so in 1786 Estachería commissioned new investigations. This time Antonio del Río, a captain in the Spanish Army was sent; an artist, Ricardo Almendáriz accompanied him.

Antonio del Río enlisted the help of Calderón, who provided labor from the area, and the structures were cleared to some extent. Almendáriz drew some of the decorative panels, although his depictions of the glyphs seem crude today. Neither he nor del Río had much idea of what they were looking at, but del Río perhaps suspected that the glyphs were a form of writing. He took measurements, made some excavations, and removed parts of some bas-reliefs to be sent to Muñoz, who had given him a list of questions to be answered and a request for artifacts. Del Río returned to Guatemala and gave his report to Estachería in 1786 (some authorities say 1787). Estachería had a copy of the report made for his files, forwarding another copy, plus the drawings and artifacts, to Spain.

Somehow, a copy of this report was brought to England by a certain Doctor McQuy, who sold it to London bookseller Henry Berthoud. Berthoud had the report translated and published some thirty-six years after del Río had presented it to Estachería. Some of the reports of earlier investigators eventually found their way into print. In 1822, when del Río's was published, it was the first detailed report to reach print, although a short description of the ruins was mentioned in the *History of Guatemala* by Domingo Juarros, published in that country in 1808. In the interval between the issuance and publication of del Río's report, however, others visited Palenque.

In 1804, Charles IV of Spain ordered investigations of aboriginal remains in New Spain, and Guillermo Dupaix—a retired captain of the Dragoons—was selected to investigate. He had lived in Mexico for twenty years and had developed an intense interest in pre-Hispanic culture, studying it extensively. This and his above-average education made him well suited for the appointment. Dupaix investigated Palenque in 1807 and had with him the artist José Luciano Castañeda. His report, like that of del Río, was published only many years later. In this case, it was partially reproduced in England by Lord Kingsborough in 1831 and completely reproduced in Paris in 1834.

An account of Palenque by Juan Galindo—the governor of the Petén in Guatemala—who had made a short visit to the site in 1831, was published later that year in England.

The colorful Count Jean Frédéric Waldeck became intrigued with pre-Hispanic remains when he copied the drawings of the del Río expedition for the 1822 publication of that work. Ten years later he arrived at the site, and remained a little over a year. He explored the site and made numerous drawings, which were published in Paris in 1866.

In 1840, two important pairs of visitors reached Palenque. The first to arrive were Patrick Walker, a politician from Belize, and his draftsman, John Herbert Caddy. Their expedition was conducted because of the jealousy aroused in Belize when it was learned that John Lloyd Stephens and Frederick Catherwood planned a trip to the site.

Stephens and Catherwood arrived at Palenque some four months after Walker and Caddy, but publication in 1841 of *Incidents of Travel in Central America, Chiapas, and Yucatán* by the former overshadowed the work of the latter.

The Frenchmen, Arthur Morelet, visited Palenque in 1846 and in 1871, and an English translation of his work was published in New York. Another Frenchman, Désiré Charnay, visited Palenque in 1858 and again some years later. He published his work in Paris in 1863 and 1885.

Some of the finest work published on Palenque, and still a standard reference, is that by Britisher Alfred P. Maudslay. The photographs and drawings provided in his monumental *Biologia Centrali Americana* (1889–1902) remain unsurpassed. In 1974, this five-volume set was reissued in facsimile form.

Other expeditions for various sponsors were undertaken during the following years. Of importance were those by Edward H. Thompson, who brought along the artist William Holmes, followed by those of Marshall Saville and Teobert Maler. Eduard Seler, Sylvanus Morley, Alfred Tozzer, and Herbert Spinden visited Palenque in the early twentieth century.

In 1923, Frans Blom was sent to Palenque by the Mexican government "to determine what could be done for the preservation of the ruined buildings." Blom collected new data and mapped the outlying groups of the site. While inspecting the Temple of Inscriptions, he noticed holes in the floor slabs and commented, "I cannot imagine what these holes were intended for." It was these holes noticed by Alberto Ruz Lhuillier twenty-six years later that led to the discovery of the tomb below the temple. One wonders if Blom would have investigated further had he the means to do so.

More recently, work was carried out at Palenque by Miguel Angel Fernández and Alberto Ruz Lhuillier for INAH and excavation and restoration continued into the 1970s.

Due to the efforts of several scholars, we now know something about the rulers of Palenque; when they were born and ascended to the throne, and when they died. Prominent among those working on the decipherment of Palenque's hieroglyphic texts, which provided this information, are Floyd G. Lounsbury, Linda Schele, and Peter Mathews. Their continuing studies will surely provide us with even more most welcome information.

## CONNECTIONS

1. 5 miles by paved road from the town of Palenque,
2. 94 miles by paved road from Villahermosa, or
3. 230 miles by paved road from Campeche.

## GETTING THERE

In addition to the good road connections to Palenque, you can fly in from Villahermosa or San Cristóbal de las Casas in a light plane. There is also bus service and taxi service from Villahermosa.

Since you should really stay for two days, it would be best to stay in the town of Palenque. But if time is limited, you could drive or fly in and out from Villahermosa in one day. Villahermosa may be reached by road or plane from Mexico City or Mérida.

To reach Palenque from Villahermosa by road, head east on Highway 186 to Catazaja. Turn right (south) for 17 miles to the town of Palenque. From Campeche head south to Champoton, then take Highway 261 to Escárcega, and Highway 186 to Catazaja and on to Palenque.

From the town of Palenque the road heads southwest to the archaeological zone.

The situation in the town of Palenque has changed drastically in the last few years. In 1968 there were two hotels in the town and you could simply drive up and get a room. Now there are a dozen in the town and nearby, but they are sometimes filled. Large tour groups in huge buses are now crowding the town on a regular (though perhaps not daily) basis, so for this reason I am listing the names of available places. Not all will answer correspondence.

In town are the Hotel Palenque, Tulija, La Cañada, and La Croix. On the new road to Ocosingo, a few miles from town, is the Nututun, and on the road to the ruins are the Chan Kah, Motel de las Ruinas, and the Mayabel Trailer Park. If all these fail, there are the Hotel Regional, Avenida, and, if you are absolutely desperate, the Casa de Huéspedes León, all in town. Apparently Palenque has been unable to cope with the recent tremendous influx of tourists.

There are a few small (and unattractive) restaurants in town, but your best bet for food is at the Chan Kah or La Cañada. There is an ice cream vendor's supply house in town where you can buy ice.

There are soft drinks and food available at the ruins.

Hiking boots would be better than tennis shoes. Bring insect repellent, plenty of film, and a sun hat.

There is a new INAH guide for Palenque, but it is not always available at the site. Try to pick up a copy before you arrive.

★★★

## PALENQUE MUSEUM

Palenque's only carved stela is exhibited on the outside of the museum; inside are displays of other objects from the site. Most notable are the carved stone slabs from various structures, decorated clay cylinders, which may have been used for burning incense, and fragments of stucco decorations. It is worth a half hour or so to visit.

*The only known carved stela from Palenque, in front of the Palenque Museum. Late Classic period.*

★★

# *Toniná and Toniná Museum*

(toh-nee-*nah*)

DERIVATION: John Lloyd Stephens gives Tonilá as the name for the site in use at the time of his visit. He was informed that in the region this was the name for "Stone Houses."

ORIGINAL NAME: Unknown.

CULTURE: Maya.

LOCATION: Central part of the state of Chiapas, Mexico.

---

## THE SITE

Toniná is notable not only for its pre-Columbian remains but also for its lovely situation on a terraced hillside overlooking some spectacular scenery. As you approach the site by road, you get some fleeting glimpses of the higher structures from miles away.

On the lower level of the hill there is one partially excavated but unrestored building. The remains include the lower walls, formed of slablike stones, and four circular altars on the south side. A band of glyphs is carved along the circumference of three of the altars and two of these are in almost pristine condition. The third is broken, although all the fragments are in place, while the fourth is badly damaged.

Immediately south and southeast of the structure are over a dozen sculptured monuments from the site. They are found propped up against trees with wooden stakes to keep them in place. None are whole and some are eroded, but all are worth a look, and a few are worthy of careful scrutiny.

Some of the monuments are three-dimensional

*Circular altar with carved glyphs, Toniná. Late Classic period.*

stelae, depicting figures in a frontal view, an unusual feature in Maya sculpture, but one that Toniná has in common with Copán and Quiriguá. The Toniná stelae, however, are much smaller than those from the other two sites. The oblique treatment of the feet on these stelae is another feature found at Copán.

Another monument is the top fragment of a stela showing the head of a figure wearing an elaborate headdress; others of this type have been reported from the site.

Some of the monuments bear carved glyphs and an especially interesting one (originally from Rancho Pestac, 1 mile south), has outsize numerals in the Maya bar-and-dot system on one side, but lacks the usual period ending glyphs. The monuments date to the Late Classic period and are carved of sandstone rather than the limestone used in most of the Maya area. There are also grass-covered mounds on this lower level.

From here, head north and climb the terraces—partly natural and partly man-made, and originally faced with stone—to the upper levels.

Excavation in these upper levels has revealed several features of interest. One is a tomb that contains a sarcophagus, apparently carved out of a single block of stone. It may be reached by descending a modern ladder. To the west of the tomb, on the same terrace, is a mask panel. It is made of stone and stucco, and, although incomplete, the lower portion retains some of the original details. A wide-angle lens is good here to eliminate some stones in front of the mask that would partly block the view in a photograph taken with a normal lens.

The treatment of the nose and eyeballs is similar to that found on the Chac masks on Temple 22 at Copán. The major difference is that at Copán the masks form the outer corners of the structure—making a 90-degree turn—while at Toniná the mask occurs in a single plane.

East of the tomb, on a slightly higher level, are the remains of another stone-and-stucco decoration, this time on either side of a small doorway. It is located in the lower section of a mound that forms the substructure for one of Toniná's better-preserved buildings.

The structure above has some of its walls intact, but much has collapsed. There is evidence of an inner chamber and stepped vaults—another feature found at Copán. On a still higher level, a short distance to the west, is another partially preserved building with a stepped vault, and a few remnants of stucco and paint on its exterior surface. The plan of the two structures is similar to temples at Palenque. The last structure is on the top level of the hill, and from here you get a gorgeous view of the surrounding countryside.

There are some mounds to the north of the highest structure, but, according to the *guardián* of Toniná, nothing of special interest.

*Monument T-20, Toniná. One of the three-dimensional stelae characteristic of Toniná. Late Classic period.*

*Stucco mask panel discovered in the early 1970s, on one of the upper terraces, Toniná. Late Classic period.*

## RECENT HISTORY

Toniná has been known in the literature for many years, sometimes as Ocosingo—the name of the nearby town.

One of the earliest reports on the site was that of Guillermo Dupaix, who visited Toniná in 1807 on his way to investigate Palenque.

In 1832, Jean Frédéric Waldeck made a side trip to see Toniná while he was working at Palenque, and in 1840, John Lloyd Stephens and Frederick Catherwood visited the site. Stephens was aware of Dupaix's visit (published in 1834) and credits Dupaix with making the site known to the outside world.

Stephens wrote an extensive description of the site and Catherwood did a drawing of a stucco ornament—since destroyed—and a plan and elevation of one of the temples.

In 1870, E. G. Squier published a paper on a cache of jades from Toniná. The jades—now housed in the American Museum of Natural History—are known as the "Squier collection." A comparative study of this collection was undertaken by Elizabeth K. Easby and her findings were published in 1961.

Eduard Seler and his wife recorded the monuments at Toniná and published their data in 1900 and 1901. In 1926–27, Frans Blom and Oliver La Farge published the results of an exploratory expedition made for Tulane University, which included a visit to Toniná.

The most extensive work at the site was that by a group of French scholars, who excavated there in 1972 and 1973. During this time the stone and stucco decorations on the upper levels of the terrace were discovered.

## CONNECTIONS

1. 74 miles by road (61 miles paved, 13 miles dirt—see text) from Palenque to Ocosingo, or
2. 60 miles by road (22 miles paved, 38 miles dirt) from San Cristóbal de las Casas to Ocosingo, then 8.2 miles of poor and narrow dirt road to the site.

## GETTING THERE

The road from Palenque to Ocosingo and San Cristóbal is relatively new and is constantly being repaired and improved; so far it is unnumbered. The first 61 miles from Palenque to Temo are paved, but the low spots—of which there are many—have deteriorated drastically and are full of potholes and mud; there are also occasional detours.

The rock-dirt part of the road from Ocosingo south is a succession of potholes, only inches apart and impossible to avoid. This alternates with some dirt areas that get muddy when it has been raining, and spots where the sides of the road have washed away. It makes for a very bumpy and unpleasant ride. There is a 5.5-mile paved stretch just south of Oxchuc, and the last 9.5 miles to Highway 190 are also paved.

Driving time from Palenque to Ocosingo is about 2¾ hours; from San Cristóbal to Ocosingo takes a bit longer. Although new sections of pavement will gradually be completed, considering that they tend to deteriorate rapidly, the driving time will probably not be greatly reduced for some time to come.

If you leave from Palenque (town), take the paved road that heads toward Palenque ruins. The cutoff for Ocosingo is a short distance out of town, is on your left, and is well marked.

From San Cristóbal, take Highway 190 southeast (toward Guatemala). The cutoff for Ocosingo is on the left 7 miles away.

If you want to stay in Ocosingo, try the Posada Margaritas, just a block off the plaza. It looked fairly decent and the restaurant upstairs serves good food.

Once you are in Ocosingo, it will take 30 minutes to drive to Toniná, if you do not have to stop and ask directions.

As you approach Ocosingo from Palenque, leave the main road and enter Ocosingo by the first cutoff on your left. Follow this road to the Main Plaza in town.

Starting from in front of the church, across from the Main Plaza, and with your car headed south: (1) proceed ahead following the road—it curves around a bit—for 1.7 miles to a fork, which occurs shortly after you pass a ranch. (2) Take the left branch of the fork and proceed for 5.7 miles. This brings you to another ranch and a side road marked with a sign saying Zona Arqueológica, 1 K. (3) Turn left on to this road and go 0.8 mile. First you pass a gate—you may have to open and close it—and later you pass a house (on your left) and, across the road, the museum. Continue 300 yards to a parking area shaded by trees where the road ends.

At this point the *guardián* or his assistant will probably arrive and offer to show you around. If they do not, then follow the foot trail from the parking lot downhill to a stream, and cross the small bridge. The trail then heads uphill a bit to a pasture that is the lower level of the site.

If you approach Ocosingo from San Cristóbal, take the cutoff on your right and enter Ocosingo. Go to the plaza, turn your car around so it is pointing south, and follow the directions given above. This will cause you to do a little backtracking, but will save you time in the long run since you will probably not have to ask directions. It should be mentioned that not everyone in Ocosingo knows about the ruins of Toniná, and that those who do are not always sure of how to reach the site.

Allow about 2 hours to visit the site and museum. Tennis shoes are adequate as the site is kept cleared. There is no food or drink at Toniná, so at least bring cold drinks along.

You can get to Ocosingo by bus and, once you are there, it may be possible to hire a taxi or private car to drive you to the site. No buses run this last part and few vehicles use the road from Ocosingo to Toniná.

★★

## TONINÁ MUSEUM

The museum at Toniná is a sort of shed open on two sides, apparently a recent enterprise. The collection is composed of sculpture from the site. Some impressive pieces are displayed on stone and mortar platforms; others are arranged on crude wooden benches. Nothing is labeled and there is no artificial lighting, but with two sides open, there is enough natural light for photography.

One especially interesting piece is a bas-relief panel depicting a semireclining figure—perhaps a captive since there is a rope around each arm. There are glyphs on his thigh and on the background. The naturalistic and graceful pose is portrayed in the best sculptural tradition of such sites as Piedras Negras, Yaxchilán, and Palenque.

To the right of this panel is another very different one. A grotesque mask forms the major motif and the undercutting in some places is extremely deep. This gives the work a certain sharpness and angularity that is unusual.

There are remains of circular altars—some with exceptionally clear glyphs that make interesting detail photographs—and other fragmented sculpture.

The museum is definitely worth a visit while you are at the site.

*Bas-relief panel with semireclining figure, Toniná Museum. Late Classic period.*

★

# *Chiapa de Corzo*

(chee-*ah*-pah deh kohr-soh)

ORIGINAL NAME: Unknown.
CULTURE: See text.
LOCATION: West-central part of the state of Chiapas, Mexico.

---

## THE SITE

Chiapa de Corzo is one of those sites that is extremely important archaeologically, but visually unexciting.

The architectural remains seen today are in a cleared area bordered by *milpas* and consist of platforms with stairs and the lower walls of range-type buildings. Some are faced with boulders and others with roughly cut stone. Most of the structures date from 100 B.C. to A.D. 200, although remnants of other construction periods are visible.

Chiapa de Corzo was occupied almost continuously from Early Preclassic times (1500–1000 B.C.) through the time of the Spanish conquest, and it is still occupied today.

There is evidence that during its early history (1500–550 B.C.) there were ceramic ties with La

*Partly restored structure, Chiapa de Corzo. Late Preclassic period.*

Venta. Ignacio Bernal considers this period at Chiapa de Corzo Olmecoid. From 550 to 450 B.C. there was a greatly reduced population and evidence of an intrusive culture, with ceramic traits related to those in Guatemala.

Shell earplug pendants depicting the plumed serpent were found at Chiapa de Corzo and date from 450–100 B.C. During this time the site was influenced by the Maya lowlands, and Monte Albán trade ware was imported.

During the period 100 B.C.–A.D. 1, connections with the Maya lowlands become less pronounced, but those with highland Kaminaljuyú increased. Also at this time there were ceramic ties with southern Veracruz, Oaxaca, and El Salvador. A burial from this period contained some interesting carved bones resembling the Miraflores style of Kaminaljuyú, but they may date to an earlier time and may have been imported. Ignacio Bernal feels that the most evident relationship, however, is with La Venta and Izapa.

An early stela found at the site—if the interpretation of the missing digits is correct—dates to 35 B.C., which would make it the oldest Long Count date known.

From A.D. 1 to 200 a strong local culture, called Isthmian, developed, and there is evidence of influence from Tehuantepec and, to some extent, from the Gulf Coast. In the following period, 200–350, the first real stone-faced pyramid complex was constructed, although stone terrace platforms were built as early as 1000–550 B.C.

During A.D. 350–550 there were no architectural endeavors and the site is considered to have been generally abandoned. This period is known only from three burial offerings of Teotihuacán-like vessels.

During the Late Classic period there was a large influx of population, probably from the highlands and Pacific Coast of Guatemala and from A.D. 1200 to 1350 ceramics from Tabasco were imported.

Chiapa de Corzo is a well-stratified site with a well-developed chronology that has been linked to that of most of the rest of Mesoamerica, and this accounts for its archaeological importance.

## RECENT HISTORY

A large southwest section of the State of Chiapas was poorly known archaeologically until the investigations of Heinrich Berlin in the 1940s. In the 1950s, in-depth study of the area was undertaken by the New World Archaeological Foundation, whose work continued for several years. One of their major efforts was concentrated at Chiapa de Corzo, and many scholars took part in the project.

The northeastern part of Chiapas, with the important sites of Yaxchilán, Bonampak, and Palenque, is logically considered an extension of the lowland Maya area, but the southwestern part of the state poses more of a problem. According to Gareth W. Lowe and J. Alden Mason, who worked in the area, it "has not lent itself so well to inclusion in any of the usual Mesoamerican culture areas, though it has in part been broadly labeled as belonging to the highland Maya territory." They refer to Chiapa de Corzo as being part of an Isthmian culture; it is surely not typically Maya.

## CONNECTIONS

1. 10 miles by paved road from Tuxtla Gutiérrez, or
2. 42 miles by paved road from San Cristóbal de las Casas, then a few blocks of dirt streets to the site.

## GETTING THERE

Take Highway 190 east from Tuxtla Gutiérrez or west from San Cristóbal to the town of Chiapa de Corzo. The archaeological site is on the east edge of the town. A small site indicates the cutoff, which heads south from the highway. Once you take the cutoff, you are in the town and no other signs point out the way. You may have to ask directions several times.

Entry to the site is through someone's front yard, with nothing to indicate that this is the way. Apparently, the house belongs to a part-time caretaker and you will be asked to sign a registration book. The caretaker or his wife will then indicate a path along the edge of a *milpa* that leads to the site a couple of blocks away.

There is no food or drink at the site, but cold drinks are available in town and you will need one after your visit. Bring insect repellent and a sun hat. Tennis shoes are adequate. A guide is not necessary—other than to point out the path to the site—since everything of interest is in a small area. Allow 1 hour for a visit.

★★★

# *Yaxchilán*

(yahsh-chee-*lahn*)

| | |
|---|---|
| DERIVATION: | Mayan for "Green Stones," according to Teobert Maler. The site is named after a nearby arroyo. |
| EARLIER NAMES: | Menche or Menche Tinamit (used by Alfred P. Maudslay). Lorillard City (used by Désiré Charnay). |
| ORIGINAL NAME: | Unknown. |
| CULTURE: | Maya. |
| LOCATION: | East-central part of the state of Chiapas, Mexico, on the border with Guatemala. |

## THE SITE

Yaxchilán is a romantic's dream. There is a brooding quality about the site due to the luxuriant vegetation, and this, plus the exquisite architecture and sculpture, make Yaxchilán one of the most fascinating of Maya centers. I guarantee a visit will be a long remembered experience.

It is a large site, located on the bank of the Usumacinta River, with clusters of buildings arranged on natural terraced hills and some on flatter land near the river. Recently some of the low bush was cleared from part of the site, making its original appearance somewhat easier to discern.

Many of the structures at Yaxchilán are in a good state of repair—probably due to the use of stone rather than wooden lintels. Wood lintels tend to rot eventually, which can cause partial collapse of the masonry above them. Some restoration has been done at the site and more is planned, which should make it even more interesting.

Some of the buildings at Yaxchilán have the mansard-style roof seen at Palenque and some have interesting perforated roof combs originally decorated with stucco figures, although little of the stucco remains. There are no tall pyramids, such as those at Tikal, but the temples at Yaxchilán are larger, some with several doorways and multiple chambers. The natural elevation on which many structures rest may have acted as a pyramidal base.

When you visit Yaxchilán, you will be shown around by Señor de la Cruz, the *guardián* of the site or by one of his descendants. His family has lived in this isolated area for generations. His grandfather guided Teobert Maler to the site in the late

*Temple 19 (the Labyrinth), front (east) side, Yaxchilán. Late Classic period.*

nineteenth century. Some of his children and grandchildren continue to live there.

You will first visit Structure 19, the Labyrinth. This temple has multiple doorways and the remains of the lower part of a roof comb, and has been recently consolidated. There are some interesting interconnected rooms on two levels and in front of the structure are a couple of altars. The carving on one is well preserved.

A short distance southeast is Structure 30, with three doorways and two long rooms. It sits on a tiered base and has a stairway on the northeast side. Some of the corbeled vaults within are intact. Again going southeast, you come to the real gem of the site, the well-preserved and recently consolidated Structure 33, the House of Hachakyum.

This god of the Lacandón Mayas is said to dwell in a headless statue, which used to be seated in front of the central doorway of the temple. During recent work at the site, the statue was moved back inside to its original location. The head was also moved inside, and both it and the statue have been cleaned, though they have not been rejoined.

The Lacandones believe that when the head is reunited with its body, the world will come to an end and jaguars will descend and devour the people. The world can be saved from destruction by the Lacandones, who are the only ones who know how to pray to Hachakyum.

*Carved altar in front of Structure 19 (the Labyrinth), Yaxchilán. Late Classic period.*

*Structure 33 (the House of Hachakyum), Yaxchilán. This temple has recently been cleared and consolidated. Late Classic period. Note the stalactite (Stela 31) at right.*

Until very recently the Lacandones would travel on foot to Yaxchilán from their jungle dwellings and burn incense in this temple. They still visit the site, but now they fly in.

The statue of Hachakyum is unusual in that it is carved in the round, whereas in the bulk of Maya sculpture relief carving is the rule. (Notable exceptions are Copán, Quiriguá and Toniná.)

Structure 33 has much of its roof comb intact and some remains of a figure in a central niche. All three doorways are topped by beautifully carved stone lintels. It is altogether an exquisite structure.

You can photograph the lintels with a wide-angle lens by resting your camera on the floor pointed straight up. A self-timed shutter release is useful in this situation. You can also lie on your back in the doorways to get a shot.

The lintels in Structure 33 indicate a dedication date of A.D. 756, and depict three scenes in the life of Bird Jaguar, one of the center's rulers. In one lintel he is seen with a woman, in another with a young male (a descendant of the previous ruler, Shield Jaguar), who was possibly Bird Jaguar's successor, and in the third with an adult male. Bird Jaguar's depiction is also found on other lintels at the site. During his reign, from A.D. 752 to 786, some of Yaxchilán's most beautiful sculpture was produced.

A new and exciting find at this structure is a step composed of thirteen carved blocks. They depict ball game activities and are accompanied by glyphs. The step is the top one before you enter the temple, and the carvings are protected by a plastic roof. At the base of the platform in front of Structure 33 is a stalactite with well-preserved incised glyphs on the lower portion. This monument (now designated Stela 31) was reported by Maler in 1903 and was recently rediscovered.

Near the north corner of the stairs of Structure 33 is a carved but eroded circular altar.

Proceeding east, you come to Structure 20. Originally, this structure had three doorways. Only the one on the right (as you face the structure) remains intact. It is topped by the beautifully carved and well-preserved Lintel 14. Lintel 13, which originally topped the center doorway, is found propped up on the ground nearby and Lintel 12, which originally topped the left doorway, has been moved to the Mexico City Museum.

Above the remaining doorway, in an upper sec-

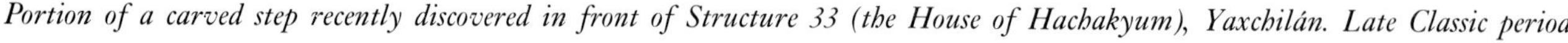

*Portion of a carved step recently discovered in front of Structure 33 (the House of Hachakyum), Yaxchilán. Late Classic period.*

*Temple 20, the front (northeast) side, Yaxchilán. Late Classic period.*

tion of the façade, is a niche, and around the corner on the northwest side is another with remains of a figure.

You now descend the terrace upon which Structure 20 rests. At the bottom you will find some carved stelae (numbers 5, 6, and 7). Portions of Stela 7 are well preserved even though the monument is fragmented. These stelae lie at the southwest side of a fair-sized plaza.

To the south of the plaza and on a higher elevation, more carved monuments are found under protective roofs. Some of these are lintels from ruined structures.

You return to the plaza, in the center of which is the reerected Stela 3 and an accompanying altar. Farther to the northeast side of the plaza is another shelter housing the lovely Stela 11. This stela was originally located in front of Structure 40, but was removed from the site to be sent to Mexico City. When the stela reached Agua Azul—a lumber camp on the Usumacinta—it was found to be too heavy to fly out. Through the efforts of Gertrude Duby Blom, the monument was returned to Yaxchilán in 1965.

Continuing to the west along the edge of the plaza you come to a hieroglyphic stair, but, unhappily, the glyphs are eroded and covered with moss. Still farther west is the recently consolidated Structure 6, with a solid wall facing the plaza. A depiction of the frontal view of a human head is found on this side. The front of this temple has three doorways and faces the Usumacinta River (and away from the plaza). The lower part of a roof comb tops the structure. Immediately west of Structure 6 is the badly ruined Structure 7.

From here you head west and enter another plaza, where Stela 1 has reen reerected. One side of this stela is well preserved and there are other carvings found near the platform on which the stela rests.

A short walk to the south, and then to the northwest, brings you to even more carved monuments, notably Stela 2 and Lintels 21, 22, and 27. Also in this area is the partially preserved Structure 23, from which three beautiful lintels were removed

*Stela 7, Yaxchilán. Late Classic period.*

many years ago. One is in the Mexico City Museum and the two others are in the British Museum.

Northeast of Structure 23 are more carved lintels that belonged to Structure 10. To the west a ball court marker is still imbedded in the ground. From here you head west again to the Labyrinth and the exit from the site. This finishes the "normal" tour.

In 1978, certain areas of Yaxchilán were restricted to visitors because of work in progress and so were not a part of the "normal" tour. Since it is likely that these areas will become open to visitors in the future, they will be mentioned. Señor de la Cruz will be able to tell you whether you may visit them when you reach the site.

The first area is near the Labyrinth and is reached by an uphill hike (which is tiring though the trail is not too difficult). Several structures cluster on the top of a hill and most are in ruin. Structure 42, however, has a carved lintel in place in a doorway, and Structure 44 has some carved steps and two beautifully carved though broken lintels. A part of Stela 14, which once stood in front of Structure 44, is found on the ground a short distance away. A trail from this area heads back to the airstrip.

The second area is 400 yards southwest of the central part of the site, and is reached by a long and tiring uphill climb. Three structures crown one of the highest hills at Yaxchilán; two are well preserved. Structures 39 and 40 each have three doorways, a mansard style roof, and a few remains of the lower portion of roof combs. The doorways in Structure 39 are stepped at the top, while those in Structure 40 are straight across. There are no carved lintels in any of the structures in this group, but several stelae and altars were originally found in the area. Some of these have since been moved.

Use fast film at Yaxchilán, as many of the monuments are sheltered and the tall trees in the area filter out much of the light. A flash unit is also a good idea.

The carved monuments at Yaxchilán date from A.D. 454 to 807, but no doubt the site was occupied before that and perhaps afterward for a time. Most of the architecture seen at the site dates to the Late Classic period, but doubtlessly we will know more about Yaxchilán when the work in progress is published.

## RECENT HISTORY

In 1696 a Spanish expedition under Jacobo de Alçayaga discovered the remains of an unnamed ancient city on the Usumacinta River. At one time it was thought to have been Yaxchilán; however, most modern scholars do not believe so.

Since the early nineteenth century the existence of Yaxchilán was a rumor among settlers in the area. It was only in 1881, however, that Edwin Rockstroh, of the National College of Guatemala, visited the ruins and wrote a description of them. From Rockstroh Alfred P. Maudslay learned of the site, which he scientifically investigated the following year.

Oddly enough, two explorers visited the site at exactly the same time in 1882. Frenchman Désiré Charnay arrived—to his dismay—shortly after Enlishman Maudslay, but the latter graciously shared with Charnay the honor of exploring the site and proclaimed himself "an amateur," not interested in publishing (as he knew Charnay planned to). They parted the best of friends. Eventually, in 1889–1902, Maudslay published an account of this and his other travels, but that was five years after Charnay's work appeared. Maudslay did, however, read a paper in London in 1882, which included his explorations at Yaxchilán and other sites. The paper was published in the *Proceedings of the Royal Geographical Society* in 1883. Charnay's account included accurate engravings of some of the temples. Maudslay produced some excellent photographs. A more thorough investigation was undertaken by Maler some years later, and his report and photographs were published in 1903 by the Peabody Museum of Harvard University. A site plan was also included. His work is still a fine source of information on the site.

Other scholars who studied Yaxchilán and its monuments in the early twentieth century were Alfred M. Tozzer, Sylvanus Morley, Linton Satterthwaite, and Herbert Spinden.

More recently Tatiana Proskouriakoff conducted a thorough study of monuments at Piedras Negras, Yaxchilán, and Naranjo, and concluded that many of the carved figures depict the current rulers rather than deities or priests, as was formerly believed. Her views are generally accepted. Because of her efforts, we know something about at least three individuals who reigned at Yaxchilán; Shield Jaguar, Bird Jaguar, and Shield Jaguar's descendant.

Surprisingly enough, although Yaxchilán has been well known in the literature for its carved monuments—approximately 120 inscriptions have been found on stelae and lintels and other monuments—and also for its architecture, excavation at the site began only in 1973 when the National Institute of Anthropology and History instituted a restoration program. This continuing program is under the directorship of Roberto García Moll.

## CONNECTIONS

1. 80 air miles from Palenque.
2. 115 air miles from San Cristóbal de las Casas, or
3. 150 air miles from Villahermosa.

## GETTING THERE

The grass airstrip at Yaxchilán can accommodate light aircraft, and the easiest way to reach the site is to fly in. Flying time to Yaxchilán from Palenque is about 45 minutes; from San Cristóbal de las Casas, about 1 hour and 10 minutes; and from Villahermosa, about 1 hour and 20 minutes. Go to the airport at any of the places mentioned and ask about arrangements. Often you can go the next morning. Generally a deposit will be required. You will find that it is virtually impossible to make arrangements from home. In addition to Yaxchilán, you can make the short hop to Bonampak before you return, at little extra cost, and this is recommended. You can also include a Lancandón village as an extra stop if you like. The cost will vary, of course, depending on your point of departure, the number of stops, the time spent (above the normal allotment), and the number of people in your party. The price is for the trip and is the same whether there is one passenger or four. Some of the aircraft can accommodate five passengers. Obviously, it is chaper per person if you have companions along. While the trip is not inexpensive, it is worth it.

The normal allotment of time at Yaxchilán is 2 hours, and that is a factor in the basic price. If you think you might want more time there, mention it when you make arrangements. There is an added charge for extra waiting time. One hour is normally allotted for Bonampak and is sufficient.

For me, 2 hours at Yaxchilán is cutting it pretty close, but if you do not visit the restricted areas or dawdle, it may be sufficient. I personally prefer to have 3 hours, and since you are already spending the money to get there, the cost of a little extra time is probably worth it. For a casual visitor who is not taking a lot of photos, the regular 2-hour visit is enough.

Bring an ice chest with cold drinks in the plane, and carry a canteen of water while you visit the site. Also carry snacks, if you think you will need them; there is no food or drink at the site, except for sour oranges from the trees. Bring insect repellent and wear boots.

It should be mentioned that there are other ways to reach Yaxchilán, but at this time they are not feasible:

(1) You can hire a dugout in Sayaxché in the Petén of Guatemala and get to Yaxchilán by river (see "Dos Pilas" for details of dugout rentals). This would be a rough trip lasting several days, and would require a good deal of provisioning. Therefore, it is not recommended.

(2) You can get to Yaxchilán from the Guatemala side by taking a newly cut road from El Subín to the Usumacinta River just opposite Yaxchilán, and then taking a dugout (if one is available) across to the site. See "A Note on the Petén and Belize" for details. This would also be a rough trip.

(3) Get in touch with Mrs. Gertrude Duby Blom at Na Bolom, Avenida Vincente Guerrero, San Cristóbal de las Casas, Chiapas, Mexico, and see if she can take you. This is how we reached Yaxchilán in 1972 on our first visit, and it was a truly memorable experience. We flew from San Cristóbal de las Casas to Agua Azul. We then proceeded to Yaxchilán by dugout, returned to Agua Azul the same way, then flew to Bonampak and back to San Cristóbal de las Casas. The trip took two days and we slept in the visitors' huts at Yaxchilán.

In 1978 we received information that indicated that while work was in progress at Yaxchilán, visitors were not allowed to stay overnight. Indeed, the visitors' huts were no longer there. Mrs. Blom would know of any changes in regulations. She still makes these trips.

These last three methods of reaching Yaxchilán have one advantage over flying in: you have more time at the site. The last of the three has the additional advantage of having Mrs. Blom's interesting company along on the trip.

★★★

# *Bonampak*

(boh-nahm-*pahk*)

DERIVATION: Mayan for "Painted Walls." Named by Sylvanus G. Morley.
ORIGINAL NAME: Unknown.
CULTURE: Maya.
LOCATION: East-central part of the state of Chiapas, Mexico, near the Guatemala border.

## THE SITE

The airstrip at Bonampak is a short walk from the ceremonial center. You enter the site at the north end of the Main Plaza, and everything of interest is visible at once. Señor Pedro Pech, the pleasant caretaker of Bonampak, or one of his assistants, will show you around, and they will remove the screen doors that were recently placed in the doorways of the temple with the murals.

Bonampak is a small site, with temples built on terraced hillsides south of the Main Plaza, and some low mounds on the other sides. More mounds, still unexcavated, lie in the surrounding jungle.

The first object of interest that you come to is the fragmented but beautifully carved Stela 1, the Warrior Stela, which dates to around A.D. 780. This unusually large monument—about 16 feet tall—was found broken into eight pieces, but it was recently restored and reerected. It is found in the center of the Main Plaza. Its large bottom fragment depicts a gigantic, elaborate mask, a glyph panel, and one of the most sensitive Maya profiles (on the viewer's left) ever created. The other main fragment depicts the warrior figure. The stela is worth some detail photographs because of the excellent state of preservation of its carving and its quality.

From the Main Plaza a broad stairway leads to

*Over-all view, Bonampak. Structure 1 containing the murals is on the right and the recently re-erected Stela 1 is in the foreground on the left. Late Classic period.*

*The main fragment of Stela 1, the Warrior Stela, Bonampak. This stela was recently restored and re-erected. Late Classic period.*

the first level of the terrace. Along the stairway are Stela 2 (A.D. 790) on your left and Stela 3 (A.D. 785) on your right. Stela 2 is noteworthy for the detailed delineation of fabric textures in the garments of the two female figures flanking the central male figure. This probably represents brocaded cotton. Forming the border on the hem of the dress of the figure on the viewer's left are depictions of Tlaloc and the Mexican Yearsign—indications of influence from central Mexico. Stela 3 has a kneeling bound captive —with his left arm to his shoulder, in a sign of submission—in addition to the standing principal figure.

Some years ago, each of these stelae was accompanied by an "altar." These "altars" are early carvings (A.D. 625 and 650) that are believed originally to have been panels, which were later moved. Unhappily, they have been moved again—this time into storage. They were not on view in 1978, but one hopes that they will soon be replaced at the feet of the stelae, as both are interesting monuments.

Bonampak's two major temples are located a few steps above the stelae on the first level of the terrace. On the left is a small, well-preserved temple with a double-columned doorway. A plain stela is found nearby.

To the right is the larger Structure 1, containing the murals. Structure 1 is the only building at Bonampak that has more than one room; it has three,

*Stela 2, Bonampak. Late Classic period.*

each with its own doorway and without inside connections. There are niches on the outside in the upper part of the structure, one above each doorway, and in the central niche are remains of a figure. Just to the right of this niche is part of a stucco figure—all that is left of a frieze. This structure is covered by a metal roof to protect it from the rain, but the exterior gets enough light for photography.

Each of the doorways is spanned by a carved and painted stone lintel depicting a warrior chief capturing a prisoner; those at either end are in an excellent state of preservation and show some color. The center lintel is somewhat eroded. The lintels and the murals date to around A.D. 790–800. Each room is encircled by a low bench.

The entire surfaces of the three rooms, including the vaulted ceilings, are covered with paintings. They were done in true fresco technique; pigment mixed with water was applied to wet lime plaster. When it dries, the painting actually becomes a part of the wall. This is a difficult technique at best. It is noteworthy that experts have been unable to detect joints in the plaster, which implies that the murals (at least in each individual chamber) were painted in one fell swoop, probably as a community effort, with the apprentices filling in the flat background after the forms were delineated by the master artist. Thirteen different pigments and their mixtures were used, providing a rich palette for painting on wet lime plaster, which destroys many colors. All were mineral colors, except for the black, which was charcoal. A few areas were overpainted with opaque color, applied after the wall was dry.

Unfortunately, the murals are covered with a layer of crystallized calcium carbonate, deposited over many centuries by infiltration of rain water. This partially obscures the paintings but provides a protective layer. Also unfortunate is the fact that you are not allowed to photograph the murals nor the lintels in Structure 1.

Depictions in the murals range from a ceremonial procession with dignitaries, servants, women on thrones, musicians, and dancers to ferocious battle scenes, replete with captive prisoners. A great festival celebration is also shown. Painted glyphs accompany the scenes.

The discovery of these paintings greatly increased our knowledge of Maya life and culture. According

*Sculptured lintel in the center structure on the upper level, Bonampak. Beginning of the Late Classic period.*

to Miguel Covarrubias, this discovery "corrects many former dogmas, such as their abhorrence of warfare and human sacrifice, the low position of their women, and an over emphasis on religion. It shows that the Maya feudal class was as ruthless and military-minded as its contemporaries in the rest of Middle America."

In addition to their cultural and historic importance, the murals are of great artistic merit. They demonstrate a dynamic quality and sophisticated handling of color that is unprecedented in an art generally considered static. Reproductions of the Bonampak murals are found in the Mexico City Museum and in the Villahermosa Museum.

Although most visitors come to Bonampak to see the murals, the site would be worth a visit simply because of the carved stelae and lintels. Behind the lower structures and on a higher level is a group of small temples in varying degrees of ruin. These are reached by a steep rocky path. In the central temple is another beautifully carved and well-preserved lintel dating to around A.D. 600, the earliest recorded date known at Bonampak. This one you may photograph. There are a few remains of painted stucco on the outside of some of these small temples.

Bonampak was influenced during the early part of the Late Classic period by the sculptural style of Piedras Negras. In the late part of the Late Classic period, a stronger influence from Yaxchilán is evident. It is probable that Bonampak was an outpost of sorts, of Yaxchilán, and under its political and cultural control. The Yaxchilán emblem glyph appears in the murals of Bonampak associated with one of the prominent women.

## RECENT HISTORY

Some accounts credit the unofficial discovery of Bonampak to one Charles Frey (sometimes Carl Fry or Carlos Frey), a young expatriate American who lived with the Lacandón Indians and gained their confidence. The Lacandones made annual pilgrimages to Bonampak, a holy center, to burn copal incense. They reportedly took Frey and John Bourne to the site in February, 1946, but Frey and Bourne did not see the murals.

In May of the same year, Giles G. Healey—a photographer-archaeologist who was working on a documentary film about the Lacandones—was also taken to the site by the Indians, and he discovered and photographed the murals. The announcement of the discovery of the murals by Healey in 1947 was one of those spectacular events that archaeological dreams are made of. Although there are many remains of Maya sculptural art, most of their paintings have been lost to time and the elements, so the discovery of three entire rooms full of paintings in a fair state of preservation was exciting. It ranks as one of the major recent discoveries in Maya archaeology.

In 1955 a definitive report on the site was published by Karl Ruppert, Sir J. Eric S. Thompson, and Tatiana Proskouriakoff for the Carnegie Institution of Washington.

The site has been only partly excavated.

## CONNECTIONS

1. 80 air miles from Palenque,
2. 100 air miles from San Cristóbal de las Casas, or
3. 125 air miles from Villahermosa.

## GETTING THERE

Since the completion of the airstrip a number of years ago, Bonampak is relatively easy to reach. Before that it was a difficult dugout-and-mule (or foot) trip, requiring extensive planning. It can still be reached that way from Sayaxché in the Petén of Guatemala, but there is nothing to recommend the latter method. For direct flights, arrangements must be made at the places listed after you arrive there. There is no regularly scheduled service.

A visit to Bonampak can be combined with a visit to Yaxchilán or a nearby Lacandón village. See "Yaxchilán" for information on flights, time allowed at the sites, food, and drink.

There are no accommodations, food, or drink at Bonampak. Wear boots and bring insect repellent.

Light on the Warrior Stela is best in the afternoon, so if you visit both Yaxchilán and Bonampak, save Bonampak till last.

Unfortunately for photographers, Stelae 2 and 3 are now protected with metal roofs and it is difficult to get good photographs without strong directional light. So far, the Warrior Stela is not covered.

*Note:* Recent maps show a road to Bonampak from Palenque. In 1978, when we inquired about it, we were told that indeed a road had been cut through but that bridges had not yet been installed. Until this is accomplished, flying in is the only recommended way of reaching Bonampak.

★★

# *Moxviquil Museum of Maya Archaeology (Na Bolom Museum)*

(San Cristóbal de las Casas)

The Na Bolom Museum is housed in a large room at Na Bolom, Avenida Vincente Guerrero, on the northeast edge of San Cristóbal. Na Bolom is the beautiful colonial home of Gertrude Duby Blom, an archaeologist and photographer, and the widow of archaeologist Frans Blom. Her name is well known to ruin buffs. She maintains Na Bolom as a center for the study of Mexican archaeology and anthropology. It houses an extensive reference library as well as the museum. She also takes in guests who have a serious interest in these subjects, if she is notified ahead and has room. Please note, though, that this is not a hotel.

The museum is named after a Late Classic Maya site located on a hilltop near San Cristóbal. Moxviquil was excavated by Frans Blom in the early 1950s, and many of the finds are on display in the museum, including ceramics, tools, and human remains. In addition, there are photo displays and maps. Other exhibits are mostly artifacts from Chiapas—some were donated to the museum and some were purchased to keep examples in the area.

While you are at Na Bolom, you will find it worthwhile also to visit the Lacandón Museum, a room housing ethnological materials from this nearly extinct group. Plans are under way to devote two more rooms to the indigenous costumes of the Indians of Chiapas, and this should make an outstanding and colorful display.

Tours of Na Bolom are conducted daily, except Mondays, between 4:00 and 6:00 P.M. In addition to the museums and library, the tour includes the lovely gardens, which are well worth a visit. If you are staying at Na Bolom, then you can visit the museums and library at other times.

★★

# *Chinkultic*

(cheen-kool-*teek*)

CULTURE: Maya.
LOCATION: East-central part of the state of Chiapas, Mexico, near the Guatemala border.

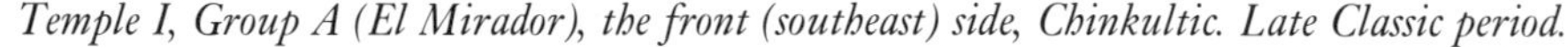

## THE SITE

As you walk along the dirt trail to the site, you will see straight ahead, in the distance, a partially restored temple on a mound atop a natural elevation, backed by a tree-covered bluff. It is easy to spot the light structure in the midst of dark green foliage. This is Temple 1 of Group A, called El Mirador, and it is the tallest structure at Chinkultic. The foot trail leads directly to it.

Along the trail you first pass some overgrown masonry constructions, including well-formed corners. You will have to keep a sharp eye out for them. They form part of another group at Chinkultic and lie to the right (northeast) of the trail shortly before the Río Naranjo. Continue along the main trail, cross the wooden bridge over the river (it can be in a state of disrepair, but, if so, a plank will get you across), and begin the steep, rocky climb to El Mirador.

From this temple you have beautiful views of some of the surrounding small lakes, part of a chain that extends all the way into Guatemala. The lovely Cenote Agua Azul is located next to the rear (northwest) of El Mirador, 150 feet below the steep cliffs on which the temple stands. The pyramidal base of the temple has been partially restored, and it rises in several tiers. Although the architecture is not terribly impressive, a couple of interesting stelae are found nearby.

When you climb back down, recross the river and retrace your steps along the main trail; continue

*Temple I, Group A (El Mirador), the front (southeast) side, Chinkultic. Late Classic period.*

*Stela 8 on the lower level, Chinkultic. Late Classic period.*

until you pass a bluff on your right (northwest) and circle around it on another trail. This will take you to the other areas of interest. If anyone is around, ask them to point out the way.

One spot has some carved stelae, mostly lying on their sides, and nearby is a ball court, with more carved stelae on its west wall. The ball court, somewhat cleared, is impressive—more than 175 feet long. From the ball court, head back to the main foot trail and on to the highway.

There are about 200 mounds scattered at the site of Chinkultic. They are clustered in six main groups, but little is currently cleared, other than what already has been mentioned.

Ceramic evidence indicates that Chinkultic was occupied from the Late Preclassic period into Postclassic times, and it is considered a Maya site, though it lies on the periphery of what is generally designated the Maya area. Like other sites in the Comitán Valley, Chinkultic had ties with the highland and lowland Maya areas. A Classic-period effigy-censer from the site (now in the Mexico City Museum) has a depiction of Tlaloc, hinting at some influence from central Mexico.

Pottery sherds and deformed skulls in nearby caves, and solid figurine fragments found at the site, mostly date to the Late Classic period. Chinkultic's densest pre-Columbian population was during this period, and the carved monuments date from A.D. 591 to 897. The earliest of these, the famous ball court floor marker, now in the Mexico City Museum, actually does not come from Chinkultic proper, but from the small nearby village of Colonia La Esperanza.

## RECENT HISTORY

Chinkultic was first reported in 1901 by Eduard Seler, the German archaeologist, who had visited the site with his wife in 1895, at which time he discovered two carved stelae. A sketch map of the site was made by Frans Blom and Oliver La Farge after their 1925 visit for Tulane University. They illustrated and described six additional carved stelae in a 1926–27 publication. In 1928, Blom returned to the site, resurveyed it, and found three additional stelae. A brief survey of the site was published by Rafael Orellana Tapia in 1954, and a more comprehensive one was undertaken the following year by Edwin M. Shook, who published his work for the New World Archaeological Foundation in 1956.

In 1966, and again in 1968, the Milwaukee Public Museum undertook brief reconnaissance of the Comitán area and of Chinkultic in particular. The latter survey was primarily concerned with studying the various possibilities of exploring Cenote Agua Azul. Both trips were reported by Stephan F. de Borhegyi in 1970, in a Middle American Research Institute publication by Tulane University.

## CONNECTION

1. 88 miles by paved road from San Cristóbal de las Casas.

## GETTING THERE

From San Cristóbal take Highway 190 southeast toward Guatemala. After passing the town of Comitán (55 miles), continue for about 9 more miles. Then take the cutoff to the left, heading due east (shortly before the town of La Trinitaria). This cutoff is Chiapas 17, a state highway, and it dead-ends 25 miles away at the Lagunas de Montebello.

Highway Chiapas 17 passes Chinkultic shortly before it reaches the lakes, and a sign marks the archaeological zone, which is on your left (northwest). You will see a dirt car trail that goes part of the way to the site, and it will save you some walking. Unless you are certain that there is not the *remotest* chance of rain, you will be safer parking on the side of the paved road and walking in. The trail looks like black cinder, but with even a light drizzle it can turn into the slipperiest clay imaginable, from which it is extremely difficult to extricate one's vehicle. Better to walk those extra blocks than take a chance. The whole walk from the paved road to El Mirador is about 1 mile.

The Lagunas de Montebello are also worth a look while you are in the area. Buses run to the lakes several times a day from Comitán and can drop you off at Chinkultic.

If you are coming in from Guatemala, Huehuetenango is the closest good stopover on that side. Chinkultic is about 4,800 feet in elevation, and has a pleasantly cool climate, so bring a sweater or windbreaker. It is free of flying insects for the most part, but watch out for anthills.

There are no accommodations, food, or drink at the site, but drinks are available at the lakes. Boots would be best if you plan to climb to El Mirador.

Two or 3 hours are adequate to visit the site—unless you get stuck in the mud. In that case, allow a couple more.

★★★

# *Izapa*

(ee-*sah*-pah)

CULTURE: Izapan.
LOCATION: Extreme southeastern part of the state of Chiapas, Mexico, near the Guatemala border.

## THE SITE

For some reason—perhaps its location away from other areas of touristic interest—Izapa is seldom visited by foreign tourists, even ruin buffs. That is a shame, because it is a most interesting site.

*Note:* There are two parts of Izapa, one to the north and one to the south of the highway that cuts through the site. The south section will be covered first.

When you arrive at the south section, you will see the caretaker's house, where you will be asked to sign the registration book. Several people live along the dirt road to the site, so it will be easy to pick up a small boy as a guide. This is recommended as there are three areas of interest in the south section, two of which you will not find on your own.

The architectural remains in the south section are simply grass-covered mounds, but the numerous carved stelae, altars, and other stones make it more interesting than the better-known north section.

The first spot of interest in the south section is a large grassy plaza with a number of carved stelae and altars, mostly located around its perimeter. Unfortunately, most of the carvings are of dark stone and have protective thatch shelters, making photography difficult.

The caretaker's wife may come along with a bucket of water and offer to splash some on the monuments. Accept her offer. The water produces glare, which helps bring out the designs. Note: Do *not*

*Plaza with stelae, altars, and three pillars topped with stone balls, south part of the site, Izapa. Late Preclassic period.*

*Monument 2 in the south part of the site, Izapa. It depicts a figure in the open jaws of a jaguar. Late Preclassic period.*

use a polarizing filter.

A few minutes by foot trail will get you to another smaller plaza and more carved monuments. In addition to the carvings, there are three pillars with stone balls on top, a unique feature that may have some astronomical symbolism.

After another short walk, you come to the third area of interest in the south section of the site. There is only one carving here—Monument 2—depicting a figure within the open jaws of a jaguar, but it is definitely worth a look.

From here return to your car, drive back to the highway, and go on to the north part of the site.

There is some restored architecture in the north section, mostly platforms, mounds, and a ball court, all faced with boulders. There are only a few carved monuments, but they are interesting and easier to photograph than those in the south section. A guide is not necessary for the north part of the site since the area is cleared and everything is centrally located. You will be asked to sign another registration book.

As you enter, on your right are some altars crudely carved to represent frogs, and a plain stela.

In front of the first architectural assemblage is the lower part of Stela 22—recarved in 1960 or 1961 by "a vandal-art dealer"—and behind this is a stone bowl and another simply carved stone.

Just roam around the platforms—they look pretty much alike—until you come to the ball court, lo-

*Restored boulder-faced platforms in the north part of the site, Izapa. Classic period.*

*Stela 67 in the north wall of the ball court in the north part of the site, Izapa. Late Preclassic period.*

cated farthest from the entrance. At the east end of the court are the remains of Stela 60, and embedded in the low side wall of the court—near the center—is Stela 67. These bas-relief carvings are filled with interesting motifs and are good for detail photographs. At the west end of the ball court is a large rectangular throne with an animal head.

Off to the right (north) of this end of the court is a tall stone column, with remains of a kneeling figure on top. Although the upper part of the figure is missing, there is enough left to verify that it is a pedestal sculpture of a type found in the highlands of Guatemala and elsewhere. It may be one of the later pieces of this type, and is perhaps a Classic-period monument.

Also of interest in the north section are a large stone basin, set into the plaza floor near one of the mounds, and a plain stela.

Izapa is a large site—with over eighty mounds—and is also an extremely important one, especially in its relationship to other Mesoamerican cultures. Izapa has been considered an intermediate in time and space between the Middle Preclassic Olmec culture of the Gulf Coast and the Early Classic Maya. Indeed, it was long thought that one of the distinguishing features between Early and Late Classic Maya sculpture was the presence of Izapan influence in the Early Classic and its absence in the Late Classic. This view of the relationship between Izapa and the Early Classic Maya is now changing, however. A 1976 publication on Izapa sculpture, by V. Garth Norman, stated that "strong roots of the Maya are now evident in the rich iconographic record at Izapa . . . but the more direct ancestors of the lowland Classic Maya may be from neighboring Guatemala as evidenced in closer sculptural stylistic ties with sites on the Pacific slopes such as El Baúl and Abaj Takalik."

Recent work at Abaj Takalik—located about 40 miles southeast of Izapa—by archaeologists from the University of California, under the direction of John Graham, resulted in the discovery of many Late Preclassic monuments, some with hieroglyphic inscriptions and Initial Series dates. These finds indicate that Abaj Takalik was probably a more direct antecedent of the lowland Classic Maya than was Izapa. (It should be pointed out that Olmec monuments were also discovered at Abaj Takalik.) When the final reports on Abaj Takalik are published, we should have a clearer understanding of the matter.

Olmec traits in Izapan art are the Saint Andrew's Cross and the U element, scrollwork skies or clouds, scenes contained within stylized jaguar mouths, realistic depictions of well-fed human forms, and the flame-scroll brow. These traits were thoroughly studied by Jacinto Quirarte in *Studies in Pre-Columbian Art and Archaeology*, published by Dumbarton Oaks in 1973.

Traits that connect the Izapan style to the later Classic Maya are stela and altar complexes, portrayal of the long-lipped god—apparently a development of the Olmec were-jaguar and a forerunner of the Maya rain god, Chac—a baroque style, and calendrics (from Izapan-style Stela 1 at El Baúl). There are few calendric notations on the monuments of Izapa itself, and no Initial Series dates.

Ceramic evidence indicates that Izapa was occupied from the Early Preclassic period into Late Classic times. Its peak occurred during the Late Preclassic period (300 B.C.–A.D. 300), according to Michael Coe. Other authorities prefer somewhat earlier dates, however, and include part of the Middle Preclassic period.

Izapa's major monuments—there are dozens of carved stelae, altars, and other sculptures—date mostly to its peak period, as do, probably, the bulk of the constructions. The boulder-faced structures in the north part of the site, however, are of the Classic period.

Izapan-style carvings are found in a number of places besides the type site, most notably along the Pacific Coast of southern Mexico and Guatemala, in the Guatemala highlands at Kaminaljuyú, on the Gulf Coast of Mexico at Tres Zapotes, and perhaps at Dainzú in Oaxaca. Some early stelae at Yaxhá in the Petén are also in this style. Undoubtedly there was much cultural interchange among these centers.

## RECENT HISTORY

The site of Izapa was known locally for a long time, but it was not until the early 1940s that investigation was begun. On one of his numerous expeditions to southern Mexico, sponsored by the National Geographic Society, Matthew Stirling heard of a site with stone monuments from Mexican archaeologist Miguel Covarrubias, who had seen photographs of them. The site had been inspected a few years before by A. V. Kidder and Karl Ruppert.

Stirling decided to visit the site, and spent a week there in 1941. He described Izapa as "an interesting and imposing site with numerous large mounds and curiously carved stelae with altars." He located thirty monuments and felt "well repaid for our efforts." He mentioned Izapa briefly in an article published in the *National Geographic Magazine* in 1941, but he published the first detailed report on the site in 1943, in the *Smithsonian Institution Bulletin.*

A report on the site, similar to Stirling's, was published in Spanish by Rafael Orellana Tapia in 1952. In 1961 a five-year program of investigation was undertaken by the Brigham Young University–New World Archaeological Foundation, which resulted in a number of published reports. This was the most thorough work at Izapa and it involved several scholars, including Gareth Lowe, V. Garth Norman, Susanna Ekholm, Thomas Lee, Jr., and Eduardo Martínez.

## CONNECTION

1. 7 miles by paved road from Tapachula, then a few blocks of poor dirt road to the south part of the site, and 0.5 mile more by paved road to the north part of the site.

## GETTING THERE

Getting to Izapa is no problem once you are in Tapachula, but Tapachula is a bit off the beaten path for most foreign visitors. If you are driving from Mexico to Guatemala, you can take Highway 200 (the coastal road), which goes through Tapachula, rather than Highway 190 (the older, mountainous route).

You can also fly to Tapachula from Mexico City, and then rent a car or taxi, or take a bus to the site. You can reach Tapachula by bus from Mexico City, but this takes a couple of days. If your base of operations is Guatemala City, then it is an easy one-day drive from the capital to Tapachula, although you will have to figure on losing an hour crossing the international border.

From Tapachula take Highway 200 east and go 6 miles past the Río Tapachula (on the east edge of town). The cutoff you are looking for is a dirt road on your right (south). Take this road and drive in as far as you can (it can get muddy). Walk the remaining distance.

After you visit the south part of Izapa, return to your car, head back to the highway, and again go east for 0.5 mile. The north part of Izapa is right on the highway (on your left), and is well marked. This is the only section that most people see; there were several other visitors, mostly local people, while we were there, but we were the first people in four days to visit the south part of the site.

The best overnight stop near Izapa is, of course,

Tapachula. It is a bustling commercial center and rather pleasant city with good hotels and all the necessary amenities.

There are no accommodations, food, or drink at Izapa. At least bring cold drinks along.

You can see both parts of Izapa in 2½ to 3 hours. Tennis shoes are fine. Bring insect repellent.

*Note:* If you drive to Izapa from the direction of Tehuantepec, you will pass through the towns of Arriaga and Tonalá (both on Highway 200) along the way. The Parador on the eastern outskirts of Arriaga is a good lunch stop; it has an air-conditioned dining room. The accompanying hotel looked far better than anything in Tehuantepec. In fact, it appeared to be the best stopover between Oaxaca City and Tapachula.

When you reach Tonalá (13 miles past Arriaga), keep an eye out to the left (north) as you pass the Main Plaza. There is an interesting carved stela on display there. An accompanying sign identifies the figure on the front as Tlaloc. The goggle eyes would seem to substantiate this. There is a Mexican Yearsign, or imbricated trapeziform, in the headdress, which would also indicate influence from central Mexico. The sign further states that the monument comes from Horcones in the Municipio of Tonalá, but I have never seen a picture of the stela in the literature. Nevertheless, it is in excellent condition and is very photogenic.

*Note:* It was reported in the literature as late as 1969 that there was a stela at the train station in Tonalá. This stela, depicting a ball player and ball court, is now in the museum in Tuxtla Gutiérrez.

*Stela with figure reportedly representing Tlaloc, Tonalá Plaza. The Mexican Yearsign appears in the headdress.*

## MEXICO

### Yucatán

*Stone mosaic mask depicting Chac, the Maya rain god, in place in the upper façade of the back of the main structure at Xlapak. Late Classic period.*

★★

# *Museum of Archaeology and History (Mérida Museum)*

The Mérida Museum is on the Paseo de Montejo and Calle 43. It is housed in the basement of an elegant building, originally constructed as the governor's residence before the turn of the century.

The collection includes a Chac Mool and other sculptures from Chichén Itzá, a Chac mask from Kabáh, and carvings from other sites in the state. There are displays of jade jewelry, ceramics, a drawing of the bas-relief at Loltún cave, and other exhibits, all of which are labeled.

A few interesting but unlabeled stelae are found in the patio outside.

Allow about 1 hour to view the collection.

ADDED EXTRA

On Calle 61, near the corner of Calle 58, is the old Convent of San Juan de Dios. This building houses the Office of Historic Monuments, where some pre-Columbian sculptures are on display. Some are from Chichén Itzá, but the provenance of others is not listed. The monuments are generally dated.

Publications in Spanish on archaeological subjects are sold there and the place feels like a library more than anything else. If you are in the neighborhood, it is worth a 20-minute stop to see the artifacts.

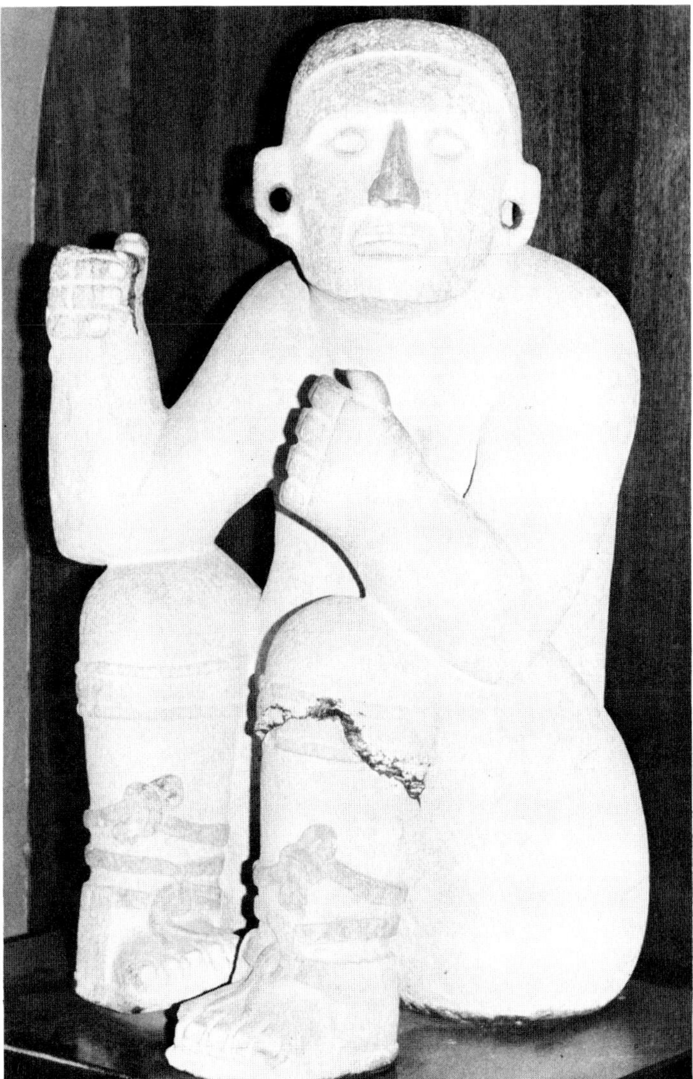

*Standard-bearer from Chichén Itzá, Mérida Museum. Early Postclassic period.*

★★

# *Dzibilchaltún and Dzibilchaltún Museum*

(tseeb-eel-chahl-*toon*)

DERIVATION: Mayan for "Where There Is Writing on Flat Stones."

CULTURE: Maya.

LOCATION: Northwestern part of the state of Yucatán, Mexico.

---

## THE SITE

Dzibilchaltún is a very large site, and an extremely important one archaeologically, because of its almost continuous occupation from 500 B.C. to the present. It had its ups and downs, and was nearly abandoned for many years, but its stratigraphic sequence is clearly defined.

As you enter the gate to the site, take the trail heading south. The trail passes the small restored temple (Structure 38-sub) and the remains of Structure 38, which once covered it. They are in an enclosure, which contains a few remains of other temple bases. Structure 38-sub dates to the first half of the eighth century, and its simple design is pleasing. A large unrestored mound lies adjacent to the south side of the enclosure.

A bit farther on, the trail is marked with a sign pointing east (left) to the Temple of the Seven Dolls. There are some architectural remains along the way.

Shortly after the turn, on the left (north), there is a restored platform and lower temple walls, and next to it a fair-sized, four-stage pyramid (Structure 36), with a central stairway facing south toward the Main Plaza. Structure 36 dates to the Late Classic period.

Stela 19 (now in the Dzibilchaltún Museum) was found set in the basal terrace of Structure 36, and a copy has been placed in its original location. Stela 18 was also found set in the terrace and it, and the copy of Stela 19, may be seen by descending the modern stairway at the southwest corner of Structure 36.

Part of the Main Plaza, southwest of Structure 36, is occupied by a small, restored open chapel, built by the Spaniards, probably in the 1590s. Some of the stones from the pre-Columbian city were used in its construction.

The trail continues east and passes a restored platform with a plain stela, and goes on to the

*Structures 38-sub and 38, Dzibilchaltún. Late Classic period. Early Spanish chapel on the right.*

*Temple of the Seven Dolls, Dzibilchaltún. Late Classic period.*

Temple of the Seven Dolls (Structure 1-sub), the principal restored structure at the site. There are remains of other structures near this temple. They, and the platform and stela, are part of the Seven Dolls Group.

The Temple of the Seven Dolls was built during the early part of the Late Classic period. Later in that period, it was filled and covered with more construction. It then seems to have fallen into disuse and was probably abandoned for 200 years. Then around A.D. 1200–1450, the Maya tunneled into the later construction, to the floor of the earlier temple, and cut a hole into the rubble below. In this they placed seven crude clay figures, each exhibiting some deformity. These figures, or dolls, give the temple its name. Perhaps they were used in connection with ceremonies for curing diseases, although this is far from certain.

E. Wyllys Andrews IV first saw this structure as a large mound whose superstructure had collapsed, revealing buried chambers. Most of the later construction was removed, exposing the partially intact temple below. Its restoration ensued.

The design of the Temple of the Seven Dolls is unusual for the Maya area because of its truncated tower and unique functional windows. It is possible that it was an experimental form of northern Maya architecture. Some interesting stucco decorations remain on the upper façade.

Although the visitor today may hardly realize it, the approach to the Temple of the Seven Dolls is over an ancient Maya *sacbé*, one of two major *sacbeob* at the site, both of which extend from the Main Plaza.

When you return from the Temple of the Seven Dolls, instead of turning right at the cutoff (back toward the entrance), take a left and go for a short distance to the Cenote Xlacah (shlah-*kah*), the largest of several cenotes at Dzibilchaltún. It is 100 feet across at its widest point, at least 140 feet deep, and it goes down at a slant. Numerous artifacts were recovered from its depths. It is a nice place to relax and have a picnic lunch. There are shade trees in the area. Swimming in the cenote is allowed, but a sign informs you that you *must* wear a swimsuit.

From the cenote, go north for a short distance to the *sacbé* that heads west. This *sacbé* goes over

1,000 yards to a terrace complex (unexcavated) that is similar to the Seven Dolls Group. The *sacbé*, however, is only cleared as far as Structure 57, 250 yards from the turnoff.

Structure 57 lies north of the *sacbé*, and was the only structure with a standing vault at Dzibilchaltún when the site was first visited by archaeologists. Since then, it has been consolidated. It probably dates to the first half of the ninth century.

Discovering the exact extent of an ancient city is difficult at best, and this is particularly true of Dzibilchaltún. About 8,400 structures have been mapped in a 7.3-square-mile area, and it is estimated that during its peak period, there was a population of 40,000 people. The agricultural sustaining area for Dzibilchaltún, however, extends far beyond the mapped section, and probably included 38 square miles.

The area of Dzibilchaltún was apparently first occupied about 500 B.C., by inhabitants with a pottery tradition related to that in the Petén of Guatemala. Constructions at the site dating to the Middle Preclassic period were platforms, which probably supported perishable buildings, although these are located some distance from the central part of the site as it is known today. There was a rapid population growth from the late part of the Middle Preclassic period into the Late Preclassic, and a peak was reached around 50 B.C. Several villages west of Dzibilchaltún developed ceremonial architecture at their cores. After this, activity sharply decreased, and until A.D. 250, the only constructions were low platforms nearer the center of the site.

From the following Early Classic period only one structure is known, and it is in an outlying area. A second period of rapid growth began after this, and 90 percent of the mapped structures are believed to have been occupied during this period, from A.D. 600 to 1000. Most of the structures the visitor sees today date to this period. During the latter part of this period Dzibilchaltún reached its maximum population peak.

During the early part of the following period (A.D. 1000–1200), construction ceased, although small groups of squatters continued to occupy the site. Population dropped to less than 10 percent of its former size. Beginning late in this period and continuing through the next (1200–1540), construction resumed in a modest way.

## RECENT HISTORY

The existence of Dzibilchaltún was never forgotten since it was almost continuously occupied up until the Spanish conquest. The open chapel that was erected in the middle of what had been the Main Plaza is one of the earliest colonial structures in Yucatán.

The pre-Columbian structures at Dzibilchaltún were cannibalized for building materials for use in several nearby haciendas, towns, and roads. This went on until the 1950s. The archaeological discovery of the site, however, was by Andrews and George Brainerd, who first visited Dzibilchaltún in 1941. They discovered, near the Hacienda of Dzibilchaltún, "a large group of hitherto unreported mounds." Brainerd collected pottery sherds and Andrews explored and recorded the architectural remains. The few weeks they spent there convinced them that they had "stumbled upon the remains of a truly extraordinary city."

World War II interrupted work until 1956, when the Middle American Research Institute (MARI) of Tulane University sponsored excavations. During the next couple of years the National Geographic Society, the National Science Foundation, and the American Philosophical Society helped fund the project, which continued until 1965 under Andrews's direction. Andrews presented a progress report in 1965, published by MARI. A more comprehensive report with coauthor E. Wyllys Andrews V was published in 1980.

The Mexican government maintains the site and provided funds for some of the restoration.

## CONNECTION

1. 12 miles by paved road from Mérida.

## GETTING THERE

From Mérida take Highway 261 north for 9 miles. Then take the paved cutoff to the right (east) for 3 miles, to the entrance to the site. The cutoff to Dzibilchaltún is just past (north of) the kilometer 15 marker on Highway 261.

The site can be reached by private car, taxi, bus, or on conducted tours from Mérida.

There are no accommodations or food at the site, but soft drinks are available at the entrance, and sometimes the caretaker has an ice chest with drinks at the Temple of the Seven Dolls. This is most welcome as it is a long, hot walk to the temple.

The logical overnight stop is Mérida, but there are a couple of hotels on the north coast. They are east of Progreso in Chicxulub, about 16 miles from Dzibilchaltún.

Bring a sun hat. Tennis shoes are fine and a guide is not necessary. Allow 2 hours to see the site and museum.

★★

## DZIBILCHALTÚN MUSEUM

The small but well-arranged museum at Dzibilchaltún is located at the entrance to the site. It displays artifacts from the site as well as photos taken during excavation. Notable are two fragments of Late Classic stelae (Stelae 9 and 19), the seven clay figures discovered in the Temple of the Seven Dolls, and inscribed bones recovered from the Cenote Xlacah. The museum is well worth a visit while you are at the site.

*Stela 19 from the site, Dzibilchaltún Museum. Late Classic period.*

★

# *Oxkintok*

(ohsh-keen-*tohk*)

CULTURE: Maya.
LOCATION: Western part of the state of Yucatán, Mexico.

## THE SITE

Oxkintok is a large but unrestored site. First off, you will be impressed by the numerous steep mounds in the area—all of very respectable size. These are the remains of large pyramidal bases, which originally supported temples, mostly Early Classic in date. If you climb one of them, you will see even more mounds in the distance and other evidence of architectural remains. The mounds are easy to spot as most of the surrounding area has been cleared for *milpas.* Be careful if you decide to climb one because the outer surface is loose rubble, which tends to shift and slide beneath your weight. A stinging plant called Malmujuer also grows on some of the mounds.

Drive to the mound area first (the western or far side of the site), since a climb part way up one of the mounds will give you a view of the whole area and will show the location of the other structures you will want to visit. From here turn around and drive back the way you came in.

Unfortunately, there is little preserved standing architecture, but two spots are accessible and worth a look. Both lie north of the dirt road.

From the mound (or the road) you can easily spot the remains of a ruined portal vault lying about 100 feet off the road (on the left, as you are leaving the site). To get there you have to walk through tall weeds. A machete would be of help.

Farther along the road, as you are leaving the site, and harder to spot, is a complex of rooms partially overgrown with trees. They lie on the far side of a couple of milpas, perhaps 200 feet left of the road.

After crossing the milpas, it is necessary to climb

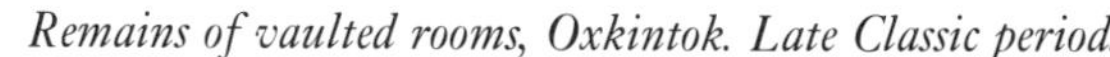

*Remains of vaulted rooms, Oxkintok. Late Classic period.*

a short but steep incline to get to the structures. There are some remains of vaulted rooms, but much has collapsed. This complex is of Late Classic construction. Take care in walking around this area as there are openings in some lower rooms where the vaults have caved in. They form holes that make dandy boobytraps.

Oxkintok is an important site archaeologically, and has some unusual features for northern Yucatán. A lintel from one of the buildings records an Initial Series Date of 9.2.0.0.0, equivalent to A.D. 475. This is the earliest Long Count date found in northern Yucatán, falling in the middle part of the Early Classic period. Ceramic evidence indicates that the site was probably occupied from Preclassic through Late Classic times. Its rise to prominence came during the Early Classic. The latest date recorded at the site is A.D. 849, found on a stela.

Two types of architecture are found at Oxkintok; the Early Classic buildings, which have a relationship to the Petén style, and the Late Classic Puuc-style structures. Different parts of the site were connected by *sacbeob.*

Some of the carved monuments from Oxkintok, including stelae and columns, show non-Classic traits that may indicate late foreign influence. The earlier monuments are in a style related to that of the Petén.

We did not see any of these monuments. Some have probably been removed from the site. After our visit, however, we learned that some are still there, lying in the bush.

## RECENT HISTORY

It is possible that John Lloyd Stephens saw the mounds at Oxkintok on his trip from Maxcanú to Uxmal during his second visit to Yucatán in 1841, but this is not certain. Work at the site was begun almost a century later by Edwin Shook, who reported his findings in 1940. Ceramic studies in Yucatán by George Brainerd, published in 1958, included specimens from Oxkintok.

## CONNECTIONS

1. 24 miles by paved road from Uxmal to Calcehtok (kahl-keh-*tohk*),
2. 42 miles by paved road from Mérida to Calcehtok via Highway 180, or
3. 53 miles by paved road from Mérida to Calcehtok via Muna on Highway 261, then 3.5 miles of dirt road to the site.

## GETTING THERE

The best overnight stops and points of departure for Oxkintok are Uxmal and Mérida.

From Uxmal head north on Highway 261, to Muna. Turn left (west) following the sign for Opichén. This narrow but paved road connects Highway 261 at Muna and Highway 180 a bit north of Maxcanú, and is not shown on all maps. Continue west through Opichén to the town of Calcehtok, 14 miles from Muna.

In Calcehtok there is a good dirt road heading south. Ask in the village to find the correct cutoff. Go south for about 1 mile, till you see a narrower dirt road heading right (west). Follow this road for 2.5 miles to the site.

From Mérida there are two choices. You can take Highway 261 south to Muna, then west to Calcehtok, or Highway 180 south to just before Maxcanú, then 3 miles east to Calcehtok. The second choice is 11 miles shorter.

Pass up Oxkintok if you do not have your own car.

There is no food or drink at the site, or even a caretaker, for that matter. Boots are recommended. A guide is not necessary, but if you prefer having one, try to hire one in Calcehtok. He may be able to locate the stelae lying in the weeds.

Also of interest in the area are the Grutas (Caves) of Calcehtok—a nice place for a picnic. The dirt road that heads south from the village of Calcehtok continues past the Oxkintok cutoff for about 1 mile, where it ends at the caves. They are worth a look. There is a sturdy metal ladder that gets you to the floor of one cave, and a couple of other openings are visible from ground level.

1 Parking lot
2 El Adivino
3 Nunnery Quadrangle
4 Ball Court
5 Cemetery Group
6 Platform of the Stelae
7 North Group
8 Great Pyramid
9 Dove-Cotes Building
10 South Temple
11 Chenes Temples
12 House of the Turtles
13 Governor's Palace
14 House of the Old Woman
15 Temple of the Phalli

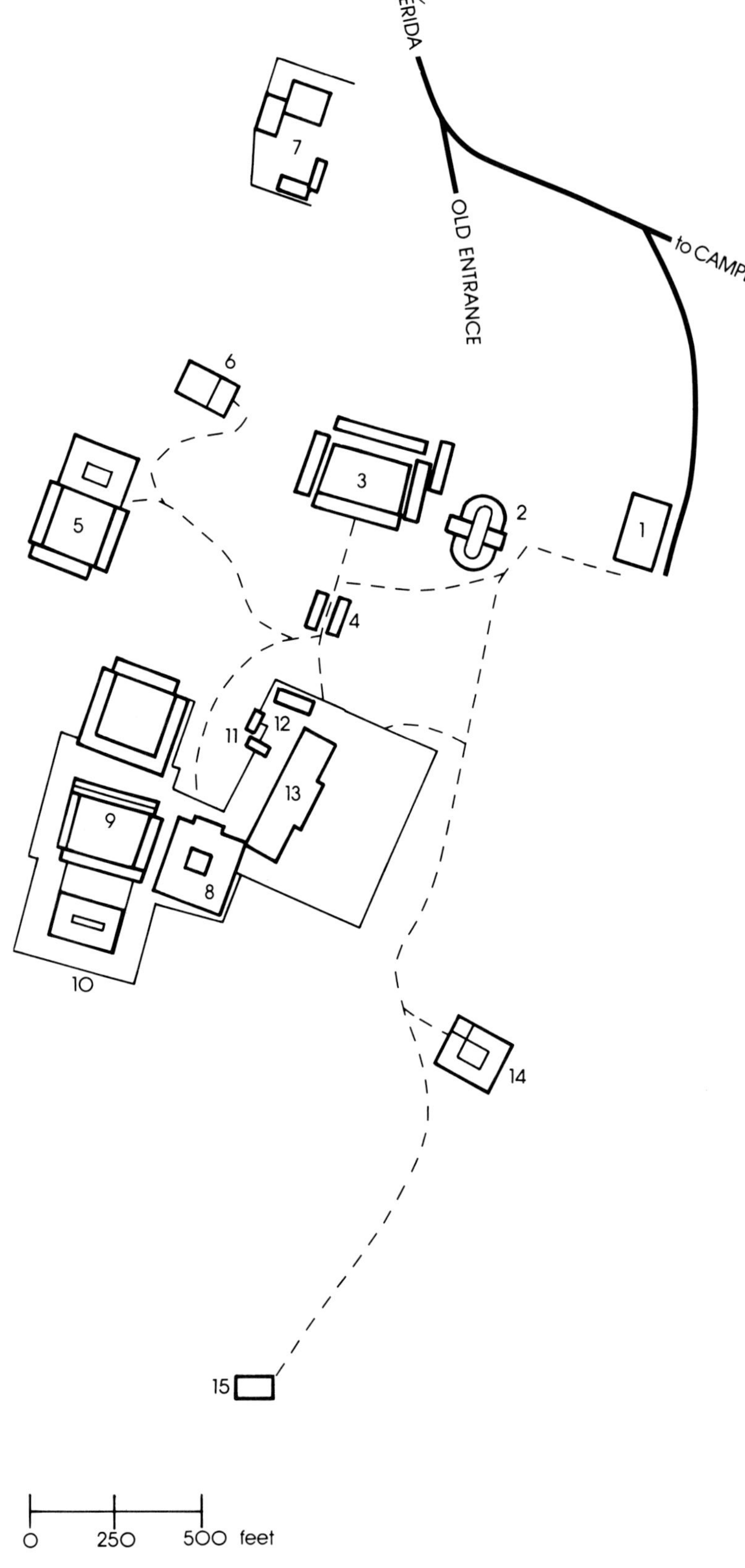


N

UXMAL

★★★★

# *Uxmal*

(oosh-*mahl*)

DERIVATION: Often given as Mayan for "Oxmal" meaning "Thrice Built." Sometimes as "Three Times" or "Three Passed." Ralph Roys finds these derivations unconvincing. Uxmal is, nevertheless, a very old place name.

CULTURE: Maya.

LOCATION: West-central part of the state of Yucatán, Mexico.

---

## THE SITE

Uxmal is one of the most popular of the really big sites, and one of the easiest to reach. Almost all visitors to Yucatán visit Uxmal (and Chichén Itzá). Certainly, it is a major attraction for the ruin buff.

Uxmal is a more compact site than Chichén Itzá. It measures over 0.5 mile from north to south and 700 yards from east to west, with a few buildings scattered outside this main area, mainly lying to the south.

For the most part, the architecture at Uxmal dates to the Maya Late Classic period and is in typical Puuc style (except for a few Mexican motifs and three structures in Chenes style). Apparently the central Mexican motifs arrived before the Toltecs occupied Chichén Itzá, because Uxmal was abandoned shortly before their arrival, or perhaps because of it. The Toltecs never occupied Uxmal.

The latest recorded date at the site is A.D. 909, painted on a capstone in the Nunnery. The stelae from Uxmal all date to the end of the Late Classic period.

The Puuc style is also found at Sayil, Kabáh, Labná, and other sites. It is characterized by imposing buildings of masonry, finished by a veneer of well-cut stone. Generally, only the upper portions of the structures are decorated. Decorative elements include snakes with barlike rigid bodies, stone lattice work with frets, panels of Chac masks made of stone mosaics, and simple engaged columns. Round stone columns are also sometimes used in doorways. There is a certain sharp crisp quality in Puuc stonework not generally seen in other styles.

When visiting Uxmal, some backtracking is necessary to visit the outlying groups. The following sequence is one of several possibilities.

The first major structure near the entrance to the site is the recently restored, monumental El Adivino (also called the Temple, Pyramid, or House of the Magician, Soothsayer, or Dwarf). Its base is often referred to as oval or eliptical, but since its east and west faces are on a straight line, perhaps it is better described as a rectangle with severely rounded corners.

El Adivino was built during five separate construction periods. The top structure, Temple V, is, of course, the latest, and it brings the building to its final height of approximately 100 feet. The earliest, Temple I, can be seen beneath the lower portion of the stairway of the west face, and a Tlaloc mask with a Mexican Yearsign in the headdress—implying some Mexican influence—was found there, but is not visible today. Temple I was almost totally covered by later construction and its rooms were filled with rubble beforehand, but portions of two well-preserved Chac masks can still be seen over the central door.

Temple II is no longer visible from the outside of the pyramid, but may be reached by climbing the east stairway and entering a chamber made during excavation. This temple has only been partially excavated, but its central chamber is supported by columns, and it is topped by a roof comb that is visible in a trench in the floor of Temple V above.

Temple III (no longer visible) was attached to the west side of Temple II. Later, Temple IV was added on in the same direction. Temple IV is visible from the outside of the pyramid on the west side. This temple has an open-mouth mask forming its doorway, and is referred to as the Chenes temple for that reason. H. E. D. Pollock, nevertheless, considers Temple IV a Puuc copy of a Chenes façade. Certainly the crisp quality of the stone work would seem to substantiate this view. When the crowning Temple V was constructed, it effectively buried the earlier Temples II and III, as well as the rear and part of the sides of Temple IV. The Magician or Dwarf who gave his name to this structure is a character in Maya folklore.

If you decide to climb El Adivino, you might

*El Adivino, from the southwest, Uxmal. Late Classic period.*

*The Nunnery Quadrangle, looking west from El Adivino, Uxmal. Late Classic period.*

*Detail of decorations on the north building of the Nunnery Quadrangle showing hut-type niche, Uxmal. Late Classic period.*

*Nunnery Quadrangle (left), El Adivino (right), and the remains of the ball court (foreground), Uxmal. Late Classic period.*

*The partly restored west building of the Cemetery Group, Uxmal. Late Classic period.*

want to go up one side and down the other. There are interesting Chac masks flanking the west stairway up to the level of Temple IV.

West of El Adivino is another of Uxmal's more impressive structures, the Nunnery Quadrangle, or Casa de las Monjas. This is actually a complex of buildings surrounding a large, roughly rectangular courtyard or plaza. The individual buildings are labeled the North Building, the East Building, and so forth. In addition, two smaller structures at plaza level flank a broad stairway, which leads to a terrace fronting the North Building. The one on the left (west) is called the Temple of Venus, while the smaller one on the right remains nameless.

The entrance to the Nunnery Quadrangle is through a large corbeled vault in the center of the South Building—there are remains of red hand prints in the top of the vault. It is also possible to enter the Quadrangle from any of its four corners as the buildings do not join each other.

*Skull-and-crossbones motif decorating the sides of a platform in the plaza of the Cemetery Group, Uxmal. Late Classic period.*

*Stela 2 at the Platform of the Stelae, Uxmal. Late Classic period.*

Each building has its own individual decoration. This is a great place for detail photographs taken with a telephoto lens. It is of interest that the feathered-serpent motif on the West Building—indicative of Mexican influence—may have been added after the original decoration was complete. The same may also be true of certain figures—seemingly warriors—found on the same structure. The decorations of the upper façades of the buildings constituting the Nunnery are fantastic in their variety and quantity.

A path heading south from the Nunnery Quadrangle goes between the two sides of a small unrestored ball court, which at present has little visual interest due to its ruinous condition. One branch of the path then heads right (west) to the Cemetery Group. This group has several structures surrounding a square plaza, but most are in a poor state of preservation. The most interesting is the recently restored, relatively early, simple temple on the west side, supported by a moderately high pyramidal base. The temple has three rooms and some remains of a roof comb.

In the plaza below are four small platforms decorated with skull-and-crossbones motifs, giving the group its name. These skull racks (Tzompantilis) are another indication of central Mexican influence. Hieroglyphs form the top border on the platforms.

From the Cemetery Group, the path heads northwest for a short distance before it branches off to the right. This branch curves around a bit, but eventually takes you to the Platform of the Stelae. The fifteen or so stelae originally found scattered around the top of the platform were placed on their sides by Sylvanus Morley to facilitate a study of them, and they are still found in this position today.

If you have seen the stelae at Copán and Tikal, these will be a disappointment. They are mostly broken, eroded, and covered with lichen, but you will still want to take a look. Certain central Mexican traits are evident in some of the stelae.

From the Platform of the Stelae you can see the remains of the North Group 200 yards to the northeast. There is no foot trail leading to this group, but

*The Great Pyramid (left), the Dove-Cotes Building (right), and the remains of the South Temple (right background), from the northwest, Uxmal. Late Classic period.*

*Chac step mask in the temple atop the Great Pyramid, Uxmal. Late Classic period.*

you can walk through the bush to get there. The North Group has not been excavated or restored, but there are remains of several structures, including one in Chenes style. You can get photos of them from the Platform of the Stelae.

From here you must retrace your steps almost to the ball court, where a path branches south to the Great Pyramid and the Dove-Cotes Building.

The Great Pyramid has had its north stairway and temple restored in recent years, and it gleams a brilliant white against the green vegetation. It is an easy climb to the top, a great vantage point for viewing and photographing the rest of the site. This spot is especially good for telephoto shots of the west temple of the Cemetery Group, which rises above the vegetation.

The huge step-mask on the interior of the temple is most impressive, as are the Chac masks on the exterior corners. Generally overlooked in the profusion of decorations are some smaller heads that appear to be depictions of the sun god. They are frontal views, are framed by what seem to be profile bird heads, and are located on the corners just below the curling snouts of the rain god. Do not miss them.

Adjacent to the west of the Great Pyramid is the Dove-Cotes Building (Casa de las Palomas). It is part of a complex that was originally similar to the Nunnery Quadrangle, but it is in a poorer state of preservation and unrestored. The main feature is the stepped roof comb, which is in excellent condition. Its fancied similarity to dove-cotes gives the building its name.

South of the Dove-Cotes Building is a large unrestored mound called the South Temple.

From the Great Pyramid you can follow the back of the Governor's Palace along its terrace (heading northeast) to the Chenes Temples that lie on the west edge of the terrace. They were mostly covered by the later construction of the terrace, but one is worth a look, as some interesting designs in stone mosaic are visible. As the name implies, the architecture is Chenes style.

Continue along the terrace to the House of the Turtles. This small but nicely proportioned structure of typical Puuc style has been restored and gets its name from representations of turtles, which adorn its upper molding. That, plus engaged columns and a simple medial molding, form the only decorations on the temple. Its sobriety is an interesting contrast to the more elaborate decorations on other structures at Uxmal.

From the House of the Turtles walk around to the front of the Governor's Palace—one of the real gems of Maya architecture. This exquisite structure lies atop a man-made terrace, which is built upon a natural elevation. A broad stairway leads to the Palace. The structure was originally built as three separate units—a long central building flanked by a smaller building on either end. Originally the three were joined by two roofed passages with a high vault. At a later date, the passages were blocked up with cross walls, and small rooms with columned porticoes were built on each side. The major motif on the upper façade of the Governor's Palace is the

*Chac masks on the northwest corner of the temple atop the Great Pyramid, Uxmal. Small, humanized faces of the sun god are just below the snouts of the Chac masks. Late Classic period.*

*The Dove-Cotes Building as seen from the Great Pyramid, Uxmal. Note the remains of vaulted rooms. Late Classic period.*

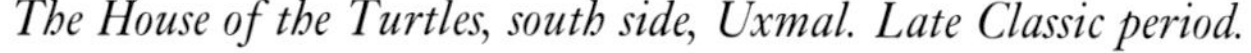

*The House of the Turtles, south side, Uxmal. Late Classic period.*

*The Governor's Palace, the front (east) side, Uxmal. Late Classic period.*

depiction of Chac, but stepped fret and latticelike designs are also incorporated to form a harmonious whole.

A small platform lies on the terrace in front of the Palace and supports a piece of sculpture. It probably depicts halves of two jaguars and may have been used as a throne. From this spot (or farther back on the terrace) you can get a good photograph of the Governor's Palace with a wide-angle lens. It is a very long building—322 feet—and the front catches the morning light, which best brings out the detail.

To get to the next area of interest, you have to get off the terrace. There is a rocky path down on the north side. Follow the trail heading south past the terrace of the Governor's Palace, and take a left branch to the House of the Old Woman. The Old Woman is the mother of the Dwarf—already mentioned—in Maya folklore.

There are several structures in this area, but all are in a ruinous condition. The House of the Old Woman originally had more than one story, but the exact number has not been determined as the whole is now a mound of rubble. There are some remains of another building at the base of the mound.

The path that takes you to the House of the Old Woman continues south for about 0.3 mile to the Temples of the Phalli. This small, poorly preserved structure, has some sculpture in the form of phalli, which protrude from the upper part of the building and which may have served as drains for water collecting on the roof. These sculptures are supposedly nonerotic in nature, but are symbolic of fertility of the soil.

Phallic sculpture is found in other parts of the site and at other sites in Yucatán as well; this trait may have emanated from southern Veracruz or the Huasteca farther north. It is frequently found in both those areas, but is generally lacking in the southern Maya lowlands.

From here retrace your steps back to El Adivino and on to the parking area.

*Note:* A freestanding arch has been reported at Uxmal and is shown on most site plans. It is possible that it marked the beginning of a *sacbé* that extended to Kabáh. Nevertheless, the location of the Uxmal arch is unknown today.

## RECENT HISTORY

Uxmal is one of those sites whose existence was probably never lost to man's knowledge. It is mentioned in early colonial documents, and is shown on a map dating to only fifteen years after the Spanish conquest. According to a genealogical tree, a member of the Xiu family founded Uxmal. Legend relates that Uxmal was one of three centers forming the League of Mayapán (the others were Mayapán and Chichén Itzá). This is not supported by the archaeological evidence, which indicates that Uxmal was abandoned long before the founding of Mayapán. It is possible that Uxmal was reoccupied by the Xiu dynasty many years after its original abandonment, accounting for its late date in the native chronicles. Some of the names for the structures used today were given them by the early Spanish conquerors.

Jean Frédéric Waldeck visited Uxmal for eight days, and he published his information and some fanciful drawings in 1838 in Paris. Waldeck knew of the site from a brief mention of it in an atlas of the two Americas, by Alexandre Buchon. Waldeck's volume came to the attention of John Lloyd Stephens, but Stephens and later investigators were unable to find some of the things reported by Waldeck.

Stephens and Frederick Catherwood visited Uxmal briefly at the end of their first trip to Central America and Yucatán but returned a couple of years later for a more thorough investigation. Stephens's measurements and Catherwood's illustrations are much more accurate than the information published by Waldeck.

At the end of the nineteenth century, Uxmal was studied by Augustus Le Plongeon and Edward H. Thompson. Eduard Seler reported on the site in 1913 and 1917. The first systematic modern exploration of Uxmal was undertaken by Frans Blom in 1929 for Tulane University. A site plan was one of the results of his research. Since 1938, Mexico's National Institute of Anthropology and History (INAH) has been in charge of the almost continuous restoration at Uxmal. Directors of the INAH work were José Erosa Peniche, Alberto Ruz Lhuillier, and César Sáenz. In 1941 Sylvanus Morley studied the stelae at the site, under the auspices of the Carnegie Institution of Washington.

## CONNECTION

1. 48 miles by paved road from Mérida.

## GETTING THERE

From Mérida take Highway 261 south. The ruins lie to the west (right) of the highway and can be reached by private car (rental cars are available in Mérida), taxi, bus, or on conducted tours from Mérida.

There are a large new parking area at the site and some new buildings housing a souvenir shop, a soft-drink stand, rest rooms, and a ticket office. The official INAH guide for Uxmal is sold only at the ticket office; other publications are available at the shop.

There are good hotels nearby. The Hacienda Uxmal is across the highway from the archaeological zone. The Hotel Misión Uxmal is on the west side of the highway 1 mile north, and the Hotel Uxmal (one of the Archaeological Villas that have sprung up at several sites) is near the entrance to the ruins. There are coffee shops and dining rooms at the hotels, and the Restaurant Rancho Uxmal, 2.5 miles north of the site, serves good regional food. It is on the west side of Highway 261.

You can visit Uxmal from Mérida and return the same day, but this does not really allow enough time at the site.

The major areas of Uxmal are kept cleared, so tennis shoes are fine. If you plan on visiting some of the outlying groups, wear a long-sleeved shirt and bring insect repellent. You will need a sun hat for the main part of the site.

Allow at least a full day to see everything; a day and a half is better.

If you have the INAH guidebook or a site plan, a personal guide is not necessary. Guides abound at Uxmal, however, since this is one of the most visited sites in all of Mexico. Finding one who speaks English is no problem. Bring plenty of film.

A light-and-sound pageant is presented in the evening and lasts about 45 minutes. You can buy tickets at your hotel in town or make arrangements in Mérida for a bus trip that returns after the pageant. You can also buy tickets at the site itself. In 1980 the schedule included a 7:00 P.M. presentation in Spanish and a 9:00 P.M. English version, but verify the times. The audience is seated on the terrace of the North Building of the Nunnery Quadrangle for the pageant; plastic chairs are provided and cameras are allowed. Try fast color film (daylight or tungsten) and use the recommended exposure for floodlighted buildings or one stop less exposure. There is not enough light for direct metering with most light meters, and you are too far away from the structures for flash to be useful. Use your fastest normal lens, set on infinity, and open it up all the way. Improvise some sort of support (with your foot propped up on your chair, your knee will serve the purpose, or use another chair if one is available). Be ready to shoot because the lighting changes rapidly. With luck, you may get a few good photos.

★★

# *Mul-Chic*

(mool-*cheek*)

ORIGINAL NAME: Unknown.
CULTURE: Maya.
LOCATION: West-central part of the state of Yucatán, Mexico.

## THE SITE

Mul-Chic is a small site that was discovered fairly recently. Nevertheless, some restoration has been done, making a visit worthwhile. The restored architectural remains face three sides of a small plaza. Some remnants of steps can be seen on the fourth side, but they are unrestored.

The largest and most interesting structure at Mul-Chic is a six-tiered pyramid with a stairway facing the plaza. The pyramid was apparently built on top of an earlier structure—a one-room temple with a vaulted roof and a perforated and decorated roof comb. The roof comb rises from the front of the temple over the single doorway as a sort of flying façade. Some of its stucco decorations may still be seen. The temple seems to have been built on the level of the plaza. A simple molding forms a border around this building and rises to clear the doorway. There were originally murals in this vaulted room, but no trace of them remains today. During the restoration, a skylight was installed to illuminate the interior.

Although building over earlier construction was

*Principal structure, the tiered pyramid, Mul-Chic. Note part of the roof comb of the inner structure at upper right. Late Classic period.*

*Detail of the roof comb of the inner structure, Mul-Chic. Late Classic period.*

a common feature in the Maya area, here at Mul-Chic it seems a bit unusual in that the earlier structure was a totally different type from the later.

The remaining architecture on the other two sides of the plaza are, for the most part, the lower walls of small buildings, with some columns in the doorways. One structure has what appears to be a small altar set into the rear wall.

Mul-Chic is not a very visited site; you will be the only one there. It seems sad that already vegetation is beginning to overtake the recently restored structures.

## RECENT HISTORY

Work at Mul-Chic was undertaken by Mexican archaeologist Román Piña Chan, who reported his findings in Mexico in 1962.

## CONNECTIONS

1. 7.6 miles by paved road from Uxmal, or
2. 55 miles by paved road from Mérida, then 1 mile of poor dirt road to the site.

## GETTING THERE

The best overnight stop and jumping-off point for Mul-Chic is Uxmal, though Mérida is close enough to be another possibility. Take Highway 261 south in either case.

The only problem is finding the correct cutoff; it is not marked for Mul-Chic. You can check your odometer reading starting at Uxmal. As another check, the cutoff is 0.4 mile (0.7 kilometer) north of the sign saying Santa Elena and it heads west. To use this check, you will have to go past the cutoff as far as the sign and check the odometer reading on the way back. In 1980 there was a yellow sign with a black figure (indicating pedestrians in the area) at the cutoff. The sign faced north. If all this fails, ask locally. If nobody is around, you can probably get a guide in Santa Elena to point out the cutoff.

Once you have located the cutoff, you will have to decide whether to drive or walk the 1 mile of dirt road. It is passable for Jeeps and sometimes for cars. If you decide to walk, it will take about 20 minutes. The structures are visible from, and lie to the right of, the dirt road.

There is no caretaker at the site, but you do not need a guide as everything of interest is in a small area. There is no food or drink, of course.

Allow about 30 minutes to visit the site once you get there. Bring insect repellent and wear boots if the trail is muddy and you are going to walk it.

If you drive in, don't let the narrowness of the road frighten you. When you reach the site, there is a wide spot where you can turn around. Driving in will take you almost as much time as walking.

★★★

# *Kabáh*

(kah-*bah*)

ORIGINAL NAME: Unknown.
CULTURE: Maya.
LOCATION: West-central part of the state of Yucatán, Mexico.

---

## THE SITE

The ruins of Kabáh straddle a modern highway. Most of the cleared structures are located on the east side of it. Closest to the road on the east, and one of the most impressive structures at the site, is the well-known Codz-Pop (Coiled Mat) named for a supposed resemblance between the curled trunks of the rain-god masks that decorate the building and a rolled mat. Today the structure is also known as the Palace of the Masks.

The Codz-Pop is 151 feet long and rests on a small platform atop a high terrace, which acts as a court in the front. There are two rows of rooms (five in each), one behind the other, the rearmost being on a higher level. They are reached from the lower rooms by a step in the form of a rain-god mask.

The entire façade of the Codz-Pop is a mass of more rain-god masks. This is unusual in Puuc-style architecture; generally only the upper façades of structures are decorated. It does seem a bit overdone when compared with other structures at the site and with palace-type buildings at Uxmal and Sayil.

The Chac masks reportedly number 250, each being constructed of 30 separate pieces. In much of this area, identical pieces of carved-stone decoration are found, and a central "factory" has been postulated. One wonders whether the factory didn't overproduce certain designs and sell them at discount to Kabáh's architects.

The structure is surmounted by a roof comb forming a stepped fret pattern. Some restoration

*The Codz-Pop, view from the southwest, Kabáh. Late Classic period.*

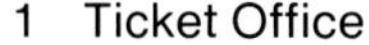

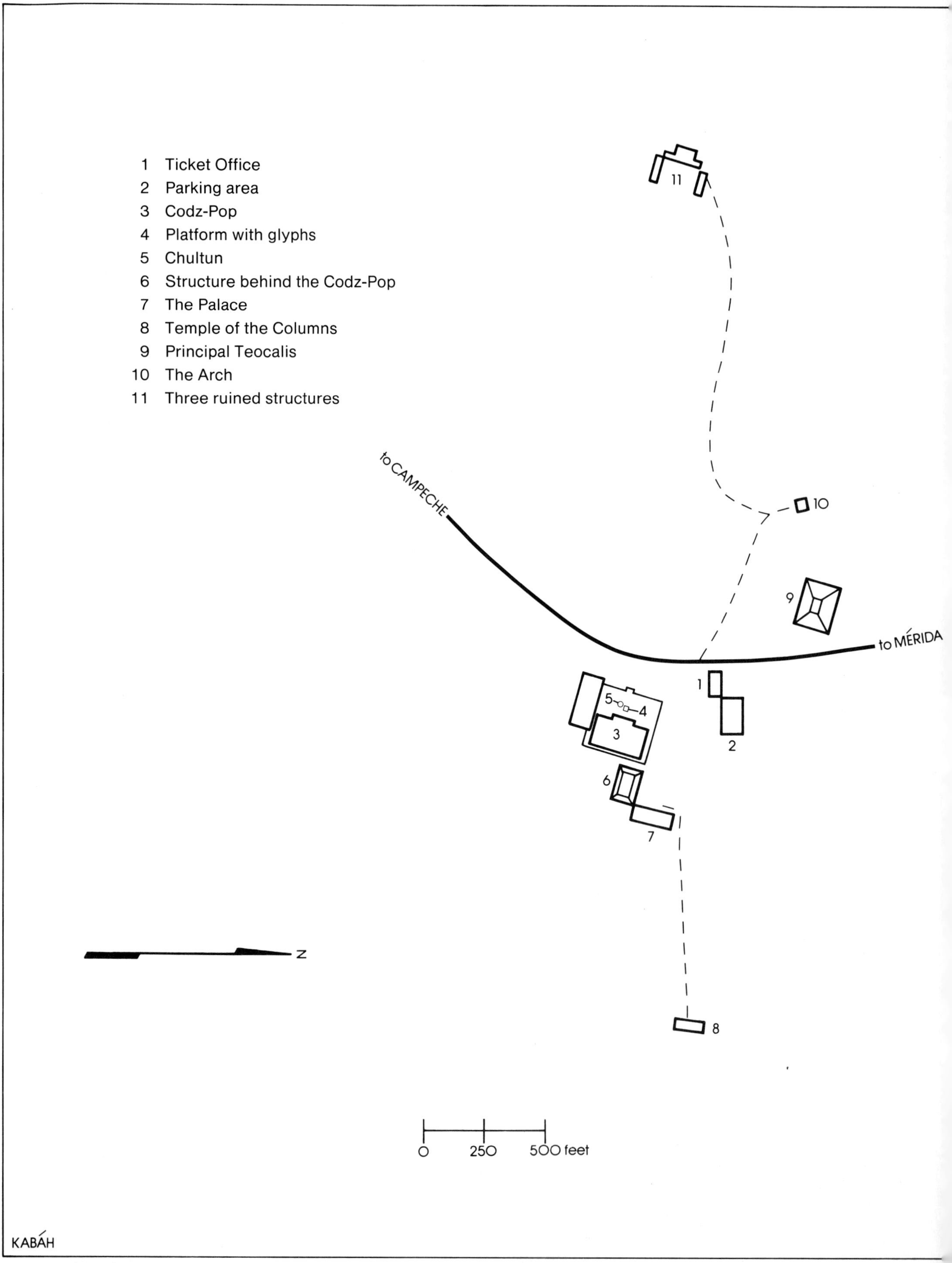
1 Ticket Office
2 Parking area
3 Codz-Pop
4 Platform with glyphs
5 Chultun
6 Structure behind the Codz-Pop
7 The Palace
8 Temple of the Columns
9 Principal Teocalis
10 The Arch
11 Three ruined structures
to CAMPECHE
to MÉRIDA
N
0 250 500 feet
KABÁH

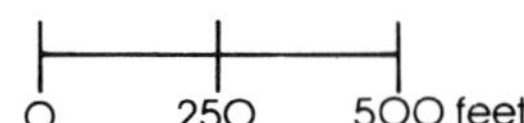

has been done, but many pieces of carved-stone decoration lie on the ground awaiting incorporation.

In front of the Codz-Pop is a small platform bearing hieroglyphs on its sides, and nearby is a chultun sunk into the terrace.

Behind the Codz-Pop is a structure in a more ruinous condition that is, nevertheless, interesting. There are columned doorways on the lower level, and it is worth some time to walk around the base of the whole building. The upper section is little more than a mound of rubble, but it is worth climbing. From the top of the mound you get good views of the back of the Codz-Pop as well as of the Palace, which lies adjacent to the north. This is also a good spot for some telephoto photographs of some ruined structures visible on the other side of the highway.

The Palace is a multiroomed, two-story structure exhibiting two columned doorways (out of seven) on an upper level. The decoration is much simpler than that on the Codz-Pop, although the Palace also has remains of a roof comb. A stairway leads to the second story, but it is pierced at ground level, forming half of a typical vault. More columned doorways are near the stairway at ground level.

*The Codz-Pop, detail of the Chac masks on the façade, Kabáh. Late Classic period.*

*The Codz-Pop, detail of the Chac mask used as a step to one of the entrances, Kabáh. Late Classic period.*

*The Palace, the front (west) side, Kabáh. Late Classic period.*

A path from the Palace leads a few hundred yards to the Temple of the Columns, the last major structure on the east side of the highway. The Temple of the Columns is 113 feet long and has five doorways. Its name comes from the relief columns in between the doorways and short columns that decorate the upper façade.

The site of Kabáh has ruined buildings covering 0.4 square mile. On the east side of the highway only those structures already mentioned have been cleared; the others are simply rubble mounds covered with vegetation.

Now head to the west side of the highway. Kabáh's large Arch is the only restored structure in the west

*Detail of the Temple of the Columns showing banded columns on the upper façade, Kabáh. Late Classic period.*

*The Arch, view of the south side, Kabáh. Late Classic period.*

section, but some unrestored remains in two areas are worth a look. As you head along the trail toward the Arch, you pass a tall pyramidal mound on the right (north). This is the tallest structure at Kabáh and was called the Principal Teocalis by John Lloyd Stephens. The few remains of the temple on top would probably not be worth the difficult climb. Now follow the trail to the Arch.

The Arch spans 15 feet and is very plain when compared to the one at Labná. It also differs in that it has no other structures attached. A *saché* leads from the arch and presumably extends to Uxmal, 9 miles away.

When you leave the Arch to head back toward the highway, watch for a trail to the right (south). It leads about 0.3 mile through the bush to a group of three ruined structures facing a plaza. This whole group is very overgrown as this area of Kabáh is not often visited. If you climb up the structure where the trail ends, you will find an intact room with a corbeled vault and remains of stucco decoration. You can climb to the roof of this structure over a steep rocky path for good views of the other two buildings in this group as well as distant views of the Principal Teocalis and structures on the east side of the highway.

There are other ruined buildings on this side of the highway. From one of them Stephens removed a carved wooden lintel and a couple of carved stone door jambs. The jambs depicted warriors and show influence from central Mexico, but probably were carved before the Toltecs established themselves at Chichén Itzá. Other carved jambs found in the Codz-Pop (but not visible today) show even more Toltec-like traits. A date of A.D. 879 occurs on two of the door jambs.

The visible remains at Kabáh are all Maya Late Classic in date, although some ceramic sherds found in trenches date to the Late Preclassic period. Apparently Kabáh was at its peak from the eighth through the tenth centuries, after which it was virtually abandoned.

## RECENT HISTORY

Stephens and Catherwood visited Kabáh in 1842, on their second trip to Yucatán. They first heard of the site from Father Estanislao Carrillo, the curate of Ticul. Father Carillo told Stephens that until the opening of the road to Bolonchén (a town farther south), nothing was known of the ruins by the white inhabitants of the area. Stephens speculated that perhaps the Indians knew of them.

Even after the opening of the road, which went right through the site, no one but the priest bothered to visit it. Stephens and Catherwood recorded Kabáh in text and illustrations published in 1843, and a rough sketch map of the site was included.

The history of Kabáh in the following years parallels that of Sayil and Labná in that it was studied by Teobert Maler, Edward H. Thompson, and Sylvanus Morley, and photographed by Henry N. Sweet, on an expedition for Peabody Museum of Harvard University.

Later Alberto Ruz Lhuillier explored the site and ceramic studies were undertaken by George W. Brainerd and Robert E. Smith. Some restoration has been undertaken by the Mexican government, and the more important structures are kept cleared.

## CONNECTIONS

1. 14 miles by paved road from Uxmal.
2. 62 miles by paved road from Mérida.

## GETTING THERE

From Uxmal or Mérida take Highway 261 south. Kabáh is located near the kilometer 120 marker on the highway. The site can be easily reached by private car, taxi, bus, or on conducted tours from Mérida.

A guide is not necessary, but if you take one of the bus tours to see Sayil, Xlapak, and Labná, a visit to Kabáh may be included (see "A Note on Sayil, Xlapak and Labná" for why I think this is a bad idea).

There are no accommodations at the site, but soft drinks and packaged snacks are available. Nearest overnight stopovers are Uxmal and Mérida.

Tennis shoes are adequate. Wear a long-sleeved shirt and bring insect repellent if you plan to visit the Temple of the Columns on the east side of the highway, or the three ruined structures on the west side.

# *A Note on Sayil, Xlapak, and Labná*

Until recently the only recommended way to reach Sayil, Xlapak, and Labná was to take a Jeep tour. These began at Uxmal, and the driving time alone was about 5½ hours, 4½ of which were over an execrable road composed of limestone outcrops and muddy ruts—or heavy dust in the dry season.

At one time it was possible to do the tour as an overnight trip. This had the advantages of: (1) breaking the bone-shattering ride into 2 separate days, (2) allowing you the romance of sleeping in a ruin (Labná), and, most important, (3) allowing you sufficient time to see each site. When this tour was discontinued due to lack of interest, the day tour was the only choice. Unfortunately, the day tour did not allow enough time to see Sayil and Labná properly.

For over a decade road improvements were promised, and I found it difficult to understand why access remained so poor for such important sites, especially since a fair number of tourists made the trip—often not really knowing what they were in for, I suspect. Finally, on December 2, 1978, the Camino Zona Puuc was dedicated. This is a beautiful, wide, paved, 19-mile road that connects Highway 261 with Cooperativa (a town on an unnumbered highway that connects with Oxkutzcab on Highway 184).

The Camino Zona Puuc passes right by Sayil, Xlapak, and Labná, and there are paved parking areas at each site.

The best jumping off place for the three sites is still Uxmal. From there go south on Highway 261 for 17 miles, to the Camino Zona Puuc. The junction is marked with a sign saying Sayil 5 (3 miles), Xlapak 13 (8 miles), and Labná 17 (10.5 miles). (Actually it is more like 2.7 miles to Sayil, 6 miles to Xlapak, and 7.8 miles to Labná.) The Camino Zona Puuc joins Highway 261 near kilometer marker 115 and it heads left (east).

After you have visited the sites and are ready to return, you can go back to Uxmal the way you came (25 miles) or continue to Cooperativa on the Camino Zona Puuc, turn left (north) to Oxkutzcab, left (northwest) to Muna on Highway 184, and left (south) to Uxmal on Highway 261 (52 miles). This second route takes you past Loltún Cave (13 miles after you leave Labná). See "Loltún" for more information.

If you are at Uxmal without a car, you can take a bus tour to Sayil, Xlapak, and Labná. It generally leaves Uxmal at 8:30 A.M. and returns at 1:00 P.M. Check at your hotel at Uxmal for more details. Like the former Jeep tour, this does not really allow enough time at Sayil and Labná for serious ruin buffs—especially for those who plan to take a lot of photos—although it is sufficient for average visitors.

The old Jeep tour also sometimes stopped for a visit at Kabáh (perhaps the new bus tour does, too). That always struck me as a bad idea, since one really cannot see all four sites in one day except in the most casual way. It would be better to spend any extra time at Sayil and Labná and to save Kabáh for another day. If you plan to take a conducted tour, make arrangements the day before at your hotel. Another improvement in the area is the recent clearing of three additional structures at Sayil, which means more time is needed there than in years gone by. See "Sayil" for details. If you are visiting the sites on your own, allow 2 to 2½ hours at Sayil, 30 minutes at Xlapak, and 2½ to 3 hours at Labná.

All three sites have cold drinks and packaged snacks, but you should bring something more substantial along from your hotel if you plan to make it an all-day trip. Tennis shoes will get you by unless it has been very rainy, in which case boots would be better as the trails at Sayil can get muddy. A sun hat is useful for Labná and the more open areas of Sayil. Bring insect repellent and lots of film. Although some film is sold at the sites, the selection is limited and all three sites are very photogenic.

*Note:* If you want to make arrangements for a tour and your base of operations is Mérida, check with Barbachano Travel Service or Yucatán Trails to see what kind of package they can offer. These packages used to include a visit to Uxmal and a night or two at one of the hotels there.

★★★

# *Sayil*

(sah-*yeel*)

DERIVATION: Mayan for "Place of the Ants."
CULTURE: Maya.
LOCATION: West-central part of the state of Yucatán, Mexico.
*Note:* Sayil is sometimes said to be located on the border of the states of Yucatán and Campeche. Current maps show it well within the borders of Yucatán.

## THE SITE

Sayil is a fairly large site with remains of structures covering an area of about 1 square mile. Until the recent clearing there, only two structures were shown to visitors, the Palace and the Mirador. Now, wide, well-marked trails lead to other structures, and all are worth a visit.

From the parking area, two trails lead to the Palace (take your pick). The Palace of Sayil is certainly one of the jewels of Maya architecture. It rises in three stories and has about seventy rooms. A wide central stairway divides the structure into two wings, which balance each other without being symmetrical.

The second and third stories are set back, so that the roofs of the first and second stories act as terraces for the second and third. You will need a wide-angle lens to get the entire structure in a head-on photo.

The second story has wide doorways supported by two columns, and the upper façade is decorated with stylized masks of Chac and depictions of the "diving god" (see "Cobá" and "Tulum" for more on this deity). This is the most interesting of the three stories and it contrasts nicely with the other two, which are simpler. The double-columned doorways give a feeling of lightness to the whole structure, which measures 275 feet wide and 130 feet deep. The Palace also shows a rare example of columns used on the interior of a room, although the outer rooms may have been added later. Gen-

*The Palace of Sayil, over-all view of the front (south) side, Sayil. Late Classic period.*

*Detail of the western half of the front (south) side of the Palace of Sayil. Late Classic period.*

erally, this method of construction appears later and indicates strong Toltec influence, as at Chichén Itzá. Tatiana Proskouriakoff said: "This forthright simplicity of arrangement, combined with the casual disregard of minor imperfections of symmetry and a freedom from the oppressively monotonous intricacy of ornament that mars many Puuc structures, makes the Sayil Palace one of the most satisfactory compositions that the Maya ever created."

There has been some restoration of the Palace, and we know that part of the first story is earlier than the rest of the structure, which is generally dated about A.D. 850. A catch basin and cistern are found near the back of this structure.

When you leave the Palace, walk past the far end and look for a trail to the right (south). This is the trail to the Mirador, and it is marked with a sign indicating the distance is 300 meters. Before reaching the Mirador, you will find two side trails to other structures.

The first side trail is marked for Temple 2 and heads left (east). Although the distance is not stated, it is about 250 yards. Temple 2 is a small structure with three doorways on its best preserved face. A simple molding runs above the doorways, and if an upper façade decoration ever existed, it has since fallen. From here return to the main trail and head left (south). You will soon come to the second side trail, which is marked Los Dinteles for the Temple of the Lintel (300 meters). The second side trail heads right (southwest), but before reaching the Temple of the Lintel, branches again. It heads left (approximately south) for 700 meters and is marked Juego de Pelota for the Ball Court. Pass this up for the moment and continue to the Temple of the Lintel.

The Temple of the Lintel is badly ruined and its façade has fallen, but it is noteworthy for some carved glyphs that decorate the front of the lintel (on your right as you face the structure). This stone lintel connected two rooms, and is plain on the underside. The face of the jambs supporting it are carved with glyphs.

Return now to the trail marked for the Ball Court and turn right for a 7-minute walk. When you reach the end of this trail, you may be surprised that the impressive structure you are looking at is most

*Palace-type structure near the ball court, Sayil. Late Classic period.*

assuredly not a ball court. Rather it is a large palace-type structure, with ranges of rooms on four sides forming a rectangle. The east façade is in excellent condition, and has seven doorways leading to five rooms; the three central doorways enter the center room. The entire lower façade is decorated with banded columns—almost all in perfect condition—and the upper façade displays shorter versions of the same motif. A different design once adorned the area above the center doorway, but this has fallen. The other ranges of rooms of this structure are poorly preserved.

Although the low bush in front of the east façade has been cleared, numerous small trees remain. Even with a wide-angle lens, it is impossible to get a really definitive photo of the structure. This building is one of three shown by John Lloyd Stephens (see "Recent History") and it seems to have suffered little in the intervening years.

What about the sign saying Ball Court? On the site plan of Sayil, the structure just described is about 100 yards west of the ball court, so perhaps this general area of the site goes by that name.

Return now the way you came, turn right at the junction with the trail to the Temple of the Lintel, and right again at the junction with the trail to the Mirador. Proceed a short distance to this structure, which is a temple atop a pyramid.

When you reach the Mirador, you will be facing the back (north side) of the structure. The north façade has fallen, but an inner wall and a perforated roof comb with projecting stones remain. Stucco decorations were supported by these stones when the temple was constructed. The pyramidal base has not been restored, but a rocky path gives access to the temple.

Eight of the nine known stelae at Sayil were set up on a platform, separate from the architecture, and generally were not dated, although their style indicates they were carved in the Late Classic period. There is a depiction of the "Manikin Scepter" on one of the stelae. Columns carved with figures also occur at Sayil and are related to the late decadent monuments found to the south. We saw only one of the carved stelae and none of the columns at the site.

The one stela currently visible at Sayil is a crudely carved frontal view of a very phallic figure. It is

*The Mirador, over-all view, Sayil. Late Classic period.*

unlike other stelae reported from Sayil, and is totally un-Maya in feeling. A connection has been suggested with other crude sculpture from Pustunich in west central Campeche and Telantunich in the southern part of the state of Yucatán. It is thought to be very late and the work of "marginal groups" not sharing in the higher intellectual achievements of Maya civilization.

As you face the back of the Mirador, look for a trail leading from the left side of its base. The trail goes a few hundred feet to the stela, which is propped up on a cement base and is covered by a protective thatch shelter.

Sayil's architectural and monumental remains date to the Late Classic period, although in the Puuc sector of which Sayil is a part, ceramics dating to as early as the Preclassic period are found. This area supported a population of about 30 people per square mile during its heyday, and was apparently abandoned around the tenth century.

*Phallic stela, Sayil.*

## RECENT HISTORY

The ruins of Sayil were reported by John Lloyd Stephens in *Incidents of Travel in Yucatán* in 1843. He used the spelling "Zayi" and gave "Salli" as an alternate. He cleared a few structures, and Frederick Catherwood did drawings of them, reproduced in the text. Stephens first heard of Sayil, as well as Kabáh, during his search for ruined cities from a priest named Estanislao Carrillo, the Franciscan curate of Ticul, who was interested in Maya antiquities. The name of the site was apparently in use locally at the time, and its location was known to hunters and farmers in the area.

He saw the figure of the so-called diving god on the façade of the Palace and described it as "the figure of a man supporting himself on his hands, with his legs expanded in a curious rather than delicate attitude" (he later saw the figure at Tulum and made the connection with the one at Sayil).

Stephens also reported that his workmen believed there was a well or other water source at the site that had supplied the ancient inhabitants. They hoped he could find it with his instruments. They even offered to cut down all the trees to help him locate it since it would have been of great use to the local inhabitants. Apparently the search was not undertaken. No further mention of it is made. A cistern does exist at Sayil, however, proving their belief was correct.

Teobert Maler visited Sayil and reported on it in 1895, at which time he mentioned three stelae not mentioned by Stephens. The site was also briefly visited in 1907 by Sylvanus Morley. In 1946 a beautiful restoration drawing of the Palace by Tatiana Proskouriakoff was published by the Carnegie Institution of Washington, which funded her 1940 trip to the area.

As with Labná, little in-depth work has been done at Sayil, although the Mexican government has undertaken some restoration and keeps the major buildings cleared.

See "A Note on Sayil, Xlapak, and Labná" for "Connections" and "Getting There" and for accommodations in the area.

★★

# *Xlapak*

(shlah-*pahk*)

## *(Maler-Xlabpak)*

DERIVATION: Mayan for "Old Walls" or "Old Ruined Walls."
ORIGINAL NAME: Unknown.
CULTURE: Maya.
LOCATION: West-central part of the state of Yucatán, Mexico.

### THE SITE

There is one major structure at Xlapak that has been nicely restored, a small one-story building in typical Puuc style, dating to the Late Classic period. The upper façade is decorated with the stepped fret pattern and with stylized Chac masks. The masks are in the center of the north and south sides and on the corners, and some of them are well preserved. The lower portion of the building is plain, is pierced by simple doorways, and has cylindrical columns with simple capitals on the corners of the structure. Although two doorways and parts of a room have collapsed, the structure is mostly intact. Near the center of the south side is a catch basin that drains into a chultun, and a bit southeast are remains of a ruined structure with remnants of stone mosaic decoration.

### RECENT HISTORY

Teobert Maler reported Xlapak under the name of Maler-Xlabpak in 1902, in a publication covering several sites in the area. A photograph of the main structure is included in his report. In 1913, in *A Study of Maya Art,* Herbert J. Spinden published a similar photograph of the structure by Henry N. Sweet. Karin Hissink included Xlapak in a study of masks on buildings in Yucatán in a 1934 publication.

Over the years the structure became overgrown, but it was recleared and partly restored in the late 1960s. It is now well maintained.

See "A Note on Sayil, Xlapak, and Labná" for "Connections" and "Getting There" and for accommodations in the area.

*Over-all view of the front of the main structure, Xlapak. Late Classic period.*

★★★

# *Labná*

(lahb-*nah*)

DERIVATION: Mayan for "Old Ruined Buildings."
ORIGINAL NAME: Unknown.
CULTURE: Maya.
LOCATION: West-central part of the state of Yucatán, Mexico.

---

## THE SITE

Labná is a thoroughly delightful site. Its three major structures are the Palace, and, across a large plaza, the Arch and the Mirador. Another palace-type structure, called the East Building, has been cleared in recent years, and there are many unexcavated mounds in the area.

The Palace is a large two-story structure set on a terrace that is 535 feet long. The first story was originally a group of separate buildings that were later joined together by the platform built to support the second story. One section of the first story, on a slightly lower level, runs perpendicular to the rest of the building, and has a simple molding for decoration. It is in one of these rooms that we slept when we took the overnight tour.

Many interesting motifs are found on the Palace. Bundles of columns in relief flank some of the doorways, and the ubiquitous masks of Chac are found on the upper façades. Some of the masks are simplified and alternate with the stepped-fret design, all of which is done in Puuc-style stone mosaic.

The first story of the Palace has a few jogs in its front—rather than running in a straight line—and on one of the outer corners is an interesting serpent with an open mouth containing a human head. The second story is made up of three separate structures, of which only the easternmost is in a decent state of repair. Even here the ends of the structure have collapsed, but the center portion retains its two large doorways with two columns in each, supporting the lintels.

An interesting feature at the Palace is a chultun, which is built into the structure. The circular catch basin that drains into the chultun is located on the terrace that supports the second story, near the structure just described.

About 150 yards east-southeast of the Palace is the East Building; it is of similar construction, but much more sober in its decoration. Several rooms

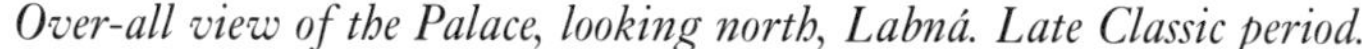

*Over-all view of the Palace, looking north, Labná. Late Classic period.*

*Detail of a Chac mask on the Palace bearing the date* A.D. *862, Labná.*

compose the remains of this L-shaped structure, which sits on a terrace. The upper façade is decorated with a row of small columns and a simple molding, and the lower façade is plain.

About 250 yards south of the Palace is a group of structures dominated by the pyramid-temple called El Mirador, or El Castillo. When John Lloyd Stephens saw this structure in 1842, more of it was standing. According to his description, the temple originally had three doorways and measured 43 feet in front, although an 8-foot section and one doorway had already collapsed. As he predicted, another section has since fallen.

The pyramidal base of the temple has not been restored, but its shape is rectangular. A rocky path leads to the temple and its small restored platform, and from here there are good views of both the Palace and the east side of the Arch.

The roof comb of the Mirador is above the front, forming a sort of flying façade. It is perforated by

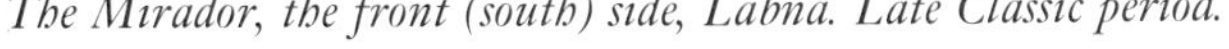

*The Mirador, the front (south) side, Labná. Late Classic period.*

*West face of the Labná Arch, Labná. Late Classic period.*

rectangular slots, and has projecting stones and remains of stucco decorations. It must have been quite impressive when intact.

The Labná Arch—also called the Portal Vault or Gateway—is one of the gems of this type of structure. It is near the Mirador and is flanked by other structures of the palace-type, but they are in ruinous condition.

The west face of the Arch is the most interesting. Above its two doorways is a decorative molding, and above this are depictions of Maya thatch huts with niches in the lower sections. Figures of some sort are thought originally to have existed inside the niches. Flanking the huts are latticelike patterns, and the whole is surmounted by the remains of a roof comb. Only a few courses of stone were found and restored, but we know that the roof comb was in three separate sections and was pierced by rectangular openings, and probably had stucco figures as decoration.

On the northwest corner of the upper façade is a mask of Chac. The east face of the Arch is more sober in decoration—having the stepped fret and geometric designs as its motifs. The Arch connected two courtyards.

A *sacbé* at Labná runs north–south through the center of the plaza and connects the Palace and the group including the Mirador and the Arch.

Labná's structures all date to the Late Classic period. The date A.D. 862 is inscribed on the elongated proboscis of the rain god, Chac, in the Chac mask in the upper façade of the lower story of the Palace (above the doorway in the west façade of the east wing).

## RECENT HISTORY

Stephens first heard of Labná from the brother of a priest from the nearby village of Nohcacab, but his informant had not personally visited the site. Stephens had the major structures cleared, and they were duly recorded by Frederick Catherwood. An engraving of the front of the Palace was used as the frontispiece for *Incidents of Travel in Yucatán.*

The site was studied—especially the chultunes—by Edward H. Thompson near the turn of the century. Thompson was appointed American consul to Mexico, stationed in Yucatán, but was under instructions to investigate Maya sites in the area. He is better known, however, for dredging the Sacred Cenote at Chichén Itzá. He wrote a book about his work among the Maya in 1932, but his more scholarly reports were published by the Peabody Museum of Harvard University and the Field Columbian Museum of Chicago between 1897 and 1904.

Sylvanus Morley visited Labná as well as other sites in the area in his early days in the field. The ceramics of this site and others in Yucatán were reported upon by George Brainerd in 1958. Herbert J. Spinden published photos of the major structures in 1913. These were taken by Henry N. Sweet and Thompson for the Peabody Museum Expeditions.

Although Labná was visited often, little in-depth work has been done. Some restoration by the Mexican government has taken place and the main area is kept well cleared.

See "A Note on Sayil, Xlapak, and Lanbá" for "Connections" and "Getting There" and for accommodations in the area.

★

# *Xcavil de Yaxché*

(shkah-*weel* deh yahsh-*cheh*)

DERIVATION: Xcavil is Mayan for "Second Sowing," (land that is sown with seed). Yaxché is Mayan for "Ceiba." It is also the name of a hacienda that once stood nearby. *Note:* Xcavil is the spelling used in the literature. The pronunciation shown, however, is that used in the area.

ORIGINAL NAME: Unknown.

CULTURE: Maya.

LOCATION: Western part of the state of Yucatán, Mexico, near the Campeche border (see note in text).

---

## THE SITE

The Temple-Palace at Xcavil de Yaxché must have been a splendid building when intact; even in partial ruin it is impressive. This large structure faces a bit north of west, and the first story is composed of a double range of very wide rooms that run north-south. Dividing the west façade in the center is a stairway that ascends to a smaller, partly intact, second-story structure. On the first level, other rooms extend to the rear (east) and on this level, there are a few intact doorways.

When the site was first reported, there was a mask panel above a doorway on the east side of the structure, but the mask has since fallen, though the doorway remains. On the north side of the rear section is an extremely narrow doorway—barely shoulder width. This doorway is also very low, though this is due in part to rubble on the floor.

Decorations on the Temple-Palace are plain and banded columns, two- and three-member moldings, and squared spiral motifs.

## RECENT HISTORY

Xcavil de Yaxché was first reported by Teobert Maler in 1902, and he included a photo of the mask panel mentioned above. In 1911 Henry A. Case reproduced Maler's photo in *Views on and of Yucatán,* where it is labeled "Yaxché," although neither Xcavil de Yaxché nor Yaxché-Xlapak is covered in the text. He explains this by saying that "our investigations could not elicit any information respecting them [some of the ruins he illustrates]," and "We have never heard of any person, except the photographer, visiting them, consequently they are only known to a few." He does not say who the photographer was.

In 1934 Karin Hissink, in a study of masks in Yucatán, presented a drawing of the same mask, done from Maler's photo.

The location of Xcavil de Yaxché is shown on a 1940 map, "Archaeological Sites in the Maya Area," by the Middle American Research Institute of Tulane University, and the site is included in an index of sites intended to be used with the map.

*Note:* Although the location of the site is shown on this map within the state of Yucatán, access today is from the state of Campeche. That is, the place where you take the cutoff onto the dirt road is on the Campeche side of the border.

Although there has been no in-depth work at the site, the style of the architecture indicates a Late Classic date.

## CONNECTIONS

1. 23.5 miles by paved road from Uxmal,
2. 71.5 miles by paved road from Mérida, or
3. 85.5 miles by paved road from Campeche, then 3.7 miles by poor dirt road and 0.5 mile by foot trail.

## GETTING THERE

From Uxmal or Mérida take Highway 261 south; from Campeche take the same highway east and then north.

The cutoff for Xcavil de Yaxché is 9.8 miles north of the center of Bolonchén and heads east. The road is narrow, bumpy, and rutted, and it will take you about an hour to drive the short distance.

In the rainy season you may need four-wheel drive to get in. If the road is too bad for your particular vehicle, you could walk in all the way from the highway about as fast. If you do, carry a canteen of water. If you drive in all the way, you can park and turn around in a cleared area at the end. From here it is a 10-minute walk to the site. Allow about an hour to see the Temple-Palace once you reach it.

A guide is essential to reach Xcavil de Yaxché. See "Itzimté" for where to find one, and for other recommendations concerning the area.

*Temple-Palace, the front (west) side, Xcavil de Yaxché. Late Classic period.*

★

# *Yaxché-Xlapak*

(yahsh-*cheh* shlah-*pahk*)

DERIVATION: Yaxché is Mayan for "Ceiba," Xlapak is Mayan for "Old Walls" (see text).
ORIGINAL NAME: Unknown.
CULTURE: Maya.
LOCATION: Western part of the state of Yucatán, Mexico, near the Campeche border (see note in text).

## THE SITE

As you walk to Yaxché-Xlapak, you pass a propped-up stone. It appears that it was once carved, but it is so eroded that it is difficult to be sure.

Although five structures are reported at Yaxché-Xlapak, visitors today are shown only one, Structure III (El Castillo). This rather large structure faces west, and though part of it has collapsed, the west façade still retains four intact doorways and remains of a central stairway that leads to the roof. There are currently no remains of second-story rooms. The lower walls are plain, but the upper façade is decorated with a continuous row of banded columns and the stairway is pierced at its base by a narrow passage. This row of rooms is well preserved.

Additional rooms extend to the rear of the structure (east), and some of these are also well preserved; you will see them as you circle the structure. The most interesting of these is a room that opens to the north. Its doorway is supported by two intact columns with capitals, and the vault of the room is pointed rather than having capstones. The central part of the façade above the doorway is decorated with groups of three columns, separated by plain sections.

## RECENT HISTORY

Teobert Maler visited Yaxché-Xlapak in March, 1887. He reported the site under this name because Yaxché was the name of a nearby hacienda. His report included a photograph of the west face of Structure III, and was published in 1902. The structure seems to have suffered little since that time. In his report he describes four other structures at Yaxché-Xlapak, but does not show photographs of them.

The site is briefly mentioned in a 1943 publication by Alberto Ruz Lhuillier, and its location is shown on a 1940 map, "Archaeological Sites in the Maya Area," by the Middle American Research Institute of Tulane University. Yaxché-Xlapak is also included in an index of sites intended for use with the map.

*Note:* Although the location of the site is shown on the map within the state of Yucatán, access today is from the state of Campeche. That is, the place where you park on the highway and begin the foot trail is on the Campeche side of the border.

There has been no in-depth work at the site, but we know that it dates to the Late Classic period and is Puuc style.

## CONNECTIONS

1. 24 miles by paved road from Uxmal,
2. 72 miles by paved road from Mérida, or
3. 85 miles by paved road from Campeche, then just under 2 miles by foot trail.

## GETTING THERE

From Uxmal or Mérida take Highway 261 south. From Campeche take the same highway east and then north.

The trail to Yaxché-Xlapak begins at the highway, 9.3 miles north of the center of Bolonchén. The only problem is finding a safe place to park. There is no real shoulder to the road, but there is a limestone outcrop. Pull onto this very carefully. If your vehicle has high clearance, you can pull off the road a bit farther and park under the shade of a tree. From here it will take about 30 minutes on foot to reach the site; the last part is very uphill. Allow about 35 minutes for a visit and 25 minutes to return to your car. It is easier on the way back.

A guide is essential to reach Yaxché-Xlapak. See "Itzimté" for where to find one, and for other suggestions about the area. In addition to those recommendations, you should wear a sun hat and carry a canteen of water when you walk to Yaxché-Xlapak.

*Structure III (El Castillo), the front (west) side, Yaxché-Xlapak. Late Classic period.*

★★

# *Loltún (Cave)*

(lohl-*toon*)

DERIVATION: Mayan for "The Rock of Flowers."
ORIGINAL NAME: Unknown.
CULTURE: Maya.
LOCATION: West-central part of the state of Yucatán, Mexico.

---

## THE SITE

For the ruin buff the primary reason for a visit to Loltún is to see the well-preserved bas-relief sculptured figure on the outside rock wall, near the Nahkab (or Hunacab) entrance to the cave. This bigger-than-life-sized figure of a man in profile with an elaborate costume is believed to date to the late middle Preclassic or Late Preclassic period, making it perhaps the earliest known sculpture not only in Yucatán but in all the Maya lowlands.

The figure is holding a lance in his right hand and may represent a warrior, though some authorities believe that the relief is related to Maya deities. A row of vertical glyphs is carved above and to the left of the figure; these are the earliest reported from Yucatán and the central Maya area. The numeral 3 accompanies the top glyph, but no date has been deciphered; the relief is dated by its style. A drawing of the relief in the National Institute of Anthropology and History (INAH) guide, lists it as Preclassic Maya.

The cave itself has recently become a tourist attraction and is worth a visit. Lighting (some colored) has been installed and tours are conducted at 9:30 A.M., 11:30 A.M., and 1:30 P.M., Tuesdays through Sundays.

You are shown through several caverns, some of which are gigantic. In several spots there are remnants of paintings, including both positive and negative painted hands, a motif seen in many parts of the Yucatán Peninsula.

The Loltún Head, discovered in the cave in 1960 by Jack Grant and Bill Dailey, was for several years in the Mérida Museum. Recently it was returned to the cave and can be seen when you take a tour. The head is about two feet tall and is rather crudely carved. When displayed at the Mérida Museum, it was labeled as in Olmec style or showing Olmec influence.

In a large chamber that you visit near the end of the tour are several carvings on boulders and wall surfaces. Although they have been recorded and were reported many years ago, they have not been dated, nor have the paintings. The carvings include spirals, crude faces, and geometrical designs.

The chamber in which these carvings appear has an opening to the surface, so there is some light. You need fast film for available-light shots; a flash is also useful here and to shoot the "paintings," where there is no natural light.

A nearby chamber with another opening to the surface has a ladder and steps carved into the rock, and this is your exit to the surface. From there you walk about a mile aboveground to where you parked.

Recent excavation at Loltún shows that the cave was used from very early times. Some lithic artifacts, associated with animal remains, have been dated 2500 to 1200 B.C. or perhaps earlier, and the earliest ceramics date to 1200 to 600 B.C. Ceramics from succeeding periods were also discovered, and analysis, by Fernando Robles and Eduardo Toro, indicates that a climax was reached during the Late Classic period. Little material from the Postclassic and colonial periods was found.

## RECENT HISTORY

Loltún Cave was first studied by Edward H. Thompson, who reported his findings in 1897, while working for Peabody Museum of Harvard University. He worked at Loltún on two occasions. The first expedition was during the 1888–89 season, and the second was two years later. He explored the cave and discovered several inscriptions (carvings) on the walls and boulders of one of the chambers. He also excavated in that area and found fragments of pottery and stone implements at various depths. Photographs of these items and of the sculptured figure on the outside wall appear in his publication.

A few years later Henry C. Mercer explored the cave, undertook some excavation, and published

*Late Preclassic bas-relief carving at the entrance to Loltún Cave.*

photographs of the carvings inside the cave. Oddly enough, he made no mention of the Preclassic figure at the entrance.

Drawings of the sculptured figure are reproduced in *A Study of Classic Maya Sculpture*, by Tatiana Proskouriakoff (1950), and *Indian Art of Mexico and Central America*, by Miguel Covarrubias (1957).

Recent work at the cave was sponsored by INAH.

## CONNECTIONS

1. 33 miles by paved road from Uxmal to Oxkutzcab, or
2. 62 miles by paved road from Mérida to Oxkutzcab, then a little over 4 miles by paved road to the cutoff, and a few yards to the parking area.

## GETTING THERE

Although Uxmal and Mérida are the best nearby overnight stops, if you do not mind something less than luxury accommodations, you might try one of the hotels in Ticul or Tekax. They are about 10 and 11 miles from Oxkutzcab, respectively.

If you leave from Uxmal, take Highway 261 north to Muna, then Highway 184 east to Oxkutzcab. From Mérida take Highway 261 south to Muna, then on to Oxkutzcab.

When you arrive in Oxkutzcab (heading east), drive through the town and go 2 blocks past the Main Plaza. There you will see a sign for Loltún indicating a paved road to the right (south). Take this road until you come to the sign for Grutas de Loltún and turn right to the parking area. From there a path of rock steps leads down to the entrance of the cave. The sculptured figure is on the rock wall to the left of the main entrance, a bit above eye level. There is another opening to the left of the sculpture.

Once you get to the sculpture, a few minutes is adequate to see and photograph it. Avoid the use of flash; it washes out the figure and emphasizes the discoloration in the rock. This is especially true if the sculpture is wet, as it sometimes is. When it is wet, good photos are extremely difficult to get. Try fast film and available light. There are trees you can lean against for support. The sculpture never gets direct sunlight.

If you decide to visit the cave, you will begin at this entrance. On the way to the entrance you pass through a gate that is kept locked before and after visiting hours. I do not know whether it is left open continuously during the day. If it is, you could see the sculptured figure anytime from 9:30 A.M. to 1:30 P.M. If it is not, you will have to enter with the tours.

For a tour of the cave and the walk back to your car, allow about 1½ hours. Tennis shoes are adequate since the footing in the cave is pretty good, for the most part. A little climbing is involved.

Bring along your own flashlight for extra light in the cave and for reading your camera dials when setting up for flash shots in dark areas.

A trip to Loltún can be easily combined with a visit to Chacmultún 21 miles away. Try Loltún first, for there is likely to be more ambient light in the morning, especially in the rainy season.

There is no food or drink at the cave. See "Chacmultún" for suggestions on food, and "A Note on Sayil, Xlapak, and Labná" for information on the new Camino Zona Puuc, which provides another route to Loltún.

★★★

# *Chacmultún*

(chahk-mool-*toon*)

DERIVATION: Mayan for "Mounds Made of Red Stone."
CULTURE: Maya.
LOCATION: South-central part of the state of Yucatán, Mexico.

## THE SITE

Chacmultún is a real sleeper. There is some standing architecture in a fair state of repair, with much of its decoration remaining. In addition, there are remnants of polychrome frescoes. The site has been known for some time and is not difficult to reach, yet it attracts few visitors.

It is currently kept cleared by a caretaker. Perhaps it is not equal to, but is nevertheless in a class with, the more popular Sayil and Labná.

There are three groups of structures at Chacmultún, all of which should be seen. As you enter the site, the road passes the first group, a complex of buildings on the right (west). This group is called Chacmultún, the same as the site as a whole. Pass it by for the moment and continue about 200 yards to the end of the road. Facing you is the second group, called Edifice 5 or Cabalpak (meaning something like "Lower Terrace"). This is a multistoried structure, although that fact is not apparent at a glance.

Its lower story has twelve rooms, with some of the corbeled vaults intact. It is divided by a partly ruined but climbable stairway in the center. The stone veneer of the lower walls has mostly fallen or been removed by local inhabitants for their own use, but some of the banded columns on the upper façade remain. You can reach the top of this lower section by the stair or by walking around to the east (left as you face the structure) and climbing over rubble from a collapsed room. On the east side of the large terrace atop the lower structure there is an opening to a chultun.

Walk to the right side (west) and you will see a trail going uphill. As you climb this trail, you will see architectural remains on higher and higher levels. Only then can you appreciate the fact that the structure is multistoried. The first three stories are built on terraces on the side of a natural hill; the fourth story is on top of the hill itself. The upper levels are hidden from view by trees when

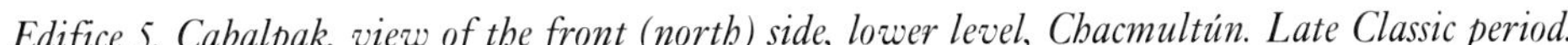

*Edifice 5, Cabalpak, view of the front (north) side, lower level, Chacmultún. Late Classic period.*

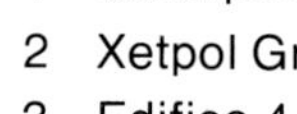

1 Cabalpak
2 Xetpol Group
3 Edifice 4
4 Room with remains of paintings
5 Upper structure
6 Small building
7 Chacmultún Group
8 Edifice 3
9 Room with murals
10 Edifice 1
11 Edifice 2

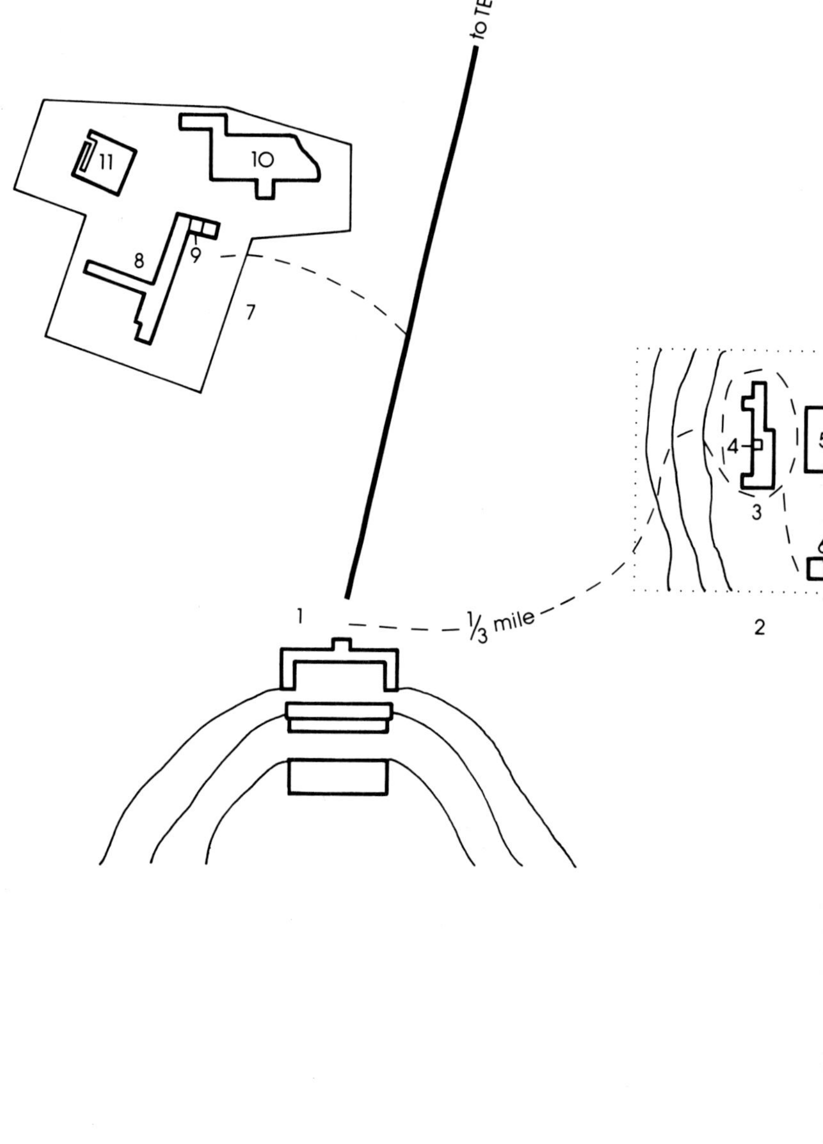


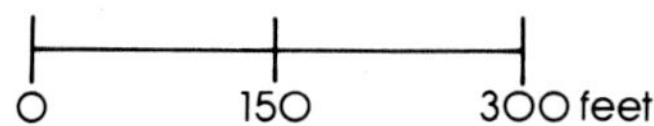


CHACMULTÚN

*Edifice 4, Xetpol Group, Chacmultún. The long central section has remains of projecting rooms at either end. Late Classic period.*

you are standing at ground level or on the terrace above the lower story.

The remains of the other levels are in a more ruinous condition than the first, but are worth a look. There are four ranges of rooms above the first, for a total of five in all. Two ranges are on one level, however, so Edifice 5 is generally called a four-storied building, but sometimes a five-storied one.

There are some intact vaults and in-place stone lintels in the upper stories. Another interesting feature is the crudely carved, foot-shaped stones projecting from the vaults in one of the upper rooms. The soles of the feet face out, and the toes point up. They appear to be too high to function as convenient hooks, and one wonders about their use.

When you return to ground level, look for a foot trail heading east (left as you face Edifice 5) that takes off from the front of the structure.

The trail leads about 0.3 mile to the Xetpol—the third group of Chacmultún. The last part of the trail is up a hill (over 100 feet high), making it a rather tiring, but not too difficult, climb.

At the top of the hill is a long building (Edifice 4) with five doorways in a central section, flanked by two projecting rooms. Most of this structure is remarkably intact. There is an altar or bench in the far left room of the central section of the structure. Even more interesting are fragmented remains of wall paintings, found in the center room, on the rear wall on either side of the doorway that leads to an upper chamber. Little remains except black line-work, but the sure flow of the lines indicates the hand of a master artist. The exterior decoration on Edifice 4 is a simple molding.

You can get to a higher level with more architectural remains by going around either end of Edifice 4. The upper structure is set back from the lower, and the terrace in front of the upper forms the roof over the lower structure. From this terrace you can see the other two groups at Chacmultún below in the distance.

The upper structure is in a ruinous condition, but contains a number of vaulted rooms on a lower floor. The amount of debris above it may indicate the existence of a second story that has collapsed. There are some stone lintels in place in the lower

*Edifice 1, Chacmultún Group, view of the southwest corner, Chacmultún. Note the width of the room seen at the collapsed corner. Late Classic period.*

story and you can walk around part of the back of the structure.

As you face the upper structure, a trail leads off to the right (south) for a short distance to a small, partly ruined building. It is simple in design, but worth a few minutes to visit.

Now return to ground level and your car, where you have an ice chest filled with cold drinks. You will need one.

After a rest, drive back to the Chacmultún Group that you saw when you came in. Across the road from this group are a couple of small mounds, but they have no standing architecture.

The Chacmultún Group has the most extensive architectural remains at the site, consisting of three separate buildings; Edifice 3 on a lower level, and Edifices 1 and 2 on a higher terrace.

Edifice 3 is composed of many rooms, and remains of mural paintings are found in one of them. They are located on the back wall of the second room on your right as you walk up the terrace. The opening to this chamber faces south. The murals

*Edifice 1, Chacmultún Group, detail of the west side with hut-type niche above the doorway, Chacmultún. Late Classic period.*

are in poor condition, but figures in a processional, wearing ritual regalia, can still be discerned. The rooms of Edifice 3 have many intact vaults and are decorated with carved moldings.

Climb now to the upper level of the group. Edifice 1 is a large building with a central stairway, banded columns decorating the upper façade, and columned doorways. Projections in the upper molding are believed by some authorities to have phallic significance.

On the upper west side of the structure is a well-preserved hut-type niche. For this and other reasons, Edifice 1 (as well as Edifice 5) reminds you most of Labná.

The rooms in Edifice 1 are unusually wide, and one of them has six of the projecting foot-shaped stones mentioned earlier in the upper levels of Edifice 5.

The right side of the structure (as you face the stairway) is mostly collapsed, and all over the terrace in front are carved stones that may have fallen from the façade. It must have been a truly outstanding piece of architecture in its heyday.

The fragments of tenoned, three-dimensional sculpture lying around must originally have been incorporated into the decoration.

The other structure on this upper level, Edifice 2, is a most unusual one. Its east face has an inset central stairway, flanked by remains of vaulted rooms—one on each side. This is backed by a large core of a solid mass of rubble. It is theorized that this solid core was meant to support an upper story that was never built. The north and south sides have no openings in the exterior walls, but there is a small opening in the west wall, which enters, makes a 90-degree turn, and extends as a narrow gallery almost the width of the structure. The purpose of the chamber has not been determined; it seems to go nowhere in particular.

## RECENT HISTORY

Teobert Maler described Chacmultún in works published in 1895 and 1902, and he gave the structures such fanciful names as "The Chamber of Justice" for Edifice 2. Edward H. Thompson, working for Peabody Museum of Harvard University, explored and mapped the site in 1899 and did a watercolor copy of the murals. This is fortunate, for when he returned two years later, they had been greatly defaced. He reported his findings in 1904.

There have been no ceramic studies at the site that would indicate its beginnings, but the architecture is in the Puuc style, indicating a Late Classic date.

## CONNECTIONS

1. 44 miles by paved road from Uxmal to Tekax, or
2. 73 miles by paved road from Mérida to Tekax, then 5.5 miles of dirt road to the site.

*Edifice 2, Chacmultún Group, view of the southwest corner with remains of vaults on the east (right) side of the structure, Chacmultún. Late Classic period.*

## GETTING THERE

The best stopovers and points of departure for Chacmultún are Uxmal and Mérida, though Ticul and Tekax are also possibilities.

From Uxmal head north on Highway 261 to Muna. From Mérida take Highway 261 south to Muna. From Muna head east on Highway 184 to Tekax.

About 0.7 mile after you pass the sign for Tekax, you will see a billboard on the right (it may be faded). It indicates the turnoff for Chacmultún and states that it is only 10 minutes away. That is optimistic; plan on about 20 minutes. The road is rutted and rough, though passable for standard cars. Turn right (south) at the billboard and go a long block to a cemetery. Then turn left—the only choice—and go another block or two to a sign for Kancab. Turn right at the sign and go through the village of Canek (unmarked), and on to Kancab, a bit less than 4 miles from Tekax. In Kancab is a pyramid sign, where you make a left turn. The sign indicates that it is 1 kilometer to Chacmultún: it is actually 3 kilometers (2 miles). Just follow the road to the site. The road from Tekax to Chacmultún is not shown on most road maps.

A bus can get you as far as Tekax, where you may be able to get a taxi to take you to Chacmultún.

Bring cold drinks and wear climbing boots. While a guide is not a necessity at Chacmultún, if the caretaker offers to show you around, let him do so. You are likely to see more in a shorter period of time. In 1980 the caretaker was Auturo Canche Atzul, a very pleasant, knowledgeable, and informative gentleman.

Allow 3 hours to see Chacmultún.

I did not suggest bringing food along; you should treat yourself to a lunch of *poc-chuc* when you return to Tekax. This regional specialty is a marinated and grilled pork steak, served with side orders of grilled chopped tomatoes, chili peppers, and pickled onions. It is delicious.

Try any of the better restaurants in Tekax, such as the one in the Hotel Perraza.

★★

# *Xkichmook*

(shkeech-*mook*)

DERIVATION: Mayan for "The Buried Beauty" (see text).
ORIGINAL NAME: Unknown.
CULTURE: Maya.
LOCATION: Southwestern part of the state of Yucatán, Mexico.

## THE SITE

Xkichmook is actually a very good two-star site. There are three or four (depending on how you count them) well-preserved structures, all with interesting decorations.

As you climb to the site from the north, you first come to the rear of the Palace (Edifice 1), a structure of unusual plan, and the largest at Xkichmook.

The main façade of the Palace faces south. In the center is a stairway (now in ruin) from a plaza to a two-room temple on top; the rest of the structure is one story. On either side of the fallen stairway are remains of decorations.

Rooms project from each side of the stairway and, on the west, additional rooms extend south. The corners of the two-story section are decorated with projecting Chac masks reminiscent of those on Structure XX at Chicanná. To get a good view of the masks, climb the rubble covering the stairway and head left (west). The masks on the northwest corner are well preserved. The rooms that extend to the south also face the plaza (with one exception),

*Mask panel on the upper façade of one of the rooms of the Palace (Edifice 1), Xkichmook. Late Classic period.*

*Two well-preserved rooms with medallion decorations in the upper façades, Xkichmook. Late Classic period.*

and the upper façades are highly decorated. There are remains of mask panels and other motifs; the façade of the room farthest right as you face this row is the best preserved. To the southeast of the two-story section of the Palace are two well-preserved rooms that face west onto the same plaza.

In Edward H. Thompson's site plan of Xkichmook, these rooms are numbered consecutively with the rooms of the Palace, but most visitors would consider them part of a separate structure.

The lower façade is plain, and is separated by a three-member molding from the upper façade, which is decorated with circular designs called medallions by Teobert Maler.

You now leave the area of the Palace the way

*Structure with triangular decorations, Xkichmook. Late Classic period.*

you came in and take a trail to the right (east). A short distance away is a small structure, partially ruined, with triangular decorations in the upper façade. The trail continues to another structure decorated with frontal view mask panels in both upper and lower façades.

Although several other structures have been reported at Xkichmook—only the lower portions remain—they are not shown to visitors today and may be in areas that are overgrown.

## RECENT HISTORY

Xkichmook was discovered in 1886 by Edward H. Thompson, who first reported it—under the name Kich Moo—in 1888 in a publication of the American Antiquarian Society.

Thompson returned to the site in 1891 and conducted excavations over a period of several years. His detailed report on Xkichmook was published by the Field Columbian Museum of Chicago in 1898, for whom he was working, with the sponsorship of Allison V. Armour. In this report Thompson says that the natives called the site Xkichmook, although he believed that "it was not the intention of the native namegiver to call it thus, but rather *Xkichmul*, a word formed of *Ichil* (between) and *mul* (hill)—a very suggestive and appropriate name, for the place is surrounded by ranges of high hills." He then explains that, according to the rules of Mayan language, *Ichmul* would be prefixed by an *X* and *k*, forming Xkichmul. Nevertheless, he continued to call it Xkichmook, and this is the generally accepted name today in the literature, although the variations listed above, as well as Xkichmool, Xkichmol, and Kichmool, are sometimes encountered. Locally the site is called Kichmo.

Oddly enough—in view of Thompson's extensive exploration of the site—he did not report two of the structures the visitor sees today; the structure with the triangular decorations and the one with the frontal mask panels in the upper and lower façades.

Maler also visited Xkichmook, and three of his excellent photos were used in *Arquitectura Prehispânica*, by Ignacio Marquina (1951).

In 1979 some clearing of the structures was undertaken. The structures seen today at Xkichmook date to the Late Classic period, and H. E. D. Pollock sees the style of the architecture as "something of a blend of Puuc and Chenes traditions, but basically Puuc."

## CONNECTIONS

1. 45.5 miles by paved road from Uxmal to Xul,
2. 78.5 miles by paved road from Mérida to Xul (via Oxkutzcab), or
3. 93.5 miles by paved road from Mérida to Xul (via Uxmal), then 16.1 miles by fair rock road, 1.9 miles by poor to fair dirt road, and 0.5 mile by foot trail.

## GETTING THERE

From Uxmal head south on Highway 261 to the cutoff for Sayil, Xlapak, and Labná (near kilometer marker 115). Turn left onto this beautiful new Camino Zona Puuc and continue to Cooperativa, about 19 miles east. At Cooperativa turn right and go 10 miles to Xul.

From Mérida take Highway 261 and head south to Muna. Here you have two choices: (1) you can turn left on Highway 184, go to Oxkutzcab, then turn right, and continue to Xul; or (2) you can continue south from Muna to Uxmal and follow the route given above.

When you reach Xul, drive straight through town and pick up the rock road that continues straight ahead (south). This road is rough but passable for standard cars. After 14.1 miles you will reach the small community Benito Juárez (marked with a sign); continue straight ahead for another 2 miles. Then turn right onto an unmarked dirt road and proceed to the Ejido (communal farm) of Xkichmook. There are a couple of bad spots in the dirt road, but it can often be driven in a standard car.

When we visited Xkichmook, we were taken there by Miguel Uc Medina, the caretaker of Sayil. I would recommend going to Sayil first, to see whether he is there and can take you. If you leave from Mérida, this would mean taking the longer route via Uxmal, rather than the shorter route through Oxkutzcab. If Miguel cannot take you, he may be able to reccomend someone else. Other possibilities are (1) checking with the caretaker at Xlapak or Labná or (2) asking around for a guide at Xul.

Although I have given the distance to the dirt cutoff, it would be safer to have someone along to point it out. He would also be likely to know the condition of the dirt road.

Once you reach the Ejido of Xkichmook, whoever you have brought along should secure permission to visit the site. Since the trail to the site is through ejido fields, someone from the ejido will accompany you. I doubt that the people of the ejido would appreciate unknown visitors walking through their fields.

Wear boots, bring insect repellent, and have a wide-angle lens for your camera. Have cold drinks in your car for your return and pack a lunch; there is no food or drink at the site.

Driving time from Uxmal to the Ejido of Xkichmook is about 2¼ hours. If you come from Mérida via Oxkutzcab, add another 45 minutes, or if from Mérida via Uxmal, add 1 hour.

Driving your own vehicle is the only recommended way to reach Xkichmook. Rental cars are available in Mérida. A bus can get you to Xul—and possibly as far as Benito Juárez—but it would be a long hike from there.

The walk to the site from the ejido takes about 10 minutes. Allow an hour for a visit once you reach the site. When you begin your walk, you will be able to see part of the Palace on the south on a hill.

★★

# *Acancéh*

(ah-kahn-*keh*)

CULTURE: Maya; see text.
LOCATION: West-central part of the state of Yucatán, Mexico.

## THE SITE

There are two structures at Acancéh; both are in the town of that name. The first is a pyramid facing an open area near the Main Plaza in the center of town, and the other is the Temple of the Stucco Façade, a couple of blocks away.

The pyramid rises in four tiers, and has an inset central stairway and apron moldings of the typical Petén Maya type. This Early Classic structure has been compared to the famous Late Preclassic pyramid E-VII-sub at Uaxactún. It is faced with roughly cut stones, and must have been plastered originally. Only the side facing the Main Plaza has been restored, and even that is somewhat overgrown with weeds. I recommend climbing the pyramid as there are a couple of pieces of sculpture and carved decorations lying around near the top.

The Temple of the Stucco Façade (Structure 1) is part of a poorly preserved acropolis comprising structures from several periods. There is evidence of a Late Preclassic beginning in this complex, although Structure 1 was built during the Early Classic period. It was then filled with rubble and another structure was built over it. Ceramic evidence also indicates that Acancéh was occupied from the Late Preclassic to the Late Postclassic period.

The most interesting feature of Structure 1 is the well-preserved remains of some carved stucco on the upper portion of the building. Its preservation is due to its being covered over by later construction. This stucco relief depicts humanized and anthropomorphic animals: bats, birds, and a squirrel are represented. Each is surrounded by a terraced border, forming separate panels. Speech scrolls are found with some of the animals and some glyph-like elements are interspersed between the panels.

*Early Classic pyramid on the Main Plaza, Acancéh.*

*Detail of decoration from the Temple of the Stucco Façade, Acancéh. Early Classic period.*

All the decorations are distinctly non-Maya. Current opinion is that they were done in the style of Teotihuacán, and especially relate to the mural painting from that site. These interesting reliefs are really the main reason for a visit to Acancéh. Very few other architectural remains are to be found in the acropolis. The reliefs are protected by a tin roof, which makes photography a bit of a problem, as strong directional light is needed to bring out the design.

## RECENT HISTORY

The reliefs at Acancéh were discovered in the early years of the twentieth century. They were brilliantly colored when first uncovered, as recorded by Adela Breton. No real evidence of color remains today.

The site was visited and reported upon by Eduard Seler in 1911, but most of what we know about Acancéh comes from the work done by E. W. Andrews IV in 1941 and 1942, for the Carnegie Institution of Washington.

## CONNECTIONS

1. 17 miles by paved road from Mérida, or
2. 19 miles by road from Mérida (13 miles paved, 6 miles dirt).

## GETTING THERE

The all-paved route to Acancéh from Mérida leaves the city on Calle 28, heading southeast, and goes through Kanasin and Tepich. It is narrow and curved. The other route leaves Mérida on Highway 180, heading east. Thirteen miles out of Mérida is a well-marked cutoff to the right (south) going to Acancéh. The first route is a few minutes faster.

When you arrive in Acancéh and find the Main Plaza, you will see the stepped pyramid behind a locked gate. To climb the pyramid and visit the Temple of the Stucco Façade (behind another locked gate), you must get keys for the gates or have the caretaker go with you and unlock them.

The caretaker, Anatolio Narvaez Medina, lives in the town of Acancéh at Number 94 on Calle 23; his office and registration book are next door on the left. The office, on a corner, has wooden doors and a small sign saying "Zona Arqueológica."

When you are standing in the open area near the plaza with the pyramid on your left and the covered market straight ahead, Calle 23 will be on your right. If the doors to the office are closed, knock. If there is no response, try knocking at the door to his house.

Acancéh can also be reached by bus or taxi from Mérida. Allow about an hour to see both structures. Tennis shoes are fine. Soft drinks are available in town.

A visit to Acancéh makes an interesting half-day trip out of Mérida when combined with a visit to Mayapán.

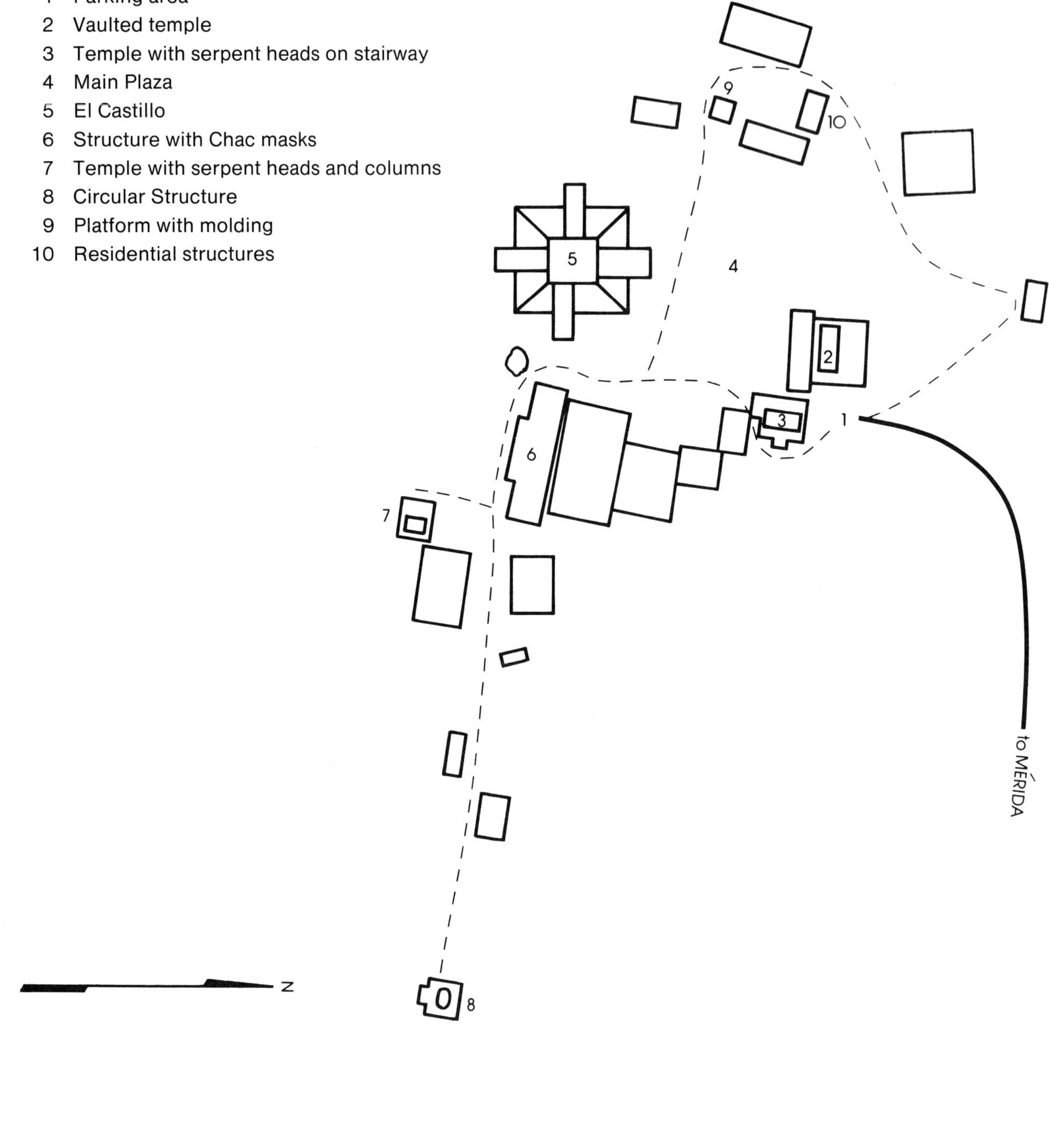
1 Parking area
2 Vaulted temple
3 Temple with serpent heads on stairway
4 Main Plaza
5 El Castillo
6 Structure with Chac masks
7 Temple with serpent heads and columns
8 Circular Structure
9 Platform with molding
10 Residential structures
1
2
3
4
5
6
7
8
9
10
10
to MÉRIDA
N
0
75
150 feet

MAYAPÁN

★★★

# *Mayapán*

(mah-yah-*pahn*)

DERIVATION: Mayan for "Standard of the Maya."
ORIGINAL NAME: Mayapán.
CULTURE: Maya.
LOCATION: West-central part of the state of Yucatán, Mexico.

## THE SITE

Although the Late Postclassic site of Mayapán is often described as a sad imitation of Chichén Itzá, exhibiting poor workmanship and showing a decadence in all the arts, it is, nevertheless, an interesting site to visit. Perhaps I enjoyed it more because I was expecting less.

The part the visitor sees today is only the small ceremonial center that stood in the heart of the city—and Mayapán was a true urban center.

A wall, more than 5 miles long and up to 2 yards high, encircled the city, enclosing an area of 1.6 square miles. Within the confines of the wall some 3,600 structures have been mapped, most of which were residential. Population estimates for Mayapán's heyday vary from 6,000 to 15,000 people, most authorities settling on a figure around 10,000.

Mayapán is in an infertile region of Yucatán, and was supported by tribute from neighboring areas, whose nobles were forced to live as hostages within the city walls, thus insuring payment from their "home towns."

Most of northern Yucatán was under the control of Mayapán from A.D. 1200 or 1250, when it was founded by the tribe of Cocoms, until its looting and destruction around A.D. 1440. The destruction is credited to the rebellion of excessively exploited tribes, led by a member of the rival Tutul Xiu family. The city was burned, and the ruling Cocom and all but one of his sons were slain. The survivor was on a trading expedition to Honduras.

Mayapán was built over or near an earlier city, which served as a quarry for some of the finely cut Puuc-style stone. Perhaps this also accounts for the Chac masks found on one of Mayapán's structures that could almost be a direct import from Kabáh, which flourished several hundred years earlier. The stone elements forming the mask are practically identical to those from the latter site. None of the buildings of the earlier city remain today.

You can see Mayapán without a guide, but having the caretaker or his young son along will ensure that you do not miss any of the interesting features.

When you arrive at the site, the first structure you see on your right is a mound with some remains of a vaulted temple on top, entangled with tree roots that seem to be supporting it. At the base of the mound a sign tacked to a tree proclaims NO SMOKEEN.

A trail leads from the mound to a partly restored temple, a short distance southeast. Its pyramidal base rests in two terraces, and the lower wall and portions of columns remain, but the most interesting feature is a carved serpent head decorating the top of the stairway on the left.

From here the trail leads southwest and enters the Main Plaza. The plaza itself is of interest for the many pieces of sculpture and carved decorative architectural elements lying around. All are worth a look.

Facing the plaza on the south is the stepped pyramid called El Castillo—the largest structure at Mayapán. This pyramid originally had stairways on all four sides and is obviously a copy of the larger and better preserved El Castillo at Chichén Itzá. Its north side, facing the plaza, is the best preserved. There are no remains of a temple on top, nor did it ever support a vaulted structure.

The trail leads along the east side of El Castillo and turns to the left (east), where it immediately passes one of the most interesting buildings at the site. This long, low structure is decorated with Chac masks in purest Puuc tradition. Remains of numerous columns and small altars are other features. Just behind the mask on the southwest corner, is a slab in the exterior wall with an interesting carving of a bird.

The main trail continues east, and soon you come to a cutoff to the right (south) that leads to a small ruined pyramid some yards away. It is worth climbing to see the carved serpent heads and columns, the only remains of a small temple that stood on top.

Return to the main trail. By following it east, you

*El Castillo, northeast corner, Mayapán. Late Postclassic period.*

pass a number of overgrown mounds. A bit farther, at the end of the trail in a clearing, is a circular two-chambered structure on a rectangular base. Access is up the partly restored stairway on the south side. This building was an observatory—one of four reported at Mayapán.

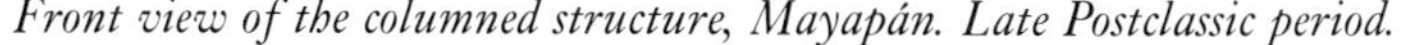

*Front view of the columned structure, Mayapán. Late Postclassic period.*

*Detail of the Chac mask from the front of the columned structure, Mayapán.*

*The two-chambered circular structure and its partly restored base, Mayapán. Late Postclassic period.*

Two other features in this area are a sculptured figure on a base—a few feet to the west of the structure—that you see upon entering the area, and a stela lying at an angle near the base of the east side of the structure. Both are in a poor state of preservation.

From here you return to the Main Plaza facing El Castillo and continue west. The trail leads to a small platform with well-preserved molding, a stairway, and a few remnants of the lower portion of a temple. Many small mounds surround this platform.

Other structures are found a bit farther north, some of which were clearly residential. One of the features of Mayapán is the large number of rather elaborate residences, their proximity to the main ceremonial precincts, and the relative paucity of religious structures. Authorities explain this by saying that by the time Mayapán was built, religion had lost its predominant place in Maya culture; it had become more secular and militaristic, a characteristic of Late Postclassic Maya culture in other areas.

## RECENT HISTORY

Since Mayapán was destroyed only a hundred years before the Spanish conquest, memory of it lingered among the natives. It is mentioned in native documents and was reported upon by Bishop Diego de Landa in 1566, from information he gathered.

Its description and location check with the known facts, but some of the data reported in these early sources cannot be substantiated archaeologically. For instance, it is reported that a Triple Alliance among Uxmal, Chichén Itzá, and Mayapán existed during the period A.D. 987–1185. Archaeological evidence, however, shows that Uxmal was abandoned for the second half of that period and that Mayapán had not yet been founded.

Little note is taken of Mayapán thereafter until John Lloyd Stephens visited the site and reported his findings in 1843. Although the site was mentioned by historians and was known to a few people in the locality, Stephens felt that "ours was the first visit to examine these ruins."

The next visitor of note was Sylvanus Morley, almost a hundred years later, but it was only in the 1950s that investigations were begun. The work was sponsored by the Carnegie Institution of Washington and publications by several prominent archaeologists were issued during the following ten years. These included works by A. Ledyard Smith, Morris Jones, H. E. D. Pollock, Ralph Roys, Tatiana Proskouriakoff, Robert Smith, Karl Ruppert, and Sir J. Eric S. Thompson.

## CONNECTIONS

1. 30 miles by paved road from Mérida, or
2. 32 miles by road from Mérida (26 miles paved, 6 miles dirt).

## GETTING THERE

See "Acancéh" for getting that far; there are two choices. From Acancéh a paved road heads south through the town of Tecoh—where there is an interesting (huge) church and convent—and continues south through Telchaquillo. About 1 mile past this last town, (and 13 miles south of Acancéh), there is a short dirt cutoff to the right (west), which goes to the caretaker's house and which continues a bit farther to the main part of the site of Mayapán.

Mayapán may be reached by taxi from Mérida, and a bus can probably get you as far as Telchaquillo.

There is no food or drink at the site. Tennis shoes are adequate. Best stopover is Mérida.

Allow an hour or a bit more to visit the site.

★★

# *Aké*

(ah-*keh*)

CULTURE: Maya.
LOCATION: North-central part of the state of Yucatán, Mexico.

## THE SITE

Aké is one of those sites that is a real sleeper. It has interesting remains, is easy to reach, and has been long known, but it attracts few visitors.

The principal structure at Aké is a large pyramidal base supporting a platform and remains of thirty-six stone columns. The structure faces a plaza and is approached by a stairway on the south side. The stair was reported by John Lloyd Stephens to be 137 feet wide, and it is made of huge stone blocks more than 4 feet long. These and other blocks used as facing on the substructure have slightly rounded corners. The columns, which range from 14 to 16 feet high and are 4 feet wide, are composed of individual drum-shaped stones with smaller stones filling in the gaps.

Although unrefined, the sheer massiveness of the structure and its gigantic facing stones are quite impressive. Aké is a good two-star site.

From the top of the principal structure you can see a couple of other huge mounds to the southwest, which also border the plaza, and more distant mounds that are covered with vegetation.

The mound immediately southwest of the principal structure is worth a visit, though it is not so well preserved. A foot trail leads to the top, where there is what appears to be a large chultun that can be entered by a modern ladder. There are also remains of a wall and some large stone facing blocks. This is a good vantage point for photographs of the principal structure.

There is evidence of more modern construction abutting the north and east sides of the second structure; perhaps this was added in colonial or more modern times. This construction is decidedly different from the large facing stones used in the original construction.

The plaza area is fenced off with barbed wire and is covered with weeds and young henequen plants. Near the center of the plaza a large white-stone shaft is easily spotted amid the greenery. It could be an uncarved stela, though Désiré Charnay reported it as a *picoté,* or punishment stone, to which an offender was tied before being whipped.

When you leave this area of Aké, return to the modern town plaza. Across from the east side of

*The structure with the columns, the front (south) side, Aké. Early Classic period.*

the plaza and north of the church is a stepped pyramidal base that is apparently part of the ancient site.

The Hacienda of Aké and the town are built right up to the ruins.

## RECENT HISTORY

Stephens and Catherwood visited Aké in 1842—the last ruin they saw on their second trip to Yucatán. Stephens was the first to report the site, and Catherwood did a drawing of the structure with the columns. It appeared then much as it does now, except that the vegetation has since been cleared. Charnay reported upon Aké in his 1885 publication on his explorations of the New World. Although Aké was visited by Augustus Le Plongeon, Sylvanus Morley, and Marshall Saville, among others, no excavation has ever been undertaken.

We do know, however, that there was an ancient *sacbé* connecting Izamal with Aké, and it is possible that it continued on to Tiho (the location of modern Mérida). It is also reported that the columns atop the principal structure never supported a roof.

## CONNECTIONS

1. 23 miles by paved road from Mérida, or
2. 55.5 miles by road from Chichén Itzá (48 miles paved, 7.5 miles fair rock).

## GETTING THERE

Leave Mérida as though you were taking Highway 180 to Chichén Itzá. On the eastern outskirts of the city there is a Pemex station where the road branches. The right branch is Highway 180; the left branch is unnumbered, but is marked for the town of Tixpeual. This is the road to Aké, and it passes through the towns of Tixpeual and Tixkokob along the way; it is the best route from Mérida, though it is not shown on most maps. The paved road ends at the modern town plaza in Aké. At the far end of the plaza, take the dirt road heading right and then left until you come to a gate. You can park here or, if the dirt road looks too bad, you can park on the plaza and walk to the ruins, which are a short distance away. Actually, you will spot the principal structure when you enter the town.

From Chichén Itzá take Highway 180 west to Tamek. The rock road cutoff for Ruinas de Aké is plainly marked and heads north. Before leaving the town of Tamek, the road turns left, and there are *topes* to make sure that you drive slowly (*Topes* are deliberate bumps in the road, but this is the only place I can recall that has them on a rock road). The road then proceeds to Aké. You will reach a paved road as you enter the town, which is the road to Mérida already described. To reach the ruins, turn right on the paved road and head to the plaza.

If you are going to visit Aké while driving between Mérida and Chichén Itzá, use the routes described above. It is much shorter than retracing your steps back to Mérida on the paved road to pick up Highway 180 at the Pemex station. The rock road is not too bad or long.

Allow about 45 minutes to visit Aké. Tennis shoes are fine. Cold drinks are available in the town, but I did not see any likely eating places.

While you are in Aké, you might want a couple of photographs of the old mill (still in operation) that processes henequen. It faces the south side of the modern town plaza.

★

# *Izamal*

(eeh-sah-*mahl*)

DERIVATION: Mayan name for the god Itzamná, "Dew of Heaven."
ORIGINAL NAME: Izamal.
CULTURE: Maya.
LOCATION: North-central part of the state of Yucatán, Mexico.

---

## THE SITE

The Pyramid of Kinich-Kakmo in the town of Izamal is one of the largest in Yucatán. As you drive to the town, you can see it rising from the plain. It is also visible from the Main Plaza in Izamal, and so it *should* be easy to get to. It is not. It is only a couple of blocks west of the center of town, but its base is hidden by modern buildings. Ask directions and then look for an open gate with stone steps leading up. The steps ascend right from the street, and from this level you cannot see the top of the pyramid, so its size is not apparent. When you find the steps, you may still wonder whether you are in the right place. You are. The steps have been restored, and it is an easy—if hot—climb. The pyramid rises in terraces, and part of it is faced with huge stones. Other unrestored areas are grass-covered.

It is rather a surprise when you reach the top of the stairs to discover not only that the flat top of the pyramid is so large but that another pyramid of respectable size rises from it.

This partly restored second pyramid is set over the rear of the first, leaving a large open area in the front. This gives you the feeling that you are at ground level, which is only dispelled when you turn and look at the town below. Only then does the size of the whole structure register.

You are not allowed to climb the second pyramid. It rises in several terraces, has rounded corners, and is faced with small boulders. You may walk around

*Second, or upper, pyramid, Izamal. The area in front is the flat top of the massive first pyramid. Early Classic period.*

it, although the path narrows and gets steep at the rear, probably due to excavation—licit or illicit.

Although there is no remaining sculpture at Izamal, the sheer size of the Kinich-Kakmo makes a visit worthwhile for the ruin buff.

## RECENT HISTORY

Izamal is mentioned in the native chronicles and by Bishop Diego de Landa, who said that there was at Izamal "a building of such height and beauty that it astonishes one."

There were several pyramids at Izamal and in the nearby area. One was partly leveled, and the Franciscan monks built a church and convent over it in 1553. This church, one of the oldest in Mexico, stands today in the center of town. The other pyramids are overgrown, unrestored, and difficult to discern. Some have been torn down to provide building materials.

John Lloyd Stephens and Frederick Catherwood visited the site in 1842, near the end of their second trip to Yucatán, and described and drew an illustration of a large stucco head. This and other stucco decorations that Stephens mentions have since disappeared, but they were not part of the Kinich-Kakmo.

Désiré Charnay also visited Izamal, and in an 1885 French publication he described and illustrated the site. In 1887 an English translation appeared.

Little work has been done at Izamal, but we do know that the pyramids date to the Early Classic period, during which time Izamal was the greatest religious center in northern Yucatán. It retained its importance until it was conquered in the Postclassic period by Hunac Ceel, the founder of Mayapán.

Thereafter Mayapán dominated Izamal in religious matters, though Izamal remained a living city until the conquest of Mayapán in A.D. 1440.

During its heyday Izamal was an important shrine and place of pilgrimage, dedicated to Kinich-Kakmo, a manifestation of Kinich Ahau—the sun god—and of Itzamná. It was connected to Aké by a *sacbé*, which may have continued to Tiho (Mérida).

Izamal was also an important trading center for salt found on the nearby coast.

## CONNECTIONS

1. 45 miles by paved road from Mérida, or
2. 43 miles by paved road from Chichén Itzá.

## GETTING THERE

A visit to Izamal will cost you only 14 extra miles when you are driving between Mérida and Chichén Itzá.

If you leave from Mérida, take Highway 180 east for 30 miles to the town of Hoctun. Then take the paved cutoff to the left (north), and go 15 miles to Izamal.

If you are heading on to Chichén Itzá, you can get back to Highway 180 by taking the alternate route, which connects with the highway at Kantunil. This is shorter. It is not necessary to return to Hoctun. Try bus or taxi if you are without a car.

If you start from Chichén Itzá, you would, of course, do this in reverse.

Best stopovers would be Mérida, Chichén Itzá, or nearby Pisté. There are a couple of small restaurants in Izamal, across the street from the pyramid, providing food and drink. Tennis shoes are adequate. Allow about 30 to 40 minutes for a visit to the pyramid, after you find it.

★★

# *Ikil*

(ee-*keel*)

DERIVATION: Mayan for "Place of the Wind."
ORIGINAL NAME: Unknown.
CULTURE: Maya.
LOCATION: Central part of the state of Yucatán, Mexico.

---

## THE SITE

Ikil is worth a visit only if you plan to make the rather difficult climb to the top of the pyramid. The trail is rubble, dirt, and roots, but there are some small trees that afford a handhold.

Although the site of Ikil has not been mapped, it is known that there are some low platform mounds surrounding the pyramid. The mounds, however, do not support standing architecture, and so the pyramid—or, more precisely, the summit temple atop the pyramid—is the feature of most interest.

The pyramid-summit temple known as Structure I is 80 feet high, one of "the largest architectural monuments of the northern Maya area," according to E. Wyllys Andrews IV, who studied the site. The pyramidal base rises in three stories, and there are stairways on each of the four sides, though none today afford access to the summit temple.

As you climb the rocky trail ascending the pyramid, you pass a portal vault that runs beneath one of the stairways. Later you see remains of another vault that is apparently part of a room. As you near the top, you can see the huge rounded corner stones that are part of the summit temple.

The temple consists of a rubble core surrounded by a vaulted corridor, although the effect today is of two rooms, the east and west chambers. The extreme weight of the core has caused it to subside, with the result that all but one small section of vault has collapsed and the capstone atop this section (in the west chamber) tilts toward the core at an odd angle.

Each of these chambers has a niche built into the core and the niches were originally spanned by glyph-carved stone lintels. In the west chamber, a section of the lintel with five glyph blocks and a fraction of a sixth remains in place; in the east chamber only two glyph blocks remain. Originally each lintel contained ten glyph blocks and the portions in place are well preserved.

To the left of the niche in the east chamber is a large stone ring tenoned into the wall of the core. It is assumed that originally there was another ring to the right of the niche. They perhaps functioned as rod holders or tie-rings for curtains, although the remaining ring seems very massive for such a purpose.

The outer walls of the summit temple were constructed of huge stone blocks, some weighing as much as 3,000 pounds, and remains of these can be seen in both the east and west chambers. According to Andrews, "No such [other] megalithic walls are known from the Maya area," although he notes that similar huge stones are used in substructure facings at Aké and Izamal.

## RECENT HISTORY

Ikil seems first to show up in the literature in Sylvanus Morley's *The Inscriptions of Petén* (1937–38), where it is listed in the appendixes, and in a later work by the same author, although the site is not described in either publication.

Under the name "Iki," the site is shown on a 1940 map, published by Tulane University, but the source of information is not listed.

In 1954 an account of the site and sketches of the glyph blocks that were in place was published by Alberto García Maldonado, a Yucatecan artist, in Mérida's newspaper *Diario del Sureste.* García was first brought to Ikil in 1951 by the Dorantes brothers of a nearby town, and he sent drawings of the glyph blocks to César Lizardi Ramos, a Mexican epigrapher, who identified them as noncalendric glyphs and noted "a number of resemblances to early forms." It was through García that Andrews's attention was brought to the site.

Andrews received permission to search for the missing fragments of the two lintels, and all but two glyph blocks were recovered and recorded in 1956; the two missing ones were assumed to have been pulverized in the collapse of the lintels. The un-

*The east chamber of the summit temple (Structure I), Ikil. Probably early Late Classic period.*

covered fragments were reburied for protection, and shortly afterward were dug up by García, who made and published additional drawings.

In 1966, Andrews, George E. Stuart, and Richard Furno returned to Ikil to gather architectural information. Structure I was almost entirely cleared, and enough data were collected to permit a restoration drawing. Although no extensive excavation was carried out, a small sample of ceramics was collected—mostly from the surface. This work was sponsored by the National Geographic Society and the Middle American Research Institute of Tulane University, and in 1968 the latter published the information.

Some interesting observations were made during this work. There were at least two phases of construction at Ikil. The summit temple and its original three-tiered base were probably built during the early Late Classic period. In later times, rooms were added to the outside of each of the three tiers (six on each side, for a total of twenty-four) and the four stairways were added.

Although mask elements, other decorations, and columned doorways are reported by Andrews and Stuart, they are not discernible today.

There is some evidence that the core of the summit temple once supported a roof comb or some sort of superstructure. If indeed it did, this would have added considerably to the height of the structure.

It is thought that perhaps Ikil was an old shrine whose base was added to during the period of dominance by Chichén Itzá.

## CONNECTIONS

1. 22 miles by paved road from Chichén Itzá, or
2. 64 miles by paved road from Mérida, then about 300 yards by foot trail.

## GETTING THERE

First proceed to the town of Libre Unión on Highway 180. It is 16 miles west of Chichén Itzá and 58 miles east of Mérida. In Libre Unión take the well-marked paved cutoff south toward Yaxcaba. There are small kilometer markers on this road, but they are hard to spot. A little past kilometer 9 is a sign on the left (east) saying San Isidro and a dirt road on the right (west) leading about 300 yards to the small rancho. Ask at the house for someone to show you the way to the pyramid. The residents of the house are familiar with the ruins, but they do not know them by the name of Ikil. When we inquired, we were told that there was no special name for the site.

You will be directed back to the paved road, where you can park on the west side. The foot trail is directly opposite on the east side. The trail soon passes a gate and is easy to follow, but it would be difficult to find the best access route up the pyramid without being shown. For this reason you need a guide.

Once you begin your climb, you will find a machete useful to cut back the vegetation for better photographs. Ikil is not a very visited site and the trail can become overgrown, as is the pyramid. Wear boots and bring insect repellent and definitely a wide-angle lens for your camera.

Allow about an hour to walk to the pyramid, climb it, look around at the summit temple, and return to your car. There is no food or drink here. If you are packing a picnic lunch, however, there is a nearby cenote that would be a pleasant place to eat.

Head north (toward Libre Unión) on the paved road for about 4.5 miles. At this point there is a well-marked rock road to Cenote Xtojil; it goes east for a little over 0.5 mile. Although the area is not very developed, there is a cement stairway leading down to the cenote.

If you are without a car, you can taxi to the rancho from Chichén Itzá, but you will still need a local guide; taxiing from Mérida is possible, but expensive. A bus can get you as far as Libre Unión, but connections from there are questionable.

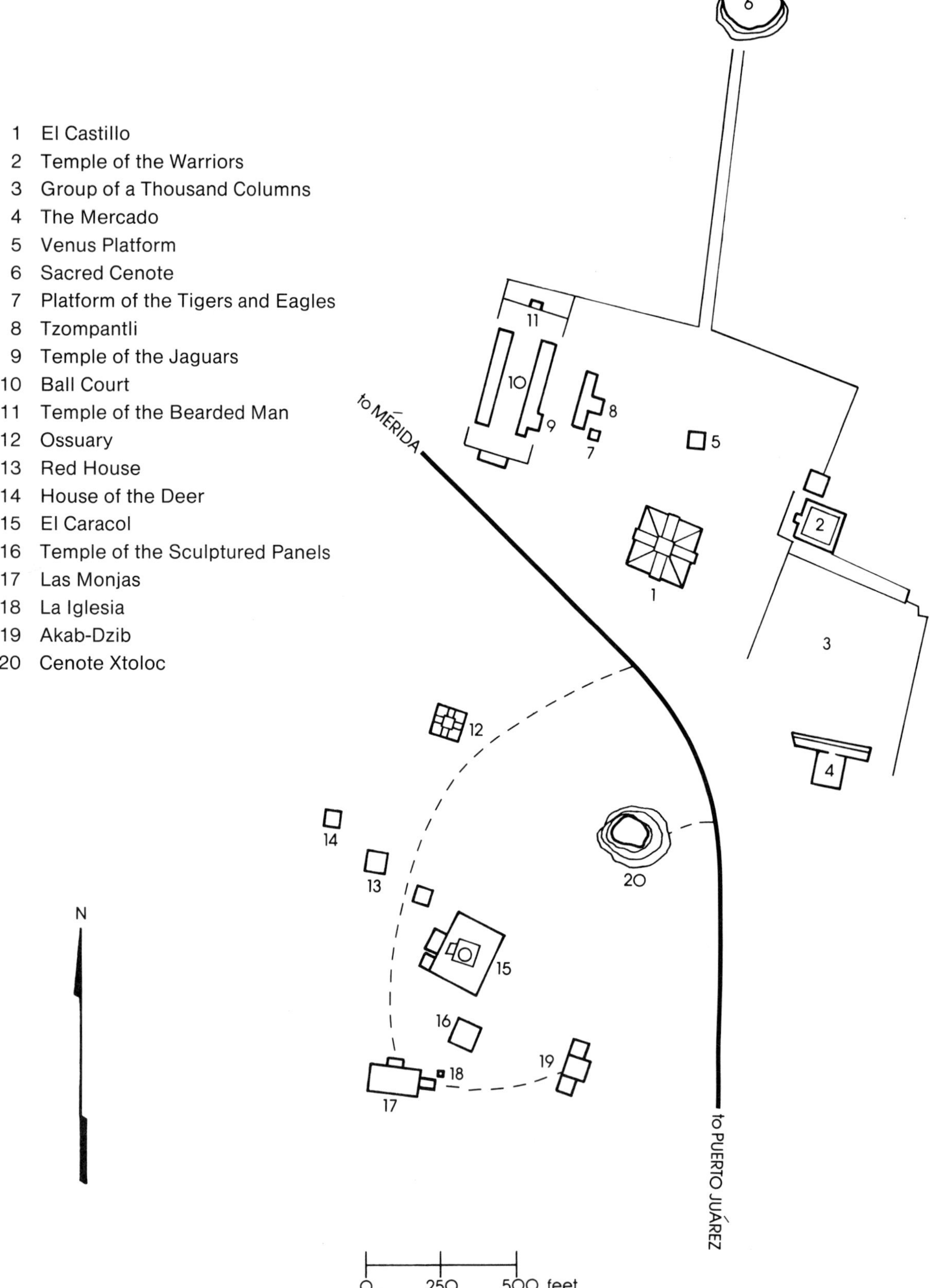


CHICHÉN ITZÁ

★★★★

# *Chichén Itzá*

(chee-*chehn* eet-*sah*)

DERIVATION: Mayan for "The Mouth of the Well of the Itzás."

EARLIER NAME: Uucil-abnal ("Seven Bushes"), according to Michael Coe; Uuc-hab-nal ("Seven Bushy Places"), according to Ralph Roys.

ORIGINAL NAME: Chichén Itzá for the later part of its pre-Columbian history.

CULTURE: Maya and Toltec.

LOCATION: Central part of the state of Yucatán, Mexico.

## THE SITE

Chichén Itzá—one of the most visited sites in Mexico—is noted for its large assemblage of buildings in a reasonably good state of repair. Many have been restored. It is a place of major interest for the ruin buff.

The ruins of Chichén Itzá can be most easily covered by breaking them into three areas; (1) structures north of the highway, (2) those immediately south of the highway, and (3) some outlying groups farther south in the bush, misnamed "Old Chichén." Some maps and guidebooks show area (2) as "Old Chichén" and area (3) as "Old Old Chichén."

As you approach Chichén Itzá from the west, the large structure El Castillo—also called the Temple of Kukulcán—towers above the vegetation and is visible from some distance away. It is north of the highway and is centrally located in a large open area called the North Terrace, or the Central Plaza. El Castillo is a square-based, stepped pyramid about 75 feet tall, crowned by a temple. It originally had stairways on all four sides, and two of these have been restored.

The visible structure covers a smaller, earlier one (of similar plan), and some interesting sculpture is found on the inside of the latter. An inner stair was discovered during excavation, and through it the inner structure can be visited. The entrance is at the base of the north side of El Castillo, but the inner temple can be visited only during certain hours. Check as you enter the site as the schedule

*El Castillo, the north side, Chichén Itzá. Early Postclassic period.*

is subject to change. Also, check on the open hours for the interior structure of the Temple of the Warriors and the painted chamber of the Temple of the Jaguars. The open hours of the three spots do not overlap; you can probably work all three into your schedule if you plan ahead.

One word about the interior of El Castillo; the steep stair leading up is very narrow, and it is generally hot, steamy, and jammed with people inside. If you are the least bit claustrophobic, you had better pass this up.

If you do go, you will see a Chac Mool and a throne in the shape of a jaguar at the top of the stair. Unfortunately, they are protected by bars, which interfere with picture taking. If you want some photos anyway, bring a flash unit and a wide-angle lens (for the Chac Mool just beyond the bars), and a normal or slightly long lens for the Jaguar Throne some feet behind. The jaguar is painted red, and has jade incrustations depicting the jaguar's spots and representing the eyeballs. A turquoise mosaic disc was found on the seat of the throne.

Climbing the exterior of El Castillo is much more pleasant and affords delightful views of the north section of the site. It is a good spot for photos of the Temple of the Warriors. This latter temple lies west of El Castillo and also exhibits two construction stages. The earlier inner temple has pillars sculptured in bas-relief, which retain much of their original color, and murals once adorned its walls. There are also a Chac Mool and the heads of serpent columns inside.

The Temple of the Warriors is worth a bit of time to see the sculptured serpent and warrior columns, mosaic and carved façade decorations, the Chac Mool, and the small Atlantean figures that support an altar at the rear of the temple. All these traits are typically Toltec, except the Chac masks on the outside wall.

A large courtyard, adjacent to the south of the Temple of the Warriors, is surrounded by numerous ruined buildings known collectively as the Group of a Thousand Columns. The many columns were originally roofed over, forming a colonade part way around the courtyard. The one structure of special note in this area is the Mercado, or Market, on the south side of the courtyard, built on a slightly elevated platform. There is an interesting carved altar

*The Temple of the Warriors, from the southwest, Chichén Itzá. Early Postclassic period.*

*Serpent columns on top of the Temple of the Warriors, Chichén Itzá. Early Postclassic period.*

in this area and a square patio surrounded by tall columns with simple capitals. The perimeter of the patio was probably roofed with thatch; no stones that could belong to a roof have been found. Other structures in the Group of a Thousand Columns are unrestored, but include two ball courts and a sweat bath.

From here head north to the Venus Platform.

This square platform has a stair on each of its four sides, and may have been used as a dance platform. It is decorated with bas-relief sculpture and three-dimensional serpent heads.

Due north of the Venus Platform you come to a Maya road than continues north 300 yards to the Sacred Cenote. Although the cenote is a natural formation, it may have been altered by man to achieve its nearly circular shapc. It is about 180 feet in diameter and its sides rise 80 feet above the water level. The Sacred Cenote was apparently not used as a water supply, but was reserved for rituals and human sacrifice involving the rain god. The notion that the sacrificed victims were all beautiful young virgins was disproved when human remains of young children and older adults, both male and female, were discovered. The Sacred Cenote is in a depression and the surrounding dense vegetation cuts off most of the air. On a still day, the heavy atmosphere and buzzing insects can create a hypnotic effect, and one can easily imagine this as a place of human sacrifice. It makes you want to get back to the open-air feeling of the Central Plaza. There are remains of a small temple on the edge of the cenote.

When you return, head west (right) and visit another dance platform, the Platform of the Tigers and Eagles. This is similar to the Venus Platform, but smaller, and its decorative motifs of tigers and eagles holding human hearts in their claws are almost identical to some bas-reliefs at Tula. A Chac Mool was excavated from this platform in the late nineteenth century.

North of the Platform of the Tigers and Eagles is the Skull Rack, or Tzompantli. The sides are covered with bas-reliefs; some depict skulls in profile, except for the corners, where they are shown full face. Oddly enough, each is different from the other and has its own personality. Other reliefs show warriors in full regalia. Two Chac Mools were excavated from the platform.

Now head west to the ball court, the largest in Mesoamerica—its walls measure 272 feet long. The playing area extends some distance beyond. There are interesting bas-relief carvings on the lower walls of the ball court depicting ball game activities and ritual sacrifice. A small temple lies at each end of the ball court, and from in front of the north temple (the Temple of the Bearded Man) a person speaking in a natural voice reportedly can be heard at the other end of the court about 150 yards away.

The Temple of the Bearded Man gets its name from some bas-relief carvings on the inside of the temple. There are two columns at the entrance to the one-room temple, and these, the interior walls, and the remaining portion of the vault are completely covered with bas-reliefs. In the vault there are some remains of red paint, and this emphasizes

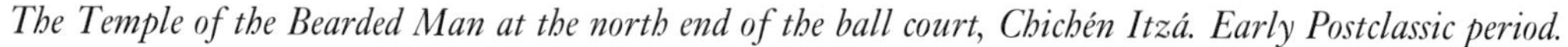

*The Temple of the Bearded Man at the north end of the ball court, Chichén Itzá. Early Postclassic period.*

*The Temple of the Jaguar and the ball court, from the southeast, Chichén Itzá. Early Postclassic period.*

the carvings. The larger temple at the south end of the ball court also has remains of columns with carvings, but the walls and vault surfaces are plain.

Even more interesting is the Temple of the Jaguars on top of the south end of the east wall of the ball court, and reached by a steep stair. The roof of the temple is supported by carved serpent columns similar to those at the Temple of the Warriors, and in an inner chamber there are a few fragments of murals that can be seen during the hours when this room is open. Unfortunately, the murals are poorly lighted and are hard to make out. A carved wooden lintel spans the doorway to the inner room. From this level you can walk along the top of the east wall of the ball court for a closer look at the stone ring set high in the wall.

When you return to the plaza level, you can enter a chamber below the Temple of the Jaguars that faces east. It has polychromed bas-reliefs on pillars, walls, and vault in a good state of preservation and a simple three-dimensional sculpture of a jaguar, possibly a throne.

After a visit to this northern section of Chichén Itzá it is time for a lunch break before you continue to the southern section.

The first structure that you come to on the south side of the highway is the Ossuary, or Grave of the High Priest, west (right) of the trail. One of the later constructions in the area, the grave is dated to the Toltec period architecturally. Although mostly ruined, it is similar in design to El Castillo, though

*Carved pillar in the chamber below the Temple of the Jaguar, Chichén Itzá. A crying rain deity and aquatic animals are depicted. Early Postclassic period.*

*The Chichán-Chob, or Red House, the front (west) side, Chichén Itzá. Late Classic period.*

*El Caracol from the south, Chichén Itzá. The structure shows both Classic Maya and Toltec traits. El Castillo rises in the background at left of center.*

built on a smaller scale. There are remains of serpent columns on top, pillars carved with human figures, and the temple walls. Near the outside base of the Ossuary are some carved-stone panels that are worth a look.

Follow the trail south to the Red House, or Chichán-Chob, on the west (right). This small temple is built on a platform with rounded corners and is reached by a stairway on the west side. A simple molding, a perforated central roof comb, and a flying façade with Chac masks form the exterior decorations. The walls are plain above and below the molding, giving a feeling of sober restraint. The Red House (so called because of a red strip painted on a wall) dates to the Maya Classic period and shows no Toltec traits. Its other name, Chichán-Chob, is Mayan and probably means something like "small holes," referring to the latticework in the roof comb. A band of glyphs is found on the vault of the interior of the structure.

Northwest of the Red House, and off the main foot trail, is the House of the Deer, named for the depiction of a deer on a mural that once existed in one of the rooms. The style of the House of the Deer is similar to the Red House, and it belongs to the same period.

Follow the main trail south to El Caracol, which lies on the left (east). This is one of the most imposing structures in this area and is worth some time to visit. *Caracol* means "snail" in Spanish and, by extension, "spiral," referring to the stairway found inside the structure. El Caracol probably served as an observatory, and it is the only round structure found at Chichén Itzá. It is now believed that this is the earliest structure that shows Toltec traits at Chichén Itzá, but Classic Maya features are also evident, especially in the Chac masks used as exterior decorations. It is believed that Toltec influence reached Chichén Itzá before the site was actually occupied by that group. The upper terrace of El Caracol has some three-dimensional sculpture of human heads. This is a good place for photographs of some of the other buildings.

Due south of El Caracol is the Temple of the Sculptured Panels. The panels are on the north and south exterior walls of the lower portion of the buildings and are in Toltec style, as is the architecture. A rocky path leads up to the temple from the south side. This is a good vantage point for photographs of El Caracol and other structures.

A short distance southwest of the Temple of the Sculptured Panels are two of the most interesting buildings in the area. The largest is Las Monjas, or the Nunnery, with its annex; it is 210 feet long, 105 feet wide, and more than 50 feet high. This structure saw several building stages leading to its present impressive size. The architecture and sculptured decorations are typically Classic Maya. There is much interesting detail here, especially in the form of Chac masks. A doorway in the east face of the annex forms the open mouth of a monster, a feature associated with the Chenes style, although the rest of the structure is Puuc style. The upper level of Las Monjas has some carved lintels still in place.

Near the annex of Las Monjas is the diminutive La Iglesia, the Church. The lower walls are plain, but the upper façade and roof comb are a riot of Chac masks, many complete with curling snout. These are accompanied by the stepped fret pattern

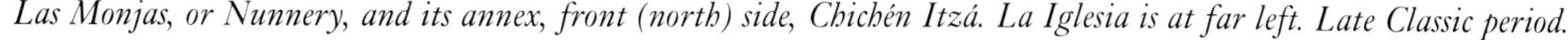

*Las Monjas, or Nunnery, and its annex, front (north) side, Chichén Itzá. La Iglesia is at far left. Late Classic period.*

*La Iglesia, the front (west) side, Chichén Itzá. Late Classic period.*

and other interesting designs. Both La Iglesia and Las Monjas are worth some detail photographs as well as over-all views.

About 100 yards east by foot trail is the Akab-Dzib (Obscure Writing), named for some undeciphered hieroglyphs appearing on a lintel. This Classic Maya structure was built in at least two stages. The central portion was constructed first, and the flanking north and south wings were added later. It is undecorated except for simple cornices and moldings.

The only other feature in this section of Chichén Itzá is the Cenote Xtoloc, which reportedly has the remains of a small temple on its rim. This area is very overgrown. I never did see the temple. The easiest way to reach the cenote is from the highway. Use the entrance to the Mayaland Lodge as a reference point. From there proceed along the highway toward the archaeological zone for about 50 feet. On the left side of the highway is a narrow trail that leads directly to the cenote, which is only 2 minutes away on foot. When you reach the cenote, you will see a side trail that branches down to the water level; the main trail goes on and later comes to the rear of the platform that supports El Caracol.

The cenote itself is really not too attractive; there are remnants of plastic foam ice chests and other debris floating in the water. If you skip it, you will not have missed too much.

The third section of Chichén Itzá is "Old Chichén," which actually dates to the same time period as the rest of the site, having both Classic Maya and Toltec remains. The structures are scattered in the bush, but are connected by trails, which begin south of Hacienda Chichén (now a hotel). This entails a hot steamy hike into the bush, but some of the structures are worth the effort.

It is best to have a guide along to see "Old Chichén." Some of the trails are easy to follow, but there are a few branches—not all of which are marked—and the very beginning of the trail is sometimes hard to find because of overgrown conditions. Check at the ticket office at the north part of the site or at the Mayaland Lodge to secure a guide. Bring along a canteen of water.

The Date Group is the most important and interesting in "Old Chichén." The names come from a Classic Maya lintel with an Initial Series date of

*The Akab-Dzib, the front (west) side, Chichén Itzá. Late Classic period.*

A.D. 879. It is the only Initial Series date known from Chichén Itzá, and the lintel was reused in a later Toltec construction. It is found spanning the top of two Atlantean figures, of typical Toltec style, which form the doorway of a small temple; only the lower walls of the temple remain. A small Chac Mool is found at the base of the mound that supports the temple.

A bit south is the Temple of the Phalli. The architecture is Classic Maya, but the phallic sculptures were a later Toltec addition. Behind this are remains of several structures, Atlantean figures, and carved columns. A short distance northwest is an enclosure with more Atlantean figures, and a bit farther on, a crude sculpture of a serpent. Just west of the Temple of the Phalli is another structure called Telecotes, with remains of carved columns depicting owls and other motifs. The trail to the next area of interest leaves from the Telecotes and heads southwest.

You come first to the Temple of Four Lintels. Little remains of this structure, except for the four carved lintels and the upright stones that support them. The lintels are carved on some of their edges and on the undersides. The glyphs on the edges of the two lintels that face north are especially well preserved and are very photogenic. Try to do this trip in the morning when they receive the best light.

A short distance southwest is the Temple of the Three Lintels, the only restored structure in "Old Chichén," and a gem. It is a typical Puuc structure, faced with the thin veneer masonry associated with the style. Although other structures at Chichén Itzá are also in Puuc style, they generally lack this particular feature. Chac masks decorate the upper façade and are interspersed with engaged columns and a lattice pattern; the lower walls are plain. Two of the lintels are carved on their front surfaces. The whole has a feeling of quiet dignity.

Another structure in this area, called the Temple of the Lintel, is reportedly totally overgrown and not worth visiting. This seems also to be true of other structures in more distant areas of "Old Chichén," including the Temple of the Sculptured Jambs and the Temple of the Hieroglyphic Jambs.

From the Temple of the Three Lintels, you retrace your steps part of the way before taking a side trail to the left. This brings you to two structures that are kept reasonably well cleared. The one you reach first is mostly a rubble mound, but it is worth climbing to see the remains of carved rectangular columns on top. A bit southwest is the Castillo of "Old Chichén." It is also mostly rubble, but there are remains of carved facing stones on the west side, a stairway on the north side, and carved columns and jambs on top. The structure dates to the

*Atlantean figure in the Date Group, Chichén Itzá. Early Postclassic period.*

*Detail of the Temple of Four Lintels showing the two lintels facing north, Chichén Itzá. Late Classic period.*

*The Temple of Three Lintels, Chichén Itzá. Late Classic period.*

Toltec period at Chichén Itzá, and from the top of it Las Monjas and El Castillo of "new" Chichén are visible (northeast, in the distance). There is a serpent head near the base of the Castillo of "Old Chichén" that presumably was part of the original construction.

From there you return to Hacienda Chichén.

We were told that many years ago a mule-drawn cart, which operated on narrow-gauge railroad tracks, was used to transport visitors from the hacienda to "Old Chichén," and the tracks are still visible in many spots along the foot trail. The story is that on one excursion the mule became startled and bolted, overturning the cart and seriously injuring a couple of passengers, after which the trip was discontinued. The cart can still be seen near the main building at the hacienda.

After you finish your hike, and if you are staying at one of the hotels near the site, you will be ready not only for some cold liquid refreshment but also for a swim.

Ceramic evidence indicates that Chichén Itzá was occupied from the Late Preclassic into the Late Postclassic period. Much of the rest of the history of the site is wrapped in legend.

Some native chronicles state that a group called the Itzás founded Chichén Itzá around A.D. 435–455, occupying it for 200 years. There seems to be little to substantiate these early dates for the Itzás, however. It is probable that the Itzás (Putun Mayas) occupied (the chronicles say "reoccupied") the site around A.D. 918 and that the famous Kukulcán with his Toltec followers (plus perhaps another and more Mexicanized group of Putun Mayas) arrived around 987.

Kukulcán is Mayan for "Feathered Serpent," a direct translation of the Nahuatl (Mexican) "Quetzalcóatl." This deity of central Mexico dates back to the Preclassic period, but one of his priests, Ce Acatl Topiltzin, took the name Quetzalcóatl in the tenth century.

Legend says that at one point this later Quetzalcóatl left his capital in Tula and moved southwest with his followers, eventually arriving in Yucatán. There are many variations in the legend, and the chronology also varies. Nevertheless, it is possible that this central Mexican culture hero (or one of his immediate followers) did get to Yucatán and introduce the cult of the deity Quetzalcóatl, with the name changed to the Mayan version. Chichén Itzá was probably abandoned some time in the thirteenth century (although some authorities prefer a date two centuries later), but it remained a place of pilgrimage.

About all that can be said with any certainty is that during the Late Classic period Chichén Itzá was already a rather typical Maya ceremonial center. Later it was occupied by Toltecs from central Mexico, who exerted great influence in the area, especially in architecture and religion. Toltec influence in Yucatán, however, arrived before the occupation of Chichén Itzá by that group, and is evident in El Caracol and in certain motifs found at Uxmal and Kabáh. These last sites were abandoned by (or at) the time that Chichén Itzá was occupied by the Toltecs.

It is the earlier Maya group that probably called the site Uucil-abnal (or Uuc-hab-nal) and the later arrivals who called it Chichén Itzá. Although the Toltecs and the Itzás are considered separate groups, they apparently arrived about the same time. Sir J. Eric S. Thompson considered the Itzás a group of Putun (Chontal Maya) people from the Gulf Coast area, who had relations with Mexican groups living nearby and who had, therefore, already picked up some Mexican traits.

## RECENT HISTORY

The existence of Chichén Itzá was never lost to man's knowledge. Although it was unoccupied at the time of the Spanish conquest, its location was known to the local inhabitants, who still considered it a holy place.

For a time Francisco de Montejo, the conqueror of Yucatán, established himself at Chichén Itzá, but the hostility of the natives forced him to leave. Bishop Diego de Landa wrote of Chichén Itzá in 1566 as a "very fine site." He gave its location and related the history of the place as given to him by local informants. Another Spanish cleric, Diego López de Cogolludo, mentions the site in his 1688 publication *Historia de Yucatán.* The books of Chilam Balam (native chronicles written in the Mayan language, but using the Spanish alphabet) record the history of Chichén Itzá. These early documents plus Landa's work are the principal sources of historical information about the site. Unfortunately, the chronology of the native documents is confused and bathed in legend, and it is difficult to put the pieces together accurately.

In more modern times, John Lloyd Stephens and Frederick Catherwood explored the site, but Stephens credited the first visit by a "stranger" to a certain John Burke of New York, who was working as an engineer in Valladolid. Stephens also mentioned a visit to Chichén Itzá by Baron Friederichsthal in 1840. Stephens said that the baron was the first to bring notice of the site to the public. A much wider audience, however, read Stephens's 1843 publication.

In Stephens's time, the road from Mérida to Valladolid passed through the ruins much as the modern highway does today, and he commented that, "The great buildings tower on both sides of the road in full sight of all passers-by, and from the fact that the road is much traveled, the ruins of Chichén are perhaps more generally known to the people of the country than any other in Yucatán."

He and Catherwood spent some time at the site, and recorded it in text and drawings. Catherwood also produced a map, but for some reason it does not extend far enough north to include the Sacred Cenote, although Cenote Xtoloc, which they used for bathing, is included.

In 1863 Désiré Charnay and E. E. Viollet-le-Duc published a work in Paris, *Cités et Ruines Américaines*, and in 1885 Charnay published another work. Both publications include information on Chichén Itzá.

In 1873 the mysterious Augustus Le Plongeon first visited Yucatán. He and his young wife spent seven years there, three months of which they devoted to the investigation of Chichén Itzá. He drew up plans, copied murals, and photographed the site, but his contribution is perhaps lessened by the fantastic theories he proposed.

Alfred P. Maudslay briefly visited Chichén Itzá in 1889. During his stay he surveyed, measured, and photographed the site. He had as his assistant Edward H. Thompson, the American counsul in Yucatán, who later returned to the site after buying Hacienda Chichén Itzá with funds provided by Allison V. Armour, a patron of scientific research. Thompson rebuilt the ruined hacienda and moved his wife and children there from Mérida, intending it to be a profitable enterprise as well as to serve as a home near the ruins. For thirty years he lived at Chichén Itzá and carried out investigations. Some of his reports remain unpublished, although others have found their way into print. His best-known popular account is the autobiographical *People of the Serpent: Life and Adventures among the Maya*, a book published in 1932.

Thompson is best known for dredging the Sacred Cenote, where he recovered artifacts of copper, gold, jade, clay, and human bones. Some of these items were given to visiting friends to take back to the Peabody Museum of Harvard University, for whom Thompson was working. The Mexican government learned of this traffic and attached Thompson's hacienda. In 1958 many of these items in the Peabody's collection were returned to Mexico.

Thompson spent his remaining years a poor man back in the United States, but he had proved his point—that the Sacred Cenote was indeed a place of human sacrifice, as legend said.

After Thompson's work, professional archaeologists took over research at Chichén Itzá. Sylvanus Morley first visited Chichén Itzá in 1907, as a guest of Thompson, and returned to do extensive work for the Carnegie Institution of Washington and the Mexican government. He began his work in 1924 and continued for two decades. In 1926, Sir J. Eric S. Thompson joined the field staff. In 1961 the Sacred Cenote was again dredged. This time a modern air pump was used, and divers explored its depths. About 4,000 artifacts were recovered in four months' work. The project was undertaken by Mexico's National Institute of Anthropology and History (INAH) in cooperation with the National Geographic Society and the Exploration and Water Sports Club of Mexico (CEDAM). The site is maintained by INAH.

## CONNECTION

1. 74 miles by paved road from Mérida.

## GETTING THERE

From Mérida take Highway 180 east to Chichén Itzá. The site straddles the highway and can be easily reached by taxi, bus, or on guided tours from Mérida, as well as by private car.

There are good hotels near the site and in Pisté a couple of miles west. If you are heading to the east coast, another stopover is Valladolid, 25 miles east.

Cold drinks and packaged snacks are sold at roadside stands on the highway. Lunch can be purchased at one of the nearby hotels or in Pisté (La Fiesta restaurant in Pisté serves good regional food, and their beer is ice cold).

Bring a sun hat and, if you plan to visit "Old Chichén," wear a long-sleeved shirt and slacks. Tennis shoes are adequate. Bring insect repellent, a lot of film, and the INAH guidebook to the site.

A guide is not necessary for the two parts of the site immediately adjacent to the highway. If you prefer to have a guide, you can bring one with you from Mérida or hire one at the entrance to the site on the north side of the highway. Allow 2 full days if you want to see the site properly, including "Old Chichén," which takes a tiring 3 hours in itself.

★★

# *Balankanche (Cave)*

(bah-lahn-kahn-*cheh*)

DERIVATION: Mayan for "Throne of the Jaguar Priest" or "Hidden Treasure of the Jaguar."
CULTURE: Maya-Toltec.
LOCATION: Central part of the state of Yucatán, Mexico.

---

## THE SITE AND RECENT HISTORY

The caves of Balankanche have been known for hundreds of years, but in 1959 José Humberto Gómez, a tourist guide, discovered a sealed section at the end of one of the chambers. He opened it and followed a long passage to a circular cavern. In the center of the cavern was a huge stalagmite resembling a tree trunk with small stalactites forming the "leaves." Around the base of the stalagmite he discovered a treasure trove of pottery, jewelry, and carved artifacts. These items remain in place today, and can be seen by the visitor. Many date to the Toltec period of Chichén Itzá. In a nearby area of the cave is a group of miniature metates with their accompanying manos, and farther on is an underground cenote.

## CONNECTIONS

1. 3 miles by paved road from Chichén Itzá, or
2. 77 miles by paved road from Mérida, then 0.3 mile of dirt road to the entrance.

## GETTING THERE

From Chichén Itzá or Mérida take Highway 180 east. The cutoff for the Balankanche Cave is marked and heads north (left).

A sign at the cutoff says that tours of the cave are conducted at 8:00, 9:00, 10:00, and 11:00 A.M. and at 2:00, 3:00, and 4:00 P.M., but do not count on getting in at those exact hours. Tours are conducted only if there are at least three visitors, or you can pay extra to make up the difference. They will take in no more than fifteen people at one time. Even if you arrive early but are number sixteen, you will have to wait until the next tour. It also seems that the tours leave ahead of time when they become fully booked.

Get there 30 minutes beforehand, buy your ticket, and wait under the thatch shelter—and hope you aren't number sixteen. Soft drinks are available at the ticket office.

The caves are adequately lighted, but the descent at the entrance can be extremely slippery in wet weather, and at these times boots would be better than tennis shoes. There are also some low overhangs in spots. You are rushed through at a frantic pace; the entire tour lasts only half an hour, which is not enough time to photograph the artifacts properly. Do bring a flash unit for your camera and a flashlight to read the dials. You may get a chance for a few photos.

For accommodations and food see "Chichén Itzá."

# *The Cobá-Yaxuná Sacbé*

(koh-*bah* yah-shoo-*nah*)

CULTURE: Maya.
LOCATION: East-central part of the state of Yucatán, Mexico.

## THE SITE

Many Maya *sacbeob* have been traced, and a good deal has been written about them, but they are seldom discernible today. This is perhaps the best place to see one.

The Cobá–Yaxuná Sacbé is not terribly impressive visually. You see only a clearing in the trees with weeds on top, but if you stop for a look, you will realize that the *sacbé* is actually a raised roadway made of rough limestone boulders. See "Cobá" for more details.

A modern, recently paved road crosses the *sacbé* at right angles and the junction is marked by a sign saying Mirador Camino Maya (if you are heading south) and simply Mirador (if you are heading north).

## CONNECTION

1. 13.5 miles by paved road from Valladolid.

## GETTING THERE

If you are traveling Highway 295 between Valladolid and Felipe Carrillo Puerto, you will cross the *sacbé* south of Valladolid; you may want to stop for a couple of minutes. Otherwise, it really is not worth the detour of 27 miles from Valladolid and back just to see it.

The *sacbé* is a little over a mile south of the town of Tixcacalcupul. There are no accommodations, food, or drink at the Mirador. Tennis shoes are adequate unless you want to walk along the *sacbé;* if so, wear boots.

## MEXICO

### Campeche

*Mask panel in place at Río Bec B, on the back or west side of the south tower, at the top of the "false" temple. Late Classic period.*

★★★

# *Museum of Archaeology (Campeche Museum, Campeche City)*

In order to see the entire collection of the Campeche Museum, it is necessary to visit two places. First is the courtyard in front of a seventeenth-century fort that faces the Main Plaza of the city. The large monuments displayed here are carved stelae, columns, and figures, some mounted on pedestals or against the walls of the structure. They come from various remote sites in the state such as Xcocha and Calakmul, and are very impressive; some are labeled. Outside the fence of the courtyard, in a sometimes dry fountain, are more sculptured monuments. Under the arches of the fort, lying on the ground, are additional fragmented stelae, many from Itzimté. These and the ones in the fountain are not labeled, but are well worth a look. The interior of the fort now houses an arms museum, which is also worth a look while you are there.

The second place to visit is about 2.5 miles away. On August 7, 1978, the official "new" Campeche Museum was opened in Fort San Miguel, on a hill on the outskirts of the city. Several rooms of the fort are used for interesting displays. The collection includes ceramics, diagrams, photo displays, and, in the last room you visit, the small sculpture once exhibited inside the fort in town. Several of the pieces are from Xcalumkin, the most interesting of which is a carved door jamb.

Fort San Miguel, with its drawbridge and cannons, is worth a visit in its own right. From the top of the fort there are delightful views of the fishing boats in the bay and the city in the distance.

To reach Fort San Miguel, leave Campeche on Highway 180–261, heading southwest. The hill and fort are visible to your left as you are leaving town. The turnoff is at a sign indicating a scenic road. The traffic flow is one way, both up to the fort and on the way down.

There is a book shop at the fort, and a few publications are also sold at the museum in town.

I have combined these two places under one heading since together they make up one collection that for many years was housed under one roof, so to speak. If I were rating them separately, they would each be 2 stars; together they are a rather impressive 3 stars. Most of the important sculptured pieces have never been published in the popular literature.

Allow half an hour to see the monuments in town and an hour to see Fort San Miguel and the collection it houses.

*Carved column with glyph-carved capital from the Glyphic Band Building at Xcocha in northern Campeche, Campeche Museum. Late Classic period.*

★★★

# *Etzna*
# *(Edzna)*

(ehts-*nah*, eds-*nah*)

DERIVATION: Mayan for "House of the Grimace (or Visage)."
ORIGINAL NAME: Unknown.
CULTURE: Maya.
LOCATION: North-central part of the state of Campeche, Mexico.

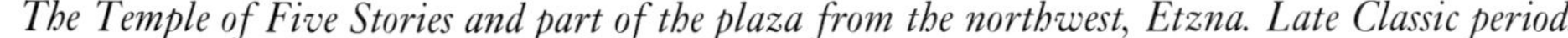

## THE SITE

It is really a shame, but Etzna is a bit of a stepchild. This lovely site is often overlooked in favor of the sites that cluster near Uxmal (Kabáh, Sayil, and Labná), yet Etzna is easy to reach if you are driving.

After you park and enter the archaeological zone, you walk past some interesting carved stelae. These are under thatch shelters near the caretaker's house—and are definitely worth a look and some photos. A path continues past a small platform topped by the lower part of a temple with columns in the doorway. From here you can see the broad stairway that leads up to a large plaza, surrounded by some restored architectural remains, forming the Main Acropolis. Pass this up for the moment and follow the path past the stairway to some carved stelae fragments in the bush, a few hundred feet away. You definitely need insect repellent in this area, but the stelae are worth it, even though some are eroded and lying in weeds.

Then return to the Main Acropolis. When you climb the stairway, you come face to face with the most interesting structure at Etzna, the beautiful Temple of Five Stories, or Templo Mayor, with a height of 100 feet to the top of its roof comb, and 126 feet above general ground level.

The first four stories are composed of rooms flanking the central stairway, and the fifth story is the temple with a roof comb. On the first and fourth stories, the doorways are supported by columns; the steps at the plaza level are carved with some interesting glyphs.

The whole feeling of the structure is one of restraint. Simple moldings form the most prominent decorative feature, although projecting stones may indicate that stucco figures once adorned the façade. This is especially true of the perforated roof comb, which was both literally and figuratively the crowning glory of the structure. The temple faces west, so the afternoon is the best time to photograph it.

Access is up the front stairway, the left side of which has been recently restored. The Temple of Five Stories covers an earlier Petén-style pyramid-temple. From the top of the temple you have a gor-

*The Temple of Five Stories and part of the plaza from the northwest, Etzna. Late Classic period.*

*The Temple of Five Stories from the southwest, Etzna. Late Classic period.*

geous view of the other recently restored structures surrounding the plaza and of some overgrown mounds beyond. Etzna must have been an impressive site in its heyday.

It is worth climbing the other structures for a visit and for good views of the Temple of Five Stories. One long building on a sizable stepped pyramidal base is especially interesting. It borders the south side of the plaza and, when first restored, was fitted with a thatch roof, presumably like its original roof. The thatch is now gone, but perhaps a new roof will be added in the future.

Of the carved stelae found at Etzna, five are dated with some certainty to the period from A.D. 672 to 810, although the site's beginnings were much earlier.

Ceramic evidence indicates that Etzna began as a small agricultural hamlet during the late Middle Preclassic period (600–300 B.C.). At this time the ceramics were related to those of the Petén, as they were in the Late Preclassic. During the Early Classic period the architecture at Etzna was influenced by the architectural style of the Petén, and the site became a city of considerable importance.

Most of the structures seen at Etzna today were built in the Late Classic Period, sometimes over earlier construction, and the style of the architecture was influenced by the style of Central Yucatán (Río Bec-Chenes), and, some authorities believe, also the Puuc. The site continued to be occupied until around the beginning of the Postclassic period.

## RECENT HISTORY

The name Etzna was given the site by scholar Nazario Quintana Bello in 1927, although its existence had been known for many years to people living in the area. In 1928 Frederico Mariscal published some drawings and plans of Etzna; later, Sylvanus Morley and Enrique Juan Palacios deciphered some of the dates on the stelae.

Mexican historian Héctor Pérez Martínez changed the name of the site from Etzna to Edzna because there is no word "etz" in the Mayan language, but both spellings are found in the literature today.

The first extensive exploration of the site was undertaken by Alberto Ruz Lhuillier and Raúl Pavón Abreu in 1943. They determined the extension of

*Recently restored structure on the south side of the Main Plaza of the Acropolis, Etzna. The thatch roof has since been removed. Late Classic period.*

the principal ceremonial center and the characteristics of the Temple of Five Stories, and the information was published by Ruz Lhuillier in 1945. Pavón Abreu conducted further work in 1958 and 1962, and the Temple of Five Stories was partly restored. In 1968 a survey of the main area and some peripheral areas was made by the University of Oregon, and it was reported by George F. Andrews in 1969. In 1970 additional excavation and restoration was undertaken by Pavón Abreu and others for the National Institute of Anthropology and History (INAH) and in 1972 the New World Archaeological Foundation investigated a long canal that extends south from the ceremonial center. INAH sponsored additional work at Etzna at the end of 1975 and the beginning of 1976.

## CONNECTIONS

1. 41 miles by paved road from Campeche,
2. 92 miles by paved road from Uxmal, or
3. 140 miles by paved road from Mérida.

## GETTING THERE

From Campeche take Highway 261 east for 29 miles. Take the cutoff (well marked) to the right (south) for 12 miles to the site. The cutoff is near the kilometer 14 marker.

From Uxmal or Mérida take Highway 261 south for 80 or 128 miles respectively, to the cutoff.

Private car is the only recommended way of getting to Etzna. A bus can drop you off at the cutoff, but I do not know that any run to the site.

There are no accommodations, food, or drink at the site. Bring cold drinks along. Tennis shoes are adequate. Allow 2 hours for a visit. A guide is not necessary.

*Note:* In the mid-1970s another access route to Etzna was completed, although it is useful only if you plan to bypass Campeche.

This bypass joins Highway 180-261 10 miles north of Champoton and 30 miles south of Campeche, near the community of Haltunchén. The cutoff is well marked, heads east, and is paved all the way. It is 35 miles from the junction to Etzna. From Etzna you can then use the 12 miles of road already mentioned to connect to Highway 261, heading to Uxmal. Of course, you will do this in reverse if you are heading south.

★

# *Tohcok* *(Tohkok)*

(toh-*kohk*)

ORIGINAL NAME: Unknown.
CULTURE: Maya.
LOCATION: North-central part of the state of Campeche, Mexico.

## THE SITE

Tohcok is just a few feet off Highway 261, from which it is easily visible. It is not a spectacular site, but one structure has been cleared. If you are driving past, it is worth half an hour to visit.

The cleared structure has remains of vaulted rooms and columned doorways. An extension goes into the bush at a right angle to the road, and more vaulted rooms are visible from the collapsed tops. The extension then seems to turn again and parallel the road.

## RECENT HISTORY

Tohcok is shown on a 1940 map, published by Tulane University. According to H. E. D. Pollock, the site is incorrectly placed north of Hopelchén, rather than west, on this map.

Edwin Shook and Tatiana Proskouriakoff, in a 1951 work published by the Carnegie Institution of Washington, described Tohcok as having architecture that is "of neither the distinctive Chenes nor the Puuc style; it appears rather to be a blend of the two." In any case, the remains are Late Classic.

Tohcok is mentioned in Florencia Muller's atlas

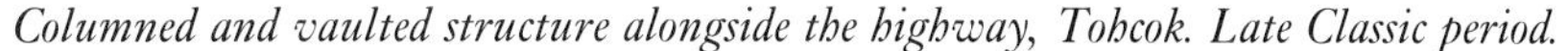

*Columned and vaulted structure alongside the highway, Tohcok. Late Classic period.*

of Campeche (1960), and is shown on a National Geographic archaeological map (1968). It is also shown on a map published by Pollock (1970). Apparently the structure near the highway was cleared in the late 1960s or early 1970s.

## CONNECTION

1. 52 miles by paved road from Campeche.

## GETTING THERE

From Campeche take Highway 261 east to the site; if you start from Uxmal or Mérida, take the same highway south and then west at Hopelchén.

The best check is that the site is 3 kilometers (a little less than 2 miles) west of the west edge of Hopelchén and is on the north side of the highway. The highway apparently cuts through the site.

The best stopovers are Campeche, Uxmal, and Mérida. There is no food or drink at the site. Tennis shoes are fine unless you want to explore the overgrown sections that run off into the bush. In this case, boots would be better.

Buses pass the site and can drop you off, or you can get a taxi in Hopelchén. Tohcok can be easily combined with a visit to Etzna, Hochob, or Dzibilnocac if you are driving.

★

# *Itzimté*

# *(Itzimté-Bolonchén)*

(eet-seem-*teh*)

DERIVATION: Mayan name for a plant used to flavor *posole*, a beverage of ground maize and water).
ORIGINAL NAME: Unknown.
CULTURE: Maya.
LOCATION: Northern part of the state of Campeche, Mexico.

---

## THE SITE

Itzimté is a fairly large site, but unfortunately most of its structures are in a very ruinous condition. This is partly due to removal of the cut-stone facings (by people living in the area) that has been going on for over a century. Nevertheless, there are three spots that are worth a look.

You first climb to Structure 1, a large building that bounds the south side of a raised plaza. This structure originally rose in three levels and had stairways on both the north and south sides. It is noteworthy for a well-preserved room with an intact vault under the north stairway. Northeast of Structure 1 is Structure 4, only one wall of which is standing. Just below the spring line of the vault are remnants of a painted band of hieroglyphs.

From here you climb back down to the road and proceed east, where another uphill trail will get you to Structure 63. This structure, which faces west, is the largest at the site and the tallest, with a maximum height of 71 feet. The front of the structure is formed of artificial terraces, while the back is part of a natural hill. A stairway (in ruin) leads up the west side to a platform that supports a row of ten rooms (mostly collapsed), and above this, in the center, is a pyramidal base that supports the remains of the topmost structure.

Many other structures have been mapped at Itzimté, and as you wander around, you will see the remains of some of them looming above the surrounding fields.

There is a dispirited air about the site because of its near destruction, and it would take a very fertile imagination to picture it in its prime.

## RECENT HISTORY

In 1842, John Lloyd Stephens visited Itzimté and was the first person to record the site. His brief description is found in his 1843 publication, *Incidents of Travel in Yucatán.* At the time of his visit many cut stones had already been removed from the structures, and even though the site had been cleared so that he could study it, he commented, "it was melancholy that when so much had been done for us, there was so little for us to do." The site is not illustrated in his text.

Toebert Maler visited Itzimté in March, 1887. He reported his findings and included one photograph in a 1902 publication. Unfortunately, the structure that he showed, with a well-preserved Chac mask above the doorway, has since collapsed.

Although mention of the site was made in some later publications, it was only in 1973 that the existence of inscribed stelae and a lintel was ascertained. These are beautifully recorded and presented by Eric von Euw in the *Corpus of Maya Hieroglyphic Inscriptions.* They are now in the Campeche Museum.

Von Euw calls the site Itzimté-Bolonchén to distinguish it from a site in Guatemala called Itsimté, which also has inscribed monuments. The latter is generally spelled with an "s," however, and is sometimes called Itsimté-Sacluk.

Although there has been no extensive work at the site, H. E. D. Pollock considers Itzimté "essentially a Puuc city" on the basis of its architecture, which would date the visible remains to the Late Classic period.

## CONNECTIONS

1. 32 miles by paved road from Uxmal,
2. 77 miles by paved road from Campeche, or
3. 80 miles by paved road from Mérida, then 0.2 mile by dirt road, and a few hundred feet by foot trail.

## GETTING THERE

From Uxmal or Mérida take Highway 261 south, or from Campeche take the same highway east, and then north to the cutoff. The cutoff is 1.5 miles north of the center of Bolonchén and 0.5 mile north of the kilometer 90 marker, and it heads east.

There is a wide place where you can park before continuing on foot. From the time you leave on foot until you return to your car, allow about 1¾ hours.

It is best to have a guide to visit Itzimté. First try contacting Pedro Pacheco Dzul, *hijo* ("son"—Jr.), in Bolonchén. If you are unable to find him, or if he is unable to take you, ask around the town for someone else.

As you drive through Bolonchén, you will pass the Main Plaza. Behind it is a row of connecting houses that extends beyond the plaza in either direction. Only two of these houses have thatch roofs; Pedro's is the thatched-roof house farthest on the left as you face the plaza, and it is the larger of the two. If you cannot spot it, ask for Pedro, and someone will direct you to his house. If he is not there, check at the Grutas (Caves) of Xtacumbixunán, 1.7 miles south of Bolonchén on Highway 261, and 0.6 mile west of the highway by a good rock road. The road to the cave is marked, and the cave itself is interesting.

If you find Pedro early in the morning, he will be able to take you to Itzimté and two other sites (Yaxché-Xlapak and Xcavil de Yaxché), both north of Itzimté, in one day. If you wish to see all three sites, allow 6 hours from the time you leave Bolonchén with Pedro until you return him there. That includes the driving and walking time and a visit to each site.

The trip from Uxmal to Bolonchén is about 45 minutes each way, which would make it 7½ hours, a rather full day, considering the heat and distances to be walked, so Uxmal is the best stopover in the area.

Driving time from Campeche or Mérida to Bolonchén is about 1¾ hours each way, so if you use one of these cities as your base, it makes it a long 9½ hours.

For all three sites you should wear boots, carry insect repellent, and have fast film and a wide-angle lens for your camera. Have cold drinks along in your car and pack a lunch. Carry matches and newspaper in case Pedro needs them to get rid of wasps.

See "Yaxché-Xlapak" and "Xcavil de Yaxché" for additional information pertaining to those sites.

★★

# *Hochob*

(hoh-*chohb*)

DERIVATION: Mayan for "Place Where Ears of Maize Are Stored," according to Teobert Maler.
CULTURE: Maya.
LOCATION: East-central part of the state of Campeche, Mexico.

## THE SITE

Hochob is one of the best preserved and most studied of all the Chenes-style sites. Although it is relatively small, the distinctive architectural remains make a visit very worthwhile for the ruin buff.

Several structures are arranged around a plaza, and together they occupy most of a low natural plateau that dominates the surrounding plain. Of prime interest is the Principal Palace (Structure 2), which bounds the plaza on the north. This building is composed of a central section and two lateral wings, each containing one vaulted room. Much of the west wing has collapsed, as has the eastern part of the east wing, but the central section is mostly intact.

The entire façade of the central section (south or main face) is decorated with an incredibly intricate mask of an open-mouthed dragon or serpent—typical of Chenes sites. The design was constructed of stone and stucco, and there are a few remnants of red paint in the eyes of the serpent. A roof comb, or flying façade with perforations, rises above the front façade and originally supported stucco figures. Little of this remains today. Some interesting graffiti have been reported from inside the central room of Structure 2, but we were unable to find them, and our guide knew nothing of them.

The lower wall of the main façade of the east wing is plain, while the upper portion is decorated with the serpent-mask motif similar to that on the central portion. Originally wooden lintels spanned the tops of the doorways of all three rooms.

There is a fair-sized hole in the back wall of the central room, which served as our access to the structure and the whole site. It is reached after a short but steep climb up the north side of the structure, which is formed in part by the natural plateau.

Some question exists concerning the sequence of construction of Structure 2. It may be that the

*The Principal Palace (Structure 2), the front (south) side of the central section, Hochob. Late Classic period.*

central room was built first, then the lateral wings, and then the walls and fill that join them together, although it is possible that the three rooms were constructed simultaneously and then joined together. Although authorities agree that there was a sequence of construction, archaeologist H. E. D. Pollock believes that they were only phases in the work, and that the structure was conceived as a unified whole.

Bounding the plaza on the east is Structure 1, similar to Structure 2, but in a more ruinous state and heavily overgrown.

Another noteworthy building is Structure 5—located a short distance southeast of Structure 2. It rises on a steep pyramidal base, which is now mostly rubble. The temple is almost square in plan, and contains two small rooms and a central perforated roof comb. The lower façade is plain, but there are stone tenons in the upper façade and in the cornice molding, which originally supported stucco decorations. The design of Structure 5 is sober when compared to the heavily decorated Structure 2.

A little west of Structure 5 is Structure 6, seemingly similar, but in a more ruinous condition. It is worth climbing, however, for photographs of Structures 2 and 5.

## RECENT HISTORY

The first scientific report on Hochob was published in 1895, in German, by Teobert Maler although he had discovered the site some eight years earlier. He explored Hochob and produced photographs, a site plan, and elevations of Structures 2 and 5. He also recorded the graffiti in Structure 2. Other German works were published by Eduard Seler in 1916 and by Karin Hissink in 1934. The last was a study of masks in the Yucatán Peninsula in which Hochob was included. The site is also mentioned in a 1945 report by Alberto Ruz Lhuillier, and in a 1956 publication by Ricardo de Robina, both published in Mexico.

The first important English-language report on the site was that of H. E. D. Pollock in 1970. He had visited Hochob and other Chenes sites on a reconnaissance mission for the Carnegie Institution of Washington in 1936.

*Structure 5, view from below showing projecting stone tenons, Hochob. Late Classic period.*

Practically all of the work at Hochob has been exploratory and descriptive. Little (if any) excavation has been attempted, and no restoration or even consolidation has been undertaken. Nevertheless, we know that the visible remains at Hochob date to the Late Classic period.

## CONNECTIONS

1. 80 miles by paved road from Campeche, or
2. 80 miles by paved road from Uxmal, then 4.7 miles by very poor dirt road, and about 1 mile by foot trail.

## GETTING THERE

Hochob is best reached from Campeche or Uxmal, although using Mérida as a base adds only 48 miles of paved road or about an hour of driving time (each way). All three places have good accommodations.

First proceed to Hopelchén on Highway 261 (east of Campeche and south of Uxmal). Here you head south to Dzibalchén. Driving time from Campeche or Uxmal to Dzibalchén is about 2 hours.

Here the fun begins. I will relate our experience in getting to Hochob, which will give you the information you need to do the same. We arrived in Dzibalchén in a rented Volkswagen Beetle at exactly 11:11 A.M. and drove once around the plaza. On this circuit we asked a man where we might find the comandante (we had been advised to find this man—the *jefe político*, or political head of the town—by the caretaker at Etzna). The comandante's office in the Municipal Palace—facing the plaza, of course—was pointed out to us, and we proceeded there. We asked some men sitting outside and were told that the comandante was not in his office but was coming. Sure enough, he showed up a few minutes later. I never was sure whether he was due to arrive anyway or did so because we were there. Foreign visitors are rather a rarity in Dzibalchén.

He invited us into his office. I explained that we were eager to visit Hochob. A few pleasantries were exchanged. I asked whether there was someone with a truck *(camioneta)* who could take us. He verified what I already knew—that we could not make it in a Volkswagen. I explained that we would like to go "Now." A few more pleasantries ensued. He asked (jokingly, I hoped) if I spoke Mayan. I laughed and told him "only three words." He laughed, I asked again—hoping that I wasn't being rude by my persistence—if he could find us a guide with a truck. I got the drift that he would try. We left the office and he indicated that we should wait for him outside.

He went off, and Jerry and I donned our heavy socks and boots in preparation, feeling hopeful about the trip. The populace looked on with mild amusement.

A while later the comandante returned to his office, and I followed him in. I asked whether he had had any luck and was most disappointed to learn that the road was so bad that even trucks could not get in. I was not about to be deterred that easily. I asked whether we could get there on foot—I knew that the distance was about 8 kilometers (5 miles). He said yes but indicated that it would be a long trip and we probably wouldn't get back until 5:30 P.M. or so, even if we left right away. I said that was fine and asked whether he could find us a guide.

We left his office. He talked to a man outside, and between them they concluded that they might be able to get a *muchacho* to take us. Since we learned long before that little boys make excellent guides, we said that that would be *fantástico.*

The two men walked to a house a block and a half away while we parked our car in the shade of a tree on the plaza, as they indicated we should. We followed them to the house and were introduced to Mario Ansenio Uc Santos, a young man of about fifteen—a bit older than the *muchacho* guides we generally ran into. We thanked the men for their assistance while Mario got his machete.

At 11:50 A.M. we took off on foot for Hochob, exactly 39 minutes after we first drove into Dzibalchén. As you can see, it is possible to show up somewhere and make arrangements on the spot.

Mario estimated the walk would take 1 hour; with us along it took 2. The road was muddy—I understood why trucks could not make it. When we neared Hochob, we left the road for a foot trail that passed through a milpa just behind the site and then made a steep climb over rubble and tangled vegetation to the back of Structure 2. A view of the Chenes mask on the other side made it all worthwhile.

The whole site is very overgrown, and Mario made good use of his machete in clearing the vegetation so we could take photos. We spent 1½ hours at the site, which included a few minutes to rest and have some crackers and canned tuna. We also carried bottled water. That is essential—even if it means that you have to leave one of your cameras behind (don't, however, load yourself down with an ice chest).

A squall came through while we were at the

site, bringing temporary relief from the heat, but increasing the humidity (if that was possible). The added wetness made getting around in the bush a bit more difficult and slowed down travel on the way back.

All in all it took us 5½ hours to walk in, see Hochob, and return to Dzibalchén. The commandante's estimate was right on the button. It was good to get back to some cold drinks.

Do not try to do this one in tennis shoes. Even if you are able to drive in, there is still the 20 minutes of foot trail and the overgrown condition of the site itself. Boots are definitely necessary.

In a nutshell, a visit to Hochob can be an exhausting trip, but for the ruin buff who is in decent physical condition, the visual rewards will be adequate payment for the effort. He will also be one of the few people to have seen the site. Mario estimated that there are only about seven visitors a year.

*Note:* Four years after our first trip to Hochob, we returned to Dzibalchén in a van with four-wheel drive, again in the rainy season. Within a few minutes we located Mario—even though he had moved a few blocks away—and drove to Hochob. Although the condition of the road was a little better than on our previous trip, it was still bad enough to require four-wheel drive, and, at one point, a winch. The driving time from Dzibalchén to the stopping place for the site took a bit over 1 hour.

Another possibility for reaching Hochob is to check with travel agents in Campeche. A few of their guides know how to reach the site, and if you can get one with a high clearance vehicle, you may be able to drive in if it has not been too wet. Obviously, your chances would be better in the dry season. If your guide does not know the route from Dzibalchén to Hochob, you could ask around for Mario, or get someone else from Dzibalchén to accompany you.

★★

# *Dzibilnocac*

(tseeb-eel-noh-*ahk*)

DERIVATION: Mayan for "Painted Vault."
*Note:* The spelling and derivation given above are those used in the literature. The pronunciation, however, is that used in the area, where the second-to-last *c* is not pronounced. When the name is spelled the way it is pronounced locally (Dzibilnohac), the meaning changes to "Large Turtle That Writes" or "Large Turtle With Writing on It."

ORIGINAL NAME: Unknown.

CULTURE: Maya.

LOCATION: East-central part of the state of Campeche, Mexico.

## THE SITE

Although Dzibilnocac is a large site, there is really only one structure of interest, even for the enthusiast. But that one—or at least a part of it—is superb. Dzibilnocac is also the easiest to reach of all the Chenes sites.

The Temple-Palace (Structure A1) is the structure that concerns us here. The building is roughly 225 feet long, by 65 feet wide, and consists of a double range of vaulted rooms surmounted by three towers with small temples, one in the center and one on each end. The central temple may have been a bit larger than the other two originally, but

*The Temple-Palace (Structure A1), the eastern temple, west face, Dzibilnocac. Late Classic period.*

it is mostly collapsed. The western temple is in a ruinous state, but the eastern temple, especially its east and west façades, is well preserved. Some authorities believe that the lower structure was built first, and the towers and temples added later.

The eastern temple contains two small rooms (as did the other two temples originally) and all four façades bear relief sculpture of the open-serpent-mouth type made from stone and stucco. The east and west façades have false doorways, while the north and south faces supported the real doorways that gave access to the back-to-back rooms. The real doorways have now fallen.

You can walk around the north, east, and south sides of the eastern tower and temple at ground level, and climb over rubble for a closer look at the west façade. Below the temple proper, on the west, is more relief sculpture, some bearing traces of original paint. There are also remains of serpent masks projecting from three of the four corners of the eastern temple. Those on the southwest corner have fallen.

Most of the lower range of rooms is not accessible, as rubble covers the entrances, but there is one opening to a vaulted room on the east side of the collapsed central temple.

Other remains at Dzibilnocac include seven major pyramids (overgrown) and numerous minor ones, as well as structures of collapsed architecture. The proximity of the town of Iturbide has resulted in extensive damage to the site.

## RECENT HISTORY

John Lloyd Stephens and Frederick Catherwood visited Dzibilnocac on their second trip to Yucatán. Catherwood did a drawing of Structure A1, which shows the remains of the three towers, but no details of the relief sculpture. They had heard of the site on an earlier visit to the village of Nophat and made note of it for future reference. They explored the other ruined mounds and Stephens commented that, "Beyond [Structure A1] were towering mounds and vestiges, indicating the existence of a greater city than any we had yet encountered."

Teobert Maler visited the site, and his photograph and notes were used by Eduard Seler—who also visited there—in a 1916 publication. Further mention of the site was made by Hissink, Ruz, Robina, and Pollock. See "Hochob" for dates of their publications.

In 1949, Karl Ruppert and George W. Brainerd, sponsored by the Carnegie Institution of Washington, visited the site. Brainerd collected ceramic samples, but Brainerd died, and the ceramics were never studied. A map of the site was produced, however.

The New World Archaeological Foundation (NWAF) of Brigham Young University became interested in the area and sponsored work at Dzibilnocac from 1968 through 1970. The site was remapped and proved to be larger than originally thought. Many test pits were dug to study the

*The Temple-Palace (Structure A1), the eastern temple, southeast corner, showing collapsed south face and interior vault, Dzibilnocac. Late Classic period.*

ceramics, and six eroded stelae were discovered. These finds were reported by Fred Nelson, Jr., in a 1973 publication by the NWAF. This work shows that Dzibilnocac was occupied at the end of the Middle Preclassic period and that the population grew in the Late Preclassic period. At the end of the Late Preclassic, the population declined drastically, and there is scant evidence for occupancy during the Early Classic. Again in the Late Classic, there is evidence for a large population and the structures visible at the site today date to this period, although in some cases these cover Late Preclassic construction. The site was abandoned around A.D. 950–1000.

Since no thorough architectural excavations have been undertaken, a great deal is yet to be learned about Dzibilnocac.

### CONNECTION

1. See "Hochob" for getting to Dzibalchén, then 12 miles of good rock road from Dzibalchén northeast to Iturbide, and a few blocks of poor dirt and rock road.

### GETTING THERE

*Note:* In 1978 the rock road to Iturbide had recently had its surface graded and plans were under way to pave it.

Dzibilnocac is on the eastern outskirts of Iturbide. As you near the town, ask for Pablo Canche Dzul, the genial *guardián* of Dzibilnocac. Canche's house is on the left side of the road, about 2 blocks before you reach the Main Plaza. He will be happy to take you to the site. If you cannot find him, drive on to the plaza and ask for someone to show you the way. The road to the site takes off from the northeast corner of the plaza (diagonally from the way you entered it), and heads east for a few bumpy blocks. There are a couple of other branch roads that connect with it, and you should have someone along to point out the way. You can park a few feet away from Structure A1.

When you return to the plaza, take a look at the structure on the east side. The pyramidal base is pre-Columbian, although the stair and guardhouse on top are modern additions. Part of Iturbide overlies the ancient site.

There are no accommodations at Iturbide, but soft drinks are available. See "Hochob" for the best nearby accommodations. Boots are recommended, and you may need insect repellent.

Allow 1 hour to visit the site and 30 minutes for the drive from Dzibalchén to Iturbide (or a bit less if the road has been paved by the time you get there).

---

## *A Note on Southern Campeche and Quintana Roo*

Southern Campeche and Quintana Roo were very isolated areas until 1972, when Highway 186 was paved. This highway crosses the states of Campeche and Quintana Roo at the base of the Yucatán Peninsula, and the kilometer markers run from Escárcega, Campeche (on the west), to Chetumal, Quintana Roo (on the east), for a total of 276 kilometers (171 miles). Although the area is still virtually unknown to most visitors, you can drive there in comfort, and the rewards are great.

The village of Xphuil lies roughly midway along the highway (driving time is 1½ hours from Chetumal and 2 hours from Escárcega) and is the only gas stop between the two cities.

Ten sites in the region are rated in the text, and nine of them form a cluster within a 22-mile radius of the village of Xpuhil. The tenth, Kohunlich, is 44 miles by paved road from Xpuhil. This is really fertile territory for the ruin buff.

Since this area is touristically undeveloped, there is one small problem—there are no hotels closer than Chetumal or Escárcega. Since the area is gradually becoming developed, perhaps some sort of facility will be built in the coming years. It is sorely needed.

There is a small guest house in the lumber town of Zoh Laguna, but when we tried to get a room there, we were told that it was only available to employees of the lumber company. Perhaps you could get a room if they are really empty, but I must stress that you cannot count on this. Zoh Laguna is 6 miles north of the village of Xpuhil by a fair rock road.

If you wish to see all the sites covered in the text, plan to sleep in your vehicle. Between the village of Xpuhil and the ruins of Xpuhil, there are a couple of cleared areas alongside the highway that were used as rock quarries when the highway was built. They are safe and suitable for an overnight stop. It is assumed you will be driving your own or a rental car. Cars can be rented in Chetumal, Campeche, and Mérida.

At the village of Xpuhil there is El Oasis restaurant. It serves simple but fairly decent food. It is across the highway from the Pemex station.

If sleeping in your car does not appeal to you, you can still enjoy the area and see the four most interesting sites in one day by traveling from Escárcega to Chetumal. Chicanná, Becan, and Xpuhil are each less than 0.5 mile by good rock road off the highway, and Kohunlich is 6 miles by paved road off the highway. Admittedly, this would be a long and strenuous day. A guide is not necessary to reach these four sites.

Reaching the other sites requires longer travel over roads that range from fair rock to very bad dirt, or walking varying distances, generally through the bush. Nevertheless, Manos Rojas and Puerto Rico are not difficult to reach. Visiting Culucbalom is more of a problem because of the condition and length of the trail, and reaching Payán entails a long, hot walk.

A visit to Río Bec B or Hormiguero is best undertaken only by adventurous souls. Your best bet for reaching these sites would be to go in the dry season, although sometimes a Volkswagen can make it in the rainy season if it has not been too wet and if the big lumber trucks have not churned up the roads. If it has been wet, the trips should not be attempted unless your vehicle has four-wheel drive and a winch. You will need both.

Whatever time of year you visit Río Bec B or Hormiguero, and in whatever kind of vehicle, be prepared for a rough trip. It will be long and bumpy, and sometimes you will find your car sliding along muddy ruts.

On the way to Río Bec B, you will also drive through tunnels of vegetation so dense that at times you will scarcely be able to see the road. On both trips you will also encounter trees lying across the road that will have to be cut back in order to get through—unless someone else has recently been through and removed them.

A guide is essential to reach Manos Rojas, Puerto Rico, Culucbalom, Río Bec B, Hormiguero, and Payán. Check with Juan de la Cruz Briceño, the *guardián* of Becan. Juan has permission from the National Institute of Anthropology and History to take visitors to these outlying sites, knows the area thoroughly, and will know (or will be able to find out) the condition of the roads and trails. He is also an amiable companion to have along on a trip and a real comfort on the more adventurous ones. Juan is also familiar with the use of a winch and will help you use it if you get stuck. He is a good man with a machete and an ax (being a former *chiclero);* machete work will be needed for all the outlying sites—either to reach them or to clear the vegetation to get photos. On the way to Río Bec B an ax is often also needed. As you may have guessed, these sites are seldom visited.

There is no food or drink at any of the sites, and you should at least have cold drinks and water along. Soft drinks are available at the village of Xpuhil and a few other places along the highway.

Buses run along the highway, with a regular stop at the village of Xpuhil, and there is a dirt airstrip there that can accommodate small planes.

*Note:* When you drive between Chetumal and Xpuhil, you will come across an *aduana* ("customs") station about 54 miles west of Chetumal. Have your tourist card and car papers ready for inspection. If you are traveling west (away from Chetumal), you are required to stop; if eastbound, it is not necessary to stop unless they flag you down.

In the past many of the sites in this region were described as displaying the Río Bec style, and a distinction was made between structures in this area and those in the Chenes area farther northwest. This distinction was based upon apparent architectural differences, but in 1973, David Potter, who studied the architecture of both areas, arrived at a different conclusion. He postulated that "the Central Yucatán Region, roughly Pollock's combined Río Bec–Chenes area, has one characteristic architectural style that prevailed during a major portion of the Late Classic period. The distinctions between the two portions of the region are, at most, not regionally significant." Only time will tell whether other authorities will come to agree with Potter's conclusion, but certainly he makes some excellent points. He also had the advantage of more abundant data than were available when the Río Bec style and the Chenes style were first separated into distinct entities.

★★★

# *Chicanná*

(chee-kah-*nah*)

DERIVATION: Mayan for "Serpent-Mouth House."
ORIGINAL NAME: Unknown.
CULTURE: Maya.
LOCATION: Southeastern part of the state of Campeche, Mexico.

## THE SITE

Chicanná is not a large site, but some of its monumental architecture is in an excellent state of preservation, making a visit most worthwhile. It is one of the most photogenic sites in the area.

When you arrive at the site, you first see Structures I and II, which border the west and east sides of the Main Plaza, respectively, the other two sides being defined by low structures—in a state of collapse—that remain unstudied. This is the only well-defined plaza at Chicanná.

Structure I, though in a sadly ruinous condition, can still be perceived as a typical example of the Río Bec twin-tower style. The towers are joined by a one-story, ten-room building with a stairway facing the plaza. The façade is decorated with monster-mask profiles in four panels. The towers themselves are stepped, have rounded corners, steep nonfunctional stairways, and once supported ornamental false temples. Structure II, in a much better state of preservation, was completely excavated, consolidated, and partly restored in 1970 by Jack Eaton. This structure dates to A.D. 750–770, slightly later than Structure I.

Structure II alone would make a visit to Chicanná worthwhile. Its highly ornamental main façade depicts profile monster masks flanking the doorway, which features an open-monster-mouth of typical Chenes style. These are quite similar to the decorations on Structure 2 at Hochob in the Chenes region, 65 miles to the north. It is Structure II at Chicanná that gives the site its name.

Although the open-monster-mouth doorway is more typical of the Chenes–Río Bec region, it is also found in other areas; for example, at Uxmal in the Puuc region, at Chichén Itzá in northern Yucatán, and even at Copán in Honduras, 250 miles away.

The styles of the doorways, as well as the basic architecture, vary a great deal from one area to another, which suggests a common Late Classic decorative religious theme. Sir J. Eric S. Thompson suggests that the motif probably represents Itzamná, the heavenly monster god (also the creator god).

*Structure II, front (west) side showing Chenes-style mask on the central portion, flanked by simpler lateral wings, Chicanná. Late Classic period.*

In any case, the experts agree that the motif is reptilian in character, although the caretaker at Chicanná may tell you that it represents a jaguar.

In Structure II there is one story containing eight rooms; the front row with three, and the rear with five. There are also the remains of a roof comb above the medial wall. Most of the wall surfaces and the roof comb were originally painted red, as shown by traces of paint. Flanking the decorative open-monster-mouth doorway in the center of the façade are two, relatively plain lateral wings. A broad, low stairway faces the plaza from the front of Structure II. Some of the original plaster remains on the interior walls, and interesting graffiti are found there. One is assumed to portray the facing Structure I with its towers, stairways, and small false temples.

Structure II is where you will want to spend a lot of your time. For really dramatic photographic results, try for a late afternoon visit when the Chenes monster mask is catching the sunlight. It is spectacular.

There are three other groups at Chicanná that can be reached from the Main Plaza. Structure VI—the only standing building of Group B—lies about 80 yards southeast of the Main Plaza and is notable for some intact façade relief sculpture, a partly intact though sagging lintel, and a perforated roof comb, much of which remains. The perforations were partly lined with marine shells. Slabs projecting from this roof comb presumably supported stucco figures. Structure VI has two rooms, though the upper portion of the front one has collapsed.

About 70 yards southwest of the Main Plaza is Group C, which contains Structures X and XI. Structure X has three rooms facing onto a broad terrace and some remains of façade decorations. Structure XI has eleven or twelve rooms on one level, and was intensively excavated in 1970. It has no remaining sculptural decoration but shows a developmental type of vaulting that fits with its relatively early date. Stone lintels are in place in some of the interior rooms. Structure XI-sub, underlying the visible building, is the earliest structural unit examined at the site.

Farthest from the Main Plaza, about 300 yards northwest, is Group D, which has only one standing building, the well-preserved Structure XX. This is the latest construction recorded at Chicanná, and

*Structure II, central portion of the main (west) side, Chicanná. Late Classic period.*

*Structure VI, view of the front (south) side showing panel with relief sculpture and perforated roof comb, Chicanná. Late Classic period.*

it is composed of two levels. The lower rooms are mostly collapsed or filled with debris, but the upper rooms are largely intact. On this latter portion are some interesting sculptural remains of the open-serpent-mouth motif, flanked on the corners by vertical rows of long-nosed masks. Little remains of the decoration on the lower portion of the building. A telephoto lens will get you good detail photos of the sculpture.

Both ceramic and architectural evidence indicate that Chicanná was occupied during the same general time as Becan. There are only minor differences in their chronologies. For instance, there is no evidence for Preclassic structural activity at Chicanná, and ceramic evidence indicates that occupation during this period (A.D. 150–250) was neither long nor extensive. There is a surprising gap in the ceramic sequence during the early part of the Early Classic period, with no evidence of occupation of the site from about 250 to 400.

Structural activities at Chicanná began between A.D. 400 and 550, though these constructions are not

*Structure XX, southeast corner showing Chac masks, Chicanná. Late Classic period.*

*Structure XX, north side, Chicanná. Late Classic period.*

visible today. The following period, 550–750, was the time of major construction; much of the standing architecture seen today dates to that period.

In the next period, 750–830, more architectural activity took place—notably the construction of Structure II; therefore, all the currently visible remains date to the Late Classic period. After that time construction ceased, though the site continued to be occupied until around 1100, presumably by simple agriculturists who perhaps came from northwestern Yucatán. There is evidence of some ritual activity during this late period, demonstrated by the presence of censers.

The major observable difference between Chicanná and Becan is one of scale. While Becan is grand and massive and has large, well-defined plazas, Chicanná has a more human scale, and its structures reflect a certain refinement and elegance. Perhaps more of this elegance would also be found at Becan if its standing structures were in as good a state of preservation as those at Chicanná.

The motifs of serpent mouths and Río Bec–style towers do not have a special chronology. The towers were built early at Chicanná and late in the history of Becan, while the reverse is true of the serpent-mouth relief facades.

## RECENT HISTORY

Chicanná was discovered in 1966 by Jack Eaton during exploration of the area before the formal start of the extensive project jointly sponsored by the National Geographic Society and the Middle American Research Institute of Tulane University (see "Becan" for more details on this work). Though Eaton discovered other sites, this find is perhaps the most noteworthy.

It is surprising that Chicanná was not discovered earlier during the Carnegie Institution's extensive reconnaissance of this area in the 1930s, especially considering its proximity to Becan. This says something about the density of the vegetation in the area.

We learned of the existence of this site in 1968 from E. Wyllys Andrews V, the son of the director of the project, before our first trip to Yucatán. At that time Highway 186 was a rough and rutted unpaved road, though even then the kilometer markers were in place. Our instructions were to stop at kilometer 143.1 (we determined the 0.1 with our odometer) and walk due south for about 300 meters. We were to be rewarded with the sight of an impressive Chenes-style mask in a good state of preservation. There was supposedly a track through the bush leading to the site.

We stopped at the—we hoped—correct spot on the highway but saw nothing resembling a track. Either we had missed it, or it had become overgrown. Since we had a machete along, Jerry tried to cut a path through the bush. Machete wielding is a very specialized art, in which he had had no experience. In addition, the machete had not been sharpened, and we had no means of remedying that problem. He hacked away for some minutes, not getting anywhere, and after having penetrated the bush for about 20 feet, he gave up the endeavor.

I can only say in retrospect, after finally having seen Chicanná in 1973, that if we had hacked our way through to the site in 1968 and had come across the Chenes monster mask in the middle of the bush, I would probably have fainted. I wonder what effect it had on Jack Eaton when he discovered it.

One of Chicanná's structures—the well-preserved Structure XX—was not discovered until 1970, during the year that Chicanná was excavated.

## CONNECTIONS

1. 80 miles by paved road from Chetumal, or
2. 91 miles by paved road from Escárcega, then 0.5 mile of good rock road.

## GETTING THERE

From Chetumal head west on Highway 186, or from Escárcega head east on the same highway to the Chicanná cutoff. The cutoff is between kilometer markers 144 and 145 and goes south. It is marked with a sign.

When you arrive at the site, the caretaker will greet you. In 1979 this was Felipe Osorio Licona. He will be happy to show you around. I recommend having him or one of his children along, for you are likely to miss some features on your own.

See "A Note on Southern Campeche and Quintana Roo" for information on food, drink, and accommodations in the area.

Allow about 2 hours for a visit. Tennis shoes will get you by.

★★★

# *Becan*

(beh-*kahn*)

DERIVATION: Mayan for "Ditch Filled with Water."
ORIGINAL NAME: Unknown.
CULTURE: Maya.
LOCATION: Southeastern part of the state of Campeche, Mexico.

---

## THE SITE

The rock road to Becan ends at the house of the site's caretaker, the pleasant, knowledgeable, and now rather famous Juan de la Cruz Briceño (see "Río Bec" for more on Juan). He or his son will take you around Becan, and you will see more if you have one of the two along.

Becan is built on a limestone outcrop that is as much as 30 feet higher than the surrounding countryside and is visible from the top of the temple of Xpuhil about 4 miles away.

From Juan's house you climb the edge of the outcrop to the site proper, entering the Southeast Plaza. This plaza is surrounded by Structures I through IV, three of which date to the latest construction period at the site.

Structure I, bounding the plaza on the south, has two lateral towers, which rise in tiers and have rounded corners, a feature in itself typical of Río Bec style. These towers are more massive than those at Xpuhil or Río Bec and bear no sculptural decorations. Limited excavation also indicates that the towers probably never supported templelike structures found atop the towers at other nearby sites. Structure I is not restored, but some facing remains on the south corners of the west tower. The towers were joined by a solid mass, with no apparent openings facing the plaza, although some rooms in the mass open to the south.

Structure II, on the west, is in a poor state of repair, and Structure III, on the east, is a featureless mound.

Structure IV, on the north of the plaza, was the most intensively excavated of this group and is by far the most interesting. Facing the plaza is a monumental south stairway—perhaps the widest in the Maya area. The lower flight of steps and some of the upper stairs are still in their original position—the rest has been restored.

The building on top has some intact relief sculpture on the south façade, to the right of the doorway as you face it, and several unroofed rooms around a courtyard. After seeing this, return down the south stairway and walk around the west side of the structure. Keep an eye out for a fragment of relief sculpture on the west side near the top, and continue around to the north façade of the structure. This façade supports several terraces and many doorways opening into numerous rooms. Some interesting sculptural decorations are intact on either side of a doorway on Terrace 2-1.

As an aside, several months after seeing and photographing the sculptured panels, I did a drawing of two of them and then made my first—and only—archaeological discovery. A step in the form of a frontal mask is centered below a doorway. On either side are sculptured panels of stylized profile serpent heads and above this, adjacent to the doorway, are more of the same. All the profile heads are abstract or "conceptual"—a term used by Potter—and rather difficult to make out. All of them face in, toward the doorway; those on the left are mirror images of those on the right, except for the lower left panel (as you face it). The design was obviously meant to be symmetrical. Therefore, this panel has the serpent head profile facing the wrong way. It made me wonder if any Maya sculptors or masons lost their heads because of this faux pas. Perhaps it went unnoticed. I did not notice the discrepancy when I saw and photographed the panels, or even when I looked at my slides. It was only when I did the drawing of the panels that the inconsistency became apparent, so perhaps those responsible got off scot free.

A short distance north of Structure IV is another building. It faces east and rises from a low platform. There are remains of the lower walls of several rooms, and the front of the structure is decorated with panels of a latticelike design.

From here follow the trail that leads to Structure VIII. Structure VIII bounds the east end of the great Central Plaza. This twin-towered building, though investigated, was not intensively excavated, but it

*Structure IV, the front (south) side, Becan. Late Classic period.*

*Inset panels and step mask, Structure IV, north side, on Terrace 2-1, Becan. The profile serpent mask on the lower left panel is reversed. Late Classic period.*

is known that originally a monumental stairway led from the plaza level up the west face of the structure. On the lower portion of the south side of Structure VIII, there is a small entrance that leads to a number of connected rooms. You have to crawl through the opening on all fours for a few feet before it enlarges and you are able to stand. Take along a flashlight and a flash unit for your camera—it is pitch black inside. The rooms are plain, but are worth a few minutes to visit.

From Structure VIII, walk west through the Central Plaza, passing Structure IX, on your right (north). At 100 feet high, it is the tallest at Becan. Although unexcavated, it is an impressive mound. It probably had a stairway facing the plaza and a temple on top.

Facing Structure VIII across the Central Plaza is Structure X, which bounds the west end. Only limited investigations were carried out here, but again we have a monumental stairway facing the plaza—this one in two flights.

The upper building has two rows of three rooms each, and remnants of a roof comb. The front façade has some remains of well-preserved relief sculpture, bearing traces of red paint. An exploratory trench dug north of the doorway revealed that the lower part of the sculpture is the profile serpent jaw—a typical Chenes motif—although simple and stylized when compared to the sculpture of Structure II at Chicanná. The sculpture was carved in stone, then covered with plaster—which provided the fine detail—and, finally, painted.

To the west of Structure X is the West Plaza, which has a small unrestored ball court, one side of which is attached to the rear of Structure X. At the west end of the West Plaza is a group of buildings designated Structure XIII. This group is poorly preserved and has not been excavated. Within the West Plaza is found an eroded plain stela.

Just behind Structure XIII, you can get a look at a portion of the huge moat that surrounds the site—a most unusual feature. The moat is quite overgrown, but it is possible to discern when it is pointed out to you. It is difficult to get a descriptive photograph of the moat.

Recent work at Becan has uncovered a ceramic complex that dates to the Middle Preclassic period, and lithic evidence for this period was also found. It is thought that settlers pushed northward from the Petén during this time as there are close ceramic ties between Becan and the Petén area. It is assumed that these people practiced slash-and-burn agriculture.

During the Late Preclassic period (between 50 B.C. and A.D. 250) there was a sudden proliferation of architectural undertakings. A building inside Structure IV, and several others at the site, date to this period, and the huge defensive earthworks at Becan were probably constructed between A.D. 150 and 250.

This was followed by an abrupt decline in population during the first half of the Early Classic period, and then an increase in population for the latter half of this period and the early Late Classic period. This increase may have been associated with an influx of people from southern Quintana Roo and Belize. Around A.D. 550–600 the regional Río Bec architectural style makes its appearance. For the most part, all the buildings seen today at Becan were erected during Late Classic times—more specifi-

*Structure X, the front (east) side, Becan. Late Classic period.*

cally, from A.D. 550 to 830. By A.D. 600 the moat, in part, was being used as a refuse dump. The moat is actually a kidney-shaped ditch, 1.2 miles in circumference, that encloses the 46 acres of the site. It conforms well to the edge of the limestone outcrop on which Becan was built. There is ceramic and lithic evidence of contact with Teotihuacán or Teotihuacán-associated people, though exactly how this ties into the construction of the moat is a matter still being considered.

It is known that there was Teotihuacán influence in the Tikal area, and David Webster sees three possibilities concerning the defensive earthworks at Becan: (1) that the earthworks were built to protect Becan against Petén Maya influence, (2) that Becan was fortified as an outpost of the Petén Maya, and (3) that the construction of the earthworks had nothing to do with influences from the Petén, under Teotihuacán influence.

Irwin Rovner, on the basis of his lithic evidence, sees Teotihuacán contact around the second century A.D. This would be corroborated by a find at Altun Ha, made by David Pendergast, which suggests highland contact with the lowlands around A.D. 150–200.

Richard E. W. Adams feels that "the already extant fortress of Becan may have been taken over by a Teotihuacán allied elite or that the elite of Becan allied themselves to the great central Mexican city. A third possibility is that the Teotihuacanos shut themselves up in a redoubt built with corvee labor."

Joseph Ball's ceramic data indicate contact with Teotihuacán during the period A.D. 400–550. One of the more interesting pieces of ceramic evidence brought to light was a hollow, two-piece terra-cotta statuette, and ten solid figurines, found associated with a cylindrical tripod vessel. The statuette and figurines are typical of Teotihuacán art, while the vessel (the shape of which is also typical of Teotihuacán) portrays Maya deities.

Most of the dating for Becan and the surrounding area is from ceramic, lithic, and architectural evidence, as there are no usable inscribed stelae like those found to the south. In fact, few stelae of any kind are found in the Río Bec region. Carbon-14 determinations were made from materials at Becan and Chicanná, but the results were erratic.

Another influx of new people, this time from northwestern Yucatán, occurred around A.D. 830, and is indicated by ceramic evidence; but major building activities ceased.

Becan continued to be occupied during the Early Postclassic period, but by A.D. 1200 it was once again in the hands of shifting agricultural tribesmen. From then until the early twentieth century, the area was virtually unoccupied.

## RECENT HISTORY

From 1932 through 1938 the Carnegie Institution of Washington sponsored explorations in the Río Bec region and adjacent areas. The results of these efforts were published by Karl Ruppert and John Denison in 1943. During their reconnaissance, they discovered many sites, including Becan in 1934.

An accurate survey showed that the entire site was surrounded by artificial earthworks, consisting of a ditch and embankments, crossed by seven causeways. Ruppert and Denison identified these earthworks as formal fortifications—to the consternation of some of their fellow Mayanists—and further speculated that the ditch was originally filled with water, forming a true moat. (With this in mind, they gave the site its name—which remains—although recent work on the fortification by David Webster proves that the ditch or moat was never filled with water. Nevertheless, it would have been an effective defense system.)

The consternation of their fellow scholars was caused because at that time (in the 1930s) the prevailing theory was that fortified Maya sites were not constructed until the Postclassic period (or, at the earliest, at the very end of the Late Classic), yet Becan was obviously occupied during the whole of the Late Classic. Most Mayanists preferred to think of Maya society as peaceful throughout the Classic period, yet here was evidence of warfare appearing earlier than it should, according to their theory.

E. Wyllys Andrews IV was project director of work carried out in the Río Bec region (including Becan) from 1969 through 1971, sponsored jointly by the National Geographic Society and the Middle American Research Institute (MARI) of Tulane University. Under his directorship, a great deal of new information was gathered. Extensive ceramic analysis was undertaken by Joseph Ball (who returned in 1973 for additional research), the lithic assemblages were studied by Irwin Rovner, the fortifications by Webster, the architecture by David Potter, and the cultural ecology by Ingolf Vogeler. In addition, Jack Eaton, of the field staff of MARI, undertook extensive reconnaissance, discovering numerous sites and relocating sites previously reported.

The prehistoric settlement of Becan was studied by Prentice Thomas, Jr., for a joint University of Tennessee–National Geographic Society expedition in 1972 and further work was projected for 1973. The preliminary report published by MARI in 1974 was compiled by Richard E. W. Adams, who was also director of the work at Becan during the 1970 season.

Final reports by Webster, Ball, Potter, James B. Stoltman, and E. Wyllys Andrews V were published by MARI from 1976 through 1978, and other reports on Becan are in press.

## CONNECTIONS

1. 78.5 miles by paved road from Chetumal,
2. 92.5 miles by paved road from Escárcega, then less than 0.5 mile of good rock road.

## GETTING THERE

Take Highway 186 to the Becan cutoff. This is west of Chetumal and east of Escárcega. The cutoff is marked with a sign and heads north. It occurs between kilometer markers 146 and 147.

See "A Note on Southern Campeche and Quintana Roo" for information on food, drink, and accommodations in the area.

Allow 2 hours for a visit. Wear boots and bring insect repellent.

★★★

# *Xpuhil*

(shpoo-*heel*)

DERIVATION: Mayan for "Place of the Cattails." Named after a nearby *aguada* ("waterhole").

ORIGINAL NAME: Unknown.

CULTURE: Maya.

LOCATION: Southeastern part of the state of Campeche, Mexico.

---

## THE SITE

The lovely Late Classic temple of Xpuhil is a rather typical example of the Río Bec style of architecture, with tall towers joined by a lower range of rooms. One unusual feature here, however, is the incorporation of three towers, rather than the two generally encountered.

The temple faces east, but the best preserved portions are on the west face, so the afternoon is the best time to photograph it.

The central tower on the west façade is the most interesting because of its better state of preservation. Much of the facing stone is intact and the rounded corners and steep ornamental stair give a good impression of what the other two towers must have looked like originally. The stairs, according to Tatiana Proskouriakoff—who did a restoration drawing of the temple—incline only 20 degrees from the vertical. For this reason, the risers had to be given a reverse batter to provide the indication of steps.

Three ornamental relief masks decorate the stair from top to bottom; the top one is the best preserved. According to David Potter, the masks are "obviously feline." This is an interesting point; most of the mask decorations in the Río Bec region are reptilian in nature.

Atop the three towers, but best seen on the central one, are small simulated temples with the Chenes open-serpent-mouth motif. There may or may not have been roof combs above originally. You will want your telephoto lens here for detail photos of the masks and false temples. Another point of interest is the remains of a narrow inner stairway in the south tower.

The one-level structure that joins the towers together originally contained twelve rooms, but, unhappily, it is little more than a pile of rubble today. When first discovered, it was in a better state of repair, making possible the restoration drawing. There is some question, however, about the accuracy of the elaborate relief sculpture on the upper east façade as shown in the drawing.

*Structure I of Group I, the back (west) side, Xpuhil. Late Classic period.*

*Detail of the mask panel and false temple on the upper part of the west tower, west side, Xpuhil. Structure I of Group I. Late Classic period.*

You should climb the central area of the structure —access is up the east side over the rubble—for a photo of Becan to the west. Use your longest telephoto lens, with an extender, if you have one. The entire outcrop upon which Becan is built is plainly visible on the horizon.

## RECENT HISTORY

Xpuhil was discovered by Karl Ruppert and John Denison in the 1930s, while they were working for the Carnegie Institution of Washington. They reported this find as well as others in 1943, and Proskouriakoff's drawing accompanied their volume.

This drawing, plus photos and a model of Río Bec B, were the main sources of information on Río Bec–style architecture until the recent work in the area sponsored by the National Geographic Society and Tulane University. (See "Becan" for more details of this recent work.) The temple was cleared in the late 1960s by E. Wyllys Andrews IV, and the clearing has been maintained. In 1977 some additional clearing and minor restoration was undertaken.

It should be mentioned that there are several archaeological groups in the area called Xpuhil; they are differentiated by Roman numerals. Some were discovered by Ruppert and Denison in the 1930s, and others were discovered more recently by Jack Eaton. The temple described here is properly designated Xpuhil, Group I, Structure I—by far the most impressive of the lot. Xpuhil is also the name of a nearby village.

## CONNECTIONS

1. 75 miles by paved road from Chetumal, or
2. 96 miles by paved road from Escárcega.

## GETTING THERE

Xpuhil is between kilometer markers 152 and 153, though it is closer to 152. Take Highway 186 west from Chetumal or east from Escárcega. The site is marked; you cannot miss it, for a wide trail has been cut to the temple, which is visible on the north from the highway.

You do not need a guide at Xpuhil. There is only the one temple to see, and you can easily cover that on your own.

See "A Note on Southern Campeche and Quintana Roo" for information on accommodations, food, and drink.

Allow 45 minutes to see the temple. Tennis shoes are fine.

★

# *Manos Rojas*

(*mah*-nohs *roh*-hahs)

DERIVATION: Spanish for "red hands" (see text).
EARLIER NAME: Kilometer 132 (see text).
ORIGINAL NAME: Unknown.
CULTURE: Maya.
LOCATION: Southeastern part of the state of Campeche, Mexico.

## THE SITE

The name Manos Rojas was given this site because of red-painted hand prints found in one of the structures. This is the name by which the site is known locally. It was previously called Kilometer 132, since it is located near this kilometer marker on the Escárcega-Chetumal Highway (Highway 186).

Manos Rojas is reported to be a "scattered site," with several structures and a stone-lined *aguada* ("waterhole"), but it is the Structure of Group C that is of interest to the visitor. This structure is the northernmost at the known site and is closest to the highway. It is a large building on several levels, and is much destroyed or buried, but there are some remains of corner masks, in a vertical row, made of stone and plaster. They are similar to those on Structure XX at Chicanná. To the left of the masks (as you face them) are a few remains of relief carving. Some carved stones, which were once a part of the building, are found on the ground nearby.

There are two small vaulted corridors running at right angles to each other and they begin on each side of the corner masks. They appear to pierce the

*Structure of Group C showing the corner masks and the vaulted corridors on each side, Manos Rojas. Late Classic period.*

bases of now destroyed stairways, but of this I am not certain. The vault on the left is made of well-cut stone and is particularly well preserved. Some remains of larger vaults—originally a part of rooms—may also be seen on another corner of the structure.

## RECENT HISTORY

Manos Rojas was discovered in 1971 by Jack Eaton during a reconnaissance conducted for the Middle American Research Institute (MARI) of Tulane University. See "Becan" for more information on MARI's work in the area.

Although Manos Rojas has been recorded, and the existing architecture studied by David Potter, no excavation or restoration has been undertaken, so little can be said about the site except that the architectural remains date to the Late Classic period and the corner masks are typical of the Central Yucatán (Río Bec–Chenes) style.

## CONNECTIONS

1. 82 miles by paved road from Escárcega, or
2. 89 miles by paved road from Chetumal, then about 200 yards by foot trail.

## GETTING THERE

Take Highway 186 east from Escárcega or west from Chetumal to a spot on the highway between kilometer markers 131 and 132. Park and walk south to the structure with the corner masks.

Although the structure is close to the highway—when you are there you can hear the highway traffic—it is not visible because of the very dense vegetation, and the trail to the structure is equally invisible, except to those who know its exact location. I must stress that there is no way you will find it on your own. See "A Note on Southern Campeche and Quintana Roo" for information on getting a guide.

Wear boots, bring insect repellent, and have cold drinks in your car. Allow 30 minutes to see the structure with the corner masks and 5 minutes each way for walking there and back.

★

# *Culucbalom*

(koo-look-bah-*lohm*)

ORIGINAL NAME: Unknown.
CULTURE: Maya.
LOCATION: Southeastern part of the state of Campeche, Mexico.

---

## THE SITE

Culucbalom is principally composed of a plaza with five structures arranged around it, although another structure and a low mound are also reported. The site is totally overgrown, and, although we were told the plaza was 50 meters wide, we could not see across it because of the vegetation. Today only two of the plaza structures are of interest to the visitor.

Structure I, the larger and better preserved of the two, bounds the plaza on the north. It is reportedly composed of six rooms, although only the two center rooms are easily discernible today since much has collapsed. The center rooms—one behind the other—are on a high platform and are reached by a rocky foot trail up the south side. On each side of the central doorway are two inset panels, with applied carved columns, and each column bears the depiction of two seated figures, one above the other. Only three of the original columns remain, and they are rather eroded. A fourth—reported to be the best preserved of the lot—has been removed from its place, and is believed to have been stolen. Above and below the columns are short sections of a three-part molding, which give the effect of capitals. There is a perforated roof comb on Structure I, with a few remains of projecting figures. Graffiti—both ancient and modern—is found on the interior plaster walls of the center rooms.

To the southwest of Structure I is Structure V, set atop a low platform. Three rooms are reported, but only the center one is easily visible today, and much of its vault has collapsed. The most interesting feature is a pair of inset carved panels flanking the central doorway. They depict stylized profile masks similar to those on the north side of Structure IV at Becan. Propped up next to the north panel (on the right side of the doorway) were two loose stones with geometrical designs. They seem to have been deliberately placed there, but I do not know if they were originally a part of this structure.

There was also evidence of recent digging—presumably illicit—at Structure V, at the base of the north panel, at the back wall, and into the floor of the center room.

Another mound lies to the south of Structure V but there appeared to be no standing architecture. The other mounds were not seen in the dense vegetation.

## RECENT HISTORY

Culucbalom was discovered in the 1930s during extensive exploration sponsored by the Carnegie Institution of Washington. This site and many others were reported upon by Karl Ruppert and John Denison in a 1943 Institution publication. The site is also mentioned by Alberto Ruz Lhuillier in a 1945 publication. No serious excavation has been undertaken at the site, though the visible architectural remains are fairly typical of the area and date to the Late Classic period. I have never seen Culucbalom mentioned in the popular literature.

## CONNECTIONS

1. 74 miles by paved road from Chetumal to the village of Xpuhil, or
2. 97 miles by paved road from Escárcega to the village of Xpuhil, then 3.5 miles of rock road, 0.8 mile of dirt trail, and 2.5 miles of foot trail.

## GETTING THERE

To reach Culucbalom, a guide is essential. Check with Juan de la Cruz Briceño, the caretaker at Becan to arrange a visit. (See "Becan" for getting to Juan's house.)

To get to the village of Xpuhil, take Highway 186 west from Chetumal or east from Escárcega. From the west side of the Pemex station in the village of Xpuhil, there is a rock road that heads north; it is well marked and goes about 6 miles to Zoh Laguna. Take this road for 3.5 miles. Then turn left (west) onto an unmarked dirt car trail (Juan will point it out), and proceed 0.8 mile to the caretaker's house.

*The inset panel on the north (right) of the doorway of Structure V, Culucbalom. Late Classic period.*

Drive this part *very* slowly because limestone outcrops are hidden by vegetation. Nevertheless, this part can generally be negotiated in a regular car.

From the caretaker's house proceed on foot to the site. This sounds relatively easy, but it is not. Culucbalom is not a visited site. Sometimes years go by without a single visitor. The trail, therefore, is often completely overgrown in parts, and not too well defined in other parts.

The first section is generally in fairly decent shape, but it soon gets worse, and then much worse. Perhaps it would be more accurate to say that in some areas there *is* no trail and a new one has to be cut. Most of the way you are traveling through dense second-growth vegetation. There is no way to describe this to someone who has not experienced it. Suffice to say that it requires constant machete work.

It took us 2 hours and 20 minutes on foot to reach the site. Of course, if a trail has been recently cut, you could make it much faster. On the return trip it took us only 1 hour at a fast pace. The vegetation can completely obliterate the trail in a matter of a few months. This is unquestionably the worst foot trail I have ever traveled.

Wear boots and a long-sleevėd shirt because there are many thorn bushes and some wasps. It is also a dandy place to pick up *garrapatas* ("ticks"). Bring a canteen of water, plenty of insect repellent, fast film, and a wide-angle lens for your camera. You do not need a sun hat, but having your own machete along to help clear the trail is a good idea. Also have matches available; Juan needs them to set fire to the newspaper he carries to get rid of the wasps.

Have cold drinks in your car for when you return.

Allow 1 hour to visit the site once you reach it.

See "A Note on Southern Campeche and Quintana Roo" for information on accommodations and food in the area.

★

# *Puerto Rico*

(poo-*ehr*-toh *ree*-koh)

DERIVATION: Spanish for "Rich Port."
ORIGINAL NAME: Unknown.
CULTURE: Maya.
LOCATION: Southeastern part of the state of Campeche, Mexico.

## THE SITE

The main feature of interest at Puerto Rico is an almost solid, large cylindrical tower. It rests on a circular platform, which is now mostly destroyed, although the tower itself is well preserved. It reaches an impressive height of about 20 feet, but bears no decoration.

The facing stones on the tower are carefully cut and are intact, for the most part. The tower is pierced by a few small holes, but there are no rooms on the inside. The original function of the tower remains uncertain, although it has been speculated that the holes were used in some way for astronomical determinations. This, however, has not yet been demonstrated.

About 160 feet east of the tower is a plaza surrounded by remains of ancient structures, but these are simply mounds today. There are openings into the plaza in the center of the mounds on the north and west sides, and reportedly on the other two sides as well. The details of the construction of the tower date it to the Late Classic period.

## RECENT HISTORY

Puerto Rico was discovered by Jack Eaton and Loring Hewen in 1967, and the tower was reported upon by E. Wyllys Andrews IV in 1968, in a work published in Mexico. The tower was also described by David Potter in a Middle American Research Institute publication in 1977. There has been no significant excavation at the site.

## CONNECTIONS

1. 74 miles by paved road from Chetumal to the village of Xpuhil, or
2. 97 miles by paved road from Escárcega to the village of Xpuhil, then 11 miles of fair rock road, and 0.6 mile of dirt road.

## GETTING THERE

Take Highway 186 to Xpuhil by heading west from Chetumal, or east from Escárcega. At Xpuhil, take the rock road that heads north to Zoh Laguna (6

*Solid cylindrical tower, Puerto Rico. Late Classic period.*

miles). Continue on this road for another 2 miles, past Zoh Laguna, and take a rock cutoff to the right (east) for about 3 miles. This brings you to a dirt (better grass) road on the right. Take the grass road and drive as far as you can. Sometimes you can drive all the way to the site, although we were stopped by a large tree trunk across the road about 500 feet from where the grass road began. From this point it took us 8 minutes on foot to reach the tower, which means it was approximately 0.5 mile farther. If it has been rainy, and the dirt (grass) road looks bad, you can easily walk the 0.6 mile. The rock road all the way to the junction with the dirt (grass) road is generally in fair condition, though the last part is bumpy. It will take about 40 minutes to drive the 11 miles from Xpuhil village to the junction with the dirt (grass) road.

Do not attempt to reach Puerto Rico on your own. There are cutoffs in addition to those mentioned and you will never find the right ones by yourself. See "A Note on Southern Campeche and Quintana Roo" for information on getting a guide and for general information about the area.

Allow ½ hour to see the tower and visit the plaza once you get there.

Wear boots, bring insect repellent, and have cold drinks in your car.

★★

# *Río Bec B*

(*ree*-oh *behk bee*)

DERIVATION: Río is Spanish for "River" and Bec is Mayan for "evergreen oak" (see text for details).
ORIGINAL NAME: Unknown.
CULTURE: Maya.
LOCATION: Southeastern part of the state of Campeche, Mexico.

## THE SITE

The recently rediscovered Temple B at Río Bec is magnificent. Many sites are merely rubble heaps until they are excavated and restored, but here is one that, once cleared of its jungle vegetation, was found to be intact for the most part. (Since its rediscovery, a lintel above the doorway in the medial wall has been restored.) This rarely seen gem of world art sits in a small clearing encircled by the green of towering trees and trailing vines. Temple B has six rooms on one level, two in the center (one behind the other), and two smaller ones on each end. Some of the corbeled vaults supporting the roof over the rooms have collapsed, but essentially the feeling of the whole is preserved. When you look at it, you know exactly how some Maya architect wanted it to look when he designed it.

There is a central doorway on the front or east side, and a doorway on each of the north and south sides. Even more interesting are the towers, one at each end of the front façade. These 55-foot-high towers have rounded corners and false steps leading to false temples decorated with open-mouth-monster masks. The steep towers—with steps that incline only about 8 degrees from the vertical and have the same outward batter seen at Xpuhil—seem purely decorative, but may have been incorporated into the design in imitation of the large pyramid-temples found in the Petén.

An interesting recent speculation by David Potter

*Temple B, the front (east) side, Río Bec B. Late Classic period.*

is that the pyramid portion of the twin-pyramid complexes found at Tikal (and recently at Yaxhá) "could have been fused with the intermediate linear structure to develop into the Río Bec twin-towered structure." He adds, however, that "the forms make this seem reasonable, but the date given [about A.D. 771 for Complex Q at Tikal] suggests contemporaneity with the Río Bec structures or even the priority of the latter." The false doorways in the tower temples are topped by wooden lintels, as are the real doorways in the lower part of the structure. Some of the original lintels are still in place today.

Above the medial wall of the central part of the structure, and in between the towers, is a two-part perforated roof comb. The lower portion is decorated with stylized masks of stone; above this there are three-dimensional human figures made of plaster. The figures are poorly preserved, but the masks are mostly intact. You can climb up the rear of Temple B over a rubble trail for a good close-up view of the roof comb. There are some interesting graffiti on the plaster walls on the interior of the rooms. A moss covering has been removed from the walls in these areas, so the graffiti are not difficult to photograph, although you may need relatively long exposures if you are using slow film. Most of the graffiti are of a type commonly found at other Maya sites, and include depictions of temples, processions, and typical—if rather crude—Maya-style profiles. All are worth a photograph. The most unusual graffito, however, is a naturalistic, two-foot high, nude, female torso that is quite contemporary in feeling. It was dubbed the "Botticelli Nude" by Hugh Johnston, who discovered it and apparently believed it to be quite old. Some authorities, however, feel that it was probably done in the last century. In any case, it is completely un-Maya in feeling.

Río Bec is the type site of the area and gives its name to the architectural style of the region. Although recent ceramic analysis of this area (primarily Becan and Chicanná) by Joseph Ball was completed before the rediscovery of Río Bec B, it is safe to say—according to E. Wyllys Andrews V—

*Temple B, detail of the southern part of the roof comb, Río Bec B. Note remains of the mask panel at lower right. Late Classic period.*

that the visible remains of Temple B are datable to A.D. 700–850. Further work may pinpoint the date even more closely.

## RECENT HISTORY

As with Xpuhil, there are several groups called Río Bec. They are lettered A through E and numbered I through VIII. Our concern, of course, is Río Bec B.

Río Bec B has—to me at least—one of the most interesting histories of all the sites in this guide. In 1906–07 French archaeologist Maurice de Périgny explored the Río Bec region, and was the first person to record the existence of pre-Hispanic buildings in the area. One of the structures he found had square towers with rounded corners, and was unlike other known Maya structures in the Petén or Yucatán. He named it Río Beque, after a small stream (or dry watercourse) in the area—of which there are precious few.

In 1912 Raymond E. Merwin and Clarence L. Hay, under the auspices of the Peabody Museum of Harvard University, visited the area and relocated the structure discovered by Périgny. In addition, they discovered several others. One of these was near Périgny's building, was similar to it in design, but was in a much better state of preservation. To distinguish the two, Périgny's structure was called Río Bec A, and the one found by Merwin and Hay Río Bec B.

Merwin and Hay spent some time at the site and cleared it of its mantle of vegetation. Hay then took some excellent photographs of the temple; one classic shot has been widely reproduced.

Merwin's work formed part of his doctoral dissertation, but was never published. It wasn't until 1935 that Hay published an article in *Natural History Magazine* about Temple B; this was occasioned by the completion of a model of the temple, produced by Shoichi Ichikawa for the American Museum of Natural History. The model was produced from Hay's photographs and Merwin's field notes and at the time was considered "the finest reproduction of a Maya temple ever constructed."

After Merwin and Hay's discovery of Temple B, several other expeditions to the area were sponsored by the Carnegie Institution of Washington in the 1930s. During these expeditions, one of Merwin and Hay's groups was relocated and new groups at Río Bec were discovered, but Río Bec B was not to be found. You could look at photographs and a model of this large temple, but no one really knew where it was. It seemed almost inconceivable that once found it could be lost again. That, however, is exactly what happened.

In 1971 Jack Eaton of the field staff of the Middle American Research Institute of Tulane University, working under the sponsorship of the National Geographic Society, methodically cut a grid system through much of the area. Using Merwin's information on the location, and reports of local residents who claimed to have seen it a few years earlier, he fruitlessly attempted to relocate Temple B.

In the same year Hugh and Suzanne Johnston—a documentary film team from Princeton, engaged by WNET/13 to do a film on "Mystery of the Maya" for television viewing—visited the area and were shown around by Eaton. The Johnstons returned to the area in 1972 and 1973. On their third trip they were accompanied by Gillett Griffin, pre-Columbian art historian at Princeton University, and Andrea Seuffert, an artist with the Mexico City Museum.

In between trips the Johnstons had studied Merwin's field notes, and they drew their own map from his data. The field notes and dissertation were contradictory. The dissertation located Temple B and other structures in a north-south direction from a given point. The field notes, which turned out to be correct, pointed east-west.

With this preliminary work, the aid of workmen in the area, and with Juan de la Cruz Briceño (the current caretaker of Becan) as their chief guide, they rediscovered Río Bec B in May, 1973. This was a truly exciting find for the world of archaeology. It became known that the elusive Temple B lay but a stone's throw away from one of the trails previously cut by Eaton. The discovery was reported in June, 1973, and Río Bec B rejoined other sites in the annals of Maya archaeology.

The temple was cleared once again and filmed by the Johnstons. It was presented on television as a part of "Mystery of the Maya" in April, 1974.

## CONNECTIONS

1. 74 miles by paved road from Chetumal to the village of Xpuhil, or
2. 97 miles by paved road from Escárcega to the village of Xpuhil, then 12 miles of fair-to-poor rock road, and 9 miles of variable dirt road.

## GETTING THERE

To reach the cutoff for Río Bec B, take Highway 186 west from Chetumal or east from Escárcega to the village of Xpuhil. At Xpuhil take the rock road that heads south—it begins just east of El Oasis restaurant. (See "A Note on Southern Campeche and Quintana Roo" for recommendations on finding a guide for Río Bec B and for other information about the area.)

About 1.8 miles south of Xpuhil there is a low spot in the rock road that becomes terribly rutted in wet weather. In 1978 this was nicely repaired, but a year later it had already deteriorated and four-wheel drive was necessary to get through. It should be mentioned, however, that the condition of these rock and dirt roads can change almost daily, depending on the amount of rain and sunshine. What is impassable one day may have been passable the day before, and may be passable again in a couple of days.

If you can get through this bad spot, the rest of the rock road will pose no undue difficulties, though it will be bumpy. Once you turn onto the dirt road, however, the situation changes. There are a few low spots on this road that are filled with water or soft mud in the rainy season—dandy places to get stuck, even with four-wheel drive. In some places *desviaciones* ("bypasses") have been cut and, with a little enlargement, can be used.

Later, you reach higher ground, where trees across the road and encroaching vegetation become the problems. Driving time from the village of Xpuhil to Río Bec B is about 2 hours—if you don't get stuck.

*Note:* In 1978 we were told that there is a shorter route to Río Bec B, but this could not be used because of the lack of a bridge at a certain point. In 1980 the bridge still had not been installed, but when it is, the trip from Xpuhil to Río Bec B will be considerably shorter.

Have cold drinks along for the trip, bring insect repellent, and wear boots—in case you get stuck on the road and have to walk in the mud. For the site itself, tennis shoes are adequate. Allow 1 hour to see Río Bec B once you get there.

*Note:* On our first trip to Río Bec B in 1973, it was necessary to walk in the last couple of miles. The foot trail passed near Río Bec A and we made a detour to see it. On a subsequent visit in 1978, after the road was cut through all the way to Temple B, we did not see Temple A. Juan made no mention of it and I do not know how close the road passes to it. On this second trip, however, we did stop for a look at Río Bec II. This is just a few minutes on foot from the dirt road and is worth a look since you are in the area. This spot has three stelae—one plain and the others eroded—and three mounds, which are the remains of Structure I.

The trail to Río Bec II is encountered 3 miles before you reach Río Bec B, but it is better to stop and see it on your way back. Since Temple B faces east, the morning hours are the best for photography, so you should get there as early as possible.

If the shortcut to Río Bec B eventually gets its bridge, the route will no longer pass the area of Río Bec II. On the other hand, it may put you near some of the other Río Bec groups, and if it does, Juan will be sure to mention it.

★★

# *Hormiguero*

(ohr-mee-*geh*-roh)

DERIVATION: Spanish for "Anthill" (see text).
ORIGINAL NAME: Unknown.
CULTURE: Maya.
LOCATION: Southeastern part of the state of Campeche, Mexico.

## THE SITE

Hormiguero is an unheralded site—at least in the popular literature—and is rated two stars only because access is rather difficult. Otherwise, it would certainly be three stars. The existence of Hormiguero, while known to professionals, is virtually unknown to most others—even serious ruin buffs. This is perhaps explained by the fact that photos of the site are rarely seen in general books on Maya art and archaeology. When anything is shown, it is Structure V. While this structure is quite interesting, it is far surpassed by Structure II—a spectacular building in a generally good state of preservation.

Hormiguero covers an area of 900 feet from north to south, by 650 feet from east to west, and is one of the major sites in the Río Bec subregion. It is formed of three groups, although the layout is informal. There are eight numbered structures at the site and several unnumbered ones.

Structure II is a large and complex building, and is described by David Potter as "one of the most distinctive buildings in the Río Bec subregion."

The central portion of the south façade displays a typical Chenes open-serpent-mouth motif, formed of stone and covered with plaster. Much of the fine

*Structure II, the central part of the south façade, Hormiguero. Note the part of the Río Bec–style tower with rounded corners on the right. Late Classic period.*

*Structure II, the eastern part of the south façade with inset mask panels, Hormiguero. There are remains of an applied column on the right and a Río Bec-style tower on the left. Late Classic period.*

*Structure V, the north side, Hormiguero. Late Classic period.*

detail in plaster is intact. The original wooden lintels at the top of the central doorway, which forms the mouth of the serpent, are still in place. This part of the façade recalls Structure II at Chicanná and Structure 2 at Hochob, but the individual elements forming the additional serpent profiles adjacent to the doorway are larger and, therefore, the effect is bolder.

On either side of the central façade are tall Río Bec–style towers with typical rounded corners, banded tiers, and steep false stairways. The towers project in front of the central façade. Each is pierced at its base by a vaulted passage. Some of the steps are in place near the top of the east tower (on the right, as you face the structure). Although not visible from ground level today, it is reported that four large masonry blocks lie on top of each tower, and it is believed that they may have been part of simulated temples.

Beyond the towers are sections of façade made of a plain wall, with a vertical row of inset mask panels in frontal view. Flanking the panels are plain applied columns, which originally formed the jambs of doorways for the two end rooms, but these rooms have mostly collapsed. Structure II originally had eight rooms and one of these still has an intact vault.

According to Potter, the plan of Structure V at Hormiguero "is exceedingly difficult to understand." There is a tall platform that supports a one-room temple and an adjacent tower, but there seems to be no evidence for a second tower.

The main façade of the temple faces north and supports a typical Chenes open-serpent-mouth motif. This small structure has vertical rows of serpent heads on the north corners, and is similar to Structure XX at Chicanná and Structure A1 at Dzibilnocac. The relief sculpture is in stone, covered with plaster, and is well preserved. The temple also has its original wooden lintel in place over the doorway, and this is said to be of zapote.

The tower at Structure V has rounded corners and banded tiers, but lacks the false stairway and simulated temple typical of Río Bec–style towers.

Another structure at Hormiguero has some remains of stone and plaster masks at present ground level, but there is little else of interest to be seen there. Nevertheless, it is worth a few minutes time and a couple of photographs.

A short distance away are the remains of a portion of a wall of Structure VI, and nearby, on a lower level, is an opening into a large chultun. The visible structures at Hormiguero are of Late Classic date, but nothing is known of the site's beginnings. Visually, however, it is a most exciting site to visit.

## RECENT HISTORY

In 1933, during one of the Carnegie Institution of Washington's extensive reconnaissance missions in Campeche, the existence of some well-preserved ruins was reported to the members of the expedition by the workmen's cook. The site was then visited by the expedition, from April 4 through April 14 of the same year.

The name Hormiguero was in local use at the time for an *aguada* ("waterhole") near the ruins and was applied to the ruins as well. This probably refers to the many anthills found in the area.

The exploration of Hormiguero was reported, along with the results of other expeditions in the area, by Karl Ruppert and John Denison in 1943. The site was partly cleared and photographed, and a site plan was drawn. Additional mention of the site is made by Alberto Ruz Lhuillier in a work published in Mexico in 1945. The architecture at Hormiguero is covered in a 1977 publication by Potter for the Middle American Research Institute of Tulane University, in which he postulates a Central Yucatán style rather than regionally distinct Río Bec and Chenes styles. Certainly Structure II at Hormiguero, with its Chenes mask flanked by Río Bec towers, lends credence to his ideas.

Although there has been no extensive excavation at Hormiguero, it is reported that the National Institute of Anthropology and History has plans for work at the site. In 1978 some clearing had been done, and in 1979 a large area in front of Structure II was further cleared, allowing one to see the entire structure at once.

## CONNECTIONS

1. 74 miles by paved road from Chetumal to Xpuhil, or
2. 97 miles by paved road from Escárcega to Xpuhil, then 9 miles of fair to poor rock road, and 5 miles of fair dirt road.

## GETTING THERE

See "A Note on Southern Campeche and Quintana Roo" for general information about the area and for where to find a guide to Hormiguero, and "Río Bec B" for specific information about the location and condition of the rock road that heads south from the village of Xpuhil.

After 9 miles on the rock road, you reach the dirt cutoff on the right (west) for Hormiguero. The dirt road is in fair shape since the surface is mostly pretty solid, but it gets narrower and steeper as you go along. Generally, there are stops to be made to cut away fallen trees, and the road can be bumpy. Driving time from Xpuhil to Hormiguero is about 1½ hours (if you do not get stuck or have other problems).

Wear boots, and bring insect repellent, cold drinks, and a wide-angle lens for your camera—you will find lots of use for it—and fast film.

Allow 2½ hours to visit Hormiguero, once you get there.

*Note:* There is a problem concerning what is the best time of day to visit Hormiguero. Structure II is best lighted in the afternoon, while Structure V is best lighted in the morning. In the rainy season, the trip is best made in the morning since rain is less likely. If you reach the site early, you might try taking a brief look at Structure II, going on to the others, and returning to Structure II later when the light will be better. Even an hour or so can make a difference.

★

# *Payán*

(pah-*yahn*)

DERIVATION: Mayan for "First" (see text).
ORIGINAL NAME: Unknown.
CULTURE: Maya.
LOCATION: Southeastern part of the state of Campeche, Mexico.

---

## THE SITE

The explored portion of Payán reportedly includes several widely scattered mounds and a high pyramid faced with large stone blocks. There is some evidence of the former existence of a building atop the pyramid.

A number of other structures are found to the southeast, but only Structure I is in fair condition, and this is the main one visitors see today. On the way to Structure I, however, you pass some mounds and the remains of another small building.

Structure I has sixteen rooms on one level, and it is reported that there are suggestions of six others at a lower level. Much of the structure has fallen, but the front (west) façade has some bas-relief sculpture that is well preserved. This façade is broken by three doorways (perhaps originally there were two other smaller doorways in projections at either end), and the relief sculpture is located on each side of the central doorway. The lower portion of the sculpture depicts stylized profile serpent heads in two panels that are inset into plain sections of the wall. The motif is repeated twice vertically. The two panels are mirror images of each other and the heads of the serpents face away from the central doorway. They are similar to the relief sculpture found on Terrace 2-1 on the north side of Structure IV at Becan, but more detail is preserved at Payán, especially in the south panel (the one on the right, as you face the structure).

Above the panels, on an inclined upper-wall zone, is more relief sculpture of a different type. The upper wall zone above the central doorway has fallen, but from the design above the panels and the amount of debris in the central doorway, it seems possible that the upper-zone sculpture may have continued above the doorway. Remains of wooden lintels (reportedly zapote) are found in the doorways.

The other feature of interest at this structure is some graffiti on the plastered walls of one of the interior rooms. Enter the north doorway of the front of the structure (the one to the left as you face it). You will have to duck to get through because the doorway is partially filled with rubble. Proceed straight through the remains of two rooms and into the third, then turn left and enter a small chamber. As you enter, look to the wall on your right (east). Most of the graffiti are found on this wall and include a rather fat jaguar, a geometrical design that looks like a stylized profile serpent head, geometrical human heads, what appears to be a canoe, and a large platted design. On the opposite (west) wall, at the level of the debris, are remnants of small circular designs.

## RECENT HISTORY

Payán was explored by the Fourth Campeche Expedition sponsored by the Carnegie Institution of Washington in February, 1938. The site was named Payán ("first") as it was the first site visited on this expedition.

This site and many others were reported upon in a 1943 Carnegie Institution publication by Karl Ruppert and John Denison.

Payán is included in David Potter's comparative study *Maya Architecture of the Central Yucatán Peninsula, Mexico,* published by the Middle American Research Institute of Tulane University in 1977.

There has been no extensive excavation at the site, but it is known that the remains seen today are of Late Classic date.

## CONNECTIONS

1. 69.5 miles by paved road from Chetumal to San José Rancho, or
2. 101.5 miles by paved road from Escárcega to

*West side or front of Structure I showing inset relief panels, Payán. Late Classic period.*

San José Rancho, then about 4.5 miles on foot by rock road, and 0.5 mile by foot trail.

## GETTING THERE

You must have a guide to reach Payán. See Juan de la Cruz Briceño, the caretaker at Becan. (See "Becan" for getting to Juan's house.)

To reach San José Rancho, take Highway 186 west from Chetumal or east from Escárcega. The ranch is on the north side of the highway, near kilometer marker 161, about 4.5 miles east of the village of Xpuhil.

Permission must be secured at the ranch to enter the property, but Juan will see to this. You can park on the side of the highway in front of the ranch.

You proceed on foot through the ranch and a couple of gates, following the rock road. When you reach a high point at the first gate, look to the north. You will see a peak covered with vegetation in the distance, and this is where you are headed. It looks as though it is a long way off; it is. Later you will pass a ruined structure in a milpa, to the left (west) of the road, and afterward you take a foot trail to the right to reach Structure I.

Allow 1½ hours each way for the walk from the highway to Payán, and 45 minutes to see Structure I. Bring a canteen of water, and wear boots and a sun hat. The walk, in part, goes up and down low hills and through open country. Bring a wide-angle lens for your camera for over-all photos of the front of Structure I, and fast film or a flash unit to shoot the graffiti. Also have insect repellent, and matches for Juan to set fire to the newspaper he carries to get rid of the wasps—there generally are some. Have cold drinks in your car for when you return.

Be prepared for sore leg muscles the next day. The walk to Payán is tiring, though no longer than some others, but it is the only one that has ever left me with sore muscles in the shin area of my legs. Maybe it has something to do with the slope of the hills we climbed.

See "A Note on Southern Campeche and Quintana Roo" for information on accommodations and food in the area.

## MEXICO

### Quintana Roo

*Stucco mask panel depicting the sun god, in place at Kohunlich, on the lower level on the south side of the stairway, at the pyramid with the mask panels. Late Classic period.*

★★★

# *Kohunlich*

(koh-hoon-*leech*)

| | |
|---|---|
| DERIVATION: | Possibly "Cohune Ridge" or "Cohune Rich." Cohune is a species of palm. |
| ORIGINAL NAME: | Unknown. |
| CULTURE: | Maya. |
| LOCATION: | South-central part of the state of Quintana Roo, Mexico. |

## THE SITE

Effort is under way to make Kohunlich an interesting attraction for the benefit of Mexican residents and tourists alike. The grounds are being landscaped and a new administration building is being constructed for the comfort of visitors; there is an adjacent spacious parking area. From there it is a short distance on foot to the ruins.

The first area of interest as you enter the site lies left (north) of the road. It is composed of a plaza surrounded by four structures; the one on the east is the largest, most interesting, and best preserved. This is a pyramidal base with a western stair and remains of walls on the top; there is evidence of several rooms. The other structures surrounding the plaza are long, low platforms. There are some remains of standing architecture on the structures on the north and south sides of the plaza, while the west side is bounded by a rubble mound.

Climb the eastern structure for good views of its plaza and, more important, for a comprehensive view of the larger Ceremonial Plaza, which lies to the south.

The Ceremonial Plaza is bounded on the east and west by massive ruined buildings, which rest on top of broad, low, stepped platforms. On the south of the Ceremonial Plaza is a long stepped platform with few remains of a superstructure.

Follow the road east to what appears to be a sunken plaza. There are extensive remains of what appears to be a stucco floor, bounded by a low platform with a stair on the east side. On the south is another low platform with a short, solid, circular construction. Perhaps this is an altar; the diameter seems too great for it to be the remains of a column.

You now leave the road and head east to the pyramid with the mask panels, the real gem of the site. This pyramid sits atop what appears to be a natural elevation, and its central stair and the lower portion of its base have been partly restored. Little remains of its crowning temple. What you really came to Kohunlich to see, of course, are the fantastic mask panels flanking the stairway; there are three on each side. These panels certainly rank as some of the finest and most sensitive Maya sculptures ever produced. They are in an excellent state of preservation, and have been restored where needed.

The four lower panels depict very humanized masks of the sun god, with elaborate decorations on either side. The two upper panels are smaller and depict the same deity in a more grotesque form. The panels are made of carved stucco over a stone base. Remnants of paint are visible on some of the panels. Each is a bit different from the other.

There are thatched shelters protecting the panels, and, recently, sheets of plastic were placed in front

*Structure on the east side of the Ceremonial Plaza, Kohunlich. Late Classic period.*

*Pyramid with the mask panels, Kohunlich. Solid circular construction and part of the sunken plaza are at the bottom. Late Classic period.*

*Pyramid with the mask panels, Kohunlich. This panel is north of the stairway on the second level. Late Classic period.*

of the panels. These protections are obviously needed, but they make photography a bit difficult. A wide-angle lens is essential to get a complete panel in one shot and to keep the thatch from showing. Fast film is a good idea.

From the pyramid, head southwest by foot trail to the ball court. This court is well preserved and, though it is simple, its size is impressive. It seems to be open on both ends—at least no end enclosures are seen today—and its sides are composed of gently sloping sections topped by vertical sections.

From the ball court, you can return to the road by entering the Ceremonial Plaza at its southeast corner.

## RECENT HISTORY

Kohunlich was reportedly discovered by looters in 1967. Fortunately an informer notified the Mexican government, and protective action was taken in time to save the panels from removal or destruction.

Mexican archaeologist Víctor Segovia has directed excavations at the site for several seasons, beginning in the early 1970s, and work is continuing. So far, little has entered the English-language literature about Kohunlich, but perhaps this will soon be rectified. It is known that the mask panels and most of the architecture date to the Late Classic period; it would be interesting to learn more about the site's beginnings.

The mask panels at Kohunlich are very similar to a panel on display in the Mexico City Museum. This panel is listed (at the museum) as coming from Campeche or Quintana Roo. A guide pamphlet issued by the state government of Quintana Roo says that the panel belongs to the "zone" of Kohunlich, but I am uncertain whether that means the actual site or the general area. This enormous panel was stolen from Mexico and offered for sale to the Metropolitan Museum in New York for half a million dollars. It is to the museum's credit that it was instrumental in returning the panel to Mexico.

## CONNECTION

1. 42 miles by paved road from Chetumal.

## GETTING THERE

From Chetumal take Highway 186 west for 37 miles to the Kohunlich cutoff. The paved cutoff is near kilometer marker 214; it is well marked and heads south (left). Driving time to Kohunlich is ¾ hour from Chetumal, a few minutes more from Xpuhil, and 2¾ hours from Escárcega.

See "A Note on Southern Campeche and Quintana Roo" for accommodations in the area. Allow 2 hours at the site. Tennis shoes are fine. A guide is not necessary.

---

# *A Note on the Quintana Roo Coast and the Offshore Islands*

The Caribbean coast of Quintana Roo can be easily reached by paved highway in several ways. This area—virtually inaccessible for the visitor until the completion of coastal Highway 307 in 1972—is being rapidly developed. It is covered with the remains of small Maya temples, some of which have only recently been studied. There are also remains on the islands of Mujeres and Cozumel. In addition, the area can boast the two large and important sites of Tulum and Cobá.

Since all the sites covered are reasonably close together, the connections and accommodations mentioned apply to all, and since Tulum will be the prime target for all visitors, general mileages will be given to that site. It will also be used as a point of reference for the other sites.

The archaeology of Tulum and Cobá will be covered in individual sections, and that of Cozumel will be found under that heading as a part of the section "The Small Coastal Sites from North to South and the Offshore Islands." The archaeology of the other small sites will be grouped together here, since the little that is known generally applies to all.

The standing architectural remains along the coast and on the islands, for the most part, date to the Late Postclassic period. One exception is Tancah, which has some remains that probably date to the Classic period.

Ceramic evidence found along the coast, however, indicates that at least some areas were occupied during earlier periods. Evidence for the earliest period of occupancy in the central part of the coast was found at Tancah, and dates to the Middle Preclassic period. Late Preclassic ceramics were found at Xcaret, and Early Classic ceramics at Xelha. The substructure of the building with the painted decorations at Xelha may also predate the Late Postclassic structures at the site.

The style of the typical Late Postclassic temple is similar to that of Tulum (see "Tulum" for details), although the structures are generally smaller. The corbeled vault was used in some buildings, but beam-and-mortar roofs are common. Other characteristics are the use of simple moldings, columns in doorways, and the extensive use of stucco for decorations and to cover the surface of the structure. Certain architectural features in the east-coast buildings are also found at Chichén Itzá and Mayapán.

In addition to the archaeological investigations listed in "Tulum," recent work has been carried out at some of the smaller sites. The most important are, the work by Arthur Miller at Tancah (and Tulum) for the University of California, and a preliminary study of Xcaret (and a survey of other coastal sites) by E. Wyllys Andrews IV and Anthony P. Andrews for the Middle American Research Institute of Tulane University. Reports on these investigations were published in the 1970s.

The buildings listed in the section on the small coastal sites are those that are most accessible, though many more exist. Anthony P. Andrews estimates that there are approximately 500 masonry structures in the stretch of coast between Playa del Carmen and Tulum, and there are more north and south of the area. Some of the sites covered in the section on the small coastal sites—such as Playa del Carmen, Xcaret, Chakalal, Akumal, Xelha, and Tancah—have additional groups of structures some distance from those described. A guide would be necessary to visit these outlying groups.

## CONNECTIONS AND GETTING THERE

From Mérida—the most common starting point—there are three ways to get to Tulum:

1. By Highway 180 west to Puerto Juárez, then Highway 307 south to Tulum (275 miles),
2. By Highway 180 west to Valladolid, Highway 295 south to Felipe Carrillo Puerto, and Highway 307 north to Tulum (249 miles), or
3. By Highway 261 south to Muna, Highway 184 southeast to Felipe Carrillo Puerto, and Highway 307 north to Tulum (242 miles).

Any of these routes will get you from Mérida to Tulum in less than 6 hours since all the roads are paved.

Tulum can also be reached by paved road from Chetumal by taking Highway 186 west to the junction with Highway 307, then 307 north to Tulum (155 miles). This takes less than 4 hours.

Places to stay along the coast, from north to south, are Cancún, Cabañas Capitán Lafitte, El Márlin Azul, Hotel Molcas in Playa del Carmen, Pamul, and Club Akumal Caribe. All are north of Tulum and only a short distance off coastal Highway 307. There is a place for camping at El Paraíso and, reportedly, a hotel south of Tulum. They are on a partly paved road that parallels the coast to the seaward side of Highway 307. A new hotel is now open at Cobá ruins.

Cancún is a new development, just south of Puerto Juárez, and it is spectacular. Many hotels are now in operation, and more are under construction. Golf courses and boating, fishing, and diving facilities have also been built. All of this is on a lovely sand spit facing the Caribbean and backed by a lagoon. It is worth a few minutes to drive through just to see what is going on there. An airport to accommodate large jets has been constructed to service Cancún, which is envisioned as Mexico's new Acapulco. Cancún is 1 mile south of Puerto Juárez and 78 miles north of Tulum.

The cutoff for both El Márlin Azul and Capitán Lafitte's is 39 miles south of Puerto Juárez (4 miles north of Playa del Carmen) and 40 miles north of Tulum. The cutoff is well marked and is near kilometer marker 296. A rough dirt road leads left (east) for a little under 2 miles to El Márlin Azul and turns north for another half mile to Capitán Lafitte's.

Both places have individual cabins and adequate facilities. Although there is no restaurant at El Márlin Azul, the guests are welcome to eat at Capitán Laffite's. They are both right on the beach.

The Hotel Molcas in the town of Playa del Carmen faces the sea, and makes a good stopover if you are planning to take the early-morning ferry to Cozumel. Playa del Carmen is 43 miles south of Puerto Juárez and 36 miles north of Tulum.

Primitive but spacious accommodations can be rented at Pamul. There are four cabins with two units each, and each unit can accommodate eight or ten people. Sometimes, however, their *bomba* ("pump") is not working, and there is no running water. In this case, you have to haul your own from a drum. Check on the situation before you rent a room. There is a good swim spot here.

Ther cutoff for Pamul is between kilometer markers 274 and 273, is well marked, and goes half a mile to the cabins. The cutoff is a good rock road.

Farther south is the Club Akumal Caribe, 64 miles south of Puerto Juárez and 15 miles north of Tulum. This spot is the nicest of all, but is expensive. It has both cabañas and higher-priced bungalows facing the sea, its own small quiet bay, which is ideal for swimming, a large thatched-roof dining room with good food, and an underwater museum, which you can visit by snorkling. The club also rents snorkling and diving equipment, and will arrange boat trips and fishing and diving parties. Other extras are a number of interesting pre-Columbian sculptures, reportedly from the Veracruz area, and a museum of objects brought up from the sea by the divers of the Exploration and Water Sports Club of Mexico (CEDAM), headquartered at Akumal.

If you are equipped for it, you can camp in your recreational vehicle or tent at El Paraíso. There are also a few rooms for rent. They are attractive from the outside but contain three small cots and *nothing* else—no tables, chairs, shelves, or even sheets. There are shared baths at the end of the row of rooms. Rates are reasonable, however. To reach El Paraíso, go first to Tulum ruins. Then take the unnumbered paved road along the coast. El Paraíso is 1 mile south of Tulum. A hotel is reportedly in operation near Tulum, but it may not be open all year round. Take the coast road to El Paraíso and continue south for another 8.5 miles to the hotel. The new hotel at Cobá ruins will be useful if you are visiting that site. See "Cobá" for getting there. If you are traveling Highway 307 between Tulum and Chetumal, there is the Hotel Chan Santa Cruz, in Felipe Carrillo Puerto, that can be used as an overnight stop.

Most of the hotels listed above serve food. Other restaurants in the area are found along Highway 307 at the cutoffs for Xcaret, Tulum, and Muyil, and in Felipe Carrillo Puerto.

Isla Mujeres and Cozumel have been tourist havens for some time and have accommodations and restaurants in all price ranges.

Isla Mujeres is 6 miles off the Quintana Roo coast, and passenger ferry service from Puerto Juárez is scheduled about every 2 hours. The trip takes about 35 minutes.

There is also a car ferry, which leaves the mainland from Punta Sam (5 miles north of Puerto Juárez). Three or four trips a day are made, and they take about ½ hour. Check locally for the schedule. Sometimes the last ferry from Isla Mujeres to Punta Sam does not take cars. Check on this, too.

Cozumel is 12 miles off the Quintana Roo coast, and can be reached by ferry in two ways. A passenger ferry leaves from Playa del Carmen three times a day (generally in the early morning, at midday, and late in the afternoon—but check times, for schedules change). The trip lasts 1¼ to 1¾ hours, depending on which ship you get and the condition of the sea. A car ferry leaves Puerto Morelos once a day (check the schedule locally) and takes the passengers of the vehicles, but apparently not passengers on foot. The trip takes about 2½ hours.

If you want to have a vehicle on Cozumel and plan to use it for one or two days, it would be better to rent one when you arrive. If you plan a longer stay, it would be cheaper to bring your own vehicle across on the car ferry. There are parking areas at Puerto Juárez and Playa del Carmen where you can leave your car when you go to the islands. Parking rates are reasonable.

In general, rooms along the coast and on the islands are higher priced than their equivalents inland.

There are service stations at Puerto Juárez, 3 miles south of Puerto Juárez along the highway, and at Tulum, and gas from a drum can sometimes be purchased at Puerto Morelos and Playa del Carmen. No gas is available in the 61-mile stretch between Tulum and Felipe Carrillo Puerto. Gas is available on the islands.

Car rentals are available in Mérida and in the Puerto Juárez–Cancún area, as are taxis, which travel the coast. There is also bus service from Mérida to the coast and along the coast in both directions. Along the coast, however, the buses do not run with the frequency found in other parts of Mexico.

Until recently there were three different sets of kilometer markers along Highway 307; two have now been discontinued, though you may still occasionally spot one. The new numbering begins in the south at the junction of Highways 186 and 307 near Chetumal and runs to the north to Puerto Juárez.

There are air connections between Mérida and the islands and interisland flights, as well as flights to Cancún and Tulum. Most flights are daily or oftener.

Carrying soft drinks or water can be a nice luxury and is recommended. Ice is available in Puerto Juárez and sometimes at Playa del Carmen.

Tennis shoes are adequate for the major part of Tulum and the small coastal sites.

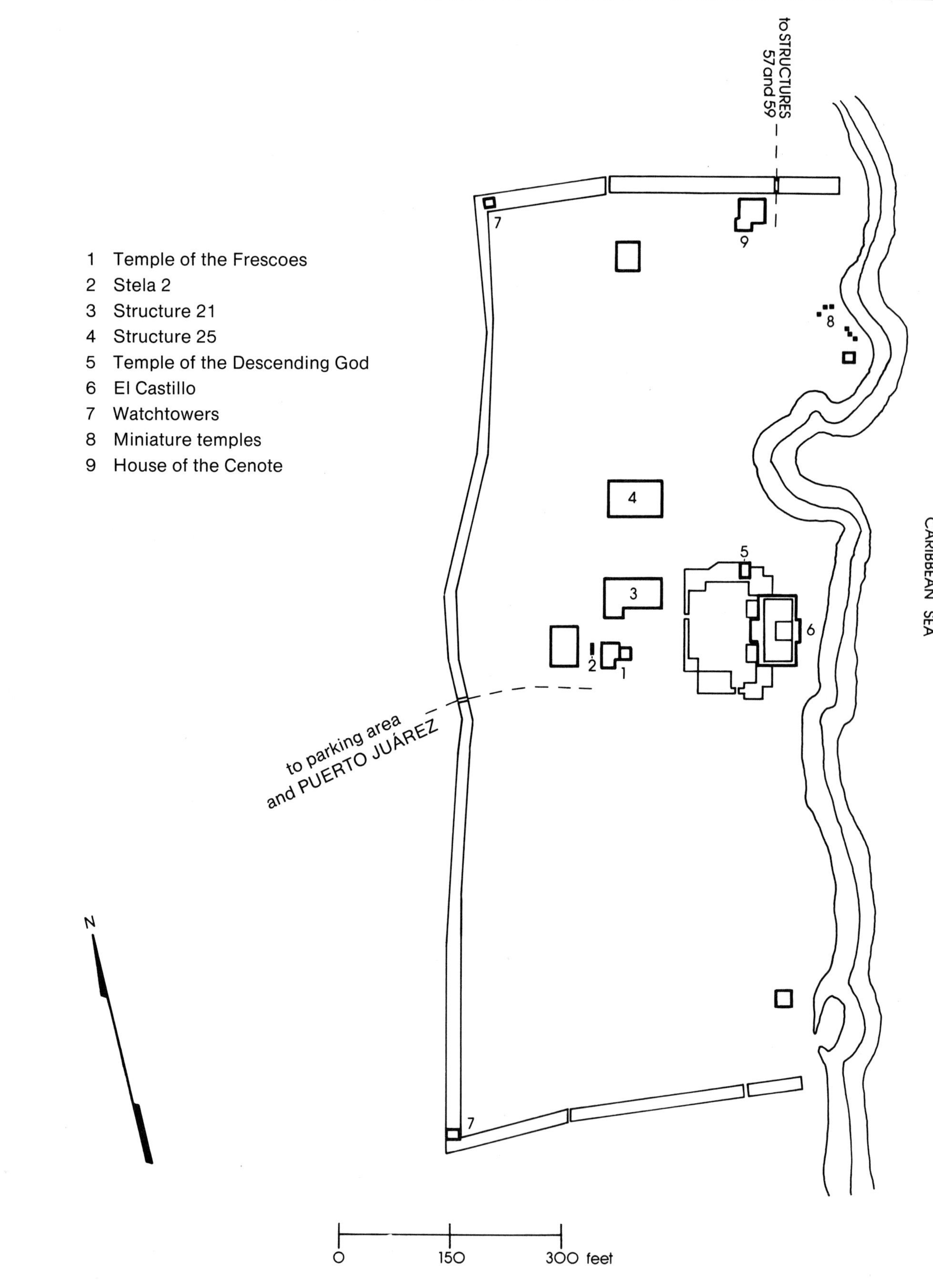

1 Temple of the Frescoes
2 Stela 2
3 Structure 21
4 Structure 25
5 Temple of the Descending God
6 El Castillo
7 Watchtowers
8 Miniature temples
9 House of the Cenote
to STRUCTURES 57 and 59
CARIBBEAN SEA
to parking area and PUERTO JUÁREZ
N
0
150
300 feet


TULUM

★★★★

# *Tulum*

(too-*loom*)

DERIVATION: Mayan for a "Wall" or "Fortification;" a "Fortress." A modern name.
ORIGINAL NAME: Possibly Zamá.
CULTURE: Maya.
LOCATION: Northeastern part of the state of Quintana Roo, Mexico.

---

## THE SITE

One of the most impressive features of Tulum is its exquisite setting. It is perched on a cliff above the turquoise waters of the Caribbean and is surrounded on three sides by a wall.

It was long thought that the wall was a defensive feature, and perhaps it was, though E. Wyllys Andrews IV makes the point that the construction may have been more symbolic than tactically defensive. The wall has five entrances—one of which is used today as access to the site—and it encloses about 16 acres. It averages 18 feet thick, and 9 to 15 feet high. Michael Coe suggests that no more than 500 to 600 people lived within the enclosure, but Tulum is thought to have been an important trading center. The wall is dated to A.D. 1200–1450, and the structures within are all Postclassic in date. At some points visible structures cover earlier ones, but even those are of late date. For example, there is an earlier temple beneath El Castillo, the tallest and apparently the most important structure at the site.

One puzzling factor at Tulum was the discovery of Stela 1, dated to A.D. 564, since removed to the British Museum by Thomas Gann. This date is several hundred years earlier than the structures at the site, and that much earlier than the ceramic evidence would indicate. It was long postulated that the stela was moved to Tulum from some other site. Andrews feels that it is almost certain that it came from the nearby site of Tancah, whose history goes back to the Classic period.

Another notable feature at Tulum is the mural paintings, especially in the Temple of the Frescoes. There are striking similarities with the Mixtec codices from the Mexican highlands (Santa Rita in Belize had similar murals), but the themes are clearly Maya. It is possible that the murals represent the spread of a new religion. The style has been called the Late Postclassic International Style by Donald Robertson. The Tulum murals are quite different from the Classic Maya murals at Bonampak and Chacmultún, and from those of the Maya-Toltec period at Chichén Itzá. Tulum's frescoes also differ markedly from Classic Maya vase painting and late Maya codices.

Robertson believes the International Style originated in the Mixteca and radiated to Mexico, Santa Rita, and ultimately to Tulum. This style is also found in ceramics, some from the Cholula area. The style was still spreading at the time of the Spanish conquest, and continued until about A.D. 1600 in manuscript painting.

The Late Postclassic style of architecture found at Tulum and most other east-coast sites is quite different from earlier Classic traditions. There was a pronounced degradation in the building arts in the Postclassic period. Ceremonial centers were less extensive in area and individual structures were smaller. Some truly miniature temples—just a few feet high—are found at Tulum, Xelha and other east-coast sites.

Stone cutting was poorly developed and thick coats of plaster were relied upon to cover rough masonry. "The vault, so long a standard form of roofing, was largely replaced by the beam-and-masonry roof," according to H. E. D. Pollock. Stucco was extensively used for decorative elements.

Since almost everything of interest is enclosed within the wall, and since the site is rather small and well cleared, no special sequence is recommended in visiting it. Just roam around and enjoy.

The more important structures at Tulum are as follows: Structure 1, El Castillo, has two serpent columns in the doorway of the temple. They are similar to the serpent columns used earlier at Chichén Itzá and show Toltec influence. Structure 5, the small Temple of the Descending God, has an interesting outward batter to the walls, stucco decorations on the outside, and remnants of mural paintings on the inside. The descending god, also called the diving god, may be in reality a bee god.

*Structure 1 (El Castillo), center, and Structure 5 (Temple of the Descending God), left, from the northwest, Tulum. Late Postclassic period.*

*Structure 5 (Temple of the Descending God), front (west) side, Tulum. Late Postclassic period.*

*Structure 16 (Temple of the Frescoes) with Stela 2 in front, from the northwest, Tulum. Late Postclassic period.*

*Structure 16 (Temple of the Frescoes), detail of the mask at the southwest corner, Tulum. Late Postclassic period.*

*Detail of the frescoes on the interior of Structure 16 (Temple of the Frescoes), Tulum. Late Postclassic period.*

This deity is found on several structures at Tulum and other east-coast sites, as well as at Cobá in the interior, 30 miles northwest of Tulum. (See "Cobá" for more on this deity.) Sayil, far across the Yucatán Peninsula has a representation of this god that dates to the Late Classic period—a few hundred years before the Tulum depiction. The figure is part human, but has winglike attachments. Structure 16, the Temple of the Frescoes, lies roughly in the center of the site. The frescoes belong to the earliest stages of construction of this temple.

In Structures 5 and 16, the frescoes are protected by flimsy barricades, but you can get photographs through the openings. You are not allowed to use flash equipment.

The badly eroded Stela 2 has recently been re-erected on a small platform in front of the Temple of the Frescoes.

Other structures of interest are Structure 25, noted for its excellent depiction of the diving god, in a niche above the central doorway of the inner chamber, and Structure 21, which has X-shaped crossbars in its small exterior windows.

The many other structures inside the wall, including the watch towers on the wall, are also worth visiting. Allow about 2 hours to cover the site.

Tulum is a most photogenic site and no special photographic problems are encountered. Since most of the interesting structures face west, the afternoon hours are best for photography.

*Temple with the roof comb (Structure 59), outside the wall, Tulum.*

There are two other well-preserved structures at Tulum, located outside the wall, along the coast, north of the main part of the site. It is possible that they are older than most of the structures in the main part of Tulum. Reaching them entails a rather rough walk over limestone outcrops and loose boulders, and through spots with thick vegetation.

The first structure you reach is Structure 57, a one-room shrine. Its walls and roof are intact, and it is unusual in that its single doorway faces inland rather than toward the sea. The structure is overgrown with vegetation and difficult to photograph, but you can climb to the roof from the southwest corner and get some nice over-all views of the main part of Tulum. This structure is approximately 0.3 mile from the north wall.

About 0.3 mile farther north is the second temple, Structure 59, which is more interesting. It is a one-room structure with remains of a roof comb—the only roof comb reported from Tulum. The roof comb is made of slablike stones placed at an angle, which leave triangular-shaped openings. Parts of two levels of the roof comb remain in place and they rise from the center of the roof. It is thought that perhaps a third level existed at one time. The area around the structure is cleared, so it is easy to photograph.

You can actually see a third structure outside the north wall at Tulum—or at least what is left of it. It appears to be the remains of a miniature shrine, but only a small part of a wall with a doorway are left standing. Two thin slabs rest against each other on top and they are reminiscent of the roof-comb slabs mentioned above. They are not bonded to the wall, so I do not know if this is their original position. This shrine is located between the north wall and the first structure described above, and you will pass right by it.

A guide is not necessary for the main part of

Tulum, and tennis shoes are adequate. You will definitely need sunglasses and a sun hat. Bring along your swimsuit if you want to take a dip at the beach.

If you decide to visit the structures outside the wall, ask for a guide at the ticket office when you enter the site. A trail leaves the north wall through its easternmost gate, near the structure called the House of the Cenote, but the trail soon vanishes, so you may not be able to find the structures on your own. Boots would be better than tennis shoes on this hike, which will take about 1 hour from the time you leave the wall until you return.

## RECENT HISTORY

Though still not certain, it is possible that Tulum was one of the "cities" sighted by Spaniard Juan de Grijalva's expedition in 1518, when it sailed the Caribbean Coast of Yucatán. A walled city, known as Zamá, was also reported in *Relación de las Cosas de Yucatán* by Bishop Diego de Landa in 1566, and the description and location fit Tulum. Thereafter, little is mentioned about the site until the middle of the nineteenth century, when credit for its discovery is said to go to one Juan José Gálvez.

As with many other ruined cities, Tulum was first made known to the world at large by those intrepid travelers John Lloyd Stephens and Frederick Catherwood. The account of their visit and illustrations of the structures were published in *Incidents of Travel in Yucatán* in 1843. They were the first to clear and explore the site.

Stephens reported a fragmented stela (Stela 1), and in 1910, George Howe deciphered the date and buried the fragments for protection. Sylvanus Morley was unable to locate the stela fragments on his first visit to Tulum in 1913 but later learned their location from Howe. In 1916, Morley returned to Tulum, found the fragments, and confirmed Howe's interpretation of the date. Morley and his personnel also cleared and photographed the site, traced some of the murals, and gathered information for a map. The Carnegie Institution of Washington underwrote these trips, and continued to support work at Tulum for the next few years. Samuel K. Lothrop reported the data from the later expeditions in 1924.

Tulum was also studied by Mexican archaeologist Miguel Angel Fernández in 1938 and the following years, during which time some of the buildings were consolidated. In 1955, W. T. Sanders, working for the Carnegie Institution, reported on a reconnaissance of northern Quintana Roo, and in 1960 presented his study of the ceramics of the area, including Tulum.

## CONNECTIONS AND GETTING THERE

General connections for Tulum and nearby accommodations are covered in "A Note on the Quintana Roo Coast and the Offshore Islands." The cutoff for Tulum is 79 miles south of Puerto Juárez and 61 miles north of Felipe Carrillo Puerto. The cutoff to the site is paved, heads east, and runs about half a mile.

Soft drinks are available at the entrance to Tulum.

★★★

# *Cobá*

(koh-*bah*)

DERIVATION: According to Michael Coe, the name means "Ruffled Waters," but other authorities equate the name with Chachalaca, a bird that cries continually while flying.

ORIGINAL NAME: Possibly Cobá (see text).

CULTURE: Maya.

LOCATION: Northern part of the state of Quintana Roo, Mexico.

---

## THE SITE

Cobá is actually a number of separated sites that go collectively under the one name. Over all, it is a huge site, as you will realize when you walk from one area to another.

Cobá proper is designated Group B and is located between Lakes Cobá and Macanxoc. Nohoch Mul is Group C, and Macanxoc, with its many stelae, is Group A. Other small ruins in the area have their own names. All the structures are located amidst five small lakes, an unusual feature in the almost waterless plain of northern Yucatán.

In the area of Cobá (all groups included), more than sixteen *sacbeob* are known. They connect various parts of the site, and some actually go through a portion of one of the lakes (which may have been smaller when the *sacbeob* were built). Some *sacbeob* lead to more distant sites. By far the most impressive is the one that goes due west for an astounding 62.5 miles, to connect with the minor site of Yaxuná. This is the longest known *sacbé* in the Maya area, and it varies in height from 2 feet, to 8 feet where it crosses swampy areas; its average width is 32 feet (see "The Cobá-Yaxuná Sacbé" for details on where best to see it). The walls of the *sacbé* are roughly dressed stone, and the bed is composed of boulders topped with small stones laid in cement. A stucco or cement layer formed the surface, though it is now badly disintegrated.

A five-ton stone roller was found on the *sacbé* and at one time was thought to have been used in connection with the road's construction (to compact the surface into a hard layer). Now, however, this interpretation seems to be in question. There is reason to believe that the Cobá-Yaxuná Sacbé continued past Cobá and connected with Xcaret on the Caribbean Coast, and that it then branched south to the Tancah-Tulum area.

Whether Maya *sacbeob* in general, and this one in particular, were used for ceremonial or commercial purposes or both remains a debated point. At any rate, since the Mayas lacked beasts of burden and wheeled vehicles, we can be sure that only foot traffic traversed these ancient roads.

Unfortunately, most of the structures at Cobá are in a poor state of preservation, but recent excavation and restoration of a few have made their original appearances clearer.

The easily followed main trail at the site leaves from the parking area and passes near Group B, which may be reached by a short side trail. The cutoff is marked Grupo Cobá.

Group B is the largest architectural assemblage at Cobá and the structures there are designated by letters. The area was totally cleared in the early 1970s, but most of it is once again overgrown. The exceptions are Structure I and its abutting platform, Structure A.

Structure I is an imposing seven-tiered pyramid, with slightly rounded corners and a broad stairway on the west side. There are a few remains of a temple on top. Other rooms may be seen flanking the stairway at the lower level, and you can enter those on the north side. The structure has been excavated and partially restored, and is kept cleared.

Structure A joins Structure I on the west and is approached by an even broader—though shorter—stairway. At the rear of the platform there is a low enclosure housing an eroded stela.

The next branch from the main trail is marked Juego de Pelota. This ball court is a short distance north of Structure A, but is best reached by returning to the main trail and taking the marked cutoff. There is really little to see here as the court is very overgrown, but the two mounds that formed the sides of the court can be seen.

Farther along the main trail you come to another side trail, which leads a fair distance to the Conjunto las Pinturas. The Conjunto las Pinturas is a small, one-room temple, sitting atop a stepped pyramid. The temple has two small doorways on

*Structure I of Group B, the front (west) side, Cobá. Late Classic period. Note stela at lower left.*

the west side, separated by a column of drum-shaped stones, an architectural style similar to the Late Postclassic temples at Tulum and along the coast. Remnants of plaster adhere to the area above the doorways and some remains of paintings are found there, giving the temple its name. There is also a single doorway on each of the north and south sides, and from the one on the north you get a gorgeous view of the Nohoch Mul in the distance. Inside the temple is a chunk of stone and stucco lying on the floor; it retains a few remnants of painting. One small painting that I saw in 1973 on the inside wall of the temple to the right of the main doorway is no longer there.

The pyramidal base supporting the temple has a western stair that faces other structures. There are remains of low walls, drum-shaped columns, and an enclosure at the foot of the stairway that houses the bottom portion of a carved but eroded stela. The Conjunto las Pinturas and adjacent structures were cleared and partially restored in recent years.

A nice touch at Cobá is the labeling of the various kinds of trees. The signs indicate the Latin as well as the Mayan name, and several may be seen in this area.

From the Conjunto las Pinturas, there is a short cut back to the main trail, which will save you some walking. Considering the oppressive heat and the distances to be covered, you will welcome this. The trail is narrower than the one you came in on, but is easy to follow. It leaves the area from the northwest corner of the base of the pyramid, in other words, to the left as you face the stairway. It is but a short distance back to the main trail.

When you reach the main trail, turn right. On both sides of the trail you will see large rubble mounds. Just past one of these, an unmarked and easily missed side trail (on your right) leads a short

*Conjunto las Pinturas, the front (west) side, Cobá. Postclassic period.*

distance to three stelae. Two are fairly well preserved and are protected by thatched shelters; a third is eroded and unprotected. You will need a wide-angle lens here.

The first stela is squarish, and depicts a single figure holding what appears to be a cross in his right hand. There are twelve glyph blocks on the left (as you face it). The back of the stela is plain, but on one of its narrow sides and top are some delicately incised glyphs. The second stela lies on its back, and has a single figure and some glyphs on its face.

Continue now along the main trail to the massive temple pyramid called the Nohoch Mul, a name given this structure and group by Sir J. Eric S. Thompson. This Mayan name means "Great Mound," and was the term used for it by one of Thompson's Maya guides.

The Nohoch Mul is 120 feet tall, and its pyramidal base is terraced in seven sections. A 35-foot-wide stairway ascends the south side to a well-preserved temple with an intact roof. The temple has a single doorway. There were originally three niches in the upper façade of the temple; one has been destroyed. The two remaining niches contain depictions of the diving god—or descending god—also found at Tulum and Sayil. The figure in the central niche bears some remnants of paint.

According to Ralph L. Roys, the modern Yucatec Mayas believe in bee gods, who appear in the story of creation. They further believe that these gods dwell at Cobá. This, plus the fact that the diving position of the figures is the same as the one found in the apiculture section of the *Codex Madrid*, leads to Roys's belief that the deity represented is a bee god.

The southwest corner of the pyramid and the stairway have been restored, but it is a long and tir-

*Stela with figure holding a crosslike object, Cobá. Late Classic period.*

*Nohoch Mul (Group C) with intact temple on top, Cobá. Late Classic period.*

ing climb to the top. It is worth the effort, though, to see the temple and niche figures, and for views of the area. Near the top of the stairway, and flanking it on the left (west), is part of a stone-and-stucco decoration. It is badly weathered and I could not make out the design. There are remains of rooms flanking the stairway at the lower levels.

The Nohoch Mul faces a large plaza, and though this was completely cleared a few years ago, it is now overgrown with small trees, except for the trail that leads to the base of the structure.

There is a large unrestored conical mound south of the Nohoch Mul, which apparently faces the same plaza, and this is best seen from the top of the Nohoch Mul.

Another structure that faces the plaza on the east side (to your right, as you face the Nohoch Mul) has been cleared and partially restored. It has a broad stairway ascending to a platform with remains of lower walls on top. A niche in the stairway houses a stela with an interesting history. The broken lower portion of the stela was discovered by Thompson in 1930, and recent work at the site uncovered the missing upper portion of the monument. It has since been restored and reerected, and is protected by a thatch shelter. This large stela is one of the best preserved at Cobá. It depicts four captive figures, in addition to the main figure, and dates to A.D. 780.

At one time it was possible to visit a structure

behind the Nohoch Mul that has remains of a corbel-vaulted chamber in the lower section. This area is now overgrown, and I did not see a trail leading to it.

When we first visited Cobá in 1973, we had the caretaker as a guide and he took us to the Macanxoc area, where we saw five stelae. One was in a niche that appeared to be the lower part of a structure, and the rest were atop small platforms. All of the stelae were somewhat eroded, but were worth a look. Macanxoc is about 1.3 miles south of the Nohoch Mul. On a visit in 1977, we did not attempt to revisit Macanxoc, but I did look for a marked trail leading there since there are several others pointing out the main features at the site. I could not find one. I do not know if Macanxoc has become overgrown, as have other parts of the site, or if it is still accessible to visitors.

Some authorities believe that the Nohoch Mul and other temple pyramids at Cobá are architecturally more related to sites in the Petén than to most other structures in northern Yucatán. Upon first viewing one of them, Sylvanus Morley told Thompson: "Eric, this can't be a Yucatán site. We must have traveled south for ten days and landed up in the middle of the Petén."

Nevertheless, David Potter—who recently studied the architecture of the Central Yucatán area and related his information to other areas of Yucatán—feels that, "Despite the assortment of influences attributed to the site of Cobá from the Petén and elsewhere, what little is known of the architecture here does not suggest any major disjuncture from the style of the other buildings of the same time period in northern Yucatán." Current research will, one hopes, clarify this matter and others.

Another point of similarity between Cobá and sites in the Petén is the depiction of captives on some of Cobá's stelae. This motif is much more prevalent in the south, although three stela at Etzna and one at Dzilám on the north coast of Yucatán also show the same subject matter. Thompson commented on the advanced state of carving of some of the early Macanxoc stelae compared to those of certain southern sites from the same time period.

An unusual feature at Cobá is the use of wooden lintels made from *chintok,* instead of the generally used zapote. We were told that *chintok* is a harder wood and superior to zapote.

On the basis of ceramic evidence it is known that Cobá was occupied at least from the Early Classic period, although the site's peak was during the early part of the Late Classic period, when over twenty sculptured stelae (dating from A.D. 623 to 780) were erected. Several plain stelae have also been discovered.

The association of the inscribed stelae and ceramic deposits with the architecture suggests construction dates from about A.D. 613 to 682, or a bit later for most of the structures. There are some structural remains, however, such as the Conjunto las Pinturas, which date to the Postclassic period, and ceramic evidence shows occupation at that time.

## RECENT HISTORY

Shortly after the Spanish conquest of Mexico some of the natives of Yucatán were taught to write in their own language, using letters of the Spanish alphabet. A body of literature developed, some of which survives today, giving us some knowledge of Postclassic times. These documents are known collectively as *The Books of Chilam Balam,* which, according to Morley, may be freely translated as "The Books of the Soothsayer of Hidden Things." Some of these writings are translations of pre-Columbian Maya codices, the originals of which are now lost. In one of the books the name Cobá is mentioned; therefore it is possible that this is the original name of the site.

In more recent times Cobá was mentioned in *Incidents of Travel in Yucatán,* by John Lloyd Stephens published in 1843. Although Stephens was unable to visit the site, he learned of it from a priest in Chemax. The priest, who had never visited the site, was recording information about "objects of curiosity and interest" from the area under his jurisdiction, by government order. Stephens copied the priest's notes, which included the location of Cobá, its setting on several lakes, a description of some of the architecture, and the existence and direction of the main *sacbé,* all of which was fairly accurate. With regard to the *sacbé,* the priest's notes said that "some aver that it goes in the direction of Chichén Itzá," as indeed it does. Yaxuná is just 13 miles southwest of Chichén Itzá.

Until fairly recently modern Mayas burned incense at the feet of some of the stelae at Cobá, doubtless in veneration of the gods of their forefathers.

Near the end of the nineteenth century Teobert Maler visited Cobá and photographed a figure of the diving god. In early 1926, Thomas Gann briefly visited the site and reported it to Morley, Thompson, and others who were working at Chichén Itzá. Later that year the last two visited the site, as did

A. V. Kidder and Jean Charlot, who made drawings of the sculpture. They were accompanied by local Mayas, who showed them additional sites in the area. Thompson returned in 1930 with his bride and H. E. D. Pollock for further study of Cobá, and in 1932, with Pollock and Charlot, he published a preliminary study of the site, including a map. The ceramics of the site, were studied by George W. Brainerd, along with the ceramics of other parts of Yucatán, and these data were published in 1958.

In the late 1960s excavation and restoration were undertaken by Mexican archaeologist Norberto González Crespo for the National Institute of Anthropology and History, and this continued for several years. In the early 1970s, the National Geographic Society sponsored additional work by George Stuart, technically working under González Crespo.

## CONNECTION

1. 30 miles by paved road from Tulum.

## GETTING THERE

From Tulum take Highway 307 south for a little over a mile to the cutoff for Cobá. The cutoff is on your right (west), is marked with a large sign, and goes directly to the site.

As you approach Cobá, the road crosses some of the ancient *sacbeob*, which are marked with signs. Also in this area you will see a branch road on your right, marked "Nvo Xcan." Nuevo Xcan is a small town in Quintana Roo, on Highway 180, near the Yucatán border. It is about 25 to 30 miles north of Cobá. The road has been cut through to Nuevo Xcan, but has not yet been paved. Inquire about its condition before taking it. When it is paved, it will offer a good shortcut to visitors driving from Mérida to Tulum.

There are a hotel and restaurant at Cobá, and soft drinks are sold at the ticket office, but by all means carry a canteen of water with you when you visit the site. Wear boots and carry insect repellent.

Allow about 3 hours to cover the site and to climb the restored structures. This will entail a walk of about 5 miles. If you plan to visit Macanxoc, add another hour.

A sign at the ticket office asks you to take a guide along. You can easily follow the main trails on your own, but without guidance you might miss the turnoff for the three stelae between the Conjunto las Pinturas and the Nohoch Mul. Of course, you will need help to reach Macanxoc, it indeed that is still visitable.

For other nearby accommodations and restaurants see "A Note on the Quintana Roo Coast and the Offshore Islands."

# *The Small Coastal Sites from North to South and the Offshore Islands*

All the coastal sites covered here are only a short distance from Highway 307. This area is in a state of flux. Some structures that were cleared have become overgrown, while others have had more clearing, so the conditions mentioned here may have changed by the time you visit the sites.

*Note:* I have been unable to learn the derivation of the names of the small coastal sites. Some are named after nearby settlements. All of the sites are Maya.

★

## *Playa del Carmen*

(*plah*-yah dehl *kahr*-mehn)

There are two small temples here. The larger and better-preserved structure has columns supporting the original wooden lintels that span the doorways; the smaller temple is in a more ruinous condition. Both have small interior shrines, and remnants of stucco and simple moldings.

The cutoff to Playa del Carmen from Highway 307 is 43 miles south of Puerto Juárez and 36 miles north of Tulum, and it is well marked. Turn east to the town of Playa del Carmen and head for the dock. As you approach the sea, there is a military compound on your right. The two temples are just beyond the compound and are visible from the road. Ask permission at the compound, and the officials will let you walk through or around it to get to the temples. The temples actually lie outside of the barbed-wire fence enclosing the compound. The temples are a little less than a mile from the cutoff. Allow about 20 minutes to see the ruins and return to the highway.

*Structure B-II with columned doorway and intact lintel, Playa del Carmen. Late Postclassic period.*

★

## *Xcaret*

(shkah-*reht*)

This is one of the more extensive "small" sites and is worth a visit. There are several structures here of the usual type. Special features are a few remnants of paint on the inset panel above the doorway of one structure and some decorative latticelike upper molding on another.

In addition to the archaeological remains two other features at Xcaret are worth seeing. As you enter the area with the temples, there are two trails. The one on the left leads to two cenotes with crystalline water, a few hundred feet away. A second trail continues straight from the way you came in and leads downhill to a *caleta* on the sea, also a few hundred feet away. This is a nice place for a swim. Allow about half an hour to see the ruins, cenote, and *caleta*—unless you decide on a dip in the sea.

The cutoff to Xcaret is between kilometer markers 284 and 283 and is 47 miles south of Puerto Juárez (a bit less than 4 miles south of the Playa del Carmen cutoff) and 32 miles north of Tulum. It is marked by a restaurant and an almost invisible sign. A dirt road heads east for about a mile and gets you to a parking area. From there you walk through gates and follow a trail a few hundred feet to the ruins.

★

## *Chakalal*

(chah-kah-*lahl*)

If you have time to see only one typical small coastal site, this may be your best bet. It is a lovely example of a one-room temple, perched on the edge of a beautiful *caleta.* The temple has a vaulted roof and simple exterior molding and is very well preserved. There are remnants of paintings on the interior walls, depicting a serpent (difficult to make out), a jaguar (easier to see), and both positive and negative painted hands.

The structure is called the Caleta Temple to distinguish it from the inland groups at Chakalal, and it is a delight. It is kept cleared of vegetation by Aníbal de Iturbide, the owner of the property, and it is easy to photograph from several vantage points.

The cutoff for Chakalal is between kilometer markers 269 and 268 and heads east. There are two cutoffs in this area about 50 feet apart. The more northerly one is marked with a sign saying Rancho Cuatro Hermanos, and a gate is visible from the highway. The cutoff a little south of this is the one that leads to the temple. It is a very rough and rocky road that passes a small house after leaving the highway and continues on to a gate about 0.4 mile from the highway. It can be driven in a Jeep or Volkswagen, but take it *very* slowly. Park at the

*Caleta Temple, Chakalal. Late Postclassic period.*

*Small shrine and enclosure, Yalku. Late Postclassic period.*

gate, and continue on foot for about 2 minutes to the temple. The cutoff for Chakalal is 56 miles south of Puerto Juárez and 23 miles north of Tulum.

Allow about 45 minutes from the time you leave the highway until you return to it.

★

## *Yalku* (yahl-*koo*)

There is a one-room shrine a little over 4 feet tall at Yalku. It is partly surrounded by a circular wall, to which it is connected at the rear. Both the shrine and the wall are constructed of crude masonry, although the shrine and its vaulted roof are well preserved. There is a small altar in the rear of the shrine that once supported a stucco idol, which has been dstroyed. The shrine and wall are built on bedrock, without any platform.

The cutoff for Yalku is near kilometer marker 256. It is a good road, well marked, and heads 0.4 mile east to a *caleta*, where you can park. The *caleta* has a small northern extension at the parking area. Follow this extension to its end, and continue northeast for about 50 yards to the shrine. The walk is over limestone bedrock, loose boulders, and vegetation, and there is no definite trail. The vegetation in this area is mostly low, but you cannot see the shrine until you are almost there. With care, you will not get lost.

Allow about 45 minutes to walk from your car to the shrine, see it, and return. Add a little extra time if you decide on a swim at the *caleta.*

The cutoff for Yalku is 63 miles south of Puerto Juárez and 16 miles north of Tulum.

## *Akumal* (ah-koo-*mahl*)

The only thing to be seen here is one small temple, with intact roof, visible from the highway. It is a few hundred feet west (inland) from the highway, and no road or trail leads to it. You can walk through the bush, but a machete would be a help. This area has quite a few mosquitos.

The temple is overgrown, and hard to spot if you are driving south—easier if you are going north. It is located about 64 miles south of Puerto Juárez and 15 miles north of Tulum, between kilometer markers 255 and 254. A better reference point, however, is that it is about 100 yards north of the cutoff for the Club Akumal Caribe.

★

## *Xelha* (shehl-*hah*)

Xelha is known to most visitors as a delightful swim spot rather than as an archaeological site. There is no reason why you cannot enjoy both. The recreational facilities have seen some development in recent years and there is now a small charge to enter the area.

If money were absolutely no object, and I were going to design the world's most beautiful swimming pool, I would simply reproduce Xelha. The lagoon of exquisitely clear, blue-green water is dotted with small islands of limestone outcrops. This is a great place for swimming and snorkling, and you can now rent foot-operated pedal boats to roam around the lagoon. A new restaurant is in operation, and some small thatch shelters provide shade if you wish to bring a picnic lunch. Be careful when swimming; the area abounds with sea urchins. Stepping on one is definitely not recommended, for the spines are almost impossible to remove from your feet. The spines are not poisonous, but they can cause some temporary discomfort.

There are two accessible structures at Xelha, one at the lagoon and one right along the highway. Two trails go from the new parking lot to the restaurant area. Take the one that goes along the far side of the lagoon; it passes near a miniscule shrine only a couple of feet tall.

The other accessible structure lies a few feet west (inland) of the highway and a few hundred feet south of the cutoff to the Xelha Lagoon.

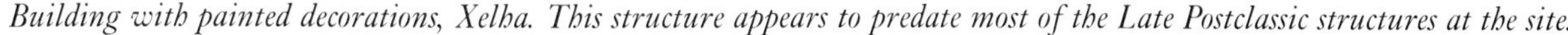

*Building with painted decorations, Xelha. This structure appears to predate most of the Late Postclassic structures at the site.*

This fair-sized structure is badly ruined but has remnants of red painted decorations. It is worth a few minutes to see, if you can spot it; it has become very overgrown.

The cutoff for Xelha Lagoon in 70.5 miles south of Puerto Juárez and 8.5 miles north of Tulum, and is well marked. The half-mile road to the lagoon is paved, and is between kilometer markers 245 and 244.

★

## *Tancah* (tahn-*kah*)

There are two main structures at Tancah that are worthwhile—one on each side of the highway—although only one is now easy to reach.

The structure on the east side of the highway is right on the road, was recently excavated and consolidated, but has since become partially overgrown. The pyramidal base rises in three tiers. Access is by a stairway on the east side. There are remains of a small ruined temple on top.

*Mural depicting the corn god at the top and another figure below, Tancah. Late Postclassic period.*

There are several overgrown mounds in the nearby bush that may be seen, and some have a few remnants of standing architecture.

The second structure lies about 150 feet west of the highway, directly across from the other structure. This building has a low corbel-vaulted roof, partially intact, and two intact doorways on both east and west sides. The most interesting features, however, are remains of murals—mostly black linework—on the inside of the east wall near the center doorway. A couple of figures are discernible, including a depiction of the corn god. These were discovered by archaeologist Arthur Miller in recent years.

Unfortunately, this structure and the trail leading to it have become totally overgrown. You will need a guide with a machete to reach it, unless they should clear the trail again.

Tancah is 77 miles south of Puerto Juárez, 2 miles north of Tulum, and a little south of kilometer marker 235. The structures we are covering are just a few yards north of the cutoff for Tancah Coconut Plantation, which is marked by a small sign. Allow about 45 minutes to see the two structures and the mounds, or about 10 minutes, if you plan to see only the structure east of the highway.

★★

## *Muyil* (moo-*yeel*)
## *Chunyaxché* (choon-yahsh-*cheh*)

There is some confusion about the nomenclature of this site. Sometimes Muyil and Chunyaxché are considered two separate sites. Sometimes, however, they are shown as one site with two names, and that is how it will be considered here.

There are three areas of interest here and a fourth that you may want a look at. The first is a few yards from the highway and is made up of several mounds around a plaza. Some standing architecture remains. As you drive in farther, you come to the caretaker's house, and can park in this area. He will probably offer to show you around. Let him, or at least get directions to the other groups.

The second area is a short distance away by foot trail. This includes a rather tall structure, with a pyramidal base and remains of a temple on top. Parts of the lower section of a stairway remain, but overall, it is in a ruinous state. It is quite steep and climbing it is not recommended.

*The third structure with remains of a stairway and partly intact temple, Muyil. Possibly Late Classic period.*

A foot trail from the second structure leads a few hundred yards through the bush to a third structure. This is the best preserved of all. A pyramidal base supports a partially intact multichambered temple. The temple has remains of corbeled vaults and appears originally to have had columns in the main doorway. An inner room is reached through a very low doorway with intact lintel.

There are bush covered mounds around this structure, but nothing of really notable interest.

You now return to the second structure, and head east for the lagoon about half a mile away.

As you near the lagoon, you come to a cleared area on the left. In this fourth area you will find a pile of rocks and tree roots—the only remains of a small structure. It is worth seeing only if you also want to see the beautiful lagoon and perhaps have a swim. Otherwise, this fourth area is not worth the long, hot walk.

The cutoff for Muyil (Chunyaxché) is 16 miles south of the cutoff for the ruins of Tulum and 45 miles north of Felipe Carrillo Puerto. The cutoff is between kilometer markers 206 and 205, and is marked with a sign saying Chunyaxché.

## Limones (lee-*moh*-nehs)

I do not know the archaeological name for this structure, but it is in the town of Limones, and I have used that designation.

The structure is a rather tall pyramid, apparently rising in terraces, with no obvious remains of a temple on top. It is in a ruinous condition and is located just a few yards off the highway (east side), from which it is visible.

Limones is 39 miles south of Felipe Carrillo Puerto and 43 miles north of the junction of Highways 307 and 186. The pyramid is between kilometer markers 70 and 69.

In addition to the accommodations mentioned for

the other coastal sites, Chetumal is a good possibility, if you get this far south.

★

## *Isla Mujeres* (*ees*-lah moo-*hehr*-ehs)

A lovely, well-preserved, small Maya temple is found on the extreme southern tip of Isla Mujeres, just south of the modern lighthouse. It is sometimes called the Temple of Ix Chel, a moon goddess, who was patroness of women and was widely worshipped in this area. Isla Mujeres gets its name from the many female figurines found there by the early Spanish explorers.

The temple, which sits on a platform, has the usual simple exterior molding. Some original lintels are in place. Its beautiful setting, perched on a cliff above the sea, makes it most worthwhile. The easiest way to reach the temple is to take the paved road that heads south from the town and follow it to its end. It is then a short walk south to the temple. If you do not have your own vehicle, you could rent a motorbike or bicycle, or hire a taxi.

If you are planning to take one of the boat tours around the island, a visit to the temple can be included as part of the trip. These trips include a visit to the turtle pens, and diving for conch (your boatman does this, but you can too, if you like). Your boatman then prepares the fresh conch as *ceviche de caracol*, by marinating it in fresh lime juice, and adding chopped tomato, onion, and chili pepper. This plus crackers and cold beer make a most delicious lunch. From the beach area where he prepares the conch it is a few minutes on foot to the temple. If you like snorkling, you will also be shown an area where literally thousands of fish congregate. This is all part of the boat tour. You might want to ask your boatman beforehand about a visit to the temple, since it is not a regular part of the trip.

## *Cozumel* (koh-soo-*mehl*)

(A Note on the Archaeology and Roads)

Cozumel was an important place of pilgrimage, honoring the cult of Ix Chel in pre-Columbian times. Access to the island was by canoe from the mainland. This was facilitated by a *sacbé* on the mainland, which ran from the important inland site of Cobá, to Xcaret, the point of embarcation for Cozumel. Another branch of this *sacbé* may have connected with Tancah and Tulum. There are over two dozen archaeological sites on the island, some of which have been recently studied by Jeremy Sabloff and William Rathje for Harvard University.

Cozumel was occupied by the Maya from around the time of Christ. It began a climb to prominence around A.D. 800–1000, and reached its peak about 1400. During its apogee, its occupants were Putun Maya traders who used the island as a storage point for goods. Large inland storage platforms, connected to the coast by causeways, have been recorded. The main route of the Putuns was from the lowlands of Tabasco on the Gulf Coast, around the Yucatán Peninsula to Honduras. Cozumel was a good midpoint. Most of the structures seen on Cozumel today are of the type found on the east coast of the mainland of Quintana Roo.

There are two paved highways and one dirt road on Cozumel that are of concern here. The only other road of note on the island is a paved one that goes a short distance to the airport and hotel area. Both paved highways have kilometer markers, and both begin in San Miguel, the only town of any size on the island. Neither highway has a number. The longest highway is what I call the Southern Loop Highway. From San Miguel, on the west side of Cozumel, the highway goes south and then loops around to the north, following the coast for a little over 48 kilometers (30 miles). Second is the Transverse Highway (which runs northwest to southeast in a straight line). This goes from San Miguel for 14.5 kilometers (9 miles) to the east coast of the island, where it joins the end of the Southern Loop Highway. About 100 feet before (west of) this junction there is a dirt road that connects to the Transverse Highway on the left. The dirt road heads northeast for 15 miles, and goes to the northern tip of the island, where it ends at the Punta Molas Lighthouse. This road does not have kilometer markers.

Jeeps can be rented in San Miguel. This is the best way to get around the island, though many visitors opt for less-expensive rented motor scooters. Scooters would be adequate to reach El Cedral and "La Ruinita," but I cannot in good conscience recommend them for a trip to the east-coast temples. Nevertheless, some people use them for this purpose.

A guide is not necessary to see any of the sites on Cozumel that are covered here.

★

### COZUMEL MUSEUM
(San Miguel de Cozumel)

In the municipal building that borders the east side of the Main Plaza in the town of San Miguel de Cozumel, there is a one-room museum that houses a small collection of artifacts. Although a sign above the door clearly proclaims Museo de Arqueología, few people in the area will be able to tell you where it is—or maybe they cannot believe that this is what you are looking for. The collection includes ceramics and some bas-relief stone carvings. There is not much labeling. Some of the more interesting displays are excellent black-and-white photos by Loring Hewen of rarely published ruins in Quintana Roo.

Fifteen minutes is ample time to view the collection and take a few photos. The museum is closed on Sundays.

★

## *El Cedral* (ehl seh-*drahl*)

There is a two-room temple with a single exterior doorway in El Cedral. The doorway was enlarged and framed with wood in modern times, when the structure was reportedly used as a jail. The pre-Columbian temple is located just a few feet away from a modern thatched roof church of similar size.

El Cedral is in the southern part of Cozumel. Take the Southern Loop Highway south from San Miguel for a little over 11 miles. Here you take the well-marked dirt cutoff to the left (east), for a little less than 2 miles. The cutoff is located between kilometer markers 17 and 18, and the road is passable for regular cars.

## *"La Ruinita"* (lah roo-een-*ee*-tah)

Along the Southern Loop Highway, halfway between kilometer markers 34 and 35 (the highway is heading north along the east coast of the island at this point), there is a part of a wall of a small shrine overlooking the sea. It is about 40 feet east of the highway, directly opposite a dirt road that heads west. I do not know the real name of this structure; "La Ruinita" is my name for it.

## *Four East Coast Temples*

There are four Maya temples adjacent to the dirt road that runs along the east coast of Cozumel. All are fairly easy to spot. I am only sure of the name of one of these, so they will simply be numbered in the order that you reach them.

Distances along the dirt road (from the junction with the Transverse Highway) will be given in both miles and kilometers; if you rent a vehicle on Cozumel, the odometer reading will be in kilometers. The distances given here in kilometers are accurate; the mileage conversions have been rounded off to the nearest tenth of a mile.

From San Miguel take the Transverse Highway toward the east coast. Near the end of this highway, you will see the dirt cutoff on your left. All four temples lie east of the dirt road, between the road and the sea. Although other structures have been reported near the dirt road, the four described here are the only ones we were able to find.

The first couple of kilometers of the dirt road are fairly good, hard-packed sand. Then there are about 1.5 kilometers of very rough limestone outcrops. The next few kilometers are poor, but not as bad as the outcrops. At this point, you have reached Temple 1. From there to Temple 2 is also pretty bad, but after that it is a bit smoother.

Unfortunately, you must return by the same bumpy dirt road to the Transverse Highway. Allow about 3½ hours from the time you leave the Transverse Highway until you return. That will give you ample time to see all four temples and the lighthouse.

Bring cold drinks along on this trip and maybe a picnic lunch. There is a large thatch shelter on the dirt road with a lovely view of the sea, where you can eat. It is between Temple 2 and El Real. There is generally a nice breeze.

★

### TEMPLE 1

This is a one-room structure, with a single doorway facing the sea. The walls are mostly intact, but the roof has collapsed into the interior of the temple. There is a stone-lined opening in the ground in front of the temple that looked like a small chultun.

Temple 1 is 5.2 miles (8.3 kilometers) from the junction and about 40 feet from the dirt road. It is situated in a cleared area, and you can drive right to it.

### TEMPLE 2

Only the rear wall and part of one side wall of this structure remain standing. The rest has collapsed toward the sea. It appears to have been a simple one-room structure.

Temple 2 lies about 50 feet from the dirt road, from which only the top part of the structure is visible. It is 7.5 miles (11.9 kilometers) from the junction and 2.3 miles (3.6 kilometers) from Temple 1.

*Two-room temple and enclosure, the front (east) side, El Real. Late Postclassic period.*

★

## TEMPLE 3 EL REAL (ehl reh-*ahl*) also CASTILLO EL REAL

This is the most interesting of the lot. It is a rather large two-room structure, with a single exterior doorway facing the sea. It has a roof vaulted in steps and a few remnants of paint above the exterior doorway. The temple sits on top of a platform that is partly enclosed by a wall in the front.

There is a bad crack above the doorway, and a slim tree trunk has been placed on the south side of the temple for support, though, considering the apparent weight of the structure, it is hard to imagine that the support does much good. The temple is intact except for two holes in the rear wall. The center hole affords the best access to the interior of the structure.

El Real lies about 100 feet from the dirt road, and is harder to spot than the others because of intervening vegetation. The stopping place is 10.8 miles (17.2 kilometers) from the junction, and 3.3 miles 5.3 kilometers) from Temple 2. As the dirt road crosses a cattle guard, look to the right to see El Real.

## TEMPLE 4

The front of this small structure is overgrown, but it appears that there was a single doorway facing the sea and that the temple had only one room. The roof has collapsed, but from the debris it appears to have been of beam-and-mortar construction. Most of the walls are intact.

Temple 4 is about 30 feet from the dirt road and its back is cleared and easily visible. It is 12.4 miles (19.7 kilometers) from the junction, and 1.6 miles (2.5 kilometers) from El Real.

About 2.5 miles (4.1 kilometers) past Temple 4 you come to the Punta Molas Lighthouse. It is painted a garish pink, but is still rather photogenic.

# GUATEMALA

## Pacific Coast

*Bas-relief stone carving from Bilbao, possibly representing Tlaloc, at Finca El Baúl. Classic period.*

★★

# *Finca El Baúl*

(*feen*-kah ehl bah-*ool*)

There are many sites on the Pacific Coast and slope of Guatemala. Most are characterized by earthen mounds, rather than by stone architecture, although some stone rubble and dressed-stone blocks occur. Nevertheless, the area is more notable for its carved-stone monuments from various periods and in various styles.

Many of these monuments are found today on several sugarcane and coffee fincas, clustering near the town of Santa Lucía Cotzumalhuapa. Some of the monuments have been moved to the finca headquarters, and these you can reach without a guide. To reach those still in place in the fields, you will need a guide. You can bring one along with you from Guatemala City, or try to find one at the finca headquarters. The latter method may not be feasible if it is the busy season at the fincas.

At Finca El Baúl headquarters all but one of the monuments are rather haphazardly displayed on the edge of a garden in front of a house. They are three-dimensional and bas-relief carvings that date to the Classic period. There are depictions of deities, figures, large human heads—some with tenoned backs—and animals. Some of the sculptures show evidence of influence from Teotihuacán and El Tajín.

Stela 1—the most impressive monument at Finca El Baúl—is protected by a thatched shelter, located some yards away from the other monuments. Stela 1 has caused a great deal of controversy over the years; its discoverer attributed it to the Aztec culture. Now it is accepted as bearing a Long Count date of A.D. 36 in the Maya system. This Late Preclassic monument is in Izapan style and is related to sculpture from that site and from Kaminaljuyú.

A little past Stela 1 we saw a more recent antique—a decaying steam tractor retired from use on the finca. This is worth a couple of photos, too, if it is still there.

Some of the earliest carvings from the Pacific Coast of Guatemala are boulder sculptures found at several sites, primarily Monte Alto. (See "La Democracia Plaza" for more on Monte Alto.) Later works from the area include many monuments in the Cotzumalhuapa style, found at sites culstered near Santa Lucía Cotzumalhuapa, including El Baúl. These works show influence from central Mexico, and a preoccupation with death and the ritual ball game.

Sir J. Eric S. Thompson considered most monuments in this style to date to the Late Classic period, but Lee Parsons and others found many of the sculptures in direct association with Late Preclassic and Early Classic ceramics. Obviously, a great deal is still to be learned about the archaeology of the Pacific Coast of Guatemala. Monuments in the Santa Lucía Cotzumalhuapa area were recorded by S. Habel and Adolph Bastain in the late nineteenth century. Shortly thereafter, several were shipped to Germany. Just before the turn of the century the area was investigated by Eduard Seler and his wife, and information was published in 1901. In 1923, T. T. Waterman discovered Stela 1 (the Herrera Stela) at El Baúl. Thompson, working for the Carnegie Institution of Washington, studied the monuments of El Baúl and, later, the ceramics of the site; he published reports in 1943 and 1948. This area was also included in reports by A. Ledyard Smith and A. V. Kidder, working for the Carnegie Institution in 1943. More work in the Cotzumalhuapa region was conducted somewhat later by the Milwaukee Public Museum, and reports were issued by Lee Parsons, Stephan de Borhegyi, Peter Jenson, and Robert Ritzenthaler in 1963, by Parsons and Jenson in 1965, and by Parsons in 1967.

To reach Finca El Baúl from Guatemala City, take Highway CA 9 southwest to Escuintla (34 miles). Then turn west (right) on Highway CA 2 and go to the town of Santa Lucía Cotzumalhuapa (21 miles). Both of these highways are paved. In Santa Lucía Cotzumalhuapa, ask directions to make sure you get the right cutoff to the finca. You are looking for a dirt road that heads north from the highway; it goes about 7 miles to the finca. Driving time is a little less than 2 hours from Guatemala City.

The best stopovers are Guatemala City or Escuintla. There is no food or drink at El Baúl; bring your own or stop in Escuintla for lunch, perhaps at

*Classic-period sculpture from El Baúl, Finca El Baúl. Monument 13 is on the left. Photograph by author.*

the Texas Restaurant or the dining room of the Motel Sarita.

Allow about half an hour to see the sculptures. If you plan to try to see the sculptures in the fields, wear boots. If you are only going to the finca headquarters, tennis shoes are adequate.

A visit to El Baúl can be easily combined with a visit to Finca Pantaleón and La Democracia. The three make a good one-day trip from Guatemala City.

★★

# *Finca Pantaleón*

(*feen*-kah pahn-tah-leh-*ohn*)

See "Finca El Baúl" for general information and for the archaeology of the region.

At Finca Pantaleón there are over a dozen carved monuments displayed at the "motel." The "motel" is used as housing for some of the employees at the finca, and most of the sculptures are exhibited on pedestals in front of it. One is on the ground at the end of the building, and more are found on a facing lawn.

Most are three-dimensional sculptures of grotesque human heads or fantastic animals, and they appear to be of Classic date; they show evidence of some Mexican influence. Most are well preserved. One particularly gory specimen shows a human head with one eyeball hanging on its cheek. Most of the human heads wear large circular earplugs and have lined faces, apparently indicating wrinkles and implying age.

The large piece at the end of the "motel" is the most interesting, although it seems to be only the top part of a monument. It depicts the frontal view of a human head wearing an elaborate headdress, which curls forward at the top. The head and headdress are three-dimensional, while the rectangular slablike background is carved in very low relief.

Finca Pantaleón can be reached in 1¼ hours from Guatemala City. Take Highway CA 9 to Escuintla; then Highway CA 2 west for a little over 18 miles. Keep an eye out for a large bridge; the cutoff for the finca is just before the bridge. The entrance to the finca, on your right (north), is marked with a sign. Turn in here through the gate; it is then a little over 0.5 mile of good dirt road to the "motel." Ask along the way, as there are a couple of turns to be made.

A bus can drop you off at the gate.

*Stone monument at the far end of the "motel," Finca Pantaleón.*

★★★

## *La Democracia Plaza (The Monte Alto Heads)*

(lah deh-moh-*krah*-see-ah)

When you arrive in the small town of La Democracia, head for the Main Plaza; ask for "El Centro" if you cannot find it.

Arrayed around the pleasant plaza, with its benches and bandstand, are a number of interesting, large boulder sculptures, most of which come from the nearby site of Monte Alto. A couple of pieces, however, apparently discovered as recently as 1968, were found at another nearby finca.

Monte Alto was probably at its peak between 500 and 300 B.C., though, according to Lee Parsons and Peter Jenson, ". . . it is distinctly possible that some of the boulder sculptures could have been carved as early as 1000 B.C." The sculptures depict figures and heads carved in a "crude but decisive fashion." There are potbellied figures, with arms and legs wrapped around their bodies, and heads with puffy faces and wide noses. Most are shown with their eyes closed.

One unusual head, however, wears a jaguar mask, in "a striking Olmecoid style," according to Ignacio Bernal, who also believes that the other sculptures are in a general style that "conforms to Olmec norms." He feels the sculptures show a somewhat remote Olmec influence. Although the Monte Alto Heads are much cruder than the pure Olmec sculptures from the sites of San Lorenzo, La Venta, and Tres Zapotes, somehow you feel an inherent relationship.

*Potbellied figure from Finca El Transito, La Democracia Plaza. Middle Preclassic period. Photograph by author.*

Monte Alto was excavated by Lee Parsons and Edwin Shook for the Peabody Museum of Harvard University and the National Geographic Society. For more on work in the general area, see "El Baúl."

La Democracia is 65 miles by paved road from Guatemala City and can be easily reached by car in 1½ hours. Take Highway CA 9 southwest to Escuintla (34 miles). Then head west on Highway CA 2 to Siquinalá (16 miles). From there, take Highway 2 south to La Democracia (6 miles). A bus can get you to Siquinalá, but connections to La Democracia may not be too frequent.

Allow 1 hour to see the heads and the indoor museum at La Democracia.

There are no accommodations in the town, but soft drinks are available. Recommended stopovers are Guatemala City or Escuintla, and the latter makes a good lunch stop.

★

## *La Democracia Museum*

While you are photographing the boulder sculpture on the plaza, someone will probably ask if you want to see the museum. It is apparently kept closed except when possible visitors arrive in town. It is housed in a small building just off the plaza and contains artifacts from the surrounding area. It is not very well organized, but you might want to stop in for a few minutes.

## GUATEMALA

### Central Highlands

*Idol of Pascual Abaj, on a hilltop above Chichicastenango. Date undetermined but possibly pre-Columbian.*

★★★★

# *National Museum of Archaeology and Ethnology (Guatemala City Museum)*

The Guatemala City Museum is at the south end of the capital, near the airport. It is only a few minutes away from the central area of the city and is easily accessible by private car, taxi, or city bus.

The museum described here is the one I saw in 1970. It closed sometime thereafter for renovation and was still closed in 1975. Plans for reopening were further delayed because of damage to the collection from the February, 1976, earthquake. No doubt when it reopens it will be even better than before.

The collection included many sculptures and jade and ceramic artifacts from throughout the republic, as well as models of the more important sites. A huge scale model of central Tikal was particularly impressive.

Of special interest were some beautifully carved stelae from the remote site of Piedras Negras, and sculptures from Kaminaljuyú and the Pacific Coast areas. Also of note was a huge boulder of unworked jade excavated at Kaminaljuyú. The museum was well arranged, lighted, and labeled. The ethnological section had displays of costumes and artifacts used by the present-day Indians. There was a small shop that sold books and pamphlets, which, one hopes, will be enlarged.

There were also some interesting sculptures on the outside, in front of the museum and in the patio. There were no photographic prohibitions, though I did not learn whether a tripod would be permitted.

*Detail of the upper portion of Stela 40 from Piedras Negras in the Petén, Guatemala City Museum. Late Classic period.*

★★★

# *Zaculeu and Zaculeu Museum*

(sah-koo-*leh*-oo)

*Early Postclassic Structure 1, top, and the ball court, bottom, Zaculeu.*

DERIVATION: Quiché Maya for "White Earth."
ORIGINAL NAME: Zaculeu.
CULTURE: Mam-Maya.
LOCATION: Southwestern part of the department of Huehuetenango, Guatemala.

---

## THE SITE

Zaculeu is in the western highlands of Guatemala, on a defensive plateau surrounded by deep ravines. Mountain ranges ring the area, providing a lovely setting. It was occupied continuously from Early Classic times up to the Spanish conquest, and several superimpositions of construction are found there.

The major building at the site, Structure 1, was built in seven separate stages, and the one visible today dates to the Early Postclassic period (A.D. 900–1200). This restored structure—the tallest at the site—rises to a height of 39 feet in eight terraces. The temple on top is entered by three doorways, approached by a divided stairway.

During the Postclassic period, when militarism increased, many of the sites in the Guatemala highlands were built on easily defensible hilltops or plateaus, but Zaculeu had been in such a location from an earlier time. The Postclassic period is noted for a growth of nationalism and emphasis on urban living, and the sites of that period took on the dual role of administrative and commercial capitals, as well as places of refuge and festive gatherings.

Zaculeu is a relatively small site, with simple architecture and no monumental stone sculpture, but it is certainly one of the most interesting Postclassic sites in the Guatemala highlands, partly because of its restoration.

In addition to Structure 1, there are several other restored buildings—Structure 4, with a small circular enclosure behind a two-roomed temple, and a ball court. All are worth a look.

There are over forty structures at Zaculeu, but many are now simply unrestored grass-covered mounds.

Split stairways apparently first came into use during the Late Classic period at Zaculeu and continued

*Structure 4, right, and another small temple, lower left, Zaculeu.*

in vogue throughout its remaining history. Several are still standing at the site. A number of platforms are also found, and the larger ones may have been used for ceremonial dances.

The corbeled vault so typical of Maya architecture is not found at Zaculeu and is rarely seen in temple construction in the Guatemala highlands. In some parts of the highlands, however, vaults were used in tombs. Roofs were of beam-and-mortar construction, as seen in Structure 1. In earlier periods and in other areas of the Guatemala highlands, perishable temples of wood and thatch were used to top the pyramidal bases. The architectural remains seen at Zaculeu today are of stone, covered either with lime plaster or with adobe and a thin lime coating. Some remains of polychromed painting were found, but today the structures are white—painted during reconstruction. It is probable that, originally, stucco decorations were used extensively on the exterior of the buildings.

Many of Zaculeu's architectural features show influence from central Mexico, such as beam-and-mortar roofs, divided stairways, dance platforms, and so forth. Luxury trade items from Mexico, including alabaster vases, were also discovered during excavation. Other important items uncovered were objects of copper, silver, gold, and their alloys. These show influence from, or were imported from, Mexico and lower Central America. Pyrite-encrusted mosaic plaques were discovered that may have been used as symbols of wealth and power on state occasions. The pyrite plaques and others of nicely worked jade date to the Early Classic period, while the metal objects date to a later period.

## RECENT HISTORY

Zaculeu was a living city at the time of the Spanish conquest. The Mam group of the Mayas valiantly attempted to defend their capital, but they were ultimately defeated by Gonzalo de Alvarado—brother of the more famous Pedro—in 1525, after a bloody campaign and siege.

Knowledge of the site was never lost, and it was visited by John Lloyd Stephens and Frederick Catherwood in 1840. The ruins were in such a poor state that Catherwood did not produce a drawing of them, though he did depict some vases that they uncovered while excavating one of the mounds. Stephens gave a description of the remains and a diagram indicating a stepped-pyramid shape for the main structure.

Major excavation and restoration at Zaculeu was undertaken by Aubrey Trik, Richard Woodbury, and John Dimick for the United Fruit Company in the mid-1940s. Woodbury and Trik's 1953 publication of this work is the major source of information on the site.

## CONNECTIONS

1. 2 miles by fair dirt road from Huehuetenango, or
2. 166 miles by road from Guatemala City (164 miles paved, and 2 miles fair dirt).

## GETTING THERE

In Huehuetenango ask directions for the road to Zaculeu; it heads northwest from the town.

From Guatemala City take Highway CA 1 west for 160 miles to the cutoff for Huehuetenango (at kilometer marker 262) and then into the town and on to the site.

Zaculeu can be reached from Huehuetenango—the best stopover—in a few minutes by private car, bus, or taxi, or from Guatemala City in about 4 hours by private car. Buses also connect Guatemala City and Huehuetenango, but you have to change at Quetzaltenango.

If you are driving in from Mexico, the closest stopover to Huehuetenango on the Mexican side is Comitán 111 miles away. From there take Mexico's Highway 190 southeast to the Guatemala border, then Guatemala's Highway CA 1 to the cutoff for Huehuetenango. Allow 3 hours' driving time and 1 hour to cross the international frontier.

In Huehuetenango stay at the pleasant Hotel Zaculeu. It serves good food.

There are no accommodations, food, or drink at the site. The site is cleared and is in the coolish highlands, so tennis shoes are fine, but bring a sweater if it is cloudy. Allow about 2 hours to see the site and museum. A guide is not necessary, and no special photographic problems are encountered, but bring a wide-angle lens for some over-all shots. The mountains form a nice backdrop for the structures.

★★

## *Zaculeu Museum*

(sah-koo-*leh*-oo)

There is a small but well-kept museum at Zaculeu, and it is worth a visit while you are at the site. Many artifacts excavated at Zaculeu are on display, including an interesting urn burial, other ceramics, and jewelry.

★★

# *Utatlán*

(oo-taht-*lahn*)

DERIVATION: Nahua for "Place of Reeds." Name by which the site was known in Mexico. A close translation of Kumarcaaj.
ORIGINAL NAME: Kumarcaaj. Quiché Maya for "Place of Old Reeds."
CULTURE: Quiché Maya.
LOCATION: Southwestern part of the department of Quiché, Guatemala.

---

## THE SITE

Like many other sites in the Guatemala highlands, Utatlán was built in a defensive position on a hilltop surrounded by ravines. The whole area received strong influence from central Mexico, and Utatlán is no exception.

Little remains to be seen at Utatlán today, and what is left is not terribly impressive. The site was burned by Pedro de Alvardo when he conquered the town, and since then much of the stone used in the original construction has been removed for building purposes to the modern town Santa Cruz del Quiché. The main structure was a steep pyramidal base, rising in several terraces. The temple on top was approached by stairs on three sides of the base. All that remains of this temple of human sacrifice is the core of its base. A niche has been dug into the core and is covered with black soot from the many candles burned within by the Quichés of today. Many mounds at Utatlán—and on neighboring hilltops—are all that remain of once-lavish palaces and ball courts.

## RECENT HISTORY

Utatlán was founded around 1400, and was the capital of the Quiché Mayas—the most powerful highland nation—at the time it was conquered by the Spaniards in 1524. Early colonial documents give glowing descriptions of the site.

In 1834, Miguel Rivera y Maestre explored the site under a commission from the Guatemalan government, and in 1840 he kindly gave a copy of his manuscript report to John Lloyd Stephens, who was then visiting the region. Stephens considered the report "full and elaborate" and, therefore, felt it unnecessary to devote much of his own time to the site. Frederick Catherwood, who accompanied Stephens, produced a map of the site and a drawing of the main structure. Alfred P. Maudslay visited Utatlán in 1887, made a survey of the site, and later published a plan.

In the twentieth century, the ceramics of the site were studied by Samuel Lothrop and Robert Wauchope. Though some date to the Preclassic period, the bulk shows that Utatlán's most active era was in the Late Postclassic (A.D. 1200–1524). Wauchope also did some excavating at the site, discovering a total of three periods of construction and remains of a mural on a clay wall. In the early 1970s excavations were carried out by the State University of New York at Albany. Some data were summarized in a monograph published in 1977, and other reports are in preparation. In 1981, *The Quiché Mayas of Utatlán*, by Robert M. Carmack, was published by the University of Oklahoma Press. This comprehensive study presents much new information on the archaeology of Utatlán, the origin of the Quichés, their social structure, the reigns of their rulers, and the symbolism of their buildings.

## CONNECTIONS

1. 11 miles by paved road from Chichicastenango to Santa Cruz del Quiché,
2. 34 miles by paved road from Panajachel (on Lake Atitlán) to Santa Cruz del Quiché, or
3. 97 miles by paved road from Guatemala City to Santa Cruz del Quiché, then a few miles of rutted dirt road to the site.

## GETTING THERE

From Chichicastenango—the best stopover—head north on the paved road (sometimes numbered 15) to Santa Cruz del Quiché.

From Panajachel head north on Highway RN 15 for 11 miles. Then follow Highway CA 1 northeast for about 2 miles, to a junction called Los Eucuentros. Then take Highway 15 north for 21 miles, to Santa Cruz del Quiché.

From Guatemala City go west on Highway CA 1 for 76 miles to Los Encuentros, and north to Santa Cruz del Quiché.

Although paved, the stretch between Los Encuentros and Chichicastenango is steep, narrow, and curved. Drive with extreme caution.

From Santa Cruz del Quiché, take the dirt cutoff to Utatlán. This is not easy to find. There are several choices to be made while on the dirt road, and it is best to bring along a guide. Generally small boys can be found in Chichicastenango who will be happy to get you there for a couple of dollars, or try to pick one up in Santa Cruz del Quiché.

There are no accommodations, food, or drink at the site.

This highland area can be cool, so bring a sweater. Tennis shoes are fine. Allow about 45 minutes for a visit.

★★

# *Chichicastenango Museum*

Chichicastenango Museum is on the Main Plaza and houses many artifacts from the area and the Pacific Coast of Guatemala, including part of the Rossbach Collection. Ildefonso Rossbach was a priest who worked for many years in Chichicastenango, during which time he collected pre-Columbian antiquities.

The museum is fairly well laid out, and most of the items are labeled. There are some pieces on display outside in the back of the museum. Allow about 45 minutes for a visit.

Although this guidebook is concerned primarily with archaeological sites and museums, a few words about Chichicastenango must be included, for there is anthropology in action. The town has one of the most interesting markets in Guatemala, and it should not be missed. If I were rating towns, Chichi—as it is affectionately called—would be four stars.

The largest market is held on Sunday, but there is another on Thursday. Try to arrive on Saturday afternoon. You will find it fascinating to see the descendants of the ancient Mayas and Toltecs arrive with their wares and set up their temporary stalls with long poles, rope, and canvas.

Indians in their colorful costumes (and mestizo merchants in western dress) converge on the town on Saturday in preparation for the big social and economic event of the week, as did their forefathers a thousand years ago at their ceremonial centers. By Sunday morning the main square and adjacent areas are packed with people and merchandise of every conceivable kind.

Although the market has become a major tourist attraction, it is really conducted for the local people. The Indian housewife buys her clay cooking pot and bits of lime for softening corn kernels. The young married couple carefully selects a crude wooden table or hand-painted chest with hard-earned centavos. Men and women burn incense to their ancient deities and Christian saints on the steps of the Catholic church. You are welcome if you do not intrude.

It is an incredible place for photography, but be delicate about it. Some of the people do not like having their pictures taken. Try your telephoto lens or a mirror attachment, if you have one. The latter gadget allows you to take pictures off to the side when it appears that you are shooting straight ahead. I admit this sounds a bit sneaky, but you can get some sensitive unposed shots that are impossible to get otherwise, and it does not disturb the populace. If you decide to try this, practice ahead of time; it takes a bit of experience. Sometimes dance groups perform, and they do not seem to mind being photographed.

For all the crowds, hustle, and bustle, the market is an amazingly quiet and orderly affair. Even the occasional drunk is discreetly sleeping in a doorway or is being led away and gently scolded by his wife or mother-in-law. I doubt that there are many markets so well conducted.

Mestizo merchants feature merchandise that will appeal to the tourist, mostly beautiful hand-woven blankets, jackets, and the like. Sometimes interesting inexpensive jewelry can be purchased from walking vendors. Altogether it is quite an experience.

If you can get in, stay at the Mayan Inn, one of the most charming places in Guatemala. It is often booked well in advance (especially for Saturday and Sunday). If so, there are other hotels in town.

On a hill above Chichicastenango is the Idol of Pascual Abaj. It is a steep climb, and you will have to ask directions a few times along the way to find it. This crude stone carving of undetermined age—but possibly pre-Columbian—is still being venerated by the people of the area, who bring offerings of incense, flowers, and thin white candles to burn before it.

From the top of the hill there is a good view of the town below, and so there are two reasons to make the climb if you don't mind puffing a bit.

★★

# *Iximché*

(eesh-eem-*cheh*)

ORIGINAL NAME: Iximché.
ANOTHER NAME: Sometimes Patinamit meaning "The City" in Cakchiquel.
CULTURE: Cakchiquel-Maya.
LOCATION: Northwestern part of the department of Chimaltenango, Guatemala.

## THE SITE

As at other highland sites, strong Mexican influence is seen in the architecture at Iximché, and its location on an easily defensible hill surrounded by ravines is typical of the Postclassic period. Stepped pyramidal bases were surmounted by buildings of perishable materials, which have long since decayed. The remains seen at the site today date to the Postclassic period. There is evidence, however, of Toltec influence perhaps as early as A.D. 800. It is known that Iximché paid tribute to Moctezuma in Tenochtitlán for some years. In addition to the pyramidal structures, there are small platforms and two ball courts, one of which has been restored. A few remains of murals in a Mixtec style are found on the exterior base of one of the structures.

During excavation at the site several burials were discovered, one of which contained the largest cache of gold objects ever found in the Maya area, except for those dredged from the Sacred Cenote at Chichén Itzá. The tomb dates to less than a hundred years before the Spanish conquest, and also contained objects of copper, jade, turquoise, and engraved shell. Human sacrifice is indicated by the three skeletons accompanying that of the principal personage in this burial, and another offertory cache had as its gruesome contents forty-eight human skulls.

No sculpture is seen today at Iximché, though

*Structure 3, the front (west) side, Iximché. Postclassic period.*

*Structure 2, right, view of the front (east) side, Iximché. Postclassic period.*

John Lloyd Stephens reported two badly eroded pieces. One boulder sculpture, of the type seen at Kaminaljuyú and on the Pacific Coast, apparently was also found at Iximché.

## RECENT HISTORY

Iximché was the capital of the Cakchiquel Mayas when it was conquered by Pedro de Alvarado in 1524. Somewhat later it was chosen as the site of the capital of Guatemala, but before building began, another location was selected.

Iximché and other sites in the highlands were described—rather fancifully—by Francisco Antonio Fuentes y Guzmán in 1690 in his *History of Guatemala.* Like other sites occupied at the time of the Spanish conquest, knowledge of its existence was never lost.

Stephens and Frederick Catherwood visited Iximché in 1840, and Stephens used the name Patinamit. He described the site, but Catherwood apparently did no drawings of the structures—at least none were published. Stephens commented that for many years Indians carried stones from the site to build the modern town of Tecpán. In 1887, Alfred P. Maudslay visited Iximché. He surveyed the site and produced a site plan, which was published later.

The ceramics of the site were studied by Robert Wauchope for the Middle American Research Institute of Tulane University in the 1940s. His work was published in 1948 and 1949.

More recently the Guatemalan government supported work at the site directed by Jorge F. Guillemín, who published a report in 1959. Additional work has been conducted since 1970. The site was cleared, and some restoration has taken place.

## CONNECTION

1. 52 miles by paved road from Guatemala City to

Tecpán, then 2 miles of dirt road to the site.

## GETTING THERE

From Guatemala City take Highway CA 1 west to Tecpán; then take the dirt road south to the site. Iximché can easily be reached by private car from Guatemala City in 1½ hours, and a bus can get you to Tecpán.

Overnight stops in addition to Guatemala City are Antigua (34 miles away), Panajachel on Lake Atitlán (38 miles away), or Chichicastenango (36 miles away). There is also a hotel on the highway near Tecpán.

There are no accommodations, food, or drink at the site, but there is a pretty good restaurant on the highway near Tecpán, the Katok. In 1970 it had an English-speaking manager who was happy to give directions to Iximché. If you do not stop here, ask directions from someone in the town of Tecpán to make sure you find the right dirt road.

Iximché is kept cleared, so tennis shoes are adequate. A guide is not necessary. Allow 1½ hours for a visit.

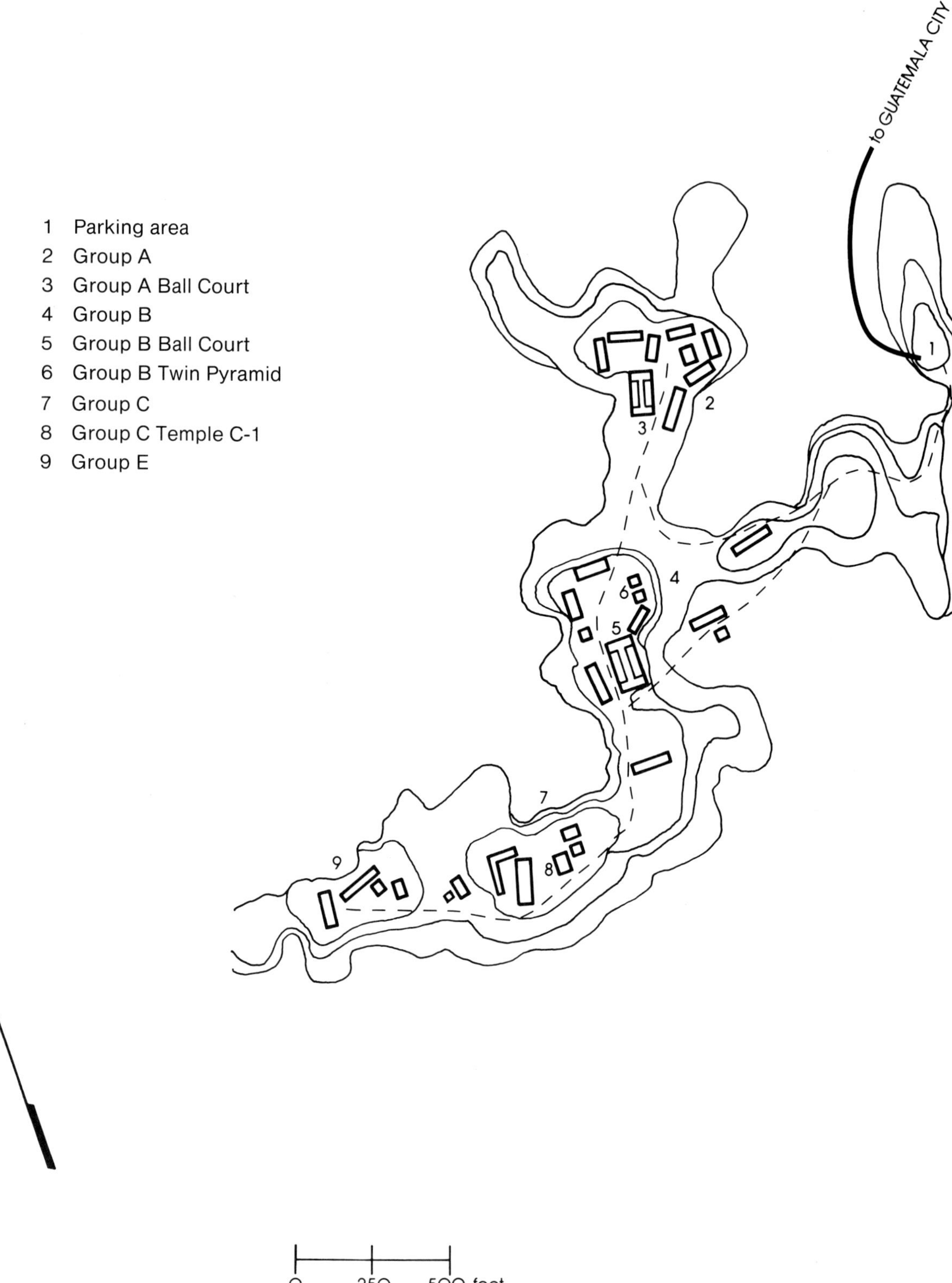

1 Parking area
2 Group A
3 Group A Ball Court
4 Group B
5 Group B Ball Court
6 Group B Twin Pyramid
7 Group C
8 Group C Temple C-1
9 Group E
to GUATEMALA CITY
1
2
3
4
5
6
7
8
9
N
0
250
500 feet


MIXCO VIEJO

★★★

# *Mixco Viejo*

(*meesh*-koh vee-*eh*-hoh)

DERIVATION: "Mixco" means "Place of the Clouds." "Viejo" is Spanish for "Old."

CULTURE: Pokomam Maya.

LOCATION: Extreme northeastern part of the department of Chimaltenango, Guatemala.

## THE SITE

For some inexplicable reason Mixco Viejo is sometimes overlooked by guidebooks and visitors alike, which makes it a real sleeper. In my view it is one of the most interesting sites in the Guatemala highlands, and it is not really difficult to reach. It does, however, require more travel over dirt roads than is necessary to reach the other highland sites. It is worth the effort. In addition, the structures are fairly well preserved, and several have been restored, though there was some damage in the 1976 earthquake. There is a large relief map of the site near the entrance and a general map of the whole area; both are well done. Take a look at the relief map to become oriented before you tour the site.

There are over 120 structures at Mixco Viejo, including temple bases, altars, ball courts, and platforms. They are grouped in several clusters atop small hills that form the top of a steep larger hill. The large hill is surrounded by ravines, making the site easily defensible. The view from the top of the hill is superb.

Mixco Viejo is considered primarily a Postclassic site, although its beginnings date back to Late Classic times. Several layers of construction are visible in many of the buildings, and some are built with almost slate-thin layers of stone. The groups of buildings are designated by letters; the most interesting are Groups A, B, C, and E.

A logical tour would begin with the northernmost Group A. Then go south to Group B, and west to groups C and E. On your return you can visit two structures of Group B that lie on a lower level. All are interesting and the paths are easily followed.

Of special interest are the two ball courts, one in Group A and an even more impressive one in Group B. The latter has the only sculpture at Mixco Viejo, in the form of human heads inside a serpent mouth. Only one such sculpture was found during excavation, and it was removed to the Guatemala City Museum. Today two cement replicas are installed

*Ball court in Group B with copies of sculptured markers on each wall, Mixco Viejo. Late Postclassic period.*

*Structure C-1 with remains of intact stucco, Mixco Viejo. Late Postclassic period.*

as markers on opposite sides of the ball court. Near the ball court of Group B is a twin pyramid, perhaps dedicated to the Mexican rain god. As with other highland sites, the architecture at Mixco Viejo shows strong Mexican influence.

The only remains of stucco facing are found in Group C, the most interesting at the site. Temple C-1, which shows several construction stages, has much of its white stucco intact, but indications are that it was originally painted. From the top of Temple C-1, you get beautiful views of the rest of the site and the surrounding countryside. About the only remaining part of a superstructure at the site is a column on top of this temple. Most of the temples at Mixco Viejo were made of perishable materials.

## RECENT HISTORY

Mixco Viejo, the capital of the Pokomam Maya, is similar to other Postclassic sites in that it was occupied at the time of the Spanish conquest in 1525.

Work at the site has been relatively recent. Mixco Viejo was included in a reconnaissance study by A. Ledyard Smith, published by the Carnegie Institution of Washington in 1955, and in 1958 Jorge F. Guillemín published a study of one of the structures. From 1954 to 1967 major excavations were undertaken by the Museum of Man (Musée de l'Homme) of Paris, under the direction of Henri Lehmann.

## CONNECTION

1. 31 miles by road from Guatemala City (19 miles paved, and 12 miles fair dirt).

## GETTING THERE

Mixco Viejo can be reached from Guatemala City by private car in 1½ hours. Either rent a car or hire one with a driver. Getting there by bus would not be practical. A good road map is essential, since there are two cutoffs to be taken.

Take Highway 5, the paved road from Guatemala City to San Juan Sacatepéquez (15 miles). Continue on this road for 4 miles past San Juan, and then take the dirt cutoff on the left (oddly enough, the first

*Over-all view of part of the site with structures on several levels, Mixco Viejo. Late Postclassic period.*

cutoff is still shown as Highway 5 on road maps). Proceed 5.5 miles on this road to another cutoff, also on the left, onto a poorer, unnumbered dirt road. You pass through the town of Montúfar shortly before the second cutoff. The second cutoff leads a little over 6 miles to the site.

The only logical overnight stop is Guatemala City. There are no accommodations, food, or drink at the site, but there is a nice restaurant on the highway at kilometer 23.5. It is called the Montesano and is near San Juan Sacatepéquez. Nearer Mixco Viejo, just before you cross the river on your way in, is a rather primitive place that has a refrigerator with cold drinks on the porch of a house. This whole area was badly damaged by the 1976 earthquake, and I do not know whether the restaurant and the place with the cold drinks are still in operation. There are a couple of sheltered picnic tables at Mixco Viejo if you want to bring your own lunch.

The drive to Mixco Viejo is lovely. You begin climbing on the outskirts of Guatemala City and get several good views of the capital. The road continues through pine forests and interesting villages and is mountainous throughout.

The site is well cleared, so tennis shoes are adequate, but wear a long-sleeved shirt, and bring insect repellent. There is a nasty little gnatlike creature that can raise huge welts with its bites.

Photography is no problem at Mixco Viejo, but bring along your longest telephoto lens for over-all shots of the site from the road. There are several spots a few miles away where you can see the entire site.

Bring Henri Lehmann's guide to Mixco Viejo or buy a copy when you arrive. A personal guide is not necessary. Allow 2½ to 3 hours for a visit; this makes a nice half-day trip from Guatemala City. It would be best to do it in the morning if you are traveling during the rainy season, for showers are less likely then and the dirt roads are easier to negotiate.

You will enjoy the beautiful scenery as well as the site.

★★

# *Kaminaljuyú*

(kah-mee-nahl-hoo-*yoo*)

DERIVATION: Quiché Maya for "Hills of the Dead."
ORIGINAL NAME: Unknown.
CULTURE: Maya; see text.
LOCATION: Central part of the department of Guatemala. On the western outskirts of Guatemala City.

## THE SITE

Kaminaljuyú is one of those sites that are extremely important archaeologically but have few visual rewards.

Over 200 mounds have been recorded, but most have been destroyed by encroaching real estate developments. Kaminaljuyú is virtually surrounded by suburbia. It has been estimated that less than 10 percent of the site has been saved from destruction. Today you see grass-covered mounds, excavations protected by modern roofs, and some sculptures that were discovered at the site. You are allowed to visit the covered sections, where there are remains of pyramidal bases and tombs, and these are worth a look.

Kaminaljuyú's fame lies in its early beginning and lengthy occupancy, the high quality of its early sculpture, and the richness of its grave goods. One unusual find was a boulder of unworked jade discovered under a stairway of one of the pyramids. It weighs over 200 pounds. There is evidence that many small pieces had been sawed from it, perhaps for making into ornaments. The boulder and other important finds have been removed to the Guatemala City Museum.

Occupancy of Kaminaljuyú began in the Early Preclassic period with a culture called Arevalo, dating to 1500–1000 B.C., according to some authorities, although others place Arevalo around 850 B.C. This phase is represented by pottery.

Following Arevalo is the Middle Preclassic Las Charcas phase, when the whole Valley of Guatemala was occupied. Las Charcas remains at Kaminaljuyú are represented by sophisticated pottery, figurines (mostly female), and clay temple mounds of considerable size.

Perhaps the greatest period at the site was the Late Preclassic Miraflores (300 B.C. to A.D. 200), when most of the mounds were constructed. During

*View of some unrestored mounds and an excavated area covered by a modern roof, center, Kaminaljuyú. The suburbs of Guatemala City are in the background.*

this time Kaminaljuyú probably supported a population of 25,000 to 50,000, and some of the mounds from this period show seven superimposed structures.

The buildings erected during this period were painted-adobe substructures, which supported temples of perishable materials. Plain columnar basalt stelae were produced and were found associated with the mounds. More impressive, however, are some beautifully carved stelae and other monuments in Izapan style, at least one of which bears an early form of Maya hieroglyphs. According to Stephan F. de Borhegyi, "The stone sculpture of this period is without question the finest ever produced in the highlands."

Other discoveries dating to this period were boulder sculptures of potbellied figures, similar to those found on the Pacific Coast—an area that also has Izapan-style carvings—and mushroom stones. These stones may have phallic connotations, but more likely are related to a cult that used hallucinogenic mushrooms in their rituals.

Lavish burials also date to the Miraflores phase, and are found inside the mounds, indicating a funerary function for Maya pyramids that dates to Preclassic times.

Kaminaljuyú went into decline at the end of the Late Preclassic period and was probably no more than a ruin for a century or so. Its star rose again during the Esperanza phase of the Early Classic period, after the Mexican intrusion from Teotihuacán, around A.D. 400. The most interesting architecture seen at the site today dates to this period; some of these structures are covered with modern protective roofs. The style is the *talud-tablero* of central Mexico, and some of the structures were faced with volcanic pumice blocks, covered with clay, and plastered in white. Ball courts were introduced at this time, and thirteen were found at Kaminaljuyú.

Monumental stone sculpture—so prominent in earlier times—is found in greatly diminished quantities in the Esperanza phase, and the figurine and mushroom-stone cults disappear. Also absent are calendrics and hieroglyphic notations.

At this time Kaminaljuyú is very Mexicanized, though typical Maya pottery from the Petén was imported. The Esperanza-phase culture is best thought of as representing a hybrid Maya-Mexican culture. Influence from Monte Albán and El Tajín is also present.

Although tombs were still constructed, they were located in front of the structures rather than inside of the mounds. They were still lavishly stocked, however, with jade, obsidian, and pyrite plaques or mirrors, locally produced pottery of Teotihuacán style and direct imports from Teotihuacán. The important deceased were interred with sacrificed servants or family members.

The central Mexican cults of Tlaloc and Xipe Totec, the god of spring, are represented, as are other deities from Teotihuacán. It is possible that the Teotihuacán influence seen at Tikal and other sites in the Petén during the Early Classic period emanated from Kaminaljuyú. It is also possible that Teotihuacán religious ideas and architecture were accepted only by the elite class in the highlands and not by their peasant neighbors.

At the end of the Early Classic period, there was a decided falloff in Mexican influence in architecture and ceramics, probably due to the destruction of Teotihuacán. During the Late Classic period, there was a return to earlier Maya styles, although a few traits from central Mexico are found, probably coming from sites that were occupied in central Mexico after the fall of Teotihuacán.

The Kaminaljuyú area was occupied into Postclassic times, but it never regained the glory of its earlier periods; the fortified hilltop sites of the highlands had gained ascendency by this time.

## RECENT HISTORY

Kaminaljuyú has been known for a long time and was visited by Alfred Maudslay near the turn of the century. He later published a plan of the site and a photograph of the mounds. Extensive excavations were undertaken at Kaminaljuyú by the Carnegie Institution of Washington in 1936, and continued for several years. Publications by A. V. Kidder, J. D. Jennings, and Edwin M. Shook in 1946, and by Shook and Kidder in 1952 reported on this work.

More recently, Pennsylvania State University entered the picture. In 1969 W. T. Sanders and J. W. Michels reported on work done in the 1968 season. In the 1970s, Charles Cheek studied the Teotihuacán-style structures at Kaminaljuyú. Some mounds at the site remain unexcavated.

## CONNECTIONS AND GETTING THERE

Since Kaminaljuyú is on the edge of Guatemala City, it can be easily reached from anywhere in the capital—the logical stopover—by private car, taxi, or city bus.

There is no food or drink at the site. Tennis shoes are adequate. Allow about 1½ hours for a visit.

## GUATEMALA

### Eastern and Northern Lowlands

*Stucco mask panel depicting a long-nosed god, in place at Tikal, in the North Acropolis in Structure 5D-33 beneath later structures. Early Classic period.*

★★★

# *Quiriguá*

(kee-rhee-*gwah*)

ORIGINAL NAME: Unknown.
CULTURE: Maya.
LOCATION: South-central part of the department of Izabal, Guatemala.

## THE SITE

Quiriguá is a small ceremonial center whose glory is its many massive sculptured monuments. The Main Group at the site is made up of three plazas—and their bordering structures—arranged in a roughly north–south line. The most northerly is the Main Plaza—the largest of the three—followed by the Ceremonial Plaza. The carved monuments are found in these two plazas and include nine stelae (all in the Main Plaza), four zoomorphic boulder sculptures, and four altars. Farther south is the small Temple Plaza, which is surrounded by the largest architectural assemblage at Quiriguá.

The entrance to the Main Group is at the north end of the Main Plaza. From here you can see nearly a dozen fantastic carved monuments decorating the neatly cut lawn. No special sequence is recommended because everything is plainly visible.

The carving of many of Quiriguá's stelae is very three-dimensional, a feature also found at Copán. In several cases, elaborately attired figures are found on the two main faces of the stelae, while glyphs—some in the rare full-figure form—cover the sides.

The largest carved Maya stela ever discovered is the monumental Stela E found at Quiriguá. It is 35 feet tall—about 8 feet are underground—and weighs 65 tons.

Stela H has glyphs in the rare "mat" pattern, another feature that forms a link with Copán.

You will want to spend a good bit of time examining the monuments in the Main Plaza. Then head to the Ceremonial Plaza for a look at even more. Most impressive here are the intricately carved Zoomorphic Boulders O and P and their accompanying altars, at the south end of the plaza, but do not overlook the smaller altars on the east side of the plaza.

The Quiriguá sculptors were fortunate in having excellent sandstone nearby. This material is somewhat soft when first quarried and is easily carved with stone tools—the only kind available to the artists. The sandstone later hardens, after exposure to air. In addition, it has a close and even grain, making results predictable. This no doubt—at least in part—accounts for the intricacy of the carvings on the monuments.

*Stela D, the upper section of the east side showing full-figure glyphs, Quiriguá. Late Classic period.*

The carved monuments in the Main Group all date to the Late Classic period, and were erected between A.D. 731 and 805. Recently an Early Classic stela (possibly dating to A.D. 493, but no later than 573) was discovered just north of the site core. This and the redating of another monument have extended the previously known occupancy of Quiriguá, as has the uncovering of Postclassic ceramics of a type simi-

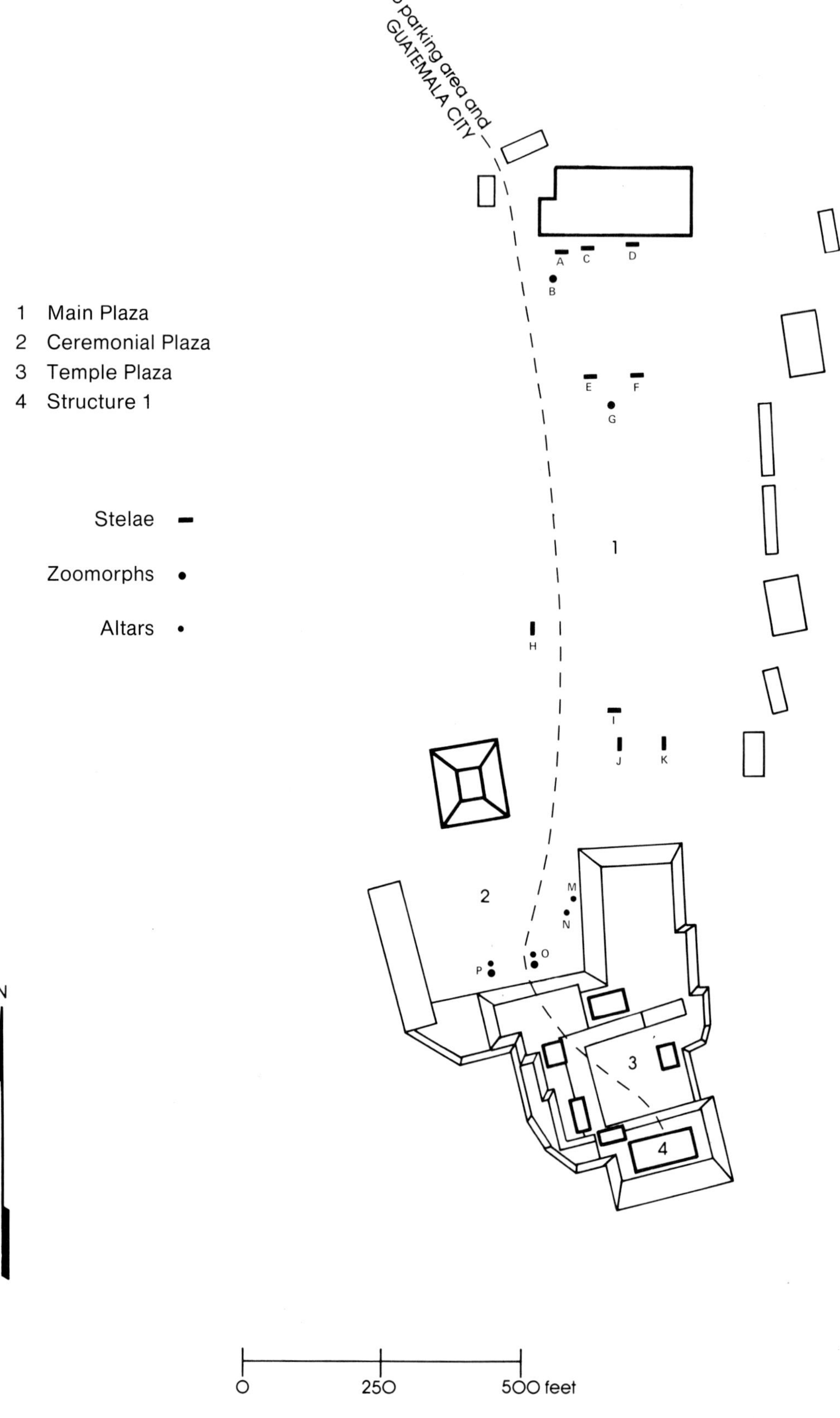

to parking area and
GUATEMALA CITY
1 Main Plaza
2 Ceremonial Plaza
3 Temple Plaza
4 Structure 1
Stelae
Zoomorphs
Altars
A
B
C
D
E
F
G
H
I
J
K
M
N
O
P
1
2
3
4
N
0
250
500 feet


QUIRIGUÁ

lar to some found on the east coast of the Yucatán Peninsula.

One of Quiriguá's rulers, Cauac Sky, may have come from Copán. He was inaugurated in A.D. 724 and captured the ruler of Copán in 737. Many of the monuments at Quiriguá were carved during his reign. New evidence indicates that Quiriguá may have been Copán's rival rather than its subordinate.

Unfortunately many of Quiriguá's monuments are surrounded by low metal fences. A wide-angle lens will eliminate some of them in photographs. Considering that the monuments are carved on all four sides, it would be advantageous to plan for some morning and some afternoon hours for best photographic results.

Architectural remains at the south end of the Ceremonial Plaza and in the adjacent Temple Plaza are being excavated and restored. When the work is finished, this area will be even more interesting.

Climb the stairway behind Zoomorphs O and P to reach the Temple Plaza. As of 1976, underground excavations protected by metal roofs were visible in this area. One of the roofs covers a well-preserved mask panel in a structure on the west side of the plaza. This panel—recently discovered by William Coe—represents the sun god.

The south end of the Temple Plaza is bounded by Structure 1—a building with three doorways and the remains of lower walls. Of interest here is a series of glyphs carved on the top step in each of the doorways. The glyphs carry the date A.D. 810, the latest recorded date found at Quiriguá.

In addition to the Main Group just described, there are three other groups at Quiriguá located a mile and more away (Groups A, B and C), which we did not visit.

*Stela D, detail of the upper section of the east side showing a full-figure glyph, Quiriguá. Late Classic period.*

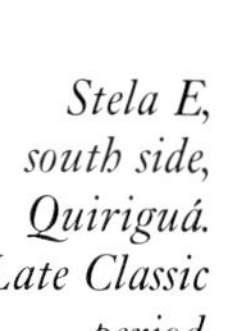

*Stela E, south side, Quiriguá. Late Classic period.*

*Zoomorph G, view of the northwest side, Quiriguá. Late Classic period.*

*Stela H, west side, showing the rare mat pattern of the glyphs, Quiriguá. Late Classic period.*

Two other early stelae from Quiriguá, probably dating to A.D. 495 (redated from 711) and 692 were found in Group A, and in Group B a stela with a date of 746 was found.

## RECENT HISTORY

Shortly before 1840, a vast tract of land was divided among three Guatemalan brothers named Payés, with an eye to development as an agricultural settlement. During the subdivision of the land, the ruins of Quiriguá were discovered.

In 1840 John Lloyd Stephens and Frederick Catherwood heard about the site. Catherwood visited it with one of the Payés brothers, while Stephens attended to other duties in El Salvador.

In *Incidents of Travel in Central America, Chiapas, and Yucatán,* published in 1841, Stephens gave an account of Catherwood's visit and reproduced two of Catherwood's drawings of stelae.

Alfred P. Maudslay began intensive work at Quiriguá on his first visit in 1881. He returned on three other occasions, up through 1894, and during these trips he felled the large trees, cleared the bush, photographed the monuments, and made molds of the sculptures. Drawings of the figures and glyphs were made, and were carefully compared with the originals. In addition, the Main Group was surveyed and partially excavated.

Further work was done at the site from 1910 through 1914 under the direction of Edgar Lee Hewitt for the School of American Research at Santa Fe. Shortly thereafter, the Carnegie Institution of Washington entered the picutre and supported work, off and on, from 1915 through 1934. Important contributors during that time were Sylvanus G. Morley, Oliver G. Ricketson, Earl H. Morris, and Gustav Stromsvik. The United Fruit Company bought the area for their banana plantations in 1919 and set aside 30 acres for the archaeological zone, leaving the jungle untouched.

Quiriguá was one of the first Maya sites to be so thoroughly studied, though little restoration of the architecture was undertaken. The structures that had been cleared and excavated by Maudslay and Morley once again became overgrown with jungle vegetation.

During the many years of work carried out at Quiriguá, the stelae have been reerected where necessary and the other monuments have been repaired and set upon cement bases. Some have been treated with preservative.

In 1975, a five-year restoration project was begun under the direction of William Coe. This venture is being jointly sponsored by the University Mu-

*Zoomorph P, west side, Quiriguá. Late Classic period.*

seum of the University of Pennsylvania, the National Geographic Society, and the Guatemalan government. One of the first endeavors was the recleaning of the monuments. This may have to be done periodically; moss and lichen grow rapidly where the sculptures are shaded by large trees.

## CONNECTION

1. 128 miles by paved road from Guatemala City to the cutoff, then 2.2 miles of poor dirt road to the site.

## GETTING THERE

Quiriguá can be reached in a little over 3 hours from Guatemala City by car. Take Highway CA 9 northeast. The cutoff to Quiriguá is on the right (east), just past a Texaco station. The cutoff is marked with a sign for the archaeological zone and the road leads directly to the site. If it has been particularly rainy, the road to the site will be bad in the low spots. You can walk in, if necessary. It is possible to visit Quiriguá and return to Guatemala City in the same day.

Other closer stopovers are; (1) the Longarone Motel on Highway CA 9 near Teculután, 49 miles before (southwest of) the Quiriguá cutoff, (2) the town of Puerto Barrios, 56 miles northeast of the Quiriguá cutoff, and (3) the Marimonte Motel near the Río Dulce ferry crossing on the highway to the Petén. This is 43 miles from the Quiriguá cutoff (25 miles northeast on Highway CA 9, then 18 miles of fair dirt road northwest to the hotel). See "Tikal" for details on the Longarone and Marimonte Motels, and for information on Highway CA 9.

Buses from Guatemala City also pass the Quiriguá cutoff, but none run to the site.

There are no accommodations or food at Quiriguá, but soft drinks were sold there at one time. The stand was later dismantled, but perhaps another will take its place. Just in case, bring your own refreshments.

Tennis shoes are fine for Quiriguá, but bring a sun hat and insect repellent. Allow 3 to 4 hours to visit the Main Group; a guide is not necessary to see this area. Bring lots of film, and if possible, Morley's *Guide Book to the Ruins of Quiriguá.*

## A Note on the Petén and Belize

The Petén is the largest, northernmost, and least populated department in Guatemala. It is well known to ruin buffs—at least from the literature—as an area abounding in ancient Maya sites. By most standards the Petén would still be considered remote, though it has been connected to the southern part of the republic by road since 1969, when the remaining portion of the Petén Highway was cut through. There have been road connections with Belize for even longer.

Major roads in the area are (1) the Petén Highway, which runs northwest from Highway CA 9 near Morales, through the departments of Izabal and Petén to Flores, the capital of, and largest city in, Petén, (2) the Flores–Melchor de Mencos Highway running east–west between the two cities, (3) a branch road connecting Flores and Sayaxché, and (4) a cutoff from the Flores–Melchor Highway that goes north from El Cruce to Tikal.

All these roads are dirt and rock, and are generally passable in the dry season for regular vehicles. In the rainy season, regular vehicles might be satisfactory, but a high-clearance vehicle would be better. You should check locally about road conditions, in any case, especially for the Petén Highway.

The condition of dirt roads—even major dirt roads—can change from one day to the next. A hard rain can make the low spots impassable, though a day or so of sunshine can dry them out enough so that you can get through.

In August, 1976, after a period of particularly heavy rains, the roads were in a worse than normal condition, but we were able to drive all of them in a van with fairly high clearance. Nevertheless, reports were—and our personal observations tended to confirm—that some spots had been impassable a couple of weeks before. The worst areas were (1) between Río Dulce and the Izabal-Petén border on the Petén Highway and (2) the last few miles before Sayaxché. Other areas were worse than we remembered from previous trips, but would have been passable for regular cars.

Even when the roads are in "good" or "regular" condition, they are rough and bumpy. You will have to drive slowly.

The highways in Belize that are of concern here are (1) the Western Highway, between Belize City and the Belize-Guatemala frontier (near Benque Viejo), and (2) the Northern Highway, connecting Belize City and the Belize-Mexico frontier. The Western Highway is paved for 49 miles west of Belize City; the rest is dirt. The highway is much improved over its condition a few years ago. The Northern Highway is paved for 48 miles north of Belize City. Then there is a 13-mile dirt stretch, followed by 39 miles of paved road to the Mexican border. Parts of the Northern Highway are narrow and bumpy, but this Highway and the Western Highway are passable for standard cars year round. Buses run on all the highways mentioned.

A new highway from Belize City to the Mexican border is due to open in 1981. The first 18 miles north of Belize City will be the same as the Northern Highway, then the routes diverge. The new highway way will reduce the road distance to the Mexican border by 15 miles.

There is a shortcut connecting the Northern Highway with the Western Highway—it saves 13 miles—if you plan to bypass Belize City. From the connecting junction on the Northern Highway to Burrell Boom it is a little over 3 miles of good, though narrow, asphalt. From Boom to Hattiville (on the Western Highway) it is a little less than 10 miles of good dirt. If you take this bypass, you will cross the Belize River near Boom on a new bridge, formerly a small hand-cranked ferry was used.

By using the roads in the Petén and Belize, it is possible to drive from Mexico into Guatemala, north to the Petén, east to Belize, and north to Mexico again, making a circle tour. You will encounter very little traffic on any of these roads. If you are somewhat adventurous and do not mind bumping along dirt roads, you will probably enjoy the remoteness of the area and the close-up views of the tropical vegetation and small towns. I guarantee that it will not be dull.

Gasoline is available in Guatemala on Highway CA 9, 1 mile before (southwest of) the cutoff for the Petén Highway; near Río Dulce and at San Luis on the Petén Highway; in Flores, Sayaxché, Tikal, and Melchor de Mencos. In Belize, gas is available at a number of places along the Western and Northern highways.

There are also short stretches of minor dirt roads in the Petén and Belize that lead to individual archaeological sites. The condition of these roads is covered in the sections on the particular sites, but, in general, these minor roads are not as good as the "major" dirt roads.

If you wish to roam the Petén without driving all the way there, you can fly from Guatemala City to Flores and use that as your base of operations. From there you can drive or bus to the various sites.

Flores is on an island in Lake Petén Itzá and is connected to the mainland by a causeway. On the lake-shore mainland opposite Flores are Santa Elena and San Benito, which run together. Most visitors lump the three towns together as Flores, while the local inhabitants make the distinction among them. The airport, for instance, is actually in Santa Elena, while the best liquor store around is in San Benito, as is the best ice house (Fábrica de Hielo San Benito). The best hotels are in Santa Elena or on the island of Flores, but there are also some in San Benito.

"Tikal" contains many details on hotels, buses, Jeep rentals, airlines, and various ways to get to the sites. I suggest reading "Connections" and "Getting There" in the "Tikal" section before reading about the other sites in the Petén and Belize, since much of the information relates to the whole area.

While you are in Flores, there are a few things you should see. A road circles the island and a couple of side streets lead uphill to the center. At the top of the hill, crowning the island, is a plaza or park bordered on two sides by a church and government buildings. Across the plaza from the church is a carved but eroded stela, and a little below the plaza, set in the side walls of a basketball court, are two more Maya relics. One is a large fragment of Stela 2 from the site of Ixlu, on the east end of Lake Petén Itzá. This stela is dated to A.D. 879 and depicts a main figure (badly eroded) and four smaller figures. The one in the upper left corner is particularly well preserved. The other monument is an eliptical altar, and its surface is covered with glyphs.

We also spied another monument propped up in front of the government building closest to the church. This was a fragment, with only the lower part of a figure remaining. Perhaps a more permanent location will be found for this fragment.

We asked at the police station next door if there were any other monuments around and were taken inside a room behind the last fragment described. The room was used as a sort of warehouse, and behind some dusty shelves and ledger books piled 4 feet high, was a lovely small stela lying on its side. It was impossible to photograph, but was well worth taking a look at. We were told that it had been found at the location of the modern church. One wonders why this hidden monument is not on display in the plaza. It is in a better state of preservation than any of the monuments currently found in the vicinity of Flores.

Other monuments in the area are three stelae and an altar found on the grounds of a school on the mainland. The school is in the center of the area where Santa Elena and San Benito meet, and the stelae are located on two levels of a grassy terrace, between rows of school buildings.

The stela on the lowest level is an Early Classic monument from Tres Islas, a site on the Río Pasión south of Seibal. It is fragmented, but restored, and

*Stela from Tres Islas, Flores. Early Classic period.*

depicts a figure on the left wearing a chin guard and carrying darts—features implying influence from central Mexico. The figure is accompanied by numerous glyphs.

On a slightly higher level of the terrace is the large top fragment of the Late Classic Stela 1 from Cancuén, another site on the Río Pasión, south of Tres Islas. This stela has a rectangular projection on the top—as do other monuments from Cancuén—and the projection and the upper left corner of the stela are perforated with large holes.

Behind the second stela is a third, with an altar in front. The upper portion of the stela is eroded or destroyed (or perhaps was never carved), but the bottom section has a well-preserved scroll-like design that seems to be a stylized profile of a serpent or deity. The accompanying altar has a border of glyphs around the edges, though its top surface is too pocked and eroded to make out.

The first time you go to Flores—especially if you have flown in from Guatemala City—it may seem like the boondocks. On subsequent visits—or if you drive in—it will seem like the center of civilization. It is being rapidly developed, as is the Petén in general.

Two new roads important to the ruin buff are being worked on. One goes from Flores to Uaxactún—bypassing Tikal. See "Uaxactún" for details. The other connects El Subín—a town on the Flores-Sayaxché branch road about 9 miles north of Sayaxché—to the Guatemala-Mexico frontier on the Usumacinta, opposite Yaxchilán, a distance of 68 miles.

In 1976 we were told by some local people that 11 miles were passable for cars from El Subín and that the rest had been cut through to the river. No doubt this road will become an important access route to Yaxchilán as its condition improves.

Although development is occurring in the Petén, it is not likely to become "overtouristed" in the foreseeable future. While it is still unspoiled, there are enough amenities available to make visiting the area reasonably comfortable. If you do not mind a bit of roughing it, you will find the Petén immensely rewarding.

★★★★

# *Tikal and Tikal Museum*

(tee-*kahl*)

DERIVATION: A traditional name of unknown meaning, according to William Coe. "Place Where the Spirit Voices Are Heard," according to Pál Keleman.
ORIGINAL NAME: Unknown.
CULTURE: Maya.
LOCATION: Northern part of the department of Petén, Guatemala.

---

## THE SITE

Tikal is—in a word—overwhelming. The sheer number and massiveness of its buildings leave one with open mouth.

According to William Coe, in the small section (about 6 square miles) of central Tikal that was mapped, over 3,000 separate constructions were recorded, including temples—five more than 125 feet tall—palaces, and shrines. Over 200 stone monuments—stelae and altars—both carved and plain are found in and about the ceremonial precincts. It is possible that 10,000 earlier constructions lie beneath the buildings already mapped. Miles of surrounding territory are still being mapped and studied. Population estimates for Tikal during its peak, range from 40,000 to 75,000 people. The architecture at Tikal suffered a great deal less at the hands of time than did some other Maya sites, because of superior construction methods. The restoration enhances its grandeur.

We now know that Mirador, approximately 35 miles northwest and only 4 or 5 miles from the Mexican border, has a greater number of large constructions, and more massive ones than Tikal's. Those, however, are in a sadly ruinous state, probably owing to the use of mud in the mortar, which has been leached out and which may have caused the general collapse of the buildings. Thus while Mirador may prove to be bigger, it cannot compete visually with the remains at Tikal.

The pre-Columbian history of Tikal dates back to at least 600 B.C. Pits cut into the bedrock below the North Acropolis indicate traces of occupation from that time on, although the earliest buildings date to 300 B.C. For over 1,000 years construction was continuous.

The length of time you have at Tikal, and whether you have your own vehicle, will determine how you can see the site most efficiently, and so I will not recommend a specific tour but will simply describe the various groups and their relative locations.

The heart of Tikal is found in the Great Plaza and the surrounding structures. The plaza is bounded on the north by the North Terrace and, above this, the North Acropolis, on the east by Temple I, on the south by the Central Acropolis, and on the west by Temple II. All these structures face the plaza itself. Many stelae and altars are found in the Great Plaza and the adjoining North Terrace, and many hours can be spent in this one area.

The plaza is now a grassy area kept closely clipped, but it was originally plastered. In fact, four plaster floors dating from 150 B.C. to A.D. 700 are found just a little below the present surface.

In the North Acropolis, a hundred buildings lie buried—one on top of the other. This interesting but confusing complex contains fine examples of Early Classic temple construction. One of the finest is the small Temple 5D-23. Most temples or other buildings from this or earlier periods are buried beneath later construction. Indeed, by far most of what is visible today of Maya ruins in general dates to the Late Classic period. Other vestiges of Early Classic construction in the North Acropolis are the underlying structures and mask decorations of 5D-22 and 5D-33. Do not miss the masks.

Temple I is 145 feet tall. It is a steep climb to the top over worn limestone and can be a bit slippery in damp weather, which is most of the time, but a chain has been installed that facilitates the climb. This is actually a construction stairway, which was used while the temple was being built. Later, a grander one was superimposed and was used for ceremonies after the temple was completed. Only a small portion of this final stairway still exists at the base of the pyramid. It is estimated that a structure the size of Temple I could have been built in a period of two years. Taken into account in this estimate were the construction methods employed and the availability of materials and labor. Marvelous views are to be seen from the top of Temple I.

1 Central area enlarged below
2 Great Plaza
3 Temple I
4 Temple II
5 North Acropolis
6 Temple 5D-23
7 Temple 5D-22
8 Temple 5D-33
9 Great Plaza Ball Court
10 Central Acropolis
11 Maler's Palace
12 Five-Story Palace
13 Structure 5D-43
14 East Plaza Ball Court
15 West Plaza (parking area)
16 Temple V
17 South Acropolis
18 Plaza of the Seven Temples
19 Triple Ball Court
20 Pyramid 5C-54
21 Palace of the Windows (Bat Palace)
22 Temple III
23 Complex N
24 Temple IV
25 Maudslay Causeway
26 Group H
27 Structure 3D-43
28 Complex P
29 Maler Causeway
30 Rock sculpture
31 Complex R
32 Complex Q
33 Méndez Causeway
34 Group G
35 Temple of Inscriptions
36 Immigration Station
37 Museum
38 Tikal village
39 Jungle Lodge
40 Camping area
41 Aviateca Office
42 Jaguar Inn
43 Hotel Tikal Inn


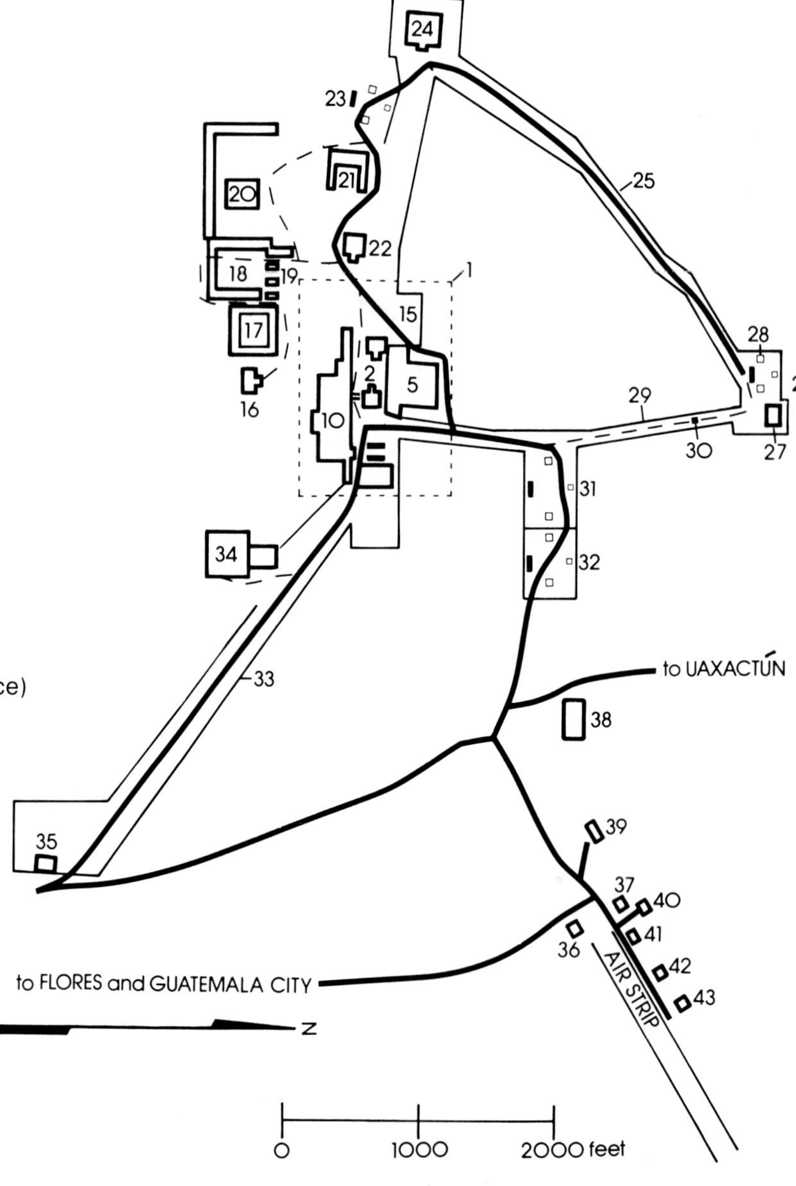

to UAXACTÚN
to FLORES and GUATEMALA CITY
AIR STRIP
N
0
1000
2000 feet


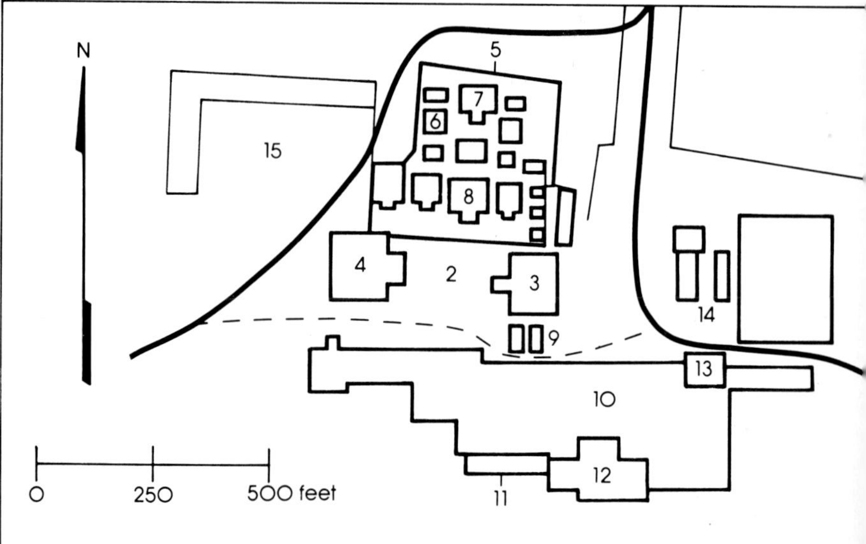

N
0
250
500 feet


TIKAL

*North Acropolis as seen from Temple I, view from the southeast, Tikal. Early and Late Classic periods.*

The Central Acropolis is another rather confusing assemblage of buildings that grew over many centuries, as did the North Acropolis. They differ, however, in that the buildings are more the palace-type (or better, range-type) structures arranged around courts, while those of the North Acropolis are of the pyramid-temple construction. Plan to spend some time in the Central Acropolis investigating its many interesting buildings. Do not miss the Five-Story Palace, with its spindle-shaped vault beams. Most of the visible remains of the Central Acropolis date to the Late Classic period.

Some interesting graffiti are found in this area, particularly in the so-called Maler's Palace, on the south side of Court 2. Another interesting, but sometimes overlooked, structure is 5D-43, near the northeastern end of the Central Acropolis and facing the East Plaza Ball Court. This Late Classic platform and temple show an architectural style that is reminiscent of Teotihuacán. It is one of three such structures found at Tikal, and the only one that has been restored. Other evidence of influence from central Mexico is found at Tikal in some Early Classic pottery and, more notably, in Stela 32 (now in the Tikal Museum), depicting the face of Tlaloc. Recent studies show that Tlaloc had at least dual aspects. One is that of the well-known rain god, but another represents a war god. Stela 32 apparently depicts this latter aspect of the deity and is differentiated by the inclusion of tassels or spear-heads in the headdress.

The small Great Plaza Ball Court (restored) is found between Temple I and the Central Acropolis. It seems strange that Tikal, one of the largest sites known, would have such a small ball court.

Temple II—125 feet tall—is the most completely

*Temple I, the front (west) side, Tikal. Late Classic period. Photograph by author.*

*The Central Acropolis, Temple V rising in the background, view looking south, Tikal. Late Classic period. Photograph by author.*

*Structure 5D-43 showing Mexican influence, view from the northeast, Tikal. Late Classic period.*

*Temple II, Tikal. Late Classic period. Part of the North Terrace and the North Acropolis are at right. The roof combs of Temple III (left) and Temple IV (center) rise above the tropical vegetation.*

*Stela 18, Tikal. Early Classic period. In the Great Plaza at the steps to the North Terrace.*

restored of all the tall pyramid-temples and is, therefore, the easiest to climb.

For best photography in the area, I would suggest climbing Temple I in the morning for front-lighted shots of Temple II. Do the reverse in the afternoon. The two flanking Acropolises have good light most of the day.

West of the North Acropolis is the West Plaza. Of interest here are some stelae and altars; not all have been reerected. A short distance south and southwest of the Great Plaza are a number of structures accessible by foot trails. Some excavation has been done in this area, but there has been little restoration. Temple V—190 feet tall—is still covered by jungle vegetation, unlike the other four tall pyramid-temples, which have been restored to some degree. Immediately west is the large South Acropolis, which has not been excavated.

West of the South Acropolis is the Plaza of the Seven Temples, which, though unrestored, is in a good state of preservation. The central temple on the east side of the plaza is decorated with a skull-and-crossbones motif on its rear face, and an unusual triple ball court bounds the plaza on the north.

Again to the west is the large Late Preclassic Pyramid 5C-54, surely one of the largest structures in Mesoamerica when it was built.

North of this structure is the Bat Palace, though the newer name is the Place of the Windows. It is listed by the latter name on the trail signs, although the Bat Palace is the nomenclature used in the guidebook and map by William Coe. This building was being restored in 1973. Much interesting graffiti is to be found within. The low windows undoubtedly give the structure its present name.

A bit to the east of this is Temple III—185 feet high—and though something of a difficult climb, it is nevertheless worth it, both for the view and the intact carved zapote-wood lintel inside the temple. (There is another carved lintel surviving in place in Temple I.) Other carved lintels, such as those in Temple IV, were removed many years ago.

I recommend an early-morning climb if you want to get a photograph of the lintel, for light enters the doorway then. Do not hesitate to lie on your back and shoot straight up. You will probably be the only one there at the time. A wide-angle lens and fast film will be helpful.

As you follow the car trail west from Temple III, past the Place of the Windows, you will come across Complex N—most notable for its exquisite Stela 16 and Altar 5. Both are Late Classic and are in an excellent state of preservation. The large altar has been tilted upward and is, therefore, easier to photograph than if it were lying flat, as most of them are.

Continuing west along the car trail, you arrive at the base of Temple IV. This is the largest of all the temples. It soars 212 feet and is presently the tallest pre-Columbian structure in America. The Pyramid of the Sun at Teotihuacán in central Mexico may have originally been a bit taller, but its temple is no longer in existence. Structure 1 at Mirador has a substructure that is 20 percent higher than that of Temple IV, but its temple has also disappeared. It may have been taller than Temple IV originally. Its base is six times greater than that of Temple IV.

If you decide to climb Temple IV, you will probably feel that it is even taller than 212 feet.

*Temple IV, the front (east) side, Tikal. Late Classic period.*

The temple on top has been consolidated and partially restored, although the pyramidal base has not been. Access is up the slightly cleared northeast corner of the base, over stones and tree roots. A chain has been installed at one point to help. Coe describes it as "a difficult climb, but well worth it." It is the only structure I have ever climbed that really made me nervous. After reaching the top and relaxing in the single doorway of the temple, I started to become panic-stricken at the thought of getting back down. I tried to distract myself by contemplating the gorgeous view. A few minutes later, I was made to feel quite silly when a truckload of Guatemalan students laughingly scampered up and back down, and without even breathing hard.

If you are up to still more—and we were—you can climb a metal ladder at the rear of the temple (south side) and get on the roof at the base of the roof comb. Stay close to the roof comb, as the roof slants outward. Needless to say, there are no protective guard rails.

My husband talked me into climbing the ladder, and just as my eyes cleared the roof level, a horrendous roar let loose. A couple of thoughts flashed through my mind as I frantically clung to the ladder. One was, "Jaguars!" Second was, "Thank God, I'm up here! They are probably at ground level." Then came the less consoling thought: "I wonder if jaguars are likely to climb pyramids?"

I was made to feel silly for the second time in a matter of a few minutes when I realized that it was only a cavorting family of raucous howler monkeys. The sound was unbelievable, especially from our vantage point above tree level, where it was not muffled by the vegetation.

When I gained a bit of composure, I climbed upon the roof but was happy to get back down in a few minutes. The view was just about as good from the doorway of the temple, and the outward slant of the roof did nothing for my sense of insecurity.

At any rate, the best time of the day for this climb would be the afternoon, when the sun hits the beautifully decorated backs of Temples II and III, and the front of Temple I in the distance. If you can manage it, take a telephoto lens along. You will find a lot of use for it. This is indeed the best spot for a comprehensive view of central Tikal.

In addition to the many buildings erected at Tikal, the Mayas also constructed causeways joining the more important groups. These *sacbeob* are in a sense still in use today, for the car trails follow their routes. The original surface is not generally discernible, however.

From the base of Temple IV, the Maudslay Causeway (supporting a car trail) heads northeast to Group H, or the North Zone, about 0.6 mile away. Group H includes a large plaza bordered by mostly unexcavated Late Classic temples. The most interesting is the massive 3D-43, with its three large interior rooms and graffiti.

Complex P, a part of Group H, has two interesting monuments, Stela 20 and Altar 8. This altar depicts a bound captive and is also set more-or-less upright for ease of viewing and photography.

From Group H it is not possible to drive directly back to the Great Plaza over the Maler Causeway; the northern half of the causeway supports only a foot path. Along the Maler Causeway, there are two areas of interest. One is a large bas-relief carved in limestone bedrock, and it can be reached on foot. It lies west of the causeway, less than a block south of Group H.

This somewhat eroded Late Classic sculpture shows two individuals with bound limbs. Its horizontal position, large size, and covering of lichen make it difficult to photograph. You might try sitting on someone's shoulders to gain additional height, or use your monopod as described in "General Advice—Camera Gear." A wide-angle lens is really needed here.

East of the Maler Causeway, and about midway between Group H and the Great Plaza, are the two twin-pyramid complexes R and Q. At least seven of these complexes are known at Tikal, and for a time they were thought to be unique to the site. Recent work at Yaxhá, however, has uncovered one there as well, with the same east-west orientation of the pyramids.

Complex R abuts the Maler Causeway and has been only partially excavated. Complex Q, adjacent to the east, and of the same size, has been largely restored and its monuments have been reerected. Carved Stela 22 and Altar 10 are in place in the northern enclosure and are additional examples of fine Late Classic sculpture, even though the figure on the stela has a mutilated face, and both captives on the top of the altar are somewhat eroded. Plain stelae and altars stand in front of the east pyramid.

From the central area it is possible to drive to Complexes R and Q, and the road then continues to the hotels.

The Méndez Causeway supports a car trail, which is steep in spots, and it runs southeast for 0.8 mile between the central area and the Temple of Inscriptions, where the causeway ends. It passes Group G (to the south of the causeway) along the way. A marked foot trail leads a short distance to this group. Some recent excavation and restoration in Group G make this area very worthwhile. The structures here are of the palace type and date to the Late Classic period. It is one of the largest clusters of this type of construction known at Tikal. The entrance to Group G is through a vaulted tunnel in the rear of one of the structures. The tunnel is surrounded by a huge fantastic mask, but, unfortunately, much of it is eroded. Follow the tunnel to the interior courtyard.

The structures facing the courtyard are all worth a look, and there are graffiti in several of the rooms. One unusual feature is the use of vertical grooves as decorations on the palace walls.

Last but not least is the Late Classic Temple of Inscriptions. This temple is best visited in the morning when the sun hits the back of the roof comb, which is covered with hieroglyphs. Panels of glyphs also cover the sides of the roof comb.

*Stela 20 in the Twin Pyramid Complex P of Group H, Tikal. Late Classic period.*

*Altar 8 in the Twin Pyramid Complex P of Group H, Tikal. Late Classic period.*

*Interior courtyard of Group G, presently being restored, Tikal. Late Classic period.*

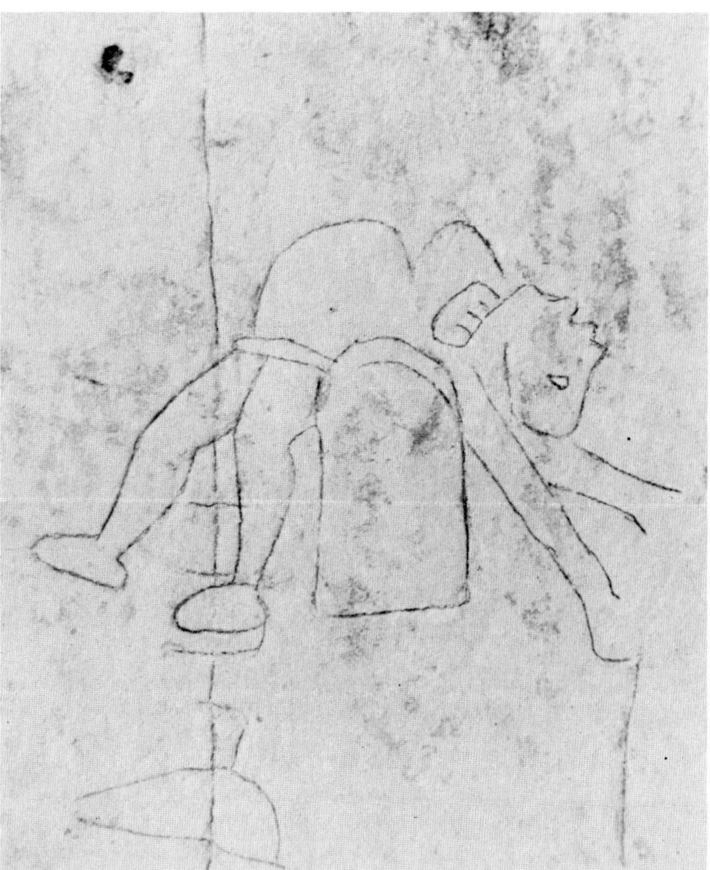

*Graffito in one of the rooms in Group G, Tikal.*

The front of the building is somewhat in ruin, but at its base are the remains of two interesting monuments, although only the bottom fragment of Stela 21 is intact—the rest having been mutilated, probably in Late Classic times. The carving of the glyphs and the feet of the personage are a superb example of the sculptor's art. The stela is accompanied by Altar 9, the top of which depicts a bound captive—a motif found frequently at Tikal.

Another car trail leads from the Temple of Inscriptions back to the hotels. The ruins close late in the afternoon, but it is possible to return after dark. You can walk in or take one of the tours conducted by the hotels. You will be checked by a guard along the trail to the site. If you wish to drive in in your own vehicle, you must get a permit ahead of time. Check at the hotels for particulars.

## RECENT HISTORY

Although the people living in the general area around Tikal were probably always aware of its existence, the first official expedition to the area took place in 1848. It was undertaken by Modesto Méndez, commissioner of the Petén, along with the governor of the Petén, Ambrosio Tut. They were accompanied by the artist Eusebio Lara, and their adventure was published in 1853 in German.

A list of later investigators at Tikal reads like a who's who of archaeology and includes Gustave Bernoulli, Alfred P. Maudslay, Teobert Maler, Alfred Tozzer, Raymond E. Merwin, Sylvanus Morley, and Edwin Shook. Publication of data, maps, and beautiful photographs ensued through the years, thanks to their work.

In 1951 an airfield was built, and five years later the University Museum of the University of Pennsylvania undertook an eleven-year program of excavation and restoration, with the cooperation of the Guatemalan government. This became known as the Tikal Project and was one of the largest of its kind ever attempted.

After the termination of the program by the University of Pennsylvania, Guatemala's Institute of Anthropology took over the site and continued the work. Restoration ensued under the direction of C. Rudy Larios and Miguel Orrego Corzo. The Institute is currently working on Group G.

The ruins are now centered in what has become the Tikal National Park—the first national park in Central America—which encompasses 222 square miles of preserved area. The roads, trails, and maintenance of the cleared areas are supervised by the director of parks under the Institute of Anthropology of Guatemala.

In 1964 a small but excellent museum was completed, and is definitely worth a visit. A nearby bookstore sells a variety of pertinent publications and maps.

## CONNECTIONS

1. 162 air miles from Guatemala City to Flores, then 40.5 miles by fair dirt road to the site,
2. 339 miles by road from Guatemala City (153 miles paved, and 186 miles dirt),
3. 141.5 miles by road from Belize City (49 miles paved, and 92.5 miles fair dirt), or
4. 190 air miles from Guatemala City.

## GETTING THERE

See "A Note on the Petén and Belize" for details of road conditions and other general information.

There are now several ways to get to Tikal. Unless you are driving all the way to Guatemala in your own car, I would recommend method 1.

1. Fly Aviateca from Guatemala City to Flores (daily morning flight) and rent a Suzuki (Jeep type) at the Hotel Maya International near the airport. You can write ahead to Señor Rodolfo Vettorazzi, in care of the hotel, and reserve a vehicle. This is recommended since he only has a couple. He will want a deposit to reserve one for you.

On the mainland in San Benito is the Posada Mayaland. The proprietors also have Jeeps and advertise tours, but I did not learn whether they would rent a Jeep without a driver.

From Flores head east and then north on the Flores-Melchor Highway to El Cruce (17.5 miles). From there take the cutoff north to Tikal (23 miles). Plan for a little over 1½ hours for the drive from Flores to Tikal.

2. You can drive to Tikal from Guatemala City in something over 12 hours; it is possible to do it in one day, if you get a very early start.

Take Highway CA 9 northeast to the junction with the Petén Highway (153 miles) (one mile before the junction is a service station, and I recommend that you gas up there). The junction is on your left and is unnumbered. The Petén Highway heads northwest for 148 miles, where it connects with the Flores-Melchor Highway (2.5 miles east of Flores). Turn right (east) at this junction—unless you plan to stop in Flores—and go 15 miles to El Cruce. Then take a left (north) and go 23 miles to Tikal.

*Note:* On Highway Ca 9, about 19 miles out of Guatemala City, there is a large bridge that was badly damaged in the February, 1976, earthquake. A one-lane wooden replacement was constructed to facilitate movement of traffic along the highway, but you could lose up to an hour as traffic is let through in only one direction at a time. It may be a while before the regular bridge is repaired or a new one constructed.

If you want to break up the trip between Guatemala City and Tikal, there are three reasonable stopovers:

*a.* The Longarone Motel: This is 79 miles out of Guatemala City and 3.5 miles past the town of Teculután. This sprawling layout is nice, has air-conditioned rooms, pretty good food, and an Olympic-sized swimming pool. There is no hot water. The owner is a pleasant and helpful man.

*b.* The Marimonte Motel: This is on the Petén Highway, 171 miles out of Guatemala City and 18 miles after you take the Petén Highway cutoff, shortly before you reach the Río Dulce. The motel is a few blocks off the highway (right side), and the cutoff is just past a service station. It is adequate, though not fancy (no hot water). It has a pool and a good dining room, and is frequented mostly by local tourists. It can get crowded on weekends.

*c.* Flores: There are several hotels here, the best of which is the Maya International. It has a nice dining room with parrots sauntering around, a pool, hot water, and helpful personnel. Tours to various Petén sites can be arranged there.

3. Tikal can be reached from Belize City, Belize (formerly British Honduras), in 4½ to 5 hours' driving time. Allow an additional hour to cross the international frontier.

From Belize City take the Western Highway to the Guatemalan border (78.5 miles). There an unnumbered highway (the Flores–Melchor Highway) continues straight ahead to El Cruce (40 miles). At El Cruce take the cutoff to the right (north), which goes directly to Tikal.

*Note:* If you enter Guatemala from Belize, you can get a Guatemala tourist card from the Guatemala consul in Benque Viejo near the border (on the Belize side). Ask directions to his office. You will save time, however, by getting a Guatemala tourist card before you leave home. They are available from your nearest Guatemala consul.

On the Belize-Tikal run, the only stopover is the Golden Orange Hotel in Cayo, about 10 miles before the Belize-Guatemala frontier. There are only a few rooms, and they are nice, although expensive. Good food is served in the dining room. We saw a couple of hotels in Benque Viejo, but I did not try them.

It is also possible to rent a car in Mérida, Yucatán, or Chetumal, Quintana Roo, drive to Belize, and on to Tikal. There are no regular car-rental agents, such as Hertz or Avis, in Belize, and although it is possible to rent cars from individuals, it may be difficult to get permission to take the vehicle into Guatemala.

4. By far the most popular way to get to Tikal is to fly in on Aviateca from Guatemala City. You then have a couple of choices, depending on your interests. You can take the regular half-day tour of the site by Jeep or minibus. This also includes a visit to the museum, lunch, and a return flight to Guatemala City in the afternoon. The whole trip can be arranged as a package in Guatemala City. The tour stops at the major areas but misses other areas

altogether; thus while it is probably adequate for the casual visitor, it will hardly suffice for the serious enthusiast.

If you want to spend more time at the site, you can fly in, take the regular tour (or not), and stay over at Tikal. You can then see more of the site on foot or on private tours arranged at your hotel at Tikal.

*Note:* If you fly in and plan to do the regular tour, make sure you eat an early breakfast before leaving Guatemala City or carry snacks along; you are not fed on the plane and have no time to eat at Tikal before your tour begins. You will want all the energy you can muster.

The main advantage of the first three ways of getting to Tikal is that you have your own vehicle at the site, the importance of which cannot be overstressed. This allows you total freedom to go where you want, when you want and to linger in the spots that interest you most.

Tikal is a huge site, and walking from your hotel to the site itself can be exhausting. You will want to save your energy for climbing some of the temples. Most of the groups of buildings—some far apart—can be driven to. This saves not only energy but time. Having your own vehicle—rented or otherwise—also allows you the luxury of carrying the ice chest you have prudently brought from home (and filled with ice and drinks at Flores or Belize). Ice is not sold at Tikal. A cold drink whenever you want one will extend your endurance for several hours. Cold drinks are available from vendors at the site, but having your own will be more convenient.

Buses run from Guatemala City to Flores, and another line runs from there to Tikal. You can bus from Mérida to Chetumal, but you will probably have to taxi from Chetumal to the Mexico-Belize frontier (6.5 miles) and from there to Corozal (7.5 miles), where you can get a bus for Belize City. Buses run from Belize City to the Belize-Guatemala frontier and from Melchor de Mencos on the Guatemala side to Flores. The buses are second class except for the Mérida–Chetumal and the Corozal–Belize City sections, which have first-class service.

If you drive or bus in to Tikal, you must stop at the immigration station just before the airfield. The officials will want to check your papers and have you sign the register.

On your first visit to Tikal allow at least 2 full days—more, if you can. There are several possibilities if you plan to stay over at Tikal. The best accommodations by far are at the Jaguar Inn, and the price is reasonable. The only problem is that it has only two bungalows (twin-bedded with private bath). If you want to stay here, I would recommend that you make reservations ahead. There is also a good dining room, which is open to the public. The beer is cold, and they have a bar of sorts. They are helpful in arranging tours of Tikal and other sites. Discuss plans with Patty Solis, the British wife of the owner.

The Jungle Inn (or Jungle Lodge) was the first hotel at Tikal. It consists of several individual bungalows with private baths and a multiunit building with shared baths. It is a bit expensive for the accommodations. There is also a dining room, but the food is only fair.

The Hotel Tikal Inn is newer, somewhat more primitive—strictly shared bath—but is quite a bit cheaper. The small rooms are separated by featheredged boards, which have large cracks in between and do not extend to the ceiling. This probably helps for ventilation, but hope that you do not get a room next to someone who snores. The roof leaks in some of the rooms; protect valuables with plastic covers in case it rains during the night. The food here is pretty good, and the place boasts a swimming pool, but after a look at its murky water, you will probably be satisfied with a cold shower. There is no hot water anywhere at Tikal, and the electricity is turned off between 9:00 and 10:00 P.M., often without much warning.

There are also camping spaces at Tikal for vans and other vehicles, and some thatched shelters where you can sling a hammock. Both are allotted on a first come, first served basis.

If you plan only the regular half-day tour of Tikal, then tennis shoes are adequate. If you plan to go it on your own, heavy socks and climbing boots will keep your feet happier. Bring extra socks, for a freshly washed pair will not dry overnight. The humidity probably never falls below 100 percent. A light sweater or windbreaker will be useful on cool, misty mornings. Take along a flashlight in case you get caught in the shower when the lights go out. Also carry insect repellent, lots of film, and William Coe's guidebook for Tikal. If you do not have a copy when you arrive, you can get one at the bookstore, the museum, or one of the hotels.

★★★

# *Sylvanus G. Morley Museum (Tikal Museum)*

The Tikal Museum is named for the great Mayanist scholar Sylvanus G. Morley, who visited the site four times and devotedly recorded the inscriptions of Tikal, as well as those of other sites in the Petén. The museum contains stelae and altars placed there for preservation, including Stela 29, the earliest known inscribed lowland Maya monument, dated A.D. 292.

A remarkable collection of pottery is attractively displayed, as are some fascinating inscribed miniature bone artifacts. Try photographing these with the camera lens resting on the horizontal surface of the glass case. This steadies the camera, and glare is no problem.

Other objects of interest are the stuccoed figures originally identified as the long-nosed Maya rain god Chac. Recent studies, however, show that there were at least two long-nosed deities besides Chac. These stuccoed figures are now believed to represent God K, patron of the Manikin Scepter.

A replica of a tomb—known as Burial 116—that was found beneath Temple I forms a spectacular display. Included, among other offerings in this burial are 108 pieces of worked jade weighing 16½ pounds. This is quite a sight. It has been calculated that 70 percent of Tikal's temples were used as burial monuments.

Recent research by Clemency Coggins has shown that glyphs on pottery interred with dead rulers record historical information on the ruler's reign. Three of Tikal's rulers who reigned in succession have now been identified. The first was Double-Comb, who ascended to power in A.D. 682. He built Temple II, apparently honoring his wife, and Temple I, beneath which he was buried around A.D. 730. He was between 60 and 80 years old when he died. It is a replica of his tomb that is on display in the museum.

You are generously allowed to photograph all the exhibits in the museum. The museum is open only during certain hours. Check locally.

*Stela 1 from Tikal, in the patio of the Tikal Museum. Early Classic period.*

*Pyramid E-VII-sub, the front (east) side, Uaxactún. Late Preclassic period. The Early Classic period Stela 20 is at the foot of the stairway.*

★

# *Uaxactún*

(wah-shahk-*toon*)

DERIVATION: Mayan for "Eight Stone." Named because of a Cycle-8 stela found at the site.
ORIGINAL NAME: Unknown.
CULTURE: Maya
LOCATION: Northern part of the department of Petén, Guatemala.

---

## THE SITE

The ancient center of Uaxactún was formed of groups of buildings atop several low hills. The airstrip at Uaxactún—and the modern village that borders it—cuts through part of the archaeological zone. Most of the site is heavily overgrown, and most of the architecture appears as rubble mounds.

There are three areas of interest for the visitor. The most impressive is the recently recleared Pyramid E-VII-sub, located a few hundred yards east of the airstrip and accessible by Jeep trail. E-VII-sub is perhaps the most famous structure at Uaxactún. It is best known for its softly undulating lines and large mask panels of two types found on all four sides. One type depicts a stylized serpent and the other is anthropomorphic. Authorities still debate whether there is Olmec influence in the masks.

E-VII-sub dates to the Late Preclassic period, and was discovered in excellent condition beneath a later structure, which had protected it. The later structure—Pyramid E-VII—was in a ruinous condition and its remains were removed to reveal the earlier pyramid. When first excavated, E-VII-sub was brilliantly white, but with time and lack of maintenance it became overgrown. The reclearing has again revealed the structure, but its stucco surface is now a mottled gray-brown. For this reason, the details of the mask panels are not as clear as they were when the pyramid was first excavated. Nevertheless, the structure is a real gem, and somehow larger than I had expected it to be from having seen published photos. It is roughly square in plan, with stairways on all four sides leading to a platform on top. The platform has a single stair on the east side. It is thought that a building of perishable materials originally crowned the top. Early Classic Stela 20 is located at the base of the eastern stair of E-VII-sub and shows a figure in frontal view.

East of E-VII-sub—a short distance by foot trail—is a group of three ruined buildings, E-I, -II, and -III (in a north-south line), and some eroded and fragmented Early Classic stelae lie near the west base of the central building. This group and E-VII-sub formed an astronomical observatory. From an observation point on the east stairway of E-VII-sub, the sun could be seen rising behind E-I, -II, or -III. Its relative position marked the summer and winter solstices (longest and shortest days of the year) and the vernal and autumnal equinoxes (when day and night are of the same length). Since the discovery of this group at Uaxactún, several similar assemblages have been identified at other Maya centers.

The best preserved—though unrestored—building on the west side of the airstrip is Structure A-XVIII. It is located a few minutes from the airstrip by foot trail. Getting there entails a climb up the hill on which it is situated. This Early Classic temple has two stories, an interior stairway, and unusual bottle-shaped vaults. Some zapote lintels and much of the original interior plaster are still in place. The front of the structure has collapsed, but it is still possible to climb to the top. From here you get a view of the village and airstrip below. The area on the west side of the airstrip is overgrown, except for a few trails.

From Structure A-XVIII, it is a few minutes on foot to Group B, which lies to the north. There is little standing architecture in this area, though rubble mounds can be discerned. Of more interest are a couple of carved stelae. The best preserved (and still standing) is the Early Classic Stela 5. It is one of several Cycle-8 stelae found at Uaxactún—the site with more of these early monuments than any other. The style of Stela 5 is unusual in several respects, notably in that the figure seems to be carrying an atlatl, which hints at foreign influence. The other stela is nearby, lying on its back. Its main surface is eroded, but remnants of glyphs can be made out on its sides.

*Stela 5, on the west side of the airstrip, Uaxactún. Early Classic period.*

## RECENT HISTORY

The first archaeologist to see Uaxactún was Sylvanus G. Morley, when he headed an expedition for the Carnegie Institution of Washington in 1916. It is not clear how he first heard of the unnamed site, but he was guided there by a trustworthy man named José. Although Morley and his staff were at the site for only six days, they examined, photographed, and did drawings of the glyphs that were found on several carved stelae, took measurements for a site plan, and did sketch plans of the structures. Uaxactún was also studied by Oliver G. Ricketson and his wife E. B. Ricketson, and by the brothers A. Ledyard Smith and Robert E. Smith, all sponsored by the Carnegie Institution of Washington, which supported extensive excavations from 1926 to 1937.

Uaxactún is one of the most studied Maya sites. The ceramic sequence that resulted from work there laid the foundation for the whole of lowland Maya chronology. This chronology was then linked to that of most of the rest of Mesoamerica. Therefore, Uaxactún is a most important site, as well as one of the earliest. Its ceramic sequence begins in the early part of the Middle Preclassic period, from which evidence of platforms was found. The first pyramid construction began in the Late Preclassic, and is exemplified by Pyramid E-VII-sub. Uaxactún continued to be an active center into the Late Classic period; one of the latest dated stelae of the southern Maya lowlands was erected there in A.D. 889.

After the intensive work at Uaxactún, the jungle was allowed to reclaim the structures until 1974, when the reclearing of Pyramid E-VII-sub was undertaken by Edwin Shook. One hopes that this time it will be possible to maintain it. Perhaps this work will also instigate an eventual improvement in road conditions from Tikal to Uaxactún for the benefit of archaeologists, workers, and visitors alike.

## CONNECTION

1. 11 miles by air, or a few miles more by poor dirt road from Tikal.

## GETTING THERE

See "Tikal" for getting that far and for accommodations there.

At one time it was possible to reach Uaxactún directly from Tikal by air. There was a daily morning flight—lasting 7 minutes—with a return flight to Tikal in the early afternoon of the same day. In 1973, on our first visit to Uaxactún, this is how we got there. The plane we were waiting for arrived at Tikal at 9:15 A.M. and unloaded the passengers from Guatemala City, who had come in for the half-day tourist visit. When it was ready to leave for Uaxactún, we discovered that we were the only passengers except for an armed guard. We were standing there in jungle clothes, carrying only camera gear and a plastic bag with soft drinks when the call for Uaxactún came over the airport loudspeaker. An American lady, who had just arrived at Tikal, heard the call and misunderstood. As we got ready to board, she looked at us and back at the plane—a well-used DC-3—and gasped, "My God! They're not going to Washington in *that*!" Several people within hearing distance had a good laugh. By 1976 this flight had been discontinued, but I mention it in case it should be resumed. It is worth checking into as this is the best way to get to Uaxactún.

In 1976 it was possible to fly to Uaxactún from Flores (2 or 3 flights a week), but it was necessary to wait a day or so to get out—a less-than-delightful prospect. See "Tikal" for hotels in Flores.

It is also possible to drive to Uaxactún from Tikal, but you need a vehicle with four-wheel drive. Check at your hotel in Tikal or in Flores for a Jeep-and-driver package. I would definitely recommend hiring an experienced Jeep driver to take you, rather than renting a Jeep and trying it on your own. Check at Tikal about the condition of the road before attempting the trip. The road is always bad, but often the trip can be made without undue difficulty. If the rains have been particularly heavy (as they were in August, 1976, when we drove in), the road can be an absolute horror.

As soon as we left Tikal village, we hit a bad spot that caused the Jeep to slide sickeningly and lean at a precarious angle. Things did not improve. In addition, we had to stop several times because of trees lying across the road. Each time a bypass had to be cut through the jungle vegetation (by hand with a machete) to get around the fallen trees. We had to take detours around some particularly muddy spots, and there seemed to be a thousand of them. On the detours, we bumped over tree roots and stones. In all it took us 3½ hours to reach Uaxactún but only 2 hours back, since we did not have to cut bypasses. I cannot really say we *drove* to Uaxactún—we *slithered* there! Without question this is the worst road I have ever been on, and I suspect that the driver would have declined to make the trip if he had known how bad the road was. We got stuck twice but managed to get out thanks to our driver's determination and some pushing, prayers, and luck. Altogether it was an interesting, though hair-raising, experience. The road from Tikal to Uaxactún is variously listed as being 11 to 15 miles in length, and after taking it, I can understand why. If it is relatively dry and you do not have to leave the main road to take the bypasses, it is shorter; with each bypass you take, a little is added to the mileage. I planned to check the distance on our Jeep's odometer, but it was inoperable.

Another way to reach Uaxactún is to hike in from Tikal. I have not tried this, nor am I inclined to. It would be a difficult trip, taking 5 or 6 hours each way, plus the time spent at the site.

There are no accommodations at Uaxactún, but bottled drinks and canned food can be purchased at stores along the airstrip. Carry your own only if you drive in; otherwise, depend on the stores. Wear boots and carry insect repellent. Allow about 3 hours to see the structures on both sides of the airstrip.

Regardless how you get to the village of Uaxactún, you will need a guide to get to the ruins—especially those on the west side of the airstrip. Someone may be able to direct you to the Jeep trail that goes to Pyramid E-VII-sub. If you have not brought a guide along, check at the Uaxactún airport, if it is open. Otherwise, ask around at the stores.

*Note:* In 1978 a new access to Uaxactún was reported. This is a road that goes from Flores around the west end of Lake Petén Itzá. It then heads northeast to the town of San Andrés, and then goes north. Farther along there is a cutoff to the east that goes to Uaxactún. Sometimes the trip can be made without four-wheel drive, but in wet weather it would probably be necessary. Nevertheless, road graders were working on the road, indicating that improvement can be expected. Although I have not yet taken this road, it sounds much better than the direct route from Tikal to Uaxactún. Check in Flores for a Jeep-and-driver package.

*Stela 11, the Tlaloc Stela, Yaxhá. Early Classic period.*

# *Yaxhá*

(yah-*shah*)

DERIVATION: Mayan for "Green Water." Named for Lake Yaxhá.
CULTURE: Maya.
LOCATION: East-central part of the department of Petén, Guatemala.

---

## THE SITE

Yaxhá, the third-largest Maya site in Guatemala, covers several square miles on a ridge overlooking Lake Yaxhá. Recent work at the site was largely devoted to exploring and mapping the more than 500 structures found in its precincts. Included are several immense pyramid temples and monumental acropolislike building complexes. One large group includes a number of palace-type structures arranged around six courtyards. A twin-pyramid complex was also discovered at Yaxhá, the only one known outside Tikal. Some forty stelae are known from the site, and about half of these are carved. In addition to the structures there are four causeways and several streets, the first to be found at a lowland Maya site. The architectural remains have been partly cleared, but none are restored. Getting one's bearings, even with the aid of a site plan, is not easy.

The most interesting area for the visitor includes the East Acropolis and Plazas B and C. In 1974 one huge pyramid temple (Structure 216) in the East Acropolis could be climbed by a narrow, steep trail. There were some remains of graffiti on the walls, of the temple on top.

*Note:* In February, 1976, a severe earthquake struck Guatemala, and it was reported by Nicholas M. Hellmuth that the back vault of the temple atop Structure 216 collapsed and the rest of the temple was badly cracked. It is recommended that you do *not* climb the structure, both for your own safety and for the preservation of the remains of the temple.

In Plaza B, adjacent to the west side of the East Acropolis, is the Early Classic monument, Stela 11. This stela depicts a frontal view of Tlaloc, the Mexican deity. He is shown in the guise of a warrior, or war god, rather than in his better-known aspect as a rain god. The stela was discovered in 1914 and the style is a variation of that of Teotihuacán. The Tlaloc stela is near the base of the structure that bounds Plaza B on the east side. The stela rests on its side and is protected by a thatched shelter, making photography a bit difficult. It is possible to part the thatch and push a camera through. A wide-angle lens is best here.

Other outside influence evident at Yaxhá is a building with six columns—across Plaza B from the Tlaloc stela—and in two other structures at the site. Buildings with columns are unusual in the Petén. According to Hellmuth, "A recent increase of interest in the influence of the central Mexican site of Teotihuacán on the lowland Maya led to the choice of Yaxhá for investigation."

Plaza C lies south of Plaza B and contains carved stelae showing traits related to the early Izapan style.

Other thatch-covered carved stela are in the central area of the site and can be reached from Plaza C via the Lincoln Causeway.

Also of interest are some unusual large carvings on an outcrop of bedrock. These would be difficult to find without a guide.

Yaxhá was active from the first to the tenth centuries A.D., and was found to have a greater density of structures than most other lowland Maya sites (about 36 percent greater density than Tikal). Unfortunately, most of these appear only as mounds today. Nevertheless, if you are in the Petén visiting Tikal or Seibal and have access to a vehicle, you will find Yaxhá rewarding.

## RECENT HISTORY

Teobert Maler explored Yaxhá in the early years of the twentieth century, and the Peabody Museum of Harvard University published his findings in 1908. Sylvanus Morley and Frans Blom visited the site briefly, and it was partly mapped in the 1930s by architect William Lincoln. In the 1960s, Merle Greene and Ian Graham documented the stelae.

In 1970, Hellmuth directed a project at Yaxhá, sponsored by the Foundation for Latin American Anthropological Research, Inc., that lasted for

*Stela 4 showing Izapan traits, Yaxhá. Early Classic period.*

several seasons. Preliminary reports have been published. Assisting in this work were Guatemalan archaeologists C. Rudy Larios, who discovered the twin-pyramid complex, and Miguel Orrego Corzo, who excavated the West Group.

## CONNECTIONS

1. 37.5 miles by fair dirt road from Flores to the Yaxhá cutoff,
2. 43 miles by fair dirt road from Tikal to the Yaxhá cutoff,
3. 30 miles by fair dirt road from Cayo to the Yaxhá cutoff, or
4. 98.5 miles by road (49 miles paved, 49.5 miles fair dirt) from Belize City to the Yaxhá cutoff, then 5.5 miles by poor dirt road to the south shore of Lake Yaxhá, and 3 miles of Jeep road to the site.

## GETTING THERE

The stretch of road from the Yaxhá cutoff to Lake Yaxhá can *generally* be made in a regular car, but at times can be impassable even for Jeeps. There are two bad spots—one at the beginning and one at the end. The road from the lake to the site is strictly for Jeeps and can become impassable for even these vehicles at times. Check locally on conditions of these last two stretches before attempting the trip.

If you can get as far as the lake but not all the way to the site, there are two other possibilities: (1) you *might* be able to get a boat at the south shore of the lake to take you across to the site, but this is not always possible, and (2) if no boats are available, then you could walk the last 3 miles to the site.

Buses run from Melchor de Mencos to Flores, and can drop you off at the cutoff, but you will have to hike in the 8.5 miles to the site. Few vehicles use this road.

When road conditions are reasonable and you are driving a vehicle with four-wheel drive, you can make it to Yaxhá from Flores or Tikal in 2 to 2¼ hours; from Cayo in 1¼ hours, or from Belize City in 3½ hours. If you leave from Cayo or Belize, you will also have to add the time spent in crossing the Belize-Guatemala frontier. See "Tikal" and "Altun Ha" for hotels in the area, Jeep rentals in Flores, airlines, and buses.

From Flores head east on the Flores-Melchor Highway to the Yaxhá cutoff. The cutoff heads north to Lake Yaxhá, but is no longer marked with a sign. A small, isolated tree marks the junction. There are few roads in the area, and you are not likely to miss it.

From Tikal head south to El Cruce, situated on the Flores-Melchor Highway (23 miles), then east to the cutoff (20 miles).

From Cayo or Belize City, head west on the Western Highway to the Belize-Guatemala frontier. From Melchor de Mencos on the Guatemala side continue west to the Yaxhá cutoff (20 miles).

When you reach the lake (actually two lakes), bear to the right at first. Then cross to the north shore between the two lakes and bear left along the shore of the left (west) lake. The lakes are not visible at all points. Keep going until you reach a large thatched shelter—left by the archaeologists who worked at the site—and the caretaker's house behind it.

There are no accommodations at Yaxhá, except for the shelter with benches and tables, but the caretaker will be happy to let you use it to eat lunch. Bring your own food and drink. You could also use the shelter to sling a hammock, if you want to stay overnight.

There is a cutoff to another part of the site before you reach the shelter and the caretaker's house, but you will save time by finding the caretaker, or you might try bringing a guide along with you from Flores or Tikal. Check at your hotel—you could arrange a guide-and-Jeep package.

Allow 3 hours to visit Yaxhá, plus time for a lunch break. Wear boots.

A visit to Yaxhá can be combined with a visit to Topoxté on Lake Yaxhá. This makes a good one-day trip from Flores.

*Note:* If you drive some of the trails around Yaxhá, you may see a small sign tacked to a tree pointing to Nakum (Nakun), 20 kilometers or so north. We inquired about this road, and the information we received indicates that there is a road from Yaxhá that goes 9 miles toward Nakum. From the point where the road ends, it is 3 miles to the site, and this part must be done on foot. The road is passable for Jeeps in the dry season and sometimes, but not always, in the rainy season. We were told that February or March would be the best time to try the trip and that a competent guide would be necessary to get there. There is a fair bit of standing architecture at Nakum, and, from published photos, it would appear to be a most interesting site.

*Plain stelae found at the west side of Structure D, Topoxté. Late Postclassic period.*

★

# *Topoxté*

(toh-pohsh-*teh*)

DERIVATION: A Mayan name for a bush, according to Teobert Maler, who gave the name to the site.
ORIGINAL NAME: Unknown.
CULTURE: Maya.
LOCATION: East-central part of the department of Petén, Guatemala.

---

## THE SITE

Topoxté is a Maya site in Lake Yaxhá, and the ruins are on three small hills—called "islands" in the literature—in the western part of the lake. The most impressive remains are on the easternmost island, or First Island. It was the only island we visited. (See "Getting There" for more on the "islands.")

The main ceremonial precincts occupy the highest part of the First Island, and the best-preserved structures border the east and north sides of a plaza. On the west the ground slopes downward as a terrace to a lower level.

Structure C (the Main Temple) is the southernmost structure on the east side of the plaza and is the most interesting. Most of the walls of this two-room temple are still standing, though the beam-and-mortar roof has collapsed. The temple rests on top of a stepped pyramidal base that rises in four tiers and is approached by a western stair. The stair is now badly ruined, but the temple can be reached by a steep climb up the north side of the substructure. Structure C was originally completely plastered and a few remnants of this surface still remain.

Structure D (north of Structure C) is poorly preserved, but at its base, on the west side, are a couple of small plain stela, and others are reported from this area.

North of Structure D is Structure E, which has some remains of standing architecture, as does the nearby Structure G, on the north side of the plaza.

There are remains of other buildings in the area on various terrace levels, but most are in a ruinous condition. Structure A—impressive for its size—is worth a look. It is now a tall rubble mound and it is located on a lower level, 50 yards to the southwest of Structure C.

Two carved but eroded stelae were reported on the slope on the west side of the plaza, but we were unable to locate them and our guide knew nothing of them. Perhaps they have become covered with soil and vegetation. (Two other carved stelae are reported on the Third Island.)

Topoxté is basically considered a Late Postclassic site, but it was occupied in earlier times. There is ceramic evidence—including figurines—for a heavy occupation during the Late Preclassic period, and this continued into the Early Classic. There was a falloff during Late Classic times. Veneer masonry—used in a retaining wall and dating to that period—was discovered, though, on the First Island. So far no evidence has been found for an Early Postclassic occupation of the site. Topoxté was reoccupied during the Late Postclassic, and it was during this time the currently visible structures were erected. During the Preclassic and Classic periods Topoxté was probably subordinate to the major center of Yaxhá across the lake.

The carved stelae are of Late Classic date and are assumed to have been reused by the later occupants of the site during the Late Postclassic period. It is thought that the stelae either came from Yaxhá or relate to an earlier occupation period at Topoxté.

Some details of the architecture at Topoxté—square columns in doorways, stairway balustrades with vertical upper zones, and beam-and-mortar roofs—are also characteristic of the Late Postclassic Maya architecture at Mayapán and Tulum, while other features at Topoxté appear to be a local development. Late Postclassic figurine censers found at Topoxté are also closely related to those produced in Yucatán and Quintana Roo during the same period. The plain stelae are also Late Postclassic, and some, at least, originally bore designs in stucco.

Topoxté is the only site known in the Petén with preserved remains of architecture dating to the Late Postclassic period.

## RECENT HISTORY

Juan Galindo—one-time governor of the Petén and an early visitor to Palenque and Copán—published the first report on Topoxté in 1834. There is some question about whether he personally visited the site or relied on reports of someone in his employ. Included in his report is a description of Structure C, mentioned as a "five-story tower," apparently referring to its four-tiered base plus the temple on top.

In 1904, Teobert Maler visited Topoxté. He photographed Structure C, and made a map of the plaza; his work was published by the Peabody Museum of Harvard University in 1908. On brief visits, the site was subsequently investigated by Sylvanus Morley in 1914 and by Frans Blom in 1924. Two biologists, Cyrus Lundell and L. C. Stuart, visited Topoxté in 1933 and discovered the four carved stelae. They also produced a new map of the main group and gave letter designations to the structures.

The most intensive work at the site was that conducted by William R. Bullard, Jr., and published by Peabody Museum in 1970. Bullard visited Topoxté briefly in 1956 and made additional visits in 1958 and 1959. In 1960 he spent two and a half weeks at the site with two workmen. Trenches were dug in various parts of the site to collect ceramic specimens, and the structures were photographed. No extensive excavations were undertaken, however, nor was any restoration attempted. Although Topoxté had been known to archaeologists for many years, until Bullard's investigations, it was not known that the remains were of Late Postclassic date.

## CONNECTIONS

1. About 30 minutes by motorized dugout from the end of the Lake Yaxhá road, or
2. A little over 3 miles on foot (1¼ to 1½ hours) from the end of the Lake Yaxhá road.

## GETTING THERE

See "Tikal" for getting to Flores and other general information, and "Yaxhá" for getting to the south shore of Lake Yaxhá.

When you get to the lake, ask at one of the houses at the end of the road about a boat with a motor, since this will afford the easiest access to the site. If only dugouts without motors are available, you would be better off walking to the site; it would be faster and safer. The lake has a reputation for becoming very choppy.

The people living in the area do not know Topoxté by that name. Locally the site is called *la ruina en el cerrito*—"the ruin on the little hill." Use this nomenclature whether you make boat arrangements or ask directions to get there on foot.

Although I give directions on how to get there on foot, you will still want to ask on the spot and have the way pointed out.

There are actually two possibilities for walking to the site. If you are at the end of the main road that goes to the lake, take a left turn (west) onto a side road that ends on the shore of the lake a couple of hundred yards away. There is a small open area right on the lake where you can park. From here you can look west across the south shore of the lake and see a finca—made up of several thatch and wooden buildings—some 1.5 miles away in a straight line. The finca is on the way to the site. Closer to you are a couple of thatch houses a little inland from the lake shore; these are on the way and you come to them first.

From the parking area follow the very edge of the lake along a rocky trail for about 0.3 mile. Then keep an eye out for a foot trail that heads inland and uphill a little. Follow this foot trail; it winds around a bit—at one point heading south and then making a U turn and heading north to bypass a small inlet. Somewhat farther along, it comes to the thatch houses, where it connects with a dirt car road. The trail is through high weeds in places (after it leaves the lake shore), but you will not get lost if you keep heading in the general direction of the thatch houses.

From the houses, simply follow the car road to the finca—I call this the finca road. It runs near the south shore of the lake. Try to get a guide at the finca—if you do not already have one along—to take you the rest of the way. It is about 0.3 mile from the finca, west through a savanna to a ranchito, and another 0.3 mile northwest to the *cerrito* on which the ruins are located. This last 0.3 mile takes you near the Arroyo Ixtinto, a small stream that runs into the lake. The *cerrito* is covered with tall forest, and the site itself is overgrown, so your guide should have a machete along.

The other possibility for walking to the site is to use the finca road for the whole way rather than taking the trail that skirts the lake. The finca road connects the finca and the thatch houses already described to the Yaxhá cutoff on which you drove to the lake. The junction is 1.3 miles south of the lake and the finca road heads west. If you find that no boat with a motor is available at the lake, you can drive to the junction with the finca road and walk in from there.

In 1976 when we visited Topoxté, the finca road was being worked on, but was passable for Jeeps. If you have a vehicle with four-wheel drive, you should be able to drive all the way to the finca, thus saving some time and effort.

At the time of our visit we did not know that it was possible to walk to the site. We assumed that it was a true island that would require a boat. When we arrived at the lake and settlement, we asked about a motorized dugout and were told that the only one in the area was at the finca, and the direction was pointed out. The people we talked to mentioned the ruins at Yaxhá (which we had visited in the past) and ruins on the *cerrito* (of which I knew nothing). We drove west a short distance till the road ended, found another house, and asked again. We got the same story—there may be a motorboat at the finca. From our present vantage point the finca was visible in the distance, and we decided to walk there (after getting directions) in hopes of finding a boat. Again ruins on a *cerrito* were mentioned in the conversation.

When we got to the finca, we came across an elderly man who worked there, and we asked him about a boat. The upshot of the conversation was that, yes, the finca owned a boat with a motor, but it was off delivering *pimienta* ("allspice"); we could ask the *dueño* ("owner") of the finca for assistance, but, on second thought, he was not there but in Flores; there were some ruins on a nearby *cerrito.*

At this point we gave up the idea of seeing Topoxté, since we could not get a boat. It was too late in the day to plan for anything else, and we decided to find out about that ruin on the *cerrito.* At first the the old gentleman tried giving us directions, but when we were obviously having difficulty understanding the details, he offered to take us. I wondered what "unreported" site we were going to see.

I had a map of the lake along and followed it as we walked. Partway there I realized that we were heading right for Topoxté; the only difference was that the area shown as swamp (or water) on my map was bone dry and 15 feet or more above the level of the Arroyo Ixtinto and the lake. When we arrived at the site, the site plan I carried removed any lingering doubts. We were, indeed, at Topoxté, but it was not a true island.

We later questioned our guide about the reportedly swampy area that joined the *cerrito* to the mainland—and the vegetation did look like the type you would expect to find in a swamp—but he insisted that that part was never wet, much less under water.

The level of Lake Yaxhá reportedly fluctuates cyclically about 10 feet for unknown reasons. In 1976 it was obviously at an extremely low level. Even a rise of 10 feet, however, did not look like it would really wet the swamp area, and certainly it would not have made the *cerrito* a true island. Nevertheless, the implication in Maler's report is that the site was on a true island at the time of his visit. I would guess that for the next few years, at least, you will still be able to walk to the site.

Wear a sun hat and boots, if you walk there. Carry water in a bottle or canteen, and have food and cold drinks in your vehicle, since there are none available in the area. Bring fast film, for the site is well shaded; even so, you will not be able to get really good shots because of vegetation that obscures the structures. Allow an hour to visit the site once you get there.

If you have facilities to sleep in your vehicle, Lake Yaxhá is a delightful place to spend the night. Set up on the lake shore, at the parking area where the road ends.

*Structure A-III, view from the northwest, Seibal. Stela 9 is at the base of the western stair. Late Classic period.*

★★★

# *Seibal* *(Ceibal)*

(say-*bahl*)

DERIVATION: "Place of the Ceiba Tree."
EARLIER NAME: Sastanquiqui.
ORIGINAL NAME: Unknown.
CULTURE: Maya; see text.
LOCATION: South-central part of the department of Petén, Guatemala.

## THE SITE

Although Seibal is not a very large site—the entire building area occupies less than one-half square mile—more than forty-three structures have been excavated. Of these, only two have been restored; (1) Structure A-III, a three-tiered pyramidal base with stairs on all four sides, surmounted by the remains of a temple with a corbeled vault and (2) a three-tiered round structure with a jaguar altar in front. The other architectural remains are now rubble and vegetation-covered mounds.

The road to the site ends near a couple of neat thatch-roofed houses with plastered walls—used by archaeologists while working at the site. A few interesting fragments of carved stelae are found around one of them. They are worth a look and a few frames of film. There is also a nice picnic area nearby.

The trail to the ruins proper leads off from the picnic area, passes both restored structures, and loops back to the picnic area. If you begin your tour by taking the trail to the left, you will come to Structure A-III first, then to the round structure. If you prefer to save the best till last, start by taking the trail to the right, and see the round structure first.

Structure A-III is a block or so away from the picnic area and is the most interesting part of the site. The structure sits in the middle of a cleared area. There are also several stelae in the vicinity—five of which are directly associated with Structure A-III. For the visitor, it is really the stelae that are of the most interest at Seibal. They are unusual in that they show strong influence from central Mexico. In fact, it is possible that there was actually a foreign penetration into the area.

The stelae have been cleaned, treated with preservative, and reerected where necessary, so photography is easy. A short walk by a side trail to the left from this area (as you enter) takes you to some other carved monuments. See these before leaving the general area for the longish hike to the round structure. The trail that connects the two restored structures passes another interesting carved stelae. The carved jaguar altar near the round structure is also worth some study. The trails at Seibal are kept well cleared, and getting around, even without a site plan, is no problem. A guide is not necessary.

*Stela 13, just northwest of Structure A-III, Seibal. Late Classic period. The use of Mexican speech scrolls and a non-Maya figure implies foreign influence.*

*Detail of upper portion of Stela 14, beside the trail between Structure A-III and the circular structure, Seibal. Late Classic period.*

All the visible remains at Seibal date to Late Classic times, although the site had its roots in the Middle Preclassic period. It was active during the Late Preclassic, inactive (it may have been temporarily abandoned) during the Early Classic, and flowered during the Late Classic. Most of the stelae date to the late part of the Late Classic period.

Seibal is a very rewarding site visually and photographically because of the quality of its carved monuments. We found and photographed fifteen stelae at the site. Stela 3 and some of the others originally found there have been removed.

Teobert Maler considered the limestone used for the stelae very hard. Perhaps that accounts for their excellent state of preservation.

## RECENT HISTORY

According to Maler, the ruins of Seibal were discovered while a woodcutters' camp was being established. He was advised to visit the site to see the fine sculptures that had been uncovered some time before, and did so in July, 1895. He spent four days. He photographed the stelae (including one he personally discovered) and made a rough site plan. In August, 1905, he revisited Seibal and corrected some details on his plan, but he discovered no new monuments, "so thorough had been my research at that time [1895]." He was working for Peabody Museum of Harvard University on both of these visits.

Sylvanus Morley visited Seibal in 1914 for the Carnegie Institution of Washington, to study the glyphs for his work on Maya chronology.

In 1964, Peabody Museum reentered the field and conducted extensive research at the site. Publication of data was begun in the 1970s, and some work is still in press.

Ian Graham mapped the site. Other archaeologists involved in the project were Gordon R. Willey, A. Ledyard Smith, Gair Tourtellot, John A. Graham, and Jeremy A. Sabloff.

*Stela 2 from La Amelia, at the east end of the government building, Sayaxché. Late Classic period.*

## CONNECTION

1. 41 miles by fair dirt road from Flores to Sayaxché, then 11 miles of poor dirt road to the site.

## GETTING THERE

To get to Seibal, you must first go to Flores and then to Sayaxché. (See "Tikal" and "Dos Pilas" for information on airlines, Jeep rentals, buses, hotels, and dugout-canoe arrangements.)

*Note:* A Late Classic monument—Stela 2 from the site of La Amelia—is in Sayaxché, although not all the townsfolk know of its location or even of its existence. As you enter the town from the ferry landing, go 1 block straight ahead. Turn left and go 2 blocks and then bear to the right. This brings you to a long wooden government building. There is an overgrown plaza area north of the building and a soccer field south of it. The stela is at the far end (east) of the building. Although fragmented, the stela has been restored, and the bas-relief carving is well preserved. It is definitely worth a look while you are in Sayaxché.

At Sayaxché get explicit directions to Seibal; there are several roads leaving the town. You might pick up a boy to serve as a guide. The road to Seibal is very poor and rutted, but we made it without having to resort to four-wheel drive. If the rain has been particularly bad, four-wheel drive might be needed. In any case, there will be times when you will wonder if you are on the right road. Have faith. Even though the road looks like it is going to play out, it does not until you get to Seibal. You pass the small community of Finca la Cumbre about halfway to the site. Plan on about 40 minutes for the whole 11-mile trip.

If you are in Sayaxché without a vehicle, or if you are told that the road is too bad to drive, you can get to Seibal by dugout. From the landing on the Río Pasión it is a short but steep climb to the site, which is on a range of limestone bluffs at a bend in the river.

If Seibal is your only goal in the area, you could drive back to Flores before dark. If you plan to see Dos Pilas or Aguateca, then an overnight stop at the Hotel Guayacán in Sayaxché is indicated. You might tell the hotel staff when you pass through on your way to Seibal that you will be returning later to spend the night.

Tennis shoes are adequate for Seibal if you drive in. Boots would be better if you arrive by dugout and have to climb the embankment to the site. Insect repellent is a must. Take your own food and drink; neither is available at the site.

★

# *Dos Pilas*

(dohs *pee*-lahs)

# *(Dos Pozos)*

(dohs *poh*-sohs)

DERIVATION: Dos Pilas is Spanish for "Two Piles" or "Two Stelae." Dos Pozos is Spanish for "Two Wells."

ORIGINAL NAME: Unknown.

CULTURE: Maya.

LOCATION: Southwestern part of the department of Petén, Guatemala.

## THE SITE

The site of Dos Pilas has been cleared, and the clearing is maintained, but no restoration has been undertaken. There are some architectural remains—one area seemed to be a large plaza bounded by carved stairways on two sides. The structures to which these stairs led are now jungle-covered mounds. I know of no published site plans for Dos Pilas; depend on your guide to show you around.

The real glory of the site is its carved monuments. The first one you encounter when you enter the site is a large stela (numbered 16 by Ian Graham and 2 by Merle Greene and Pierre Ivanoff). It lies in several large fragments, but the quality of the carving is superb. It is some of the finest and best preserved that I have ever seen. This stela must have been a truly magnificent monument when it was upright in one piece. The details of apparel worn by the personage and certain symbols depicted on the stela indicate some degree of influence from Late Classic Mexico. An interesting comparison with Stela 2 from the nearby site of Aguateca—which

*Stela 2 (Greene's enumeration), detail depicting an owl used as part of a pectoral worn by the main figure, Dos Pilas. Late Classic period.*

*Glyph-carved stairway, Dos Pilas. The glyphs on the third step are unfinished. Late Classic period.*

shows many of the same elements—was made by Ian Graham. Stela 2 (or 16) from Dos Pilas dates to the Late Classic period, as do all the other visible remains at the site. This thatch-covered stela is difficult to photograph in its entirety because of its size and horizontal position, but the main fragment can be shot with a very wide angle lens (see "General Advice—Camera Gear"). You can easily get many fine detail shots.

There are several other stelae—also protected by thatched shelters—arranged around the plaza.

The two sets of stairs bordering the plaza are carved with figures and glyphs. On one set the glyphs were never finished. It is possible that the site was abandoned while the stairs were being carved—at least, that is one theory.

In another area an interesting stela (numbered 16 by Merle Greene) is situated partway up a large, jungle-covered mound. One fragment lies against an earth embankment, but your guide will pull it back so that you can photograph it. The larger main fragment is a beauty and retains some remnants of paint.

A short distance away are other stairs, with carvings of reclining captives and glyphs similar to those discovered at Tamarindito—another nearby site. These are all reminiscent of a figure found on the Hieroglyphic Stairway at Copán. The ones at Dos

*Glyph-carved stairway flanked by a vertical glyph-carved panel, Dos Pilas. Late Classic period.*

Pilas are badly eroded and are covered with bright green moss. Some nearby stelae are in the same condition.

The cleared portion at Dos Pilas seems to indicate that it was a small site, but further exploration and excavation may show it to be larger than is now thought.

In 2 hours you can adequately see and photograph the monuments.

## RECENT HISTORY

In 1960, an expedition led by Pierre Ivanoff discovered the site. It was named Dos Pozos for two deep wells found in the area. The name used locally, however, and the one found in the literature, is Dos Pilas, signifying Two Stelae, according to Ivanoff.

The site was later visited by Ian Graham, who photographed the monuments, and by Merle Greene, who did rubbings of some of the stelae and steps. Fortunately, the monuments were recorded; later at least one stela was stolen—theft is a serious problem in these remote areas. The stolen stela was later recovered, but the bottom section with a crouching figure was missing.

The site has not been excavated, and there is little in the literature about it. Perhaps Dos Pilas will be studied more thoroughly in the future.

*Stela 16 (Greene's enumeration), Dos Pilas. Late Classic period.*

## CONNECTION

1. 1 to 2 hours by dugout canoe from Sayaxché to the landing, then about 10 miles (2½ to 4 hours) on foot to the site.

## GETTING THERE

Getting to Dos Pilas is a bit difficult—actually it is the most difficult to reach of all the sites rated in this guide and that accounts for its rating of only one star.

Fly or drive to Flores (see "Tikal" for details). Then take the fairly good dirt road for 41 miles to Sayaxché (about 1½ hours). Sayaxché is on the far side of the Río Pasión. You can also get to the river by bus from Flores. There is a ferry that will take you across the river with or without a vehicle. If you take a bus, then a dugout can also get you across the river.

From the ferry landing on the Sayaxché side of the river, it is less than a block to the Hotel Guayacán (on the left and visible from the landing). At the hotel you can tell Julio Godoy, the accommodating owner, or one of his employees, that you wish to visit Dos Pilas the next morning. It is a grueling 10- to 14-hour trip from Sayaxché until you return, and an early-morning start is imperative. The hotel will get in touch with a dugout operator, who will visit you in the evening to make arrangements. Try asking for Adelaido Paau—a very reliable and competent boatman. His boat is a typical dugout, outfitted with an outboard motor. It may look primitive, but it is an efficient craft and the kind universally used as the native means of transportation in this part of the world. If Adelaido is not available, other boatmen will be. You can pick up a boatman around the ferry landing, but try Adelaido first.

Plan to spend the night before your trip at the Hotel Guayacán. The rooms there are austere, cheap, and primitive but adequate. There are two shared baths. Lights go out about 9:00 P.M. The food is surprisingly good.

There are also a couple of restaurants in Sayaxché. The Montaña—about 2 blocks up the street from the Guayacán—serves good food. At another place—across the street diagonally from the Guayacán—eggs seem to be the only fare.

You are guaranteed to meet some interesting people at the Guayacán. The ambience of the place makes it a pleasant and interesting experience. If the Guayacán is filled, there is a place around the corner on the left run by the Méndez family, which can take a few guests. It has army cots and shared baths. There is also a small lodge some distance south of Sayaxché on Lake Petex-batún. It is run by Ray Starr and Charles Boogher, and reservations and trip arrangements can be made through Expeditions Extraordinary, Apartado Postal 63, Guatemala City, or through Turismo Kim Arrin, in Guatemala City. The only way to reach the lodge is by boat.

If you would feel more comfortable, you could bring a guide with you from Flores—ask at the Hotel Maya Internacional—but there would still be the cost of renting a dugout. If you go to Sayaxché alone, knowledge of Spanish will be helpful for making dugout arrangements.

The cost of a trip from Sayaxché to Dos Pilas will vary, depending on the size of the dugout and the number of guides who accompany you. On our visit we had a large dugout with hide-covered chairs for the two passengers and three guides. There were Adelaido; his assistant, Víctor; and the *guardián* of Dos Pilas, who met us at the spot where the dugout landed. If you go in a small dugout, without chairs, and with one guide, it will be cheaper. In either case the cost is reasonable. The size of the dugout and its motor will determine how long it takes you to reach the landing.

The hotel will make sandwiches for you to take along, and Adelaido will fill his canteen with "good" water there. The men provide their own food. Unless you leave it in the dugout, do not take an ice chest.

Streamline your camera gear as much as possible. You can leave your telephoto lenses at the Guayacán, unless, of course, you need them for photos of birds. You do not need them for the ruins, but do bring a wide-angle lens. We found a waterproof backpack for camera gear ideal on this trip. Wear boots.

Adelaido will pick you up early in the morning for the pleasant trip by dugout along the Río Petexbatún, which flows into the Río Pasión a few feet downstream from Sayaxché. You may find some mist on the river at this time of day, but it adds to the beauty and mystery of the surrounding jungle.

A landing is made a little past a small island—the only one encountered on the trip. Then begins the rough part on foot. If it has been raining, the trail can be in execrable condition, with large, unavoidable puddles and hidden tree roots to contend with. If no one has been through recently, then your guide will have to spend some time cutting detours around the fallen trees and bad spots and clearing the trail. These delays will determine how long it takes you to get there on foot.

While you are on the trail, it is all too easy to seize hold of small thorn-ridden tree trunks to keep from slipping. If this should happen, pull the spines out and remove your rings immediately, for your hands will swell. The injury is not serious, but it can be mildly painful temporarily. Exercise extreme caution.

Some of the trail is fairly easy going, but never for very long. Here is another note of caution. Do *not* leave the trail. Even on the trail, keep in sight of each other. This holds true for any jungle trip. Sounds get muffled by the vegetation, and visibility is rarely more than 20 feet. It is easy to become lost quickly. On our trip to Dos Pilas, the *guardián* shot and winged a *faisán* ("pheasant"), and it fell or flew into the jungle. The *guardián* and Víctor left the trail to look for it. Jerry decided to help and followed them. I wondered about the prudence of this, but assumed that they would keep each other in sight. I found a dry log and sat down to rest until they returned.

Some 20 minutes later the *guardián* and Víctor returned, having given up the search for the *faisán.* Before I had a chance to worry about Jerry, I heard him call, and I called back so that he could find his way back to the trail. It sounded as though he was farther along the trail than I was, but he emerged a little later from the opposite direction. While off the trail looking for the *faisán,* he got completely turned around, though he generally has an excellent sense of direction, and this was not his first jungle trip. He had retraced his steps, thinking that he had inadvertently recrossed the trail, and when he finally got back, it was hard for him to believe that we were heading in the right direction when we resumed our hike. Left to his own devices, he would have headed the other way—back toward the dugout. It is all too easy for this to happen. For all its beauty, the jungle can be confusing and treacherous for the unwary.

As an aside: A week or so later in Guatemala City we heard the story of a tourist who got lost in the jungles of the Petén. His wife offered a reward for finding him. Some time later his skeleton was found—still clutching his camera. I do not know whether the story was true, but after our experience, I found it believable.

Shortly before reaching Dos Pilas, there are a couple of thatched shelters and you will stop at one for lunch. This break will be quite a relief.

Adelaido asked us if we wanted *limonada.* We said yes, naturally, and wondered how he was going to manage that out in the middle of nowhere. He did very nicely by picking lemons from a tree next to the shelter, getting water from the canteen, and using raw sugar from a supply in a plastic bag, hung from a rafter of the shelter. This was a better thirst quencher than plain water, even though it was not cold. We disregarded the black particles floating around and refused to question the cleanliness of the old mayonnaise jar in which he mixed and served it. We suffered not at all from the experience. The men made a batch of their own, using water from a nearby pool, which seemed to be spring fed.

After your lunch break, continue to the site a short distance away.

## POSTSCRIPT

On our hike back to the dugout, we got caught in a torrential downpour, which lasted an hour. We did not mind getting wet, for it kept us cool, and our camera gear was well protected with the backpack and a sheet of plastic. Adelaido cut palm leaves for us to use as umbrellas, but we were already drenched. The puddles we had encountered on our way in ran together and became a small stream. There was no way to avoid getting our feet wet. The water was deep enough to come over the tops of our boots. At this point I just plodded along down the middle of the stream-trail. Each step was an effort as our boots got stuck in the soft mud below the water. Needless to say, it took a little longer to cover the 10 miles on the way back. We also stopped to rest more often, for all of us were exhausted. When we had almost reached the river, the *guardián* pointed out a side trail to Tamarindito and said that it was a few kilometers distant (see "Aguateca" for information on Tamarindito). At that moment I was not the least bit interested in visiting the site, nor do I think our guides would have been thrilled about taking us.

It was an unbelievable relief to arrive back at the dugout. Its hide-covered chairs felt like luxurious recliners. I took advantage of the comfort and had a nap.

I had been advised by a Texan who had a ranch near Sayaxché to bring a windbreaker for the trip. It was good advice. It was chilly on the ride back (we were still soaking wet). If it should take you 2 hours by dugout and 4 hours on foot, then you will be returning after dark, and, again, a windbreaker would be nice to have along.

When we reached Sayaxché at 5:00 P.M., I was barely able to stagger up the steps to the porch of the Hotel Guayacán. It really felt like home. If you have more stamina, you could drive back to Flores, but do not count on your ability to do so.

Don Julio informed me a bit later that it is possible to rent mules for the trip to Dos Pilas, but you must let him know several days in advance. Actually, I am not sure that that would be any easier than going on foot. I suppose it depends on which muscles you would rather have sore.

If you also plan to visit Seibal or Aguateca while you are in Sayaxché, see them first. I guarantee that after a trip to Dos Pilas you will be too exhausted for a trip to either of the others on the following day.

*Stela 7, Aguateca. Detail of the lower section showing the left leg and foot of the main figure with a grotesque mask at the ankle. A fish nibbling at vegetation is seen at right center. Late Classic period.*

★

# *Aguateca*

(ah-gwah-*tehk*-ah)

ORIGINAL NAME: Unknown.
CULTURE: Maya.
LOCATION: Southwestern part of the department of Petén, Guatemala.

---

## THE SITE

Aguateca lies on a ridge that runs along the west side of Lake Petex-batún. The site is not a large one, and the architectural remains have not been restored, though stairs can be seen in front of a couple of the structures. The rest appears as rubble mounds.

The reason for a visit is to see the carved stelae. They are in front of the structures that border a plaza on the east and south sides. Two plain stelae are in front of a structure on the west side, and there is a badly fragmented one on the north side. Unhappily, the carved stelae are also fragmented. It is difficult to get over-all photos, but some detail shots are possible. The most interesting are Stelae 1 and 2 on the east side and Stela 7 on the south side of the plaza.

Stela 1 shows a single figure in the act of scattering grain. It is thought that he was a new ruler and that the stela—dedicated in A.D. 741—commemorated his ascension to the throne. The figure is flanked on both sides by glyphs, some of which are well preserved.

Stela 2 (A.D. 736) depicts a major figure, whose attire has much in common with that shown on a stela from nearby Dos Pilas. The figures on both these stelae show influence from central Mexico in that they have a trapezoidal element—generally called the Mexican Yearsign—in their headdresses and depictions of Tlaloc on their loincloth aprons. There are other points of similarity as well. The major upper fragments of Stela 2 are lying on the ground; a bottom fragment, depicting a crouching captive, stands upright nearby.

Stela 7 (A.D. 790) is badly fragmented, and some major portions are missing. One fragment, forming the lower section of the stela, is lying on its side. This part has the clearest carving. A realistic fish and a mask that decorate the ankle of the main figure are especially well preserved.

It appears that about two-thirds of the very bottom of the stela—portraying the head and torso of a prone bound captive when it was originally recorded—has been neatly cut away. The remaining third, with the captive's legs, is still attached to the rest of the fragment. The other parts of Stela 7 lie nearby.

Carved Stelae 8, 9, and 10, on the south side of the plaza, lie on their backs and are badly eroded, and Stela 5, on the east side, is in many small fragments.

Stelae 3 and 6 (as well as the other carved stelae from Aguateca) were published by Ian Graham in 1967. Both appear well preserved from the photos. In 1976, we saw only a miniscule portion of the bottom of Stela 3—bound in the roots of a tree—and one top fragment of Stela 6. I can only assume that the major portions of both these stelae have been removed from the site, especially since looting has been reported at Aguateca.

Another feature of interest at Aguateca is a sheer-sided ravine that runs through part of the site. It is crossed by several natural bridges, and one of these serves as the present access to the site. If you want to explore the ravine, bring along a flashlight, and be careful, for it can be wet and slippery.

## RECENT HISTORY

Aguateca was discovered in 1957 by Jesús Segura, a citizen of the town of Sayaxché. Most of what we know about the site is due to the efforts of Ian Graham, who visited Aguateca briefly in 1959, for a longer period in 1960, and again in 1962. His work resulted in a site plan and descriptions, photographs, and drawings of the carved monuments. These were published by the Middle American Research Institute of Tulane University in 1967. Merle Greene did rubbings of several of the carved stelae, and these were published in 1972.

There has been no excavation at the site, but the plaza area where the monuments are situated is kept fairly well cleared. A full-time *gaurdiân* now resides at Aguateca.

## CONNECTION

1. 2 to 4 hours by dugout from Sayaxché to the landing, then 20 minutes on foot to the site.

## GETTING THERE

See "Tikal" for getting to Flores and other general information, and "Dos Pilas" for getting to Sayaxché and making arrangements for a dugout.

From Sayaxché, you head west a few yards along the Río Pasión, then south on the Río Petex-batún. This river later opens up into the lovely lake Petex-batún. Near the south end of the lake, you turn right, going through a narrow stream that eventually enters a small lagoon. The lagoon lies at the foot of the ridge on which Aguateca stands.

From the landing at the lagoon it is a steep, but not too difficult climb, to the site. You will pass the *guardián*'s house on the way, and he will ask you to register in a small notebook. We asked him how many visitors a year came to Aguateca. He began by saying twenty, then thirty, and finally fifty. If the registration book was any indication, I think his last estimate was optimistic. We were there in August, and the last visitors before us were there in May (a group of four). Before that there was a party of two in March. The *guardián* will act as your guide at the site.

Bring your own food and drink. You could leave a small ice chest in the dugout while you visit the site—you would enjoy a cold drink after your visit. If you leave Sayaxché early—as your boatman will want you to do—you will get back in time for a late lunch (if your dugout is fast enough to reach the site in 2 or 3 hours). On the other hand, the boat ride is rather long, and eating along the way gives you something to do.

Wear boots and carry insect repellent. You will need fast film, for tall trees shade the area. Allow 1½ hours at the site plus the time to make the climb from the lagoon.

If you are also a fisherman, you can combine a trip to Aguateca with fishing along the Petex-batún. The river has rinco, bass, and, in September, tarpon. Arrangements can be made through Julio Godoy at the Hotel Guayacán in Sayaxché.

*Note:* Another Maya site, Tamarindito, lies between Aguateca and the landing for Dos Pilas. We inquired about the site in 1976, and Adelaido, the boatman who took us to Aguateca, told us that everything of interest had been removed from Tamarindito. Since this report was later corroborated by two other people, we did not attempt a visit.

*Stucco frieze depicting the sun god and other astronomical motifs, in place at Xunantunich, on the east side of Structure A-6 (El Castillo). Late Classic period.*

★

# *Bliss Institute (Belize Museum, Belize City)*

The Belize Museum serves various functions, one of which is that of a repository for a few Maya relics. There are a stela, a couple of altars, and a stone head that must have been part of an architectural decoration, judging by its tenoned back.

The monuments are from Caracol, a site 25 air miles south of Xunantunich. One altar is carved with a giant Ahau glyph, a rarity elsewhere, but a feature for which Caracol is famous.

The stela is fragmented, but it is interesting to study. There is an unusual panel of incised glyphs at the bottom, on which the main figure and a subsidiary figure are standing. The rest of the stela is carved in low relief. Although the stela dates to A.D. 593, the principal figure has both feet pointing in the same direction, a feature generally seen on earlier monuments. Half an hour is adequate to see and photograph the collection.

★★★

# *Altun Ha*

(ahl-*toon hah*)

DERIVATION: Mayan for "Rockstone Pond," a nearby village. A rough translation.
ORIGINAL NAME: Unknown.
CULTURE: Maya.
LOCATION: North-central part of Belize District, Belize (British Honduras).

## THE SITE

Altun Ha is a comparatively small Maya center lying on the periphery of the central Maya area. Its central precincts are made up of Plaza A, surrounded by Structures A-1 through A-7, and, adjacent to the south, Plaza B, surrounded by Structures B-1 through B-6.

Altun Ha occupies an area of about 2.3 square miles in which 400 to 500 buildings have been found. Most of these are in the 0.4 square-mile area surrounding the central precinct. When you arrive at the site, you will see the parking area, and from there a trail leads to Plaza A.

Plaza A was originally entirely plastered. The final surface is about 10 inches below the present ground level, but at least two earlier floors were discovered beneath the last one. The most interesting structures bordering this plaza are A-1 and A-2, on the west, and A-5, on the east.

In A-1 (Temple of the Green Tomb), at least seven construction phases were found, several of which are visible today. The substructure dates to the early sixth century and is one of the few visible Early Classic temple bases not covered by later construction. The slight curvature seen at the rear is reminiscent of that in the Early Classic Temple 5D-23 at Tikal. The superstructure of Temple A-1 shows later building additions. Most of the upper portion, however, has fallen into the lower part of the chamber. A tomb that dates to A.D. 550–600—the earliest burial in the central area of the site—was found inside this structure. Among its contents were nearly 300 jade objects, which gave the tomb and temple their names. Other interesting funerary goods were the remains of a smashed codex. The paper base had disintegrated, and only the fragments of the painted stucco surface remained. Unfortunately, this rare find probably cannot be reassembled; neither can two others found at Altun Ha.

Structure A-2 abuts A-1 on the south, although they were not originally connected. A-2 is a large complex platform showing at least two construction phases, but no evidence of a superstructure.

Structure A-5 (The Bowling Alley) is later and larger than A-1, and was apparently built all at once. Its extremely narrow single chamber gives the structure its name; it was probably used for ceremonial activities.

Proceed to Plaza B, which differs from Plaza A in that there was only one surfacing of the plaza floor. The most important structure facing this plaza is B-4 (The Temple of the Masonry Altars) on the east. It lies on top of the floor—some remains of which can be seen at the base of the temple.

Of the few remains of monumental sculpture found at Altun Ha, the most interesting are at the base of B-4, in the form of mask panels. One wonders whether these seemingly crude decorations showed more refinement and detail when they had a stucco coating.

An unusual feature that you will notice is the absence of carved stelae at Altun Ha. Only one broken stela—uncarved or unfinished—has been found at the site. It was located south of the central precincts.

From 1965 through 1968 extensive excavations were carried out on B-4, and eight phases of construction were discovered. The latest six were in very poor condition and were removed. What you see today is Phase VII, dating to A.D. 600–650. The initial construction of the structure (Phase VIII), underlying the existing one, was begun around A.D. 550, at the time of the flooring of Plaza B. In Phase VIII, an altar was placed atop the temple and this was followed by three later ones giving the temple its name. The one you see today is from Phase VI, all that remains of that period.

During Phase VII a tomb was constructed in the large stair block near the top of the structure, and it contained a large jade head of Kinich Ahau, the sun god. This full-round sculpture, weighing in at 9¾ pounds, was discovered in 1968, and was the

*Structure A-1 (Temple of the Green Tomb), view from the southeast, Altun Ha. Early Classic period.*

largest carved jade known from the Maya area. Since then a larger, but much cruder, jade figure, weighing 12½ pounds, was found at San Jerónimo, in the Salama Valley of Guatemala's Baja Verapaz. The head of Kinich Ahau dates to A.D. 600–650 and is safely stored in a bank vault, but a replica is on display at the tourist board in Belize City. Since it is in a glass case, try a polarizing filter if you want a shot. Photographs are generously allowed. It is definitely worth a look.

Another spectacular carved jade was found in B-4, a bas-relief plaque with a seated figure on one side and some rather crude glyphs on the other. It was part of a burial from Phase VI that was placed against the face of the stair block in the lower stairway. I do not know the present location of this carving.

Other structures of interest are B-3 and B-5, bordering Plaza B on the south. Both have been excavated and show several construction phases. Both are multichambered and were probably residential.

The pre-Columbian history of Altun Ha shows that there was a fairly extensive settlement by perhaps 200 B.C. and that permanent buildings were erected at least by the first century B.C., although the main concentrations were not in the present central area, but south and east.

Work in the central precincts (Groups A and B) began around A.D. 300 and continued for 600 years, but there was a decline in quality and size of construction during the last 150 years. A population of 8,000 to 10,000 occupied the site during its peak, but the central-area population was probably no more than 2,500.

Although construction stopped at the end of the Classic period, the site was not totally deserted.

*Structure B-4 (Temple of the Masonry Altars), the front (west) side, Altun Ha. Late Classic period.*

There is evidence of occupation in the Postclassic period, during the tenth, thirteenth, and fourteenth centuries, but so far evidence is lacking for the eleventh and twelfth centuries.

The oldest major structure at Altun Ha is Temple F-8 (The Reservoir Temple), apparently started in A.D. 100 and added to until A.D. 200–250. It is 0.4 mile away, by trail leading south from the back of Structure B-6. We did not know of its existence at the time of our visit, and indications are that it is not very impressive visually. Its name comes from a nearby reservoir, the ancient water supply for Altun Ha. There is no indication that the reservoir was the scene of sacrifices or offerings. If you decide to visit F-8, it is recommended that you do not leave the trail as the area is covered with dense second-growth bush.

There is one interesting point about F-8 that merits mention. During excavation a postinterment offering was discovered above a tomb in the top of the structure. The offering contained a wide range of imported objects, including green obsidian eccentrics and blades, traceable directly to a Teotihuacán source. While it is not unusual to find evidence of Teotihuacán influence in the lowland Maya area, the dating of these objects to A.D. 150–200 is remarkable. Until this discovery the earliest evidence of contact between the lowland Mayas and Teotihuacán was found at Tikal and dated about 250 or 300 years later (see "Becan" for other possible early contacts).

Some tombs at Altun Ha contained shells from the Pacific, which suggest that the site may have been an important trading center in a network spread along the Caribbean coast.

## RECENT HISTORY

Altun Ha has only recently entered the archaeological literature. Although the location of the site was

*Detail of the mask panels on the front of Structure B-4 (Temple of the Masonry Altars), south of the stairway, Altun Ha. Late Classic period.*

known for many years, it was only in 1964 that work was begun there, sponsored by the Royal Ontario Museum of Toronto, Canada, under the field directorship of David M. Pendergast. The work continued through 1970. The site was selected because of its peripheral location in the Maya area, where little work had been done previously. In addition to clearing and excavation, some restoration was undertaken in the central precincts.

## CONNECTIONS

1. 30 miles by paved (but poor) road from Belize City, or
2. 75 miles by road from Chetumal, Quintana Roo, Mexico (62 miles paved, 13 miles dirt), then 2 miles of dirt road to the site.

## GETTING THERE

Altun Ha may be reached in 45 minutes by car, by taking the Northern Highway (north) from Belize City, or from Chetumal (south) in 2½ to 3 hours, not counting the time necessary to cross the international border.

The cutoff to Altun Ha (near the 30-mile marker on the Northern Highway) is marked with a small sign and heads west. The site is open to visitors between 8:00 A.M. and 5:00 P.M. You may be asked to sign a registration book on your way in or out by the occupants of a house near the site. The bus that runs from Belize to Corozal can drop you off at the cutoff.

The easiest way to get to Altun Ha is to fly to Belize and rent a car or hire a car and driver. Check at the airport or at your hotel in Belize. There are no regular car-rental agencies, and arrangements must be made with individuals.

Belize is not visited by many tourists, and hotel and car rentals can be hard to come by. By all means, make hotel reservations ahead. The best is the Fort George, then the Bellview (only fair, but with good food and accommodating personnel), and then the Bliss. There is still another place to stay, the Palms Motel on the outskirts of town, but it should be a last resort. They serve good food, but the service is extremely slow. Belize, compared with Mexico and Guatemala, is an expensive country because most items are imported. Some of the roads in Belize are poor, although there has been some improvement recently; expect to drive slowly.

There is a thatched shelter at Altun Ha where you can have a picnic lunch. No food or drink is provided at the site. Either bring your own or get an early start from Belize City and return for lunch. In any case, you will want to have cold drinks along.

Tennis shoes are adequate, but wear a long-sleeved shirt and pants and carry insect repellent. The mosquitoes during the rainy season can be annoying, but I had a report that they were not a problem in December. Allow 1 hour to visit the site. Bring David M. Pendergast's guidebook for Altun Ha if possible, or try to pick up a copy at the site. A guide is not necessary.

# *Floral Park*

ORIGINAL NAME: Unknown.
CULTURE: Maya.
LOCATION: North-central part of Cayo District, Belize (British Honduras).

---

## THE SITE

Today the only sights at Floral Park are a couple of conical mounds that lie adjacent to the Western Highway. The site is worth a 5-minute stop and a couple of photographs if you are passing right by on your way to or from Xunantunich.

## RECENT HISTORY

Floral Park is mentioned in *Prehistoric Maya Settlements in the Belize Valley,* published by Peabody Museum of Harvard University in 1965. The authors are Gordon Willey, William Bullard, Jr., J. B. Glass, and James C. Gifford.

## CONNECTION

1. 60 miles by road (49 miles paved, 11 miles fair dirt) from Belize City.

## GETTING THERE

Take the Western Highway west from Belize City. When you have gone close to 60 miles, and just after you cross a small bridge and begin a slight climb, look for the mounds on your right (north). This is 2 miles before you reach the town of Georgeville.

There is no food or drink at the site, of course, and tennis shoes are adequate since you do not have to leave the highway. See "Tikal" and "Altun Ha" for hotels, buses, and Jeep and car rentals.

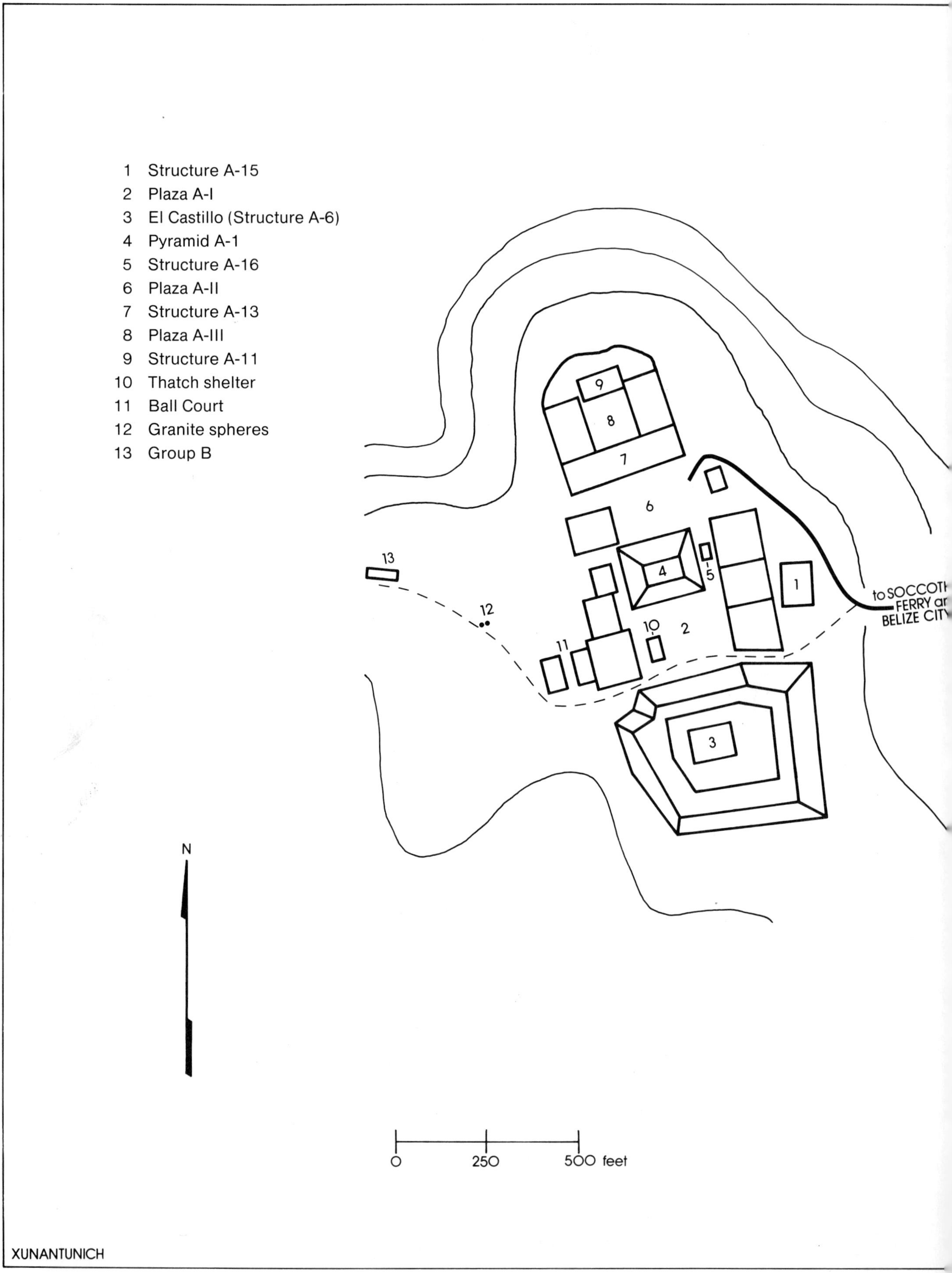

1 Structure A-15
2 Plaza A-I
3 El Castillo (Structure A-6)
4 Pyramid A-1
5 Structure A-16
6 Plaza A-II
7 Structure A-13
8 Plaza A-III
9 Structure A-11
10 Thatch shelter
11 Ball Court
12 Granite spheres
13 Group B

to SOCCOTH
FERRY a
BELIZE CIT

0 250 500 feet

XUNANTUNICH

★★★

# *Xunantunich*

(shoo-nahn-too-*neech*)

# *(Benque Viejo)*

(*behn*-keh vee-*eh*-hoh)

DERIVATION: Xunantunich is Mayan for "Maiden of the Rock." A free translation. Benque Viejo is Spanish for "Old Bank" or "Old Business Settlement," referring to a lumber camp where logs are thrown into the river. According to Teobert Maler, the word *benque* is apparently not used outside Belize.

ORIGINAL NAME: Unknown.

CULTURE: Maya.

LOCATION: Extreme western part of Cayo District, Belize (British Honduras).

---

## THE SITE

The Maya site of Xunantunich is the largest ceremonial center in the Belize River valley, but as Maya sites go, it would be considered of medium size. It is impressive, however.

Some ceramics found at the site date to the Late Preclassic period, and some structures at Xunantunich date to the end of the Early Classic period or perhaps to the beginning of the Late Classic. All of the currently visible remains are of Late Classic date.

If you drive to the site from Belize City, you get a couple of good views before you arrive. Keep an eye out toward the right (north) whenever the road climbs a bit (after Cayo and before Succoths). The towering Structure A-6, also called El Castillo, is plainly visible on the horizon and worth a couple of telephoto pictures. If you come in from the Guatemala side, you also get a good view—just as you leave the Belize immigration office—since the road climbs a little before descending to the town of Benque Viejo.

When you arrive at the site, the first structure you see is A-15, excavated and cleared but not restored. The remains of a multichambered building are visible. From there you climb to the central part of the site, by car trail or steeper foot path.

The central area of Xunantunich is laid out around three plazas, A-I, A-II, and A-III, which are aligned in a north–south row, A-I being the most southerly. The plazas were formed by leveling the top of the limestone ridge on which the site was constructed. About twenty mounds or structures border these plazas.

By far the most interesting is Structure A-6, which forms the southern boundary of Plaza A-I. Its present height is a very respectable 127 feet, and it is estimated that its roof comb was originally 10 feet higher. It is easy to climb since steps and ladders have been installed. On our visit, along the way up, we found large clusters of pale pink wild begonias.

Part way up to the top of A-6, you come across a fantastic stucco frieze (on the east side of the structure). In typical Maya fashion, this frieze was covered with later construction. It is likely that the decoration originally extended around the other sides of the building as well, but was destroyed by the action of roots and weather.

The existing frieze has been restored and is protected from the weather by a metal roof. Unfortunately—for the photographer—it was apparently also necessary to protect it from visitors, as a wire mesh fence has been installed in front of it. The effect of the mesh can be minimized by focusing carefully on the frieze and opening your lens as wide as possible. The limited depth of field will blur the mesh somewhat, making it less distracting. The elements displayed on the frieze are masks of the sun god and other motifs symbolic of astronomical matters; the moon and Venus are prominently represented. You will want lots of photos here—including details. A wide-angle lens is necessary for over-all shots of the frieze, as it is impossible to back off from it more than a few feet.

From the roof comb of A-6, you get delightful views of the surrounding lush jungle—notable for the abundance of graceful cohune palms—and the towns of Succoths, Benque Viejo, and even Melchor de Mencos, across the river in Guatemala. This is also a good spot for photos of the rest of the site, which extends north. Several vaulted rooms have been partially restored on Structure A-6, and it also supports some unrestored buildings. For the best over-all photos of A-6, climb Pyramid A-1, the centrally located (unrestored) mound between Plazas A-I and A-II. There are a few remaining steps on the north side of the pyramid, but the rest is rubble. It is a short, but rather steep, climb. This central vantage point also allows good photos of other parts of the site and probably the best photo of the small Structure A-16, a two-chambered building containing a plain stela, lying adjacent to the east.

Other excavated structures are A-11 and A-13, forming the north and south boundaries of a quadrangle surrounding Plaza A-III. The level of Plaza A-III is about 10 feet higher than that of the other plazas. The rest of the structures at Xunantunich are, for the most part, simply mounds.

The neat thatched shelter used by the workmen, and for the registration book, is located in Plaza A-I, and attached is an additional thatch roof, housing three prone stelae. Two of the stelae were found at the south base of Pyramid A-1 and, though eroded, are worth a few photos. Especially interesting is the captive figure at the bottom of one of the stelae, a motif common in this general area (at least 14 stelae depciting bound captives were found at the site of Naranjo 10 air miles away to the northwest). Several plain stelae are found in Plazas A-I and A-II.

From Plaza A-I, a trail leads to Group B, a short distance away. As the trail exits the plaza near the thatched shelter, it passes the remains of an unrestored ball court, and, farther along, two granite spheres of unknown significance.

Group B is unrestored and uncleared, but some remains of stone walls are visible. It makes a pleasant walk, if you have the time.

## RECENT HISTORY

Xunantunich was studied by Teobert Maler in the early twentieth century during his extensive work in the southern Maya lowlands. His work was published by Peabody Museum of Harvard University in 1908. Maler called the site Benque Viejo because of the nearby town, and that is the name generally found in the literature, though Xunantunich is the name used in Belize.

Thomas Gann also visited the site and did some excavation. In his book *Mystery Cities*, published in 1925, Gann relates that he first learned that the site was locally called Xunantunich from the natives in the area. Maler and Gann also reported a carved altar from the site, which has since disappeared.

Later work was done by Sir J. Eric S. Thompson, who studied the ceramics, and by Linton Satterthwaite, who in 1950 began excavating the stucco frieze.

During the 1959–60 season work was sponsored

*Structure A-6 (El Castillo), front (north) side, Xunantunich. Late Classic period.*

by England's Cambridge University Museum of Archaeology and Ethnology, and many of the structures were consolidated. A. H. Anderson completed the uncovering of the frieze in 1959, and this impressive decoration was later restored by Joseph O. Palacio. Some restoration was still going on in other areas of the site in 1974.

## CONNECTIONS

1. 75 miles by road (49 miles paved, 26 miles fair dirt) from Belize City to the ferry landing at Succoths,
2. 61 miles by fair dirt road from Flores, Petén, Guatemala to the landing, or
3. 66.5 miles from Tikal, Petén, Guatemala, to the landing, then, across the Mopán River by car ferry or dugout, and 1 mile of dirt road to the site.

## GETTING THERE

Xunantunich can be reached from Belize City in 2 hours by car, over the Western Highway, and this is the easiest way to get there. If you are without a car, a second-class bus can get you to the ferry landing at Succoths.

From Flores, head east to the Belize-Guatemala frontier and continue east to the ferry landing (2½ hours).

From Tikal, head south to El Cruce, then east to the frontier and landing (2¾ hours).

Although the road distance is somewhat shorter from Flores or Tikal, you would have to spend some time crossing the international border.

From Flores or Tikal, a bus can get you to the frontier, and from here it is a 3.5-mile taxi ride to the ferry landing. A taxi may also be able to take you all the way to the site. You could also charter a flight from Belize City to Cayo, and taxi to Succoths, 3.5 miles away, but this would be expensive. Once you get to Succoths, you have to cross the river.

In the summer of 1973, we saw a small, car ferry, but arrived too late to visit the site. When we returned in February, 1974—on a trip made especially to see Xunantunich—we arrived at the landing in Succoths and discovered that the ferry was no longer there. We were dismayed, to say the least. We learned that the ferry had "sprung a leak" about two months before, and no one was sure when it would be replaced.

We were able to get across the river, however, in a small hand-paddled dugout, after asking about transportation at some houses near the landing.

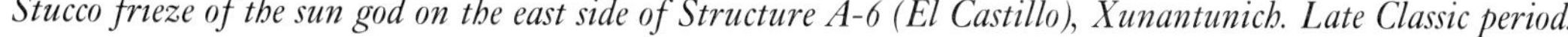

*Stucco frieze of the sun god on the east side of Structure A-6 (El Castillo), Xunantunich. Late Classic period.*

*Structure A-16 with a plain stela, Xunantunich. Late Classic period.*

This meant, of course, that we could not take our car across. The 1 mile of trail to the site was dry enough so that we could have driven it, although this is not always the case. Ask the ferry operator about the road, but drive it if you can because it is all uphill. If you walk it, keep an eye out to the left of the trail for the opening of a chultun. It is worth a photograph.

If you take the dugout across, do not worry. When you are ready to return, the same dugout or another will be waiting around at the river for you; they will not leave you stranded. By 1976 the ferry was back in operation, but if it should spring another leak, it's nice to know you can still get across the river.

You can make it from Belize City to Xunantunich and back in one day, but a possible stopover is the Golden Orange Hotel in Cayo. Cayo is also locally called San Ignacio. See "Altun Ha" for hotels and car rentals in Belize City, and "Tikal" for details on the Golden Orange, hotels in Flores and Tikal, and Jeep rentals in the area.

There is no food or drink at the site, so bring your own. Allow 2 or 3 hours for a visit, plus ½ hour each way if you are doing the climb on foot. Tennis shoes are fine unless it has been particularly wet. You can use the thatched shelter to eat your lunch.

Bring along the guide to Xunantunich and the map of Belize, which has a site plan. Both are available at the tourist board in Belize City.

We did not need insect repellent in February, but it might be advisable in the rainy season.

## HONDURAS

*Stone mask depicting Chac, the Maya rain god, in place at Copán, on the southeast corner, exterior of Structure 22 (the Temple of Meditation). Late Classic period.*

★★

# *National Museum of Honduras (Tegucigalpa Museum)*

The Honduran Institute of Anthropology and History, created in 1952, is responsible for the conservation and protection of Honduran cultural materials, and it operates the Tegucigalpa Museum. The museum is on the second floor of an interesting old home in Barrio Buenavista, near the center of Tegucigalpa, the capital city. The collection is not extensive, but enlargements are planned, and the artifacts are nicely displayed and labeled.

At the top of the stair are displays of metates from various parts of the republic. Some are of elaborate design. Nearby, cases contain ceramics from different areas and time periods, including pots, necklaces, musical pipes, whistles, and figurines. Stone hand tools are displayed in another case.

A separate room is devoted to Copán, and it is the most interesting exhibit. There is a large-scale reproduction of Tatiana Proskouriakoff's reconstruction drawing of the site during its Great Period and photos of the ruins as they are today. Ceramics, sculpture, and jade jewelry from Copán are also exhibited. The gem of the collection is a stone bench (perhaps an altar or throne) from the site. Its edges are beautifully carved with astronomical symbols and glyphs.

The museum also houses a small display of ethnological materials from the present-day Indians of Honduras, and another room is devoted to the life of Jesús Aguilar Paz. Aguilar Paz, a doctor, teacher, and explorer, drew sketch maps of various parts of the country, and these, and the instruments he used, are displayed along with other memorabilia. The information provided by his sketch maps was used to produce the first modern published map of Honduras in 1933.

A beautiful pre-Columbian jade-and-bone necklace that he acquired during his travels was donated to the museum by his family and is found in this room.

Unless you are familiar with Tegucigalpa, I would recommend taking a taxi to the museum. The city—with its twisting and one-way streets—is difficult to negotiate on your own.

Allow 1 hour to see the collection.

1 Ceremonial Plaza
2 Structure 4
3 Central Patio
4 Ball Court
5 Structure 9
6 Court of the Hieroglyphic Stairway
7 Hieroglyphic Stairway
8 Acropolis
9 Temple of Inscriptions
10 Giant head
11 Terrace 25
12 Temple 26
13 Temple of Meditation
14 Eastern Court
15 Jaguar Stairway and Venus Altar
16 Tunnel
17 Jaguar Altar
18 Structure 16
19 Western Court
20 Platform Number 13
21 Spectator's Grandstand
22 Mound 7
23 Mound 6

Stelae ▬

Altars and other sculptures • ▪

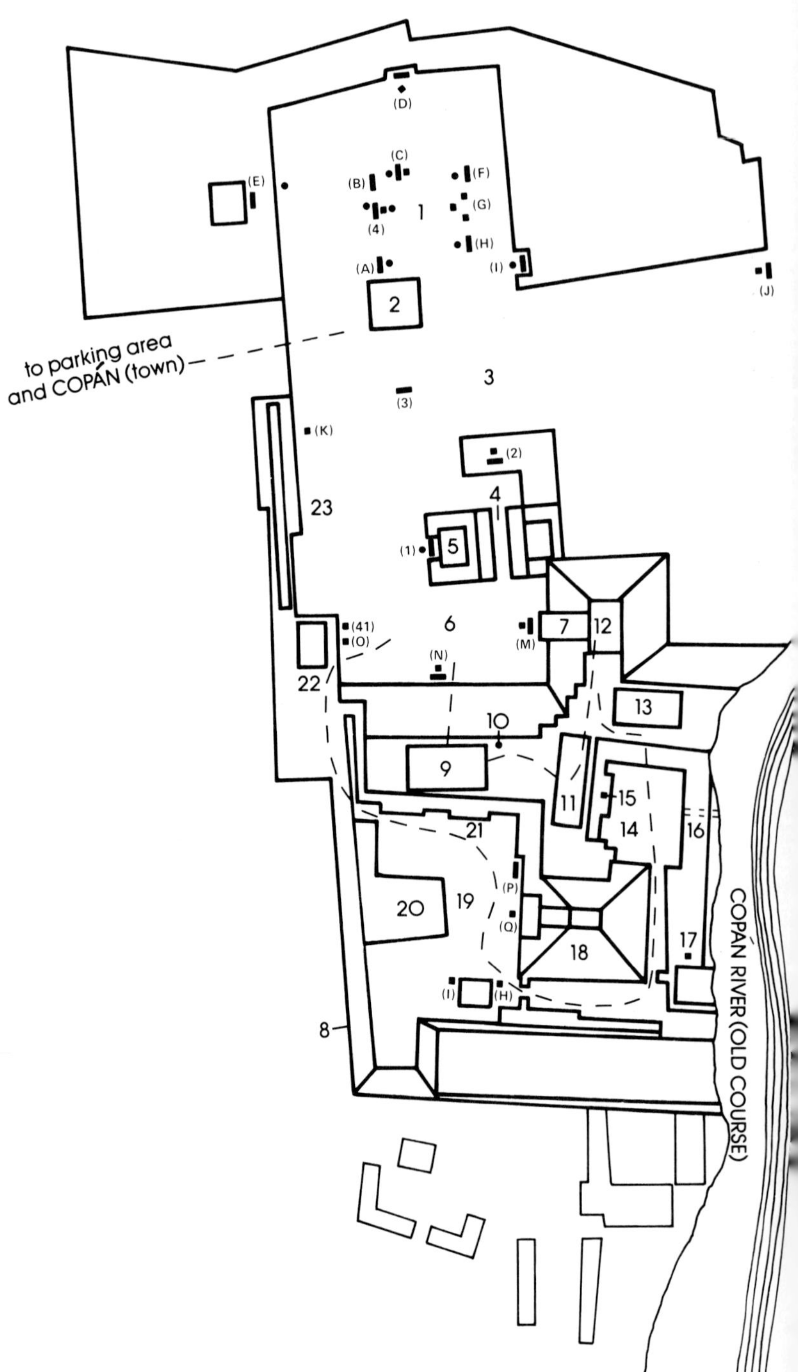

COPÁN

★★★★

# *Copán and Copán Museum*

(koh-*pahn*)

DERIVATION: There are a number of possible derivations; the first is considered the most probable.

1. Named for Copán-Calel, the chief of the region at the time of the Spanish conquest.
2. Capital of Co.
3. From the Nahuatl word *copantl*, meaning a "pontoon" or "bridge."

CULTURE: Maya.

LOCATION: Extreme-western part of the department of Copán, Honduras.

---

## THE SITE

Copán is truly one of the most impressive archaeological sites in Mesoamerica. Although its location is on the southeastern periphery of the Maya area, it is thought to have been one of the intellectual and artistic centers of that culture. It greatly influenced small centers in the Ulúa Valley, and one of its rulers and some of its people may have colonized Quiriguá. Copán's achievements in astronomy spread even farther and influenced not only all of Mayadom, but much of Mesoamerica as well.

It is set in a lovely fertile valley, with nearby pine-wooded hills, at an elevation of 2,000 feet, which makes it an ideal spot—much more logical to us perhaps than building a city in the steamy jungles of the Petén. Today, some of Honduras's finest tobacco is grown in the area.

Most interesting, of course, is the Main Group, although some outlying monuments are very worthwhile. Part of the Main Group has neatly cut grass over what originally had been a plastered floor and, even though the site is surrounded by woods, the feeling is open and airy when compared to the more jungly sites of Tikal and Yaxchilán. A certain aura of dignity pervades the place.

On the way to the site, just off the road that links the town of Copán (officially San José de Copán) to the Main Group, there are two interesting stelae (Numbers 5 and 6) with accompanying altars. They are easily spotted from the road and should not be missed.

Stelae 6 shows influence from central Mexico. There is a depiction of Tlaloc in the headdress above the main figure, and near the top of the stela the Mexican Yearsign is shown three times. While this motif is unquestionably Mexican, some authorities feel it has no calendric meaning. Stela 6 dates to A.D. 682 and, like the other outlying monuments, is earlier than most of those in the Main Group.

The earliest dated stelae from Copán (A.D. 465 and A.D. 485) were found in the area that is now occupied by the modern town. This area is called Group 9, or Old Copán, and was the first important settlement in the valley in Classic times. Some years later, the ceremonial locus shifted to what is now the Main Group.

Stela 5 (A.D. 706) lies about 50 yards east of Stela 6. Stela 5 has depictions of figures on its east and west faces and hieroglyphs on the two narrower sides. There are glyph-carved altars in front of each personage. A date of A.D. 502 is found on one of the altars.

Other stelae, notably Numbers 10 and 12, are also outside the Main Group, but are some distance away. It will be necessary to get a guide if you want to see these monuments. They are located on hills on either side of the Copán Valley, a little over 4 miles apart. It has been demonstrated that they may have acted as a giant sundial. Twice a year, on April 12 and September 7, the sun sets exactly behind Stela 10 as viewed from Stela 12. Sylvanus Morley believes that the April 12 date was the time set for the burning of the fields in preparation for planting. The priests knew when to declare the proper time by watching the sun.

When you arrive at the entrance to the Main Group, you walk across the dirt airstrip and enter a wide cleared path that leads directly to the Ceremonial Plaza. Off to the sides of this path are many overgrown mounds—yet to be investigated.

Upon entering the plaza it is easy to feel like a kid in a candy store. Half a dozen beautifully carved stelae are seen at once, and it can be unsettling trying to decide which to see first. I hope that you will have allowed enough time to see them all properly.

The stelae are carved from a greenish andesite, or volcanic tuff, a material superior to the lime-

stone used for monuments in most of the Maya area.

Bring lots of film. All of Copán's stelae in the Main Group are carved on all four sides. Photography is not a problem, as the monuments are cleared. You should allow some morning and some afternoon hours to get the best light on all sides of the monuments. This is also a great place for detail photos.

The history of Copán goes back to approximately 3000 B.C., when the first inhabitants arrived in the Copán Valley. This is represented by a preceramic phase. The earliest ceramics date to the Middle Preclassic period (1000–300 B.C.), but the real glory of Copán was during the Classic period—more specifically, from A.D. 465 to A.D. 800, when carved and dated monuments were erected.

Two sculptures from the Preclassic period were found in vaults beneath Late Classic stelae. The one discovered beneath Stelae 4 in the Ceremonial Plaza is found behind the stela; the other, found beneath Stela 5, is now in the Copán Museum. These two early sculptures are in a style that is neither purely Maya nor purely Olmec. They are reminiscent of some early boulder sculptures from the Pacific Coast of Guatemala and from Kaminaljuyú. According to Ignacio Bernal, "we could almost say that this sculpture begins to be Mayanized; at least it is not typically Olmec." At any rate, these sculptures seem quite simple and crude when compared to the later sculpture at Copán.

A logical tour of Copán would be to see the Ceremonial Plaza and the monuments in and around it first. Stelae A, B, C, F, H, and 4 are in the plaza proper, and D, E, and I are around the edge.

Stela E is at the top of the stair centered on the west side of the Ceremonial Plaza. It dates to A.D. 616, and is the earliest dated monument in the Main Group. It is believed that Stela E was moved to its present location from an earlier one. Stela D is at the north edge of the plaza, and Stela I is in a niche in the south part of the east wall.

There are also many interesting altars in the plaza. Altar G, which represents a fantastic serpent, dates to A.D. 800—the last dated monument at Copán.

All of these superb sculptures deserve careful study. Each has its own special feature. For instance, the macaw heads at the top of the front corners of

*Stela 6, right side, Copán. Late Classic period. Note the Tlaloc head and Mexican Yearsign in the headdress. The stela is on the road between the town of Copán and the Main Archaeological Group.*

Stela B were said to be elephant heads by one self-styled expert, and this led to speculation about an Asiatic origin of Maya culture, since elephants are not indigenous to the Americas.

Stela D is noted for the rare full-figure glyphs on its back face and for the double-faced altar that accompanies it; one side of the altar represents Chac, and the other, perhaps, the death god. Stela H has a figure with a long skirt and is said to represent a female, although some recent authors disagree.

At the south end of the Ceremonial Plaza is the recently cleared Structure 4. From here, head east across the north edge of the Central Patio for 200 yards to Stela J. Stela J is one of the few known stelae with the unusual basket-weave or mat design for its glyphs (found on the east side). Other stelae with this design are Stelae H at Quiriguá, and the badly eroded and fragmented Stela 10 at La Florida in the Petén.

From Stela J, return to the Central Patio and ball court. The ball court is one of the best proportioned courts to be found. Two earlier courts underlie the visible one, which uses three macaw heads on each side for markers. Some glyphs on a border at the ball court date the structure to A.D. 775.

There are two stelae associated with the ball court. Stela 2 stands atop a terrace at the north end of the court and is accompanied by an altar carved with seated figures and glyphs. Stela 1 stands in a niche in the steps of the west side of Structure 9, which bounds the west side of the ball court. It is accompanied by a circular altar.

A carved, but poorly preserved, ball court marker is propped up against the south wall of the court on the east side of the playing area, facing the Court of the Hieroglyphic Stairway.

Go to the Court of the Hieroglyphic Stairway. Climbing this stairway is prohibited. You can, however, see the sculpture at the top of the stairway and the few remains of the temple later on (see below).

The Hieroglyphic Stairway contains about 2,500

*Over-all view of the Ceremonial Plaza, view from the southeast, Copán. Late Classic period.*

*Stela A, the front (east) side, Copán. Late Classic period.*

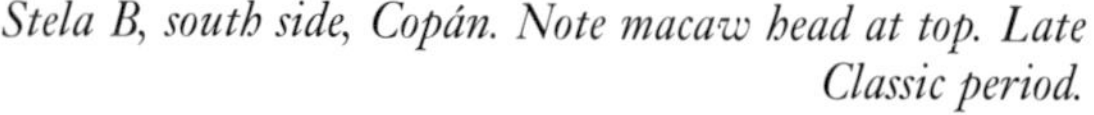

*Stela B, south side, Copán. Note macaw head at top. Late Classic period.*

*Altar in front of Stela D, view of the north side representing the death god, Copán. Late Classic period.*

*The ball court with Stela 2 at the far (north) end, viewed from the south, Copán. Late Classic period.*

glyph blocks, and is the longest Maya inscription known. It records dates from A.D. 554 to 744, but was probably dedicated in A.D. 756, when Stela M and its altar were erected at its foot. Evidence of central Mexican influence is seen in the use of depictions of Tlaloc in the headdresses of the figures that project from the steps. These motifs are not discernable from ground level, however.

Southwest of the Hieroglyphic Stairway is another huge stairway, with Stela N (A.D. 761) and its altar at the foot. Stela N is noted for being the closest thing to sculpture-in-the-round found at Copán. Both main figures on this stela show deep undercutting, which in places almost separates the figures from their backgrounds. It is sometimes called Stone Filigree. Many delightful minor figures also decorate the stela.

The southern part of the Main Group at Copán is called the Acropolis. This assemblage of courtyards, pyramids, and temples is on a higher level than the Court of the Hieroglyphic Stairway and the Ceremonial Plaza. To reach this upper level, climb the stairs and rubble behind Stela N directly to the Temple of Inscriptions (Temple 11), dated A.D. 763. There are some well-preserved figures on the steps as you near the top, thought to be done at the same time and perhaps by the same sculptor who did Altar Q (see below). There are many glyphs on the walls of the temple. At the northeast corner of the Temple of Inscriptions, overlooking the Court of the Hieroglyphic Stairway, is a huge stone head depicting an old man. Its tenoned back indicates that it once formed part of the architectural decoration.

From here, proceed east to Terrace 25, which has remains of some interesting sculpture. Head north on this same level, past the edge of the Temple of Meditation (Temple 22), to see the remains of Temple 26 and some sculpture at the top of the Hieroglyphic Stairway. Then return to the Temple of Meditation, which bounds the Eastern Court on the north. The remains of the exterior doorway

*The Hieroglyphic Stairway, view from the west, Copán. Late Classic period.*

*Carved figures on the steps leading to the south side of Temple 11, the Temple of Inscriptions, Copán. Late Classic period.*

*Three-dimensional sculpture on Terrace 25 in the Acropolis, Copán. Note* ik *signs on the cheeks. Late Classic period.*

*Temple 22, the Temple of Meditation, view of the front (south) side, Copán. Late Classic period.*

of this temple shows the open lower jaw of a serpent, with fangs and teeth intact. Another such doorway occurs at Copán, on the south face of the Temple of Inscriptions. This motif is unusual in this part of the Maya world, but is frequently encountered in that part of the Yucatán Peninsula where remains of Río Bec and Chenes architecture occur. On the two south corners of the exterior of Temple 22 are large Chac masks, also a more common feature in Yucatán.

The inner sanctuary of Temple 22 displays some magnificent sculpture surrounding the doorway. Great skulls rest on the floor and support squatting human figures. These in turn support a fantastic collection of mythological creatures. It is unfortunate that part of the sculpture is badly stained. It is difficult to make out details. It makes you wish it were uniform in color so that the designs could be more easily appreciated. Photographs of the whole (you need a very wide-angle lens to get it all) tend to be a bit disappointing, but there are some good possibilities for detail photos. Temple 22 was dedicated in A.D. 765.

On the west side of the Eastern Court is the Jaguar Stairway. It rises in three levels and has figures of two jaguars—in a rather lighthearted pose—flanking the lower level. The circular depressions in the figures once were filled with obsidian discs. There are some glyphs carved on either end of the lower stairway. Centered on a higher level is the Venus Altar. The head in the middle of the altar has been variously identified as the sun god,

*Jaguar sculpture on the left (south) of the Jaguar Stairway, on the west side of the Eastern Court, Copán. Late Classic period.*

the Roman-nosed god, or the god of the evening star. It is flanked by unquestionable symbols of the planet Venus.

The east side of the Eastern Court is faced by steps on which thousands of carved stone blocks have been placed. More than anything else, it resembles a giant three-dimensional jigsaw puzzle. The remains apparently came from temples originally built at the top of the stairway. These mostly fell into the Copán River below, before its course was changed. This is another great place for detail photographs. A small tunnel through this stairway leads to the outside of the Acropolis. It is then a sheer drop to the former riverbed below. Be careful.

As you leave the Eastern Court heading south, you will pass the Jaguar Altar at the top of some steps on your left (east). It seems to guard the entrance to the court itself. Remains of a temple with some glyphs are found nearby. Proceed south, and then west, around the base of Structure 16—the highest mound in the Copán Valley—to the Western Court. Altars H and I are found at the southeast entrance to this court, and both are carved with hieroglyphs.

Structure 16 (unrestored) bounds the Western Court on the east side, and at the base of its stairway is the fascinating Altar Q. This rectangular altar, probably dedicated in A.D. 776, is carved with hieroglyphs on the top and with four seated personages on each side. It was long thought that Altar Q commemorated an achievement in astronomy accomplished some years before. The depiction

*The Venus Altar above the Jaguar Stairway in the west side of the Eastern Court, Copán. Late Classic period.*

of the sixteen figures, thought to represent dignitaries from various parts of the Maya realm, was humorously likened to "a group photograph of the Copán Academy of Sciences." Recent research, however, makes this interpretation doubtful. It is now thought that all the figures represent dignitaries of Copán, and that no astronomical activity is represented.

It is true, nevertheless, that Copán was an important center for astronomical advances. From the middle of the fourth century A.D. on, each Maya center had its own way of correlating the lunar and solar calendars, but in A.D. 682, at Copán, a new and fantastically accurate formula for calculating the length of a lunation was developed. This formula was eventually adopted almost universally within the Maya realm. A few years later a very accurate calculation for the duration of the tropical (365-day) year was produced.

To the west of Altar Q is the unrestored platform Number 13, bounding the Western Court on the west. North of Altar Q, on the east side of the court, is the early Stela P, dated A.D. 623.

It has been debated whether this stela was originally erected in its present location, or whether it was moved there from Old Copán. There is some evidence that the Western Court dates to an earlier period than Stela P, so this may be the place where the stela was first erected.

Bounding the Western Court on the north is the massive Spectator's Grandstand, which forms the south base of the Temple of Inscriptions. Although

*Altar Q, west side, Copán. Late Classic period.*

a stairway leads to a terrace below the temple, it does not give access to the temple itself. At the top of the stair there are two impressive figures of the Ik god, designated for the "ik" symbol on the rattles they carry. There are glyphs carved on the step below the figures. On the terrace above the stairway there are gigantic three-dimensional sculptures representing conch shells.

Set in the floor of the Western Court, near the bottom of the steps, are three carved rectangular altars; other remnants of sculptural decoration are found lying around.

Leave the Western Court by the foot trail that exits from the northwest corner. The trail descends and curves around to the southwest corner of the Court of the Hieroglyphic Stairway. To your left (west), as you enter the court, are some interesting sculptures in front of Mounds 7 and 6. All are worth a look, but especially impressive are Altar 0, depicting a feathered serpent, and Altar 41, showing a double-headed monster.

From here, head northeast across part of the Central Patio for a look at Stela 3 before leaving the site.

*Note:* It is possible, of course, to go to the Western Court directly from the Court of the Hieroglyphic Stairway by the trail on which you returned, but access to the Temple of Inscriptions is easier if you climb the stair and rubble behind Stela N as recommended.

## RECENT HISTORY

The existence of Copán and a description of the site were first reported in a letter written to Philip II, king of Spain, by Diego García de Palacio, dated March 8, 1576. Palacio was a member of the Royal Audiencia of Guatemala and was under orders from Philip to report, among other things, on the antiquities of the New World. After visiting the site and studying the architecture, Palacio correctly assumed that Copán was built by the same "nation"

*The east figure of the Ik god, at the north end of the Western Court, Copán. Late Classic period.*

that erected the buildings previously discovered in Yucatán and Tabasco by the Spaniards. Much of Palacio's letter is reproduced in Jesús Núñez Chinchilla's guidebook to Copán and it makes interesting reading.

Some time around 1820, Jean Frédéric Waldeck—better known for his work at Palenque and Uxmal—spent a month sketching the ruins of Copán.

An important report on the site was that of Colonel Juan Galindo, born in Ireland of an Irish mother and a Spanish father, and named John at birth. Galindo headed the first archaeological expedition to Copán for the Guatemalan government in 1834. He published several articles in American, English, and French periodicals.

A great many more people learned of Copán, however, when John Lloyd Stephens published his popular narrative *Incidents of Travel in Central America, Chiapas, and Yucatán* in 1841. Engravings of Frederick Catherwood's drawings published with the text brought to light the splendor of Copán's sculptures. Considering the complexity of the carvings, the accuracy of the drawings is phenomenal. It is still easier to study the details of the sculpture from the engravings of these drawings than from even the best photographs. Stephens also published a map of Copán, but, oddly enough, it shows north and south reversed. He apparently used this map in reconstructing his visit, as his narrative is consistent with it.

During the remainder of the nineteenth century and into the twentieth century many archaeologists and institutions investigated Copán. Among them were Alfred P. Maudslay, who published many beautiful photographs and carefully detailed drawings. The Peabody Museum of Harvard University sent several expeditions to Copán, led by Marshall H. Saville, John G. Owens, and George Byron Gordon. The site and its monuments were studied by Eduard Seler, Herbert J. Spinden, J. T. Goodman, Sylvanus G. Morley, Sir J. Eric S. Thompson, Gustav Stromsvik, A. V. Kidder, Aubrey Trik, John M. Longyear III, Tatiana Proskouriakoff, and others. Much of this work was sponsored by the Carnegie Institution of Washington, in cooperation with the Honduran government.

During this time, the hieroglyphs were recorded and studied, the stelae were repaired and uprighted where necessary, some of the architecture was restored, and many tombs were excavated. Perhaps one of the most beneficial endeavors was the rechanneling of the course of the Copán River, which had been eating into the side of the Acropolis for many years. This project, undertaken by the Carnegie Institution, prevented further destruction of the site. Some structures reported by Stephens less than a hundred years before had already disappeared.

In 1952, the Honduran government created the National Institute of Anthropology and History, and the archaeological zone was placed under its responsibility. Honduran archaeologist Jesús Núñez Chinchilla was named curator. This agency continues to maintain the site and is carrying on further investigations.

In 1976, it was reported that some major work at the site was being planned to begin in early 1977. It was to be conducted by a French group and sponsored by UNESCO, the Central American Bank, and the Honduran government. In conjunction with this work, there were also plans to pave the section of road from La Entrada to Copán.

## CONNECTIONS

1. 110.5 miles by road from San Pedro Sula, Honduras (71 miles paved, 39.5 miles fair dirt),
2. 146 miles by road from Guatemala City, Guatemala (111 miles paved, 35 miles fair dirt),
3. 252.5 miles by road from Tegucigalpa, Honduras (213 miles paved, 39.5 miles fair dirt),
4. 89 air miles from San Pedro Sula,
5. 97 air miles from Guatemala City, or
6. 140 air miles from Tegucigalpa.

## GETTING THERE

Of all the four-star sites, Copán is the one least visited by foreign tourists. For many travelers it is somewhat off the beaten path, although there are a number of ways to get there.

1. Fly to San Pedro Sula (from Miami or New Orleans in the United States, Guatemala City, Belize, or Mexico City). In San Pedro Sula (there are good hotels there) you can rent a car, or hire a car and driver, and drive to Copán in a little over 3 hours. Buses also run between San Pedro Sula and Copán.

From San Pedro Sula, head south on National Highway 1 to Chamelecón (6 miles). Then take National Highway 18 (on your right) west, and later southwest, for 65 miles. Highway 18 is also shown as Highway CA4 on some maps. This gets you to the town of La Entrada where you pick up Department Highway 20 (on your right) and take it 39.5 miles west to the town of Copán. You pass the entrance to the archaeological zone about 0.5 mile before the town.

2. You can drive to Copán from Guatemala City in about 4½ hours. From the latter, take Highway CA9 northeast for 85 miles to Highway CA10, near Río Hondo. Take Highway CA10 south for 26 miles to Highway 21, where there is a sign reading Vado Hondo (on your right), and another reading Copán Ruinas 61 K. (on the left). The junction is near kilometer 177, although the marker is not in place. Keep a careful eye out after you pass kilometer marker 176. Highway 21 then heads east (left) for 27 miles to the Guatemala-Honduras frontier. On the Honduran side, the highway is numbered 20, and it continues 8 miles to the town of Copán. For many years the road from the frontier to Copán was in very bad condition. It has been recently improved, however, so this 8-mile section can now be driven in less than ½ hour (rather than 1 hour and 10 minutes previously required).

The only good stopover between Guatemala City and Copán is the Longarone Motel near Teculután in Guatemala. See "Tikal" for details on the motel and for information on Highway CA9.

There are also day tours conducted from Guatemala City to Copán in minibuses, but they really do not allow enough time at the site. You need at least a full day to see Copán properly—more is better. You can also reach Copán by regular bus lines from Guatemala City, although it requires a change at Chiquimula and the frontier. Transportation from the frontier to Copán is by pickup truck.

On the Guatemala side, there are several small rivers and streams to be forded. If it has been raining, be extremely careful, as the rivers can rise rapidly.

3. From Tegucigalpa, take National Highway 1 northwest for 148 miles to Chamelecón. Then see above to get to Copán. Driving time from Tegucigalpa to Copán is 6¼ hours.

4. From San Pedro Sula there are three SAHSA flights a week to Copán. Check locally for schedules, as they tend to change.

5. Special charter flights from Guatemala City to Copán can be arranged, but this is expensive unless you have a group.

6. There are no regularly scheduled flights from Tegucigalpa to Copán, although occasional charter flights for groups are conducted. If you start from Tegucigalpa, you can fly to San Pedro Sula and on to Copán.

It is also possible to drive to Copán from San Salvador, but occasional border conflicts between El Salvador and Honduras may not make this the best choice. Even though citizens of other countries are freely allowed to cross the border either way, some time may be lost in doing so.

It is convenient to have a car at Copán to drive to the site, although a taxi can drop you off and pick you up later.

There are two hotels in the town of Copán, both on corners of the Main Plaza. The best is the Hotel Marina. Lights go out about 9:00 or 10:00 P.M. The food is pretty good.

You can get a copy of Núñez Chinchilla's guidebook for Copán at the hotel, the museum, or the building at the entrance to the site. If you get a copy, you can get along without a personal guide, but if you prefer having one along, you can find one at the hotel. Some of them speak English.

You could also get a guide at the nice new building at the entrance to the site. The building houses a small restaurant (cold drinks and snacks), a souvenir shop (they have interesting hand-carved mahogany boxes and other local crafts, and also sell publications), neat restrooms, and a ticket office. When you buy a ticket to the site, keep it, as it is also good for entry into the Copán Museum in town. Conversely, if you visit the museum first, save the ticket to get into the site.

You will be asked to sign a registration book at this building and again at another small building, about a block away near the gate to the site.

*Note*: There is a regulation prohibiting you from entering the site with a backpack. You will be asked to leave one at the first building. Camera bags—which are *obviously only* camera bags—are permitted. If you normally carry your camera gear in a backpack, it would be better to transfer it to a camera bag for this trip. Apparently, removal of artifacts by some visitors has necessitated this regulation.

It would be wise to carry a canteen of water with you to the site, as the restaurant is several blocks away from the main area and you will be spending a lot of time there.

Carry insect repellent. Sometimes there are swarms of small stingless bees around, and, while they will not hurt you, their buzzing can be annoying. Tennis shoes are adequate for getting around Copán.

*Altar U from Copán, perhaps representing a "Monster of the Earth," in the patio of the Copán Museum. Late Classic period.*

★★★

# *Regional Museum of Copán (Copán Museum)*

The Copán Museum, inaugurated in 1939, is located in the town on the southwest corner of the Main Plaza. It has some interesting remains from Copán and other nearby sites. There are both indoor and outdoor sections.

Stela 7 (A.D. 613) occupies the center of the outdoor patio. It was originally erected in Old Copán about 100 yards south of where it now stands. The stela has a depiction of a figure on its main face, while its back and sides are carved with glyphs. Other important monuments in the patio are, Altar T (reminiscent of Altar Q), carved with seated humans and animals on its sides; Altar U, with a grotesque mask on one side and glyphs on the back; Altar W—which looks more like a small stela—carved with glyphs on all four sides. Additional fragments of stone carving are arranged around the edge of the patio.

On the inside is Stela 11 (with an unusual columnar shape that makes it perhaps not a true stela), depicting a figure in profile on its main face. This is the only profile treatment of a figure on a stela known from Copán. Its back is carved with glyphs. There are numerous small sculptures from the site, and glyph-carved panels, ceramics, jade, and two ball court floor markers from the second ball court at Copán. One is beautifully preserved.

In one glass case are two important, and easily missed, small artifacts. They are the lower legs and feet of a gold figurine believed to have been made in Panamá or Colombia. They were discovered as part of a cache beneath Stela H. Apparently, there is still some question about when they were placed there. Some authorities believe they were buried in the Classic period, when the stela was erected, but there is some evidence to support a later date. They could have been deposited during the Postclassic period, after the site was deserted, or even in more recent times. If indeed the legs were placed under Stela H in Classic times, they would be rare examples of metals found in Mesoamerica during this period.

Allow an hour to see and photograph the collection at the Copán Museum. Use fast film in the indoor section, where there is not much light. The more impressive pieces in the collection are labeled, but the others are not.

## EL SALVADOR

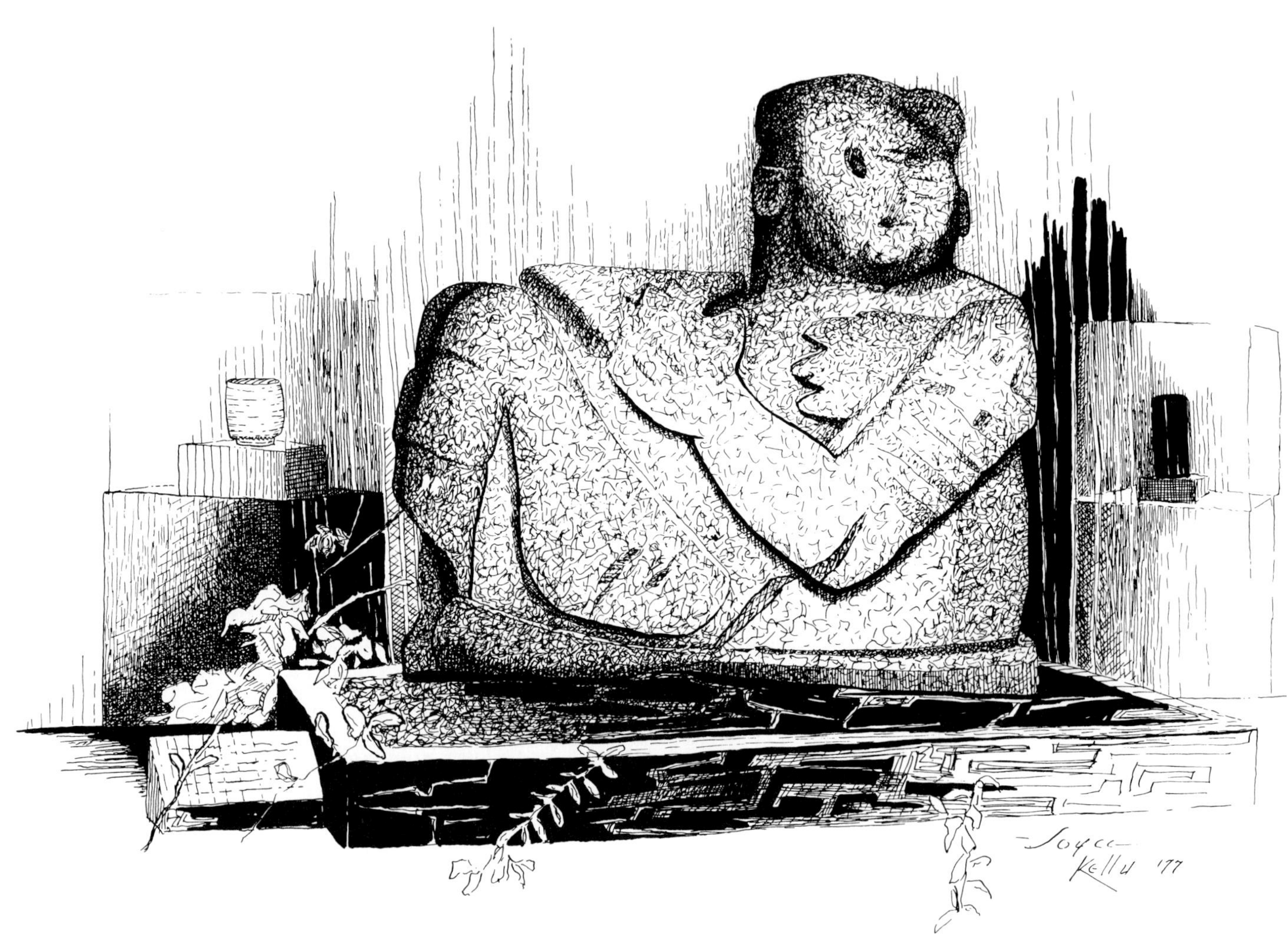

*Chac Mool from Casa Blanca, San Salvador Museum. Attributed to the Toltec Culture. Early Postclassic period.*

# *A Note on El Salvador*

El Salvador is the smallest and most densely populated of the Central American republics. All the El Salvadoran sites covered in the text can easily be reached from the capital city of San Salvador by car, in 2½ hours or less, making it the best stopover, and the one you will want to use if you fly in.

Both Hertz and Avis rent cars in San Salvador. This is the recommended way to get around, if you are not driving your own car, as buses are always jammed.

For those driving through the country, other stopovers are as follows (from west to east); (1) the town of Santa Ana on Highway CA 1, the Pan American Highway, (2) Hotel del Lago on Lake Coatepeque, 5 miles south of Highway CA 1, (3) the government-operated hotel in Cerro Verde National Park, 18 miles south of Highway CA 1, of which 9 miles are rough dirt, (4) the town of San Miguel on Highway CA 1.

In addition to the ruins and other points of interest mentioned in the individual sections, there are two other spots that are worth a visit in this lovely small country. One is Los Chorros, a tourist center with several swimming pools in a natural setting of fern-covered cliffs and waterfalls. There is a bathhouse, picnic area, and a small restaurant, as well as an abundance of colorful plants. Los Chorros is on the north side of Highway CA 1, about 9 miles west of San Salvador.

The other point of interest is El Boquerón, the mouth of the San Salvador volcano. Within the mile-wide crater is a small volcanic cone, the remains of a 1917 eruption. A rough, steep, dirt-and-rock road goes from Santa Tecla north to El Boquerón. Santa Tecla is 7 miles west of San Salvador on Highway CA 1. After you park, it is a 5- to 10-minute climb on foot uphill to the mirador that overlooks the crater. The mirador is visible from the parking area.

★★★

# *National Museum David J. Guzmán (San Salvador Museum)*

The San Salvador Museum is well laid out and lighted, and has sections devoted to the pre-Columbian archaeology of El Salvador, the colonial period, and the local costumes and artifacts of the inhabitants.

At the entrance is a large ceramic sculpture of Xipe Totec, from the Chalchuapa Zone. Other large artifacts of stone are a stela from Tazumal called the Virgin of Tazumal, a Chac Mool and an anthropomorphic jaguar from Casa Blanca, and a stone sun disc from Cara Sucia. There are also displays of ceramic pots and jade, and photo diagrams. The more important pieces are well labeled.

The spacious lawn in front of the museum exhibits a large stone jaguar altar from Quelepa, numerous petroglyphs, and several interesting stone heads. An English-speaking guide will show you around, if you so desire. The service is free. You are generously allowed to photograph all displays—both indoor and outdoor.

The museum is open from 9:00 to 12:00 A.M. and 2:30 to 6:00 P.M., and is well worth a visit.

To get there, head west on Avenida Franklin Roosevelt. When you reach a small park with a monument, bear to the left. The street then becomes Calle Santa Tecla and heads southwest. This is also Highway CA 1. Continue on Calle Santa Tecla for a bit over 1 mile until you drive under a pedestrian overpass. Take a right just past this, onto Avenida Revolución. Go for 1 or 2 blocks and loop around to the museum entrance. The museum is visible from the highway, but you have to turn right, before it comes into view. Allow 1 hour to see the collection.

*Stela from Tazumal called the "Virgin of Tazumal," San Salvador Museum. Postclassic period.*

★★★

# *Tazumal and Tazumal Museum*

(tah-soo-*mahl*)

DERIVATION: "Place of Sacrifice."
CULTURE: See text.
LOCATION: Western part of the department of Santa Ana, El Salvador.

## THE SITE

Tazumal is the most restored and most publicized site in El Salvador. It is the only one where you will run into other visitors. The shaded sides of the main structures are a popular place for students of the area, who go there to get a bit of breeze, to study, and to flirt with each other.

The major structures of Tazumal are surrounded by a fence and gate, and, to my knowledge, this is the only site covered that closes one day of the week (reportedly Monday), and for siesta between noon and 2:00 P.M. on the other days. Most of the construction at Tazumal is of adobe, or stone set in adobe, with a facing of lime plaster, and is similar to Kaminaljuyú in the Guatemala highlands and to Campana-San Andrés.

The most important and interesting building at Tazumal is Structure 1, a large stepped pyramid rising in numerous tiers, with vertical walls. Access is by stairs on the front (western) face. A temple with square columns once crowned the top. An unusual feature is a small one-room, templelike structure with a flat roof, found on the west side, part way up the pyramid. Its simple decorations are attractive. Structure 1 was rebuilt and added to on many occasions. Tazumal is part of a large archaeological zone that occupied the edge of the city of

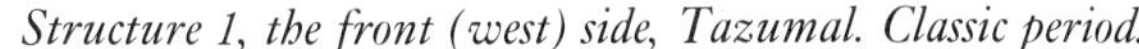

*Structure 1, the front (west) side, Tazumal. Classic period.*

*Remains on the north side of Structure 1, Tazumal. Classic period.*

Chalchuapa and is, therefore, called the Chalchuapa Zone. Although close together, the individual groups have been given separate names and are treated as separate sites in the literature. Some, including Tazumal, had beginnings in the Preclassic period.

During the Preclassic period, western El Salvador had trade links with Kaminaljuyú, and this is reflected in the ceramics of the area. During the Classic period, Tazumal was influenced by the architectural style of Kaminaljuyú, but looked to Copán for ceremonial pottery when trade with Kaminaljuyú was cut off. There was also a Postclassic occupation of the site and Mexican (Pipil) influence at this time is evident. The statue of Xipe Totec at the San Salvador Museum dates to this period. It was found about 0.5 mile east of the Tazumal Group.

Although Structure 1 was built during the Early and Late Classic periods, other structures at Tazumal are Postclassic. Generally attributed to the Postclassic is the Virgin of Tazumal. It is sometimes described as Maya because of the glyphs on its side, but authorities point out that the glyphs do not resemble those on Maya monuments. Certainly the carved figure on the stela does not appear typically Maya. It was found at the base of the west side of Structure 1. Tazumal was occupied until—or almost until—the time of the Spanish conquest.

Climb Structure 1 for a good view of the rest of the site. Other architectural remains include the restored stepped pyramid Structure 2, abutting Structure 1 on the west; a ball court-like construction on the south of Structure 1; partially restored remains of several structures on the north side of Structure 1; an excavation northeast of Structure 1, locally called the Catacumbas, with evidence of

*Structure 2, view of the northwest corner, Tazumal. Probably Postclassic period.*

steps; and an overgrown and unexcavated ball court in the modern cemetery across the street from the enclosed structures. All these structures are easily visible from the top of Structure 1.

## RECENT HISTORY

Tazumal was excavated by Stanley H. Boggs in 1942, although the site had been known to pot hunters for many years. Under the technical supervision of Boggs, the San Salvador Museum continued investigations in 1943. Additional work at the site was undertaken by William Coe, and, in the 1960s, by Robert Sharer.

## CONNECTION

1. 48 miles by paved road from San Salvador.

## GETTING THERE

From San Salvador, take Highway CA 1 west, then northwest to Santa Ana. A little less than 2 miles past Santa Ana, an unnumbered paved road connects with CA 1. This road heads west for about 6 miles to Chalchuapa. As you enter Chalchuapa, look for a dirt cutoff to the left (south). It is marked, and as soon as you turn, you can see Structure 1 of Tazumal a few hundred yards away. Chalchuapa can also be reached by bus.

There is no food or drink at the site, but sometimes an ice-cream vendor is nearby, and there are small stores in the area. Tennis shoes are fine.

Allow about 2 hours to visit the site and museum, and another 15 minutes if you want to look at the nearby Casa Blanca mounds. Driving time from San Salvador to Tazumal is about 1½ hours.

Tazumal can be combined with a visit to Campana-San Andrés. The following tour makes a nice one-day trip from the capital. It is rather long, but not too strenuous.

Leave San Salvador early in the morning, and visit Campana-San Andrés. Continue to the town of El Congo, and take the cutoff that goes to Lake Coatepeque and on to Cerro Verde National Park. From the park, you get a good view of Izalco Volcano, which sent up sparks until 1957 and which was known to mariners as the Lighthouse of the Pacific.

Return to Lake Coatepeque for a lunch of crab soup (sopa de cangrejo) at the Hotel del Lago. Then return to Highway CA 1 and on to Tazumal. This puts you at the site in the afternoon, which affords best light on Structure 1. Visit Tazumal and its museum and have a look at the Casa Blanca mounds before returning to San Salvador.

*Note:* You will be swamped by small boys wanting to guide you and watch your car as soon as you arrive at Tazumal. A guide is not really necessary, but they can be fun and will help you carry your camera gear.

★★

# *Tazumal Museum*

The Tazumal Museum is a very nice site museum, and, while not extensive, it is well lighted and labeled in both Spanish and English—a rare occurrence.

Displays include a model of the site, as well as ceramics, stone *hachas* and jade. Photographs are freely permitted. The gem of the collection is a new acquisition that is found outside the museum on a cement platform. It is the well-publicized carved boulder from the nearby site of Las Victorias, depicting four Olmec figures. It was moved to Tazumal in January, 1976. According to Ignacio Bernal (in *The Olmec World*), "Curiously—in view of its great distance from the Metropolitan [Olmec] zone—the style is one of the most characteristically Olmec in the entire Pacific watershed." A diagram in the museum dates the carving to 600 B.C. The boulder also gets best light on the most prominent figures in the afternoon.

A couple of other carved stone monuments stand outside the museum.

*Carved boulder with Olmec figure from Las Victorias in western El Salvador, Tazumal Museum. Middle Preclassic period.*

# *Casa Blanca*

(*kah*-sah *blahn*-kah)

DERIVATION: Spanish for "White House."
ORIGINAL NAME: Unknown.
CULTURE: See text.
LOCATION: Western part of the department of Santa Ana, El Salvador.

---

## THE SITE

Casa Blanca is part of the Chalchuapa Zone, near the edge of the city of the same name. It is reportedly the largest group in the zone and comprises at least sixteen mounds. Three of these rubble- and vegetation-covered mounds are clearly discernible today, but no restoration has been undertaken, so there is not really a whole lot to see.

## RECENT HISTORY

In 1926, Jorge Lardé reported on the archaeology of the Chalchuapa Zone and mentioned the existence of fifteen mounds at Casa Blanca. In 1942, the site was visited by John Longyear III, who discovered the additional mound and heard of other smaller structures in the area. He reported that two mounds had been partially excavated, but that the others remained untouched.

A Chac Mool figure from Casa Blanca is now in the San Salvador Museum, where it is attributed to the Toltec culture. It is dated from the eleventh to the thirteenth centuries A.D. An anthropomorphic jaguar from the site is also in the museum and carries a similar date.

## CONNECTION

1. 48 miles by paved road from San Salvador.

## GETTING THERE

Follow directions for getting to Tazumal. There you can hire one of the small boys to take you to Casa Blanca. It is just a few minutes away by car.

Casa Blanca is not worth a special trip by itself, but when you visit Tazumal, you might want to take a look.

The mounds are located near a railroad track.

Tennis shoes are fine. There is no food or drink, of course. Bring an ice chest with liquid refreshment.

*Note:* The El Trapiche Group is also part of the Chalchuapa Zone, and reportedly has a mound comparable in size to Structure 1 at Tazumal. We asked our guide about this, but he knew nothing of it. Maybe you will have better luck.

★★

# *Campana–San Andrés*

(kahm-*pah*-nah sahn ahn-*drehs*)

DERIVATION: Campana is Spanish for "bell," and San Andrés is Spanish for "Saint Andrew."
ORIGINAL NAME: Unknown.
CULTURE: See text.
LOCATION: Central part of the department of La Libertad, El Salvador.

## THE SITE

Campana–San Andrés is in the broad valley of the Río Sucio, which has many mounds and which was apparently thickly occupied in pre-Columbian times. Campana–San Andrés is the most interesting group in the area and the only one that has been systematically excavated. The major structures are on the east and south sides of a large platform, and some restoration has been done. Near the southeast corner of the platform, and on a lower level, are the remains of another structure, near the area where you park. This structure is composed of walls or terraces of squared stone blocks. From there climb the platform for a look at the other structures.

The major pyramid rises in several tiers and has a stair on the north side. Construction is of adobe brick, covered with lime plaster—similar to that used at Tazumal and Kaminaljuyú. There were four construction periods on this and other adobe structures, some of which are visible today. Climb this mound for good views of the other structures.

As you look north across the platform, you can see a gridlike pattern on the ground. I do not know if this was due to some original construction, but I suspect that it may be remains of evidence of trenching, done during excavation.

Several structures lie on the east side of the plat-

*The major pyramid, center, and the structures bordering the east side of the plaza, left, Campana–San Andrés. Classic–Postclassic periods.*

*Structures bordering the east side of the plaza, Campana–San Andrés. Classic–Postclassic periods.*

form with stairs facing west. One exhibits balustraded stairs, apparently from at least two construction periods. The stepped pyramidal base of the structure has been partially restored. Climb this for good photos of the main pyramid. Proceed north to the edge of the platform. On the northeast corner is a long projection running east–west, and in the cane fields below the platform are several mounds covered with vegetation.

The architectural and ceramic remains indicate that Campana–San Andrés was occupied during the Classic period and into the Postclassic period. There is evidence of influence from the Guatemala highlands, as well as from Copán, where the plaza-acropolis arrangement of the structures is similar. Ceramics of Copán type are also found at Campana–San Andrés.

## RECENT HISTORY

John M. Dimick excavated Campana–San Andrés in 1940 and 1941, and his findings were published in the latter year by the Carnegie Institution of Washington.

## CONNECTION

1. 20 miles by paved road from San Salvador, then about 0.3 mile of dirt road to the site.

## GETTING THERE

Leave San Salvador on Highway CA 1, heading west. Watch for kilometer marker 32; the dirt cutoff to the site is on your right (north), and is located shortly after the marker. As you enter the dirt road, make another right turn (paralleling the highway) and go for a couple of blocks, and then go left, through the sugarcane fields, directly to the site. The structures can be seen from the highway. Keep an eye out as soon as you pass the kilometer 32 marker.

Driving time is about 30 minutes from the capital. The road is four lanes most of the way. Campana–San Andrés can also be reached by bus or taxi from San Salvador.

There is no food or drink at the site. Tennis shoes are adequate. Allow 45 minutes for a visit. A guide is not necessary to get you to or to see Campana–San Andrés.

★

# *Cihuatán*

(see-wah-*tahn*)

CULTURE: See text.
LOCATION: Northern part of the department of San Salvador, El Salvador.

---

## THE SITE

Cihuatán is reportedly an extensive site, although the cleared portion that the visitor sees today is not huge. As you park and enter the site, you walk through the partly excavated remains of a ball court, although the fact that this is a court is not readily apparent.

A trail continues to Structure 1, a fair-sized pyramid with remains of the original stairways on the north, south, and west sides. There is some question about whether the east side ever supported a stairway; there is no evidence of one today. Climb the pyramid for good views of the other structures. Some mounds lie in the fields beyond, to the east and southeast. Of more interest are the structures to the north, which are cleared and partially restored.

About 300 feet north of the pyramid is an enclosure with a platform called the Templo de los Idolos. It supports balustraded stairways on the north and south sides. Abutting this, to the north, is a partially restored ball court. From the north end of the ball court, you can get good photos of it, with the Templo de los Idolos and Structure 1 in the background.

## RECENT HISTORY

The little that is known about Cihuatán is mostly

*The ball court, foreground; platform (Templo de los Idolos), midground; and pyramid (Structure 1), background, Cihuatán. Postclassic period.*

due to the brief investigation by the El Salvadoran government in 1929, under the direction of Antonio E. Sol. A site plan was produced by Augusto Baratta.

The ceramics that were excavated are Postclassic in date. No evidence of Classic occupation was discovered, but the size of the site indicates that it is possible that it was occupied during the Classic period. Further investigations would no doubt clarify the matter.

The Postclassic remains show evidence of Mexican (Pipil) influence, as do other Postclassic sites in the highlands of El Salvador and Guatemala.

## CONNECTION

1. 22 miles by paved road from San Salvador to the cutoff, then about 1 mile of poor dirt road to the site.

## GETTING THERE

Take Highway CA 4 north from San Salvador. This goes through the towns of Apopa and Aguilares. Look for kilometer marker 36 (located a little over 1 mile past the north edge of Aguilares). The cutoff for Cihuatán is about 300 feet past the kilometer 36 marker, and it is on your right (east). There is no sign, but there is a cement and iron fence with an iron gate at the cutoff. A small house lies just beyond the gate. The poor dirt road that passes the house continues for a bit under 1 mile to the site. Ask at the house if you are in doubt.

*Note:* Although Highway CA 4 is paved, it is rough, full of potholes, and passes through a densely populated area. Plan on driving slowly. Figure on 45 minutes driving time from San Salvador.

There is no food or drink at the site. Take an ice chest and cold drinks. Tennis shoes are adequate.

Buses run on Highway CA 4 and can drop you off at the junction. A taxi could get you there from San Salvador, but it might be expensive for the rewards received. A guide is not necessary at Cihuatán. Allow 1 hour to visit the site.

★

# *Quelepa*

(keh-*leh*-pah)

DERIVATION: Lenca for "Stone Jaguar."
ORIGINAL NAME: Unknown.
CULTURE: See text.
LOCATION: Central part of the department of San Miguel, El Salvador.

## THE SITE

Quelepa is reported to be the most important site in eastern El Salvador. It shares with Los Llanitos—a site 13 miles south—the distinction of being the easternmost ceremonial site with oriented mounds. Approximately forty structures are known at Quelepa, and they occupy an area of about 0.2 square mile. They are located along the north side of the Río San Esteban. A small stream divides the site into the East and West groups, and the latter is the one the visitor sees today.

The most interesting area of the West Group is an arrangement of mounds, mostly atop a terrace, facing a plaza in the southeastern part of the group. They are eroded, and those that were recently excavated have been re-covered for protection, so no architectural features are presently discernable.

One of the structures excavated in this area proved to be a three-tiered platform with a projecting stairway. The platform apparently supported a building of perishable materials. This structure dates to the Late Classic period, as probably do the other mounds in this group.

From this group, additional mounds—covered with cultivated henequen—are visible to the northeast.

Quelepa is believed to have been occupied from around 500 B.C., and according to E. Wyllys Andrews V, ". . . the first inhabitants clearly arrived before 300 B.C." The large and impressive jaguar altar from Quelepa—found in the West Group and now in the San Salvador Museum—dates to this early period, and shows certain stylistic ties to monuments from Izapa and Kaminaljuyú. In the Early Classic period, at least two important structures were built in the East Group. During the Late Classic period, architectural activity shifted to the southeastern corner of the West Group. The site was abandoned for unknown reasons around A.D. 1000.

During its long history Quelepa had contact with and received influence from various areas. In the earliest ceramic levels discovered, there is evidence of trade with highland Guatemala. In the Early Classic period the ceramics from Quelepa are similar to those from southern Honduras and the Chalchuapa Zone of western El Salvador.

In the Late Classic period, there is strong evidence of contact with the culture of Classic Veracruz. One cache of carved stone objects found at Quelepa included yokes, *palmas*, and an *hacha*—objects related to the ritual ball game and more commonly found in the Veracruz area. According to Andrews, "this cache marks the first time all three of these distinctive sculptured forms have been found together." It is perhaps worthy of note that the cache was found 100 yards south of the unexcavated Late Classic ball court at Quelepa.

There is also evidence of influence from Veracruz in some of the ceramics at Quelepa, including wheeled figurines. These figurines and *palmas* are exceedingly rare in the interlying areas of Chiapas, the Guatemala highlands, and western El Salvador.

Andrews believes that a group strongly influenced by the culture of Classic Veracruz moved into eastern El Salvador around A.D. 600. He holds this view, since in addition to the portable objects—which alone might have indicated trade—there was the introduction of new architectural styles and construction methods at this time.

## RECENT HISTORY

Although Quelepa has long been known in the general area as a major site, the first report seems to have been that of Doctor Atilio Peccorini in 1913. In 1926, Peccorini issued another report, and Samuel Lothrop reported on his brief visit to the site. Three years later, Antonio E. Sol visited the site and also issued a report. The first excavations at Quelepa were those of Pedro Armillas in 1949, but his work was not completed or published.

The most extensive work at Quelepa was that undertaken by Andrews. In 1967—sponsored by

*Jaguar altar, Quelepa. Now at the museum in San Salvador. Middle Preclassic period.*

the Middle American Research Institute (MARI) of Tulane University—he made a reconnaissance trip to El Salvador and undertook preliminary investigations at Quelepa. He returned in 1968–69, funded by a Fulbright-Hays Fellowship, to carry out more thorough excavations. This work was the basis of his doctoral dissertation, a later version of which was published in 1976 by MARI of Tulane University.

Quelepa, Campana–San Andrés, and Cihuatán, were recently declared national historic sites by the El Salvadoran government.

## CONNECTION

1. 80 miles by paved road from San Salvador to the cutoff, then 2 miles of dirt road to the site.

## GETTING THERE

From San Salvador, take Highway CA 1 east for 80 miles (75.5 miles past the airport). Near kilometer marker 130 there is a dirt cutoff to the left (north) that goes a bit over 1 mile to the town of Quelepa. The cutoff is marked. From the town it is a bit under 1 mile by dirt road to the site.

The site is on private property, and it is necessary to go through a gate on the way. It is, therefore, best to ask in the town of Quelepa for a guide who can accompany you to the site. You have to walk about 0.5 mile from where you park.

There is no food or drink at the site, but cold drinks are available in town. It is better to have drinks along in your car and to pack a box lunch.

You can reach the cutoff to the town of Quelepa, and perhaps the town itself, by bus, but the best way to get there would be to have your own vehicle. The site is too far from San Salvador to make a taxi practical. Tennis shoes are adequate. Allow 1 hour to visit the site once you get there, and about 2½ hours each way for the drive from San Salvador. You may lose a bit more time finding a guide. That makes it a day's trip from the capital.

# *Glossary*

Atlantes (also *Atlantean figures* and *Telemones*): Statues of men used as supporting columns for roofs and altars. Prevalent at Tula and at Chichén Itzá during the Toltec period.

atlatl: A dart thrower or spear thrower, made of a grooved stick with a handle on one end, which gives extra thrust to propel the dart or spear.

balustrades: In architecture, sloping side sections that flank stairways.

bar-and-dot system: A method of recording numerals, used by the Mayas and the Zapotecs. A bar represents 5; a dot, 1.

*caleta*: A protected bay or cove. Especially good for swimming.

Ce Acatl Topiltzin Quetzalcóatl: A Toltec priest-king and culture hero, the founder of Tula. He added the name Quetzalcóatl to his own name and promoted worship of the deity Quetzalcóatl.

ceiba: A huge tree sacred to the ancient Mayas and found in the tropical rain forest.

cenote: A natural well, formed when the top surface of limestone collapses, exposing the water below. Prevalent in northern Yucatán.

Chac: The Maya rain god.

Chac Mool: The statue of a figure in a recumbent pose, holding a receptacle on its abdomen. Used at Tula and Toltec-influenced sites. Postclassic period.

Chalchihuitlicue: The water goddess of central Mexico. Variously identified as the wife, mother, or sister of Tlaloc.

Chenes style: A Maya Late Classic architectural style found at such sites as Hochob and Dzibilnocac. Characterized by whole façades covered with a single monster mask, with a mouth as the doorway (see *Río Bec style*).

*chiclero:* A man who bleeds the zapote tree for its latex, which, when refined, forms the base for chewing gum. The raw product is known as *chicle*.

chultun: A bottle-shaped underground storage area, used to store water in some regions and food in others.

Coatlicue: The earth goddess of central Mexico. Generally depicted wearing a skirt made of serpents.

Cocijo: The Zapotec rain god.

codex (plural, *codices*): Pre-Columbian painted books, (some are of early post-Columbian date). They are made of deerskin or bark paper, and are folded like a screen.

corbeled vault (also corbeled arch): The prevalent style of roofing used in Classic Maya structures. The vault is built up from the top of a vertical wall, and each layer of stone or brick juts past the one below. When the sides of the vault approach each other closely enough, a capstone is added to bridge the remaining gap.

Danzantes (Spanish for "dancers"): Life-sized figure carved on stone slabs found at Monte Albán and thought to resemble dancers because of their fluid poses. Although they do not depict dancers, they may depict captives.

eccentric flints: Fragile chipped flints of unusual and intricate design, often depicting humans, dogs, birds, scorpions, and so on. They are probably of some ceremonial significance, and are frequently found in votive caches in the lowland Maya area.

Éhacatl: The wind god of central Mexico; an aspect of Quetzalcóatl.

finca: A farm or ranch.

*florero:* A ceramic vessel with a long thin neck and a flaring rim. Typical of Teotihuacán.

glyphs (also *hieroglyphs*): A form of ancient writing in Mesoamerica. Both pictographic and ideographic forms are used. In Maya writing some glyphs have phonetic value.

GMT correlation: A correlation between the Maya and Christian calendars proposed by Goodman, Martínez, and Thompson. This is now the generally—though not universally—accepted correlation. Another—the Spinden correlation—would place Maya dates some 260 years earlier in the Christian calendar.

*hachas* (Spanish for "axes"): Thin stone objects in the shape of an ax, and often carved. Associated with the ritual ball game. Prevalent in the culture of El Tajín.

hieroglyphs: see *glyphs*.

Huasteca: An area in Mexico occupied by the Huastecs, a group linguistically related to the Mayas. It includes portions of several Mexican states: southern Tamaulipas, northern Veracruz, and small parts of San Luis Potosí, Querétaro, Hidalgo, and Puebla.

Huehueteotl: see *Xiutecuhtli.*

INAH: Instituto Nacional de Antropología e Historia (National Institute of Anthropology and History), the Mexican government agency that is responsible for the care of ancient remains. It also sponsors excavations and publishes guides to the sites.

Initial Series (also *Long Count date*): A method of recording dates in the Maya calendar. It represents the total number of days that have elapsed from a mythical starting point, calculated at 3113 B.C., according to the GMT correlation.

Itzamná: The supreme Maya deity; the heavenly monster-god and creator-god.

Ix Chel: The Maya goddess of the moon, women, and childbirth.

Kinich-Ahau: The Yucatec name for the sun god. A manifestation of Itzamná.

Kinich-Kakmo: A manifestation of Kinich-Ahau.

Kukulcán: The Mayan name for the deity Quetzalcóatl, the feathered serpent.

Long Count date: see *Initial Series.*

long-lipped god: Believed to be a development of the Olmec were-jaguar and the forerunner of the Mesoamerican rain gods (Chac, Tlaloc, Cocijo, and Tajín). Prominent in Izapan art.

Manikin Scepter: A wand or scepter topped by a small monster figure. The scepter is held by the main figure on carved Maya stelae and panels.

mano: See *metate.*

Mesoamerica: The areas of Mexico and Central America where high civilizations arose in pre-Columbian times. It includes parts of western and eastern Mexico; all of central and southern Mexico and the Yucatán Peninsula; all of Guatemala, Belize, and El Salvador; western Honduras; and part of the Pacific Coast areas of Nicaragua and Costa Rica.

mestizo: A person of mixed Indian and European ancestry.

metate: A trough-shaped stone used for grinding foodstuffs, generally corn (maize). Accompanied by a cylindrical hand stone (*mano*).

Mexican Yearsign (also *Teotihuacán Yearsign, Mixtec Yearsign,* and *imbricated trapeziform*): A motif of overlapping geometrical elements originating in Mexico. Believed to be a sign indicating "year," though some authorities hold that there is no calendric meaning.

milpa: A plot of land cultivated by slash-and-burn agriculture. Most often used for growing corn (maize).

Mixteca: The area occupied by the Mixtecs, a portion of the western part of the modern state of Oaxaca and adjacent regions.

Nahua: A group of people who spoke a Uto-Aztecan language; also the language itself.

Nahuat: An early linguistic form of Nahua.

Nahuatl: A later linguistic form of Nahua; also the language spoken by the Aztecs.

palace-type structures (also *range-type structures*): Multichambered structures built on low platforms, rather than on tall pyramidal bases. Probably mostly residential or used for administrative purposes rather than for religious ceremonies.

*palmas:* Stone objects in the form of a fan or palm leaf, often carved. Associated with the ritual ball game. Prevalent in the culture of El Tajín.

Pipils: Nahuat-speaking groups who migrated to Central America. The name is loosely applied.

Putun: A Chontal Maya group known as traders. They occupied eastern Tabasco and southern Campeche.

Puuc style: A Maya Late Classic architectural style found at Uxmal, Kabáh, Labná, Sayil, and so forth. Characterized by facings of finely cut veneer stones, highly decorative stone mosaics of various designs, engaged columns, and round columns in doorways.

Quetzalcóatl: The major deity of central Mexico: the feathered serpent. He brought knowledge of agriculture, arts, and science.

Río Bec style: A Maya Late Classic architectural style found at such sites as Río Bec B and Xpuhil. Characterized by tall towers with "false" steps and "false" temples on top. It has recently been proposed that the Chenes and Río Bec styles be combined into one Central Yucatán style because of their similarities.

roof comb: In architecture, a stone superstructure built on the roof of a temple to give additional height and grandeur. The combs are sometimes perforated and are generally decorated. Prevalent in the lowland Maya area.

*sacbé* (plural in Mayan, *sacbeob*): An ancient road or causeway made of rough-stone blocks topped with crushed stone and then plastered.

stela (plural, *stelae*): A freestanding monolithic stone monument, either plain or carved on one or more sides. Especially prevalent in the Maya area. Often accompanied by a drum-shaped altar.

stepped fret: A design composed of a squared spiral and a step element. It is derived from the stylized head of the "sky-serpent" and is, therefore, a symbol of Quetzalcóatl. Found throughout Mesoamerica, but especially prevalent at Mitla and other sites in Oaxaca.

Tajín: The Totonac rain god.

*talud-tablero:* In architecture, a sloping lower section, or *talus (talud),* topped by a vertical, rectangular, recessed panel *(tablero).* Prevalent style at Teotihuacán.

Tepoztecatl: The god of pulque of central Mexico.

Tezcatlipoca: Smoking mirror, god of the night, deity of central Mexico associated with death and evil. Brother of Quetzalcóatl.

Tlahuizcalpantecuhtli: Quetzalcóatl in his aspect as Lord of the House of Dawn, the planet Venus as Morning Star.

Tlaloc: The rain god of central Mexico. He also has a lesser-known aspect as a war or warrior god.

*tzompantli:* A skull rack where heads of sacrificial victims were placed. A platform with depictions of carved skulls on its sides. Postclassic period.

were-jaguar: A mythical creature, presumably the offspring of the union between a human female and a jaguar. Prominent in Olmec art.

Xipe Totec: The god of spring of central Mexico. Generally depicted wearing the skin of a flayed victim.

Xiuhcóatl: The fire serpent, a deity of central Mexico.

Xiuhtecuhtli (also Huehueteotl): The old fire god, a deity of central Mexico.

*yácata:* A mound or "pyramid" of unusual shape found in the Tarascan area.

yokes: Yoke-shaped stones, sometimes elaborately carved. Related to the ritual ball game. Prevalent in the culture of El Tajín.

zapote (also *sapote* and *sapodilla*): an extremely hard wood found in the lowland Maya area. Often used for lintels in pre-Columbian buildings. The latex from this tree is chicle, the base for chewing gum. The fruit of the tree is also called zapote.

Zócalo: The Main Plaza in Mexico City and, by extension, the Main Plaza in some other cities in the republic.

# Selected Readings

The following list includes general books on Mesoamerican history, art, and archaeology, and others by and about some early explorers and archaeologists. General guidebooks for the area and guides to specific sites are listed in the "General Advice" section. The reader who wishes to delve more deeply into the subject is directed to publications by the following institutions. All will send catalogs upon request: Peabody Museum of Archaeology and Ethnology, Harvard University, 11 Divinity Avenue, Cambridge, Mass. 02138; Carnegie Institution of Washington, 1530 P Street, N.W., Washington, D.C. 20005; Middle American Research Institute, Tulane University, 6823 St. Charles Avenue, New Orleans, Louisiana 70118.


Andrews, George F.
1975 *Maya Cities: Placemaking and Urbanization.* Norman: University of Oklahoma Press.

Benson, Elizabeth P., ed.
1968 *Dumbarton Oaks Conference on the Olmec.* Washington, D.C.: Dumbarton Oaks.

Bernal, Ignacio
1969 *The Olmec World.* Berkeley: University of California Press.

Brunhouse, Robert L.
1971 *Sylvanus G. Morley and the World of the Ancient Mayas.* Norman: University of Oklahoma Press.
1973 *In Search of the Maya.* Albuquerque: University of New Mexico Press. Reprint. New York: Ballantine Books, 1974.
1975 *Pursuit of the Ancient Maya.* Albuquerque: University of New Mexico Press.
1976 *Frans Blom: Maya Explorer.* Albuquerque: University of New Mexico Press.

Carmack, Robert M.
1981 *The Quiché Mayas of Utatlán: The Evolution of a Highland Guatemala Kingdom.* Norman: University of Oklahoma Press.

Caso, Alfonso
1958 *The Aztecs: People of the Sun.* Norman: University of Oklahoma Press.

Coe, Michael D.
1962 *Mexico.* New York: Frederick A. Praeger.
1966 *The Maya.* New York: Frederick A. Praeger.

Covarrubias, Miguel
1946 *Mexico South.* New York: Alfred A. Knopf. 5th printing, 1962.
1957 *Indian Art of Mexico and Central America.* New York: Alfred A. Knopf.

Díaz del Castillo, Bernal
1956 *The Discovery and Conquest of Mexico.* Translated by A. P. Maudslay, edited by Génaro García. New York: Farrar, Straus and Giroux. 6th printing, 1972.

Dockstader, Frederick J.
1964 *Indian Art in Middle America.* Greenwich, Conn.: New York Graphic Society.

Ferguson, William M., with Royce, John Q.
1977 *Maya Ruins of Mexico in Color.* Norman: University of Oklahoma Press.

Greene, Merle
1967 *Ancient Maya Relief Sculpture.* New York: Museum of Primitive Art.

———; Rands, Robert L.; and Graham, John A.
1972 *Maya Sculpture.* Berkeley, Calif.: Lederer, Street and Zeus.

Heyden, Doris, and Gendrop, Paul
1973 *Pre-Columbian Architecture of Mesoamerica.* Milan: Electa Editrice. New York: Harry N. Abrams, 1975.

Hunter, C. Bruce
1974 *A Guide to Ancient Maya Ruins.* Norman: University of Oklahoma Press.
1977 *A Guide to Ancient Mexican Ruins.* Norman: University of Oklahoma Press.

Keleman, Pál
1943 *Medieval American Art.* 2 vols. New York: Macmillan Co. 3d ed. New York: Dover Publications, 1969.

Maudslay, Alfred P.
1889–1902 *Archaeology.* Biologia Centrali Americana. 5 vols. London. Facsimile edition. New York: Milpatron Publishing, 1974.

Mercer, Henry
1896 *The Hill-Caves of Yucatán: A Search for Evidence of Man's Antiquity in the Caverns of Central America.* Introduction by Sir J. Eric S. Thompson. Philadelphia: Lippincott. Reprint. Norman: University of Oklahoma Press, 1975.

Morley, Sylvanus G.
1946 *The Ancient Maya.* 2d ed., revised by George W. Brainerd. Stanford, Calif.: Stanford University Press, 1956.

Paddock, John, ed.
1966 *Ancient Oaxaca.* Stanford, Calif.: Stanford University Press.

Pendergast, David M.
1967 *Palenque: The Walker-Caddy Expedition to the Ancient Maya City, 1839–1840.* Norman: University of Oklahoma Press.

Peterson, Frederick
1959 *Ancient Mexico.* New York: Capricorn Books.
Proskouriakoff, Tatiana
1946 *An Album of Maya Architecture.* Washington, D.C.: Carnegie Institution of Washington. Reprint. Norman: University of Oklahoma Press, 1963.
Robicsek, Francis
1972 *Copan: Home of the Mayan Gods.* New York: Museum of the American Indian, Heye Foundation.
1978 *The Smoking Gods: Tobacco in Maya Art, History, and Religion.* Norman: University of Oklahoma Press.
Scholes, France V., and Roys, Ralph L.
1968 *The Maya Chontal Indians of Acalan-Tixchel: A Contribution to the History and Ethnography of the Yucatán Peninsula.* Norman: University of Oklahoma Press.
Soustelle, Jacques
1966 *Arts of Ancient Mexico.* Paris: B. Arthaud. New York: Viking Press, 1967.
Spinden, Herbert J.
1913 *A Study of Maya Art.* Cambridge, Mass.: Peabody Museum. Reprint. New York: Dover Publications, 1975.
Stephens, John Lloyd
1841 *Incidents of Travel in Central America, Chiapas, and Yucatán.* 2 vols. London. New York, 1854. Reprint. New York: Dover Publications, 1969.
1843 *Incidents of Travel in Yucatán.* 2 vols. New York. Reprint. Norman: University of Oklahoma Press, 1962.
Stone, Doris
1972 *Pre-Columbian Man Finds Central America.* Cambridge, Mass.: Peabody Museum.
Thompson, Sir J. Eric S.
1954 *The Rise and Fall of Maya Civilization.* Norman: University of Oklahoma Press. 2d ed., 1966.
1963 *Maya Archaeologist.* Norman: University of Oklahoma Press.
1970 *Maya History and Religion.* Norman: University of Oklahoma Press.
Vaillant, George C.
1944 *Aztecs of Mexico.* Garden City, N.Y.: Doubleday, Doran and Co. Revised by Suzannah B. Vaillant. Bungay: Penguin Books.
Von Hagen, Victor W.
1947 *Maya Explorer: John Lloyd Stephens and the Lost Cities of Central America and Yucatán.* Norman: University of Oklahoma Press.
1958 *The Aztec: Man and Tribe.* New York: New American Library of World Literature. Revised edition, 1962.
1960 *World of the Maya.* New York: New American Library of World Literature.
Wauchope, Robert
1965 *They Found the Buried Cities.* Chicago: University of Chicago Press.
———, ed.
1965–71 *Handbook of the Middle American Indians.* Vols. 2–4, 10, 11. Austin: University of Texas Press.
Weaver, Muriel P.
1972 *The Aztecs, Maya, and Their Predecessors.* New York: Seminar Press.
Westheim, Paul, et al.
1972 *Prehispanic Mexican Art.* New York: G. P. Putnam's Sons.
Wolf, Eric R.
1959 *Sons of the Shaking Earth.* Chicago: University of Chicago Press.

# Index

Note: Towns that are cited only in giving directions are not included in the Index. Those towns that are also possible stopovers are included.